Bettina Franzese, PsyD

Handbook of Psychological Treatment Protocols for Children and Adolescents

**The LEA Series in
Personality and Clinical Psychology
Irving B. Weiner, Editor**

Handbook of Psychological Treatment Protocols for Children and Adolescents

Edited by

Vincent B. Van Hasselt
Nova Southeastern University

Michel Hersen
Pacific University

 LAWRENCE ERLBAUM ASSOCIATES, PUBLISHERS
1998   Mahwah, New Jersey   London

Lawrence Erlbaum Associates, Inc., Publishers
10 Industrial Avenue
Mahwah, New Jersey 07430

Cover Design by Kathryn Houghtaling Lacey

Library of Congress Cataloging-in-Publication Data

Handbook of psychological treatment protocols for children and adolescents / [edited by] Vincent B. Van Hasselt, Michel Hersen.
     p. cm.
  Includes bibliographical references and indexes.
  ISBN 0-8058-1782-4 (alk. paper)
    1. Child psychotherapy—Handbooks, manuals, etc.   2. Adolescent psychotherapy—Handbooks, manuals, etc.   I. Van Hasselt, Vincent B.   II. Hersen, Michel.
  [DNLM: 1. Psychotherapy—in infancy & childhood.
  2. Mental Disorders—in infancy & childhood.   3. Psychotherapy—in adolescence.
  4. Mental Disorders—in adolescence.   WS 350.2 H23588 1997]
  RJ504.H3618   1997
  618.92'8914—dc21
  DNLM/DCL
  for Library of Congress   97-25173
                                                    CIP

Books published by Lawrence Erlbaum Associates are printed on acid-free paper, and their bindings are chosen for strength and durability.

Printed in the United States of America
10 9 8 7 6 5 4 3 2 1

Contents

Preface

Over the past 10 years, increasingly greater attention has been paid to the assessment and treatment of child and adolescent disorders. This upsurge of activity on both research and clinical fronts is related, in part, to improvements and refinements in diagnostic classifications that are increasingly empirically determined and behaviorally based, and, in part, to the growing realization of the need for heuristic interventions with these populations in order to prevent serious psychological dysfunction in adulthood. However, although innovative and efficacious treatment strategies now exist for these populations, most have been designed and implemented in the context of major research programs or funded research centers targeting childhood disorders, and complete protocols are rarely disseminated or replicated. Moreover, when descriptions are provided, they are typically embedded in the "Methods" section of journal articles or briefly covered within a book chapter.

The *Handbook of Psychological Treatment Protocols for Children and Adolescents* is an attempt to bridge the gap between clinical research and practice. The book is a compendium of current, state-of-the-art treatment manuals designed to facilitate the application of the various treatment methods in clinical contexts. It provides specific instructions on the utilization of approaches combined with relevant case illustrations.

The *Handbook* is divided into three parts. Part I, Introduction, includes a chapter by Ron Acierno and the editors on basic contemporary issues of accountability in treatment. Part II, Treatment of Childhood Disorders and Problems, and Part III, Treatment of Adolescent Disorders and Problems, include 15 detailed treatment manuals for use with a large variety of problems presented by children and adolescents both as outpatients and inpatients. Our goal for each chapter is to provide the reader with sufficient information so that the respective approaches can be replicated. We anticipate considerable interest in this volume from a wide range of mental health professionals, including psychologists, psychiatrists, child development specialists, family counselors, social workers, and their graduate students.

Many individuals have devoted their time and effort to this project. First, we thank our eminent contributors for providing their treatment manuals for publication. Second, we thank Burt G. Bolton for his technical assistance. Finally, we thank Judith Amsel, our friend and editor at Lawrence Erlbaum Associates, for her assistance throughout all phases of this project.

—**Vincent B. Van Hasselt**

—**Michel Hersen**

Part I

Introduction

Chapter 1

Accountability

Ron Acierno
Medical University of South Carolina
Vincent B. Van Hasselt
Nova Southeastern University
Michel Hersen
Pacific University

The development of psychological theory has always depended on efforts to empirically justify its hypothetical constructs and applied practices. But vis-à-vis applied practices, the pressure for justification has become increasingly strong. In the recent past, mandates that psychologists, psychiatrists, and other mental health professionals be accountable for their clinical actions have been issued repeatedly from both within our own ranks (e.g., Eysenck, 1952; Raimy, 1950) and by outside parties such as consumer protection organizations and insurance companies. Calls for accountability have been amplified with the realization that the practical value of psychotherapy is frequently less than had been assumed or implied. Indeed, over 45 years ago, Raimy (1950) pointed out that the basic features of acceptable science, including reliability, internal validity, and predictive validity, were lacking in clinical endeavors: "Psychotherapy is an undefined technique, applied to unspecified problems, with unpredictable outcomes" (p. 93). A primary reason for the decidedly unscientific status of clinical psychology and psychiatry five decades ago can be found in the wide gap that existed at the time (and continues to exist, though it is narrower) between basic research and applied clinical practice. Until Wolpe's (1958) reciprocal inhibition procedure, no psychological treatment had its basis or origins in empirically generated findings. As a result, clinical work proceeded independently of laboratory efforts. Wolpe's procedure was unique in two respects. First, his hypotheses were inductively formed through analysis of experimental data. As such, they contrasted with the hypotheses of contemporaneous psychodynamic theories, which were abstracted from clinical impressions. Second, effects (if not processes) of Wolpe's treatment were predictable and measurable. Declarations of success or failure were made according to operationalized, observable criteria. Thus, for the first time, therapists were able to justify their actions and theories on the basis of data instead of inference. Psychotherapists, like practitioners of other therapeutic sciences (e.g., medicine), were in a position to account for their behavior.

Public awareness of mental health options is greater now than ever before. Additionally, the increased prevalence of large-scale managed care organizations and new practices of selective reimbursement by third-party payers for only those treatments that are deemed necessary and shown to be rapidly effective, create an environment of enforced accountability. Fortunately, practitioners have been able to respond to the challenges of this new environment. Unspecified "psychological issues" and "problems" have been replaced by highly reliable (albeit not yet completely valid) systems of psychopathological classification. Wildly variable treatments with unverified and unverifiable techniques based largely on "clinical intuition" have yielded to thoroughly operationalized, reproducible interventions, such as those described in this volume. Random and baseless predictions of treatment outcome have been gradually discarded in favor of data from empirical clinical trials that purposefully illustrate efficacy of one treatment over another for different types of patients (Azrin et al., 1994; Robbins, Alessi, & Colfer, 1989).

Disappointingly, research on children has lagged behind that on adults, as has been historically the case in the clinical sciences (Ammerman & Hersen, 1993; Frame & Cooper, 1993). For example, although rates of drug use are again increasing in adolescent and preadolescent populations, only one controlled evaluation of drug abuse treatment with this age group has been reported (Azrin, Donohue, Besalel, Kogan, & Acierno, 1994). Similarly, despite widespread incidence of documented child sexual and physical abuse (Polusny & Follette, 1995), no large-scale treatment outcome studies have addressed this area. In the frequent absence of clear empirical outcome results, what are the guidelines by which child psychologists and psychiatrists are to maintain accountability?

NECESSARY ELEMENTS OF ACCOUNTABILITY

Clinicians treating children must, of course, consider relevant developmental factors, but accountable practice also requires that they *define problems* on the basis of comprehensive and accurate assessment; *select treatments* that have empirically demonstrated efficacy with child populations, where possible; and *consistently and repeatedly monitor patient progress* during, and at the conclusion of treatment. Each one of these efforts is necessary, but not sufficient to maintain accountability.

ASSESSMENT

Comprehensive assessment of psychopathology is a multidimensional and dynamic process that continues throughout a clinician's contact with patients. Moreover, measurement of symptomatology, the traditional focus of most assessment efforts, is appropriately comple- mented by both delineation of etiological pathways and specification of contextual factors that contribute to the maintenance of a disorder. Unfortunately, almost all psychological assessment research and evaluation of popular diagnostic systems focuses entirely on symptom definition, to the exclusion of maintaining and etiological factors. This focus is problematic if patients with differing psychopathological etiologies in different environments present with identical symptoms requiring dissimilar treatments (e.g., substance abuse in a child of low-in- come substance abusers vs. substance abuse in a child of high-income nonusers). Indeed, clinical researchers have inappropriately presumed patient homogeneity on the basis of similar symptomatology, thereby confounding effects attributable to treatments under study with those produced as a result of (unspecified) differences in etiology or maintaining factors (Hersen, 1981; Wolpe, 1977). Unfortunately, deficits in psychopathological classification continue to be propagated by the *Diagnostic and Statistical Manual and Mental Disorders* (DSM–IV). While highly reliable (Williams et al., 1992), this diagnostic system does not adequately address variation in age, etiology, or environmental context within psychopathology classes, such that patients with decidedly different treatment needs receive identical diagnoses. Assessment and experimental control of etiology and maintaining factors, in addition to symptomatology, overcomes this diagnostic superficiality. As mentioned, however, virtually no evaluation of differential treatment effects among symptom subtypes of disorders in children has been done. This chapter provides examples from both the adult and child literature that serve to illustrate the relevance of multidimensional assessment of symptoms, etiology, and maintaining factors to maximizing treatment efficacy and thus achieving accountability.

The overt and readily apparent nature of most child psychopathology (e.g., conduct disorder, separation anxiety) typically elevates symptomatology to a position of primacy in any assessment process. It is important that symptom assessment include data obtained through observation (i.e., behavior), patient and other self-report (i.e., cognition), and, when possible, physiological monitoring (Lang, 1968). Such tripartite assessment facilitates modification and adaption of interventions to specific needs of the patient. Öst, Johansson, and Jerremalm (1982) illustrated this point with their comparison of two treatments for claustrophobia. Following thorough tripartite symptom assessment, 34 patients were classified as either behavioral or physiological fear responders. Half of each group received an intervention designed to affect the physiological component of their anxiety, and the remaining half was given a treatment that addressed behavioral aspects of their disorder. As expected, differential treatment responses were observed, with patients classified as behavioral responders improving to a relatively greater extent with a behavior-focused treatment, and those classified as physiological responders showing greatest gains with a physiological-focused intervention. Note that all patients were similarly diagnosed, hence typical *DSM* classification would not have been sufficient to prescriptively match pathology and treatment. Instead, phenomenological categorization of symptomatology beyond that offered by the *DSM* was necessary to maximize treatment efficacy.

Treatment selection that is purposefully guided by multidimensional assessment of symptoms has also proven to be beneficial in amelioration of other forms of specific phobia. For example, although heart rate and blood pressure elevation are typical and consistent responses in phobic individuals confronted with feared stimuli, psychophysiological assessment reveals that a small subset of patients—specifically, blood phobics—evince heart rate decreases when presented with phobic objects (see Öst, Sterner, & Lindhal, 1984). Therefore, typical treatments for phobics that foster heart rate reduction appear to be inappropriate interventions for blood phobics. Indeed, applied tension, as opposed to applied relaxation, is indicated when treating this disorder.

Similar symptom-based subtypes of depression also exist and have varied treatment requirements (McKnight, Nelson, Hayes, & Jarrett, 1984; Paykel, Prusoff, Klerman, Haskell, & Dimascio, 1973; Wolpe, 1977, 1979, 1990). Specifically, Wolpe (1979) posited that behavioral, subjective, and physiological symptoms of anxiety are present in a large percentage of major depression patients, and the phenomenological experience of this disorder differs greatly from that of depressed individuals who do not suffer from concomitant manifestations of anxiety. Importantly, physiological and behavioral discrimination between anxious and nonanxious depressives has been achieved. For example, individuals with anxious depression evince above-average sedation thresholds (see Wolpe, 1986), as compared with nonanxious depressives, who demonstrate subaverage sedation thresholds, indicating that qualitative differences exist between these affective disorder subtypes. As was the case in the earlier example with specific phobias, discrimination between these two classes of depression is not possible with the *DSM–IV*. This is somewhat disconcerting in that, it is very likely that these qualitatively different forms of depression require qualitatively different types of treatment. Along these lines, Conti, Placidi, Dell'Osso, Lenzi, and Corsano (1987) reported that nonanxious depressives evinced significant improvement following treatment with antidepressant medication, whereas anxious depressives responded no better to medication than to placebo. As Wolpe (1986, 1990) maintained, interventions that reduce anxiety, as well as enhance affect, are appropriate for these patients. Given the heterogeneity of depressive disorder in adults, it is most certainly the case that children diagnosed as "depressed" also possess dissimilar treatment requirements (Robbins, Alessi, & Colfer, 1989).

Adolescent substance abusers are also benefited by focused assessment of symptoms. For example, Vaglum and Fossheim (1980) found that youth who abused psychedelic drugs responded to a greater extent following individual or family treatment, relative to a confrontational milieu therapy, whereas adolescents who abused opiates or stimulants responded most favorably to confrontational milieu therapy. Consistent with treatment of depressive disorders, assessment of substance abuse symptomatology in excess of that specified by the *DSM–IV* often facilitates positive treatment outcome. Indeed, Cooney, Kadden, Litt, and Getter, (1991) demonstrated that individuals evincing impulsivity, sociopathy, aggressiveness, interpersonally dysfunction, increased negativity, episodic binge drinking, and an external locus of control (classified as "externalizes") responded better to a structured cognitive-behavioral therapy than to an interpersonal based treatment. By contrast, patients demonstrating low dependence and aggressiveness, but relatively elevated anxiety, self-reflection, and an internal locus of control (classified as "internalizers"), improved most with an interpersonally based treatment. Similarly, Kadden, Cooney, Getter, and Litt (1989) found that alcoholics high in global psychopathology (i.e., externalizers) responded better to a structured coping skills program than to interactional group therapy, whereas for patients low in global psychopathology (i.e., internalizers), the reverse was true.

Clearly, accountability in clinical child psychology and psychiatry is enhanced by comprehensive evaluation of behavioral, subjective, and physiological parameters of patient and pathology. That is, thorough multidimensional symptom assessment increases therapeutic precision so that general treatments may be modified and directed to meet specific requirements of individual patients. However, measurement of symptomatology does not sufficiently address all criteria for appropriate treatment selection. Rather, consideration must be given to contextual factors that serve to maintain pathology as well.

Functional assessment of contextual or maintaining factors logically follows symptomatic assessment and serves to reveal the reasons constellations of psychopathological behavior persist. Strongly grounded in learning theory, the assessment of contextual factors involves specification of reinforcement contingencies and identification of discriminant stimuli in the patient's environment that reliably elicit or perpetuate problem behavior. Although specific procedural aspects involved in measurement of contextual factors are determined for the most part by an individual's symptomatic presentation, all assessments must include: specification of antecedents and consequences of problem behavior, description of the effects of problem behaviors on the patient's significant others (and their responses to these effects), and identification of environmental stimuli that vary with the presence or absence of pathological behavior. Antecedents and consequences of a behavior are clearly relevant areas of consideration when designing an intervention and require little elaboration. Knowledge of the effects of problem behaviors on significant others can be essential in constructing treatment regimens that require active collaboration of family members by assuring that their concerns and needs are also addressed. Finally, delineation of stimuli that vary as a function of target behavior permits identification and manipulation of conditions under which problem behavior is and is not likely to occur. Children are relatively more dependent on others, and hence more reactive to their immediate social environment than adults. Therefore, the measurement of maintaining factors is particularly important when designing or selecting interventions for this population. For example, symptoms of school-specific conduct-disordered behavior in a 13-year-old male who resides with drug abusing and violent parents demand entirely different treatment than an identical conduct-disordered presentation in a 13-year-old male residing with parents with no such overt pathology. For the first child, implementation of powerful school-based contingencies is short-sighted in that they fail to address problems evident in the family unit that most certainly contribute to the maintenance of problem behavior (Henggeler & Borduin, 1990), whereas similar contingency restructuring procedures may be adequate in altering negative behavior in the second child.

Azrin et al. (1996) also demonstrated the usefulness of assessing maintaining factors in their evaluation of two treatments for adolescent drug abuse. In this controlled outcome study, standard supportive counseling was compared to a behaviorally oriented intervention package that was individually tailored to address and alter factors thought to maintain drug use. Specifically, treatment included identification of those stimuli that elicited drug ingestion, followed by skills training to reduce the frequency and magnitude of time spent in the presence of those stimuli. Additionally, existing patterns of contingent reinforcement were clarified and restructured so that drug use resulted in high response cost of previously obtained reinforcement, and abstinence resulted in increased social reinforcement. Importantly, this intervention addressed both contingencies that served to maintain the unwanted operant, as well as conditioned discriminative stimuli that consistently elicited problem behavior. Predictably, subjects receiving the behavioral intervention evinced significantly greater reductions in substance abuse, both at posttreatment and at 9-month follow-up, than patients receiving standard substance abuse counseling.

Meichenbaum, Gilmore, and Fedoravicius (1971) provided further evidence for the utility of complementing symptom measurement with assessment of contextual factors in their study of two treatments for public-speaking fears. In this experiment, pretreatment assessment included characterization of public-speaking anxiety in terms of fear specificity. That is, individuals were evaluated according to whether their fears were confined to public-speaking situations (i.e., elicited by a narrow range of stimuli), or were generalized responses to a variety of social contexts (e.g., elicited by a wide range of stimuli). Subjects were then treated by either a cognitively oriented intervention involving training to attend to and alter inappropriate self-verbalizations during anxiety-producing situations (i.e., a treatment aimed at addressing factors responsible for maintaining anxiety across a variety of social situations) or by standard desensitization (i.e., a technique that intentionally confines its therapeutic focus to only those stimuli deemed relevant to the problem at hand). Predictably, patients evincing generalized interpersonal performance anxiety responded best to the cognitive intervention. By contrast, subjects with fears maintained by specific public-speaking stimuli improved most with the desensitization treatment. Note that the cognitively oriented intervention was more readily applied to overcome a wide variety of discriminitive stimuli that elicited anxiety in individuals with generalized fears: desensitization treatment was adequate to ameliorate anxiety in those patients with a limited number of well-defined fear triggers.

As mentioned, thorough assessment of maintaining or contextual factors requires that attention be directed to both the associative and instrumental aspects of the environment. Importantly though, assessment must not end with maintaining factors. Rather, identification of etiological pathways potentially enhances treatment outcome and is thus a requisite component in account-able practice (Wolpe, 1986).

A large number of contemporary psychological and pharmacological treatments produce highly focalized and specific effects. Choice among them must be preceded by precise and well-conceptualized diagnosis. Such diagnosis requires etiological assessment that compli-ments measurement of symptoms and delineation of maintaining factors (Agras, 1987; Eifert, Evans, & McKendrick, 1990; Hersen, 1981; Wolpe, 1986). Fortunately, etiological assessment is regularly undertaken in applied clinical settings, where clinicians appear to recognize the inherent value of identifying "how" as well as "what" characteristics of their patient's psycho-pathology. By contrast, researchers conducting treatment outcome studies have largely ignored the contributions of etiology to treatment response. Hence, experimental conditions in these studies are composed of heterogeneous groups of subjects and intervention effects are con-founded by etiological differences across individuals. The relevance of etiological assessment to accountable practice is best illustrated by the existing literature on the treatment of affective disorders. Most attention has been focused on differentiating endogenous (the *DSM–IV* uses the term *melancholic*) from nonendogenous depression, with the assumption that somatic interven-tions (e.g., medication, electroconvulsive therapy) are most effective with endogenous depres-sives, whereas psychological interventions (e.g., interpersonal therapy) yield greatest improvement with nonendogenous depressives. A limited number of controlled studies has been performed that supports the endogenous/nonendogenous distinction, and has yielded several methods by which to make this differential diagnosis. No technique, however, has been found to be completely reliable or valid.

The dexamethasone suppression test (DST) is the best known (and debated) method by which to discriminate endogenous from nonendogenous depression. Nonsuppression of the DST is indicative of the endogenous subtype of depression (Chadhury, Valdiya, & Agustine, 1989; Robbins, et al., 1989; Zimmerman, Coryell, & Black, 1990). Symptom correlates of DST non-suppression and endogenous depression include early or middle morning insomnia, worsened mood in the morning, reduced appetitive and psychomotor activity, and low anxiety (Robins, Block, & Peselow, 1989; Wolpe, 1979). By contrast, high anxiety is strongly associated with DST suppression or nonendogenous depression. A second objective means of identifying depressive etiology is the sedation threshold, or the level of sodium amobarbital required to produce certain nonresponding effects in patients. Qualitative differences in responding of endogenous and nonendogenous depressives have been demonstrated on this test, with the former group displaying lower than average sedation thresholds and the latter group evincing higher than average thresholds. Moreover, differential treatment response among these affective disorder subgroups has been observed. For example, Robbins, Alessi et al. (1989) treated 38 depressed adolescents with a psychosocial intervention and found that only 47% responded. Nonresponders were then treated by a combined package of tricyclic antidepressants and psychotherapy, which produced a 92% improvement rate. Importantly, nonsuppression on the DST (endogenous depression) was associated with reduced effectiveness of psychosocial treatment. Differential treatment responses among these etiological subgroups were also observed by Raskin and Crook (1976), who noted that antidepressant medication and placebo were equally effective for nonendogenous depressives, whereas endogenous depressives responded only to active medication. Though seemingly simplistic, *DSM–IV* makes no provision for such affective disorder subclassification.

Usefulness of etiological assessment has also been established with anxiety disorders. Along these lines, Öst (1985) noted that phobic patients whose fears were determined to have been acquired through conditioning were more responsive to counterconditioning or extinction-based treatments than to cognitive restructuring. Furthermore, Trower, Yardley, Bryant, and Shaw (1978) reported that social phobics with skills deficits showed greatest outcome following skills training, whereas similarly diagnosed patients with no skills deficits responded equally well to skills training or systematic desensitization. An interesting etiological subtype of nonfearful panic disorder has been described by Russell, Kushner, Beitmen, & Bartels (1991). Diagnostic markers implicating atypical panic were evident, as indicated by the fact that 100% of these nonfearful panickers evinced attacks during lactate infusion challenges, and none demonstrated this response to placebo infusion challenges. Moreover, all patients reported at least a 75% reduction in symptomatology following treatment by imipramine or clonazepam, a rate of improvement exceeding that regularly observed in fearful panickers receiving these treatments (see Mavissakalian, Michelson, & Dealy, 1983). The unusual uniform response of nonfearful panickers to both lactate and placebo challenges, and to antipanic medication, in addition to the notable lack of fear during attacks provide support for the validity of this, non-*DSM–IV* defined, etiological subtype.

Overall, these examples demonstrate the potential usefulness of extending assessment beyond that specified by the *DSM* to include consideration of etiology so that treatment selection may be refined and accountability thus maintained. Verification of psychopathological origins is even more imperative when treating children, who are more likely to present with identical symptom clusters that do not remit with identical treatments.

SELECTION OF TREATMENTS WITH EMPIRICAL SUPPORT

Selection of an empirically validated treatment in favor of interventions lacking such validation is the second criterion of accountable practice (Garfield, 1987; Wilson, 1984; Wolpe, 1990). This requirement is an accepted and obvious component of medical practice, but it has only recently been addressed by governing boards of psychologists, psychiatrists, and mental health practitioners. For example, the American Psychological Association (APA) Committee on Professional Standards (1987) Practice Guideline 1.5 stated that "all providers of psychological services attempt to maintain and apply current knowledge of scientific and professional developments that are clinically related to the services they render" (p. 715). In keeping with this point, the Task Force on the Practice and Dissemination of Psychological Procedures (September 1993) recommended that "APA site visit teams make training in empirically validated treatments a criterion for APA accreditation" (p. 8). Unfortunately, many providers of mental health treatment do not approach their work in a scientific manner. That is, a majority of clinicians fail to contribute to, or even keep abreast of, current research in their area (Cohen, 1979). Importantly, clinicians who select an intervention that lacks empirical validation over one with such support are potentially responsible for exacerbating patient suffering and costs. In a very powerful comment on this state of affairs, Rush (1993) declared that "there is a wide variation in actual practice [that]…is generally believed to reflect unnecessary diversity of practice procedures that raise the cost of care and result in sub-optimal outcomes" (p. 484). Obviously, selection of treatments with empirical support is a requirement of accountable practice.

CONSISTENT MONITORING OF PATIENT PROGRESS

The final criterion of accountable practice is repeated assessment of patient progress during treatment. Such assessment should be conducted in a manner that permits accurate and timely modification of intervention procedures, thus resulting in maximized improvement and minimized suffering. The American Psychological Association (1987) has also addressed this topic under Practice Guideline 3.3, stating simply that "there are periodic, systematic, and effective evaluations of psychological services" (p. 719). Moreover, as Smith (1989) noted, "Accountability requires that applied psychologists provide data concerning their effectiveness" (p. 169). At the very least, clinicians should employ some form of outcome assessment to both justify and guide their work. However, causal inferences supported in a manner beyond that provided by simple case report is preferable and unobtrusively accomplished. Barlow and Hersen (1984) and Barlow, Hayes, and Nelson (1984) provided excellent guides for clinicians attempting to implement moderately controlled, single-case clinical research strategies in their applied practice. Moreover, the *Journal of Consulting and Clinical Psychology* (Vol. 61, No. 3) has devoted a special issue to demonstrating applicability of single-case designs to clinical process research. Additionally, in the empirical realm, single-case designs have several advantages over standard group experiments. This is because single case, or small N research, generally involves extensive specification of subject and pathology along parameters (i.e., symptoms, etiology, maintaining factors) outlined earlier. By contrast, group designs necessarily disregard most individual subject and pathology characteristics. That is, single-case designs permit emphasis through specificity—rather than nullification through aggregation—of potentially relevant symptomatic, contextual, and etiological factors that affect treatment outcome. This focus can then be useful to consumers of research in refining future interventions with similar patients. Of course, one controlled single-case study cannot serve as the bass for future treatment selection, and as is the case with group experimental designs, replication is necessary to both establish the reliability of an effect, and delineate situations under which noted effects do and do not occur.

CONCLUSION

In the current climate of accountability, justification of therapeutically directed behavior is of paramount importance. Indeed, specialized subgroups of clinical psychologists (see Anderson, 1992; Beck & Haaga, 1992; Bishop & Trembley, 1987; Burchard & Schaefer, 1992; Cross,

1985; Furedy & Shulhan, 1987; Garfield, 1987; Smith, 1989), the American Psychological Association, other groups of mental health professionals, third-party payers, and the general consumer have all called for practitioners to provide data to support what it is they do. This pressure over all has been beneficial for a field in which practitioners have escaped basic scrutiny for so long. Whereas the use of unproven treatment constitutes malpractice in medicine, it has been commonplace in the mental health profession. Nowadays, however, therapists are no longer free to choose that treatment that best "suits them." Instead, their selection of therapeutic interventions must be guided by empirical knowledge, and they must pay attention to three specific issues. First, a comprehensive assessment of maintaining factors and etiology, in addition to symptomatology, must be made to prescriptively match patient and pathology to treatment. Second, those procedures that have been shown to effect change under controlled conditions must be selected over those lacking such empirical validation. Third, patient progress during treatment must be monitored through repeated and specific evaluations. General procedural aspects of each of these processes have been outlined previously and specified more fully elsewhere (e.g., Bellack & Hersen, 1988; Wolpe, 1990).

The courses of treatment offered in this volume have been constructed and revised through empirical evaluation of their efficacy. They represent the most specialized interventions available for the problems addressed. As a result of their specificity, however, their effects are typically circumscribed. Therefore, it is probable that multiple treatments will be applicable and appropriate for a particular patient. Moreover, despite their highly structured format, these interventions are not intended to be used with all children in an identical manner, and modification may be required for some individuals. Of course, such procedural adaptions are justifiable if they are performed in response to data gathered during a multidimensional assessment and accompanied by repeated controlled evaluations of their efficacy.

REFERENCES

Agras, W. S. (1987). So where do we go from here? *Behavior Therapy, 18*, 203–217.

American Psychiatric Association (1994). *Diagnostic and Statistical Manual of Mental Disorders* (4th ed.). Washington, DC: American Psychiatric Association.

American Psychological Association Committee on Professional Standards. (1987). General guidelines for providers of psychological services. *American Psychologist, 42*, 712–723.

Ammerman, R. T., & Hersen, M. (1993). Developmental and longitudinal perspectives on behavior therapy. In R. T. Ammerman & M. Hersen (Eds.), *Handbook of behavior therapy with children and adults: A developmental and longitudinal perspective* (pp. 3–10). Needham Heights, MA: Allyn & Bacon.

Anderson, D. (1992). A case for standards of counseling practice. *Journal of Counseling and Development, 71*, 22–26.

Azrin, N. H., Acierno, R., Kogan, E. S., Donohue, B., Besalel, V., & McMahon, P. (1996). Follow-up results of supportive versus behavioral therapy for illicit drug use. *Behaviour Research and Therapy, 34*, 41–46.

Azrin, N. H., Donohue, B., Besalel, V., Kogan, E., Acierno, R. (1994). Youth drug abuse treatment: A controlled outcome study. *Journal of Child and adolescent Drug Abuse, 3*, 1–16.

Azrin, N. H., McMahon, P., Donohue, B., Besalel, V., Lapinski, K., Kogan, E., Acierno, R., & Galloway, E. (1994). Behavior therapy for drug abuse: A controlled treatment-outcome study. *Behaviour Research and Therapy, 32*, 857–866.

Barlow, D. H., Hayes, S. C., & Nelson, R. O. (1984). *The scientist practioner: Research and accountability in clinical and educational settings*. New York: Pergamon.

Barlow, D. H., & Hersen, M. (1984). *Single case experimental designs: Strategies for studying behavior change* (2nd ed.). New York: Pergamon.

Beck, A. T., & Haaga, D. A. (1992). The future of cognitive therapy. *Psychotherapy, 29*, 34–38.

Bellack, A. S., & Hersen, M. (1988). *Behavioral assessment: A practical handbook* (3rd. ed.). New York: Pergamon.

Bishop, J. B., & Trembley, E. L. (1987). Counseling centers and accountability: Immovable, objects, irresistible forces. *Journal of Counseling and Development, 65*, 491–494.

Burchard, J. D., & Schaefer, M. C. (1992). Improving accountability in a service delivery system in children's mental health. *Clinical Psychology Review, 12*, 867–882.

Chadhury, S., Valdiya, P. S., & Augustine, M. (1989). The dexamethasone suppression test in endogenous depression. *Indian Journal of Psychiatry, 31*, 296–300.

Cohen, L. H. (1979). The research readership and information source reliance of clinical psychologists. *Professional Psychology, 10*, 780–786.

Conti, L., Placidi, G.R., Dell'Osso, L., Lenzi, A., & Cassano, G. B. (1987). Therapeutic response in subtypes of major depression. *New Trends in Experimental and Clinical Psychiatry, 3*, 101–107.

Cooney, N. L., Kadden, R.M., Litt, M. D., & Getter, H. (1991). Matching alcoholics to coping skills or interactional therapies: Two year follow up results. *Journal of Consulting and Clinical Psychology, 59*, 598–601.

Cross, D. G. (1985). The age of accountability: The next phase for family therapy. *Australian and New Zealand Journal of Family Therapy, 6*, 129–135.

Eifert, G. H., Evans, I. M., & McKendrick, V. G. (1990). Matching treatments to client problems not diagnostic labels: A case for paradigmatic behavior therapy. *Journal of Behavior Therapy and Experimental Psychiatry, 21*, 163–172.

Eysenck, H. J. (1952). The effects of psychotherapy: An evaluation. *Journal of Consulting Psychology, 16,* 319–324.

Frame, C. L., & Cooper, D. K. (1993). Major depression in children. In R. T. Ammerman & M. Hersen (Eds.), *Handbook of behavior therapy with children and adults: A developmental and longitudinal perspective* (pp. 59–72). Needham Heights, MA: Allyn & Bacon.

Furedy, J. J., & Shulhan, D. (1987). Specific versus placebo effects in biofeedback: Some brief back to basics considerations. *Biofeedback and Self Regulation, 12*, 211–215.

Garfield, S. L. (1987). Towards a scientifically oriented eclecticism. *Scandinavian Journal of Behaviour Therapy, 16*, 95–109.

Henggeler, S., & Borduin, M. J. (1990). *Family therapy and beyond: A multi-systemic approach to treating the behavior problems of children and adolescents.* Pacific Grove, CA: Brooks/Cole.

Hersen, M. (1981). Complex problems require complex solutions. *Behavior Therapy, 12*, 15–29.

Kadden, R. M., Cooney, N. L., Getter, H., & Litt, M. D. (1989). Matching alcoholics to coping skills or interactional therapies: Posttreatment results. *Journal of Consulting and Clinical Psychology, 57*, 698–704.

Lang, P.J. (1968). Fear reduction and fear behavior: Problems in treating a construct. In J.M. Shlien (Ed.), *Research in psychotherapy* (Vol. 3). Washington, DC: American Psychological Association.

Mavissakalian, M., Michelson, L. & Dealy, R. S. (1983). Pharmacological treatment of agoraphobia: Imipramine versus imipramine with programmed practice. *British Journal of Psychiatry, 143*, 348–355.

McKnight, D., Nelson, R., Hayes, S., & Jarrett, R. (1984). Importance of treating individually assessed response classes of depression. *Behavior Therapy, 15*, 315–335.

Meichenbaum, D., Gilmore, J., & Fedoravicius, A. (1971). Group insight versus group desensitization in treating speech anxiety. *Journal of Consulting and Clinical Psychology, 36*, 410–421.

Öst, L. G. (1985). Ways of acquiring phobias and outcome of behavioral treatment. *Behaviour Research and Therapy, 23*, 683–689.

Öst, L. G., Johansson, J., & Jerremalm, A. (1982). Individual response patterns and the effects of different behavioral methods in the treatment of claustrophobia. *Behaviour Research and Therapy, 20*, 445–560.

Öst, L.G., Sterner, U., & Lindhal, I.L. (1984). Physiological responses in blood phobics. *Behaviour Research and Therapy, 22*, 109–117.

Paykel, E.S., Prusoff, B.A., Klerman, G.L., Haskell, D., & Dimascio, A. (1973). Clinical response to amitriptyline among depressed women. *Journal of Nervous and Mental Disease, 156*, 149–165.

Polusny, M., & Follette, V.M. (1995). Long-term correlates of child sexual abuse: Theory and review of the empirical literature. *Applied and Preventive Psychology, 4,* 143–166.

Raimy, V. C. (Ed.). (1950). *Training in clinical psychology (Boulder Conference).* Englewood Cliffs, NJ: Prentice-Hall.

Raskin, A., & Crook, T. H. (1976). The endogenous-neurotic distinction as a predictor of response to antidepressant drugs. *Psychological Medicine, 6*, 59–70.

Robins, D. R., Alessi, N. E., & Colfer, M. V. (1989). Treatment of adolescent with major depression: Implications of the DST and the melancholic subtype. *Journal of Affective Disorders*, *17*, 99–104.

Robins, C. J., Block, P., & Peselow, E. D. (1989). Specificity of symptoms in RDC endogenous depression. *Journal of Affective Disorders*, *16*, 243–248.

Rush, A.J. (1993). Clinical practice guidelines: Good news, no news, or bad news? *Archives of General Psychiatry*, *50*, 483–490.

Russell, J. L., Kushner, M. G., Beirman, B. D., & Bartels, K. M. (1991). Non-fearful panic disorder in neurology patients validated by lactate challenge. *American Journal of Psychiatry*, *148*, 361–364.

Smith, R. E. (1989). Applied sport psychology in an age of accountability. Second annual conference of the Association for the Advancement of Applied Sport Psychology. *Journal of Applied Sport Psychology*, *1*, 166–180.

Task Force on Promotion and Dissemination of Psychological Procedures. (1993, September 15). A report to the American Psychological Association, Division 12 Board.

Trower, P. Yardley, K., Bryant, B., & Shaw, P. (1978) The treatment of social failure: A comparison of anxiety reduction and skills acquisition procedures for two social problems. *Behavior Modification, 2,* 41–60.

Vaglum, P., & Fossheim, I. (1980). Differential treatment of young abusers: A quasi-experimental study of a "therapeutic community" in a psychiatric hospital. *Journal of Drug Issues*, *10*, 505–516.

Williams, J. B., Gibbon, M., First, M. B., Spitzer, R. L., Davies, M., Borus, J., Howes, M. J., Kane, J., Pope, H. G., Rounsaville, B., & Wittchen, H. (1992). The structured clinical interview for *DSM–III–R* (SCID): II. Multi-site test–retest reliability. *Archives of General Psychiatry*, *49*, 630–636.

Wilson, G. T. (1984). Clinical issues and strategies in the practice of behavior therapy. *Annual Review of Behavior Therapy Theory and Practice*, *9*, 309–343.

Wolpe, J. (1958). *Psychotherapy by reciprocal inhibition*. Stanford, CA: Stanford University Press.

Wolpe, J. (1977). Inadequate behavior analysis: The Achilles heel of outcome research in behavior therapy. *Journal of Behavior Therapy and Experimental Psychiatry*, *8*, 1–3.

Wolpe, J. (1979). The experimental model and treatment of neurotic depression. *Behaviour Research and Therapy*, *17*, 555–565.

Wolpe, J. (1986). The positive diagnosis of neurotic depression as an etiological category. *Comprehensive Psychiatry*, *27*, 449–460.

Wolpe, J. (1990). *The practice of behavior therapy* (4th ed.). Elmsford, NY: Pergamon.

Zimmerman, M., Coryell, W. H., & Black, D. W. (1990). Variability in the application of contemporary diagnostic criteria: Endogenous depression as an example. *American Journal of Psychiatry*, *147*, 1173–1179.

Part II

Treatment of
Childhood Disorders and Problems

Chapter 2

Mental Retardation

Cynthia R. Johnson
Western Psychiatric Institute and Clinic
University of Pittsburgh School of Medicine

DESCRIPTION OF THE DISORDER

The diagnostic criteria and definition of mental retardation have met with much controversy over the past two decades. This has been the result, in large part, because of the varied professional groups involved in shaping the definition of mental retardation, the criteria used for the definition, and the diagnostic criteria of mental retardation. Two primary diagnostic systems that have set forth criteria for mental retardation include the *Diagnostic and Statistical Manual of Mental Disorders* (4th ed.; *DSM–IV*; APA, 1994) and *Mental Retardation: Definition, Classification, and Systems of Support* (AAMD, 1992). Both classification systems list below-average cognitive functioning as the fundamental feature of mental retardation. In addition, impairment in adaptive functioning in skill areas—such as communication, self-care, social skills, leisure and work, and personal safety (AAMD, 1992; APA, 1994)—is necessary to make the diagnosis. A third criteria is the onset of mental retardation before age 18.

Four degrees of mental retardation are used to designate severity of impairment in *DSM–IV* (APA, 1994). For each level, a corresponding IQ range is assigned. The *DSM– IV* lists *Mild* (IQ level of 50–55 to approximately 70), *Moderate* (IQ level of 35–40 to 50–55), *Severe* (20–25 to 35–40), and *Profound* (IQ level below 20 to 25) mental retardation. Mental Retardation, Severity Unspecified is also used in *DSM–IV* in cases where mental retardation is strongly suspected, but the administration of appropriate assessments has not yet been conducted.

These levels or degrees of mental retardation give some predictive value with regard to expected competencies and in planning for appropriate educational and habilitative services. The mild category describes the largest number of individuals with mental retardation. It is generally accepted that these persons are capable of achieving nearly full independence with appropriate instruction and support. Within the moderate range, it is expected that some level of supervision and assistance in the community will be necessary. Individuals functioning in the severe to profound range of mental retardation is generally require life-long care, though there may be mastery of some self-care, survival skills, and communication. It should be underscored that the achievements of individuals may vary considerably within all levels of mental retardation.

BEHAVIOR AND EMOTIONAL DISORDERS
IN CHILDREN/ADOLESCENTS WITH MENTAL RETARDATION

An estimated 15% to 57% of children with mental retardation and other developmental disabilities exhibit behavioral or emotional disturbance (Beitchman, Nair, Clegg, Ferguson, & Patel, 1986; Eaton & Menolascino, 1982; Gillberg, Persson, Grufman, & Themner, 1986). The presence of these behavioral and emotional problems can be one of the greatest obstacles to the normalization and education of those persons with developmental disabilities. Severe behavioral problems not only pose a significant risk to life, health, and property, but may disrupt or disable normal family function and interfere with participation in habilitative activities. The presence of behavioral problems in individuals with mental retardation and other developmental disabilities greatly influences the level of restrictiveness of educational placement (Singer & Irwin, 1987), and in later years, is associated with placement decisions and placement failures in living arrangements (Lakin, Hill, Hauber, Bruininks, & Heal, 1983; Vitello, Atthowe, & Cadwell, 1983).

For purposes of this chapter, behavioral and emotional problems refer to behavioral excesses, behavioral deficits, and atypical behaviors and emotional responses that significantly interfere with educational, therapeutic, and socialization opportunities, or that significantly interfere with normal family functioning. The following are descriptions of the most dangerous and commonly interfering behavioral and emotional problems in children and adolescents with mental retardation used in this chapter.

Aggression

Aggression has been widely defined as behavior that injures or irritates another person (Eron, 1987). Difficulty in operationalizing the concept of "intention to harm" typically results in a definition describing the child's actual overt behavior and includes hitting, kicking, biting, shoving, poking, pinching, and throwing objects. Aggression in individuals with mental retardation has been acknowledged as a maladaptive behavior that is likely to interfere with management and optimal functioning (Fo el, Lash, Barron, & Roberts, 1989; Gast & Wolery, 1987; Matson & Gorman-Smith, 1986).

Property Destruction

The destroying of property is an often-identified maladaptive behavior in individuals with mental retardation. Property destruction was identified in 24% of residents with mental retardation (Fovel et al., 1989).

Self-Injury

Self-injurious behavior (SIB) refers to chronic, repetitive actions that have the potential to result in physical injury to the self. Examples of self-injury include self-striking, headbanging, self-scratching, self-biting, eyepoking, and rumination (Bauer, Shea, & Gaines, 1988). The severity of resulting injuries may range from bruising to retinal detachment, loss of consciousness, or in some cases, death. Potentially injurious responses, such as headbanging, have been observed in normally developing children under age 4 (e.g., Delissovoy, 1961; Kravitz & Boehm, 1971), but prospective descriptions of onset and the developmental course of self-injury have not been reported in the literature. The etiology of self-injury has generated hypotheses and findings to support both environmental (e.g., Carr & Durand, 1985, Carr, Levin, McConnachie, Carlson, Kemp, & Smith, 1994) and biological (e.g., Cataldo & Harris, 1982; Sandman, 1988) influences.

Stereotypies/Self-Stimulatory Behavior

The primary feature of behaviors falling under this rubric is repetitive motor movements that appear nonpurposeful and nonfunctional. Typical topographies include hand flapping, hand and finger posturing, body rocking, eye gazing, and repetitive vocalizations. The *DSM–IV* classification for these behavior is Stereotypic Movement Disorder. For a diagnosis to be made, the stereotypical behaviors must significantly interfere with other activities of living. Like self-injury, many hypotheses have been proposed about the etiology of stereotypical behaviors. These involve a homeostatic viewpoint and a learned, operant view (see Guess & Carr, 1991). In the former, self-stimulatory behaviors are assumed to decrease or increase stimulation to a level of arousal of some optimally set homeostatic state. An operant explanation explains stereotypies as learned behaviors maintained by environmental contingencies.

Pica

Pica, the repeated ingestion of inedible or nonnutritive substances, is a behavior disorder more often seen in individuals with mental retardation. Although occasional pica behavior is considered developmentally normal in infants, it is deemed pathological when the behavior persists beyond the age of 12 to 18 months (Baltrop, 1966). Pica has been observed frequently in institutionalized children and adults with mental retardation. Prevalence estimates have ranged from 25.8% (Danford & Huber, 1982) to approximately 9% in a more recent survey (McAlpine & Singh, 1986). These rates, although quite disparate, are nonetheless alarming given the serious, even life-threatening, health and medical consequences of pica. The potential effects of pica in children are very serious. Pica has been associated with lead poisoning (Cataldo, Finney, Madden, & Russo, 1983), which may result in irreversible neurological impairment and in rare cases death. Intestinal blockage, intestinal perforation (Ausman, Ball, & Alexander, 1974), and intestinal parasites (Foxx & Martin, 1975) have all been associated with pica behavior. Most commonly ingested items included paper and cloth, cigarettes and cigarette butts, metal or plastic objects, plaster crumbs and paint chips, hair, and feces (McAlpine & Singh, 1986).

Oppositional/Noncompliant Behavior

Compliance refers to obedience to adult requests (Parpal & Maccoby, 1985), acceptance of adult requests in teaching situations (Rocissano, Slade, & Lynch, 1987), and cooperation of adult suggestions and requests (Schaffer & Crook, 1980). When children fail to follow most caregiver or teacher instructions and rules (given they are capable of hearing, comprehending and performing the tasks involved) they are said to be noncompliant. When such behavior interferes with the functioning of the child or family, it becomes a clinical concern and is the most common reason for referral of normally developing children for mental health services (Forehand, 1977). In individuals with mental retardation and other developmental disorders, noncompliant and oppositional behaviors are common and often disruptive to habilitative services (Thompson, 1984; Walker, 1993). Noncompliant behaviors, in fact, have been noted to be one of the most frequently occurring referral concerns in clients with mental retardation with problem behaviors (e.g., Fidura, Lindsey, & Walker, 1987).

Attention Deficits/Hyperactivity

Attention deficit hyperactivity disorder (ADHD) afflicts 3% to 5% of school-age children (Barkley, 1990) and is characterized by behavioral symptoms that include hyperactivity, impulsivity, and inattention in normally developing children. Although prevalence of these symptoms associated with the psychiatric diagnosis of ADHD in children and adolescents with mental retardation is less clear, these behaviors are recognized as a significant problems in this population (Cullinan, Gadow, & Epstein, 1987).

Tantrums

Tantrums are outbursts of behavior as an expression of anger, irritability, or frustration. Behaviors commonly exhibited during temper tantrums include crying, whining, falling to the floor, thrashing, kicking, throwing things, aggression, and self-injurious behavior (e.g., Bunyan, 1987; Hart, Bax, & Jenkins, 1984; Lovaas, 1987). Temper tantrums vary in duration both between and within individuals and may occur anywhere from a few minutes to over a hour at a time (Bunyan, 1987). Tantrums are reportedly more common among children with physical and developmental disabilities than in normally developing children (Bax, 1985; Beitchman, 1985); they are associated with recurrent illnesses in 2-year-olds, but not in older children who presumably have better communication skills (Hart et al., 1984).

Feeding/Mealtime Problems

Although feeding problems are commonplace in young children, there is a much higher incidence of chronic feeding and mealtime problems in children with mental retardation and other developmental disabilities (Palmer & Horn, 1978; Perske, Clifton, McClean, & Stein, 1977; Stimbert, Minor, & McCoy, 1977). Types of feeding problems most frequently described in the literature include food refusal, food selectivity, inadequate amount of food intake, inappropriate mealtime behaviors, and lack of adequate development in self-feeding skills (Berkowitz, Sherry, & Davis, 1971; Palmer & Horn, 1978; Palmer, Thompson, & Linscheid, 1977).

Elimination/Toileting Problems

Elimination and toileting problems in children and adolescents with mental retardation are quite common (Azrin & Foxx, 1971; Foxx & Azrin, 1973). *Enuresis* is the repeated urination in inappropriate places (in clothes, in the bed). Enuresis is usually specified as either primary and secondary. *Primary enuresis* is used when urinary continence has never been obtained and *secondary enuresis* refers to incontinence after a period of continence. *Encopresis* is the defecation of feces in inappropriate places. Again, the qualification of primary and secondary is used to designated whether training had occurred in the past.

Sleep and Bedtime Problems

Sleep problems appear to be quite frequent in children with mental retardation. Indeed, the number of children with mental retardation reported to have sleep problems has ranged from 34% (Clements, Wing, & Dunn, 1986) to over 80% (Barlett, Rooney, & Spedding, 1985). In a more recent longitudinal study, Quine (1991) found some type of sleep problem in children with mental handicaps. Sleep problems identified have included difficulty in going to bed, difficulty in settling and falling asleep, and difficulty remaining asleep. These sleep problems may lead to the child's poor daytime performance (Quine, 1991). An association between the daytime behaviors of self-injury and aggression has been suggested in children with mental retardation (Clements et al., 1986)

It should be strongly emphasized that whereas problematic behaviors have been described separately, it is often the case that behavior problems co-occur in the same individual with mental retardation. Hence, assessment practices should be comprehensive in determining the presence of *all* problematic behaviors.

ASSESSMENT METHODS

Diagnosis of Mental Retardation

Overall intellectual or cognitive functioning is assessed by the administration of standardized intelligence tests. A few commonly used intelligence tests employed with mentally retarded children include the Wechsler Preschool and Primary Scale of Intelligence—Revised (Wechsler, 1989) and Wechsler Intelligence Scale for Children (3rd ed., Wechsler, 1991); the Stanford–Binet Intelligence Scale (Thorndike, Hagen, & Sattler, 1986), McCarthy Scales of Children's Abilities (McCarthy, 1972), and the Bayley Scales of Infant Development–Second Edition (2nd ed., Bayley, 1993). In conjunction with the administration of an individual cognitive measure, an adaptive behavior instrument is also necessary. These include such tools as the AAMR Adaptive Behavior Scales–Revised (Lambert, Leland, & Nihira, 1992) and the Vineland Adaptive Behavior Scales (Sparrow, Balla, & Cicchetti, 1984). Additional instruments are often administered in conducting a comprehensive battery in the assessment of children to formulate the diagnosis of mental retardation. Typically, these involve the use of measures of academic achievement and other supplemental instruments to determine other specific abilities and weaknesses. For complete discussions on the assessment practices in the diagnosis of mental retardation, refer to Salvia and Ysseldyke (1985), Sattler (1988), and Anastasi (1988).

Behavior/Emotional Problems in Children/Adolescents With Mental Retardation

The development of appropriate assessment tools and practices of behavioral and emotional problems in children and adolescents with mental retardation lags far behind those for their normally developing counterparts. Nonetheless, recent interest in the valid and reliable assessment of behavioral problems in persons with mental retardation has greatly advanced and improved current practices (see reviews by Aman, 1991; Singh, Sood, Sonenklar, & Ellis, 1991). The empirical assessment of specific behavior and emotional problems should accomplish the following: describe the extent of the behaviors, identify the dimensions of the problematic behaviors, delineate variables associated with maladaptive behavior responding, determine the function or motivation of the behaviors in the child's environment, and direct treatment choices. For purpose of discussion, assessment methods are categorized as: interviews, informant behavior rating tools, self-report instruments, and direct observation methods. Also, most current assessment strategies incorporate multimethods and multisources in evaluating childhood behavior and emotional disorders.

Behavioral Interview

An intake interview is an initial step of the assessment process. The purpose of this interview is to gather specific information concerning behavior problems exhibited and the behaviors that will be a focus of behavioral treatment. In addition to obtaining an operational definition of "target" behaviors, eliciting possible information about possible antecedents and consequences of the problematic behaviors serves to initiate hypothesis formulation about the environmental influences of the behaviors. This information is also helpful in suggesting additional behavioral assessment procedures that will be most sensitive in measuring identified behavior problems. Other commonly obtained information during a behavioral intake interview is the trend of the behavior problems, and previous remedial approaches that have been carried out.

Informant Behavior Rating Scales

To supplement an interview, parents, other caregivers, and educators are often asked to complete behavior rating scales. Until recently, no standardized, psychometrically sound measures were developed specifically for individuals with mental retardation. For children and adolescents within the mild range of mental retardation, the use of behavior rating scales developed for normally developing children has proven useful. Commonly employed instruments include the Child Behavior Checklist (CBCL; Achenbach & Edelbrock, 1991), The Preschool Behavior Questionnaire (Behar & Stringfield, 1974), and the Conners' Rating Scales (teacher and parent versions) (Conners, 1989). However, these measures may be inappropriate and insensitive in the assessment of children and adolescents with more severe levels of mental retardation. A recent adaption of the CBCL is the Developmental Behavior Checklist (DBC; Einfeld & Tonge, 1989). Similar in format to the CBCL, the DBC includes items more specific to those children with mental retardation and other disabilities. The six subscales on this measure are labeled disruptive, self-absorbed, language deviance, anxiety, autistic relating, and antisocial.

One of the first psychometrically sound instruments developed solely for persons with mental retardation is the Aberrant Behavior Checklist (ABC; Aman & Singh, 1986). The five subscales on this measure are: irritability/agitation/crying; lethargy/social withdrawal; stereotypic behavior; hyperactivity/noncompliance; and inappropriate speech. The *Behavior Problem Inventory* (Rojahn, 1989) is another rating scale developed for use with individuals with mental retardation. It is narrow in scope in that it assesses only self-injurious behaviors, aggression, and stereotypical behaviors, but has specific utility in determining topographies and frequency of these behaviors. Moreover, the majority of the adaptive behavior instruments mentioned previously have a subdomain devoted to problematic or maladaptive behaviors that interfere with other areas of functioning. Although these rating tools may be helpful in initially determining problematic behaviors that warrant treatment, and may be sensitive to treatment change, they are not useful in hypothesizing the function of maladaptive behaviors in the child's repertoire.

Self-Report Instruments

Again, for those children and adolescents falling into the mild range of mental retardation, commonly used self-report instruments may be employed as part of multisource, multimethod assessment. Administration of self-informant tools such as the Child Depression Inventory (Kovacs, 1981), Children's Manifest Anxiety Scale (Reynolds & Richmond, 1978), and Self-Report Depression Questionnaire (Reynolds, 1989) have all been used with children and adolescents with mental retardation and may have value in the assessment process where an affective or anxiety disorder is suspected. The Psychopathology Instrument for Mentally Retarded Adolescents (Matson, 1988) has a self-report version appropriate for use with adolescents with mild and possibly moderate mental retardation. These self-report measures may supplement other assessments by providing insight to the individuals' internal states and perceptions about their problems.

Direct Observation

Direct behavioral observation has been the hallmark of behavioral assessment of disorders in childhood and in mental retardation. Behavioral observations may be classified as *naturalistic* and *analogue*. Naturalistic observations are those conducted in the child's environment. Analogue observations are those carried via simulations of some real-life situation. Common examples of naturalistic observations include observing a child in a the classroom or on a playground. Although these observations may provide valuable descriptive information regarding a child's problematic behavior, a functional analysis of the child's behavior may be conducted by evaluating behavioral antecedents and consequences.

The goal of a functional analysis is to identify environmental variables and stimuli that may be maintaining or controlling certain behavioral problems. Whereas applied behavior analysis has long adhered to the identification of antecedents and consequences of behavior (Baer, Wolf, & Risley, 1968), the technology of functional analysis has been greatly enhanced in recent years (Iwata, Dorsey, Slifer, Bauman, & Richman, 1982; Iwata, Vollmer, & Zarcone, 1990; Touchette, McDonald, & Langer, 1985). The essence of functional assessment observations is the systematic manipulation of variables in an analogue setting in order to develop hypotheses regarding the function of the behavior problem for that particular child or adolescent. The following are commonly used assessment conditions and procedures.

Social Attention. Following Iwata et al. (1982), this condition is designed to approximate a type of reinforcement contingency that may maintain an aberrant behavior. In the natural environment, many of the target behaviors already discussed usually attract much attention from caregivers, teachers, and peers. Verbal attention and expressions of pain and discomfort on the part of the parent may inadvertently maintain the behavior as a form of positive reinforcement.

Demand.   This session is designed to assess whether any of the target behaviors are maintained by negative reinforcement as a result of being allowed to escape or avoid demand situations (Iwata et al., 1982). Typically, in this condition, appropriate demands or requests are issued; the child is allowed to escape these contingent on the target behavior(s) of interest.

Toy Play.   This session serves as a control procedure for the presence of the parent, availability of potentially stimulating materials, absence of demands, delivery of social approval for appropriate behavior, and lack of attention to target behaviors (Iwata et al., 1982).

Alone.   This analogue condition serves to assess whether a behavior is maintained by automatic reinforcement (Iwata et al., 1982). In these sessions, the child is left in a room without stimulation/activities and receives no attention. Numerous variations of these procedures have been described in the literature. Despite the promise of conducting functional analogue observa- tions, there are shortcomings and risks involved. Obvious disadvantages involve the time commitment and needed manpower. Moreover, there is the risk of introducing a new contingency for the function of that behavior (Iwata et al., 1990). Finally, these procedures may lack sensitivity for behaviors that are being maintained by multiple, complex variables (Iwata et al., 1990). For these reasons, applying functional analysis principles in conducting naturalistic observations may be desirable. For example, in addition to simply recording the frequency and topography of aggressive behaviors, the recording of antecedent and consequent events may reveal patterns over time in order to develop hypotheses regarding the function a particular behavior. An example of an Antecedent–Behavior–Consequence Data Form used to record information about target behaviors is provided in Fig. 2.1.

More naturalistic analogue observations might also be conducted, such as observing par- ent–child interactions during free play, during clean-up, and mealtime, in a clinical setting. This type of observation allows for "controlled" but more naturalistic observations. Other types of analogue observations have included those with baited items to systematically assess a target behavior such as pica, fireplay, and other types of inappropriate and dangerous play. In these observations, stimuli or bait is placed in a room to assess the function of these behaviors, but in a safe environment.

TREATMENT/TRAINING PROCEDURES

Treatment approaches for behavior and emotional problems in children and adolescents have been derived primarily from the field of applied behavior analysis. An overview of applied behavior analysis is presented followed by specific treatment and training procedures. To avoid redundancy, general procedures are discussed, and their use with specific problem behaviors will be highlighted. It should be underscored here that it is often the case that treatment is usually composed of several different components and procedures. Finally, use of each procedure with specific target problems is examined with special attention directed to issues related to that problem.

Name_____

Date_____

Frequency Data Sheet

	Behavior	Behavior	Behavior	Behavior	Behavior	Staff Initials
Time						
Time						
Time						
Time						

Target Behavior Definitions

1._____ - _____

2._____ - _____

3._____ - _____

Record with the following

Mark a "1" for each occurrence of the behavior

FIG. 2.1. An antecedent–behavior–consequence data form.

Applied Behavior Analysis

As discussed previously, assessment and treatment of behavior problems in children and adolescents with mental retardation have relied heavily on procedures developed from applied behavior analysis. The last 25 years have brought a burgeoning of evaluative efforts to better refine behavioral treatments (Favell & Reid, 1988). Recently, there have been many promising developments in the innovative behavioral treatments for behavior problems in children and adolescents with mental retardation. These approaches are alternatives or adjuncts to an earlier reliance on consequence management strategies which often involved the use of mild punishments and the contingent presentation of aversive stimuli. Although it is not the intention to provide an in-depth discussion here of the controversy surrounding the use of aversives and punishment procedures with the developmentally disabled (for representative reviews, see Evans & Meyer, 1985; Horner et al., 1990; Lavigna & Donnellan, 1986; Matson & Taras, 1989; Mulick, 1990), there is a strong movement toward the use of other, alternative approaches to promote behavior change.

The least intrusive methods along with alternative approaches that are typically multicomponent strategies are reviewed first. Closely tied to the development of many of these alternative treatments has been the enhanced behavioral assessment methods that now include the functional analysis procedures described earlier. Interventions may be developed that are based on hypotheses derived from the functional analysis. The use of punishment procedures is then addressed.

Selecting Reinforcers

Key to the effective use of reinforcement is an assessment of reinforcers for a particular individual. A common manner in conducting an assessment of reinforcers is to either question the children or adolescents and their caregivers about preferred items or activities. The completion of a reinforcer inventory is also a customary approach. More sophisticated approaches to reinforcement assessment have been described in Mason, McGee, Farmer-Dougan, and Risley (1989) and Pace, Ivancic, Edwards, Iwata, and Page (1985). These have involved the systematic presentation of numerous stimuli (potential reinforcers) and the assessment of the individual's response (i.e., approach or avoidance). A stimuli is labeled a potential reinforcer if the children or adolescents consistently approach it. At an even finer level of selecting reinforcers, the contingent presentation of various stimuli after an already occurring behavior in the children or adolescents is conducted. For example, the comparative reinforcing value of bubbles versus a rattle may be made by determining which of two behaviors (a wave vs. a smile) increases after the potential reinforcers are introduced contingent on chosen target behaviors.

Use of Positive Reinforcement

Based on the assumption of accurate reinforcement choices, the rate of presenting reinforcement contingent on a behavior to be increased should be based on current rate of the behavior. In treating behavior problems, it may be the case that a continuous reinforcement schedule is initially used. For example, the child is reinforced for every worksheet completed. When compliance is consistently obtained, the schedule is faded slowly and systematically so that maybe every 3 to 5 worksheets are completed before reinforcement is provided. Whereas the final goal is to provide a reinforcement schedule consistent with the child's natural environment, straining the reinforcement schedule too quickly is likely to result in the lack of behavioral maintenance. Use of an array of reinforcers has also been suggested (Charlop, Kurtz, & Casey, 1990; Dyer, 1987).

Contingency Management Systems

Reinforcement systems, often referred to as *token economies*, contingency *management systems*, and *point systems*, have been successfully implemented to improve various types of behaviors with children and adolescents in numerous settings (Kistner, Hammer, D. Wolfe,

Rothblum, & Drabman, 1982; V. V. Wolfe, Boyd, & D. A. Wolfe, 1983). The mainstay of the these motivational systems is the delivery of tokens, points, or "stars" contingent on discrete, observable behavior. Accumulated tokens or points may be "cashed in" at a later time for tangible reinforcers or privileges. Loss of points, a response cost, is commonly included in the program for which points are removed contingent on specific, problematic behaviors (e.g., aggression). The point ratio should be set to maximize learning of contingencies operating and to ensure some success soon after implementation. For younger children, use of "stars" or stickers in lieu of points or tokens is the norm. For children of lower developmental levels, more frequent "cash in" times may be necessary. Since the earlier reports, design and implementation of token economies (e.g., point systems, star cards) have been widely instituted in schools and homes for the treatment of problematic behaviors in normally developing children, and children and adolescents with mental retardation. An example of a simple "star card" that is appropriate for use with children with mental retardation is provided in Fig. 2.2. The rate of the delivery of stars may be varied (e.g., every 3–5 minutes) and more boxes may be added to the card before the child earns the back-up reinforcer.

Differential Reinforcement Schedules

Differential reinforcement of other behaviors (DRO) is the less intrusive reductive method that has proven to be effective in decreasing maladaptive behaviors that include aggression and self-injury (Frankel, Moss, Schofield, & Simmons, 1976; Wong, Floyd, Innocent, & Woolsey, 1991), disruptive classroom behavior (Deitz, 1977), and inattentive behavior (Luiselli, Colozzi, & O'Toole, 1980). Variations of this procedure have also been successful, such as differential reinforcement of incompatible behaviors (DRI) and differential reinforcement of low rates (DRL). To illustrate, a DRI schedule was used to treat pica where the incompatible behavior was gum chewing (Donnelly & Olczak, 1990).

_____ 's Classroom Star Card

Completes work	Listen to teacher	Keep hands to self

Things to earn when my card is full:

_____   _____

_____   _____

FIG. 2.2. A star card.

Differential reinforcement schedules may be *whole interval,* or *momentary.* Whole interval DRO refers to the delivery reinforcement for the occurrence of "other" behaviors for the full duration of the time interval (e.g., 2 minutes). If delivery of reinforcement is provided when an "other" behavior (and not the target behavior) is occurring at the end of the time interval (e.g., at the second minute), this is referred to as momentary DRO (Sulzer-Azaroff & Mayer, 1991). Although Repp, Barton, and Brulle (1983) demonstrated the superior effect of whole interval differential reinforcement, this may be difficult to implement consistently on an inpatient unit. Of interest is that momentary differential reinforcement has been shown to be more effective if preceded by a whole interval approach (Barton, Brulle, & Repp, 1986). Hence, it may be advisable to first consider a whole interval approach but quickly revise to a momentary approach once acceptable decreases in the target behavior have been observed. Another consideration in using differential reinforcement is the rate or schedule that reinforcers will be delivered. This rate should be individualized and based on the frequency of appropriate and inappropriate behaviors observed during baseline with an initial, obtainable goal set. Examples of "other" or "incompatible" behaviors should be made explicit so that appropriate behaviors are reinforced. A timer is often used to implement a DRO schedule. As progress is made, reinforcement should be systematically faded to more closely approximate the schedule that will realistically be applied in the child's natural environment.

Extinction

Extinction refers to the withholding of reinforcement of a behavior that has previously been reinforced. The effectiveness of extinction in reducing or eliminating a problematic behavior is clearly documented (Brown & Elliot, 1965; Rincover, 1978; Williams, 1959; M. M. Wolf, Risely, & Meese, 1964). Extinction is rarely used in isolation and is most commonly implemented in conjunction with a differential reinforcement schedule. These methods taken together are often referred to as *systematic attention/planned ignoring.* Behaviors to be placed on extinction should be those that are nonharmful to others, can be consistently ignored, and where there is strong evidence from assessment results that the behavior is motivated and has been maintained by attention. Those responsible in the implementation should be reminded of the likelihood of an extinction "burst" before the target behavior decreases. Parents, educators, and other paraprofessionals commonly interpret the use of extinction as "not doing anything," and consequently a continued emphasis that extinction is a legitimate behavioral treatment for some target behaviors may be necessary. If extinction does not result in reduction in the target behavior, the therapist responsible for the development of behavioral treatment should closely observe the implementation to ensure that inadvertent attention is not being given to the child in response to the behavior.

Response Interruption/Blocking

This procedure precludes the maladaptive behavior response from occurring or interrupts the behavior when it begins to occur. The interruption or blocking may entail a physical block of another person (standing in front of a peer to block aggression), physical shadowing the person's arms and hands (e.g., interrupt hand biting, hairpulling), or using some other device to block the response (e.g., use of a foam pad to block headbanging against a hard surface). Response interruption or blocking should be considered when it is inappropriate to place a behavior on extinction but the behavior does not warrant treatment with more intrusive procedures.

Antecedent Management Strategies

Antecedent management strategies refer to approaches that alter the environment either by modifying it or by adding antecedents that decrease the probability that the behavior problem will occur (Horner et al., 1990). Antecedent strategies that have resulted in decreased behavior problems have included such manipulations as providing more preferred toys in the child's environment (Madden, Russo, & Cataldo, 1980); teaching children to play with toys (Santarcangelo, Dyer, & Luce, 1987); changes to a daily, routine schedule (Brown, 1991); allowing children to have a choice in both task and reinforcer selection; varying presentation of tasks and requests (Dyer, Dunlap, Winterling, 1990; Horner, Day, Sprague, O'Brien, & Heathfield, 1991; Winterling, Dunlap, & O'Neill, 1987); and redesigning the physical environment (Duker & Rasing, 1989). Another interesting antecedent approach is the use of physical exercise. Several single case studies have demonstrated a decrease in maladaptive behaviors in response to participation in an aerobic exercise program (Baumeister & MacLean, 1984; Kern, Koegel, Dyer, Blew, & Fenton, 1982; McGimsey & Favell, 1988). Although the specific exercise programs and the target subjects have varied, treated behaviors included stereotypies, self-injury, aggression, and negative vocalization. Similarly, participation in relaxation training has been successful in decreasing problematic behaviors in individuals with mental retardation (Calamari, Geist, & Shahbazian, 1987; McPhail & Chamove, 1989). A useful resource for conducting relaxation training with children and adolescent with mental retardation is provided by Cautela and Groden (1978).

This area is quite promising, although to date, strategies falling into this category have included small numbers with less severe behaviors than are likely to be seen in treating many children and adolescents with mental retardation. Whereas a first step in approaching all maladaptive problems should include considering altering antecedents that might at least add to the likelihood of the occurrence of the behavior, this will probably be in conjunction with other treatments. To summarize, antecedent considerations should include level of stimulation (overstimulation and understimulation may contribute to problem behaviors), physiological status (hunger, fatigue, physical illness), structural and environmental factors, introduction of choice in the routine, and adherence to daily routine.

Functional Equivalence Training

The premise of treatments that fall under this domain is the functional replacement of the aberrant behavior with a socially appropriate behavior. In other words, the goal of treatment is to teach an alternative, more adaptive behavior that will serve the same function for the individual. The most common use of this approach has been the teaching of a communicative behavior (verbal or manual sign) to request a preferred activity, to end an activity, or to obtain assistance or attention (Carr & Durand, 1985; Durand & Carr, 1991; Horner, Sprague, O'Brien, & Heathfield, 1990). The teaching of a replacement behavior is thought to be effective because this alternative behavior is less effortful and more efficient in achieving the same goal

(Horner & Day, 1991). This approach has been successful in the treatment of aggression, self-injury, and destructive behaviors.

Steps in using treatment based on this paradigm are outlined here:

1.   Following a functional assessment and a determination of the function of the problem behavior, a replacement behavior is chosen.

2.   On the premise that the behavior serves to escape a demand, a replacement behavior may be teaching the child or adolescent to sign "finish." If the behavior is determined to be used to gain the attention of a preferred teacher's aide, teaching the child to say "help please" would be an appropriate replacement behavior.

3.   The training of these replacement behaviors may initially take place out of the setting where the problem behavior is likely to occur.

4.   Once the children or adolescents have in their repertoire the chosen replacement behavior, it will be exhibited in the target setting by either prompting the children to use it while placing the maladaptive behavior on extinction or blocking the maladaptive behavior.

5.   When the children are consistently using the replacement behavior in lieu of the maladaptive behavior, the addition of requests (in the case of a demand situation), or increasing delay for a response (in the case of receiving assistance), these should systematically be added with reinforcement for the absence of the maladaptive behavior and/or compliance with the demand. (For a more thorough discussion of treatment options and procedures using these interventions, see Carr et al., 1994.)

Discrimination/Rule Training

The premise of discrimination training in treating problem behaviors is that an inappropriate behavioral response is occurring in the presence of a particular set of stimuli. Variations of discrimination training have been used in the treatment of pica, firesetting, and other dangerous behaviors, whereby different discriminations are taught (i.e., what stimuli to touch and not to touch, what stimuli to put in the mouth and not put in the mouth) and then an appropriate behavior response is reinforced. Specific examples are discussed in the individual behaviors section later in the chapter.

PUNISHMENT PROCEDURES

Timeout

A commonly employed behavioral intervention is timeout from positive reinforcement. This mild punishment procedure has been successfully used to reduce an array of behaviors from mild to extremely severe behavior problems (Bostow & Bailey, 1969; Mace, Page, Ivancic, & O'Brien, 1986), despite ongoing controversy over its use (Foxx & Shapiro, 1978). There are several variations of timeout that have been carried out, ranging from the least restrictive (nonexclusionary timeout) to more restrictive (exclusionary) to the most restrictive (seclusionary timeout). Nonexclusionary timeout refers to moving children away from a group or situation, although they remain in view of the group or activity (Porterfield, Herbert-Jackson, & Risely, 1976). A variation of this form of time out was used by Foxx and Shapiro (1978). In their investigation, children with ribbons in a classroom received edible reinforcers. Contingent on misbehavior, a child's ribbon was removed and the delivery of reinforcement was withheld. This nonexclusionary timeout procedure drastically reduced classroom behavior problems. Variations of this procedure include "time in" bows, baseball hats, and special "jewelry" to apply the same principles.

Use of exclusionary time out includes removal of the child to an area, such as a timeout room (Wilson, Robertson, Herlong, & Haynes, 1979; M. M. Wolf, Risely, Johnson, Harris, & Allen, 1967) or a corner (Olson & Roberts, 1987), away from the group. However, caution should be used when deciding on such a treatment procedure. A functional analysis of the behavior should have demonstrated that the child's behavior is not motivated by escape (i.e., the desire to get out of the situation or demand). Otherwise, timeout could be reinforcing and therefore increase the behavior it is intended to decrease. Parameters in the use of a seclusionary timeout should be clearly delineated to prevent it being abused. Operational definitions of the behavioral response(s) for use of seclusionary timeout and length of time secluded should be clearly specified.

Restitution Overcorrection

This punishment technique has been extensively used to suppress numerous maladaptive behaviors, including pica (Foxx & Martin, 1975; Singh & Bakker, 1984), aggression, and disruption (Ollendick & Matson, 1978). Contingent on the target behavior, the individual is required to "overcorrect" the effects of the behavior and also may include the practice of an appropriate behavior. In developing an overcorrection procedure for a particular behavior, Foxx (1982) advised that it must be related to the target behavior. Moreover, it needs to be implemented swiftly. A fuller account of the use of overcorrection is provided by Azrin and Besalel (1980).

As with all other behavioral procedures, overcorrection procedural steps should be clearly delineated in a behavioral protocol. In training parents and staff, modeling of the overcorrection procedure is essential in ensuring the integrity of the procedure. It should be remembered that rarely should overcorrection be used in isolation. If overcorrection is necessary for behavioral change, reinforcement procedures to strengthen other behaviors should be implemented simultaneously.

Positive Practice Overcorrection

In implementing this intervention procedure, the child or adolescent is required to engage in a behavior, often repeatedly, which is incompatible with the target behavior. Positive reinforcement is provided for compliance to complete the steps of the positive practice procedure.

Negative Practice

In this less-often-used reductive behavior procedure, the child or adolescent is instructed to engage repeatedly in the identified maladaptive behavior. Obviously, the behavior to be repeated should not be dangerous in any way.

Contingent Exercise

Similar to overcorrection, contingent exercise is a mild punishment procedure in which the patient is asked to perform a specified physically effortful exercise contingent on occurrence of the target behavior. This procedure has been effective in reducing verbal and aggressive behaviors in children diagnosed as seriously emotionally disturbed (Luce, Delquadri, & Hall, 1980).

Behavioral Physical Restraint

As evident from the name, this procedure involves the brief restraint or immobilization of a patient's limbs (e.g., hands held to the side or on flat surface) or body for a prespecified time period contingent on the occurrence of the target behavior. Use of a physical restraint procedure has been effective in decreasing pica (Bucher, Reykdal, & Albin, 1976), tantrums (Swerissen & Carruthers, 1987), and self-injury (Favell, McGimsey, & Jones, 1978).

Use of Aversive Stimuli

The contingent presentation of an aversive stimulus as a punisher of a specified behavior as a treatment has raised many ethical and humanitarian issues, particularly in children and individuals with developmental disabilities (see LaVigna & Donnellan, 1986; Matson & DiLorenzo, 1984; Matson & Taras, 1989). Nonetheless, empirical data show that such approaches may be effective in reducing or suppressing severe behavior problems. Some aversive stimuli that have been applied contingently include water mist (Dorsey, Iwata, Ong, & McSween, 1980), aromatic ammonia (Baumeister & Baumeister, 1978; Rojahn, McGonigle, Curcio, & Dixon, 1987), lemon juice (Sajwaj, Libet, & Agras, 1974), and contingent electrical shock (Foxx, McMorrow, Bittle, & Bechtel, 1986; Linscheid, Iwata, Ricketts, Williams, & Griffin, 1990). Subjects in these studies were either mentally retarded or psychotic (Tate & Baroff, 1966) and evinced severe behavior problems. It is not the intention of this chapter to promote in any way the use of aversive stimuli. However, given the equivocal view among experts in the field, the use of these procedures deserves mention.

Despite the fact that aversive treatment is never a first choice or used in isolation, its use may be appropriate in certain situations and under certain conditions. These include: documentation that the maladaptive behavior is a serious threat to others or the child; minimal effect of other treatments that have been consistently tried; the behavior precludes the child from participating in activities essential for development; and the child is being managed only by the use of either chemical or physical restraint (see Foxx, Plaska, & Bittle, 1986; Martin, 1975). The chapter strongly advocates the recommendation by Lovaas and Favell (1987) that such techniques be implemented only under the supervision of a trained and experienced professional in the use of aversives. Similarly, procedural safeguards (see Matson & Kazdin, 1981) should be closely adhered to, and informed consent should be obtained.

OTHER TREATMENT APPROACHES TO BE CONSIDERED

Self-Control/Self-Regulation/Self-Management Training

Procedures falling under this category share behavioral components but are unique in the focus on more reliance on internal control versus external controls. These procedures assume some level of self-awareness and ability to self-observe. *Self-control techniques,* as described for children, typically incorporate any or all of the following components: self-monitoring, self-instruction training, cognitive modeling, role playing, self-evaluation, and self-reinforcement (Kendall, 1984; Meichenbaum & Goodman, 1971).

Self-monitoring simply refers to the monitoring of one's own behavior. Despite the reactive nature of self-monitoring, this strategy should be considered as an option when children or adolescents with mental retardation have the ability to observe their own behavior and have a means of communication to record this.

The impetus and rationale for *self-instructional training* evolved from the work of Luria (1961), who proposed three stages by which behavior comes under the control of covert speech. Briefly stated, this theory asserts a developmental sequence by which behavior is initially governed by the speech of others; however, after employing overt speech as a behavior regulator, covert speech assumes a self-control function. Hence, the assumption is that children and adolescents with mental retardation and who present with such behaviors as aggression, overactivity, and distractibility, may lack verbal mediation skills or use verbal mediation in an ineffective manner. The goal of self-instructional training is thus to either teach verbal mediation skills or to remediate faulty existing covert speech. The typical sequential steps for the self-instructional procedure include the following: therapist models task performance while talking out loud—Cognitive Modeling; child performs the task while instructing himself out loud—Overt Self-Guidance; therapist models task performance while whispering to himself—Faded Overt Modeling; child performs the task while whispering to himself—Faded Overt Self-Guidance; therapist performs the task using covert self-instruction with pauses and behavioral gestures of thinking (e.g., stroking chin, raising eyes toward ceiling)—Covert Modeling; the child performs the task using covert self-instruction—Covert Self-Instruction (Kendall & Finch, 1978; Meichenbaum & Goodman, 1971). The specific content of the self-instruction typically includes a problem identification statement, a problem approach statement, a statement to focus attention, and a self-evaluation and reinforcement statement when applicable (Kendall & Braswell, 1982; Kendall & Finch, 1978).

Burgio, Whitman, and Johnson (1980) successfully used this type of sequence to increase on-task behavior in five children with mental retardation. In training the use of self-instruction steps, social reinforcement was issued contingent on correct responding. An added component of the training provided in this study was the use of a "distraction-inoculator" procedure whereby extraneous stimuli where introduced, and the subjects were trained to ignore distractions by making self-statements. Again, necessary prerequisite skills must be assessed in individual children before embarking on this type of treatment approach.

Special Treatment Considerations for Behavior Problems

Aggression/Property Destruction.   The severity and intensity of aggression and property destruction must be taken into consideration when developing treatment. For aggression or property destruction that is only mild and exhibited by a younger, smaller child, a very different approach might be taken than when treating aggression in large adolescents with a long-standing history of intense aggressive behaviors. In both cases, a functional assessment should be conducted before making treatment decisions.

Self-Injury.   As with aggression and property destruction, the approach with self-injurious behaviors is dependent on several variables, including the intensity, the potential for damage or injury, the different topographies of the self-injurious, and, of course, the assessment function of the behavior(s). As mentioned earlier, the training of a communicative response to replace the self-injurious behavior has resulted in impressive decreases in this maladaptive behavior. When the self-injury is determined to be maintained by negative reinforcement (used to escape or avoid a task or situation), the training of a replacement behavior may be saying "I done," or manual signing "finish." Choice of the replacement behavior should be made based on the child's cognitive and language skills. Similarly, if the self-injury is being maintained by social attention, teaching the child to gain attention by another means would be an effective treatment choice. Again, this could be to verbalize a brief statement, use of a manual sign, or shaking a bell. Allowing a child to escape a particular situation or gain attention immediately may not be accepted by parents and other caregivers. Hence, it should be explained that once decreases in self-injury are consistently noted, either demands will be added before escape is allowed, or there will be a delay in time before attention is delivered. The use of functional communication training is likely to be most effective when a component of other treatment approaches. This could include a differential reinforcement for incompatible behavior (i.e., reinforcing using the hands to complete a prevocational task in lieu of hand-biting). When self-injury remains severe despite the use of alternative approaches, employment of a punishment procedure is a consideration. This may involve the use of a brief hand restraint contingent on engaging in hand-biting.

A special consideration in the treatment of self-injury is the use of protective devices such as helmets, arm splints, and protective gloves. Although protective equipment may be indicated in some cases of children with self-injury, extreme caution is warranted in their use for several reasons. First, in some cases where protective equipment prevents one self-injurious response, the result is that the child engages in another more serious or difficult to treat behavior. Second, the child may become dependent on the device in the absence of learning an alternative behavior. Finally, the wearing of protective equipment is stigmatizing. For the therapist treating a child with severe, long-standing self-injurious behavior, eliciting consultation from a colleague with expertise in this area is strongly advised.

Stereotypical/Self-Stimulatory Behavior.   The decision to treat stereotypical behavior should be carefully deliberated. When the decision is made to treat stereotypes due to their disruptive nature, a functional assessment of possible environmental contingencies contributing to the behaviors is needed. As discussed earlier, it highly probable that the behavior is motivated by internal variables. Hence, typical treatment approaches may be antecedent approaches (maintaining certain level of stimulation) while choosing other appropriate functionally derived treatments if the self-stimulatory behaviors are also maintained by other factors (such as social attention).

Pica.   Treatment choices should be made after assessing the function of pica behavior. Once medical causes have been ruled out, and hunger is not a factor, a first line of intervention is the antecedent management strategy of ensuring the appropriate level of stimulation (Madden et al.,

1980). A differential reinforcement schedule for the absence of pica behavior should also be an initial treatment consideration. If in fact, the child or adolescent appears not to discriminate food items from those that are inedible, some form of discrimination training is required. In children and adolescents with mild mental retardation, this may simply be conducting teaching trials of what you do not put in your mouth. When the children respond correctly, they should be reinforced. For lower functioning children, the teaching of a different discrimination rule may be warranted. (e.g., teaching them to eat only from a certain place). A detailed illustration of this type of training is provided later in Case Illustration 2.

Oppositional/Noncompliant Behavior.   Methods for increasing compliance include reinforcing compliance, issuing the request a second time with an additional prompt for noncompliance after the first request, and then imposing a consequence if the child fails to comply (Forehand & McMahon, 1981; Parrish, Cataldo, Kolko, Neef, & Egel, 1986). The consequence for noncompliance could be a timeout procedure or the use of physical prompting to gain compliance. This sequence of steps is often collectively referred to as *compliance training*. Interspersing commands or requests that are likely to be followed with those less likely to be followed has also been demonstrated to increase the overall rate of compliance. In combination, the use of a contingency management system whereby specific daily tasks and chores are reinforced for their completion may be implemented.

Attention Deficits/Hyperactivity.   Children and adolescents who meet criteria for Attention Deficit Hyperactivity Disorder (APA, 1994) present with a number of behavioral features that may be the focus of nonpharmacological treatment. Typically contingency management systems (token economies, point systems) have been utilized to reinforce on-task behaviors, work completion, and work accuracy. These reinforcement systems may also target other behavioral problems in children with attention problems and high activity level, including noncompliance and aggression. Measures to decrease extraneous stimuli that might be distracting should be an antecedent approach to be considered. Similarly, use of a structured, consistent routine is a common strategy with ADHD symptoms.

Tantrums.   The constellation of tantrum behaviors are most often treated with a combination of a differential reinforcement schedule of other, appropriate behaviors and extinction of the tantrum itself. In prescribing the use of extinction or "planned ignoring," as part of a treatment strategy to decrease the frequency and duration of tantrums, those adults responsible for implementing treatment should be well apprised of the likelihood of the "extinction burst." Another approach has been to use negative practice, in which the child is instructed to engage in tantrumming behaviors at scheduled times (citations).

Feeding/Mealtime Problems.   The employment of an array of behavior procedures have been successfully employed to treat mild to severe feeding and mealtime problems. Most treatments have again involved multiple elements with the use of positive reinforcement of some target eating response. For food refusal and food selectivity, the reinforcement of the acceptance of food in general or of select food types or textures is a typical starting point in treatment. Specifically, reinforcement is contingent on the acceptance and swallowing of the target food item. This may be in combination with the extinction of disruptive mealtime behavior. For children whose food intake is inadequate, the reinforcement of a specific amount of food is appropriate. This "clean plate" contingency may be devised whereby the child receives reinforcement initially for eating all food on a plate with only small portions. The amount of food may gradually be increased until an appropriate meal is consumed before the delivery of reinforcement. Punishment procedures, such as overcorrection, may be a consequence of inappropriate mealtime behaviors (i.e., throwing food, throwing utensils) whereby the child is made to correct the environment.

Elimination/Toileting Problems. Common first line strategies for addressing toileting problems have been the implementation of a consistent toileting schedule (e.g., every 30 minutes) along with the use of positive reinforcement for successful voids and bowel movements. A simple restitution or overcorrection procedure may also be used. This typically involves having the child participate in all or a portion of the cleaning following an enuretic or encopretic incident. When these interventions are unsuccessful, and for individuals that are more resistant to the common steps in toilet training, Foxx and Azrin (1973) described intensive bladder and toilet training procedures. These procedures involve the following training sequence: giving as much liquid as the child or adolescent will take, having the child sit on the toilet soon after the liquid intake, having the child sit on the toilet for an extended period of time, conducting dry pants checks every 5 minutes with reinforcement delivered for dry pants, and delivering reinforcement for both staying dry in between toileting and for successful voids and bowel movements. Use of overcorrection for accidents might also be added to treatment. Depending on the age and skills of the child, this might involve placing responsibility for cleaning up, washing out soiled clothes, and other aspects of cleaning with the child.

Sleep and Bedtime Problems. Despite the wide acknowledgment that sleep problems are quite common in children with mental retardation, few intervention studies have been conducted. For bedtime problems, general treatment recommendations include: establishing consistent bedtime routine, using reinforcement for appropriate behavior, and systematically using extinction for behavior problems (e.g., tantrums, crying). A "graduated" extinction procedure has been successfully used to treat bedtime tantrums (Adams & Rickert, 1989). In this adapted use of extinction, the parent enters the bedroom of the child to ensure the child's safety on a regular schedule (e.g., every 10 minutes) and interacts with the child minimally. Hence, the adult's attention is not contingent on the child's behavior but on the time interval. An innovative approach used on four children with profound mental retardation and severe sleep problems (e.g., delay sleep onset, night waking, early morning waking, and disruptive bedtime behaviors) involved: setting a bedtime based on information about when the children fell asleep, and removing the children from the bed for 1 hour if they had not fallen asleep within 15 minutes (Piazza & Fisher, 1991). If the children fell asleep, their bedtime was made 30 minutes earlier the next night. Conversely, the child was put to bed 30 minutes later if sleep onset did not occur within the 15 minute time period.

MAINTENANCE AND GENERALIZATION STRATEGIES

The issues of maintenance and generalization of behavioral change to different settings have proven problematic in individuals with mental retardation. Because of the failure for change to generalize beyond the treatment setting, and with the specific change agent in that setting, maintenance in real-world settings may be jeopardized. Whereas clinical researchers initially directed minimal attention to the problem of maintenance, the essential need in programming for the maintenance and generalization is well accepted. Specific strategies to promote maintenance and generalization have been suggested. These include systematic fading of reinforcement to a schedule that is more likely to be maintained, use of reinforcers readily available in the child environment, utilization of multiple trainers in the implementation of treatment procedures, training in multiple settings in which treatment is implemented, use of a functional equivalence approach whenever possible, and employment of self-control or self-management procedures to decrease reliance on external control whenever appropriate.

PROBLEMS IN IMPLEMENTATION

As may be apparent from the discussion of the aforementioned interventions, treatment of many behavior problems in children and adolescents with mental retardation involves considerable individual time to train particular responses. Hence, accessing the necessary intensive services may be problematic or altogether unrealistic, depending on available resources and supports.

Moreover, a unique factor in the treatment of children and adolescents is that it is often the parent(s) who is targeted as the change agent. This is even more so the case when treating behavior problems in children and adolescents with mental retardation. In many cases, children and adolescents with mental retardation may reside in an alternative placement (group home, residential setting) where the change agent may also be staff members. Consequently, treatment involves training caregivers in the previous procedures for implementation in their respective settings. Training parents, staff, and teachers brings about special problems and considerations. First, therapists, are essentially training someone else to be a therapist. The following suggestions are offered for providing parent and staff training:

1. Develop operational definitions of each target behavior to be treated to ensure all adults responsible for treatment are addressing the same behavior problem (e.g., What does "aggression" entail for a particular child?).
2. Adults should be trained in the use of a data/record keeping system in order to evaluate the effectiveness of the treatment procedures.
3. The acceptability of the treatment protocols should be determined in order to promote compliance. This may be done informally by inquiring about the adult's reactions to a suggested procedure. There are also treatment acceptability measures (see Kazdin, 1980; Miltenberger, Suda, Lennox, & Lindeman, 1991) that may be helpful in assessing views of different behavior procedures.
4. Direct observation of the implementation of the procedures should be a priority. This may be achieved while conducting in vivo observations. Role playing may also have value in determining competency in implementing specific procedures.

CASE ILLUSTRATION

The two cases discussed illustrate the treatment of a young child with mild mental retardation and an older adolescent with profound mental retardation.

Case 1

Edward was a 9-year-old male diagnosed with mild mental retardation and cerebral palsy. Although ambulatory, Edward relied on the use of a wheelchair for distances of any length. Edward was admitted to a behaviorally oriented psychiatric inpatient unit for aggression, tantrums, and noncompliance. Functional assessments indicated that Edward's aggression and tantrums were motivated by escape/negative reinforcement (i.e., the removal of a peer from the area around his wheelchair, and in academic demand situations when he was fatigued). A functionally equivalent response was trained whereby Edward was taught to hold up a stop sign with a bell attached when he wanted a peer to be removed from his space and when he wished to cease an academic activity. The bell was used so that those adults present would become quickly aware of Edward when he held up the stop sign. This procedure was deemed effective based on the decrease in effort on Edward's part in communicating given his labored, inarticulate speech. Use of functional equivalence training was in combination with a "star card" system in which Edward received stars for the completion of work, absence of aggression, and following adult requests. Additionally, the interspersal of academic tasks to minimize fatigue and frustration resulted in increased compliance and a concomitant decrease in inappropriate behaviors.

Case 2

Walt was a 15-year-old male with diagnoses of profound mental retardation, pica, and Class II plumbism (severe lead poisoning). Walt had three prior hospitalizations for lead poisoning. X-rays provided evidence that Walt had consumed staples, paperclips, and paint chips. Though essentially nonverbal, Walt used several manual signs appropriately, including "eat," "drink," and "toilet."

Observations of Walt's baseline rates of pica were made in three settings in the hospital (dining room, group activity room, and alone in an individual therapy room) under analogue conditions (settings were baited with "pica items"). Walt engaged in pica behaviors 35% of interval during baseline. The treatment package involved reinforcement, discrimination training, functional equivalence training, and punishment components. Walt was taught to eat only food from a placemat, taught to sign "eat" to have more food, reinforced for eating from the placemat, and punished for putting any other inedible or inappropriate food items in his mouth. Hence, the discriminative stimulus to eat was the placemat and Walt was also provided with a functional equivalent response to gain access to what he wanted (more food). Verbal praise was provided contingent on eating from the placemat and the use of a face-wipe was the punishment implemented contingent on pica behavior. As shown in Fig. 2.3, the multicomponent treatment package resulted in substantial decreases in pica behavior.

Maintenance of treatment effects promoted by providing Walt's parents, siblings, and school staff with simple written descriptions and demonstrations of the treatment procedures. During follow-up visits, decreases in the home and school were maintained.

CONCLUSIONS

Children and adolescents with mental retardation by definition present with intellectual and adaptive behavior deficits of varying degrees. Behavior and emotional disorders in these individuals are two to five times that of their normally developing peers (Matson & Frame,

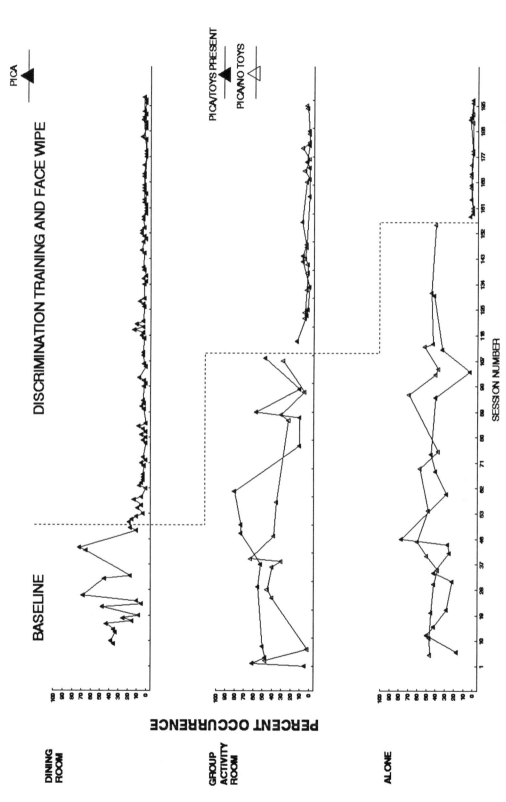

FIG. 2.3. Percentage occurrence of pica for Case 1 across setting. From Johnson, Hunt, and Siebert (1994). Copyright 1994 by Sage Publications. Reprinted with permission.

1986). Problematic behaviors described have been successfully treated with interventions primarily derived from the field of applied behavior analysis. Treating children and adolescents with mental retardation (and concomitant with behavior and emotional problems) can prove to be challenging and rewarding. Decreases in behavioral excesses (aggression, tantrums) with simultaneous increases in behavioral deficits (elimination problems) may lead to improvement in adaptive behavior, greater participation in integrative community activities, and improved family functioning.

Treatment approaches are likely to include multiple components with behavioral treatment protocols addressing more than one problem. Treatment should be approached in a systematic fashion to include a functional assessment of target behavior problems and inclusion of all significant caregivers. In developing and implementing treatment protocols, the acceptability of treatments by those actually implementing them (parents, group home staff) should be determined. Moreover, an evaluation plan to clearly determine the effects of the treatment protocols should be developed. Only with ongoing assessment can the achievement of treatment goals be evaluated. Conversely, the lack of treatment response should then lead to modification in treatments being implemented.

REFERENCES

Achenbach, T. M., & Edelbrock, C. S. (1991). *The Child Behavior Checklist.* Burlington: University of Vermont Department of Psychiatry.

Adams, L. A., & Rickert, V. I. (1989). Reducing bedtime tantrums: Comparison between positive routines and graduated extinction. *Pediatrics, 84,* 756–761.

Aman, M. G. (1991). *Assessing psychopathology and behavior problems in persons with mental retardation: A review of available instruments.* Rockville, MD: U.S. Department of Health and Human Services.

Aman, M. G., & Singh, N. N. (1986). *Aberrant Behavior Checklist: Manual.* East Aurora, NY: Slosson Educational Publications.

American Association on Mental Retardation. (Eds.). (1992). Diagnosis and systems of support. *Mental retardation: Definition, classification, and systems of support* (9th ed., pp. 23–34). Washington, DC: American Association on Mental Retardation.

American Psychiatric Association. (Eds.). (1994). Mental retardation. *In Diagnostic and statistical manual of mental disorders* (4th ed., pp. 39–46). Washington, DC: Author.

Anastasi, A. (1988). *Psychological testing* (6th ed.). New York: MacMillian.

Ausman, J., Ball, T. S., & Alexander, D. (1974). Behavior therapy of pica with a profoundly retarded adolescent. *Mental Retardation,* Dec., 16–18.

Azrin, N. H., & Besalel, V. A. (1980). *How to use overcorrection.* Lawrence, KS: H & H Enterprises.

Azrin, N. H., & Foxx, R. M. A. (1971). A rapid method of toilet training the institutionalized retarded. *Journal of Applied Behavior Analysis, 4,* 89–99.

Baer, D. M., Wolf, M. M., & Risley, T. R. (1968). Some current dimensions of applied behavior analysis. *Journal of Applied Behavior Analysis, 1,* 91–97.

Baltrop, D. (1966). The prevalence of pica. *American Journal of Diseases in Children, 112,* 116–123.

Barkley, R. A. (1990). A critique of current diagnostic criteria for attention deficit hyperactivity disorder: Clinical and research implications. *Journal of Developmental and Behavioral Pediatrics, 11,* 343–352.

Barlett, L. B., Rooney, V., & Spedding, S. (1985). Nocturnal difficulties in a population of mentally handicapped children. *British Journal of Mental Subnormality, 31,* 54–59.

Barton, L. E., Brulle, A. R., & Repp, A. C. (1986). Maintenance of therapeutic change by momentary DRO. *Journal of Applied Behavior Analysis, 19,* 277–282.

Bauer, A. M., Shea, T. M., & Gaines, H. (1998). A primer on self-injury. *Education and Treatment of Children, 11,* 157–165.

Baumeister, A. A., & Baumeister, A. A. (1978). A suppression of repetitive self-injurious behavior by contingent inhalation of aromatic ammonia. *Journal of Autism and Childhood Schizophrenia, 8,* 71–77.

Baumeister, A. A., & Maclean, W. E. (1984). Deceleration of self-injurious responding by exercise. *Applied Research in Mental Retardation, 5,* 385–393.

Bax, M. (1985). Crying: A clinical overview. In B. M. Lester & C. F. Z. Boukydis (Eds.), *Infant crying* (pp. 241–348). New York: Plenum.

Bayley, N. (1993). *Bayley Scales of Infant Development* (2nd ed.). San Antonio: Psychological Corporation.

Behar, L., & Stringfield, S. (1974). *Preschool Behavior Questionnaire.* Durhum, NC: LINC Press.

Beitchman, J. H. (1985). Therapeutic considerations with the language impaired preschool child. *Canadian Journal of Psychiatry, 30,* 609–613.

Beitchman, J. H., Nair, R., Clegg, M., Ferguson, B., & Patel, P. G. (1986). Prevalence of psychiatric disorder in children with speech and language disorders. *Journal of the American Academy of Child and Adolescent Psychiatry, 25,* 528–535.

Berkowitz, S., Sherry, P. J., & Davis, B. A. (1971). Teaching self-feeding skills to profound retardates using reinforcement and fading procedures. *Behavior Therapy, 2,* 62–67.

Bostow, D. E., & Bailey, J. B. (1969). Modification of severe disruptive and aggressive behavior using brief timeout and reinforcement procedures. *Journal of Applied Behavior Analysis, 2,* 31–37.

Brown, F. (1991). Creative daily scheduling: A nonintrusive approach to challenging behaviors in community residences. *Journal of the Association for Persons with Severe Handicaps, 16,* 871–889.

Brown, P., & Elliot, R. (1965). Control of aggression in a nursery school class. *Journal of Experimental Child Psychology, 2,* 103–107.

Bucher, B., Reykdal, B., & Albin, J. (1976). Brief physical restraint to control pica in retarded children. *Journal of Behavior Therapy and Experimental Psychiatry, 7,* 137–140.

Bunyan, A. (1987). "Help, I can't cope with my child"—A behavioral approach to the treatment of a conduct disordered child within the natural homesetting. *British Journal of Social Work, 17,* 237–256.

Burgio, L. D., Whitman, T. L., & Johnson, M. R. (1980). A self-instructional package for increasing attending behavior in educable mentally retarded children. *Journal of Applied Behavior Analysis, 13,* 443–459.

Calamari, J. E., Geist, G. O., & Shahbazian, M. J. (1987). Evaluation of multiple component relaxation training with developmentally disabled persons. *Research in Developmental Disabilities, 8,* 55–70.

Carr, E. G., & Durand, V. M. (1985). Reducing behavioral problems through functional communication training. *Journal of Applied Behavior Analysis, 18,* 11–126.

Carr, E. G., Levin, L., McConnachie, G., Carlson, J. I., Kemp, D. C., & Smith, C. E. (1994). *Communication-based intervention for problem behavior: A user's guide for producing positive change.* Baltimore: Paul H. Brookes.

Cataldo, M. F., Finney, J. W., Madden, N. A., & Russo, D. C. (1983). Behavioral approaches to lead ingestion. In J. J. Chisolm & D. M. O'Hoara (Eds.), *Lead absorption in children: Management, clinical & environmental aspects* (pp. 103–111). Baltimore, MD: Urban & Schwarzenberg.

Cataldo, M. F., & Harris, J. (1982). The biological basis for self-injury in the mentally retarded. *Analysis of Intervention in Developmental Disabilities, 2,* 21–39.

Cautela, J. R., & Groden, J. (1978). *Relaxation: A comprehensive manual for adults, children, and children with special needs.* Champaign, Il: Research Press.

Charlop, M. H., Kurtz, P. F., & Casey, F. G. (1990). Using aberrant behaviors as reinforcers for autistic children. *Journal of Applied Behavior Analysis, 23,* 163–181.

Clements, J., Wing, L., & Dunn, G. (1986). Sleep problems in handicapped children: A preliminary study. *Journal of Child Psychology and Psychiatry, 27,* 399–407.

Conners, C.K. (1989). *Conners' Rating Scales manual.* New York: Multi-Health Systems.

Cullinan, D., Gadow, K. D., & Epstein, M. H. (1987). Psychotropic drug treatment among learning-disabled, educable mentally retarded, and seriously emotionally disturbed students. *Journal of Abnormal Child Psychology, 15,* 469–477.

Danford, D. E., & Huber, A. M. (1982). Pica among mentally retarded adults. *Journal on Mental Deficiency, 87,* 141–146.

Deitz, S. M. (1977). An analysis of programming DRL schedules in educational settings. *Behavior Research and Therapy, 15,* 103–111.

Delissovoy, B. (1961). Head banging in early childhood: A study of incidence. *Journal of Pediatrics, 58,* 803–805.

Donnelly, D. R., & Olzcak, P. V. (1990). The effect of differential reinforcement of incompatible behaviors (DRI) on pica for cigarettes in persons with intellectual disability. *Behavior Modification, 14,* 81–96.

Dorsey, M. F., Iwata, B. A., Ong, P., & McSween, T. E. (1980). Treatment of self-injurious behavior using a water mist: Initial response suppression and generalization. *Journal of Applied Behavior Analysis, 13,* 343–353.

Duker, P. C., & Rasing, E. (1989). Effects of redesigning the physical environment on self-stimulation and on-task behavior in three autistic-type developmentally disabled individuals. *Journal of Autism and Developmental Disorders, 19,* 449–460.

Durand, V. M., & Carr, E. G. (1991). Functional communication training to reduce challenging behavior: Maintenance and application in new settings. *Journal of Applied Behavior Analysis, 24,* 251–261.

Dyer, K. (1987). The competition of autistic stereotyped behavior with usual and specially assessed reinforcers. *Research in Developmental Disabilities, 8,* 607–626.

Dyer, K., Dunlap, G., & Winterling, V. (1990). Effects of choice making on the serious problem behaviors of students with severe handicaps. *Journal of Applied Behavior Analysis, 23,* 515–524.

Eaton, L., & Menolascino, F. (1982). Psychiatric disorders in the mentally retarded: Types, problems and challenges. *American Journal of Psychiatry, 139,* 1297–1303.

Einfeld, S., & Tonge, B. J. (1989). *Developmental Behavior Checklist (DBC).* Sydney, Australia: University of Sydney.

Eron, L. D. (1987). The development of aggressive behavior from the perspective of a developing behaviorism. *American Psychologist, 42,* 435–442.

Evans, I. M., & Meyer, L. H. (1985). *An educative approach to behavior problems: A practical decision model for interventions with severely handicapped learners.* Baltimore: Paul H. Brookes.

Favell, J. E., McGimsey, J. F., & Jones, M. L. (1978). The use of physical restraint in the treatment of self-injury and as positive reinforcement. *Journal of Applied Behavior Analysis, 11,* 137–140.

Favell, J. E., & Reid, D. H. (1988). Generalizing and maintaining improvements in problem behavior. In R. H. Horner, G. Dunlap, & R. L. Koegel (Eds.), *Generalization and maintenance: Lifestyle changes in applied setting* (pp. 171–196). Baltimore: Paul H. Brookes.

Fidura, J. G., Lindsey, E. R., & Walker, G. R. (1987). A special behavior unit for treatment of behavior problems of persons who are mentally retarded. *Mental Retardation, 25,* 107–111.

Forehand, R. (1977). Child noncompliance to parental requests: Behavioral analysis and treatment. In M. Hersen, R. M., Eisler, & P. M. Miller (Eds.), *Progress in behavior modification* (Vol. 5, pp. 111–147). New York: Academic Press.

Forehand, R., & McMahon, R. (1981). *Helping the noncompliant child: A clinician's guide to parent training.* New York: Guilford.

Fovel, J. T., Lash, P. S., Barron, D. A., Jr., & Roberts, M. S. (1989). A survey of self-restraint, self-injury, and other maladaptive behaviors in an institutionalized population. *Research in Developmental Disabilities, 16,* 377–382.

Foxx, R. M. (1982). *Decreasing behaviors of severely retarded and autistic persons.* Champaign, IL: Research Press.

Foxx, R. M., & Azrin, N. H. (1973). *Toilet training the retarded: A rapid program for day and nighttime independent toileting.* Champaign, IL: Research Press.

Foxx, R. M., & Martin, E. D. (1975). Treatment of scavenging behavior (coprophagy and pica) by overcorrection. *Behavior Research and Therapy, 13,* 153–162.

Foxx, R. M., McMorrow, M. J., Bittle, R. G., & Bechtel, D. R. (1986). The successful treatment of a dually-diagnosed deaf man's aggression with a program that included contingent electric shock. *Behavior Therapy, 17,* 170–186.

Foxx, R. M., Plaska, T. G., & Bittle, R. G. (1986). Guidelines for the use of contingent electric shock to treat aberrant behavior. *Progress in Behavior Modification, 20,* 1–34.

Foxx, R. M., & Shapiro, S. T. (1978). The timeout ribbon: A nonexclusionary timeout procedure. *Journal of Applied Behavior Analysis, 11,* 125–136.

Frankel, F., Moss, D., Schofield, S., & Simmons, J. Q. (1976). Case study: Use of differential reinforcement to suppress self-injurious and aggressive behavior. *Psychological Reports, 39,* 843–849.

Gast, D. L., & Wolery, M. (1987). Severe maladaptive behaviors. In M. E. Snell (Ed.), *Systematic instruction of persons with severe handicaps* (3rd ed., pp. 300–332). Columbus: Merrill.

Gillberg, C., Persson, E., Grufman, M., & Themner, U. (1986). Psychiatric disorders in mildly and severely mentally retarded urban children and adolescents: Epidemiological aspects. *British Journal of Psychiatry, 149,* 68–74.

Guess, D., & Carr, E. (1991). Emergence and maintenance of stereotypy and self-injury. *American Journal on Mental Retardation, 96*, 299–319.

Hart, H., Bax, M., & Jenkins, S. (1984). Health and behavior in preschool children. *Child Care Health and Development, 10*, 1–16.

Horner, R. H., & Day, H. M. (1991). The effects of response efficiency on functionally equivalent competing behaviors. *Journal of Applied Behavior Analysis, 24*, 719–732.

Horner, R. H., Day, M., Sprague, J., O'Brien, M., & Heathfield, L. T. (1991). Interspersed requests: A nonaversive procedure for reducing aggression and self-injury during instruction. *Journal of Applied Behavior Analysis, 24*, 265–278.

Horner, R. H., Dunlap, G., Koegel, R. L., Carr, E. G., Sailor, W., Anderson, J., Albin, R. W., & O'Neill, R. (1990). Toward a technology of "nonaversive" behavioral support. *Journal of the Association for Persons with Severe Handicaps, 15*, 91–97.

Horner, R. H., Sprague, J. R., O'Brien, M., & Heathfield, L. T. (1990). The role of response efficiency in the reduction of problem behaviors through functional equivalence training: A case study. *The Journal of the Association for Persons with Severe Handicaps, 15*, 91–97.

Iwata, B. A., Dorsey, M. F., Slifer, J. K., Bauman, K. E., & Richman, G. S. (1982). Toward a functional analysis of self-injury. *Analysis and Intervention in Developmental Disabilities, 2*, 3–20.

Iwata, B. A., Vollmer, T. R., & Zarcone, J. R. (1990). The experimental functional analysis of behavior disorders: Methodology, application, and limitations. In A. C. Repp & N. N. Singh (Eds.), *Perspectives on the use of nonaversive and aversive interventions for persons with developmental disabilities* (pp. 302–330). Sycamore, IL: Sycamore Publishing.

Johnson, C. R., Hunt, F. M., & Siebert, M. J. (1994). Discrimination training in the treatment of pica and food scavenging. *Behavior Modification, 18*, p. 212.

Kazdin, A. E. (1980). Acceptability of time out from reinforcement procedures for disruptive child behavior. *Behavior Therapy, 11*, 329–344.

Kendall, P. C. (1984). Cognitive-behavioral self-control therapy for children. *Journal of Child Psychology and Psychiatry, 25*, 173–179.

Kendall, P. C., & Braswell, L. (1982). Cognitive-behavioral self-control therapy for children: A components analysis. *Journal of Consulting and Clinical Psychology, 50*, 672–689.

Kendall, P. C., & Finch, A. J. (1978). A cognitive-behavioral treatment for impulsivity: A group comparison study. *Journal of Consulting and Clinical Psychology, 46*, 110–118.

Kern, L., Koegel, R. L., Dyer, K., Blew, P. A., & Fenton, L. R. (1982). The effects of physical exercise on self-stimulation and appropriate responding in autistic children. *Journal of Autism and Developmental Disorders, 12*, 399–419.

Kistner, J., Hammer, D., Wolfe, D., Rothblum, E., & Drabman, R. S. (1982). Teacher popularity and contrast effects in a classroom token economy. *Journal of Applied Behavior Analysis, 15*, 85–96.

Kovacs, M. (1981). Rating scales to assess depression in school-age children. *Acta Paedopsychiatry, 46*, 305–315.

Kravitz, H., & Boehm, J. (1971). Rhythmic habit patterns in infancy: Their sequence, age of onset, and frequency. *Child Development, 42*, 399–413.

Lakin, K. C., Hill, B. K., Hauber, F. A., Bruininks, R. H., & Heal, L. W. (1983). New admissions and readmissions to a national sample of public residential facilities. *American Journal of Mental Deficiency, 88*, 13–20.

Lambert, N., Leland, H., & Nihira, K. (1992). *AAMR Adaptive Behavior Scales—School* (2nd ed.). San Antonio: The Psychological Corporation.

LaVigna, G. W., & Donnellan, A. M. (1986). *Alternatives to punishment: Solving behavior problems with non-aversive strategies*. New York: Irvington.

Linscheid, T. R., Iwata, B. A., Ricketts, R. W., Williams, D. E., & Griffin, J. C. (1990). Clinical evaluation of the self-injurious behavior inhibiting system (SIBIS). *Journal of Applied Behavior Analysis, 23*, 53–78.

Lovaas, O. I. (1987). Behavioral treatment and normal educational and intellectual functioning in young autistic children. *Journal of Consulting and Clinical Psychology, 55*, 3–9.

Lovaas, O. I., & Favell, J. (1987). Protection for clients undergoing aversive/restrictive interventions. *Education and Treatment of Children, 10*, 311–325.

Luce, S. C., Delquadri, J., & Hall, R. V. (1980). Contingent exercise: A mild but powerful procedure for suppressing inappropriate verbal and aggressive behavior. *Journal of Applied Behavior Analysis, 13*, 583–594.

Luiselli, J. K., Colozzi, G. A., & O'Toole, K. M. (1980). Programming response maintenance of differential reinforcement effects. *Child Behavior Therapy, 2,* 65–73.

Luria, A. R. (1961). *The role of speech in the regulation of normal and abnormal behaviors.* New York: Liveright.

Mace, R. C., Page, T. J., Ivancic, M. T., & O'Brien, S. (1986). Effectiveness of brief time-out with and without contingent delay: A comparative analysis. *Journal of Applied Behavior Analysis, 19,* 79–86.

Madden, N. A., Russo, D. C., & Cataldo, M. F. (1980). Behavioral treatment of pica in children with lead poisoning. *Child Behavior Therapy, 2,* 67–81.

Martin, R. (Ed.). (1975). *Legal challenges to behavior modification: Trends in schools, corrections and mental health.* Champaign, IL: Research Press.

Mason, S., McGee, G., Farmer-Dougan, V. & Risley, T. (1989). A practical strategy for ongoing reinforcer assessment. *Journal of Applied Behavior Analysis, 22,* 171–179.

Matson, J. L. (1988). *The PIMRA manual.* Orland Park, IL: International Diagnostic Systems.

Matson, J. L., & DiLorenzo, T. M. (1984). *Punishment and its alternatives: A new perspective for behavior modification* (Vol. 13). New York: Springer.

Matson, J. L., & Frame, C. L. (1986). *Psychopathology among mentally retarded children and adolescents* (Vol. 6). Beverly Hills: Sage.

Matson, J. L., & Gorman-Smith, D. (1986). A review of treatment research for aggressive and disruptive behavior in the mentally retarded. *Applied Research in Mental Retardation, 7,* 95–103.

Matson, J. L., & Kazdin, A. E. (1981). Punishment in behavior modification: Pragmatic ethical and legal issues. *Clinical Psychology Review, 1,* 197–210.

Matson, J. L., & Taras, M. E. (1989). A 20 year review of punishment and alternative methods to treat problem behaviors in developmentally delayed persons. *Research in Developmental Disabilities, 10,* 85–104.

McApline, C., & Singh, M. M. (1986). Pica in institutionalized mentally retarded persons. *Journal of Mental Deficiency Research, 30,* 171–178.

McCarthy, D. (1972). *McCarthy Scales of Children's Abilities.* San Antonio: The Psychological Corporation.

McGimsey, J. F., & Favell, J. E. (1988). The effects of increased physical exercise on disruptive behavior in retarded persons. *Journal of Autism and Developmental Disorders, 18,* 167–179.

McPhail, C. H., & Chamove, A. S. (1989). Relaxation reduces disruption in mentally handicapped adults. *Journal of Mental Deficiency Research, 33,* 399–406.

Meichenbaum, D., & Goodman, J. (1971). Training impulsive children to talk to themselves: A means of developing self control. *Journal of Abnormal Psychology,* 115–126.

Miltenberger, R. G., Suda, K. T., Lennox, D. B., & Lindeman, D. P. (1991). Assessing the acceptability of behavioral treatments to persons with mental retardation. *American Journal on Mental Retardation, 96,* 291–298.

Mulick, J. A. (1990). The ideology and science of punishment in mental retardation. *American Journal on Mental Retardation, 95,* 142–156.

Ollendick, T. H., & Matson, J. L. (1978). Over correction: An overview. *Behavior Therapy, 9,* 830–842.

Olson, R. L., & Roberts, M. W. (1987). Alternative treatments for sibling aggression. *Behavior Therapy, 18,* 243–250.

Pace, G. M., Ivancic, M. T., Edwards, G. L., Iwata, B., & Page, T. J. (1985). Assessment of stimulus preference and reinforcer value with profoundly retarded individuals. *Journal of Applied Behavior Analysis, 18,* 249–254.

Palmer, S., & Horn, S. (1978). Feeding problems in children. In S. Palmer & S. Evall (Eds.), *Pediatric nutrition in developmental disorders* (pp. 107–272). Springfield, IL: Thomas.

Palmer, S., Thompson, R. J., & Linscheid, T. R. (1975). Applied behavior analysis in the treatment of childhood feeding problems. *Developmental Medicine and Child Neurology, 17,* 333–339.

Parpal, M., & Maccoby, E. E. (1985). Maternal responsiveness and subsequent child compliance. *Child Development, 56,* 1326–1334.

Parrish, J. M., Cataldo, M. F., Kolko, D. J., Neef, N. A., & Egel, A. L. (1986). Experimental analysis of response covariation among compliant and inappropriate behaviors. *Journal of Applied Behavior Analysis, 19,* 241–254.

Perske, R., Clifton, A., McClean, B. M., & Stein, J. I. (Eds.). (1977). *Mealtimes for severely and profoundly handicapped persons: New concepts and attitudes.* Baltimore: University Park Press.

Piazza, C. C., & Fisher, W. (1991). A faded bedtime with response cost protocol for treatment of multiple sleep problems in children. *Journal of Applied Behavior Analysis, 24,* 129–140.

Porterfield, J. K., Herbert-Jackson, E., & Risley, T. R. (1976). Contingent observation: An effective and acceptable procedure for reducing disruptive behavior of young children in a group setting. *Journal of Applied Behavior Analysis, 9,* 55–64.

Quine, L. (1991). Sleep problems in children with mental handicap. *Journal of Mental Deficiency Research, 35,* 269–290.

Repp, A. C., Barton, L. E., & Brulle, A. R. (1983). A comparison of two procedures for programming the differential reinforcement of other behaviors. *Journal of Applied Behavior Analysis, 16,* 435–445.

Reynolds, C. R., & Richman, B. O. (1978). What I think and feel: A revised measure of children's manifest anxiety. *Journal of Abnormal Child Psychology, 6,* 271–280.

Reynolds, W. M. (1989). *Self-Report Depression Questionnaire (SRDQ).* University of Wisconsin-Madison.

Rincover, A. (1978). Sensory extinction: A procedure for eliminating self-stimulatory behavior in psychotic children. *Journal of Abnormal Child Psychology, 6,* 299–310.

Rocissano, L., Slade, A., & Lynch, V. (1987). Dyadic synchrony and toddler compliance. *Developmental Psychology, 23,* 698–794.

Rojahn, J. (1989). *The Behavior Problems Inventory.* Nisonger Center for Mental Retardation and Developmental Disabilities, Ohio State University.

Rojahn, J., McGonigle, J. J., Curcio, C., & Dixon, M. J. (1987). Suppression of pica by water mist and aromatic ammonia: A comparative analysis. *Behavior Modification, 11,* 65–74.

Sajwaj, T., Libert, J., & Agras, S. (1974). Lemon-juice therapy: The control of life-threatening rumination in a 6-month-old infant. *Journal of Applied Behavior Analysis, 7,* 557–563.

Salvia, J., & Ysseldyke, J. E. (1985). *Assessment in special and remedial education* (3rd ed.). Boston: Houghton Mifflin.

Sandman, C.A. (1988). B-endorphine disregulation in autistic and self-injurious behavior: A neurodevelopmental hypothesis. *Synapse, 2,* 193–199.

Santarcangelo, S., Dyer, K., & Luce, S. C. (1987). Generalized reduction of disruptive behavior in unsupervised settings through specific toy training. *JASH, 12,* 281–289.

Sattler, J. M. (Ed.). (1988). Assessment of mental retardation and giftedness. In S. M. Sattler (Ed.), *Assessment of children* (pp. 646–685). San Diego: Author.

Schaffer, H. R., & Crook, C. K. (1980). Child compliance and maternal control techniques. *Child Development, 16,* 54–61.

Singer, G. & Irwin, L. (1987). Human rights review of intrusive behaviors for students with severe handicaps. *Exceptional Children, 54,* 46–52.

Singh, N. N., & Bakker, L. W. (1984). Suppression of pica by overcorrection and physical restraint: A comparative analysis. *Journal of Autism and Developmental Disorders, 14,* 331–341.

Singh, N. N., Sood, A., Sonenklar, N., & Ellis, C. R.(1991). Assessment and diagnosis of mental illness in persons with mental retardation: Methods and measures. *Behavior Modification, 15,* 419–443.

Sparrow, S. S., Balla, D. A., & Cicchetti, D. V. (1984). *Vineland Adaptive Behavior Scales.* Circle Pines, MN: American Guidance Service.

Stimbert, V. E., Minor, J.W., & McCoy, J. F. (1977). Intensive feeding training with retarded children. *Behavior Modification, 1,* 517–529.

Sulzer-Azaroff, B., & Mayer, G. (1991). Behavior analysis for lasting change. Chicago: Holt, Rinehart, & Winston.

Swerissen, H., & Carruthers, J. (1987). The use of a physical restraint procedure to reduce a severely intellectually disabled child's tantrums. *Behavior-Change, 4,* 34–38.

Tate, B. G., & Baroff, G. S. (1966). Aversive conditioning of self-injurious behavior in a psychotic boy. *Behavior Research and Therapy, 4,* 281–287.

Thompson, R. J. (1984). Behavior problems in developmentally disabled children. *Advances in Developmental and Behavioral Pediatrics, 5,* 265–330.

Thorndike, R. L., Hagen, E. P., & Sattler, J. M. (1986). *Stanford–Binet Intelligence Scale* (4th ed.). San Antonio: The Psychological Corporation.

Touchette, P. E., MacDonald, R. G., & Langer, S. N. (1985). A scatter plot for identifying stimulus control of problem behavior. *Journal of Applied Behavior Analysis, 18,* 343–351.

Vitello, S. J., Atthowe, J. M., & Cadwell, J. (1983). Determinants of community placement of institutionalized mentally retarded persons. *American Journal of Mental Deficiency, 87,* 539–545.

Walker, G. R. (1993). Noncompliant behavior of people with mental retardation. *Research in Developmental Disabilities, 14*, 87–105.

Wechsler, D. (1989). *Wechsler Preschool and Primary Scale of Intelligence–Revised*. San Antonio: The Psychological Corporation.

Wechsler, D. (1991). *Wechsler Intelligence Scale for Children* (3rd ed.). San Antonio: The Psychological Corporation.

Williams, C. D. (1959). The elimination of tantrum behavior by extinction procedures. *Journal of Abnormal and Social Psychology, 59,* 269.

Wilson, C. C., Robertson, S. J., Herlong, L. H., & Haynes, S. N. (1979). Vicarious effects of time-out in the modification of aggression in the classroom. *Behavior Modification, 3,* 97–111.

Winterling, V., Dunlap, G., & O'Neill, R. E. (1987). The influence of task variation on the aberrant behaviors of autistic students. *Education and Treatment of Children, 10,* 105–119.

Wolf, M. M., Risley, T. R., Johnson, M., Harris, F., & Allen, E. (1967). Application of operant conditioning procedures to the behavior problems of an autistic child, a follow-up extension. *Behavior Research and Therapy, 5,* 103–112.

Wolf, M. M., Risley, T. R., & Meese, H. (1964). Application of operant conditioning procedures to the behavior problems of an autistic child. *Behavior Research and Therapy, 1,* 305–312.

Wolfe, V. V., Boyd, L. A., & Wolfe, D. A. (1983). Teacher cooperative play to behavior-problem preschool children. *Education and Treatment of Children, 6,* 1–9.

Wong S. E., Floyd, J., Innocent, A. J., & Woolsey, J. E. (1991). Applying a DRO schedule and compliance training to reduce aggressive and self-injurious behavior in an autistic man: A case report. *Journal of Behavior Therapy and Experimental Psychiatry, 22,* 299–304.

Chapter 3

Autism

Aubyn C. Stahmer
Children's Hospital and Health Center, San Diego
Laura Schreibman
University of California, San Diego

DESCRIPTION OF THE DISORDER

For individuals unfamiliar with Autistic Disorder, the word *autism* often generates a picture of an isolated child, sitting in a corner rocking back and forth for hours. People often say they think of children "off in their own world," or "kids who are really good with numbers." In reality, children with autism are a very diverse group with a range of interests and abilities. Because of advancements in treatment models and early intervention techniques, it is rare to see a child with autism simply sitting and rocking for hours. Although there has been a substantial amount of research into the nature of autism, many aspects of the disorder remain a mystery. Although children with autism typically avoid social interaction, some children with autism appear to enjoy interacting with family members. Their interaction might be considered unusual, but it is an attempt to socialize. So, before beginning a description of the disorder, picture children who do not understand their place in the social world rather than rocking in the corner.

DSM–IV

The *Diagnostic and Statistical Manual of Mental Disorders* (*DSM–IV*; 4th ed.; American Psychiatric Association, 1994) describes a set of disorders called Pervasive Developmental Disorders, or disorders that affect all areas of a child's ability to function in the world. The particular label used depends on the severity of the characteristics in that particular child as well as age of onset of the symptoms. Many researchers and clinicians think of pervasive developmental disorders as being a spectrum of disorders along which a child can be diagnosed. A label of Autistic Disorder often represents the most severe end of the spectrum. Autism is a disorder comprised of a constellation of symptoms a child can manifest at different levels of severity. Additionally, there is no "test" for autism or any of the other pervasive developmental disorders. Parents, therefore, are often left frustrated by the various labels applied to their child by different professionals. The characteristics of the disorder as discussed here can be present in varying degrees.

Autism is a pervasive developmental disorder; consequently, it affects all areas of a child's functioning. Further, in order to receive a diagnosis of autism, a child must manifest these impairments before age 3. The three areas of development most profoundly affected are, reciprocal social interaction skills, language and communication skills, and the presence of stereotyped behaviors or interests. For ease of presentation, each of these areas is discussed separately. Note that these areas of functioning interact, and impairment in one area can exacerbate difficulties in another.

Social Interaction Skills.   This characteristic seems to be one of the most noticeable to laypersons and strangers. Often, children with autism do not fully engage with others, do not give eye contact, and opt for solitary play. This is especially apparent to individuals who do not know the child well, as the child may avoid contact with and/or ignore them. Children with autism typically do not develop reciprocal friendships with their peers (Rutter, 1978). This may be because they seem to lack the ability to express social and emotional reciprocity. Their responses to social initiations, especially those from other children, are often inappropriate. Inappropriate responding may include ignoring the other child or becoming upset. The child with autism has difficulty engaging in the complex task of interactive play, games, and make believe (e.g., Thorp, Stahmer, & Schreibman, 1995).

Children with autism seem to show some social interaction skills with familiar individuals, although these skills are still well below what would be expected for their age and ability level, or tend to be somewhat atypical. It seems that the more familiar or predictable an individual is, the easier it is for the child with autism to attempt some type of interaction. The interaction itself may be labored and not altogether appropriate, but the child will try to engage with others on some level. Therefore, it is the task of the teacher or treatment provider to build on these spontaneous attempts at interaction to expand the skills of the child with autism to include more appropriate types of interactions with increasing numbers of individuals.

Communication Skills.   Approximately half of all people with autism will never develop functional spoken language (Rutter, 1978). Those children with autism who do speak have severely delayed language development and poor communication skills (e.g., Ricks & Wing, 1977; Rutter, 1978). One of the characteristics that distinguishes autism from a language delay is the lack of attempts to compensate for the language impairment by using other forms of communication such as gesture (e.g., Rutter, 1978). Even with intervention, many of the children learn to use only single words or very simple sentences. Once words are learned, moving beyond simple labeling is often difficult. The children must be taught to use sentences, answer questions, and to talk about things that are not immediately present. These more abstract aspects of language may never be mastered by most individuals with autism. In those individuals that do learn to use complex language, conversation remains literal and concrete in most cases (e.g., Rutter, 1978). They converse about particular topics of interest to themselves, ignore the conversational needs of others, and have difficulty carrying on lengthy conversations.

Language difficulties tend to persist throughout the person's adult life and interact with the social deficits to make social situations that involve language skills (as most do) extremely difficult. Moreover, skills that require both language and social interaction abilities are impaired. One example of this is make believe, or social-imitative play. Most children with autism tend to have severe deficits in play skills (see Jarrold, Boucher, & Smith, 1993, for review). Although they may have the language ability, their play often remains repetitive, or manipulative, and rarely becomes symbolic or interactive without extensive intervention.

Stereotyped Behaviors and Interests.   Stereotyped behaviors can range from repetitive spinning of the wheels on a toy car or wanting all the books in the house lined up in a certain order, to only being willing to discuss one topic of conversation. Other examples of this behavior include resistance to change in routine of any type, including changing the furniture or using a new route to the grocery store. Severe stereotyped behavior can affect both social and language skills.

Stereotyped behaviors may also be used as a way to perform difficult skills. For example, children with autism have great difficulty with complex types of play, such as playing "house" or pretending to be a "firefighter" (see Thorp et al., 1995). However, numerous parents have reported anecdotally that their children will act out entire movies, and in fact attempt to engage others in this "game." Because the movie is unchanging and predictable, it may be easier for the child with autism to understand, unlike the complex play scenes observed when other children play. Although odd, this can provide a foundation for a treatment provider to begin teaching more appropriate skills.

ASSESSMENT METHODS

The development of any effective behavioral treatment plan depends on accurate, comprehensive, and appropriate assessment as an integral part of the process. Because parent training is typically incorporated as an important part of a child's treatment, it is advisable to obtain two types of information: assessment of relevant child variables and assessment of relevant parent and family variables.

Child Measures

Measures of child behavior are important for the identification of important behavioral targets for treatment as well as for evaluation of treatment effects. The Autism Diagnostic Interview–Revised (ADI–R; Lord, Rutter, & Le Couteur, 1994) is a semi-structured interview for caregivers (usually parents) of children for whom autism or pervasive developmental disorder is a potential diagnosis. This instrument is helpful not only for diagnostic purposes but may assist in the identification and description of important target behaviors.

It is also useful to measure the child's level of intellectual functioning. Many standardized instruments lend themselves to this purpose, including the Stanford–Binet (4th ed.), which is a standardized assessment that yields both a verbal and a performance scale.

Measures of children's social adaptation provide an index of their level of functioning relative to their social environment. One very useful measure is the Vineland Adaptive Behavior Scales (Sparrow, Balla, & Cicchetti, 1984), which is a standardized measure yielding scores relating to socialization, communication, daily living skills, an adaptive behavior composite, and level of maladaptive behavior. This measure reflects the children's competence and independence in their social environment.

Another useful assessment is a behavioral measure consisting of a structured or semi-structured situation in which the children are observed in a naturalistic play setting (e.g., a room with toys) and presented with "challenges" that allow for direct observation of the children's behavior in a variety of situations. For example, the children are observed with a therapist and with an unfamiliar adult to assess their behavior independent of their parents. Also, the children can be observed during social overtures of adults, in the absence of such overtures, and when language demands are made. These sessions are typically videotaped. Later analysis and scoring of multiple responses provide for quantitative description of the degree to which specified behaviors are present or absent in a free-play setting (e.g., Lovaas, R. L. Koegel, Simmons, & Long, 1973). Typically, four behaviors characteristic of autism are scored, including self-stimulation, inappropriate play, poor social nonverbal behavior (e.g., response to requests, imitating), and tantrums or crying.

It is also very important to obtain measures allowing for determination of the child's level of language development. Again, both standardized and behavioral assessments are useful. Appropriate standardized measures include the Peabody Picture Vocabulary Test (L. M. Dunn & L. M. Dunn, 1981), which provides a measure of the child's receptive language level; the Expressive One Word Picture Vocabulary Test (Gardner, 1990), which provides a measure of the child's expressive language level; and the Assessment of Children's Language Comprehension (Foster, Giddan, & Stark, 1973), which provides an in-depth analysis of the child's level of generalized language development with respect to population norms.

For a behavioral measure, the naturalistic setting and situations described previously can be scored according to several categories of verbal behavior. These may include appropriate imitation of speech of others, answers to questions presented by others, spontaneous speech, and other appropriate speech. It is also important to assess the presence of inappropriate speech (e.g., echolalia, neologisms, idiosyncratic language).

Parent and Family Measures

As noted earlier, assessment of family environment and interaction may be quite informative in the design of parent training programs. Information on how families budget their time over a day provides useful information regarding the effects of the child on the family and the general burden on the parents. One example is the 24-Hour Time Activity Diary (e.g., R. A. Berk & S. F. Berk, 1979), in which the parents write down all activities in which they engaged (except when away at work, etc.), how long the activity lasted, who was with them, and how they feel about the activity. This measure yields important information regarding the amount of leisure time, teaching time, custodial care, and so forth that the parents engage in on a typical day. The measure is also sensitive to changes in how parents alter the structure of their time as a function of parent training and child behavior change (R. L. Koegel, Schreibman, Britten, Burke, & O'Neill, 1982).

Another informative behavioral assessment is a home observation where the family is observed in semi- or unstructured interactions. Such observations can be scored in vivo or videotaped for later scoring. Behaviors and interactions of interest can then be scored for analysis.

Standardized assessments can also be very useful and informative. The Questionnaire on Resources and Stress (QRS; Holroyd, 1974) is a paper-and-pencil, true–false item questionnaire designed to measure variables pertinent to families with handicapped family members and provides information regarding specific areas of stress experienced by the parents. The Family Environment Scale (FES; Moos, 1974) is a pencil-and-paper assessment providing information about the atmosphere in the entire family.

It is likely that parental attitudes toward childrearing may affect parent training. For example, parents' attitudes may affect choice of target behaviors, utilization of specific techniques, or expectation of success. The Ideas About Parenting Instrument (C. P. Cowan et al., 1985) measures attitude along three subscales: authoritarian control, child centeredness, and permissive-protectiveness.

TREATMENT PROCEDURES

Optimal treatment procedures for children with autism are typically multidimensional. Because autism is a pervasive developmental disorder, many areas need to be considered when designing treatment strategies. In addition, because those with autism comprise a heterogeneous group, interventions must be individualized. Some variables that must be taken into consideration when individualizing treatment include the child's functioning level, age, environment, and specifics of the behaviors to be treated. In addition, because research indicates that parent training is a very effective treatment method for children with autism (R. L. Koegel et al., 1982), parent and family characteristics must also be considered when designing an intervention.

The child's verbal ability, nonverbal IQ, motor skills, social skills, and disruptive behavior need to be taken into account when designing a treatment package. In addition, parent variables—such as stress level, motivation to implement treatment procedures, desire for independence in their child, and parental expectations for the child—should be considered. In most cases, parents will be an integral part of the interventions, so they need to be comfortable with the strategies used. Finally, teachers often wish to use intervention strategies in the classroom setting. Schools may have limitations on the types of interventions they can implement, available resources, and trained treatment providers. Each of these factors is important to the success of treatment. This prescriptive approach can often eliminate problems with implementation of the intervention.

Several different types of treatment programs are outlined here. These treatment strategies are not mutually exclusive. In fact, the most effective intervention program combines appropriate elements of various treatment strategies. Each treatment description will include information about the particular child and environmental characteristics for which that intervention works best. Strategies for individualizing treatment packages are also discussed.

Discrete Trial Training (DTT)

This type of treatment strategy was one of the first successful interventions to be used with individuals with autism. Although the field has moved beyond simple discrete trial training (DTT) to strategies that enhance generalization and maintenance, as well as those that are more appropriate to the natural environment, DTT is a useful part of the entire treatment package. This type of intervention strategy is typically used in conjunction with, or as a precursor to, the strategies discussed next.

This intervention focuses on training specific individual target behaviors. Examples of target behaviors could include learning the word "red," learning to answer the question "What's your name?", or toilet training (which would be further broken down into component steps). This type of training has been found to be especially useful for learning new behaviors, for behaviors the child would not choose to learn, and for behaviors whose natural consequences are of no positive or negative interest to the child. Toilet training is a good example of a behavior with natural consequences that may have no impact if a child does not mind wearing a wet diaper and is not motivated by social praise.

The first step in this type of intervention is to identify the target behavior (see Lovaas, 1981, for a complete description of this training technique). An example of a target behavior may be identifying circles. In the next step, the instruction is presented to the child. Important aspects of this step include ensuring the child is attending before giving the instruction, and then making the instruction clear, concise, task-relevant, and consistent across trials. Prompts are often used to evoke a correct response from the child. An example of a direct prompt for learning to identify circles might be to help the child point to the picture of the circle. Prompts can be faded as the child learns. That is, once the child can point to the circle correctly when the instructor is pointing to it, the instructor might move the finger away from the picture, then fade it out completely.

Techniques such as *chaining* can also be used to break down the target behavior into small steps. Each successive approximation of the target behavior is then rewarded until the child can respond correctly. For example, when working on getting dressed, the child might first be rewarded for just putting on a shirt, then for a shirt and socks, and so on until the child has learned to dress completely. Each individual step is practiced and rewarded until it is mastered, at which time the child begins to learn the next step in the sequence.

Instructors also learn to provide appropriate consequences for behaviors. Positive reinforcement should be given immediately after a correct response. Reinforcers should be chosen based on the child's interests and changed frequently to ensure that the child remains motivated. It is also important that the child receive no reward for incorrect responses. Consequences should be clear, effective, and contingent on the behavior of the child.

Again, this type of training is particularly useful for acquisition of new skills. After a skill has been mastered, one of the other treatment strategies discussed here may be more appropriate for generalization and maintenance of the behavior change.

Pivotal Response Training (PRT)

One of the difficulties found with the use of DTT was that the children often failed to generalize their newly learned skills to new materials or situations (Stokes & Baer, 1977). That is, a child might learn to say "car" in response to a certain picture of a car, but would not make that same response in the presence of a real car, or a different picture of a car. In addition, DTT is often time consuming to use in teaching complex tasks such as language. Finally, children with autism did not seem to be motivated to perform the behaviors being taught to them. They did not seem to enjoy the repetition of the training, or the actual tasks involved. In order to remedy some of these difficulties, researchers developed a treatment program called Pivotal Response Training (PRT; R. L. Koegel, Schreibman, Good, Cerniglia, Murphy & L. Koegel, 1989).

The focus of treatment in this program is to increase *pivotal* components of responses such as motivation and responsivity to multiple cues. This treatment facilitates generalized behavioral change rather than focusing on individual behaviors (R. L. Koegel, O'Dell, & L. K. Koegel, 1987). When a child's motivation to participate in treatment is increased, the child is more likely to learn from the treatment procedures. Included in the process of PRT are specific steps designed to increase a child's motivation to perform in the learning environment and in generalization environments as well. PRT is implemented in the child's natural environment, which helps to facilitate generalization of newly learned skills. Another advantage is that treatment can be administered continuously throughout the child's day and across many environments.

There are two primary focus areas in PRT: *motivation* and *responsivity*. The first component includes increasing a child's motivation to learn. Lack of motivation is often a problem when teaching children with autism (see Schreibman, 1988). Traditional treatment programs often inadvertently work to decrease a child's motivation to learn through allowing repeated failure, using repetitive tasks, and utilizing complete adult control. PRT attempts to increase motivation in children with autism by including the following components in teaching situations: utilizing functional response–reinforcer relationships (R. L. Koegel & Williams, 1980; Williams, R. L. Koegel & Egel, 1981), reinforcing attempts at appropriate responding (R. L. Koegel & Egel, 1979; R. L. Koegel, O'Dell, & Dunlap, 1988), frequent variation of task and stimulus materials (Dunlap, 1984; Dunlap & R. L. Koegel, 1980), use of multiple examples (Stokes & Baer, 1977), allowing the child to choose the activity (Dunlap & R. L. Koegel, 1980; R. L. Koegel, Dyer, & Bell, 1987), and interspersing maintenance tasks the child has already mastered (Dunlap, 1984). These techniques allow a child to be successful and in control of the learning situation. Research indicates that these techniques used in combination with turn taking (Lieven, 1976) and the use of natural consequences (Bloom & Lahey, 1978) increase language use and generalization in children with autism.

Responsivity to multiple cues in the environment is also an important component of Pivotal Response Training. Research has indicated that children with autism often respond to a restricted set of cues in the environment (e.g., Lovaas, R. L. Koegel, & Schreibman, 1979). This occurs in teaching situations (Rincover & Koegel, 1975), as well as in social arenas (Pierce, Glad, & Schreibman, 1997). An example might be a child with autism who recognizes his father only when his father is wearing his glasses. The glasses are an irrelevant cue the child has chosen to use in recognizing his father. However, this will not be very useful if his father purchases contact lenses. This overselective attention to irrelevant cues leads to difficulty when learning new skills, generalizing learned behaviors, and interacting in complex social situations. Remediating this attentional deficit can have widespread effects on learning (e.g., Schreibman, Charlop, & Koegel, 1982). Pivotal Response Training addresses this issue by programming responsivity to multiple cues into the teaching procedures and requiring children to respond to a wider range of cues or components. Teaching interactions that include multiple cues require the child to attend to two or more aspects of a stimulus item. For example, instead of asking a child to "put on a sweater," a parent might ask a child to "put on your new blue sweater." In this way, the child must distinguish the new blue sweater from an old blue sweater, a red sweater, a blue t-shirt, and so forth.

Increasing both motivation and responsivity comprise Pivotal Response Training that has been successfully used to increase language skills (R. L. Koegel, O'Dell, & L. K. Koegel, 1987), play skills (Stahmer, 1995; Thorp et al., 1995) and interaction (Pierce & Schreibman, 1995) in children with autism. Pivotal Response Training includes the following steps:

1. The instruction must be clear, appropriate to the task, uninterrupted, and the child must be attending to the therapist or task.
2. Maintenance tasks (tasks the child has already mastered) need to be interspersed frequently.
3. Multiple cues must be presented if appropriate to the child's developmental level.
4. The child needs to be given a significant role in choosing the stimulus items.
5. Rewards need to be immediate, contingent, uninterrupted, and effective.
6. Direct reinforcers (reinforcers related to the task) need to be used the majority of the time.
7. The therapist should take turns with the child to allow for natural interaction and to provide multiple exemplars.
8. Rewards should be contingent on correct responses or attempts (see R. L. Koegel et al., 1989, for a complete description of the training technique).

This method can be used to target a wide array of tasks. Typically, parents and teachers are concerned about language development, so a verbal response is required from the child before consequences are administered. This method is particularly useful in the natural environment. For example, if children wish to watch television, they can be required to ask at a level appropriate to their ability. Depending on the child's developmental level, this may mean saying "May I watch television please," "TV, Mom," "tel," or a manual sign. In each case, the child is choosing the stimulus and is reinforced directly with access to the item. This encourages the use of language in the natural environment and increases generalization. Parents, siblings, and peers of children with autism have successfully mastered PRT (Laski, Charlop, & Schreibman, 1988; Oke, 1993; Pierce & Schreibman, 1995).

In addition, other social skills, such as play and interaction, have been successfully taught using PRT. Children with autism who had appropriate language ability (2.5 years) success-fully learned to engage in spontaneous, creative, symbolic, and sociodramatic play (Stahmer, 1995; Thorp et al., 1995). Interaction skills have been taught to children with autism in schools using peer tutors as trainers (Pierce & Schreibman, 1995). Research is currently being conducted to assess the particular characteristics of families, children, and behaviors that will be most facilitated through the use of PRT. Preliminary information indicates that this type of training is useful for children of most ages and functioning levels. However, if a child does not verbalize at all, initial DTT training for increasing verbalizations might be sug-gested. Additionally, for children with extremely good verbal ability, self-management training (discussed later) may be more appropriate for altering verbal idiosyncrasies such as topic preservation. PRT is particularly useful for behaviors that are social or communicative and with behaviors that have reinforcing natural consequences. Although PRT has been successfully taught to families with extremely variable characteristics, family characteristics that seem to predict superior performance include a parenting style that allows the child some shared control in the learning situation. Parents who have a high need for structure and control may have more difficulty with this type of training. In general, PRT is recommended for use in structured and unstructured settings; for teaching skills such as language, interactions, and play; as well for generalization of skills acquired in other teaching formats (e.g., DTT).

Self-Management Training

Self-management training, although not a new procedure in itself, has only recently been used with developmentally disabled populations. The use of self-management in children with autism was brought about through a growing need for generalization of treatment gains to new environments and a desire for more independence after training. Self-management fulfills these goals by allowing individuals to take some responsibility for their own treatment. The individuals are taught to choose target behaviors (when applicable), record progress toward goals, and administer their own consequences.

Recent research in this area has demonstrated that self-management can be useful for eliminating difficult behaviors and teaching a variety of new skills to individuals with autism with varying cognitive abilities (see Schreibman & R. L. Koegel, 1996). Some behaviors that have been successfully improved through self-management training include: increasing independent work skills (Sainato, Strain, Lefebvre, & Rapp, 1990); decreasing self-stimulatory behavior (R. L. Koegel & L. K. Koegel, 1990); increasing daily living skills (Pierce & Schreibman, 1994); increasing appropriate, unsupervised play skills (Stahmer & Schreibman, 1992); and increasing social skills (L. K. Koegel, R. L. Koegel, Hurley, & Frea, 1992). This body of research indicates that self-management procedures can be useful for increasing appropriate behavior of individuals with autism in unsupervised settings, thereby increasing their independence. In addition, self-management is an effective, positive approach to the management of difficult behaviors such as self-stimulation (R. L. Koegel & L. K. Koegel, 1990; Stahmer & Schreibman, 1992).

The specific procedures of self-management training have varied based on the ability of the individual using the procedures as well as the particular target behavior chosen. However, the following procedures are typically the focus of most self-management programs (see R. L. Koegel, L. K. Koegel, & Parks, 1990, for a more complete description of these techniques): Initially, the individual chooses a target behavior. If individuals cannot choose a target behavior independently, then they can be assisted by a parent or treatment provider. The children are then taught to identify the target behavior. For example, the children learn the difference between periods of *appropriate play* and *inappropriate play*. Appropriate play may include behaviors such as completing a puzzle or playing a game, whereas inappropriate play may include throwing toys, tantruming, or engaging in self-stimulation. The child is taught to identify these behaviors through modeling by the treatment provider, as well as through role playing. Once the children can reliably identify the behavior, they learn to monitor their own performance. Typically, this is done either with a wrist counter (if the frequency of a behavior can be counted) or a watch with an interval timer (to decide if a behavior did or did not occur during a specific period of time). Initially, appropriate recording of the behavior is rewarded, and later rewards are only earned if both recording and behavior are appropriate. Initially, interval durations are quite short in order to ensure success. As the children's behavior improves, the interval duration, as well as the number of intervals required to receive reinforcement, increases. Typically, successful behavior is recorded using a checkmark or a sticker. These markers can then be exchanged for tangible reinforcers. During the early stages, accurate recording as well as short intervals of appropriate behavior are reinforced. Later, the child obtains reinforcement independently after longer periods of appropriate behavior. Once a child is successfully managing and recording behavior in the presence of the treatment provider, the treatment provider's presence is slowly faded from the area. Time without direct supervision is gradually increased (treatment providers can confirm correct implementation by communicating with others in the child's environment or by doing random checks of behavior) and reinforcement schedules are reduced. The final goal is for the child to engage in appropriate behavior independent of the treatment provider, and in some cases, without dependence on self-management materials.

As indicated by the aforementioned research, self-management procedures have been used successfully with children with autism. Preliminary research has pointed to specific parent and child variables that interact to predict success with self-management training. Although self-management leads to more independence in the long run, initial training of the skills can be time consuming. Typically, parents (or other treatment providers) who implement self-management procedures must be willing to make an initial time investment. That is, the children need practice using the self-management materials and identifying target behaviors in order to gain the promised independence. Of course, a time commitment is necessary for success with any treatment method; however, self-management is a technique in which the *child* must learn the process before much behavior change is seen. In typical treatment methods, initial gains are often seen more rapidly because the parent is in charge of the technique. Although most parents who have used self-management report success, others have reported difficulty implementing the procedures. These parents, according to preliminary data, tend to be those who do not place great value on independence, have very limited time to spend with their children, or those that report low motivation to see behavior change.

Moreover, child characteristics seem to play a part in success with this type of treatment. Self-management is typically recommended for children with autism who have some verbal skills. Verbal skills equivalent to that of a typically developing 2-year-old are sufficient for success. In preliminary studies, self-management has been found to be more successful for children who have IQ scores above 50.

As mentioned previously, child and parent characteristics can interact to affect success with self-management training. For example, Pierce and Schreibman (1994) used a pictorial self-management technique to teach individuals with little to no verbal skills to engage is self-help skills, such as dressing, doing laundry, and making lunch. And children whose characteristics may not be indicative of successful self-management may do quite well if they are instructed in these techniques by a highly motivated treatment provider (or parent) who values independence and has the time to invest in the initial training. Children who seem to meet the requirements may not learn the procedures if the treatment provider cannot (for whatever reason) appropriately train the child. Therefore, it is important to look at characteristics of both the child and the treatment provider when deciding whether or not to use self-management procedures. Parents and treatment providers should be intimately involved in the decision to implement self-management procedures. These procedures can be part of a very successful treatment program if everyone involved is motivated and able to participate. However, they can also become frustrating for treatment providers who are already under undue stress, or are simply not motivated to train these techniques, and for children who are not developmentally ready to learn the techniques.

In summary, it has become clear that there is no one optimal treatment or set of intervention procedures that are equally effective for all cases. In order to get the most benefit from the available options, the entire spectrum of child, parent, and target behavior characteristics must be considered. The choice of intervention strategy should be a cooperative decision with input from the clinician, family members, and when appropriate, the child with autism. Taking these individual characteristics into consideration will ensure a more successful outcome.

MAINTENANCE AND GENERALIZATION STRATEGIES

Treatment gains do not always generalize to nontreatment environments (stimulus generalization), across untreated behaviors (response generalization), or over time (maintenance). Treatment is of little value if generalization does not occur, and this has led researchers to place an increasing emphasis on the occurrence and assessment of generalization effects.

Stokes and Baer (1977) described strategies to promote generalization of behavior change, several of which have been added to the treatment of children with autism. One approach to facilitating generalization is to make the treatment environment more similar to the natural environment. This can be done in several ways. One way is to use intermittent schedules of reinforcement during treatment in order to provide a learning environment that more closely approximates the natural environment. Several studies (e.g., Charlop, Kurtz, & Milstein, 1992; R. L. Koegel & Rincover, 1977) have suggested that intermittent schedules increase the durability of treatment gains by reducing the discriminability of the reinforcement schedules used in the treatment and nontreatment settings.

Another strategy is to use natural (direct) reinforcers during training, which will further reduce the differences between the treatment and nontreatment environments (Stokes & Baer, 1977). Thus, reinforcers should be like those found in the individual's natural environment, such as social reinforcers or preferred activities. Also, behaviors taught should be those that will access these reinforcers. To illustrate, Carr, Binkoff, Kologinsky, and Eddy (1978) taught children with autism to use sign language to request items that were likely found in the natural environment. The children were taught to spontaneously request (via signing) their favorite toys as opposed to nonfavored educational stimuli. This led to generalized spontaneous signing. In addition, this procedure incorporates another of the generalization strategies identified by Stokes and Baer (1977): the use of common stimuli (those found in treatment and nontreatment settings).

Behavior therapy often incorporates procedures that directly train generalization. Sequential modification occurs when generalization is programmed by teaching the targeted behavior in every nongeneralized condition (e.g., across people, settings, behaviors). However, it may be impractical to train a behavior in every potential situation. An alternative approach is to merely train sufficient exemplars (Stokes & Baer, 1977). This technique may also be difficult because it is usually impossible to determine beforehand the necessary number of situations or exemplars that will be required before generalization is achieved. To reduce this problem, Stokes and Baer (1977) suggested using mediated generalization. This procedure focuses on teaching a target response that is likely to occur in both treatment and nontreatment situations. The most common mediator is language. Children giving self-instructions in different environments are using this generalization strategy. Self-management procedures may also be considered mediated generalization because the target behavior (self-management) can be taken along from the training environment to other settings.

In addition to these specific strategies, generalization has been enhanced by extending the treatment environment. Thus, the incorporation of parent training programs (R. L. Koegel, Schreibman et al., 1982), teacher training programs (R. L. Koegel, Rincover, & Egel, 1982); and sibling training programs (Schreibman, O'Neill, & R. L. Koegel, 1983) have all been used to extend treatment delivery into those environments in which the child lives.

PROBLEMS IN IMPLEMENTATION

Several problems may occur when attempting to implement treatment with children who have autism. One is the inconsistency of treatment implementation. Often, these children have severe behavior problems requiring constant supervision, and treatment providers— whether they are clinicians, parents, or teachers—have difficulty responding appropriately to behaviors at each occurrence. This leads to, at best, slow progress and, at worst, increases in inappropriate behaviors and decreases in appropriate behaviors. Finally, treatment providers may become frustrated with this slow progress and abandon the program altogether. This is one reason the treatment must be prescriptive and based on the individual child. Moreover, parents can be taught to implement treatment procedures they enjoy (Schreibman, Kaneko, & R. L. Koegel, 1991) and that are easier to use in the natural setting (such as Pivotal Response Training). Teachers and parents must be willing and able to implement the intervention consistently and effectively in order for it to succeed. Even the best program will not work if there is no one to implement it.

Generalization of behavior change is also a problem for these children (Stokes & Baer, 1977), especially when attempting to teach children with autism social skills. Typically, these skills are taught by an adult; however, the hope is that the skills will be used with peers. In most cases, even if interaction increases with an adult, it does not increase with other children (e.g., Stahmer, 1995). Including other children, even siblings, in training can help remedy this problem (e.g., Oke, 1993; Pierce & Schreibman, 1995); however, so far there is no simple solution.

CASE ILLUSTRATION

Case Description

Max, a 3-year-old dark-haired, green-eyed child, was referred to the clinic by a local psychologist. Max had recently been diagnosed with Autistic Disorder after his parents became concerned about his lack of language and poor social responsivity. He had an older brother, Peter, who was 5 years old. As a baby, Max did not sleep well. He tended to cry quite often, and he could not be easily consoled. Max had never used functional language, although his father reported that they did hear an occasional word. This was typically out of context and would not be used again for several weeks, if at all. Max did not often point or gesture, but instead would drag his parents by the arm toward any desired item.

Max did not enjoy playing with his brother, and would often retreat to his room and play alone with his record player any time he had the opportunity. Max would become upset and tantrum if his schedule was upset in any way. As a result, the family rarely varied their normal routine, and they found holidays and vacations quite difficult. Max did use toys and games in his play. He had several doll figures from a favorite movie that he carried with him constantly and, on some occasions, he would use them appropriately, placing them in a bus or at a table. He also enjoyed familiar music, and any games or toys that had the alphabet printed on them.

Max's parents seemed very motivated to learn how to work with Max at home. Although they were under some stress because of the recency of the diagnosis, both of Max's parents seemed to be handling the news well, both doing well at work, and had a good marital rapport. They expressed concern with his tantrum behavior, his occasional aggression toward his brother, and his lack of ability to change his routine. However, they were most concerned with language and social skills deficits.

Assessment

After observing Max and administering the Autism Diagnostic Interview, a second diagnosis of autism was made at the clinic. Max and his family were then admitted to the program, at which time Max was given a battery of behavioral, intellectual, and language assessments; Max's parents were assessed for stress, depression, marital adjustment, and parenting style. The choice of treatment methods was to be decided based on the results of these assessments, using both Max's and his parents' characteristics to choose an optimal treatment program.

First, behavioral observations were conducted in an unfamiliar homelike setting with Max's parents, and then with an unfamiliar adult. Each adult was asked to do a series of tasks during the assessments, including observing Max without initiating toward him, attempting to elicit speech from Max, asking Max to follow verbal instructions, and playing with Max using the available toys. These tapes were then scored for language skills, social skills, and inappropriate behavior.

Max did not exhibit any functional speech during the assessment, although he did vocalize throughout by using jargon and babbling. He did exhibit some understanding of language as evidenced by his ability to follow simple, one-step instructions ("Show me the letter A," and "Bring me the telephone"). Max would engage in appropriate play with each of his parents when they prompted it. Typically, these interactions lasted about 1 to 2 minutes before Max attempted to escape the situation. He did not show affection to his parents, although he would respond better to their requests and overtures than he would to those of the stranger. When the adults did not initiate interaction, Max tended to walk around the room looking at the alphabet on the wall or carrying letters from the alphabet puzzle. He did not initiate any interaction with any of the adults, although he did notice when his father left the room.

Standardized assessments of Max's intellectual abilities, language skills, and adaptive behavior were also conducted. Intellectual ability was assessed using the Leiter International Performance Scales (Leiter, 1979) and the Stanford–Binet 4th ed. (Thorndike, Hagen, & Sattler, 1986). Max did not perform well on the Stanford–Binet (score = 63) due to its heavy emphasis on verbal ability. However, on the Leiter, a nonverbal measure, he received a standard score of 93, which is typical for his chronological age. These scores indicated that although Max had severe language deficits, his nonverbal ability was relatively strong.

A scorable response was not obtained from Max on tests of receptive language. The tests attempted included the Peabody Picture Vocabulary Test (PPVT) and the Assessment of Child Language Comprehension (ACLC). His parents reported that Max probably did understand a few of the words on the tests, but he did not seem to understand the nature of the task when testing was performed.

In addition to assessing Max's behavior, several measures were administered to Max's parents. These included the Family Environment Scale, the Questionnaire on Resources and Stress, and the Ideas About Parenting Instrument.[1] The information from these assessments indicated that Max's parents had a relatively good relationship, although both were feeling a high level of stress regarding Max's future needs, as well as the financial burden of raising a child with special needs. Max's mother, in particular, felt concerned about limitations on opportunities for the family because of Max's difficulties. According to the Ideas About Parenting Instrument, both parents valued independence in their children, and had parenting styles amenable to allowing Max some degree of control during the course of treatment selection and application.

Treatment Implementation

In order to choose the optimal treatment package for Max, all of the assessment measures were taken into account. Max's parents were well adjusted and motivated to provide treatment for Max, making them excellent candidates for parent training. Their parenting style would fit with the shared control and naturalistic procedures of Pivotal Response Training. In addition, they valued independence, indicating that self-management might be an option for this family. However, when taking Max's characteristics into account, it was clear that he was too young (only 3 years old) and did not have sufficient language ability for success with self-management skills. Both PRT and DTT training were the best options based on his abilities.

Because Max's parents were most concerned with language and interaction skills, and because gains in these skills often serve to alleviate some problem behaviors (e.g., tantruming and aggression used as communication) it was decided to begin with language training. Max already used some sounds and would occasionally use a single word. Max needed to learn that these vocalizations could be useful for him. The process began by teaching Max's parents to use Pivotal Response Training to increase Max's use of communicative vocalizations.

Max and his parents would come in to the clinic twice each week for 1-hour (consisting of two 30-minute sessions). Max's parents were asked to read *How to Teach Pivotal Behaviors to Children with Autism: A Training Manual* (R. L. Koegel et al., 1989), which described the steps used in PRT. After completing the manual, observing a therapist working with Max, and going over examples of each step with a therapist, Max's parents began training by working with Max for only 5 minutes at a time. The time spent with Max increased slowly over the next several weeks until they were working with Max for the entire 30-minute session. During each session, a therapist observed and gave immediate feedback to Max's parents. They would continue to work with Max in this way until they could perform each of the steps outlined in the PRT manual accurately during at least 80% of the session.

During the weeks that Max's parents were learning the techniques, Max worked both with therapists as well as with each of his parents. Initially, he would only choose to play with his favored toys. He learned quickly that he would need to make a vocalization in order to obtain the toys. In the early stages, Max would tantrum when his turn ended. However, he quickly discovered that if he waited and watched, he would soon receive another turn of his own. After Max could consistently make a vocalization for a desired item, he was required to use sounds

---

[1] For brief descriptions of these assessments, the reader is referred to the earlier section devoted to assessment.

that approximated the word for that item. For example, he would need to use a "b" sound to acquire a book (these more difficult trials were, of course, interspersed with maintenance trials throughout). After a few weeks, Max was beginning to use a few words (e.g., "more," "book," and "doll"). When Max's parents began using PRT at home, and training time increased, so did his use of communication skills. He began to use sounds for everything, and some of his tantrum behaviors decreased as his ability to communicate increased.

Recall that Max's parents were also concerned about helping Max get through vacations and nonroutine days without tantruming. It was decided that to work on this behavior, a variation of the behavioral principles used in DTT would be used in which Max's parents would change the antecedents and the consequences of the behavior in order to help Max get through the day without a tantrum. His parents were first asked to read *Behavior Problems* (Baker, Brightman, Heifetz, & Murphy, 1976), a manual describing how to look at a behavior as well as modify it. They were then asked to keep detailed records of Max's behavior. After reviewing the records, Max's parents realized that each time Max tantrumed, they would make every attempt to reinstate his original routine. That is, if they had decided to go to the beach instead of the park, when Max would tantrum they would change their plans and go to the park. This procedure seemed disruptive to the family and reinforced Max's inappropriate behavior.

In order to change this behavior, Max's parents felt it would be best to begin with some preventative measures. They began by putting together a booklet full of pictorial representations of common activities and routines (e.g., park, beach, car ride, bath, breakfast). Each evening before bed Max and his parents would make a chart of the activities/routines for the following day. Moreover, Max would be allowed to help choose the activities whenever possible so that he would be motivated to participate in them. If a major change in routine was expected, such as a family visit or a holiday, Max's parents would show him pictures related to the event each evening for at least a week before the event would take place. Each morning the pictures would be on Max's wall so he could remind himself of the activity of the day. In order to help Max overcome his need for routine, Max's parents decided to vary his routine slightly each day so that the problem of routines might be avoided in the future. For example, some nights they would brush teeth and then read a story and other nights they would reverse the order. During the early stages of this training, Max often became upset. When Max did tantrum, his parents were careful not to inadvertently reinforce him. They would explain to him (and show him with pictures) what had happened, and then they would ignore him until he calmed down. Max's parents revealed that the first few times they tried this they almost gave up. Max cried for almost an hour. After he was quiet for about 5 minutes they would offer some choices of activities that fit into the new routine. After a few accidental changes in routine, the data Max's parents were taking indicated that his tantrums began to get shorter and less intense. Also, he was handling routine changes more easily on a day-to-day basis, even making a game of rearranging his pictures into new routines and asking to do things like take a bath before dinner. Max's parents were glad to allow Max this bit of control over his activities in exchange for some flexibility in theirs!

Conclusion of Treatment

After about 6 months of training, Max's parents had met criterion with the PRT training and demonstrated proficiency with the behavior modification training. They were using both programs at home, and had begun to work on Max's aggression by assessing the behavior and setting up a program on their own. All of the previous assessments were completed again with Max and his family. His language skills had increased according to both the Stanford–Binet and the Peabody Picture Vocabulary Test, indicating that he had the vocabulary skills equivalent to that of a 2-year-old. Max was more responsive to his parents, playing short interactive games and responding to directions. He still did not interact well with the stranger, as he withdrew to a corner with a letter puzzle. He was also more compliant at home as he seemed to understand the verbal instructions more easily. His parents' areas of increased stress had somewhat decreased.

It was suggested that Max's family continue with the PRT to help him increase both his play and language skills. They would also continue to use the behavioral methods as needed for new skills such as potty training. It was suggested that when Max turned 5, they return to our clinic to learn self-management techniques. Because of their family profile and Max's significant language progress this family would benefit from self-management training.

CONCLUSIONS

Autism is a pervasive developmental disorder that places severe limits on language skills and social interaction. The disorder presents itself differently for each child with autism, however, training in communication and social skills will be a necessary component of training for all of these children. The treatment of choice will vary based on child and family characteristics, as well as variables related to target behaviors. The most effective treatment will be prescriptive and will include family participation in treatment choice and implementation.

Researchers have not yet found a "cure" for autism. However, treatment methods continue to improve. As "best practice" has been modified based on systematic data, researchers have begun to realize the importance of individual factors in treatment. There is no one "best" treatment method for children with autism, but instead the need for designing a "best" method for each individual family. Hopefully, by taking all of these complex variables into account, each treatment method can be made more effective by ensuring implementation and maintenance of the technique. This will, in turn, increase the chances for success for both the family and child with autism.

ACKNOWLEDGMENTS

Portions of the research reported in this chapter were supported by U.S.P.H.S. Research Grants MH39434 and MH28210 from the National Institute of Mental Health. Special thanks to Lauren Loos for reviewing an earlier draft of this chapter.

REFERENCES

American Psychiatric Association. (1994). *Diagnostic and statistical manual of mental disorders* (4th ed.). Washington, DC: Author.

Baker, B. L., Brightman, A. J., Heifetz, L. J., & Murphy, D. M. (1976). *Behavior problems*. Champaign, IL: Research Press.

Berk, R. A., & Berk, S. F. (1979). *Labor and leisure at home: Content and organization of the household day*. Beverly Hills, CA: Sage.

Bloom, L., & Lahey, M. (1978). *Language development and language disorders*. New York: Wiley.

Carr, E. G., Binkoff, J. A., Kologinsky, E., & Eddy, M. (1978). Acquisition of sign language by autistic children: I. Expressive labeling. *Journal of Applied Behavior Analysis, 11*, 489–501.

Charlop, M. H., Kurtz, P. F., & Milstein, J. P. (1992). Too much reinforcement, too little behavior: Assessing task interspersal procedures in conjunction with different reinforcement schedules with autistic children. *Journal of Applied Behavior Analysis, 25*, 795–808.

Cowan, C. P., Cowan, P. A., Heming, G., Garrett, E., Coysh, W. S., Curtis-Boles, H., & Boles, A. J., III (1985). Transitions to parenthood: His, hers and theirs. *Journal of Family Issues, 6,* 451–481.

Dunlap, G. (1984). The influence of task variation and maintenance tasks on learning and affect of autistic children. *Journal of Experimental Child Psychology, 31*, 41–64.

Dunlap, G., & Koegel, R. L. (1980). Motivating autistic children through stimulus variation. *Journal of Applied Behavior Analysis, 13*, 619–627.

Dunn, L. M., & Dunn, L. M. (1981). *Peabody Picture Vocabulary Test—Revised.* Circle Pines, MN: American Guidance Service, Inc.

Foster, R., Giddan, J. J., & Stark, J. (1973). *Assessment of children's language comprehension*. Palo Alto, CA. Consulting Psychologists Press.

Gardner, M. F. (1990). *Expressive One-Word Picture Vocabulary Test—Revised.* Novato, CA: Academic Therapy Publications.

Holroyd, J. (1974). Questionnaire on resources and stress: An instrument to measure family response to a handicapped family member. *Journal of Community Psychology, 2*, 92–94.

Jarrold, C., Boucher, J., & Smith, P. (1993). Symbolic play in autism: A review. *Journal of Autism and Developmental Disorders, 23*, 281–308.

Koegel, L. K., Koegel, R. L., Hurley, C., & Frea, W. D. (1992). Improving social skills and disruptive behavior in children with autism through self-management. *Journal of Applied Behavior Analysis, 25*, 341–353.

Koegel, R. L., Dyer, K., & Bell, L. K. (1987). The influence of child-preferred activities on autistic children's social behavior. *Journal of Applied Behavior Analysis, 20*, 243–252.

Koegel, R. L., & Egel, A. L. (1979). Motivating autistic children. *Journal of Abnormal Psychology, 88*, 418–426.

Koegel, R. L., & Koegel, L. K. (1990). Extended reductions in stereotypic behavior through self-management in multiple community settings. *Journal of Applied Behavior Analysis, 23*, 119–128.

Koegel, R. L., Koegel, L. K., & Parks, D. R. (1990). *How to teach self-management skills to people with severe disabilities: A training manual.* Unpublished manuscript, University of California, Santa Barbara.

Koegel, R. L., O'Dell, M. C., & Dunlap, G. (1988). Producing speech use in nonverbal autistic children by reinforcing attempts. *Journal of Autism and Developmental Disorders, 18*, 525–538.

Koegel, R. L., O'Dell, M. C., & Koegel, L. K. (1987). A natural language teaching paradigm for nonverbal autistic children. *Journal of Autism and Developmental Disorders, 17*, 187–200.

Koegel, R. L., & Rincover, A. (1977). Research on the difference between generalization and maintenance in extra-therapy responding. *Journal of Applied Behavior Analysis, 10*, 1–12.

Koegel, R. L., Rincover, A., & Egel, A. L. (1982). Educating and understanding autistic children. Houston, TX: College Hill Press.

Koegel, R. L., Schreibman, L., Britten, K. R., Burke, J. C., & O'Neill, R. E. (1982). A comparison of parent training to direct clinic treatment. In R. L. Koegel, A. Rincover, & A. L. Egel (Eds.), *Educating and understanding autistic children* (pp. 260– 279). San Diego: College Hill Press.

Koegel, R. L., Schreibman, L., Good, A., Cerniglia, L., Murphy, C., & Koegel, L. (1989). *How to teach pivotal behaviors to children with autism: A training manual.* Unpublished manuscript, University of California, Santa Barbara.

Koegel, R. L., & Williams, J. A. (1980). Direct versus indirect response reinforcer relationships in teaching autistic children. *Journal of Abnormal Child Psychology, 8*, 537–547.

Laski, K. E., Charlop, M. H., & Schreibman, L. (1988). Training parents to use the natural language paradigm to increase their autistic children's speech. *Journal of Applied Behavior Analysis, 21*, 391–400.

Leiter, R. G. (1979). *Leiter International Performance Scale: Instruction manual.* Chicago: Stoelting.

Lieven, E. V. M. (1976). Turn-taking and pragmatics: Two issues in early child language. In R. N. Campbell & P. T. Smith (Eds.), *Recent advances in psychology of language* (pp. 215–236). New York: Plenum.

Lord, C., Rutter, M., & Le Couteur, A. (1994). Autism Diagnostic Interview—Revised: A revised version of a diagnostic interview for caregivers of individuals with possible pervasive developmental disorders. *Journal of Autism and Developmental Disorders, 24,* 659–686.

Lovaas, O. I. (1981). *Teaching developmentally disabled children: The me book.* Austin, TX: Pro-ed.

Lovaas, O. I., Koegel, R. L., & Schreibman, L. (1979). Stimulus overselectivity in autism: A review of the research. *Psychological Bulletin, 86*, 1236–1254.

Lovaas, O. I., Koegel, R. L., Simmons, J. Q., & Long, J. S. (1973). Some generalization and follow-up measures on autistic children in behavior therapy. *Journal of Applied Behavior Analysis, 6*, 131–166.

Moos, R. H. , Insel, P. M., & Humphrey, B. (1974). *Family Environment Scale: Preliminary manual.* Palo Alto, CA: Consulting Psychology Press..

Oke, J. (1993). *A group training program for siblings of children with autism: Acquisition of language training procedures and related behavior change.* Unpublished doctoral dissertation, University of California, San Diego.

Pierce, K. L., Glad, K., & Schreibman, L. (1997). Social perception in children with autism: An attentional deficit. *Journal of Autism and Developmental Disorders, 27* (3), 261–278.

Pierce, K. L., & Schreibman, L. (1994). Teaching daily living skills to children with autism in unsupervised settings through pictorial self-management. *Journal of Applied Behavior Analysis, 27*, 471–481.

Pierce, K. L., & Schreibman, L. (1995). Increasing complex social behaviors in children with autism: Effects of peer-implemented pivotal response training. *Journal of Applied Behavior Analysis, 28*, 285–295.

Ricks, D. M., & Wing, L. (1977). Language, communication, and the use of symbols in normal and autistic children. *Journal of Autism and Childhood Schizophrenia, 5*, 191–222.

Rincover, A., & Koegel, R. L. (1975). Setting generality and stimulus control in autistic children. *Journal of Applied Behavior Analysis, 8*, 235–246.

Rutter, M. (1978). Diagnosis and definition. In M. Rutter & E. Schopler (Eds.), *Autism: A reappraisal of concepts and treatment* (pp. 139–161). New York: Plenum.

Sainato, D. M., Strain, P. S., Lefebvre, D., & Rapp, N. (1990). Effects of self-evaluation on the independent work skills of preschool children with disabilities. *Exceptional Children, 56*, 540–549.

Schreibman, L. (1988). *Autism.* Beverly Hills, CA: Sage.

Schreibman, L., Charlop, M. H., & Koegel, R. L. (1982). Teaching autistic children to use extra stimulus prompts. *Journal of Experimental Child Psychology, 33*, 475–491.

Schreibman, L., Kaneko, W. M., & Koegel, R. L. (1991). Positive affect of parents of autistic children: A comparison across two teaching techniques. *Behavior Therapy, 22*, 479–490.

Schreibman, L., & Koegel, R. L. (1996). Fostering self-management: Parent delivered pivotal response training for children with autistic disorder. In E. D. Hibbs & P. S. Jensen (Eds.), *Psychosocial treatment for child and adolescent disorders: Empirically based strategies for clinical practice.* Washington, DC: American Psychological Association.

Schreibman, L., O'Neill, R. E., & Koegel, R. L. (1983). Behavioral training for siblings of autistic children. *Journal of Applied Behavior Analysis, 16*, 129–138.

Sparrow, S. S., Balla, D. A., & Cicchetti, D. V. (1984). *Vineland Adaptive Behavior Scales.* Circle Pines, MN: American Guidance Service.

Stahmer, A. C. (1995). Teaching symbolic play to children with autism using pivotal response training. *Journal of Autism and Developmental Disorders, 25*, 123–141.

Stahmer, A. C., & Schreibman, L. (1992). Teaching children with autism appropriate play in unsupervised environments using a self-management treatment package. *Journal of Applied Behavior Analysis, 25*, 447–459.

Stokes, T. F., & Baer, D. M. (1977). An implicit technology of generalization. *Journal of Applied Behavior Analysis, 10*, 349–368.

Thorndike, R. L., Hagen, E. P., & Sattler, J. M. (1986). *The Stanford–Binet Intelligence Scale* (4th ed.). Chicago: Riverside Publishing.

Thorp, D. M., Stahmer, A. C., & Schreibman, L. (1995). The effects of sociodramatic play training on children with autism. *Journal of Autism and Developmental Disorders, 25*, 265–282.

Williams, J. A., Koegel, R. L., & Egel. A. L. (1981). Response–reinforcer relationships and improved learning in autistic children. *Journal of Applied Behavior Analysis, 14*, 53–60.

Chapter 4

Attention-Deficit/Hyperactivity Disorder

Mark D. Rapport
University of Hawaii

This chapter provides readers with a comprehensive protocol for treating children with attention-deficit/hyperactivity disorder (ADHD). This task is challenging. Children with ADHD typically present with myriad, complex, and multifaceted difficulties. These difficulties extend from academic (from performance deficits to specific learning disabilities and more nebulously defined cognitive challenges) to broad-based behavior dyscontrol problems. Experienced difficulties transcend traditional boundaries of the child's home and school. And there are no established set of procedures, specific therapies (e.g., behavioral, pharmacological), or unique strategies alone or in combination that can restore children with ADHD to a normal state of functioning. Consequently, some investigators have speculated that ADHD may represent an evolutionary different (not damaged) brain that is ill-equipped to deal with the demands of 21st-century industrialized societies, in general, and formal schooling experiences, in particular (Rapport, 1995). This point of view is derived from the principle that change is dangerous and organisms ignore predictable and everyday stimuli so that resources are ready to react to new and potentially dangerous or significant events (i.e., adaptive behavior). Mental health professionals are nevertheless being increasingly called on to provide comprehensive treatment interventions for children with ADHD, despite the aphoristic difficulties faced in attempting to make a "square peg fit a round hole." With these caveats in mind, the chapter draws on empirical works, 20 years of professional experience working with children with ADHD, and certain ideas that have not been subjected to empirical testing, but may nevertheless prove fruitful for devising innovative treatment strategies.

CHAPTER OVERVIEW

The initial sections present a brief historical overview of the disorder, followed by an exposition of current diagnostic criteria, clinical features, and pertinent findings from intermediate and long-term outcome studies of children with ADHD. The intent is to provide the reader both with a comprehensive understanding of the disorder and a vivid appreciation of the complex realities inherent in formulating a treatment plan.

The third section presents information concerning the clinical assessment of children with ADHD, which represents the cornerstone of treatment planning and must be considered fully prior to initiating intervention. Experienced, highly seasoned clinicians remember the number of misdiagnosed cases they have encountered hiding under the ADHD umbrella. Even correctly diagnosed cases are frequently comorbid for a variety of other disorders, the most common being conduct disorder (and its predecessor, oppositional-defiant disorder), learning disabilities, speech/language disorders, and mood and anxiety disorders. And, some of the core features of ADHD, such as *inattention*, are central to multiple disorders of childhood and/or acute reactions to environmental stressors, further obfuscating the diagnostic picture.

The ensuing two sections present treatment protocols for school and home/community settings. The proposed protocols involve multiple interventions (e.g., curricula, pharmacological, behavioral) that are intricately linked and must be individually titrated to each child's unique difficulties. A caveat, however, is in order. Readers expecting a review of traditionally employed behavioral and pharmacological interventions may be better served by comprehensive texts by Barkley (1990) and DuPaul and Stoner (1994).

The treatment protocol sections include several aspects of currently used treatment approaches, but intentionally transcend established empirical fact in an attempt to broaden existing clinical armamentarium. The primary reason for this departure is that innovative treatments for children with ADHD are virtually nonexistent. The field has stagnated over the past 20 years as evidenced by its overreliance on traditional behavioral therapies and pharmacological interventions. As a result, current treatment efforts may be likened to re-arranging deck chairs on the Titanic. Diminutive changes and manipulations in independent variables common to behavioral and pharmacological interventions continue to dominate the treatment outcome literature, whereas glaring deficiencies in classroom environments and curricula are condoned, resulting in academic failure for a majority of children with ADHD.

Although behavioral principles and medicines arguably represent the cornerstone of treatment for children with ADHD, a continued reliance on these reactive interventions belies the development of proactive innovative strategies such as computerized instruction and automatic feedback systems. The treatment protocol sections thus include descriptions of ideal in addition to empirically proven working environments for children with ADHD. They intentionally offer a *proactive* as opposed to *reactive* approach for working with children with ADHD. Critical issues pertinent to monitoring treatment outcome are also discussed in the two treatment protocol sections. The final section serves as a summary and explores additional directions for treatment planning and intervention.

HISTORICAL OVERVIEW

Historically, children with ADHD were referred to as having "minimal brain damage" (1947 to early 1950s). The association between brain damage and behavioral deviance was a logical one and was introduced following the 1918 encephalitis epidemics. Many of the post-encephalitic children were observed to be motorically overactive, inattentive, and aggressive, and displayed a wide variety of emotional and learning difficulties. Subsequent attempts to validate the concept of minimal brain damage, however, were unsuccessful. Neither "soft neurological signs" (i.e., objective physical evidence that is perceptible to the examining physician as opposed to the subjective sensations or symptoms of the patient), nor a positive history of brain damage or birth difficulties, were evidenced in a majority of children with a history of behavioral problems.

The concept of a clinical disorder resulting from brain damage was gradually discarded and replaced with the more subtle but nebulous concept of "minimal brain dysfunction" (MBD; late 1950s to mid-1960s). The distinction between brain damage and brain dysfunction was an important one. It implied a hypothesis of brain dysfunction resulting from manifestations of central nervous system dysfunction, as opposed to brain damage as an assumed fact in affected children. It also suggested that a wide range of learning and behavioral disabilities could accompany the hypothesized deviations of the central nervous system. These symptoms could be inferred from various combinations of impairment in attention, impulse control, gross motor activity, perception, language, and memory, among others.

The concept of minimal brain dysfunction was eventually replaced with the moniker, "hyperkinetic reaction of childhood" in the second edition of its *Diagnostic and Statistical Manual* (DSM–II; American Psychiatric Association, 1968). The change in diagnostic labels reflected a general dissatisfaction with the untestable notion of brain dysfunction and concomitantly suggested that an excessive degree of and difficulties in regulating gross motor activity best represented the core symptoms of the disorder.

The concept of an independent syndrome of *hyperactivity* prevailed between 1968 and 1979, during which time considerable effort was spent trying to validate the notion of a hyperactive child syndrome. An upsurge in child psychopathology research directly affected the evolution of thinking over this time period and resulted in a focus on *attentional difficulties*, or deficits, as the core disturbance of the disorder. Excessive gross motor activity was subsequently relegated to an associative feature role in defining the disorder, which in turn was considered to be neither sufficient nor necessary to establish a formal diagnosis. This rather dramatic shift in diagnostic emphasis was reflected in the third edition of the *Diagnostic and Statistical Manual* (DSM–II; American Psychiatric Association, 1980), wherein the disorder was renamed "attention deficit disorder" (ADD) and could occur with hyperactivity (ADDH) or without hyperactivity (ADD). *Polythetic schema* ——— vs monothetic

A second important change in the *DSM–III* nomenclature involved the conceptualization of the disorder itself. Earlier diagnostic conceptualizations of the disorder required, among other clinical criteria, that a child meet a specified number of symptoms from a prepared list to qualify for a diagnosis (e.g., any eight criteria on the list). This type of diagnostic conceptualization, in which no single behavioral characteristic is essential or sufficient for group membership and members having a number of shared characteristics or clinical features are grouped together, is referred to as a *polythetic* schema. The *DSM–III* nomenclature, however, incorporated a *monothetic* schema for the first time, wherein an individual was now required to present with a specified number of symptoms from each of three assumably independent behavioral categories for a diagnosis to be established: inattention, impulsivity, and overactivity. The difference may appear subtle, but it has important implications for diagnostic categorization and defining what constitutes a particular clinical disorder. In the case of ADDH, for example, it would be much more difficult to meet multiple criteria in three distinct behavioral domains (vs. from a single list of symptoms), which in turn would have the effect of refining the disorder to a more homogeneous (similar) grouping of children.

As a consequence of this conceptual shift, researchers began focusing their efforts on establishing whether or not inattention, impulsivity, and hyperactivity were in fact independent behavioral domains—primarily by conducting factor-analytic studies on child behavior rating scale data obtained from classroom teachers. What emerged from factor-analytic research was a mixed and often confusing picture. Most studies failed to find evidence of independent factors or behavioral domains to support the three dimensions associated with ADDH. Several found evidence for a separate "attentional disturbance" domain, whereas impulsivity and hyperactivity appeared to load together on a second factor. That is, items comprising these latter two domains were frequently inseparable from one another, suggesting that impulsivity and hyperactivity were probably different, but related, behaviors of a single dimension of behavior.

The evolution from the *DSM–III* to the revised *DSM–III–R* (American Psychiatric Association, 1987) was much quicker than was the case with previous volumes. In fact, many researchers were displeased with this rapidity of change. Information concerning critical questions was still being collected and analyzed that had a direct bearing on the independence of factors or behavioral dimensions assumed to be integral components of ADDH. And insufficient evidence was available concerning whether ADD represented a special subtype of the disorder that could occur without the hyperactivity component.

Nevertheless, the disorder was renamed in the *DSM–III–R*, with hyperactivity reemerging as a central feature of the disorder. Several other important changes were adopted in the revised 1987 nomenclature. The modified monothetic classification schema that required the presence of behavior problems in three different dimensions (inattention, impulsivity, and hyperactivity) was discarded. The new classification schema reverted back to a polythetic dimensional approach—that is, diagnosis now required that 8 of 14 behaviors from a single list be present in a child for a minimum of 6 months duration, with onset of difficulties occurring prior to age 7. ADD without hyperactivity was abandoned as a distinct subtype of the disorder, and a secondary category termed "undifferentiated attention deficit disorder" was added to subsume those children with attentional problems occurring without hyperactivity. Finally, the "residual ADDH" category, which was used in the earlier edition to describe older individuals (usually adolescents) who no longer presented with the full complement of ADHD symptoms, was discarded.

CLINICAL DESCRIPTION

Current Diagnostic Criteria

The *DSM–IV* (APA, 1994) reflects additional changes both in the formal name of the disorder and the specific criteria used in arriving at a formal diagnosis. It contains three subtypes under the "attention-deficit and disruptive behavior disorders" of childhood. These include: Attention-Deficit/Hyperactivity Disorder, predominantly inattentive type; Attention-Deficit/Hyperactivity Disorder, predominantly hyperactive-impulsive type; and Attention-Deficit/Hyperactivity Disorder, combined type (inattentive and hyperactive-impulsive). The first category is used to describe those children who were previously diagnosed as ADD without hyperactivity in the earlier *DSM–III–R* (APA, 1980) nomenclature. It requires children to exhibit at least six (from a list of nine) inattentive behaviors for a minimum duration of at least 6 months and to a degree that is considered developmentally inappropriate for their age. Moreover, the "inattentive" subtype children must not exhibit more than five behaviors from a second list of hyperactivity-impulsivity items listed under the symptom checklist for "ADHD, predominantly hyperactive-impulsive subtype." To meet diagnostic criteria for the second subtype, children must exhibit a minimum of six developmentally inappropriate behaviors from the hyperactivity-impulsivity symptom checklist, but less than six from the inattention list for a minimum duration of 6 months. For the combined subtype, children must meet criteria for both "inattention" and "hyperactivity-impulsivity." Additional changes reflected in the *DSM–IV* include requiring that symptoms (or problem behaviors) be exhibited pervasively (as opposed to situationally) across settings (e.g., in two or more settings such as at school and at home) and that the disturbance cause clinically significant impairment in social, academic, or occupational functioning. Finally, ADHD cannot occur exclusively during the course of a pervasive developmental disorder, schizophrenia, or other psychotic disorder and cannot be better accounted for by another mental disorder, such as mood disorder, anxiety disorder, or personality disorder.

The *DSM–IV* nomenclature thus departs from previous versions in several important ways: There is recognition that ADHD is a developmental disorder, probably present from birth and therefore implying a genetic linkage in family members; the disorder is pervasive and thus cannot be accounted for by environmental elements specific to certain settings (e.g., difficulties at home but not at school or vice versa); there is a recognition that many of the clinical features of ADHD (e.g., attentional difficulties) overlap with those seen in other childhood disorders. *DSM–IV* (APA, 1994) diagnostic criteria are depicted in Table 4.1.

not accounted for by environ. elements.

Expression of Primary Symptoms

Individuals with the disorder generally display some disturbance in each of the three assumed deficit areas (inattention, impulsivity, hyperactivity) and in most settings, but to varying degrees. Conversely, signs of the disorder may be minimal or even absent in novel settings (e.g., being examined in a doctor's office or clinical setting), when receiving individualized attention, or under conditions in which stimulation or interest level is relatively high.

At home, inattention is commonly displayed by frequent shifts from one uncompleted activity to another, and a failure to follow through and/or comply with instructions. The impulsivity component is often expressed by acting without considering either the immediate or delayed consequences of one's actions (e.g., running into the street, accident proneness), interrupting the conversation of other household members, and grabbing objects (not with malevolent intent) in the store while on shopping trips. Problems with overactivity are often expressed by difficulty remaining seated during meals, while completing homework or riding in the car, and excessive movement during sleep.

At school, inattention is usually evidenced by difficulty deploying and maintaining adequate attention (i.e., staying on-task), a failure to complete academic assignments, and deficient organizational and information-processing skills. Impulsivity is expressed in a variety of ways, such as interrupting others, beginning assignments before receiving (or understanding) complete instructions, making careless mistakes while completing assignments, blurting out answers in class, and having difficulty waiting for a turn in both small group and organized sport activities. Hyperactivity is frequently manifested by fidgetiness, twisting and wiggling in one's seat or changing seat positions, dropping objects on the floor, and emitting noises or playing with objects during quiet assignment periods. Be careful to note, however, that all of

TABLE 4.1

Diagnostic Criteria for Attention Deficit Hyperactivity Disorder (ADHD)

A. Either (1) or (2):

(1) inattention: six (or more) of the following symptoms of inattention have persisted for at least 6 months to a degree that is maladaptive and inconsistent with developmental level:

(a) often fails to give close attention to details or makes careless mistakes in schoolwork, work, or other activities

(b) often has difficulty sustaining attention in tasks or play activities

(c) often does not seem to listen when spoken to directly

(d) often does not follow through on instructions and fails to finish schoolwork, chores, or duties in the workplace (not due to oppositional behavior or failure to understand instructions)

(e) often has difficulty organizing tasks and activities

(f) often avoids, dislikes, or is reluctant to engage in tasks that require sustained mental effort (such as schoolwork or homework)

(g) often loses things necessary for tasks or activities (e.g., toys, school assignments, pencils, books, or tools)

(h) is often easily distracted by extraneous stimuli

(i) is often forgetful in daily activities

(2) hyperactivity-impulsivity: six (or more) of the following symptoms of hyperactivity-impulsivity have persisted for at least 6 months to a degree that is maladaptive and inconsistent with developmental level:

Hyperactivity

(a) often fidgets with hands or feet or squirms in seat

(b) often leaves seat in classroom or in other situations in which remaining seated is expected

(c) often runs about or climbs excessively in situations in which it is inappropriate (in adolescents or adults, may be limited to subjective feelings of restlessness)

(d) often has difficulty playing or engaging in leisure activities quietly

(e) is often "on the go" or often acts as if "driven by a motor"

(f) often talks excessively

Impulsivity

(g) often blurts out answers before questions have been completed

(h) often has difficulty awaiting turn

(i) often interrupts or intrudes on others (e.g., butts into conversations or games)

B. Some hyperactive-impulsive or inattentive symptoms that caused impairment were present before age 7 years.

C. Some impairment from the symptoms is present in two or more settings (e.g., at school [or work] and at home).

D. There must be clear evidence of clinically significant impairment in social, academic, or occupational functioning.

E. The symptoms do not occur exclusively during the course of a Pervasive Developmental Disorder, Schizophrenia, or other Psychotic Disorder and are not better accounted for by another mental disorder (e.g., Mood Disorder, Anxiety Disorder, Dissociative Disorder, or a Personality Disorder).

Code based on type:

314.01 Attention-Deficit/Hyperactivity Disorder, Combined Type: if both Criteria A1 and A2 are met for the past 6 months.

314.00 Attention-Deficit/Hyperactivity Disorder, Predominantly Inattentive Type: if Criterion A1 is met but Criterion A2 is not met for the past 6 months.

314.01 Attention-Deficit/Hyperactivity Disorder, Predominantly Hyperactive-Impulsive Type: if Criterion A2 is met but Criterion A1 is not met for the past 6 months.

Coding note: For individuals (especially adolescents and adults) who currently have symptoms that no longer meet full criteria "In Partial Remission" should be specified.

Note: From the *Diagnostic and Statistical Manual of Mental Disorders* (4th ed., pp. 83–85). Copyright 1994 by the American Psychiatric Association. Reprinted by permission.

these behaviors may be diminished or exacerbated by subtle changes in the environment. Teachers frequently comment, for example, that an identified child with ADHD who is absorbed in a particular activity of high interest value or who is working in a one-on-one situation with an adult can attend for normal time expectations and not move a muscle while doing so. Parents also report that their children with ADHD can sit perfectly still while engaged in high stimulation activities, such as watching movies (e.g., "Star Wars"), and while playing interactive computer or video games.

Clinical Features

The first distinction that should be noted in understanding children with ADHD is that it is not the type or kind of behavior they exhibit that is particularly deviant, but the quantity or degree and intensity of their behavior. That is, they tend to exhibit higher rates of behavior and frequently with greater intensity in situations that demand lower rates or more subtle kinds of behavior (e.g., becoming disruptive and behaving inappropriately in school or while interacting with others) and at other times, lower rates of behavior when higher rates are demanded (e.g., not paying attention and completing academic assignments in the classroom). Overall, they appear to be out-of-sync with environmental demands and expectations, especially in situations that require careful sustained attention and protracted effort at tasks that are not particularly interesting or stimulating to the child.

Children's behavior must also be viewed in an appropriate developmental context. For example, younger children typically are more active, cannot pay attention to a particular task for as long a time interval, and tend to spend less time in making decisions or analyzing problems compared to older children. Other factors, such as gender and cultural differences, may also play a defining role in determining what constitutes normality. And, it is only when a child's behavior consistently and significantly exceeds these expectations that it is considered deviant.

In ADHD, the developmental behavioral pattern typically observed is associated with an early onset, a gradual worsening of symptoms over time, and an unrelenting clinical course until late adolescence when the child is no longer in school. Most children with ADHD continue to exhibit symptoms of the disorder as adults, the severity of which depends on a number of factors.

A third feature characteristic of children with ADHD is that their behavioral difficulties tend to be pervasive across situations and settings. Most people have been "hyper" at one time or another, have experienced difficulty concentrating, and have acted impulsively in particular situations. These occurrences tend to be isolated events and usually particular environmental circumstances, situations, or contingencies can be identified as responsible for or as contributing factors associated with the behavior (e.g., feeling ill or having to study for a particularly uninteresting class). The child with ADHD, on the other hand, exhibits this pattern of behavior in most situations and settings, day after day, year after year. A gradual worsening of behavioral and academic difficulties is usually observed as the child grows older, because with increasing age the environment demands being able to pay attention, sit still, and control impulses for longer periods of time. Difficulties are especially conspicuous on entry into the fourth and seventh grades, when classroom demands and academic assignments become increasingly more complex, take longer to complete, and rely heavily on the ability to work independently.

Children with ADHD are also known for their "consistently inconsistent" behavior. That is, they tend to behave rather erratically both within and across days even when their home and school environments are relatively stable. Teachers frequently report, for example, that on some days the child appears relatively settled and able to pay attention and complete academic assignments, although most days are characterized by disruptiveness, inattention, and low work completion rates. Parents report a similar phenomena at home, even among those who are highly skilled in managing their child's behavior. The reasons for the ADHD child's inconsistent pattern of behavior are varied and may be related to a complex interaction between brain regulation mechanisms and prevailing environmental stimulation and contingencies (Rapport, 1995).

Secondary Symptoms or Associated Features

Secondary features are those behaviors and difficulties that occur at a greater than chance frequency in children with a particular disorder, but are neither necessary nor sufficient to serve as formal diagnostic criteria. Many of these symptoms or behaviors are reported early in the developmental course of the disorder and may thus represent less prominent features of the disorder. These include lability of mood, temper tantrums, low frustration tolerance, social disinhibition, cognitive impairment with associated learning disability, and perceptual motor difficulties (Barkley, 1990). Other aspects of disturbance or behavioral difficulties may be secondary to or direct and indirect consequences of the disorder. For example, disturbed peer and interpersonal relationships, academic underachievement, school failure, decreased self-esteem, depressed mood, and conduct problems are characteristic of many children with ADHD. The presence or absence of attendant aggressive or conduct features is especially important and may be of both diagnostic and prognostic value.

Longitudinal Studies

The importance of longitudinal studies in understanding children with ADHD are manifold. Some continue to argue that symptoms related to ADHD are merely a manifestation of poor or faulty parenting combined with the mental health establishment's bent on fabricating clinical disorders and a failure by educational systems to accommodate for differences in children's learning styles. There also remains a prevalent but perceptibly diminishing myth in the field that ADHD is limited to childhood and, as such, reflects a maturational disorder that is outgrown as the child approaches adolescence. Both intermediate (adolescent) and long-term (adult) outcome studies address these viewpoints and help clarify the nature of ADHD and its diagnostic significance. Of greater relevance to the goals of this chapter is their potential for illuminating serious problem behaviors that do not abate over time, which in turn can be incorporated into long-range treatment plans.

Intermediate (Adolescent) Outcome.   Follow-up studies into adolescence are unanimous in demonstrating that ADHD is not limited to childhood years. Continued psychopathology into adolescence is the rule rather than the exception. A majority of children show a continuation of symptoms and significant numbers develop antisocial behavior. In the New York study of 101 hyperactive boys, for example, nearly 70% of the children followed continued to display the full syndrome of ADDH until age 15 (Gittelman, Mannuzza, Shenker, & Bonagura, 1985). Moreover, approximately half met diagnostic criteria for conduct disorder (CD) at some point during their adolescent years.

Recent follow-up studies of children with ADHD have reported similar findings. In their 8-year follow-up study of 123 mostly male hyperactive children, Barkley, Fischer, Edelbrock, and Smallish (1990) reported that 72% of children followed into adolescence continued to meet diagnostic criteria for ADHD, with 44% meeting criteria for conduct disorder. In terms of educational outcome, 30% of the formerly diagnosed hyperactive children had been retained in at least one grade, 31% and 1.6% had been suspended or expelled from school, respectively, and 4.8% had dropped out of school. Three of the four findings were significantly elevated when both hyperactivity and conduct disorder were present at follow-up: Grade retentions remained the same, whereas 67% and 22% of subjects had been suspended or expelled from school, respectively, and 13% had dropped out of school. These statistics are particularly alarming considering the adolescents were an average of 14.9 years old at follow-up.

A recent follow-up study of 94 children previously diagnosed with ADDH buttress the findings reported by Barkley et al. (1990). Mannuzza et al. (1991) found that, on follow-up, 43% and 32% of their sample met diagnostic criteria for ADDH and conduct disorder, respectively—which ranged from 8 to 14 years after initial diagnosis. Drug use disorders were also significantly more prevalent in previously diagnosed children with ADDH, but were associated and always preceded or coincided with the development of antisocial behavior—not continuing ADDH symptomatology.

In summary, a significant majority of children previously diagnosed as hyperactive, ADD, or ADHD continue to experience problems with distractibility, concentration, and hyperactivity as adolescents. A subset of these children develop conduct disorder by late childhood, which precedes and serves as a significant predictor for substance abuse during adolescent years. Continued difficulties with school adjustment and poor academic performance across subject areas are common in adolescents with ADHD (particularly those comorbid for conduct disorder), indicating that early difficulties in academic achievement (Cantwell & Satterfield, 1978) rarely abate during adolescence and are exacerbated by antisocial behavior.

Long-Term Outcome.   Several well-controlled prospective studies have been conducted that shed light on the long-term outcome of children previously diagnosed with hyperactivity. In their 10-year follow-up of 75 hyperactive children at 17 to 24 years of age, Weiss, Hechtman, Perlman, Hopkins, and Wener (1979) reported that children previously diagnosed with hyperactivity relocated more often, experienced higher rates of automobile accidents, and were less likely to be living with their parents as compared to a normal control group. Of greater significance were their findings concerning educational outcome. As adults, formerly diagnosed hyperactive children had earned poorer grades in school, failed more grades, had been expelled from school more often, and completed significantly fewer years of schooling—the latter of which was attributed to their poor grades. Thus, it was surprising that formerly diagnosed children with hyperactivity did not differ from normal controls in terms of occupational status (for those working full time) at adult follow-up. The formerly diagnosed children offered several revealing comments concerning their childhood years. Significant numbers (41%) regarded their childhood as unhappy. Many believed that a significant adult (usually the mother or a teacher) or discovering a special talent within themselves had positively impacted their lives; and family fights (usually concerning their behavior), feeling inferior, and being criticized were regarded as behaviors that contributed negatively to their childhood and adolescent years.

Results from a recent longitudinal study by Mannuzza, Klein, Bessler, Malloy, and LaPadula (1993) are consistent with those reported by Weiss et al. (1979). Ninety-one formerly diagnosed hyperactive children were followed an average of 16 years (range = 13 to 19 years) into adulthood (mean age at follow-up = 26 years, range = 23 to 30 years). As adults, the formerly diagnosed children had completed an average of 2.5 fewer years of formal schooling with 23% (vs. 2% of controls) dropping out by the 11th grade. Only 12% (vs. 49% of controls) had completed a bachelor's degree or higher. Yet, nearly 90% of the formerly diagnosed children were gainfully employed as adults. But, consistent with their inferior formal education, fewer held professional positions, which in turn lowered their overall occupational rankings as adults. Relatively large percentages, however, were owners of small businesses (18%) or in trade fields (20%); similar percentages were unemployed (5%) compared with normal controls (4%). A small but significant percentage (5%) of the formerly diagnosed children were incarcerated at follow-up. Assessment of mental health at follow-up indicated that 33% (vs. 16% of controls) had an ongoing clinical diagnosis at adult follow-up, with the most common diagnosis being antisocial personality disorder (18%). Only 8% continued to meet diagnostic criteria for ADHD as adults. Finally, formerly diagnosed hyperactive children were nearly five times more likely than controls to have an ongoing drug abuse syndrome (primarily alcohol and marijuana abuse), which was nearly always associated with an antisocial personality disorder. Review articles (e.g., Klein & Mannuzza, 1991) and texts (Weiss & Hechtman, 1986) are available for readers interested in a more comprehensive and detailed discourse on long-term outcome in children with ADHD.

Summary.   Longitudinal studies uniformly demonstrate that 40% to 70% of formerly diagnosed children continue to display the full clinical syndrome of ADHD as adolescents, whereas a disturbing 32% to 50% show a persistent pattern of conduct problems. This latter subgroup is particularly at risk for school difficulties and adult psychopathology (substance abuse and antisocial personality disorder). Stated differently, continuation of ADHD symptoms into adolescence indicates a 50% chance of conduct disorder developing, and nearly two thirds of this latter group will go on to develop a drug or alcohol abuse syndrome.

An alarming 23% of formerly diagnosed children drop out of school by the 11th grade, owing to cumulative years of school difficulties and failures, which in turn negatively impacts their potential for advanced education, occupational choices, and upward socioeconomic mobility. The full spectrum of ADHD symptoms appears to abate in the majority of cases (92%) by adulthood, although many continue to complain of their interfering effects in everyday life. Nearly one fifth (18%) of the children are diagnosed with antisocial personality disorder as adults and 38% of these individuals are comorbid for an ongoing substance abuse disorder.

Implications from intermediate and long-term outcome studies for treatment planning are explicit. Past efforts have focused almost exclusively on reducing ADHD symptomatology (attention, hyperactivity, impulsivity) in particular and have failed to produce desirable long-term results. Innovative methods for improving academic success and reducing the risk for development of conduct disorder must be considered fundamental elements of a comprehensive proactive treatment plan.

ASSESSMENT

Overview

A chief role of clinical assessment is the identification of prominent behavioral or social, cognitive, affective, and physical signs and symptoms in the individual. Information obtained may be used subsequently to formulate initial diagnosis, select and evaluate response to treatment, and in some cases portend long-term outcome. The complexity and multifaceted nature of ADHD eludes facile efforts at clarification and measurement. Broad-based behavioral and sensory domains are affected in the disorder. Many areas of dysfunction are apparent only under certain environmental conditions or situations (Douglas, 1988; Kinsbourne, 1984; Rapport, 1983; Whalen & Henker, 1985). And to complicate matters, children with ADHD frequently exhibit an inconsistent pattern of deficits from day to day, even when tasks and other parameters are held constant. This phenomenon has been observed in both field and highly controlled laboratory settings (Kinsbourne, 1984; Rapport, 1990) to the dismay of researchers and clinicians alike.

Eliciting information from single sources and limiting or relying exclusively on certain types of information to determine diagnosis of ADHD results in a high rate of misidentified cases. A careful, thorough evaluation that assesses multiple modalities, relies on multiple informants, and incorporates a variety of instruments and methods is preferred. It is equally important to gain an experienced clinical understanding of ADHD phenomenology and its "consistently inconsistent" behavioral and cognitive manifestations. This chapter seeks to identify a developmental and aberrant pattern of behavior that is perceived as overtly disruptive to others and that interferes with the individual's ability to achieve academically; attend consistently to select environmental stimuli; regulate, and especially inhibit, behavioral and cognitive functioning in accordance with rules and situational demands; and experience positive regard from usual environmental sources, including interpersonal relationships that, in turn, contribute to development of self-esteem and adaptive functioning.

Owing to the increased precision required for reliable clinical diagnosis, the following sections are intended to serve as an overview of customary diagnostic procedures and clinical instruments used to evaluate children suspected of having ADHD. Approximate use of these instruments and recommended practice parameters are depicted in Table 4.2.

Standardized Interviews

The suggested practice of using a standardized interview format as a clinical diagnostic tool, and the recognition that parents and children frequently disagree regarding both the occurrence and severity of child dysfunction have been credited to the pioneering work of Rutter and Graham (1968). The relative merits and specific advantages associated with their use have been outlined and reviewed (Saghir, 1971; Spitzer, 1983; Weinstein, Stone, Noam, Grimes, & Schwab-Stone, 1989). Chief among them are their potential to reduce or minimize different sources of error variance that are internal (e.g., interviewer's behavior, training, and personal or professional biases) or external (e.g., informant and source discrepancies) to the interview (Weinstein et al., 1989; Weissman et al., 1987). Structured and semi-structured interviews also provide clinicians with a reliable method by which to probe, clarify, and facilitate the reporting of specific aspects of behavior and symptomatology (including history) that may be overlooked during the course of an unstructured clinical interview (Gammon, Rothblum, Mullen, Tischler, & Weissman, 1983; Rutter & Shaffer, 1980), yet are relevant to treatment (Achenbach & Edelbrock, 1978; Helzer et al., 1985; H. C. Quay & L. C. Quay, 1965). Finally, the increased uniformity by which clinicians derive diagnoses and its impact on the establishment of an empirical database for heuristic and clinical purposes may be realized.

TABLE 4.2

Clinical Assessment of Children With ADHD

Intake Referral: Is this an appropriate referral for your practice or setting?

A. If *no*, refer to appropriate agency or resource.

B. If *yes*, establish date for initial intake session.

Clinical Procedure:

A. Parent(s) complete broad-band clinical rating scales by mail or in office setting prior to appointment.

B. Structured or semistructured clinical interview with parent and child when appropriate. Interview to include comprehensive pre-, pari-, post-natal, developmental, medical, psychiatric, educational, and treatment history as well as onset, course, and duration of symptoms/behavior problems.

C. Informed consent forms signed by parent(s).

    (1) Forward broad-band clinical rating scales to classroom teacher(s). Request all school records including psychoeducational evaluations.

    (2) Forward requests for information to other appropriate agencies and treatment providers.

D. Determine whether a psychoeducational evaluation been completed recently:

    (1) If not completed recently:

        (a) Determine appropriateness and need for a current psychoeducational evaluation (e.g., questions concerning intellectual abilities, current educational functioning, and educational placement).

        (b) Administer psychoeducational battery to include intelligence and educational achievement tests.

        (c) Determine appropriateness of administering and/or referring for additional assessment such as specific academic skills disorders, speech/language/hearing evaluations.

    (2) If recently administered, collate results with information obtained by clinical interview, historical records, and broad-band rating scales.

E. Have parents complete select narrow-band clinical rating scales based on observed and reported symptomatology. Forward select narrow-band rating scales to the child's classroom teacher(s).

F. Collate all obtained information. Engage in hypothesis testing and case formulation (convergent/divergent validity of obtained information).

Differential Diagnosis:

A. Determine appropriate rule-outs.

    (1) Additional clarification by clinical interview (parent and/or child); administer additional clinical rating scales as appropriate.

    (2) Refer for additional assessment by medical professional or other service providers as appropriate (e.g., neurological complication suspected).

B. Determine possible comorbid diagnoses.

    (1) Quantify additional clinical diagnoses using follow-up clinical interview, rating scales, and/or assessment by relevant treatment providers.

    (2) Refer for additional assessment by medical professional or other service providers as appropriate (e.g., neurological complication suspected).

Final Diagnosis:

A. Schedule debriefing for parent(s) and child.

    (1) Provide comprehensive review of clinical disorder(s) and expected course for parents (including written material).

    (2) Discuss implications of clinical disorder with child at level appropriate to his/her developmental age and level of oral comprehension.

B. Discuss available treatment options, associated benefits/drawbacks (e.g., side effects), and other recommendations with parent(s).

Parent(s) Decision:

A. Parent(s) should be asked to wait a minimum of 1 week to fully consider/weigh all information provided and to ask additional questions.

B. If parent(s) refuse treatment at this time, offer additional recommendations for second opinion and/or other alternatives.

C. If parent(s) elect to pursue treatment, formulate comprehensive treatment plan and debrief appropriate others (e.g., classroom teachers, other relevant professionals).

Initiation of Treatment Plan:

A. Schedule meetings with appropriate others such as relevant school personnel.

B. Write-up and forward report of findings and recommendation to appropriate professionals (e.g., child's physician).

C. Select appropriate empirical instruments for monitoring treatment effects.

Structured Interviews. The Diagnostic Interview for Children and Adolescents (DICA; Herjanic & Campbell, 1977; Herjanic & Reich, 1982) and the Diagnostic Interview Schedule for Children (DISC; Costello, Edelbrook, Kalas, Kellser, & Klaric, 1984) are the two most popularly used structured psychiatric interviews suitable for assessing children with ADHD. Total interview time ranges from 60 to 90 minutes. Both instruments assess the major disruptive disorders of childhood as well as Axis I disorders, are suitable for interviewing children between 6 and 17 years of age, and may be administered by either a clinician or a trained lay interviewer. Computer scoring and separate versions for interviewing parents and children are available for both instruments. Primary psychometric properties have been established for both instruments, with reliability between parent and child reports typically improving with increasing age of the child.

Semistructured Interviews. The semistructured interviews permit the interviewer greater flexibility with regard to probing and follow-up questioning than do the structured interviews. Most also require that expressed symptomatology be quantified using severity ratings, as opposed to a present–absent or yes–no format. The tradeoff is that the increased reliance on clinical acumen for appropriate probing, follow-up questioning, and symptom quantification necessitates administration by a trained and experienced clinician who is familiar with childhood psychopathology and *DSM–IV* diagnostic criteria.

The three most popularly used semistructured interviews for assessing child psychopathology include the Children's Assessment Schedule (CAS; Hodges, McKnew, Cytryn, Stern, & Klein, 1982), the Kiddie–SADS (K–SADS; Chambers et al., 1985; Puig-Antich & Chambers, 1978), and the Interview Schedule for Children (ISC; Kovacs, 1982). Total interview time ranges from 45 to 120 minutes, and total number of items ranges from 128 to just over 200 for the CAS, K–SADS, and ISC. All three instruments have established psychometric properties, are suitable for interviewing children between 6 and 17 years of age, and assess all major *DSM–IV* Axis I disorders pertinent to childhood. (Note: Structured and semistructured interviews are currently undergoing field testing for *DSM–IV* criteria.) Separate parent and child versions and computer scoring are available for all three interviews, whereas the K–SADS alone allows for item-by-item summary ratings based on clinical judgment and information obtained during the parent–child interviews.

Use of Interviews for Diagnosing ADHD

Only one study has compared structured to semistructured interviews with regard to assessment of children with ADHD. Low to moderate concordance was found when comparing structured (DICA) and semistructured (K–SADS) interviews to best estimate diagnosis in assessing *DSM–III* Axis I disorders in a child psychiatry inpatient population (Carlson, Kashani, Thomas, Vaidya, & Daniel, 1987). Kappa estimates (controlling for base rate) for both interviews fell within the modest to poor range for reliability. Although the sensitivity (true positive rate) of both interviews for identifying ADHD symptomatology in particular was high (between 0.75 and 1.0), specificity rates (true negatives) were unacceptably low (.22) for the DICA. As might be expected, the primary source of confusion was in differentiating ADHD from the other two disruptive behavior disorders: conduct disorder (CD) and oppositional defiant disorder (ODD).

Sensitivity (true positives) and specificity (true negatives) rates have been used in most validation studies to estimate the probability that certain symptoms are present given the presence of a particular disorder (diagnosed positive), or absent given the absence of a disorder (diagnosed negative), respectively. For diagnostic decision-making purposes, however, clinicians may be more interested in knowing the reverse: the likelihood that a particular disorder is or is not present given the presence or absence of a particular symptom or set of symptoms. That is, which symptoms or behaviors, reported as present or absent in a child's history or current repertoire, are most useful for determining diagnosis? The statistics that address this question are referred to as positive predictive power (PPP) and negative predictive power (NPP), respectively (Daws, 1986; Widiger, Hurt, Frances, Clarkin, & Gilmore, 1984), and indicate the utility of specific symptoms as inclusionary (PPP) and exclusionary (NPP) criteria for a particular diagnosis. The information these statistics yield may be especially valuable when attempting to assign appropriate diagnosis to children within the *DSM–IV* "disruptive behavior disorders" category, because of the overlap and covariation in symptomatology among children with ADHD and CD (Hinshaw, 1987).

A single study was located that examined the relative value of different symptoms elicited during the course of a structured psychiatric interview (DISC–P) in differentiating children with ADDH from those with CD (Milich, Widiger, & Landau, 1987). Optimal *inclusion* criteria for identifying ADDH consisted of 4 (of 16 possible) *DSM–III* items: "can't sit still," "restless sleeper," "games unfinished," and "runs around" (i.e., specificity and PPP rates for these items ranged from .86 to .92 and from .76 to .79, respectively). Unfortunately, the items occurred with relatively low frequency (base rate range = .25 to .40) in the referral sample studied, thus limiting their potential usefulness as exclusionary criteria for the disorder. Only one *DSM–III* symptom was found to be useful as an exclusionary criterion: "easily distracted." It occurred frequently (base rate = .80), was a commonly found symptom in the ADDH children studied (sensitivity rate = .95), and its absence suggested that ADHD was not present (NPP = .87). The low specificity (.36) and modest PPP rates (.62), however, indicate that the presence of this symptom was not specific to a diagnosis of ADDH. Its common occurrence with other disorders of childhood thus prohibits its usefulness as a two-way pathognomic.

Interview Information: Other

Standard questions concerning a child's developmental, medical, neuropsychiatric, behavioral, and educational history are included in most structured and semistructured interviews. These factors should be explored, in combination with information relevant to family history, leisure activities, peer relations, behavior at and away from home, and treatment history, to determine whether and how they contribute to the presenting clinical picture (e.g., the onset or point at which first noticed—typically reported by parents to occur at 3 to 4 years of age, and course of ADHD symptoms are readily differentiated from most other childhood disorders). Most of this information must be derived from the parent interview, as young children are notoriously poor historians regarding their early development, and frequently minimize or are unaware of their behavioral and educational difficulties.

A routine physical examination should be scheduled to assess for the presence of physical and sexual characteristics that may be associated with sex-linked genetic disorders and to rule out hearing and vision impairment as causal or contributing factors to a child's attentional or behavioral symptoms. Although much has been written on the subject of minor physical anomalies, their presence has not proven to be sufficiently useful to qualify them as marker variables for identifying children at risk for ADHD (Firestone & Prabhu, 1983; S. E. Shaywitz, 1982). In a similar vein, the results of neurological examination of children with ADHD are usually normal and unrevealing; however, inclusion of certain aspects of a neuromaturational examination may be recommended (S. E. Shaywitz, B. E. Shaywitz, McGraw, & Groll, 1984).

Comment

Clinical and semistructured interviews usually employ more questioning and allow for more probing than do the structured interviews. As a result, they frequently yield greater information relevant to differential diagnosis. In either case, the use of and time required for both types of interviews is easily justified for diagnostic decision-making purposes. Much as a pilot needs to read off the preflight checklist before every flight despite having flown for thousands of hours, clinicians and their patients benefit similarly by taking the time to review symptoms and patterns of behavior in a systematic fashion. Clinicians should be astutely aware, however, of both the individual and collective shortcomings inherent to interviews (see Edelbrock & Costello, 1984; Orvaschel, 1985; Rosenberger & Lewine, 1982; Shrout, Spitzer, & Fleiss, 1987; Weinstein et al., 1989; Weissman et al., 1987). With respect to ADHD, both types of interviews used alone tend to overdiagnose "caseness" in general, resulting in an inflated rate of false positive diagnoses. Continued difficulty with differential diagnosis for the disruptive class of childhood disorders will also be realized (i.e., differentiating ADHD, CD, and ODD from one another). Much of this is because of efforts at applying quantitative measurements to categorical diagnosis. Consequently, additional information relevant to diagnosis must be obtained from other sources such as rating scales, historical and school records, direct observations of behavior, psychoeducational testing, and neurocognitive assessment techniques.

Checklists and Rating Forms

Behavioral checklists and rating scales play a prominent role in assessing children with ADHD. They serve as an important source of information concerning a child's behavior in different settings, how it is judged by significant others, and the extent to which it deviates from age- and gender-related norms. For some instruments, the information obtained contributes to the diagnostic process, whereas the value of others lies in their detection of and sensitivity to treatment effects. Numerous publications have been devoted in recent years to reviewing the major scales and checklists (Achenbach, 1985; Barkley, 1990; Mash & Terdal, 1981). Others have focused on discussing how they are used in diagnosing ADHD (Achenbach, 1987; Barkley, 1990; Barkley & Edelbrock, 1987; Conners, 1987; Edelbrock, Costello, & Kessler, 1984; S. E. Shaywitz & B. E. Shaywitz, 1988). Extensive reviews concerning limitations associated with rating scales and checklists have also been presented (Barkley, 1987; D. M. Ross & S. A. Ross, 1982; Sandberg, Rutter, & Taylor, 1978).

The most commonly used instruments for assessing children with ADHD are presented in Table 4.3. Descriptions and critiques of these instruments, as well as detailed information relevant to their development, inherent psychometric properties, length, factor structure, and general characteristics have been discussed (see Barkley, 1987).

TABLE 4.3

Instruments for Diagnosing, Qualifying, and Quantifying Clinical Symptomatology in Children With ADHD

Structured Clinical Interviews
  Diagnostic Interview for Children and Adolescents (DICA)
  Diagnostic Interview Schedule for Children (DISC)
Semistructured Clinical Interviews
  Children's Assessment Schedule (CAS)
  Interview Schedule for Children (ISC)
  Kiddie–SADS (K–SADS)
Broad-Band Rating Scales and Checklists
  Child Behavior Checklist (CBCL)
  Child Behavior Checklist–Direct Observation Form (DOF)
  Child Behavior Checklist–Teacher Report Form (CBCL–TRF)
  Child Behavior Chekclist–Youth Self-Report Form (YSF)
  Child Symptom Inventory (CSI)
  Conners Parent Symptom Questionnaire-Revised (CPSQ–R)
  Conners Teacher Rating Scale-Revised (CTRS–R)
  Personality Inventory for Children (PIC)
  Revised Behavior Problem Checklist (BPC–R)
  Yale Children's Inventory (YCI)
Narrow-Band Rating Scales and Checklists
  Abbreviated Conners Teacher Rating Scale (ACTRS)
  ADD–H Comprehensive Teacher Rating Scale (ACTeRS)
  ADHD Rating Scale (ADHD–RC)
  Academic Performance Rating Scale (APRS)
  Home Situational Questionnaire-Revised (HSQ–R)
  IOWAQ Conners Teacher Rating Scale (IOWA–ACTRS)
  School Situations Questionnaire-Revised (SSQ–R)
  Teacher Self-Control Rating Scale (TSCRS)
  Werry–Weiss–Peters Rating Scale (WWPAS)

Comment

Broad-band rating scale and checklists are used primarily during the initial screening or diagnostic process, whereas the strength of the narrow-band scales lies in their quantification of very specific types of dysfunction that are usually more relevant to setting or situational characteristics associated with ADHD. Most instruments were created for somewhat different purposes, and each has its own strengths and limitations (see Barkley, 1987). It is also important to keep in mind that the convergence of child psychiatric diagnoses and behavior problems quantified by checklists and rating scales is in its infancy. At present, it is recommended that both parent and teacher ratings be used as integral components of a diagnostic battery, keeping in mind that the latter are better for discriminating among ADHD and other disorders of childhood. Whenever possible, information should be obtained from both sources and used in tandem to maximize diagnostic sensitivity and specificity.

The question remains as to whether child psychopathology should be viewed as a quantitative deviation from normal or a discrete entity that is best described by categorical diagnosis (Achenbach, 1980; Edelbrock & Costello, 1988). The convergence of psychiatric diagnoses and behavior problems quantified by checklists and rating scales should be questioned and not assumed. That is, *no* parent or teacher rating scale can be used by itself with any degree of confidence to make a clinical diagnosis of ADHD (or any other disorder for that matter). The disturbing and increasingly popular trend to diagnose by rating scale is unjustified from an empirical perspective, and reflects a naivete by perhaps well-intentioned but misinformed or poorly trained clinicians. Instrument selection depends on several factors and must be determined by the specific needs and competence of the clinician. All of the narrow-band instruments presented have proven useful for measuring outcome in children with ADHD. Their ability to detect medication states and correspondence with classroom academic performance under different dosage conditions, however, is far from monolithic and must be considered separately if used for these purposes (Rapport, 1990).

Intellectual and Achievement Testing

Psychometric testing is an integral and necessary part of a diagnostic evaluation for children presenting with ADHD symptomatology, because recent estimates suggest that more than 50% of these children have learning or achievement deficiencies (Cantwell & Satterfield, 1978; McGee & Share, 1988). Information relevant to the child's overall intellectual functioning and academic achievement are used to discern not only the general level of cognitive functioning, but to elucidate specific and overall patterns of strength and weakness that may be related to classroom functioning. Testing also allows for a fuller understanding of the range of attentional deficits, their impact on cognitive performance and academic achievement, and the opportunity to observe the child directly in a one-to-one situation.

Comparisons between ability and level of achievement are also essential to ascertain whether learning disabilities are present, and if so, whether they are primary or secondary to ADHD phenomena. Whether or not a child is eligible for special assistance by resource room instructors, or in more serious cases, special education classroom placement for partial or full-day instruction, in most states depends on an ability–achievement discrepancy formula (which varies from state to state). Many, if not most, children with ADHD fail to qualify for special services despite their arduous and continuous struggle with the educational process.

The Wechsler Intelligence Scales for Children (WISC–III) test battery is currently the most popular instrument for assessing children's intelligence because of its relatively broad survey of verbal and performance repertoires. With respect to overall intellectual functioning, no compelling evidence to date indicates that children with ADHD differ in any significant fashion from normals (Campbell, Douglas, & Morgenstern, 1971; Douglas, 1988; Loney, 1974). Recent evidence suggests, however, that performance on certain aspects of neuropsychological functioning may decrease as a function of increasing age in children with hyperactive and inattention problems (Massman, Nussbaum, & Bigler, 1988).

A relatively ubiquitous misconception is that the subscales comprising the "freedom from distractibility" factor (i.e., arithmetic, coding, and digit span subscales), or including the information subscale, the "ACID" profile (Kaufman, 1975), are pathognomonic to children with ADHD. Difficulties with attention, concentration, and alertness are characteristics of most major disorders of childhood, including the developmental disabilities and academic skills (learning disabilities) disorders. As such, these profile patterns have not been shown to be associated with a specific diagnosis and should neither be relied on nor expected as confirmatory or exclusionary evidence for the present or absence of ADHD. Similarly, neither significant discrepancies or inter- or intrasubscale scatter (Kaufman, 1981) has proven particularly useful in the differential diagnosis of children with ADHD or other learning disorders.

Caution should be observed when interpreting results of group-administered intelligence batteries. Their findings are frequently gross underestimates of intellectual functioning in children with ADHD, as to a lesser extent, are individually administered instruments. Not unexpectedly, the inattention and impulsivity components inherent to the disorder may interfere with test performance to the extent that they result in an incomplete and inaccurate evaluation of a child's knowledge and level of achievement.

Academic achievement tests are routinely incorporated as part of a psychoeducational battery because of the prevalence and depth of academic achievement problems associated with ADHD that cannot be explained by lower intellect or chronological age (Cantwell & Satterfield, 1978). Standardized test scores for reading, arithmetic, and other skill domains may be obtained from any number of instruments, such as the Woodcock–Johnson Psychoeducational Battery, the Peabody Individual Achievement Test, and more recently, the Kaufman (K–TEA) battery. More analytical assessment of these areas are often warranted for purposes of developing curricula intervention that yield specific, more detailed information regarding a particular topic area (e.g., Key Math).

Neurocognitive Assessment

Because ADHD represents a constellation of behavioral and cognitive deficits, a relatively wide range of clinic-administered instruments is being used in an attempt to capture and assess various aspects of the disorder. The three neurocognitive instruments employed most often for assessing and monitoring treatment effects in children with ADHD include the Continuous Performance Test (CPT), the Matching Familiar Figures Test (MFFT), and the Paired Associates Learning Task (PAL–T). Different versions of the three instruments have been developed and some are available commercially. It should be noted, however, that no instrument can be exclusively relied on for purposes of determining diagnosis or treatment outcome. Comprehensive reviews of their psychometric properties (Barkley, 1991; Rapport, 1995) and suitability for assessing treatment effects (DuPaul, Anastopoulos, Shelton, Guevremont, & Metevia, 1992; Rapport, 1990) are available for readers interested in a more detailed discourse of the instruments and their inherent limitations.

Differential Diagnosis

ADHD Versus Other Childhood Disorders.   Differentiating ADHD from other childhood disorders is an essential but cumbersome task. There are two primary differentials inherent to the process: establishing the onset, course, and duration of symptoms; and qualifying and quantifying the symptom picture.

Establishing onset, course, and duration of symptomatology is best accomplished by structured or semistructured clinical interview in conjunction with careful history taking and review of pertinent records. It is the single most useful procedure for differentiating ADHD from other clinical disorders owing to the growing database garnered from clinical and epidemiological studies. As mentioned earlier, structured and semistructured interviews will likely result in over diagnosis of caseness for both ADHD and comorbid disorders and must be complemented by information obtained from parent and teacher completed broad- and narrow-band rating scales to qualify and quantify the symptom picture.

The typical age at which symptoms are reported for children with ADHD is 3.5 years, which readily differentiates it from a majority of other childhood clinical disorders. It should be noted, however, that this age corresponds to retrospective parental reports (usually the mother) of early problem behaviors, not with age of initial referral (which is more typically after school entry and almost always by the end of second grade). The typical onset, course, and duration of the most commonly diagnosed clinical disorders in children is depicted in Table 4.4.

Table 4.4 shows that ADHD is similar in age of onset of symptomatology with Asperger's Disorder, Autistic Disorder, Childhood Disintegrative Disorder, Rett's Disorder, Bipolar Disorder (when occurring in young children), and Early Onset Child Schizophrenia. Although a majority of these disorders share a common (chronic) course, their presenting symptomatology is easily differentiated from ADHD with the exception of mania (childhood onset).

TABLE 4.4

Onset, Course, and Duration of Major Clinical Disorders of Childhood.

Clinical Disorders	Onset[abc]	Course	Duration
Disruptive Behavior Disorders			
Attention Deficit Hyperactivity Disorder[h]	3.5[b]	chronic	adoles–lifelong
Conduct Disorder (CD)			
Childhood Onset	<10[c]	variable	adulthood[d]
Adolescent Onset	<16[c]	variable	early adulthood
Oppositional Defiant Disorder	<8[c]	variable	remits or antecedent to CD
Pervasive Developmental Disorders			
Asperger's Disorder	3–6[c]	chronic	lifelong
Autistic Disorder[e]	<3[b]	chronic	lifelong
Childhood Disintegrative Disorder[e]	3–4[b]or[c]	chronic	lifelong
Rett's Disorder[e]	1–2 & <4[c]	chronic	lifelong/or fatal
Mood Disorders			
Major Depressive Disorder[f]	5–19[b]or[c]	variable	remits or variable
Dysthymic Disorder[g]	8.5[c]	variable	remits or variable
Early Onset Mania (in context of Bipolar Disorder)[h]	5–14	variable	lifelong
Anxiety Disorders			
Acute Stress Disorder	any age[i]	1 month	2 days–1 month
Obsessive-Compulsive Disorder[j]	6–15(m)[c]	chronic	lifelong
	20-29(f)[c]	chronic	lifelong
Posttraumatic Stress Disorder	acute or delayed[i]	variable	2 months–2 years
Separation Anxiety Disorder[m]	9–13[b]or[c]	variable	adoles
Social Phobia[m]	mid-teens[b]or[c]	chronic	remits by adulthood or lifelong
Specific Phobia[k,m]	7-12[b]or[c]	variable	remits by adoles
Other Clinical Disorders			
Tourette's Disorder	7[c]	variable	lifelong
Early Onset Schizophrenia[l]	5–11[b]or[c]	variable	lifelong

Note: m = males; f = females; Adoles = adolescence; ADHD = attention deficit hyperactivity disorder; CD = conduct disorder. [a] = age of onset indicates age in years at which symptoms are most frequently first reported in children. [b] = acute onset. [c] = insidious onset. [d] = at risk for antisocial personality disorder and substance abuse disorder as adults. [e] = typically associated with mental retardation. [f] = frequently associated with an anxiety disorder. [g] = frequently associated with an externalizing disorder. [h] = frequently associated with conduct disorder. [i] = onset immediately following a traumatic event. j = commonly associated with depression, other anxiety disorders, and/or Tourette's. [k] = slightly higher rates in females and dependent upon the type of phobia. [l] = significantly higher number of males versus females prior to age 10. [m] = frequently continuous with adult anxiety disorder.

ADHD Versus Mania.   Children with both disorders experience concentration difficulties; have higher than normal gross motor activity; and often present with emotional lability, irritability, disruptive behavior, impulsivity, low frustration tolerance, poor school performance, decreased need for sleep, restlessness, talkativeness, psychopathology in family members (i.e., alcoholism, conduct disorder, and antisocial personality), denial of problems, and poor judgment. The onset of ADHD, although believed present from birth (inherited), is typically during the preschool years (3.5 years by parent report), whereas early onset mania in children is more commonly reported between 5 and 11 years of age. Mood disturbance is nearly always present in mania, with approximately 50% of children reporting a primarily elated mood and 50% primarily an irritable mood. In ADHD, mood disturbance may co-occur, but is more typically seen during later childhood and adolescent years. Decreased need for sleep is a continual and chronic problem for children with ADHD, whereas, in mania, it occurs episodically and corresponds with a manic or hypomanic episode. Persecutory delusions (70%), as well as visual (70%) and auditory (50%) hallucinations, are relatively common in children with mania, but rare and not part of the usual symptom picture in children with ADHD. Pressured speech and racing thoughts, as classically described, are common in children with mania (69%) and may be difficult to distinguish from the frequent verbal intrusiveness and disorganization characteristic of children with ADHD. Talkativeness and distractibility are common to both disorders, but occur regularly in ADHD and episodically in children with mania. Grandiose delusions are not reported in children with ADHD, but may occur in up to 20% of mania cases. Finally, up to 50% of children with mania present with a positive family history of depression, whereas no such relation exists for children with ADHD. Thus, the chronic (ADHD) versus episodic (mania) course, relative absence of abnormally expansive or elevated mood and psychotic features, and family history are the most distinguishing clinical features differentiating ADHD from mania (for details, see E. B. Weller, R. A. Weller, & Fristad, 1995).

The Mania Rating Scale (MRS; Young, Biggs, Ziegler, & Meyer, 1978) may also prove valuable for differentiating the two conditions in prepubertal children (Fristad, E. B.Weller, & R. A. Weller, 1992). Children with mania receive significantly higher total scores and higher scores on most items than do matched children with ADHD. More importantly, there is virtually no overlap between the two groups (i.e., children with mania receive scores of 14 to 39 on the MRS, whereas children with ADHD receive scores of 0 to 12).

SCHOOL-BASED TREATMENT PROTOCOL

Place yourself in the most boring setting imaginable in which you must listen to an adult and complete mundane tasks for 6 to 8 hours each day, day after day, year after year. Most of your peers appear able to function in this fashion, but for some unknown reason you find the task daunting. Your brain simply does not enable you to pay attention to the materials presented due to their nonstimulating nature. And your body squirms about in a futile effort to self-medicate itself via increased gross-motor activity. Every time you fail to listen to the charged adult, stray from these tasks, or try to engage others around you in conversation or play, you are reprimanded and informed of your shortcomings in front of your peers. Periodically, you are tested to determine how much information you have retained and feedback is provided directly to your parents. The negative feedback loop between the charged adult and your parents intensifies with each passing month, convincing you that you are different from other children and a failure. You periodically regroup and try your hardest (as significant others have attributed your difficulties to a lack of volition) but cannot sustain the effort for more than a few days at a time—even when you are bribed and/or threatened by your parents. You seek out other children to play with but are rejected by peers within 20 to 30 minutes. You have neither good friends nor lasting friendships. You are constantly in trouble for not listening. You frequently forget to follow rules that other children seem to be able to remember. You are disorganized and often act without thinking about the consequences of your behavior. No one appears to like you. No one appears to have anything positive to say about you. You are a child with ADHD attempting to obtain a public school education.

Proactive Versus Reactive Interventions

Current treatments for children with ADHD are reactive by design. Both behavioral and pharmacological interventions are geared to assist children with ADHD behave and function more appropriately within traditional classroom environments. The implicit assumption is that the classroom environment and curricula materials used therein are appropriate for most children. Those who fail to function well in school are thus considered abnormal, necessitating external means by which to bolster their ability to behave and learn. Closer examination of the most popularly used interventions for treating children with ADHD reveal a shared characteristic. They provide the child with either internal (psychostimulants) or external (behavioral interventions) stimulation, which is lacking in most classrooms. By design, they are reactive in the sense of treating the symptoms (behaviors) children with ADHD exhibit in response to a nonstimulating environment.

To further clarify the difference between a proactive and reactive treatment approach, consider the following example. When faced with typical academic exercises or assignments to complete in school, the child with ADHD strays off-task and loses checkmarks or points administered by the classroom teacher after a specified period of time; this is a *reactive* approach. Alternatively, direct changes are instituted in the classroom environment and curricula that capture the child's attention and provide continual feedback throughout the school day, thus eliminating the necessity of an after-the-fact point system; this is a *proactive* approach. The point is, the focus can be on the behavioral aftermath of placing a child with ADHD in an environment that is nonconducive to learning, or energy can be used to alter the environment that elicits the undesirable behavior in the first place. Regrettably, there are no existing comprehensive models for the latter course of action.

A Proactive Treatment Approach

Several basic assumptions are presumed in this section. The first assumption is that a moderately sized third grade classroom is being designed entirely for children with ADHD. This assumption is predicated on the consideration that appropriate learning environments for these children do not currently exist and thus must be created and subsequently subjected to empirical examination. The second assumption is that there are existing funds to purchase necessary equipment and curricula materials for the classroom. Although educational districts throughout the

United States have been plagued for years by insufficient funding, a convincing argument can be advanced that the eventual cost to society of not planning appropriate educational interventions for children with ADHD far outweighs necessary expenditures for new equipment and curricula materials. The final assumption is that teachers are willing to abandon their traditional training, assumed sapiential authority (the right to be heard by reason of knowledge or expertness), and roles as bestowers of information in favor of a combined managerial-explicator role in the classroom.

Preliminary Steps.   Several procedures are undertaken during the first week of class as an initial step in arranging a learning-conducive environment for children with ADHD. First, a comprehensive assessment of each child's abilities and academic skills is conducted (e.g., assessment of intelligence, academic achievement/functioning, preferred use of learning modalities). Second, appropriate levels are selected to represent each child's current level of functioning and existing knowledge base within areas of defined curricula. (Note: Much of this can be accomplished by means of available academic-curricular software.) For example, initial assessment may indicate that a child is currently at level 3 in the mathematics program and has accumulated basic knowledge of elementary addition and subtraction processes (computation skills), but has an inability to perform word problems (application skills) requiring these same processes. Third, estimated guidelines for involving children in different aspects of the curricula are predetermined by national curricula guidelines (i.e., expected knowledge to be learned in areas such as math, science, grammar, reading, history, and so forth, is based on established guidelines for each grade level). Fourth, optimal work periods for concentrated attention while engaged in academic computer-administered tasks are established based on developmental norms and empirically based knowledge of attention span in children with ADHD. Finally, basic computer file management, word processing, and other relevant skills are taught to and practiced by all students during the first 2 weeks of class.

Basic Design Elements of the Classroom and Curricula.   The classroom curricular approach integrates personal computers (PCs), software, and instructional and training materials. In the *teaching and learning with computers classroom* (TLCC), students rotate between three groups. The first group works with computers at individual modular stations containing preprogrammed software for history, science, geography, and discovery. The next group works independently at a second modular grouping of computer stations writing journals (word processing) and using manipulatives designed to improve mathematical, language and critical thinking skills. The classroom teacher serves as a mentor to the remaining work group, working directly with students (e.g., preparing them for particular lessons, practicing oral reading, mentoring science experiments, and teaching logic and creative thinking). An interactive system is used that electronically links each student in class to a teacher PC station, providing for real-time monitoring and immediate feedback. The system supports instruction, testing, grading, record keeping, and other routine classroom management tasks.

Each day begins with all children participating in a 15-minute session that stresses focusing, breathing, and controlled movement exercises (e.g., Tai Chi). Inclusion of controlled exercises in the treatment protocol is based in part on recent evidence indicating that antecedent exercise may promote modest reductions in disruptive behaviors among hyperactive children (Allison, Faith, & Franklin, 1995), and secondarily, to provide organized breaks between academic sessions.

Children subsequently attend their assigned grouping, log on to their personal computer (PC), and review accomplishments of the previous day's work (e.g., tasks completed, total work time, accuracy, and teacher comments). Following the review, students click on an icon marked "daily file," which contains a selection of tasks to be worked on within the specific classroom computer group station for that particular day and the approximate time required to complete each exercise. After reviewing the menu selections, students select the first task/exercise to be worked on and open the corresponding file, most of which are contained on read-only memory compact discettes (CD ROM). Students thus have the flexibility of determining the order in which they will engage in various curricula throughout the day within a given group. Comfortable headphones are worn by students while working at the computer stations to minimize distraction and because many of the learning exercises and lessons incorporate both visual and auditory instructions to maximize modality input and processing. Each PC contains a real-time clock (upper righthand corner of monitor), which provides continuous feedback regarding total time spent on task, as well as "rest" and "help" buttons. These buttons serve to temporarily suspend a given exercise if the student requires a break, and signal the teacher (or teacher aide) via a multiple server when assistance is required, respectively. The teacher (or aide), in turn, can directly attend to or communicate by electronic message with the student requesting assistance.

Cumulative recordings of students' performance accuracy and time on-task are monitored by the classroom teacher, who in turn adjusts task difficulty and required temporal parameters within a given academic assignment or learning exercise to maximize student concentration and success. At the end of a given academic exercise or lesson, feedback is provided concerning student performance (e.g., accuracy, time on-task). Students can subsequently elect to continue working by returning to the main menu and selecting "daily file" to review remaining exercises to be completed, or take a 15-minute break in the resource corner of the classroom. Table 4.5 provides a partial listing of commercially available software.

Resource Corner.   The resource corner contains a panoply of books, CD listening stations (with headphones), a rocking chair, comfortable floor mats, and drawing materials. When entering the resource corner, the children log in (enters their name) on the resource PC, which after a 15-minute interval continuously calls their name to indicate that it is time to return to their designated work group. Students terminate the resource computer message by logging off and exiting the corner. Similar to the workstation groupings, time spent in resource activities is monitored for teacher review.

TABLE 4.5
Partial Listing of Commercially Available Software and Publications Relevant
to Designing Proactive Learning Environments

Discourse Technologies, Inc., 8050 N. Port Washington Road, Milwaukee, WI 53217.
Educational Activities, Inc., P.O. Box 392, Freeport, NY 11520.
Edunetics Corporation, 105 Terry Drive, Suite 120, Newtown, PA 18940-3425.
Milliken Publishing Company, 1100 Research Boulevard, P.O. Box 21579, St. Louis, MO 63132-0579.
Pioneer New Media Technologies, Inc., 2265 East 220 Street, Long Beach, CA 90810.
Rand McNally Educational Publishing, P.O. Box 1906, Skokie, IL 60076-8906.
Terrapin Software, Inc., 400 Riverside Street, Portland, ME 04103-1068.
The Electronic Bookshelf, Inc., 5276 S. County Road 700 West, Frankfort, IN 46041-8113.
T.H.E. Journal, P.O. Box 5524, Pittsburgh, MA 01203-9260.

The Role of the Classroom Teacher.   Children rotate between the three work groups throughout the day. Regularly scheduled breaks occur every 60 minutes, during which time the entire class participates in a 15-minute exercise session emphasizing controlled movement, breathing, and focusing. A central command module enables the teacher to review each child's selected programs and progress throughout the day, providing summary graphs and hard copy for reviewing/modifying curricula. Cumulative information is also used to assess each child's rate of learning, accuracy, and/or potential need for one to one instruction. For example, consistently low accuracy results in a return to and review of previously learned information in a given lesson module and prompts the teacher to check for understanding of instructions. Academic review periods are programmed to occur periodically following learning exercises with selection of temporal parameters based on literature showing appropriate rehearsal periods that maximize recall of information.

Finally, a variety of learning exercises complement computer-assisted instruction when children are working directly with the classroom teacher and are interspersed throughout the daily curricula. These learning exercises incorporate elements from multiple domains and serve to integrate and provide for hands-on learning of relevant information. The Developmental Approaches in Science and Health (DASH) program, developed at the University of Hawaii Laboratory School, is a magnum opus of this type of approach. The kindergarten through 6th-grade program integrates science, health, and technology in a series of inquiry activities that enable students to construct their own understanding of basic concepts and skills. Children in an identified grouping, for example, might integrate math, written composition, meteorology, and plant science by means of a garden experiment. Observation of variables affecting plant growth patterns, such as prevailing weather conditions (sunlight, rainfall), soil conditions, and added nutrients, are closely monitored and recorded by students in a daily journal. Measurement of growth velocity, yield, and so on, are taken daily, and both their specific and broader (e.g., health) implications are discussed using a small group format. Students subsequently generate computer graphs with accompanying journals (using word processing) describing objectives of the experiment, manipulated variables, dependent variables, outcome, and conclusions. Results are presented to the class weekly using a computer slide show format. Other lessons promote the development of logic, reasoning, and creative thinking—such as the "40 questions game," during which children attempt to identify an unknown animal by asking pertinent questions concerning the animal's habitat, color, size, eating habits, and characteristic patterns of behavior.

Parent Involvement.   Parents meet at the school weekly during the first month, biweekly for the ensuing 3 months, and monthly for the duration of the school term. At these meetings they are provided with basic instruction and information concerning methods for improving their child's ability to learn information and complete homework assignments, as well as basic feedback regarding their child's progress in the classroom. Mnemonics, "chunking," and other basic strategies are taught to improve the child's metacognitive skills, ability to store/retrieve information, and complete homework assignments. For example, mnemonic and chunking strategies involve organized procedures for breaking down, studying, and memorizing lists of spelling words or historical facts. Parents are instructed to break down lists of historical facts into component parts (chunking), identify and associate one of the previously learned visual stimuli (e.g., animals beginning with each letter of the alphabet) with the fact to be remembered, and then practice learning and recall of the groupings at 2-hour intervals for 15 minutes and again in the morning before school to enhance memory consolidation and recall ability. Homework assignments are broken down (chunked) in a similar fashion, requiring no more than 20 to 30 consecutive minutes of sustained concentration and effort at any one sitting.

Textbooks, notebooks, and other materials used for each study topic at school and home are color coded and labeled to enhance organizational skills. The purchase of separate texts for home use is required to circumvent loss of materials. Finally, children and/or their parents who have access to a PC and modem at home are able to check on weekly assignments and communicate directly with the teacher by means of e-mail. All parents are provided with telephone numbers of other children in their child's classroom whose parents participate in one of three homework assignment study sections that were established at the beginning of the school year. Parents within an assigned study section telephone one other concerning homework assignments and/or to seek assistance in helping their child complete a given assignment.

Monthly meetings at the school also serve to facilitate clear communication regarding each student's academic progress throughout the year. Periodically, guest speakers with expertise in ADHD are invited and serve to communicate this knowledge to parents by means of informal meetings.

Summary.   The proactive learning environment described earlier relies on advanced technology and improved communication and cooperation between school personnel and parents. It differs from prevailing educational practices by design. Admittedly, it represents an ideal learning environment in which children with ADHD would succeed academically without the necessity of the usual panoply of reactive behavioral interventions. Some children with more severe ADHD-related symptomatology will nevertheless require complementary pharmacological intervention. The next section describes a complementary pharmacological treatment protocol.

PHARMACOLOGICAL TREATMENT PROTOCOL

Psychopharmacological treatment of ADHD gradually gained acceptance following Bradley's (1937) pioneering work, demonstrating the effectiveness of Benzedrine in school-age children with various learning and emotional difficulties. Methylphenidate (Ritalin) was synthesized in 1954 and rapidly became a mainstay treatment for children with ADHD during the 1950s and 1960s. It and similarly acting psychostimulants (e.g., dextroamphetamine, pemoline) are currently the most frequently used psychotropic drugs in child psychiatry.

There are essentially three *lines of defense* considered by child psychiatrists, pediatricians, and neurologists when treating children with ADHD: psychostimulants, tricyclic antidepressants, and neuroleptics. The psychostimulant class of drugs represents the first line of defense and are prescribed for an estimated 3% to 6% of elementary-age children (Wilens & Biederman, 1992). The most popular of these include methylphenidate (Ritalin), dextroamphetamine (Dexedrine), and pemoline (Cylert), with the former prescribed for an estimated 90% of cases. Because of its widespread use and documented effectiveness (i.e, approximately 70% to 80% of treated children show a positive response), the ensuing discussion focuses on methylphenidate (Ritalin).

Methylphenidate (MPH)

MPH is available as tablets of 5 mg, 10 mg, 20 mg, and in a sustained release (SR) 20-mg formula for oral administration, the latter of which is equivalent to a 10-mg twice a day (b.i.d.) dose. MPH effects can be detected behaviorally and by examining a child's performance on a variety of cognitive tasks within 30 to 45 minutes following oral administration (for a review, see Rapport & Kelly, 1991). Its behavioral half-life of 2½ hours is relatively short and means that (assuming a positive response to medication) salutary effects can be expected to begin 30 to 45 minutes following oral administration and to last 4 to 5 hours. Because of its short half-life, MPH is typically administered twice (b.i.d.) or three (t.i.d.) times daily. The timing of ingestion is integrally related to monitoring treatment response.

Titrating and Monitoring MPH in Children

Titrating MPH, on the surface, appears to be a relatively straightforward process. A 5-mg tablet is usually administered in the morning and another at lunchtime for 1 to 2 weeks. If minimal or no effects are observed, dosage is increased to 10 mg for an ensuing 1- to 2-week period. This process of gradually increasing dosage is followed until therapeutic efficacy is established (at least until 5-mg through 20 mg dosages are attempted) or untoward effects necessitate dosage reduction and/or discontinuation of the regimen. The conundrum, however, lies in deciding which behaviors to target and how best to assess these behaviors. The process is further complicated by several factors. There is substantial evidence that distinct behavioral domains may be differentially affected at discrepant dosage levels of the drug (see review by Rapport & Kelly, 1991). For example, a child's vigilance or ability to sustain attention on a Continuous Perform- ance Test (CPT) in the clinic may show optimal medication response at 10 mg, whereas weekly ratings obtained from the child's teacher may indicate that a higher dosage is required to optimize behavior in the classroom. Three recent studies have conclusively shown body weight to be unrelated to MPH response in children (Rapport & Denney, 1997; Rapport, DuPaul, & Kelly, 1989; Swanson, Cantwell, Lerner, McBurnett, & Hanna, 1991) rendering mg/kg guidelines meaningless (e.g., those offered by the *Physicians' Desk Reference*). And, nearly all of the teacher rating scales currently used for titrating psychostimulant response fall under the *Dead Man Rule*. That is, they focus on quantifying reductions observed in maladaptive behavior to the exclusion of changes in adaptive functioning (i.e., if a deceased individual can earn a good score on the rating scale, it probably lacks the necessary characteristics for monitoring changes in children's adaptive behavior). Because of these factors, the onus of monitoring treatment effects (albeit primarily resting with the prescribing physician) is frequently augmented by a clinical or school psychologist.

Psychostimulant Treatment Protocol

When a psychostimulant regimen is indicated, the first rule of thumb is to plan a fixed dosage trial of MPH, preferably using a placebo control. A fixed trial is recommended owing to the idiosyncratic response typically observed in children undergoing psychostimulant therapy. For example, a small but significant number of children will show minimal or no response to lower levels of drug (i.e., 5 mg through 15 mg), yet evidence a clear threshold response at higher dose levels (Rapport et al., 1987). Standard tablets of 5 mg, 10 mg, 15 mg, and 20 mg should be placed in opaque gelatin capsules such that a child receives each dose daily for a 2-week period of time (using either a morning only or b.i.d. daily dosing regimen). Thus, a child would be administered 5 mg daily (morning only or morning and afternoon) for 2 consecutive weeks, followed by 10 mg for 2 weeks and so on until the protocol is complete. An inert placebo can be administered for any 2-week period in between the active dosage regimen.

The reasons for using gelatin capsules to disguise dosage and taste are twofold. First, it *blinds* raters (parents and teachers) and the child to the regimen, thus providing a more objective assessment of drug response. Second, it permits use of an inert placebo to control for both expectancy and observer/patient biases. Anecdotally, parents are quite willing to have their children undergo a controlled medication assessment wherein they are kept blind to dosage so long as outcome is closely monitored by a knowledgeable professional.

Prior to beginning a psychostimulant trial, it is incumbent on the psychologist (in collaboration with the prescribing physician) to obtain baseline ratings across several domains. These include parent ratings of behavior at home, teacher ratings of behavior and academic performance in school, and baseline levels of physical complaints reported by the child. Obtained scores can be used subsequently to assess medication response across settings, raters, and behavioral domains (usually completed at the end of each week by the rater to reflect the child's behavior for the entire week).

The most popular parent and teacher rating scales used for baseline assessment and treatment monitoring are listed in Table 4.3. Other factors, such as time demands, adequate sampling of behavioral domains, and sensitivity in detecting psychostimulant effects must also be considered when selecting instruments suitable for monitoring treatment outcome. For these reasons, the following rating scales are recommended for classroom use: the Abbreviated Conners Teacher Rating Scale (ACTRS), the Academic Performance Rating Scale (APRS), and the Teacher Self-Control Rating Scale (TSCRS). Their combined use provides a reasonably comprehensive picture of the child's behavior and academic performance in the classroom, each is highly sensitive in detecting medication effects, and all three correspond to an acceptable degree with direct observations of classroom behavior (Rapport, 1990). Adoption of the APRS is especially important as it provides information concerning the child's academic performance (learning ability and academic performance factors), which does not always correspond with changes in behavior. The revised Home Situations Questionnaire (HSQ–R) is ideally suited for monitoring behavior at home. Its unique advantages are that it provides descriptions of common problems observed in the home setting (compliance and leisure situations factors), allows for quantification of both the total number of problem settings and mean severity across settings, and has proven sensitivity to medication effects. The scale also facilitates identification of specific types of problems at home that may require complementary interventions by the parents.

The Side Effects Rating Scale (SERS) is recommended for monitoring potential emergent symptoms associated with psychostimulant therapy. Assessing the frequency and severity of side effects should be undertaken during the baseline (no treatment) phase and at the end of each treatment week of the protocol. Baseline assessment of side effects is necessary because children with ADHD tend to report more somatic complaints (Barkley, DuPaul, & McMurray, 1990); and adolescents with ADHD have an increased incidence of somatization disorders (Szatmari, Offord, & Boyle, 1989) unrelated to pharmacological treatment. Failure to document these complaints a priori may thus lead to the untoward conclusion that they are related to treatment when in fact they are not.

The assessment instruments recommended previously should be administered prior to beginning the medication trial and at the end of each week of treatment. The rating scales are self-explanatory and place minimum time demands on the teacher and parent. It is essential, however, that teachers and parents be instructed to rate behavior observed during the active phase of the medication (i.e., 30 minutes to 4 or 5 hours postingestion). If MPH is being administered only in the morning, for example, the teacher rating scales should indicate that ratings reflect behavior observed up until noon each day during the week, assuming the child ingests the tablet at 7:00 a.m. For these cases, the rating scales can be customized such that weekly ratings are dichotomized into morning and afternoon sections, which in turn provides an additional within-day dimension for assessing outcome.

Parent rating scales should be completed based on behavior observed at home during the weekend, and similar to teacher observations, limited to the active behavioral life of the medication. Anecdotally, many parents present with an "antimedication" attitude and insist they do not wish their children to receive medication on nonschool days. Requiring them to observe their child on active medication during the weekend (either Saturday or Sunday), however, serves several purposes. First, this will dispel the belief that MPH adversely affects their child's "personality" or results in other untoward effects. In cases seen at the Children's Learning Clinic over the past decade, nearly half the parents have been unable to distinguish active from inactive (placebo) medication conditions at home. A home trial also serves the purpose of establishing whether a child benefits from MPH on non-school days, and if so, the appropriate dosage to be administered. Dosage for non-school days is frequently lower than for school due to the different and, usually, less demanding nature of the home setting.

All data and information collected should be graphed at the conclusion of the medication trial, taking the form of distinct dose–response curves. (Note: Several commercially available spread sheet programs are ideally suited for this purpose.) Prototypical dose–response profiles for two children are depicted in Figs. 4.1 and 4.2. Baseline (no treatment) is followed by placebo (inactive treatment) and incremental doses of active medication as one moves from left to right on the abscissa of the graph. Although placebo and active MPH doses were not administered in the order shown, they are depicted in this manner to facilitate interpretation of outcome for both the clinician and parent(s). As depicted in Fig. 4.1, GJ (left graph) evidenced considerable disruptive behavior (ACTRS) and poor self-control (TSCRS) in the classroom prior to treatment (baseline) and during the placebo control week, the latter of which was scheduled between the 15-mg and 20-mg treatment conditions. These difficulties were mirrored by low scores on the APRS learning ability and academic performance factors. Weekly teacher ratings showed improved behavior with increasing dose (indicated by upward movement on the vertical axis), indicating that GJ evinced maximum benefit across sampled behavioral domains in the classroom under the 20-mg dose condition.

Examination of GJ's behavior at home under identical dosage parameters indicated a somewhat different dose–response profile (see right graph in Fig. 4.1). Under baseline and placebo conditions, GJ evidenced difficulties in 12 of the 14 listed problem settings and obtained mean severity scores of 7.5 and 7.2 (on a 9-point Likert scale), respectively, on the parent completed HSQ– R. GJ continued to evidence difficulties across most of the problem settings assessed by the HSQ–R while receiving differing doses of MPH; however, mean severity ratings of his behavior showed a clear reduction under 5-mg and 10-mg conditions and a leveling off of benefit thereafter. Assessment of emergent symptoms (assessed using the SERS) revealed a moderate level of expressed or observed complaints during no-medication

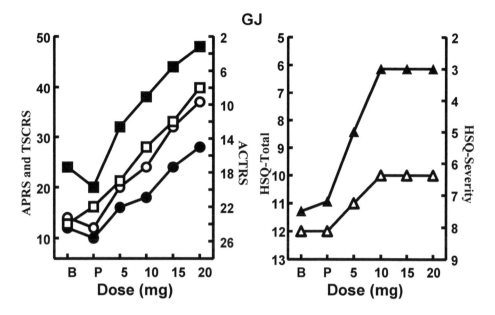

FIG. 4.1. Dose–response curves for GJ obtained from school (lefthand graph) and home (righthand graph). Baseline (B), placebo (P), and four doses of methyphenidate (MPH) are depicted on the abscissa. Improvement is indicated by upward movement on the ordinate for the three teacher rating scales (APRS: Academic Performance Rating Scale academic performance factor depicted as open circles, learning factor depicted as open squares; TSCRS: Teacher Self-Control Rating Scale depicted as closed squares; ACTRS: Abbreviated Conners Teacher Rating Scale depicted as open squares) and parent rating scale (HSQ: Home Situations Questionnaire total problem score depicted as open triangles, severity rating depicted as closed triangles).

and inactive (placebo) medication conditions and a slight diminution in complaints under MPH. It was recommended that GJ receive a 20-mg b.i.d. maintenance dosage on school days, a lower 10-mg b.i.d. dosage on Saturdays, and no medication on Sundays at the conclusion of the trial.

The dose–response graphs for a second child, SV, are shown in Fig. 4.2. SV evidenced levels of behavior problems in the classroom similar to GJ (above) under baseline (no medication condition), with a slight diminution observed under placebo (see left graph in Fig. 4.2). His behavior improved markedly under the 5-mg and 10-mg dosage conditions, followed by a leveling off under 15 mg, with additional improvement observed at 20 mg. Similar levels of improvement were documented by the parents.

Examination of SV's APRS scores, however, indicate a worsening in learning ability and academic performance (compared to lower dose levels) under higher MPH dosages. This phenomena is well documented in the literature and referred to as "cognitive toxicity," or "overfocused behavior" (Kinsbourne, 1990; Swanson et al., 1991). The phenomenon is similar to that observed in normal individuals after they ingest one too many cups of coffee. Rather than being more alert, the excess caffeine causes one to become tired, quiet, and somewhat withdrawn with a resulting overconstriction of attention. A hypothetical illustration of this effect is depicted in Fig. 4.3. The middle portion of the curve represents the zone of optimal arousal. Children with ADHD are situated on the lefthand portion of the curve. Individuals who tend to be anxious are situated on the righthand portion of the curve. As such, they tend to be chronically overaroused and behave in ways to reduce environmental stimulation (e.g., by avoiding loud music, crowds, thrill-seeking situations and settings). The arrows indicate

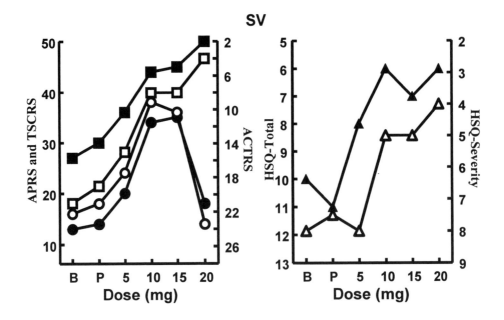

FIG. 4.2. Dose–response curves for SV obtained from school (lefthand graph) and home (righthand graph). Baseline (B), placebo (P), and four doses of methylphenidate (MPH) are depicted on the abscissa. Improvement is indicated by upward movement on the ordinate for the three teacher rating scales (APRS: Academic Performance Rating Scale academic performance factor depicted as open circles, learning factor depicted as open squares; TSCRS: Teacher Self-Control Rating Scale depicted as closed squares; ACTRS: Abbreviated Conners Teacher Rating Scale depicted as open squares) and parent rating scale (HSQ: Home Situations Questionnaire total problem score depicted as open triangles, severity rating depicted as closed triangles).

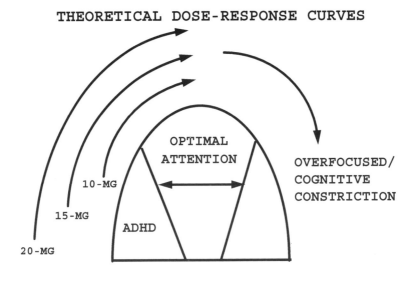

FIG. 4.3. Theoretical dose–response curves associated with methylphenidate (MPH) treatment in children. Comparatively lower doses are required to center a child's attention in the "optimal" range. Overshooting the optimal range results in overfocused, anxious behavior (cognitive constriction).

children with excessively low to moderate attentional capacities for normal schoolwork and the effects of increasing doses of MPH. As depicted, children on the extreme lefthand side of the curve eventually fall within the optimal zone at higher dose levels. Conversely, children occupying positions further to the right overshoot the optimal zone at higher doses and become overfocused, which is characterized by constricted attention and reduced cognitive efficiency and academic productivity. Parent and teacher ratings of these children typically indicate optimal improvement despite being overfocused because the children become very quiet and compliant. This is not to say that the raters prefer the children in this state as some have suggested (Sprague & Sleator, 1977). Rather, they are accurately rating the children using the instructions and descriptions of disruptive conduct provided them by the physician or psychologist. The key, then, is to include measures (e.g., the APRS) that are sensitive in detecting overfocused states in children undergoing psychostimulant treatment. In turn, these measures must be compared with obtained parent and teacher ratings to determine optimal dosage for a particular child.

Recalling the intermediate and long-term outcome studies reviewed earlier, it would appear prudent to optimize the child's academic and learning success even at the expense of having to tolerate moderate levels of continuing disruptiveness in the classroom and at home. This point is worth bearing in mind, as the literature is replete in showing that academic success during childhood is among the best predictors of long-term outcome and healthy functioning in adulthood.

Results from the largest in vivo MPH dose–response outcome study conducted to date provide additional incentive for closely monitoring children's academic performance while undergoing a psychostimulant trial. Rapport, Denney, DuPaul, and Gardner (1994) found that 76% of the 76 children undergoing a comprehensive trial of MPH showed normal or nearly normal attentiveness in the classroom with at least one of the four doses (5 mg, 10 mg, 15 mg, 20 mg) administered. Over 90% were rated by their classroom teachers as having significantly improved or normal behavior under MPH. In contrast, only 53% of the children had significantly improved in the area of academic functioning. Thus, even when a positive response to MPH is observed across multiple domains of classroom functioning, nearly half the children will require complementary interventions to augment academic performance.

Use of Neurocognitive Instruments for Titration

The neurocognitive instruments used most frequently for assessing MPH response in children with ADHD include the Continuous Performance Test (CPT), the Matching Familiar Figures Test (MFFT), and the Paired Associate Learning Task (PAL–T). These instruments are purported indices of vigilance (attention), cognitive tempo in the context of visual problem solving, and short-term memory, respectively. Comprehensive reviews concerning the clinical utility of these instruments, however, have been disappointing. All three instruments appear useful in detecting overall medication effects (i.e., drug versus nondrug states), but relatively insensitive to between-dose differences (Rapport, 1990; Rapport & Kelly, 1991).

The PAL–T has been proposed as a unique instrument for discerning overfocused phenomena associated with MPH treatment (i.e., to identify cognitive nonresponders). A recent outcome study, however, revealed that the test's most useful attribute is to identify children who exhibit improved academic efficiency in school (Rapport, Loo, & Denney, 1995). That is, when short-term memory for learning paired associations is improved following MPH treatment, it tends to portend improved academic efficiency in the classroom (positive predictive power or PPP).

Collectively, none of the available neurocognitive instruments can be recommended for titration purposes at present. Newly devised computerized batteries of neurocognitive instruments represent promising avenues for clinicians, but await empirical validation.

Recommendations for Continuing Treatment

After completing the MPH protocol, an optimal dosage regimen for purposes of ongoing therapy is recommended to the child's physician (assuming a positive treatment response). For children responding optimally at 10-mg, 15-mg, or 20-mg doses, the longer acting sustained release (SR) formula can be used as part of the daily regimen, keeping in mind that it is the equivalent to a 10-mg twice-a-day dosage. For example, SR 20-mg dosage can be administered in the morning in place of a 10-mg twice-a-day (b.i.d.) dosage; a SR 20-mg dosage combined with a 5-mg tablet in the morning can frequently be substituted for a 15-mg b.i.d. regimen; and two SR 20-mg tablets can be administered in the morning for children requiring a 20-mg b.i.d. regimen. It should be noted, however, that some children do not experience extended benefit (i.e., 6–8 hours) from the sustained release formula. In these cases, short acting tablets will have to suffice or alternative medications, such as Dexedrine spansules, be substituted.

Emergent Symptoms and Contraindications Associated With MPH

Emergent Symptoms.   Monitoring potential side effects associated with MPH therapy is an essential component of a comprehensive treatment protocol. The most common emergent symptoms include: increased frequency of urination, sleep problems (initial insomnia), reduced appetite (with potential weight loss and/or growth suppression), stomach upset, headache, elevated blood pressure, accelerated heart rate (tachycardia), depressed affect (crying, sadness), irritability, social withdrawal, constricted cognitive ability (see "overfocused phenomena" mentioned earlier), rebound effects, and emergence or intensification of tics.

Increased frequency of urination is primarily due to increased liquid consumption, which in turn is caused by MPH's desiccating (drying) effects in the mouth and on mucous membranes. Parents and teachers should be alerted to this fact and allow these children to have a water container on their desk. Periodic requests by the children to visit the restroom should be expected and permitted.

Sleep problems typically consist of difficulty falling asleep (initial insomnia) and are characteristically associated with receiving late afternoon or early evening doses of MPH. The results of the only known controlled study to date that directly address this issue, however, indicate no significant effects of MPH on initial latency to or total duration of sleep (Kent, Blader, Koplewicz, Abikoff, & Foley, 1995). Nevertheless, monitoring for initial insomnia would appear prudent, and in cases where it does occur, doses administered during the latter part of the day may need to be reduced or eliminated.

Reduced appetite and associated weight loss and/or growth suppression have received considerable attention by the media in past years. Suppressed appetite is a well-documented emergent symptom associated with MPH therapy. Its relation with growth velocity is more complex. In the most comprehensive evaluation of MPH effects on growth in children, Gittelman-Klein and Mannuzza (1988) reported that many children experience reduced appetite, corresponding weight loss, and reduced growth velocity. MPH therapy, however, did not compromise final height in the young adults who were treated with MPH in childhood (average daily dose was 45 mg; duration of treatment, 6 months to 5 years), even when it exerted an adverse effect on their growth rate during the active treatment phase. The authors concluded that compensatory growth occurs after discontinuation of stimulant treatment (i.e., growth rebound phenomenon), which in turn supports the recommendation for an extended drug holiday during summer months.

Stomach upset is reported by an estimated one third of children undergoing MPH therapy (Barkley, 1990). A primary reason for its occurrence is due to prevailing clinical lore that MPH should be administered prior to ingesting food, or stated otherwise, that MPH administered after a meal results in diminished clinical effectiveness. The only outcome study directly examining this phenomenon, however, revealed no significant differences in clinical effectiveness between children administered MPH with or before ingesting food (Swanson, Sandman, Deutsch, & Baren, 1983). To circumvent complaints of stomach upset, it is advisable to administer MPH after meals. Timing of dosage administration in this manner offers the additional benefit of circumventing commonly reported appetite suppression and associated weight loss in children. Afternoon dose and its potentially adverse effect on appetite for lunch is more problematic when medication must be administered at a prescribed time by a school nurse. In these cases, it is recommended that children be encouraged to eat a healthy snack during the usual school lunch period (e.g., carrot sticks, granola bar) and then have a more balanced meal when returning home from school.

Elevated blood pressure and tachycardia are commonly reported emergent symptoms associated with MPH treatment. Although traditional medical practice involves assessment of these parameters, the timing of measurement is critical to interpretation of results. For example, Kelly, Rapport, and DuPaul (1988) found that MPH effects on children's heart rate were related to both dosage and time of day, consistent with the phenomenon termed the *Law of Initial Values*. From a practical standpoint, their results indicate that heart rate should be measured at the same time of day when comparing active drug to baseline values. The long-term effects of accelerated heart rate (generally reported to average 5 bpm to 10 bpm with MPH and lasting a few hours) are presently unknown, but should be considered in light of common heart rate acceleration associated with physical exertion by children during a normal day's activities.

Depressed affect and irritability are occasionally evidenced with MPH treatment and are easily monitored using instruments such as the SERS. These symptoms frequently abate following several days of MPH therapy, especially when they are of a mild to moderate nature. If symptoms persist after 2 weeks, dosage should be decreased. It should be noted, however, that many children become more sensitive and attuned to the environment when receiving MPH therapy. As a result, children who previously would not blink an eye when scolded for misbehaving may become upset and exhibit more appropriate levels of emotional responsiveness to feedback received from others in the environment.

Social withdrawal is occasionally reported with MPH therapy and should be carefully investigated. Many children, finding that they can more easily attend to their environment, will elect to play quietly or occupy themselves with previously aversive activities (e.g., reading, working on a puzzle). Anecdotally, parents describe such behaviors as a "major personality change," and are unaccustomed to having their child focus on an activity for an extended period of time. Alternatively, social withdrawal may indicate an overfocused state, as described previously, and reduced dosage should be considered.

Rebound effects refer to behavior that is judged to be worse than behavior observed prior to administration of the drug. Many parents complain, for example, that their child is difficult to control and more "hyper" in the late afternoon or early evening following daytime administrations of MPH. A rigorous, placebo-controlled study of this phenomenon in a sample of 21 children with ADHD receiving .3 and .6 mg/kg MPH reported that about a third of the sample exhibited rebound effects (Johnston, Pelham, Hoza, & Sturges, 1988). Several options are available to mitigate rebound effects and include administering a lower dose of medication in the late afternoon when returning home from school (e.g., 5 mg) or reducing the noontime dosage. Alternatively, children who are unaccustomed to attending for extended periods of time will frequently exhibit cranky and irritable behavior after focusing in school for 6 to 7 consecutive hours. Other strategies should be considered before adjusting dosage. These include providing the child with a healthy snack when returning home in the afternoon and instituting a mandatory rest period (e.g., 30 minutes) during which the children engage in quiet activities by themselves in a designated area of the house.

Emergence or intensification of tics is a more serious but infrequent side effect associated with MPH treatment. Exacerbation of preexisting tics are estimated to occur in 13% of cases, and fewer than 1% of children with ADHD develop a tic disorder following initiation of MPH therapy (Denckla, Bemporad, & MacKay, 1976). Tics normally subside with discontinuation of MPH, and a personal and family history of tics or Tourette's disorder is recommended prior to initiating treatment.

Contraindications.   Potential contraindications for MPH therapy in children include a positive history of tics (including tic disorders in family members), a history of seizures (MPH may lower the convulsive threshold in some patients with a prior history of seizures), glaucoma, hypertension, hyperthyroidism, documented hypersensitivity, allergic, or adverse reactions to the drug. Comorbid anxiety and/or depressive symptomatology (internalizing symptoms) in children with ADHD have also been proposed as potential contraindications for MPH treatment. A recent study comparing children with ADHD alone and ADHD with comorbid internalizing symptoms has a direct bearing on this issue. Significantly fewer comorbid children exhibited a positive response to MPH, although an estimated 25% experienced improvement on the drug (DuPaul, Barkley, & McMurray, 1994). Thus, the presence of internalizing symptoms in children with ADHD does not contraindicate consideration for MPH treatment, but does warrant close monitoring for potential iatrogenic effects.

Maintenance

Periodic reevaluation (every 3 months) of effectiveness using the rating scales already described is recommended for children receiving ongoing MPH treatment. Because many practitioners continue to entertain the notion that MPH is related to body weight, there is an expectation that dosage will require upward adjustment with increasing age of the child. This has not been borne out by empirical investigations (Rapport & Denney, 1997). Careful initial titration of dosage is the most effective method for diminishing the likelihood of having to adjust dosage at some future point in time.

Educating parents about MPH, including appropriate expectations for treatment outcome, is highly recommended. Parents need to understand that their children will continue to experience occasional "off" days at home and at school, but reduced variability in behavior and academic performance within and between days can be expected. They should also be aware that family crisis, distressing incidents, illness, and other emotionally laden events may adversely affect MPH response. Medication may need to be temporarily discontinued in these situations after consultation with the prescribing physician.

Finally, thorough compliance with the prescribed medication regimen is central to outcome. Extensive clinical experience indicates that poor compliance by parents is typically associated with two factors: insufficient information and monitoring received during the initial medication trial, and the presence of psychopathology in family members, which is frequently accompanied by an unstable home environment. Some parents, although convinced of the benefits derived from MPH treatment, prove unreliable in administering medication owing to their own emotional problems. For these cases, it is advisable to have both the morning and afternoon doses administered at school. Conversely, reliable compliance can be expected in parents who are relatively well adjusted, have access to the clinician in times of needed support, and receive periodic reevaluations.

HOME- AND COMMUNITY-BASED TREATMENT PROTOCOL

Establishing an effective protocol for home and community life is essential for children with ADHD, regardless of whether they are receiving adequate schooling and/or ongoing MPH therapy. Results from intermediate and long-term outcome studies indicate that their inattentiveness, impulsiveness, and propensity for stimulation-rich environments increase the risk for development of conduct disorder and substance abuse during adolescence and antisocial behavior in adulthood. In response, the protocol must be developed to arrest the development of comorbid psychopathology by complementing the basic temperament and unique brain functioning of these children. This can be accomplished by incorporating three primary elements into the home and community environment: advanced planning, basic structure, and consistent monitoring (the "abc's" of treatment planning).

Basic Elements

Prior to discussing the basic elements of home/community treatment planning, it is important to emphasize that the proposed protocol assumes that the clinician has provided parents with a basic understanding of childrearing principles, appropriate developmental expectations, and basic management procedures—the latter of which are usually based on principles derived from social learning theory. Several excellent texts are available for this purpose (e.g., Barkley, 1990; Kazdin, 1989; Patterson, 1975). As opposed to reiterating these principles, the ensuing sections present basic elements that focus on proactive procedures that parents can incorporate into their daily lives to diminish the need for more formal intervention.

Advanced Planning and Structure.   Parents will need to spend a minimum of 1 hour each weekend planning for the ensuing week's activities. A weekly calendar taking the form of a large poster board to be placed on the kitchen refrigerator or other highly visible location at home is recommended for this purpose. Days of the week are posted across the top of the calendar and hours (beginning with morning wake-up time and ending with bedtime) depicted in the lefthand margin from top to bottom. Each hourly block should be filled in with a scheduled event or activity. An abbreviated (two weekdays and one weekend day) example of a prototypical weekly calendar is depicted in Table 4.6.

In reviewing the calendar, it should be apparent that every day is fully scheduled, beginning with waking up in the morning and continuing to bedtime. Parents will need to periodically review and closely follow each day's planned events with their child. The ensuing paragraphs present broad rather than specific strategies to be used by parents. It is incumbent on parents to apply these strategies to new situations and activities because of the inestimable exigencies that may arise in a given day. A discussion begins with examples of fairly typical outings and considers the potential benefits of advanced planning and structure.

Trips to the store or shopping mall, vacations, and other outings without the benefit of advanced planning increase the probability of unforeseen events and unpleasant experiences occurring for both the child and family members. When planning activities, parents are encouraged to invoke an empathic response set (i.e., that is, to think how an ADHD brain reacts and the types of activities preferred by children with ADHD). For example, children with ADHD typically detest boring, monotonous routines and situations that are low in

TABLE 4.6
Herkimer's Weekly Calender of Planned Activities

	Monday	Wednesday	Saturday
6:30	Wake-up/Get Dressed	Wake-up/Get Dressed	Wake-up/Get Dressed
7:00	Breakfast	Breakfast	Breakfast
7:30	School Bus	School Bus	Morning Chores
8:00	School	School	Prepare Shopping List with Mom
8:30			Grocery Shopping
9:00			
9:30			Bike Riding/Roller Blading Outside
10:00			
10:30			Leave for Game
			Soccer Game
11:30			
12:00			
12:30			Lunch at Home
1:00			Free Time on Computer
1:30			Leave for Karate Lesson
2:00			Karate Lesson
2:30			
3:00	Return Home on Bus	Return Home on Bus	Quiet Play in Room
3:30	Homework Session #1	Homework Session #1	Supervised Peer Activity
4:00	Soccer Practice	Soccer Practice	
4:30			Activity with Dad (e.g., sports)
5:00			
5:30	Shower	Shower	Shower
6:00	Homework Session #2	Homework Session #2	Dinner
6:30	Dinner	Dinner	Movie at Home
7:00	Prepare clothes/materials for tomorrow	Prepare clothes/materials for tomorrow	
7:30	TV Viewing or Computer Time	TV Viewing or Computer Time	
8:00	Bedtime/Optional Reading	Bedtime/Optional Reading	Bedtime/Optional Reading
8:30	Lights Out	Lights Out	Lights Out

stimulation. Thus, accompanying Mom to the grocery store or shopping mall, riding to the beach in the back seat of the family automobile with an older brother, and similar situations requiring children to wait and control themselves for extended periods of time are beset with difficulties from the start. To circumvent potential problems, parents must invoke foresight and map out a basic plan of action based on their knowledge of ADHD, in general, and their son or daughter, in particular. Trips to the grocery store, for example, can include having the children push their own basket (many stores have small, child-size carts for this purpose), actively participate in obtaining certain food items (e.g., those on low shelves located on the same aisle), and checking-off items on the grocery list while shopping. The key is to have the children actively engaged in the shopping experience rather than requiring them to passively accompany the parent. In a similar vein, scheduled trips in the family automobile can be made more stimulating by taking along various activities, such as hand-held computer games, audiocassettes with headphones, and Lego building pieces.

Planning extracurricular activities after school and on weekends is an essential component of the protocol for two reasons. First, even well-educated and emotionally stable parents require time away from their children to cope with the daily challenges of childrearing. This is especially true of parents raising a child with ADHD. Second, children with ADHD require extensive adult supervision and exposure to other children to establish age-appropriate social skills. Past studies, for example, indicate that children with ADHD are rejected by normal peers within 20 to 30 minutes of play (Pelham & Bender, 1982). Of potentially greater consequence is their propensity to seek out inappropriate playmates and activities when left on their own, paving the way for development of conduct disorder.

Extracurricular activities should ideally incorporate all three of the proposed protocol elements: extensive planning, structure, and adult supervision. As presented in the aforementioned examples, parents will achieve greater successes in planning activities if they don their facsimile of an ADHD brain—that is, think ADHD. Select small group, focused, nonsedentary activities that involve other children and are closely supervised by an adult. Examples include soccer, swimming, gymnastics, and martial arts (e.g., Judo or Karate). These activities involve gross motor movement and peer interactions, minimize passive waiting and verbal instruction, and are typically supervised by adults experienced in working with children. Conversely, activities, such as baseball, are generally ill-suited for children with ADHD owing to the passive waiting involved. Exceptions for this sport are found when the child exhibits a natural talent for one of the "active" field positions (e.g., such as pitcher or catcher). Under more usual circumstances, the child is placed in right field, misses the occasional ball hit to the outfield, and is expected to wait for 8 other players before taking a turn at bat.

Consistent Monitoring.   Children with ADHD require nearly continuous monitoring and supervision by an adult regardless of their age. Stimulating yet potentially dangerous and illicit situations attract these youngsters like iron particles to a magnet. Peer relationships are tenuous at best and require frequent adult intervention. Knowledge of rules and societal norms is adequate for most children with ADHD, but consistent application of this knowledge is lacking. The downside is that providing necessary levels of supervision for children with ADHD is emotionally draining and physically exhausting for even the most experienced professional. Consequently, parents must carefully prepare for the inevitable by establishing a support network. This is recognizably a difficult and time-consuming goal to achieve. However, the degree to which this can be accomplished is inversely related to the emotional expenditure exacted by a lack of supervision. Networking can take several forms. Recruiting extended family members, hiring older neighborhood children for afterschool care or on weekends to provide coverage for designated time periods, and arranging a neighborhood co-op for supervising small numbers of children are reasonable ways to share the burden of supervision.

Homework

Homework assignments present unique difficulties for both the children and their parents. Homework is typically uninteresting and traditionally requires initiative, organizational skills, self-control, tenacity, and an ability to concentrate for extended time intervals. Regrettably, few children with ADHD possess these attributes to the extent necessary for independent, consistent completion of daily homework assignments. Thus, it is advisable to schedule two or more homework sessions each day with the duration of each depending on the child's attention span and specific characteristics associated with the assignment. Very young and more severely hyperactive children will often require assignment periods initially lasting no more than 5 to10 minutes. Total duration can gradually be lengthened to correspond with the child's developing abilities for longer periods of concentration. The assignments themselves should be "chunked" using methods similar to those described previously. For example, an assignment requiring memorization of 20 spelling words should be broken down into chunks of five words. Method of rehearsal at home should be similar to those used at school. Specifically, if the classroom teacher requires children to write dictated words on a piece of paper during a spelling test, a preferred practice is to present each word orally, have the child spell the word orally, then write the word down on paper. (Note: Saying the word orally eventually becomes a covert process for the child during test situations.) Alternatively, if a computer is available at home the child can listen to an orally presented cassette recording of each word at 20-second intervals and utilize a word processing program. A spell checker program can be engaged subsequently to provide corrective feedback. A final oral exam should be scheduled at dinner and again during breakfast to facilitate consolidation and recall of information. Other assignments can also follow this general format. For example, completion of dittos or writing assignments by younger children can be chunked by cutting the assignment into smaller pieces with scissors, presenting one part at a time, and scheduling breaks between work sessions. For more severe cases, homework sessions will require complementary management devices such as the Attentional Training System (ATS; Gordon, 1987) or an inexpensive kitchen timer preset for a designated work time.

Access to a home-based computer is rapidly becoming a necessity for children. Of perhaps greater importance are their numerous advantages for children with ADHD. These include provision of feedback (e.g., built-in spell checkers, grammar check software), built-in stimulation, and increasing availability of sophisticated educational software. Children with ADHD prefer word processing over hand-writing assignments and playing math games over filling out dittos. Although potentially inconvenient, every conceivable assignment handed out in class can be converted by a scanner for computer adaptation.

Summary

The proposed recommendations for home and community management intentionally omit discussion of more traditional approaches such as behavior management for two reasons: Detailed presentations of these approaches are available from multiple sources; and they rely too heavily on reactive, time-consuming interventions. An alternative approach to raising children with ADHD is offered to provide an overview of the basic principles intrinsic to proactive intervention techniques. The underlying principle is straightforward: Actively plan to keep the child occupied in engaging activities that are closely monitored by knowledgeable adults.

CONCLUSIONS

Treating children with ADHD begins with an understanding of the basic nature and core features of the disorder. Existing evidence derived from temperament, genetic, epidemiological, family, and brain-based studies suggests that the disorder represents either an evolutionary different type of brain that is inherited or affected prenatally. In either case, knowledge of appropriate assessment instruments and techniques as well as differential diagnostic procedures are prerequisites to designing effective treatment strategies. This chapter intentionally offers a nontraditional and proactive approach to treating children with ADHD in an effort to promote development of new therapies. It is hoped that at least some will shake off the garments of stagnation and rise to meet the challenges of assisting future generations of children with ADHD become well-adjusted, contributing members of society. Genetic research will likely reveal the mystery of the ADHD brain in the foreseeable future, but will not alter the need for carefully designed environments conducive to learning.

REFERENCES

Achenbach, T. M. (1980). *DSM–III* in light of empirical research on the classification of child psychopathology. *Journal of the American Academy of Child and Adolescent Psychiatry, 19,* 395–412.

Achenbach, T. M. (1985). *Assessment and taxonomy of child and adolescent psychopathology.* Beverly Hills, CA: Sage.

Achenbach, T. M. (1987). How is a parent rating scale used in the diagnosis of attention deficit disorder? In J. Loney (Ed.), *The young hyperactive child: Answers to questions about diagnosis, prognosis, and treatment* (pp. 19–32). New York: Haworth.

Achenbach, T. M., & Edelbrock, C. S. (1978). The classification of child psychopathology: A review and analysis of empirical efforts. *Psychological Bulletin, 85,* 1275–1301.

Allison, D. B., Faith, M. S., & Franklin, R. D. (1995). Antecedent exercise in the treatment of disruptive behavior: A meta-analytic review. *Clinical Psychology Science and Practice, 2,* 279–304.

American Psychiatric Association. (1968). *Diagnostic and statistical manual of mental disorders* (2nd ed.). Washington, DC: Author.

American Psychiatric Association. (1980). *Diagnostic and statistical manual of mental disorders* (3rd ed.). Washington, DC: Author.

American Psychiatric Association. (1987). *Diagnostic and statistical manual of mental disorders* (3rd ed., rev.). *(DSM–III–R).* Washington, DC: Author.

American Psychiatric Association. (1994). *Diagnostic and statistical manual of mental disorders* (4th ed.). *(DSM–IV).* Washington, DC: Author.

Barkley, R. A. (1987). Child behavior rating scales and checklists. In M. Rutter, A. Tuma, & I. S. Lann (Eds.), *Assessment and diagnosis in child psychopathology* (pp. 113–155). New York: Guilford.

Barkley, R. A. (1990). *Attention deficit hyperactivity disorder: A handbook for diagnosis and treatment.* New York: Guilford Press.

Barkley, R. A. (1991). The ecological validity of laboratory and analogue assessment methods of ADHD symptoms. *Journal of Abnormal Child Psychology, 19,* 149–178.

Barkley, R. A., DuPaul, G. J., & McMurray, M. B. (1990). A comprehensive evaluation of attention deficit disorder with and without hyperactivity. *Journal of Consulting and Clinical Psychology, 58,* 775–789.

Barkley, R. A., & Edelbrock, C. (1987). Assessing situational variation in children's problem behaviors: The home and school situations questionnaires. In R. J. Prinz (Ed.), *Advances in behavioral assessment of children and families* (Vol. 3, pp. 157–176). Greenwich, CT: JAI Press.

Barkley, R. A., Fischer, M., Edelbrock, C. S., & Smallish, L. (1990). The adolescent outcome of hyperactive children diagnosed by research criteria: I. An 8-year prospective follow-up study. *Journal of the American Academy of Child and Adolescent Psychiatry, 29*, 546–557.

Bradley, C. (1937). The behavior of children receiving Benzedrine. *American Journal of Psychiatry, 94*, 577–585.

Campbell, S. B., Douglas, V. I., & Morgenstern, G. (1971). Cognitive styles in hyperactive children and the effect of methylphenidate. *Journal of Child Psychology and Psychiatry and Allied Disciplines, 18*, 239–249.

Cantwell, D. P., & Satterfield, J. H. (1978). The prevalence of academic underachievement in hyperactive children. *Journal of Pediatric Psychology, 3*, 168–171.

Carlson, G. A., Kashani, J. H., Thomas, M., Vaidya, A., & Daniel, A. E. (1987). Comparison of two structured interviews on a psychiatrically hospitalized population of children. *Journal of the American Academy of Child and Adolescent Psychiatry, 26*, 645–648.

Chambers, W. J., Puig-Antich, J., Hirsch, M., Paez, P., Ambrosini, P. J., Tabrizi, A., & Davies, M. (1985). The assessment of affective disorders in children and adolescents by a semi-structured interview. *Archives of General Psychiatry, 42*, 696–702.

Conners, C. K. (1987). How is a teacher rating scale used in the diagnosis of attention deficit disorder? In J. Loney (Ed.), *The young hyperactive child: Answers to questions about diagnosis, prognosis, and treatment* (pp. 33–52). New York: Haworth.

Costello, A., Edelbrook, C., Kalas, R., Kellser, M., & Klaric, S. (1984). *NIMH Diagnostic Interview Schedule for Children (DISC)*. Rockville, MD: National Institute of Mental Health.

Daws, R. M. (1986). Representative thinking in clinical judgement. *Clinical Psychology Review, 26*, 422–441.

Denckla, M. B., Bemporad, J. R., & MacKay, M. C. (1976). Tics following methylphenidate administration. *Journal of the American Medical Association, 235*, 1349–1351.

Douglas, V. I. (1988). Cognitive deficits in children with attention deficit disorder with hyperactivity. In L. M. Bloomingdale & J. A. Sergeant (Eds.), *Attention deficit disorder: Criteria, cognition, intervention* (pp. 65–81). New York: Pergamon.

DuPaul, G. J., Anastopoulos, A. D. Shelton, T. L., Buevremont, D. C., & Metevia, L. (1992). Multimethod assessment of attention-deficit hyperactivity disorder: The diagnostic utility of clinic-based tests. *Journal of Clinical Child Psychology, 21*, 394–402.

DuPaul, G. J., Barkley, R. A., & McMurray, M. B. (1994). Response of children with ADHD to methylphenidate: Interaction with internalizing symptoms. *Journal of the American Academy of Child and Adolescent Psychiatry, 33*, 894–903.

DuPaul, G. J., & Stoner, G. (1994). *ADHD in the schools: Assessment and intervention strategies*. New York: Guilford.

Edelbrock, C., & Costello, A. J. (1984). Structured psychiatric interviews for children and adolescents. In G. Goldstein & M. Hersen (Eds.), *Handbook of psychological assessment* (pp. 276–290). New York: Pergamon.

Edelbrock, C., & Costello, A. J. (1988). Convergence between statistically derived behavior problem syndromes and child psychiatric diagnoses. *Journal of Abnormal Child Psychology, 16*, 219–231.

Edelbrock, C., Costello, A. J., & Kessler, M. D. (1984). Empirical corroboration of the attention deficit disorder. *Journal of the American Academy of Child and Adolescent Psychiatry, 23*, 285–290.

Firestone, P., & Prabhu, A. N. (1983). Minor physical anomalies and obstetrical complications: Their relationship to hyperactive, psychoneurotic and normal children and their families. *Journal of Abnormal Child Psychology, 11*, 207–216.

Fristad, M., Weller, E. B., & Weller, R. A. (1992). The Mania Rating Scale: Can it be used in children? *Journal of the American Academy of Child and Adolescent Psychiatry, 31*, 252–257.

Gammon, G. D., Rothblum, J. K., Mullen, K., Tischler, G. L., & Weissman, M. M. (1983). Use of a structured diagnostic interview to identify bipolar disorder in adolescent inpatients: Frequency and manifestations of the disorder. *American Journal of Psychiatry, 140*, 543–547.

Gittelman, R., Mannuzza, S., Shenker, R., & Bonagura, N. (1985). Hyperactive boys almost grown up. I. Psychiatric status. *Archives of General Psychiatry, 42*, 937–947.

Gittelman-Klein, R., & Mannuzza, S. (1988). Hyperactive boys almost grown up: III. Methylphenidate effects on ultimate height. *Archives of General Psychiatry, 45*, 1131–1134.

Gordon, M. (1987). *The Attentional Training System* (ATS). Gordon Systems, Inc., P.O. Box 746, Dewitt, NY.

Helzer, J. E., Robins, L. M., McEvoy, L. T., Spitznagel, E. L., Stoltzman, R. K., Farmer, A., & Brockington, I. F. (1985). A comparison of clinical and Diagnostic Interview Schedule diagnoses: Physical reexamination of lay interviewed cases in the general population. *Archives of General Psychiatry, 42,* 657–666.

Herjanic, B., & Campbell, W. (1977). Differentiating psychiatrically disturbed children on the basis of a structured interview. *Journal of Abnormal Child Psychology, 5,* 127–134.

Herjanic, B., & Reich, W. (1982). Development of a structured psychiatric interview for children: Agreement between child and parent on individual symptoms. *Journal of Abnormal Child Psychology, 10,* 307–324.

Hinshaw, S. P. (1987). On the distinction between attentional deficits/hyperactivity and conduct problems/aggression in child psychopathology. *Psychological Bulletin, 101,* 443–463.

Hodges, K., McKnew, D., Cytryn, L., Stern, L., & Klein, J. (1982). The Child Assessment Schedule (CAS) diagnostic interview: A report on reliability and validity. *Journal of the American Academy of Child and Adolescent Psychiatry, 21,* 468–473.

Johnston, C., Pelham, W. E., Hoza, J., & Sturges, J. (1988). Psychostimulant rebound in attention deficit disordered boys. *Journal of the American Academy of Child and Adolescent Psychiatry, 27,* 806–810.

Kaufman, A. S. (1975). Factor analysis of the WISC–R at 11 age levels between ½ and 16½ years. *Journal of Consulting and Clinical Psychology, 43,* 135–147.

Kaufman, A. (1981). The WISC–R and learning disabilities assessment: State of the art. *Journal of Learning Disabilities, 14,* 520–526.

Kazdin, A. E. (1989). *Behavior modification in applied settings.* Monterey, CA: Brooks/Cole.

Kelly, K. L., Rapport, M. D., & DuPaul, G. J. (1988). Attention deficit disorder and methylphenidate: A multi-step analysis of dose-response effects on children's cardiovascular functioning. *International Clinical Psychopharmacology, 3,* 167–181.

Kent, J. D., Blader, J. C., Koplewicz, H. S., Abikoff, H., & Foley, C. A. (1995). Effects of late-afternoon methylphenidate administration on behavior and sleep in attention-deficit hyperactivity disorder. *Pediatrics, 96,* 320–325.

Kinsbourne, M. (1984). Beyond attention deficit: Search for the disorder in ADD. In L. Bloomingdale (Ed.), *Attention deficit disorder: Diagnostic, cognitive, and therapeutic understanding* (pp. 133–162). New York: Spectrum.

Kinsbourne, M. (1990). Testing models for attention deficit hyperactivity disorder in the behavioral laboratory. In C. K. Conners & M. Kinsbourne (Eds.), *Attention deficit hyperactivity disorder* (pp. 51–69). Munich, Germany: Medizin Verlag Munchen.

Klein, R. G., & Mannuzza, S. (1991). Long-term outcome in hyperactive children: A review. *Journal of the American Academy of Child and Adolescent Psychiatry, 30,* 383–387.

Kovacs, M. (1982). *The longitudinal study of child and adolescent psychopathology: I. The semi-structured psychiatric Interview Schedule for Children (ISC).* Unpublished manuscript, Western Psychiatric Institute and Clinic.

Loney, J. (1974). The intellectual functioning of hyperactive elementary school boys: A cross-sectional investigation. *American Journal of Orthopsychiatry, 44,* 754–762.

Mannuzza, S., Klein, R. G., Bessler, A., Malloy, P., & LaPadula, M. (1993). Adults outcome of hyperactive boys: Educational achievement, occupational rank, and psychiatric status. *Archives of General Psychiatry, 50,* 565–576.

Mannuzza, S., Klein, R. G., Bonagura, N., Malloy, P., Giampino, T. L., & Addalli, K. A. (1991). Hyperactive boys almost grown up. V. Replication of psychiatric status. *Archives of General Psychiatry, 48,* 77–83.

Mash, E. G., & Terdal, L. G. (1981). *Behavioral assessment of childhood disorders.* New York: Guilford.

Massman, P. J., Nussbaum, N. L., & Bigler, E. D. (1988). The mediating effect of age on the relationship between child behavior checklist hyperactivity scores and neuropsychological test performance. *Journal of Abnormal Child Psychology, 16,* 89–95.

McGee, R., & Share, D. L. (1988). Attention deficit disorder-hyperactivity and academic failure: Which comes first and what should be treated? *Journal of the American Academy of Child and Adolescent Psychiatry, 27,* 318–325.

Milich, R., Widiger, T. A., & Landau, S. (1987). Differential diagnosis of attention deficit and conduct disorders using conditional probabilities. *Journal of Consulting and Clinical Psychology, 55,* 762–767.

Orvaschel, H. (1985). Psychiatric interviews suitable for use in research with children and adolescents. *Psychopharmacology Bulletin, 21,* 737–745.

Patterson, G. R. (1975). *Families: Applications of social learning to family life.* Champaign, Ill: Research Press.

Pelham, W. E., & Bender, M. E. (1982). Peer relationships in hyperactive children: Description and treatment. In K. D. Gadow & I. Bialer (Eds.), *Advances in learning and behavioral disabilities* (Vol. 1, pp. 365–436). Greenwich, CT: JAI Press.

Puig-Antich, J., & Chambers, W. (1978). *The schedule for affective disorders and schizophrenia for school-aged children*. New York: New York State Psychiatric Institute.

Quay, H. C., & Quay, L. C. (1965). Behavior problems in early adolescence. *Child Development, 36*, 215–220.

Rapport, M. D. (1983). Attention deficit disorder with hyperactivity: Critical treatment parameters and their application in applied outcome research. In M. Hersen, R. Eisler, & P. Miller (Eds.), *Progress in behavior modification* (pp. 219–298). New York: Academic Press.

Rapport, M. D. (1990). Controlled studies of the effects of psychostimulants on children's functioning in clinic and classroom settings. In C. K. Conners & M. Kinsbourne (Eds.), *Attention deficit hyperactivity disorder* (pp. 77–111). Munich, Germany: Medizin Verlag Munchen.

Rapport, M. D. (1995). Attention-deficit hyperactivity disorder. In M. Hersen & R. T. Ammerman (Eds.), *Advanced abnormal child psychology* (pp. 353–374). Mahwah, NJ: Lawrence Erlbaum Associates.

Rapport, M. D., & Denney, C. B. (1997). Titrating methylphenidate in children with attention-deficit/hyperactivity disorder: Is body mass predictive of clinical response. *Journal of the American Academy of Child and Adolescent Psychiatry, 36*, 523–530.

Rapport, M. D., Denney, C., DuPaul, G. J., & Gardner, M. J. (1994). Attention deficit disorder and methylphenidate: Normalization rates, clinical effectiveness, and response prediction in 76 children. *Journal of the American Academy of Child and Adolescent Psychiatry, 33*, 882–893.

Rapport, M. D., DuPaul, G. J., & Kelly, K. L. (1989). Attention-deficit hyperactivity disorder and methylphenidate: The relationship between gross body weight and drug response in children. *Psychopharmacology Bulletin, 25*, 285–290.

Rapport, M. D., Jones, J. T., DuPaul, G. J., Kelly, K., Gardner, M., Tucker, S. B. & Schoeler, T. (1987). Attention deficit disorder and methylphenidate: Group and single-subject analyses of dose effects on attention in clinic and classroom settings. *Journal of Clinical Child Psychology, 16*, 329–338.

Rapport, M. D., & Kelly, K. L. (1991). Psychostimulant effects on learning and cognitive function: Findings and implications for children with attention deficit hyperactivity disorder. *Clinical Psychology Review, 11*, 61–92.

Rapport, M. D., Loo, S., & Denney, C. (1995). The paired associate learning task: Is it an externally valid instrument for assessing methylphenidate response in children with attention deficit disorder? *Journal of Psychopathology and Behavioral Assessment, 17*, 125–144.

Rosenberger, P., & Lewine, R. (1982). Conceptual issues in the choice of a structured psychiatric interview. *Comprehensive Psychiatry, 23*, 116–123.

Ross, D. M., & Ross, S. A. (1982). *Hyperactivity: Theory, research, and action* (2nd ed.). New York: Wiley.

Rutter, M., & Graham, P. (1968). The reliability and validity of the psychiatric assessment of the child: I. Interview with the child. *British Journal of Psychiatry, 114*, 563–579.

Rutter, M., & Shaffer, D. (1980). *DSM–III*: A step forward or back in terms of the classification of child psychiatric disorders? *Journal of the American Academy of Child and Adolescent Psychiatry, 19*, 371–394.

Saghir, M. T. (1971). A comparison of some aspects of structured and unstructured psychiatric interviews. *American Journal of Psychiatry, 128*, 72–76.

Sandberg, S. T., Rutter, M., & Taylor, E. (1978). Hyperkinetic disorder in psychiatric clinic attenders. *Developmental Medicine and Child Neurology, 20*, 279–299.

Shaywitz, S. E. (1982). Assessment of brain function in clinical pediatric research: Behavioral and biological strategies. *Schizophrenia Bulletin, 8*, 205–235.

Shaywitz, S. E., & Shaywitz, B. E. (1988). Attention deficit disorder: Current perspectives. In J. F. Kavanagh & T. J. Truss (Eds.), *Learning diabilities: Proceedings of the national conference* (pp. 369–523). Parkton, MD: York Press.

Shaywitz, S. E., Shaywitz, B. E., McGraw, K., & Groll, S. (1984). Current status of the neuromaturational examination as an index of learning disability. *Journal of Pediatrics, 104*, 819–825.

Shrout, P. E., Spitzer, R. L., & Fleiss, J. L. (1987). Quantification of agreement in psychiatric diagnosis revisited. *Archives of General Psychiatry, 44*, 172–177.

Spitzer, R. L. (1983). Psychiatric diagnosis: Are clinicians still necessary? *Comprehensive Psychiatry, 24*, 399–411.

Sprague, R. L., & Sleator, E. K. (1977). Methylphenidate in hyperkinetic children: Differences in dose effects on learning and social behavior. *Science, 198*, 1274–1276.

Swanson, J. M., Cantwell, D., Lerner, M., McBurnett, K., & Hanna, G. (1991). Effects of stimulant medication on learning in children with ADHD. *Journal of Learning Disability, 24*, 219–230.

Swanson, J. M., Sandman, C. A., Deutsch, C., & Baren, M. (1983). Methylphenidate (Ritalin) given with or before breakfast: I. Behavioral, cognitive and electrophysiological effects. *Pediatrics, 72*, 49–55.

Szatmari, P, Offord, D. R., & Boyle, M. H. (1989). Correlates, associated impariments, and patterns of service utilization of children with attention deficit disorders: Findings from the Ontario child health study. *Journal of Child Psychology and Psychiatry, 30*, 205–217.

Weinstein, S. R., Stone, K., Noam, G. G., Grimes, K., & Schwab-Stone, M. (1989). Comparison of DISC with clinicians' *DSM–III* diagnoses in psychiatric inpatients. *Journal of the American Academy of Child and Adolescent Psychiatry, 28*, 53–60.

Weiss, G., & Hechtman, L. (1986). *Hyperactive children grown up*. New York: Guilford.

Weiss, G., Hechtman, L., Perlman, T., Hopkins, J., & Wener, A. (1979). Hyperactives as young adults: A controlled prospective 10-year follow-up of 75 children. *Archives of General Psychiatry, 36*, 675–681.

Weissman, M. M. Wickramaratne, P., Warner, V., John, K., Prusoff, B. A., Merikangas, K. R., & Gammon, G.D. (1987). Assessing psychiatric disorders in children. *Archives of General Psychiatry, 44*, 747–753.

Weller, E. B., Weller, R. A., & Fristad, M. A. (1995). Bipolar disorder in children: Misdiagnosis, underdiagnosis, and future directions. *Journal of the American Academy of Child and Adolescent Psychiatry, 34*, 709–714.

Whalen, C. K., & Henker, B. (1985). The social worlds of hyperactivity (ADDH) children. *Clinical Psychology Review, 5*, 447–478.

Widiger, R. A., Hurt, S. W., Frances, A., Clarkin, J. F., & Gilmore, M. (1984). Diagnostic efficiency and *DSM–III*. *Archives of General Psychiatry, 41*, 1005–1012.

Wilens, T. E., & Biederman, J. (1992). The stimulants. *Psychiatric Clinics of North America, 15*, 191–222.

Young, R. C., Biggs, J. T., Ziegler, V. E., & Meyer, D. A. (1978). A rating scale for mania: Reliability, validity and sensitivity. *British Journal of Psychiatry, 133*, 429–435.

Chapter 5

Interpersonal Family Therapy for Childhood Depression

Jennifer A. J. Schwartz
Emory University School of Medicine

Nadine J. Kaslow
Emory University School of Medicine

Gary R. Racusin
Yale University

Erin Rowe Carton
Emory University

With accumulating data revealing the association between maladaptive parent–child interactions and child maladjustment, family therapy approaches for treating childhood psychopathology have become popular. Family interventions appear particularly valuable for childhood mood disorders, which are frequently developed and maintained within the context of dysfunctional family interactional processes (Oster & Caro, 1990; Sholevar, 1994; Stark, 1990). A recent proliferation of relevant research (for review, see N. J. Kaslow, Deering, & Ash, 1996; N. J. Kaslow, Deering, & Racusin, 1994; McCauley & Myers, 1992) includes theoretical writings advocating family therapy for depressives and reports describing positive outcomes. Few intervention models, however, focus specifically on family therapy with depressed children and adolescents. Development of clearly delineated, empirically grounded, theory-based treatment models for depressed youth will facilitate research and enhance clinical care.

Lack of attention to family interventions with depressed children is of concern to therapists given the literature indicating the family context and impact of childhood depression (N. J. Kaslow et al., 1994; McCauley & Myers, 1992), particularly genetic factors, family structure, and family interactional processes (Sholevar, 1994). To address this important problem, a model of Interpersonal Family Therapy (IFT) has been designed for depressed youth (N. J. Kaslow & Racusin, 1988, 1994; Racusin & N. J. Kaslow, 1991). This chapter details an expanded version of IFT. The model builds upon the research literature noted and draws on approaches advanced by other clinical researchers working with families of depressed adults. IFT is an integrative model, incorporating concepts and techniques from family systems theory, cognitive-behavioral psychology, object relations theory, and developmental psychopathology.

CHILDHOOD DEPRESSION

Despite historical controversy as to the existence of depression in young people, contemporary consensus holds that children and adolescents can experience depressive disorders, including adjustment disorder with depressed mood, dysthymic disorder, and major depressive disorder. *The Diagnostic and Statistical Manual* (4th ed.; *DSM–IV*; APA, 1994) posited that childhood and adult mood disorders are similar, albeit with some minor differences in symptom presentation and duration. Developmental psychopathologists argue, however, that children's levels of cognitive and emotional development influence the disorder's manifestations (Cicchetti & Schneider-Rosen, 1986). They further assert the influence of age and developmental level, biological endowment, and familial and sociocultural environment, and that depressed children and adolescents evidence impairments in cognitive, affective, interpersonal, biological, and adaptive behavior functioning (N. J. Kaslow & Racusin, 1990a).

In community youth samples, prevalence rates for depressive disorders range between 2% and 5% (Fleming & Offord, 1990), with higher rates reported in children of depressed parents, psychiatric populations, and children with peer problems, medical illnesses, and educational and learning problems (e.g., Kupersmidt & Patterson, 1991; Stark, 1990). Prevalence rates increase with age and appear equal in prepubertal males and females (Angold, 1988). By adolescence, however, significantly more females than males appear depressed (Petersen, Sarigiani, & Kennedy, 1991). Depressive disorders in youth persist and recur and are associated with increased risk for and co-occurrence with other psychiatric conditions in childhood, adolescence, and adulthood (Angold & Costello, 1992; Kovacs, 1989).

DEPRESSED CHILDREN AND THEIR FAMILIES

Rates of psychopathology are high among parents and extended family members of depressed children (Puig-Antich et al., 1989), and rates of affective disorders in the offspring of depressed adults are six times that reported in control families (Downey & Coyne, 1990). High-risk studies reveal that children of depressed parents exhibit similar or worse problems than children of parents with schizophrenic disorders, bipolar disorder, or serious medical illnesses (Downey & Coyne, 1990; Hammen, 1991). Specifically, children of depressed mothers are at risk for myriad emotional and behavioral disorders (e.g., mood disorders, disruptive behavior disorders, substance abuse) and deficits in interpersonal, adaptive, and cognitive functioning.

At particular risk are children of families characterized by divorce, single parenthood, and low socioeconomic status (e.g., Feldman, Rubenstein, & Rubin, 1988; Garrison, Schlucter, Schoenbach, & Kaplan, 1989; Warner, Weissman, Fendrich, Wickramaratne, & Moreau, 1992). These children's families display a disproportionately high number of negative life events, notably loss (e.g., parental death, divorce, or separation) and child maltreatment (e.g., physical or sexual abuse, neglect; Handford, Mattison, Humphrey, & McLaughlin, 1986; Hoyt, Cowen, Pedro-Carroll, & Alpert-Gillis, 1990; Kazdin, Moser, Colbus, & Bell, 1985; Koverola, Pound, Heger, & Lytle, 1993; Shapiro, Leifer, Martone, & Kassem, 1990; Warner et al., 1992).

Depressed children and adolescents manifest impairments in the relationships with their parents and siblings (Puig-Antich et al., 1985a, 1993). Compared to their nondepressed peers, they describe their families as less cohesive, supportive, and adaptable, more controlling and conflictual, and less able to communicate effectively (e.g., Barrera & Garrison-Jones, 1992; Burt, Cohen, & Bjorck, 1988; Feldman et al., 1988; Forehand et al., 1988; Puig-Antich et al., 1985a, 1985b), and they describe their families as less involved in social, recreational, and cultural activities (e.g., Stark, Humphrey, Crook, & Lewis, 1990). Depressed children and adolescents report less secure attachments to their parents than do nondepressed psychiatric patients and nonpsychiatric controls (e.g., Armsden, McCauley, Greenberg, Burke, & Mitchell, 1990; Cummings & Cicchetti, 1990). One contributing factor may be the tendency for depressed mothers' parenting behavior to interfere with development and maintenance of secure parent–child attachments (Radke-Yarrow, Cummings, Kuczynski, & Chapman, 1985).

In families in which the mother is depressed, parent-child interactions have been characterized by maternal hostility and irritability, dysfunctional problem-solving communication, limited positive affect, and difficulties expressing love and nurturance toward family members (e.g., for review, see Chiariello & Orvaschel, 1995; Hammen, 1991; N. J. Kaslow & Carter, 1991; Sholevar, 1994). This interactional style may impair the children's self-esteem and development of effective communication patterns, and increase the child's vulnerability to psychological difficulties (e.g., Chiariello & Orvaschel, 1995).

Accumulating data indicate that these dysfunctional family interactional patterns are bidirectional (Chiariello & Orvaschel, 1995), such that the child's maladjustment may be attributable to the mother's depressed and irritable mood, and the mother's symptoms may be a response to the child's temperamental predisposition (Sholevar, 1994), or the two may act in combination. For example, sons of depressed single mothers often become engaged in a coercive pattern of antisocial behavior mitigating mother's depression, which in turn reinforces the child's externalizing behavior (Patterson & Forgatch, 1990). The nondepressed parent's effecting coping skills in families with one depressed parent lessens the negative impact on the child of the compromised parenting displayed by the depressed parent (Sholevar, 1994).

TREATMENT OUTCOME RESEARCH

Since the literature on family therapy for depressed youth is limited, it is useful to draw on treatment outcome studies targeting related clinical problems. Thus, this section highlights key findings as to marital/family interventions for depression, preventive family interventions for high-risk youth, and psychosocial interventions for depressed children and adolescents that include family involvement.

Marital and Family Interventions for Adult Depression

Clinical researchers have generated marital and family therapy models targeting major depression in adults (e.g., Beach, Sandeen, & O'Leary, 1990; Clarkin et al., 1990; Coyne, 1988; Epstein, Keitner, Bishop, & Miller, 1988; Falloon, Hole, Mulroy, Norris, & Pembleton,

1988; Foley, Rounsaville, Weissman, Sholomskas, & Chevron, 1989; Gotlib & Colby, 1987; Holder & Anderson, 1990; Jacobson, Dobson, Fruzzetti, Schmaling, & Salusky, 1991; N. J. Kaslow & Carter, 1991; Klerman, Weissman, Rounsaville, & Chevron, 1984; Y. Teichman, 1986). Although such treatment approaches have their unique features, they share significant commonalities. First, these approaches are based on systemic models of depression (Coyne, 1976, 1984; Feldman, 1976), and thus focus on interactional patterns, rather than intrapsychic conflicts. According to Feldman (1976), for instance, the depressed couple's repetitive interaction patterns triggers self-deprecatory cognitive schemas perpetuating one partner's depression. Similarly, Coyne (1976; 1984) emphasized how the depressed persons' aversive behavior elicits support, yet covert hostility from the nondepressed partner, which is experienced as rejection by the depressed individuals, who in turn intensify their aversive behaviors and needs for support. The second commonality among approaches is that the therapist's active stance helps the couple/family identify and address interactional patterns maintaining the depressed behavior, leading to an amelioration of the depressive symptoms.

A limited number of well-controlled treatment outcome studies investigates effectiveness of marital therapy for depressed adults (e.g., Beach & O'Leary, 1992; Foley et al., 1989; Jacobson et al., 1991; Jacobson, Fruzzetti, Dobson, Whisman, & Hops, 1993; O'Leary & Beach, 1990; Waring, Chamberlaine, Carver, Stalker, & Schaeffer, 1995). Collective findings support the effectiveness of marital therapy for depression. However, marital therapy does not appear to be superior to pharmacotherapy, other psychosocial interventions, and multimodal treatments in ameliorating depressive symptoms. One unique contribution of marital therapy involves the reduction of relationship discord, which in turn may be associated with a better long-term prognosis. This finding is true for discordant-depressed couples as well (e.g., Beach & O'Leary, 1992; Foley et al., 1989; Jacobson et al., 1991). Thus, couples therapy targets marital adjustment and depression and its sequelae, whereas other interventions only focus on addressing individual factors associated with depressive disorders (Gollan, Gortner, & Jacobson, 1996).

Only a limited number of family therapy–oriented empirical studies addresses the treatment of depression (Prince & Jacobson, 1995). One published pilot study found that family therapy with pharmacotherapy was associated with improved family functioning and amelioration of depressive symptoms (Epstein et al., 1988). An additional study investigated a family psychoeducation approach to mood disorders among inpatients. This study found that inpatient family intervention was not associated with greater improvement at the time of discharge than was treatment as usual (Clarkin et al., 1990). There was some suggestion that those adults with major depressive disorder who received the family intervention performed more poorly at long-term follow-up than those individuals who did not receive the inpatient family intervention. The opposite pattern was found for individuals with bipolar disorder.

Prevention for High-Risk Youth

Beardslee and coworkers (Beardslee, 1990; Beardslee et al., 1992) have developed a psychoeducational preventive intervention for families with parental affective disorders. This cognitive psychoeducational approach includes assessment of all family members, education as to affective disorders, linking of educational content to family life experience, and enhancing the children's understanding of, and coping with, their parent's mood disorder. Families participating in this preventive intervention report treatment satisfaction and improvement (Beardslee et al., 1993). Furthermore, clinical improvement and treatment are more evident in families receiving a clinician-based version of the intervention as opposed to families receiving a lecture-based version (Beardslee et al., 1993).

Child and Adolescent Studies Involving a Family Component

Treatment outcome studies of depressed youth have only recently included family involvement (Lewinsohn, Clarke, Hops, & Andrews, 1990; Mufson, Moreau, Weissman, & Klerman, 1993; Stark, Rouse, & Livingston, 1991). Three studies are reviewed briefly. First, an investigation conducted by Lewinsohn and colleagues (1990) compared the relative efficacy of a cognitive-behavioral group intervention for adolescents versus this same intervention with an additional treatment module provided to the parents. Although a trend emerged favoring the concurrent adolescent and parent intervention, the between-group differences were not as great as expected. A second empirical investigation compared relative efficacy of self-control therapy versus traditional counseling for depressed elementary schoolchildren; monthly family sessions were held for the children in each condition (Stark et al., 1991). There are no data, however, as to the advantages of this family involvement. The third research program examined efficacy of interpersonal psychotherapy for depressed adolescents (IPT–A) (Mufson et al., 1993). This intervention approach, which focuses on grief, interpersonal deficits, role disputes, and role transitions, includes the depressed adolescent and, when indicated, the parents. Preliminary results from an open trial reveal that IPT–A is effective in ameliorating depressive symptoms in adolescents (e.g., Moreau, Mufson, Weissman, & Klerman, 1991; Mufson et al., 1993), but the nature and significance of parental involvement in this intervention approach is unclear.

Comments

Despite sparse and inconsistent empirical support for efficacy of marital and family therapy in alleviating depression in a family member, the need for effective family interventions remains. This assertion is based on evidence that maladaptive family patterns, particularly an unsupportive family environment, are associated with high relapse rates, depressive episodes of long duration, and an increased risk for suicidal behavior in depressed adults (Keitner & Miller, 1990). Additional support for this position comes from preliminary findings that treatments for depressed adolescents including parent involvement may be more effective than those approaches not incorporating work with parents (Lewinsohn et al., 1990).

INTERPERSONAL FAMILY THERAPY (IFT): OVERVIEW

Inclusion and Exclusion Criteria

IFT is a psychosocial model for clinical assessment and intervention with depressed elementary schoolchildren and their families. This intervention is appropriate for females and males, from age 6 to 12, who meet *DSM–IV* criteria for major depressive disorder, dysthymic disorder, adjustment disorder with depressed mood, or depressive disorder not otherwise specified. This intervention is not appropriate for youth meeting the following criteria: moderate, severe, or profound retardation; primary and active substance abuse/dependence disorders; pervasive developmental disorders or schizophrenia spectrum or other psychotic disorders; or imminently life-threatening medical conditions. Further, IFT should not be the primary intervention for youth residing in families with ongoing child maltreatment (physical or sexual abuse) or whose parents exhibit any of the following classes of disorders: delirium, dementia, and amnestic and other cognitive disorders; substance-related disorders not in remission; or schizophrenia or other psychotic disorders.

Theoretical Underpinnings

Consistent with the psychotherapy integration movement (Norcross & Goldfried, 1992), this treatment synthesizes theoretical constructs and intervention techniques from family systems theory, cognitive-behavioral psychology, object relations theory, developmental psychopathology, and Interpersonal Therapy (IPT) for depression (Klerman et al., 1984; Mufson et al., 1993). By focusing on those dysfunctional family interactional processes hypothesized to maintain the child's depressive symptoms, IFT aims to ameliorate psychological symptoms, foster more adaptive family interactional patterns, and improve family members' cognitive, affective, interpersonal, and adaptive behavior functioning. The following sections elaborate on the 16 sessions of this integrative model of brief family therapy.

SESSIONS 1 AND 2: JOINING AND ASSESSMENT

Rationale

The primary tasks of the first two sessions are to join with the family and to provide a comprehensive assessment of the family system. The joining process enables the therapist to gather the data necessary for formulating a family relational diagnosis (F. Kaslow, 1996). Joining is understood as related to enhancing the attachment process, which is particularly important in working with depressed families. Insecure attachments increase an individual's vulnerability to depression (Bowlby, 1981; Hammen, 1991), and depression may result in a reduced capacity to sustain secure and positive attachments.

Because assessment is integral to IFT, Sessions 1 and 2 entail a comprehensive assessment of the child's and family's current functioning across a broad range of domains. An assessment is also conducted in the final session of the intervention to ascertain the efficacy of the intervention. This postintervention evaluation is discussed later.

Goals

The goals of these sessions are to join with the family, and to provide a comprehensive assessment of the depressed child and their family.

Tasks

Join With the Family

In the family therapy field, *joining* refers to the process by which the therapist develops a working alliance with each family member. To permit subsequent assessment and therapeutic intervention, the therapist and family form a partnership that aims to "free the family symptom bearer of symptoms, reduce conflict and stress for the whole family, and learn new ways of coping" (Minuchin & Fishman, 1981, p. 29). Through the process of joining, therapists communicate to the family that they "understand[s] them and [are] working with and for them" (Minuchin & Fishman, 1981, pp. 31–32). Supportive and confrontative therapeutic techniques offer the family a sense of protection and hope, engendering a willingness to explore alternative interactional patterns and to change. For a more detailed discussion of joining techniques associated with various models of family therapy, see Minuchin and Fishman (1981).

When working with families with a depressed child, specific aspects of the joining process need to be underscored. The clinician must empathize with the vicissitudes of depression in the family and child, concurrently maintaining requisite clinical objectivity and communicating a sense of hope. The clinician acquires this therapeutic balance by regulating the pacing of the interview, as well as the voice quality and tone. Cognizant of depressed families' propensities to feel helpless, incompetent, self-blaming, and to fear negative evaluation, the therapist challenges generalizations of single negative acts into global definitions of individuals or families as failures. This approach communicates respect for the family's distress and belief in its potential to effect positive change via modification of distorted cognitions. Finally, joining sets the stage for repairing disrupted family attachments and developing more positive, secure, and developmentally appropriate relationships (Diamond & Siqueland, 1995). This work in turn helps reduce the current depression and family members' vulnerability to future depression, and improves interpersonal functioning within the family system.

Provide a Comprehensive Assessment of the Depressed Children and Their Family

The following guidelines frame assessments conducted from the perspective of IFT. These guidelines address session membership, constructs to be assessed, assessment procedures, disposition decisions, and feedback regarding the information gleaned from the evaluation.

Membership.   Optimally, assessment should include the index child, the parent(s) or principal caretakers, the depressed child's siblings, and other relevant family members (e.g., grandparents living in the home, stepparents, step or half siblings). This approach allows the clinician to glean information about each individual family member and their reciprocal interactions, particularly as they pertain to the onset and maintenance of depressive symptoms. Additionally, given high rates of parental psychopathology in families with depressed children, the parents' psychiatric status must be evaluated. Further, in families with a depressed parent, resources of the nondepressed parent need to be evaluated, as this information is crucial in informing the intervention process (Sholevar, 1994).

Decisions regarding membership of each assessment session depends on a number of variables, most notably the family constellation (e.g., nuclear, single parent, step family) involved in each case, the custody status of the identified patient child, the family living situation, and the age of the participants. For intact families, it is recommended that all family members residing in the home participate in the first evaluation session, although various subsystems may be asked to participate in subsequent evaluation sessions. For nonintact families, the family unit with whom the child principally resides should constitute the membership at the initial assessment session. However, whenever possible, subsequent assessment sessions should include all those family subsystems of which the child is a part. Based on the data gathered during the assessment phase, the clinician formulates a definition of the principal tasks of the intervention. This information, in turn, informs the clinician about the membership and pattern of attendance for the subsequent intervention sessions.

Constructs to Be Assessed.   Psychological symptoms; life events; and functioning across cognitive, affective, interpersonal, adaptive behavior, and biological and family domains should be assessed for each child, because these represent the key domains in which depressed children manifest impairments (Kaslow & Racusin, 1990a). In terms of psychological symptoms, it is necessary to obtain child, parent, teacher, and peer reports regarding the child's depressive symptoms, as substantial research indicates low concordance rates across informants regarding the presence and severity of a child's depressive symptoms (e.g., Achenbach, McConaughy, & Howell, 1987). Also, high rates of comorbid psychiatric conditions with child and adolescent depression (Angold & Costello, 1992) require a thorough evaluation of the full array of child emotional and behavioral problems and diagnoses. Life events must be assessed, as a growing body of research indicates an association between negative life events and the timing and course of depressive symptoms (Gotlib & Hammen, 1992). In particular, life events associated with loss (e.g., death, divorce) have been demonstrated to be strongly associated with emergence of depressive symptoms (Wallerstein & Corbin, 1991; R. Weller, E. Weller, Fristad, & Bowes, 1991).

In terms of affective functioning, the therapist assesses the child's predominant affects and capacity to experience, label, and regulate both negative and positive emotions. Key affects to be assessed include sadness, anger, guilt, shame, and the capacity for pleasure and happiness. Cognitive variables to assess include the child's view of self (self-esteem, perceived competence), information processing (self-schema, cognitive distortions), future perspective (hopelessness and hopefulness), learned helplessness (instrumental responding, locus of control, attributional style), and self-control (N. J. Kaslow, Brown, & Mee, 1994). In the domain of interpersonal behavior, it is important to examine problem-solving skills (Goodman, Gravitt, & Kaslow, 1995) and social skills with peers, siblings, parents, and teachers, given that depressed children manifest significant interpersonal deficits (e.g., Altmann & Gotlib, 1988) persisting even after the cessation of depressive symptoms (Puig-Antich et al., 1985b). Assessment of adaptive behavior functioning is required, as depressed children might evidence delays in acquisition of developmentally appropriate communication, socialization, or daily living skills. Although there are not well agreed on biological markers of child and adolescent depression, a thorough medical workup is needed to rule out physical problems of etiological significance for observed depressive symptoms (e.g., thyroid dysfunction; N. J. Kaslow, Croft, & Hatcher, in press).

Finally, since depressed youth reside in families characterized by myriad problematic interactional patterns (N. J. Kaslow et al., 1994) and to lay the groundwork for a family intervention, assessment of family structure, perception of family functioning, and observable family interactions must be conducted. Parallel constructs to those assessed in the identified patient should be examined in each family member. The modeling of depressive behaviors, influence of parental depression on parenting, and a depressive family style may reinforce and perpetuate the child's depression, providing the rationale for assessing parallel behaviors in all family members. A child's depression may be a marker for family dysfunction, so family interactional patterns should be assessed and, if deemed maladaptive, identified as a focus of treatment. These patterns need to be changed in order to ameliorate the child's current depressive symptoms to decrease the child's risk for recurrent depressive episodes.

Assessment Procedures. A multitrait, multimethod, multi-informant assessment approach enables the clinician to develop a thorough formulation of the child's depression and the social context within which it is embedded. Assessment data for psychological symptoms, functioning across domains, and interactional patterns can be collected through a clinical interview format and/or via semistructured clinical interviews, questionnaires, and observational interaction methods. Potential assessment devices are delineated in Table 5.1. Information should be gathered from a variety of informants, including the child, parents or primary caretakers, siblings, teachers, peers, and other involved health care and community service providers.

TABLE 5.1
Child, Parent, Teacher, and Family Assessment Batteries

Domain	Instrument	References
	Child Measures	
Symptomatology		
Depressive symptomatology	Children's Depression Inventory	Kovacs & Beck (1977)
Depressive symptomatology	Mood and Feelings Questionnaire	Angold, Costello, Pickles, & Winder (1987)
Depressive symptomatology	Children's Depression Scale (CDS)	Lang & Tisher (1978)
Anxiety symptomatology	Revised Children's Manifest Anxiety Scale (RCMAS)	Reynolds & Richman (1978)
Psychological symptomatology	Schedule for Affective Disorders and Schizophrenia (K–SADS)	Orvaschel & Puig-Antich (1987); Puig-Antich & Ryan (1986)
Psychological symptomatology	Personality Inventory for Children (PIC–1990 Edition)	Wirt, Lachar, Klinedinst, & Seat (1990)
Psychological symptomatology	Youth Self-Report (YSR)	Achenbach (1991c); Achenbach & Edelbrock (1987)
Psychological symptomatology	Child Assessment Schedule (CAS)	Hodges, McKnew, Cytryn, Stern, & Kline (1982)
Cognition		
Intellectual functioning	Wechsler Intelligence Scale for Children–III (WISC–III)	Wechsler (1991)
Intellectual functioning	Peabody Picture Vocabulary–Revised (PPVT–R)	Dunn & Dunn (1981)
Academic achievement	Woodcock-Johnson Tests of Achievement–Revised	Woodcock & Johnson (1989)
Self-concept	Piers–Harris Children's Self Concept Scale	Piers (1969, 1984)
Self-esteem/Perceived competence	Self-Perception Profile for Children	Harter (1985)
Social problem solving	Alternative Solutions Test (AST)	Caplan, Weissberg, Bersoff, Ezekowitz, & Wells (1986)

Domain	Instrument	References
	Child Measures	
Negative cognitive triad	Cognitive Triad Inventory for Children	Kaslow, Stark, Printz, Livingston, & Tasi (1992)
Negative cognitive processes	Automatic Thoughts Questionnaire (ATQ)	Hollon & Kendall (1980); Kazdin (1990)
Negative cognitive processes	Children's Negative Cognitive Error Questionnaire	Leitenberg, Yost, & Carroll-Wilson (1986)
Hopelessness	Hopelessness Scale for Children (HPLS)	Kazdin, Rodgers, & Colbus (1986)
Locus of control	Internal–External Locus of Control Scale (IE Scale)	Nowicki & Strickland (1973)
Perceived control	Multidimensional Measure of Children's Perceptions of Control	Connell (1985)
Attributional style	KASTAN–R Children's Attributional Style Questionnaire (KASTAN–CASQ)	Seligman, Peterson, Kaslow, Tanenbaum, Alloy, & Abramson (1984)
Interpersonal behavior		
Social adjustment	Social Adjustment Inventory for Children and Adolescents (SAICA)	John, Gammon, Prusoff, & Warner (1987)
Social skills	Matson Evaluation of Social Skills with Youngsters (MESSY)	Matson, Rotatori, & Helsel (1983)
Social anxiety	Social Anxiety Scale for Children (SASC)	LaGreca, Dandes, Wick, Shaw, & Stone (1988)
Loneliness	Loneliness Questionnaire	Asher & Wheeler (1985)
Adaptive behavior		
Adaptive behavior	Vineland Adaptive Behavior Scales	Sparrow, Balla, & Cicchetti (1984)
Affective functioning		
Emotional characteristics	Differential Emotion Scale IV (DES–IV)	Izard, Dougherty, Bloxom, & Kotsch (1974)
Emotional encoding and decoding	Diagnostic Analysis of Nonverbal Accuracy (DANVA)	Nowicki & Duke (1994)
Life events	Life Events Checklist (LEC)	Brand & Johnson (1982); Johnson & McCutcheon (1980)
	Parent Measures	
Symptomatology		
Self-report of depression	Beck Depression Inventory (BDI)	Beck, Ward, Mendelson, Mock, & Erbaugh (1961)
Anxious and depressive symptomatology	Cognition Checklist	Beck, Brown, Steer, Eidelson, & Riskind (1987)
Psychological and behavioral symptomatology	Child Behavior Checklist (CBCL; CBCL/4–18)	Achenbach (1991a); Achenbach & Edelbrock (1983)
Psychological and behavioral symptomatology	Conners' Rating Scales	Conners (1990)
Psychological and behavioral symptomatology	Revised Behavior Problem Checklist (RBPC)	Quay (1983); Quay & Peterson (1987)
Psychological symptomatology	Structured Clinical Interview for DSM–III–R	Spitzer, Williams, Gibbon, & First (1990)
Cognition		
Intellectual functioning	PPVT–R	Dunn & Dunn (1981)
Intellectual functioning	Wechsler Adult Intelligence Scale–Revised (WAIS–R)	Wechsler (1981)
Self-esteem	Tennessee Self-Concept Scale	Fitts & Roid (1988)
Hopelessness	Hopelessness Scale (HS)	Beck, Weissman, Lester, & Trexler (1974)
Attributional style	Attributional Style Questionnaire (ASQ)	Seligman, Abramson, Semmel, & von Baeyer (1979)
Self-control	Self–Control–Schedule–Self-Control Questionnaire (SCS–SCQ)	Rehm (1977)

Domain	Instrument	References
	Parent Measures (cont.)	
Interpersonal behavior		
Social adjustment	Social Adjustment Scale–Self-Report (SAS–SR)	Weissman & Bothwell (1976)
Affective expression		
Emotional characteristics	DES–IV	Izard, Dougherty, Bloxom, & Dotsch (1974)
Adaptive behavior		
Adaptive behavior	Vineland Adaptive Behavior Scales	Sparrow et al., (1984)
	Teacher Measures	
Symptomatology		
Depressive symptomatology	Teacher Rating Inventory of Depression (TRID; TRID–M)	Lefkowitz & Tesiny (1980); Bell-Dolan, Reaven, & Peterson (1993)
Psychological and behavioral symptomatology	Teacher's Report Form (TRF)	Achenbach (1991c); Achenbach & Edelbrock (1986)
Psychological and behavioral symptomatology	Conners' Rating Scales	Conners (1990)
Psychological and behavioral symptomatology	RBPC	Quay (1983); Quay & Peterson (1987)
Social behavior		
Social behavior	Taxonomy of Problematic Situations Questionnaire (TOPS)	Dodge, McClaskey, & Feldman (1985)
Adaptive behavior		
Adaptive behavior	Vineland Adaptive Behavior Scales (teacher version)	Sparrow et al. (1984)
	Peer Measures	
Symptomatology		
Depressive symptomatology	Peer Nomination Inventory for Depression (PNID)	Lefkowitz & Tesiny (1980)
Social adjustment		
Sociometric status	Positive and negative peer nominations	Coie, Dodge, & Coppotelli (1982)
Sociometric status	Peer ratings	Singleton & Asher (1977)
Social behavior	Revised Class Play	Masten, Morison, & Pellegrini (1985)
Social competence	Peer Nomination Inventory of Social Competence (PNISC)	Hopper & Kirschenbaum (1985)
	Family Measures	
Symptomatology		
Family functioning	Family Adaptability and Cohesion Evaluation Scales III (FACES-III)	Olson, Portner, & Lavee (1985)
Marital functioning	Dyadic Adjustment Scale-Locke-Wallace (DAS–LW)	Locke & Wallace (1959); Spanier (1976)
Family adjustment	Family Assessment Measure	Skinner, Steinhauer, & Santa-Barbara (1983)
Marital adjustment	Marital Adjustment Test	Locke & Wallace (1959)
Marital coping	Marital Coping Inventory (MCI)	Bowman (1990)
Family characteristics		
Family interaction	Living and Familial Environments Coding System (LIFE)	Arthur, Hops, & Biglan (1982)
Family characteristics	Family Environment Scale (FES)	R. H. Moos & B. S. Moos (1981)
Expressed emotion	Five Minute Speech Sample–Expressed Emotion (FMSS–EE)	Magana et al., (1986)
Family strengths	Family Strengths	Olson, Larsen, & McCubbin (1985)
Life events		
Life events	Family Inventory of Life Events and Changes (FILE)	McCubbin, Patterson, & Wilson (1985)

SESSION 3: FEEDBACK AND DISPOSITION

Rationale

The data collected during the first two sessions are used to guide the intervention. These data enable the clinician to tailor the intervention to the needs of each child and family treated. By sharing findings from the assessment with the family during the third session, the clinician endeavors to foster a collaborative therapeutic alliance with the family, which is both empowering and necessary for implementing the intervention. During the feedback session, the clinician reviews the assessment data and is prepared to discuss with the family the advantages and disadvantages of various treatment options using the guidelines for therapeutic modality choice presented here.

Goals

The goals of Session 3 are to ascertain the need for adjunctive treatment resources, to determine whether or not family treatment is the treatment of choice, to provide feedback from the assessment to the family and collaborate with them in devising a treatment plan, and to educate the family about depression.

Tasks

Ascertain the Need for Adjunctive Treatment Resources.   In planning interventions for the child's psychological symptoms associated with depression, it is important to evaluate the need for specialized procedures and reliance on other resources. For example, suicidal ideation may necessitate mobilization of additional community resources or hospitalization. Clearly, as soon as the need for hospitalization becomes evident in order to assure a child's safety, appropriate action should be taken immediately. Although some intervention programs for child and adolescent depression exclude suicidal youth (e.g., Lewinsohn et al., 1990; Mufson et al., 1993; Stark et al., 1991), this treatment model posits that IFT can be modified to be appropriate, either alone or in conjunction, for children across the depressive continuum. Similarly, the presence of significant neurovegetative symptoms may require evaluation by a child psychiatrist regarding possible adjunctive pharmacotherapy.

Certain comorbid conditions may also require adjunctive psychosocial or pharmacological interventions. For example, children warranting a diagnosis of attention deficit hyperactivity disorder may require parallel concurrent and/or sequential treatment that might include parent training, educational intervention and pharmacotherapy targeting ADHD symptoms on the one hand, and IFT focusing on depressive symptomatology on the other. Similar treatment plans designed to address two or more comorbid diagnoses would be indicated for depressed children with anxiety disorder, substance abuse, conduct disorder, and eating disorders.

Determine Whether or Not Family Treatment Is the Treatment of Choice.   Following completion of the assessment, the clinician provides the family with results and recommendations. If clinical intervention is indicated, several guidelines are useful for determining the treatment modality of choice based on the level of parental resources and the degree of the child's ego strength (N. J. Kaslow & Racusin, 1990b). Parents who love and care for their child, assume a developmental perspective, learn from experience, reflect on their child's thoughts and feelings, and exhibit frustration tolerance are considered to have adequate parental resources. Children who either possess or evidence potential to acquire age-appropriate adaptive behavior skills, and do not evidence serious behavioral and/or cognitive disorganization are viewed as having adequate ego strength. When there are adequate parental resources and child ego strength, family intervention is the treatment of choice. When this is the case, parents may be both partners in the treatment process and targets of intervention (Stark et al., 1991). When there are neither adequate parental resources nor reasonable ego strength in the child, individual therapy is the treatment of choice. When adequate parental resources are available or the child has a reasonable degree of ego strength, the clinician's own predilections may serve as the basis for modality choice. Consideration of several additional guidelines is required when deciding whether or not to implement individual and family therapies concurrently versus sequentially (see Racusin & N. J. Kaslow, 1994; N. J. Kaslow & Racusin, 1990b).

Provide Feedback From the Assessment to the Family and Collaborate With the Family in Devising a Treatment Plan. When family therapy is the treatment of choice, either alone or in combination with other interventions, feedback of assessment findings should be presented to all family members. Feedback underscores the conceptualization of the child's symptoms and functional difficulties as reflecting both the child's and the family's problematic negotiation of developmental tasks and maladaptive family transactional processes. In this way, the definition of the problem is expanded beyond that of the child's depression to encompass interactional patterns among all family members (Diamond & Siqueland, 1995). Thus, in providing feedback, the therapist reframes (i.e., redefines) the presenting problem in a manner that does not blame any individual family member for the child's depression.

Consistent with a systemic conceptualization of the child's depression, the therapist and family define the family's problems and treatment goals in behavioral and interpersonal terms, enabling the clinician and family to collaborate in constructing a treatment plan. Throughout treatment planning, the therapist emphasizes that change in each family member and the family unit as a whole may be required to ameliorate the child's depression (M. Shaffi & S. L. Shaffi, 1992). Collaboration during feedback and treatment planning phase fosters the joining process and empowers the family to assume greater control and hopefulness in alleviating family members' symptomatology and general family distress.

Educate the Family About Depression. In this session, the therapist begins to provide information to the family about a number of issues related to the child's depression and the treatment process. Rather than provide this information in an autocratic lecture format that may foster feelings of helplessness and incompetence, the therapist dialogues with the family in order to teach them about depressive processes and treatment interventions (Bedrosian, 1988). Thus, the clinician possesses a mental outline of information to impart to the family, and the information is communicated as the family raises questions or as issues naturally arise in the course of the conversation. This educational approach empowers families by reducing their bewilderment as to their child's difficulties and increasing their sense of hope for change (Holder & Anderson, 1990). This collaborative and respectful stance also sets the stage for future interventions aimed at facilitating changes in the child's and family's cognitive, affective, interpersonal, and adaptive functioning.

The IFT therapist educates the family about various aspects of depression and its treatment. Specific attention should be paid to discussing the psychological symptoms associated with depression, functional domains affected by depression, common precipitants of depression, and the IFT approach to treatment. When a positive family history for mood disorders suggests that the child's depression partially expresses an underlying biological vulnerability, the family also should be educated about the genetics and biological vulnerability of such disorders (Holder & Anderson, 1990; Mufson et al., 1993). Although this information may be sobering for the family, if provided empathically, it may reduce the extent to which the child is blamed and/or feels guilty for depressive symptoms.

Helping the family to develop an appreciation for the child's ongoing risk for depression can sensitize the family to the potential impact of life stressors on the family as a whole and the child in particular. Moreover, this information may alert the family to early warning signs of mood disorders in other family members. When the depressed child's parents experience significant affective disorders, Beardslee's (1990) preventive intervention strategies for such families may be instituted.

In addition to providing in-session education to the family regarding depression, additional resources may be helpful to the family. Specifically, self-help books, popular psychology references, and professional literature may be recommended. One resource that families have found to be particularly helpful is Seligman, Reivich, Jaycox, and Gillham (1995). Although not specific to childhood mood disorders, several additional reading and video materials that address issues central to work with many depressed children also can be helpful. These include, but are not limited to, the following: Goldstein and Solnit (1984), Krementz (1981), Lavoie (1990).

SESSION 4: PSYCHOLOGICAL SYMPTOMATOLOGY

Rationale

Depressed children typically present with the following psychological symptomatology: depressed or irritable mood, anhedonia, appetite and/or sleep disturbance, psychomotor retardation or agitation, fatigue, cognitive distortions (e.g., feelings of worthlessness, helplessness, and/or hopelessness; inappropriate guilt), concentration difficulties, and thoughts of death or suicide (APA, 1994). Because these depressive symptoms often impact negatively on the child's development and functioning, and because they tend to persist and recur, it is important to ameliorate the child's depression. Moreover, because depressive reactions often occur in response to major negative life events and/or to an accumulation of minor stresses (Compas, Grant, & Ey, 1994), precipitants of the child's depression need to be understood and addressed. Finally, manifestation of depressive symptoms in a child typically reflects some form of family dysfunction, so reframing of the child's depressive behavior in terms of family interaction patterns can be helpful in ameliorating and/or alleviating the child's depressive symptoms.

Goals

The goals of this session are to teach strategies to alleviate specific depressive symptoms, to identify precipitants of depressive reactions and teach the child and family more adaptive ways to cope with these stresses, and to reframe the child's psychological symptoms and decrease scapegoating of the depressed child.

Tasks

Teach Strategies to Alleviate Specific Depressive Symptoms.   Because strategies addressing the affective and cognitive symptoms of depression are elucidated in detail in later sessions,
in this session the therapist offers psychological strategies for targeting the behavioral and
vegetative symptoms of depression. For example, for those youth with insomnia, relaxation
training can be used to facilitate sleep, and the therapist should teach the child and other family
members standard progressive muscle relaxation skills. In addition, caretakers and older siblings
can be taught to serve as coaches to assist the child's use of these strategies. When behavioral
techniques fail to provide symptomatic relief, referral for medications may be appropriate.
However, given the dearth of empirical data supporting the efficacy of antidepressants in the
treatment of childhood depression, medication management should be considered after exhausting other interventions.

Another common symptom associated with depression in youth is suicidality. Although
severely suicidal youth may require hospitalization, many can benefit from implementation of a
suicide contract combined with use of cognitive and problem-solving techniques designed for
the treatment of suicidal behaviors (e.g., Berman & Jobes, 1991). More specifically, the therapist
may incorporate techniques from the Successful Negotiation Acting Positively (SNAP) brief
cognitive-behavioral treatment for adolescent suicide attempters and their families (Rotheram-
Borus, Piacentini, Miller, Graae, & Castro-Blanco, 1994). For example, behavioral contracting,
cognitive restructuring, therapist modeling, structured role playing and/or reframing may be used
to direct the family's attention onto problematic situations rather than the behavior of the
depressed and suicidal youth. This process fosters the family's learning of effective problem
solving within a positive family atmosphere.

*Identify Precipitants of Depressive Reactions and Teach the Child and Family More Adaptive
Ways to Cope With These Stresses.*   Given the significant association between stressful major and minor life events and depressive symptoms in youth, the therapist inquires about family
events that may have precipitated the child's depression (e.g., divorce, death, discord). The
therapist focuses not only on the content of the stressful event, but also the ways in which the
child may have interpreted the event. Such focus on interpretation is crucial, given data
indicating that individuals with negative schemas about the self, world, and future tend to
negatively distort their perceptions of life events, in turn rendering them vulnerable to depressive experiences (Gotlib & Hammen, 1992). Accordingly, the first step in this process is to ask
each family member to identify all possible events, changes, and/or accumulation of minor
stressors and daily hassles that occurred prior to the onset of the child's depression. Once
identified, the depressed child's and the family's interpretation of these stresses should be
queried. For those stresses and/or interpretation of stressors appearing pertinent to the onset of
the child's depression, the therapist should help the child and family see the connection between
stress and depression, and elucidate any family interactional sequences appearing to cause or
maintain stress for the depressed child. The therapist also should challenge those distorted
interpretations that may lead to self-blame or feelings of helplessness and hopelessness. And,
with the help of the therapist, the child and family should devise more effective strategies for
alleviating and/or managing these stresses. Much of this work involving distorted cognitive
styles is addressed in Sessions 5 and 6 such that the work in this session lays the groundwork

for the subsequent sessions. Finally, the therapist and family should ascertain potential future stressors both within and outside the family, and plan strategies to cope with future stresses and their impact (Clarkin, Haas, & Glick, 1988; Holder & Anderson, 1990).

Another strategy for addressing the role of precipitants involves inquiring about stressful events impacting one or both of the parents, both currently and historically. In examining these stressful situations and parents' interpretations and reactions to these stressors, a pattern of vulnerability within the family to particular kinds of stress (e.g., loss, conflict) may be manifested. In a related vein this inquiry can examine parents' experiences in their families of origin that may have rendered them vulnerable to depressive experiences. Such exploration can help all family members become more cognizant of the stress–depression link, in turn enabling them to be both more empathic about the child's depression and more able to help the depressed child cope effectively with stress. In certain instances, exploring other family members' reactions to stress may reveal that the child's depressive reaction reflects a parent's or sibling's depressed feelings that the other family member had difficulty tolerating. If this is so, the intervention needs to focus on helping family members acknowledge, modulate, and express their distressing affects.

Reframe the Child's Psychological Symptoms and Decrease Scapegoating of the Depressed Child. One underlying assumption of IFT is that psychological symptoms and deficits reflect systemic dysfunction, with priority placed on family systems dysfunction. To highlight this assumption, during this session the therapist should help the family begin to acknowledge the possibility of a correlation between the child's depressive symptoms and family dysfunction. Also, during this process, the therapist attempts to assist family members to observe that the nature of their responses to their depressed child may either mitigate or exacerbate the child's depressive symptoms and the course of the disorder (Holder & Anderson, 1990). If the family is able to begin to ascertain such relations, the therapist should assist family members in articulating and addressing their feelings associated with systemic dysfunction and family patterns that may exacerbate or maintain the child's depression. This, in turn, will set the stage for helping the family learn more adaptive ways of expressing feelings about family problems.

From a family perspective, the therapist also works to block scapegoating or blaming of the depressed child or other family members (e.g., parents, siblings) for the child's difficulties. Scapegoating may reflect parents' or siblings' frustration that their efforts to reassure the child have not resulted in rapid amelioration of depressive symptoms and that the child cannot volitionally bring about the disappearance of these symptoms (Bedrosian, 1988). Rather than blaming the child for personal or family problems, the child's depression should be framed by the therapist as emblematic of multiple determinants—including family interactional processes, individual child factors (e.g., temperament), and genetic or biological predisposition. This process of reframing serves to alleviate the child's self-blame and guilt, and as a result may enhance the child's self-esteem.

SESSIONS 5 AND 6: COGNITIVE FUNCTIONING

Rationale

Depressed children feel negatively about themselves, the world, and the future (negative cognitive triad); make maladaptive attributions for explaining events (depressogenic attributional style); and cognitively distort information (faulty information processing) as a result of dysfunctional schemata (for review, see N. J. Kaslow et al., 1994). These maladaptive thought patterns emerge from intra- and extrafamilial interpersonal contexts over the course of the individual's development (Seligman et al., 1984; Stark, 1990; Teichman, 1986). Depressed youth may have received repeated verbal or nonverbal critical, rejecting messages from family members contributing to and maintaining their negative self-schema and depressogenic thinking (Stark, 1990). Further, parents may communicate their perceptions of the social environment as critical, overcontrolling, and unlikely to improve—perceptions that when assimilated by the child contribute to negative schema about the world and the future (Stark, 1990). Because parental responses powerfully affect the way children think, it is important to enlist parents during the cognitive therapy component of the work (DiGiueseppe, 1986). Cognitive-behavioral techniques can be integrated with family therapy interventions (Schrodt, 1992), including IFT. Interventions in the cognitive domain therefore proceed from developmentally informed family systems and cognitive-behavioral perspectives.

Goals

The goals of this session are to provide education about the negative cognitive triad, depressogenic attributional patterns, and faulty information processing; to teach ways to identify depressive cognitive patterns; and to challenge and change the depressive cognitive patterns within the family system that maintain or exacerbate the child's depression.

Tasks

Provide Education About the Negative Cognitive Triad, Depressogenic Attributional Patterns, and Faulty Information Processing

Educating all family members about the cognitive patterns associated with the child's depressive feelings and behaviors prepares the child and family for developing the skills needed to alter maladaptive cognitions (Stark, 1990). To explain the negative cognitive triad, the therapist helps the family understand that depression is associated with a pervasive negative view, such that the depressed children feel badly about themselves (low self-esteem), feel the world is a negative place, and feel hopeless about the future. Maladaptive causal attributional patterns can be explained to the family as follows: Individuals who tend to blame themselves for negative events (internal) view the causes of these events as consistent over time (stable) and generalizable across situations (global), and make external, unstable, and specific attributions for positive events are more likely to be depressed than are those individuals with the opposite style. When explaining faulty information processing to the family, the therapist should inform members that depressed youth tend to make systematic errors in thinking that reinforce negative beliefs regardless of evidence to the contrary. The therapist may provide examples of commonly made systematic errors, such as arbitrary inference, selective abstraction, overgeneralization, magnification and minimization, personalization, and absolutistic and dichotomous thinking (Beck, Rush, Shaw, & Emery, 1979).

Teach Ways to Identify Depressive Cognitions

As family members begin to comprehend the cognitive theory of depression, the therapist underscores that depressive cognitive processes often occur automatically. Thus, the next step of the cognitive component of IFT is to enable family members to identify the presence of

automatic thoughts in their everyday lives. This can be accomplished by utilizing strategies enumerated by Stark, Rouse, and Kurowski (1994a); Stark, Raffaelle, and Reysa (1994b); Lewinsohn and
coworkers (1990); and Wilkes, Belsher, Rush, and Frank (1994). Specifically, the therapist attends
to each family member's descriptions and perceptions of life events and encourages each member to
be cognizant of those thought patterns associated with dysphoric affects, particularly when a
noticeable change in mood occurs. Family members are asked to keep a thought chart as to situations,
feelings, and thoughts, and parents are asked to help their children accomplish this task. Therapeutic
strategies that assist in the detection of automatic thoughts include cognitive replay (a discussion
during the therapy session designed to obtain sufficient information about a given event so as to
identify the associated automatic thoughts), cognitive forecasting (predicting thoughts and feelings
about hypothetical events in the future), and the third-person perspective (when family members are
asked to consider the thoughts and feelings of a hypothetical individual in response to a negative
event in an effort to enable them to gain perspective; Wilkes et al., 1994). In addition, tips can be
taught to facilitate the process of "catching" one's own thoughts, particularly those likely to be untrue,
such as the use of extreme words (*always* or *never*, *everyone* or *no one*; Stark et al., 1994a, 1994b).
Further, visual aids (e.g., cartoon characters) and tasks (e.g., puzzles) can be incorporated to teach
the concept of automatic thoughts and to illustrate the association between maladaptive cognitions
and depression.

Challenge and Change the Depressive Cognitive Patterns Within the Family System That Maintain or Exacerbate the Child's Depression

One of the central tasks of Sessions 5 and 6, as well as of the overall IFT program, is to challenge
and change those maladaptive cognitive processes that maintain or exacerbate the child's depression. Particular attention should be paid to modifying depressive cognitions evidenced in dysfunctional parent–child interactions, including verbal and nonverbal communications, and covert or
overt rules (Stark, 1990). Depressive cognitive processes must be addressed whenever they occur
in the family, so as to ameliorate individual depressive experiences and to alter the parents'
childrearing practices that may be reinforcing and maintaining the child's depression (DiGiuseppe,
1986). Cognitive restructuring techniques that provide genuine, realistic, and developmentally
appropriate interpretations are useful in modifying these maladaptive family beliefs and rules
(Stark, 1990). In initiating the cognitive restructuring process, it should be underscored to all family
members that changing one's thoughts to be more adaptive is equivalent to improving one's mood.
Once this relation is understood, participants in the IFT can be helped to enhance their self-evaluations and develop a more positive perspective regarding the world and the future; taught to utilize
adaptive causal attributions; and, assisted in altering faulty information processing and underlying
dysfunctional schemata. Because cognitive restructuring techniques have received considerable
attention by other authors and have been delineated in detail by Stark and colleagues (1994a,
1994b) and Wilkes and coworkers (1994), space permits only brief discussion of these strategies.

Negative Cognitive Triad.   To enhance self-esteem, cognitive restructuring techniques can
help family members make more positive self-statements and be more tolerant of their own and
other family members' behavior. To increase frequency of positive self-statements, family
members should be instructed to provide reciprocal positive feedback, and each individual
should be encouraged to rehearse these positive messages in addition to generating positive
self-statements. The therapist should encourage family members to utilize these positive

self-statements in stress-inducing contexts and to make an effort to provide one another with positive feedback in such situations. Self-perception often depends on an individual's assessment of whether personal or family standards have been obtained, so the therapy also must address family members' performance standards, which often are overly stringent and unrealistic in depressed families and strongly influence one's self-perception. When standards appear unattainable, family members are supported in developing more realistic ones, and providing positive feedback to one another for meeting these more reasonable expectations. If standards within the family system appear to be realistic, but self-evaluation remains overly stringent, participants are challenged to find the evidence to support their self-evaluations and are encouraged to self-monitor for evidence supporting a more lenient self-evaluative view.

A variety of problem-solving strategies and cognitive restructuring techniques may be taught to family members in an effort to address their negative views of the world and the future. For example, if it appears that the child and/or family are viewing the world and/or the future in an overly negative fashion, Stark's (1990) "What if" technique may be introduced. Use of this technique includes educating the family about the association between negative expectations about the world and/or future and distressing affects, as well as the potentially self-fulfilling nature of these predictions. Moreover, the therapist should underscore that sad people tend to exaggerate the potential negative consequences of a negative event. Then, the therapist encourages the child and family members to ask "what if" questions to ascertain the validity of their concerns. Specifically, they should ask themselves questions such as the following: "*What* really will happen to me *if* this negative event does occur (i.e., will it really be as bad as I had anticipated)?" This process helps the child and family decatastrophize the future. Throughout this work, the therapist must find a balance between empathizing with the child and the family's concerns while simultaneously challenging the distorted thought processes.

Attribution Retraining.   One of the most pragmatic discussions of attribution retraining for depressed youth has been presented by Seligman and coworkers (1995). For purposes of family intervention, the techniques articulated by Seligman and colleagues (1995) should be expanded to incorporate all family members. The overarching goal of attribution retraining is to help family members develop adaptive ways of explaining the causes of both good and bad events in the child's life and in the family. Visual aids, such as cartoon characters and comic books, as well as worksheets, can be useful in the attribution retraining process.

The first step of attribution retraining is to teach the child and family concepts of optimism and pessimism and to help them understand that optimistic thinkers feel good, whereas pessimistic thinkers tend to feel bad. The second step entails helping family members to think accurately about real problems. This involves supporting "nonnegative" and realistic thinking (learned optimism) as opposed to an excessively positive and unrealistic world view in which responsibility is shirked; and to encourage all family members to consider the myriad variables that may cause a negative event and then to focus their attentions on addressing only those factors subject to control. The third step is to remind the family of the three key attributional dimensions: internality (personal vs. impersonal), stability (permanent vs. temporary), and globality (pervasive vs. specific). Hypothetical and then real examples from the child and family's life should be discussed to illustrate maladaptive and adaptive causal attributions for negative and positive events on these dimensions.

Altering Cognitive Distortions.   In altering automatic thoughts, family members use their daily records of automatic negative thoughts. First, they are taught the major kinds of cognitive distortions associated with depressive thinking (e.g., overgeneralization, selective abstraction, excessive responsibility, assuming temporal causality, self-references, catastrophizing, dichotomous thinking). Second, the triple-column technique (Wilkes et al., 1994) is employed in dialogue with family members. This strategy includes listing automatic thoughts, noting the underlying cognitive distortions, and delineating more adaptive or rational responses. Third, the construction of a genogram focusing on multigenerational cognitive patterns (Wilkes et al., 1994) is a useful family therapy intervention that facilitates cognitive restructuring. This particular genogram technique involves inquiring about the perceptions of the index child's family of origin. When this genogram probe reveals that family members' beliefs may be reinforcing the depressed child's maladaptive cognitions, the therapist must use the sessions to alter both the child's and the family's belief systems. When data gleaned from the genogram probe indicate that family members already employ adaptive cognitive styles, family members may be used as "co-therapists" during the cognitive restructuring phases of the IFT intervention.

To help change cognitive patterns in families in which more than one member demonstrates depressive thinking, the therapist should model replacing negative thoughts with more positive and adaptive cognitions and encourage rehearsal of this strategy within and outside of sessions. This work can be facilitated by role plays; games involving multiple possible moves (e.g., checkers, Othello) to help people brainstorm all possibilities and consider outcomes; discussions in which participants examine evidence for negative beliefs, generate alternative and more adaptive interpretations, and institute behavioral experiments designed to provide evidence for new and more adaptive cognitive patterns; and tasks in which family members monitor cognitions associated with involvement in a pleasant activity and increase their involvement in such activities.

In those families in which cognitive distortions reside principally within the child, the therapist may teach parents to assist their child in identifying and modifying faulty cognitions (DiGiuseppe, 1986). Because parents and siblings spend more time with the child when acutely depressed than does the therapist, they can better challenge the child's depressive cognitions. This process enlists parental and sibling support in addressing the child's distorted cognitions, and educates parents and siblings about cognitive strategies for helping the depressed child cope with affectively distressing situations (DiGiuseppe, 1986).

SESSIONS 7 AND 8: AFFECTIVE FUNCTIONING

Rationale

Sad, or dysphoric, affect, the sine qua non of childhood depression (Poznanski, 1982), may be elicited by interpersonal losses, material deprivation, victimization, achievement/competence concerns, and physical illness or injury (Garber & Kashani, 1991). Because such stressors are either directly or indirectly associated with the family environment, they deserve specific attention in family therapy interventions. In addition to negative affects, depressed children display difficulties with adaptive affect regulation (Cole & N. J. Kaslow, 1988). Further, whether the family system is overly enmeshed or disengaged, depressed children's families have difficulties expressing and modulating emotions and resolving conflict (Coyne, Schwoeri, & Sholevar, 1994; Oster & Caro, 1990), and thus are characterized by emotional dysregulation (Coyne, Downey, & Boergers, 1992). These families are unable to resolve conflicts or "resist the contagiousness of each others' negative affect" (Coyne et al., 1994, p. 194). Such dysfunctional family processes contribute to dysphoric affect, anhedonia, and affect regulation difficulties in depressed youth.

Goals

The goals of these sessions are to teach family members to label and verbalize both negative and positive affects, and to educate the family regarding adaptive strategies for affect regulation.

Tasks

Teach Family Members to Label and Verbalize Both Negative and Positive Affects.   C h i l d r e n and their families first need to be instructed in basic labels for different emotions (e.g., anger, sadness, fear, happiness) and how to differentiate among various feelings. Initially, instruction should be carried out in a relatively neutral context. For example, teaching can be facilitated through the use of such board games as the "Thinking, feeling, and doing game," or Feeling Posters that depict and label a broad array of facial expressions appropriately labeled. An additional task is the use of the game "Pass the mask," in which one family member makes a face depicting an emotional state and the family member to their right mimics the face. Family members continue to mimic the face until all participants have communicated this facial and emotional expression. At the end of the process, those family members who did not initiate the face are asked to articulate their understanding of the emotion being expressed and the initiator then validates their perception.

Once all family members appear to have acquired an agreed on understanding of a range of positive and negative emotions, the family is asked to use these labels in discussing or sharing their own emotional status with one another. Family members are encouraged to utilize acquired communication skills to discuss times in their family when they have experienced various negative and positive emotions. Finally, they are supported in labeling their own emotional experiences and in expressing these feelings toward one another as they arise.

The final step in teaching family members to label and verbalize their feelings is to help them identify the links between events, thoughts, and emotions, for both positive and negative affective states. In doing so, the family therapist may incorporate strategies recommended by Stark and colleagues (1994b), including homework assignments in which situations and thoughts associated with strong positive or negative feelings are recorded.

Educate the Family About Adaptive Strategies for Affect Rregulation.   Family interventions regarding adaptive strategies for affect regulation are framed according to the assessment of the developmental capacities of the child and family members (Cicchetti & Schneider-Rosen, 1984, 1986; Cole & N. J. Kaslow, 1988), the nature of the event, and the degree of associated affective intensity. Parents are assisted in helping the child ascertain circumstances under which feelings may be expressed appropriately, toward whom, and in what way. For example, depressed children sometimes express distress in the classroom or with peers, creating social problems that only serve to perpetuate their depression. Parents can help these children identify supportive adults in the school system with whom they can meet privately, and problem solve regarding how and with whom they can share problems among peers in ways that do not overwhelm their friendships.

Therapeutic interventions should help the child acquire developmentally appropriate capacities for affect regulation. Not only should family members and other support systems be encouraged to appreciate the emotional impact on the child of life events, but they should assist the child in comprehending and coping with these events by aiding in the acquisition of cognitive, behavioral, and interpersonal strategies for affect regulation (Garber & Kashani, 1991).

Second, several approaches may be taken either simultaneously or in sequence to help children acquire regulatory skills. For instance, children learn about emotions within the context of interpersonal interactions, through observation and by direct instruction from their parents. These processes continue over the course of development. Accordingly, if children exhibit deficits in affective regulatory capacities through underexpression of feelings (e.g., anhedonia) or unmodulated expression of sadness (e.g., frequent crying spells), change must be affected in parent–child interactions. Specifically, parents must provide their children with response-contingent positive reinforcement, offer a realistic understanding of those events which the child may control, and ensure the child assumes control where appropriate. In Sessions 7 and 8, emphasis is placed on helping parents provide direct instruction with developmentally appropriate rules for affective expression and affect regulation. For instance, they may encourage their child to discuss feelings when upset, rather than act-out in behaviorally maladaptive ways or withdraw and emotionally "shut down."

In addition, because children are socialized in affect expression by observing others, parents may need to demonstrate by their own behavior appropriate conditions under which to express particular emotions, methods for expressing and regulating these emotions, and consequences accruing to such emotional expression (Garber & Kashani, 1991). For example, depressed mothers may be encouraged to tell their children when they are feeling tired or sad and to take a short rest, instead of inexplicably withdrawing or becoming critical and irritable while trying to press onward in activities with the children.

The therapist must attend to presence of parental depression and its effects on the child. In some cases, children of depressed parents imitate their parents' depressed mood state and exhibit sadness themselves. In other instances, these children may be reluctant to express distressing affects in an effort to protect their depressed parent. In either case, family intervention entails helping the depressed parent modulate affective distress more adaptively in order to provide a context supporting healthy emotional development in the child. For families with a depressed parent, IFT strategies may be indicated in conjunction with Beardslee and colleagues' (1992, 1993) psychoeducational family preventive intervention geared toward families with a depressed parent.

Concurrent with the aforementioned efforts with parents and the family unit, the child is worked with directly to develop self-regulating cognitive and personal strategies for coping with emotions and for developmentally appropriate acceptance of nurturant caretaking. This work entails encouraging children to talk about their affective states, so as to enlist significant people in their social environment to provide support and comfort, which in turn helps them to regulate their affect (Dunn & Brown, 1991). Children also can be taught to use problem-solving strategies that interrupt maladaptive expressions of behavior reflecting distressing affects, and using such skills to express feelings in a more direct and appropriate fashion. Other cognitive strategies for affect regulation include thinking positive thoughts, engaging in selective distraction when distressed, or reality testing about the validity of one's negative emotional reactions. Finally, for those youth who constrict their affective expression, permission and encouragement to verbalize feelings, both positive and negative, needs to be given. For further discussion, see Garber and Dodge's (1991) examination of the development of emotion regulation and dysregulation.

SESSIONS 9 AND 10: INTERPERSONAL FUNCTIONING

Rationale

Depressed children often exhibit deficits in pleasurable interpersonal functioning with siblings and peers, and the families of depressed children frequently have difficulties with interpersonal problem solving and communication. Thus, IFT addresses these interpersonal aspects of functioning. Social skills training within a family context can enhance a child's sense of control, leading to increased self-esteem and peer status and decreased feelings of depression (LeCroy, 1994a; Strauss, Lahey, Frick, Frame, & Hynd, 1988). Furthermore, parents and children who learn to solve problems effectively and to engage in positive communication likely will have fewer conflicts (Robin, Bedway, & Gilroy, 1994) and may be at less risk for future episodes of depression than those who do not learn such skills.

Goals

The goals of these sessions are to improve interpersonal problem-solving skills and increase positive communication within the family, to assist the child in the development of social and relationship skills in order to improve their interpersonal functioning with peers, and to increase involvement in pleasurable activities with peers.

Tasks

Improve Interpersonal Problem-Solving Skills and Increase Positive Communication Within the Family. It is important to identify specific communication skill strengths and deficits within the family by attending to the ways in which family members approach one another and communicate about difficult problems. These data then can be used by the therapist to reframe family problems in interactional terms, identifying the sequences of behaviors and miscommunications. The therapist helps the family by correcting negative communication patterns consistently, while being careful not to focus on one member disproportionately. The therapist teaches problem-solving skills through instruction, modeling, behavioral rehearsal, and feedback (Robin et al., 1994). In addition, the therapist emphasizes to the child's parents the importance of providing appropriate reinforcement for their child's accomplishments in the interpersonal domain (Kendall, Kortlander, Chansky, & Brady, 1992). Family members may role play different interpersonal scenarios while the therapist shapes appropriate communications through successive approximations. Because the nature of peer relationships and difficulties varies according to the developmental stage of the child, these role plays focus on more structured interpersonal situations for younger children and more socially ambiguous scenarios for older youth (Kendall et al., 1992).

Rather than teaching specific thoughts or behaviors, it is important to instruct families about the thinking process during interpersonal problem solving. Family members then can utilize this interpersonal problem-solving process to resolve difficulties within the family in addition to social or peer relationship problems. It is essential that the therapist provide feedback, as well as encouragement, about practicing positive communication skills outside of the sessions.

Assist the Child in the Development of Social and Relationship Skills in Order to Improve Their Interpersonal Functioning With Peers.   Once the family displays more effective problem-solving communication, parents can serve to facilitate better interpersonal functioning in their children by teaching them strategies for responding to difficult social situations, encouraging active rather than passive approaches to increasing their social networks, and challenging negative cognitions children may have about how peers view them. During this stage of therapy, the therapist and parents can work together to improve the depressed child's social skills. The nature of this work will depend on the basis of the child's social skills problems. For example, whereas anxiously depressed youth may be likely to avoid social situations secondary to anxiety, other depressed youth may have actual skill deficits or lack the motivation to engage in peer interactions (Stark et al., 1991).

Most programs designed to teach social problem solving include the following six steps: identifying the problem, determining goals, generating alternative solutions, examining consequences, choosing the solution, and evaluating the outcome (Forman, 1993). Parents are encouraged to help their children solve interpersonal problems by teaching them to apply these steps in a variety of social situations. Often, this entails using role plays. In addition, it may be important to help the child learn to read accurately the facial expressions, postures, gestures, and tones of voice of others, as nonverbal communication skills have been found to be related to positive peer relationships (Nowicki & Duke, 1994). Breaking down the different phases of a social situation to identify where the child may be having difficulty (e.g., interpreting others' intentions, generating alternative responses, evaluating the effectiveness of their responses) may also prove useful. When parents are unable to facilitate improved social functioning in their child, or when children exhibit more profound peer relationship deficits, referral for child group therapy should be considered (e.g., Siepker & Kandaras, 1985).

Increase Involvement in Pleasurable Activities With Peers.   IFT emphasizes the importance of parents providing the child opportunities to engage in age-appropriate peer activities and practice peer relationship skills. Engaging in pleasurable family activities, some involving all family members and others only the sibship, also is stressed. Activity scheduling can be used to increase the activity level of the family in which depression prevails (Stark, 1990). This strategy must incorporate input from all family members and work within the family's financial resources and practical work and school constraints (Stark, 1990). As models for peer interaction skills, the importance of parents participating in adult activities as a couple and with peers is underlined (e.g., Diamond & Siqueland, 1995; N. J. Kaslow & Racusin, 1994). If parents manifest marital or individual deficits impeding their capacity to undertake these behaviors, then it may be necessary to address these deficits prior to focusing on enhancing parenting skills.

SESSION 11: ADAPTIVE BEHAVIOR

Rationale

Depressed children often demonstrate delayed acquisition of age-appropriate adaptive behavior skills. Adaptive behavior, defined as the individual's personal and social self-sufficiency, includes skills in three areas: communication, daily living, and socialization (Sparrow, Balla, & Cicchetti, 1984). In the area of communication, depressed children typically communicate less within the family and with their peers than do nondepressed youth. In terms of daily living skills, depressed children often evidence insufficient personal hygiene. Finally, depressed youth evidence deficits in socialization. Because these latter problems are addressed in the interpersonal component of the IFT intervention, the session on adaptive behavior functioning focuses primarily on communication and daily living skills.

Goals

The goals of this session are to educate families about age-appropriate adaptive behaviors, and to facilitate acquisition and utilization of age-appropriate adaptive behaviors.

Tasks

Educate Families About Age-Appropriate Adaptive Behaviors. IFT educates parents and children about age-appropriate adaptive behaviors and how their acquisition has been compromised secondary to the child's depression and the depressive process of the family as a whole. Specifically, the child's deficits in communication skills are addressed by pointing out ways family members speak for the depressed child, ignore the child's efforts to communicate, or refute or devalue the child's assertions. The importance of all family members communicating in a clear and direct fashion, listening empathically to one another, and responding in a supportive and nurturing fashion is highlighted. In terms of daily living skills, the family is educated as to age-appropriate behaviors in this domain, so that expectations for the child's performance are neither too high nor too low.

Facilitate Acquisition and Utilization of Age-Appropriate Adaptive Behaviors. In order to address deficits in communication, this session focuses on the provision of communication training. Many of the skills and strategies taught are enumerated by Stark and colleagues (1994b). Specifically, family members are taught to state their needs succinctly, use "I" statements rather than "you" statements, communicate directly, express needs and wishes in concrete and clearly defined terms, use active and empathic listening, state clearly the impact of other members' behaviors, present options when negotiating differences rather than make demands, ask for clarification and feedback to ascertain whether or not communications have been understood, communicate in congruent verbal and nonverbal messages, and decrease critical tone and rejecting comments and increase positive and supportive statements.

Teaching the aforementioned communication skills entails a number of steps. First, didactic information regarding effective communication strategies is offered. Second, the family discusses a relatively neutral topic and applies these skills in this discussion. Whenever the therapist notes maladaptive communication patterns, these are pointed out to the family, and more adaptive modes of communicating are coached. Additionally, when family members communicate effectively, the therapist provides them with positive reinforcement. Third, once the family has gained some measure of success in using good communication skills, they are encouraged to discuss affectively laden topics with one another, including issues that appear associated with the maintenance of the child's depression. Finally, the family practices these communication strategies on a daily basis outside of the session. Given the need for ongoing practice of these skills, effective family communication continues to be a primary focus of the remaining sessions, particularly those designed to address family functioning.

The child's impaired utilization of age-appropriate daily living skills is also addressed. First, for those children who have not acquired these skills because of inadequate parenting, the parents are helped to teach their child these skills systematically. The parenting deficit associated with the depressed child's lack of appropriate daily living skills is understood to reflect the parents' own depression (e.g., lack of available energy) or a dysfunctional family system (e.g., the parents' need to sustain the child's dependence). Second, for those children who fail to utilize acquired age-appropriate daily living skills, parents are supported in developing creative strategies for encouraging and reinforcing their child's use of these skills and their increasingly autonomous functioning. Third, other family members, such as siblings, are encouraged to help the depressed child engage in more self-care activities.

SESSIONS 12 AND 13: FAMILY FUNCTIONING

Rationale

Although each session of IFT includes all family members and addresses family functioning in an ongoing manner, Sessions 12 and 13 shift focus from individuals skills and behaviors to interactional patterns and family structure. To effect improvements in psychological symptomatology, quality of family interactions, and functioning across domains, structural changes may need to occur in the family (Minuchin, 1974). Structural changes can decrease frequency and intensity of unresolved conflictual interactions and increase the family's ability to effectively problem solve, make decisions, cope with crises, and negotiate differences. In addition, such changes allow family members to develop a more positive sense of themselves and their self-efficacy, acquire a more differentiated and cohesive sense of self, experience an enhanced sense of family identity and esteem, increase their comfort with intimacy and attachment, and derive a more hopeful outlook on the future.

Goals

The goals of these sessions are to identify dysfunctional family interaction patterns, and to promote changes in the structure of the family system.

Tasks

Identify Dysfunctional Family Interaction Patterns.   IFT for the family domain identifies problematic family patterns and their origins, models ways to understand the communications, thoughts, and feelings of family members, and facilitates alternative interactional patterns leading out of the depressive cycle. Maladaptive interactional patterns are identified primarily by "mapping" the family structure, focusing on subsystems, boundaries, and family members' roles (Minuchin, 1974), and secondly by helping the family discover the intrapsychic and interpersonal mechanisms maintaining depression within the family system (Y. Teichman & M. Teichman, 1990). This information, then, is used to aid the family in developing alternative and more adaptive modes of reciprocal interaction.

As noted earlier, a variety of problematic interactional patterns characterizes families of depressed children, each of which requires unique intervention planning. Common family patterns include the depressed child's maladaptive role in the family system (e.g., mediator of parental marital conflict; triangulation of child), parental ambivalence regarding the child's achievement, and significant difficulties with attachment.

Promote Changes in the Structure of the Family System.   To address the identified maladaptive patterns, the therapist assists the family in making structural changes by strengthening the executive subsystem, restructuring the familial hierarchy, and facilitating changes in the family rules and interaction sequences maintaining undesirable behaviors (Minuchin, 1974). In-session practice of new interaction patterns allows the therapist to provide feedback, and the effects of these patterns can be discussed and understood (Holder & Anderson, 1990). The family is also encouraged to implement these new patterns and strategies outside of the therapy hour, enhancing generalization of skills and preparing for ultimate departure from therapy.

A number of specific structural problems observed commonly in families of depressed children may be amenable to the following structural interventions. First, when a family map reveals that a child's depression is a function of the role played in the family (e.g., mediator of parental marital conflict), the therapist helps the family redefine the child's role to reduce associated stresses contributing to the child's depression (Freeman, Epstein, & Simon, 1986). If the depressed youth is triangulated either by buffering two conflicting family members or by detouring conflict with another family member through a third party, the therapist helps the child disengage from the triangle and encourages the conflicting parties to fight directly (Bedrosian, 1988). The therapist also assists family members in changing their cognitions and behaviors so as to prevent the depressed child from resuming a triangulated position.

Second, parents displaying ambivalence about their child's achievement are assisted in exploring the sources of this ambivalence, which typically lie in their families of origin. As this work progresses, the child is less likely to be employed as an object of the parents' projection residual to family of origin experiences, thus freeing the parents to be more genuinely reinforcing of their child's strivings and accomplishments. Work with children focuses initially on feelings of helplessness and hopelessness in the achievement domain, and then on feeling empowered to pursue higher levels of achievement. As parents become more able to fulfill the role of empowering and rewarding their children for social, academic, athletic, and artistic achievements, the children are assisted in perceiving more accurately these changes in their parents' ways of interacting with and reinforcing them.

Third, families with attachment problems may oscillate between parental overinvolvement with and distancing from the child, parental belittling and controlling of the child, or familial resentment of the depressed child's needs. Intervention focuses on illuminating these patterns, especially as they occur within family sessions, and assisting parents in maintaining a more evenly present and positive attachment to their child. Changes in these often unconscious shifts in parental behavior can result in the child feeling more loveable, less depressed, and more supported. Parents are encouraged to increase the overall consistency of their nurturance and to reinforce positively any accomplishments and gains in developmentally appropriate adaptive behavior. It is also important to challenge the often-distorted inferences that the children may be drawing from their own behavior and performance, and fostering the children's ability to respond to differences in the parents' behavior, thus rewarding the parents for their increased support and encouragement. In addition, this work attempts to engender more integrated, developmentally appropriate internal representations of the parent in the child. In doing so, the child's capacity to sustain attachment to the parent—despite the parents' periodic expressions of negative affect—is enhanced. Such attachment in turn increases the likelihood that the child will recognize and accept nurturance and positive reinforcement when forthcoming from the parent.

SESSIONS 14–16: REVIEW, SYNTHESIS, AND POSTASSESSMENT

Rationale

The termination phase is crucial, given that separation and loss often are precipitants for a child's depression. Termination work is important in insuring that treatment gains are maintained over time and generalized across settings.

Goals

The goals of these sessions are to review information provided in prior sessions and troubleshoot about problem areas, to evaluate the family's progress, and to address termination issues.

Tasks

Review Information Provided in Prior Sessions and Troubleshoot About Problem Areas. Typically, the concluding phase entails reemergence of psychological symptomatology and dysfunction in various functional domains. An increase in symptoms is thought to represent the family's question as to appropriateness of concluding the work and/or a reemerging familywide depressive experience associated with loss and anxiety about facing the future without the therapist's support. It is helpful to note in which particular domain(s) reemergence of symptoms occurs, as particular areas of dysfunction signal components of IFT requiring further review of information, practice of previously learned skills, and problem solving regarding more effective coping.

The therapist acknowledges the family's previously demonstrated capacity to problem solve and works collaboratively with the family in enumerating changes that occurred during the intervention. Special attention is paid to alterations in specific behaviors, emotional responses, and cognitions, and helping the child and family take responsibility for the therapeutic gains.

These interventions typically suffice to prepare the family for termination. Also, in those instances in which a reemergence of dysfunctional patterns occurs, such interventions enable the family to return to a more competent and less depressed stance. IFT therapists must, however, entertain the possibility that additional interventions may be required to assist the family in dealing with the complexities contributing to their child's depression.

Evaluate the Family's Progress.   To ascertain the family's progress and IFT efficacy, a posttreatment assessment should be conducted focusing on constructs similar to those assessed during the initial evaluation phase. Specific attention should be paid to evaluating the child and family members' psychological symptoms; life events; and functioning across cognitive, affective, interpersonal, adaptive behavior, biological, and family domains. Once again, a multitrait, multimethod, multi-informant approach to the postintervention assessment allows the therapist and the family to gather a comprehensive perspective of therapeutic gains and areas requiring continued attention. Feedback about progress, strengths, and weaknesses should be provided to all participants.

Address Termination Issues.   The concluding phase of IFT derives from Klerman and colleagues' (1984) description of the termination phase of interpersonal therapy for depression, as well as from the work on interpersonal therapy with depressed adolescents (Wilkes & Belsher, 1994). The first task entails explicitly acknowledging the impending conclusion of treatment so that the additional work of the concluding phase may proceed. The second task is to focus on the grief evoked by termination of the therapeutic relationship. This grief reaction may reflect a generic response to loss of relationships with others, and a more immediate loss of the connection between the therapist and family. The third task emphasizes the family's acquired competence to deal more adaptively with distressing life events, capitalizing on the family unit as a resource for coping. IFT concludes with a "soft therapy" termination, as an open door policy is underscored.

MAINTENANCE AND GENERALIZATION STRATEGIES

Maintenance and generalization of skills acquired during IFT is a primary goal of the intervention. Thus, strategies for applying newly acquired coping capacities outside therapy sessions are incorporated throughout each intervention phase in several ways. First, when appropriate, family members are taught to "coach" one another in acquiring and practicing more adaptive behaviors and interactions within sessions. Family members then can help monitor and encourage the application of new competencies outside of sessions. Second, homework assignments provide families with structured activities for practicing new coping strategies outside of sessions. Family members also are encouraged to discuss these assignments with the therapist after they have been attempted, providing an opportunity for problem solving about the generalization of skills. Third, IFT focuses on helping families plan appropriate outside activities to augment acquisition and maintenance of adaptive behaviors, such as instituting family outings and joining social groups (e.g., Cub Scouts).

The final stages of IFT pay particular attention to ensuring maintenance and generalization after termination. The therapist informs family members that concluding sessions serve as a laboratory for practicing acquired skills prior to termination. The family also discusses with the therapist anticipated road blocks to applying newly acquired coping techniques in the family's current or future situations. Finally, booster sessions to assist with maintenance of adaptive coping are considered as a posttermination option.

PROBLEMS IN IMPLEMENTATION

The following is a brief review of some of the major issues to be considered when implementing IFT. First, although no empirical data address the question of optimal treatment duration for psychosocial interventions for depressed children, most clinicians report that longer term treatment often is required to address developmental and family issues contributing to the onset and maintenance of childhood depression. Thus, although IFT, a time-limited treatment paradigm, is consistent with the current mental health care zeitgeist, prioritizing brief, cost-efficient, and empirically based approaches, this brief intervention may not address sufficiently the needs of all depressed children and their families. In such cases, principles and techniques guiding the IFT approach may be incorporated into longer term interventions.

Second, despite their many advantages (including treatment specificity, increased validity of treatment outcome findings, and enhanced reliability of treatment methods; e.g., LeCroy, 1994b), manualized treatments such as IFT may not anticipate complexities of symptom presentation and vicissitudes of psychotherapy encountered by clinicians, leaving the practitioner in a quandary as to the appropriate steps. The IFT treatment manual is intended to be both structured enough to allow for empirical validation of the treatment approach and flexible enough to meet the specific needs of each child and family. However, for use in clinical practice, the trained mental health professional may need to modify the treatment approach based on the child's developmental level and functional capacities and the unique characteristics of each family.

Third, IFT does not address adequately certain problems often associated with childhood depression, including comorbid psychological syndromes (e.g., anxiety disorders, attention deficit and disruptive behavior disorders, eating disorders, substance abuse/dependence) and serious family problems (e.g., parental alcoholism or depression, child maltreatment, spouse abuse). When these problems are primary and/or present, IFT may not be the sole or even primary treatment of choice.

Fourth, as is the case for the majority of manualized treatment approaches to date, the IFT approach has been developed and assessed primarily with middle-income, predominantly Caucasian youth and their families. The approach delineated may require modification to be used effectively with children and families of different cultural backgrounds and across socioeconomic groups (e.g., Canino & Spurlock, 1994).

Finally, although IFT has received considerable clinical success and the preliminary empirical findings supporting this approach are encouraging, larger scale empirical findings supporting the efficacy of the approach to date are lacking.

CASE ILLUSTRATIONS

Rather than provide one detailed case illustration that encompasses all aspects of IFT, the next sections present a series of vignettes, each with a different child and family and illustrating one of the components of IFT. Not all components are addressed due to space considerations.

Sessions 1 and 2: Joining and Assessment

The mother of Brett, an 11-year-old Caucasian male, initially was concerned about her son's declining academic performance and increased argumentativeness both at school and at home. Preliminary telephone contact revealed that the parents, who had been separated for over a year, had finalized their divorce within the preceding month. Both parents stated their willingness to attend the first session with their only child to discuss their concerns about him.

In this first interview, it became clear that the parents retained a shared perspective that their son was reacting to culmination of the divorce, but that he was not articulating his feelings to either of them. Brett sullenly stated that it would not do any good to talk about his feelings, as he felt that neither of his parents backed him up when he had difficulties with teachers. This statement provided entreé for the parents, with the clinician's assistance, to probe gently the sources of Brett's perception of his parents as unsupportive. This portion of the assessment reflected the clinician's early efforts to join with the family, as he sought to define the initial locus of distress and to begin to open channels of communication between the child and each parent.

The first two interviews revealed areas of difficulty across the spectrum of assessed domains: Brett was displaying difficulty sleeping and increased irritability at home and at school, a withdrawal from previously pleasurable athletic activities, concentration problems, and low self-esteem (psychological symptoms). He was feeling a sense of hopelessness about current and future interpersonal relationships and his own ability to do well at school, and had a tendency to blame himself for these problems (cognitive functioning). Brett was experiencing strong feelings of anger and difficulty regulating the expression of all negative affects (affective functioning), decreased contact with friends and a suspension from school for fighting on the basketball court (interpersonal functioning), decreased attention to personal appearance (adaptive functioning), and increased parental conflict (family functioning). Teachers were asked to complete the classroom edition of the Vineland Adaptive Behavior Scales and the Teacher Rating Form (companion to the Child Behavior Checklist), the scores of which were consistent with the interview data noted earlier. The clinician summarized information collected and cast the perspective that Brett's behavior could be understood as manifesting a depressive episode requiring the parent's involvement. The family then discussed how to utilize their involvement while still recognizing the parents' divorce and their wish to circumscribe their contact around assisting their son.

Session 4: Psychological Symptomatology

Kym, a 9-year-old female, appeared to be dysphoric following the death of her paternal grandmother. Because Kym had not been particularly close to her grandmother due to physical distance, the family did not make an association between onset of Kym's symptoms (e.g., depressed mood, anhedonia, suicidal ideation, low self-esteem, fatigue, and psychomotor retardation) and her grandmother's death. In exploring precipitating events, it became evident that Kym's father had felt unable to acknowledge his sadness over his mother's death, in part because he felt that his second wife was not tolerant of his dysphoria. The unspoken marital tension over this matter reminded Kym of the marital discord between her biological parents prior to their divorce, an event for which she had blamed herself. Thus, Session 3 with this reconstituted family focused on ascertaining and addressing the correlation between paternal grandmother's death, father's unexpressed dysphoria, marital tension, and Kym's depression; and reframing Kym's depression as a reflection of Kym's earlier experiences with marital separation, her concern about her father's negative reaction to the loss of his mother, and her parents inability to tolerate, modulate, and appropriately express distressing affects.

Sessions 5 and 6: Cognitive Functioning

Julia, a 12-year-old Hispanic female, who was a very good student and talented athlete, was brought to therapy by her mother (a hard-working beautician and single parent) when she started to withdraw from her friends. During the evaluation, it became evident that Julia's social withdrawal occurred following receipt of her most recent report card on which she received all A's except for one B in English. Julia thought that the B was evidence that she was "dumb," a sentiment that was heightened by her mother's concern about implications of the B for Julia's future educational and occupational opportunities. Thus, Julia appeared to be making an internal–stable–global attribution for this perceived negative event, and her mother inadvertently was communicating a concern about the permanence of the cause of this event. Interventions therefore focused on providing attribution retraining to both Julia and her mother. Specific attention was paid to helping Julia take credit for her multiple successes and more realistically assess the causes and consequences of her English grade. Additionally, her mother was supported in praising Julia for her accomplishments and keeping her daughter's grade in perspective.

Sessions 7 and 8: Affective Functioning

Shaniqua, a 9-year-old African-American female, lived in a family characterized by limited verbal interactions, in general, and by a pronounced lack of verbalized expression of feelings, in particular. Her socially outgoing mother tended to focus more on her own friendships than on her relationship with her daughter, and her moody and withdrawn father tended to engage in socially isolating activities, such as solitary ocean fishing. Shaniqua was brought for clinical services because she had few friends and appeared to have little interest in forging relationships with others. Extended periods of minimal verbalization and time spent alone in her room were interspersed with episodes in which Shaniqua ragefully would destroy property in her room, scream physical threats to her brother, and simultaneously cry and yell. In addition to the social modeling of her parents, especially her father, the assessment revealed that Shaniqua lacked the vocabulary for labeling her own emotions, a lack that fueled her frustration in being able to communicate with her parents and brother, and culminated in the rageful episodes. Sessions 7 and 8 therefore focused on helping the parents assist their daughter in attaching words to emotions and on discussing ways that the family could allow Shaniqua to better communicate these feelings to her parents and brother so she would feel more understood and minimize the need for expressing her dysphoric affect through unmodulated behavior.

Sessions 9 and 10: Interpersonal Functioning

As part of his clinical picture of depression, 8-year-old Brian presented as having only one current friend, a boy 1 year younger than he. His grandmother, who raised him, reported some ambivalence on her part about this friend. Indeed, she described Brian's friend as being so unkempt that she encouraged him to shower before going to bed when he spent the night visiting her grandson. Further exploration revealed that the family as a whole had only minimal social contacts, although the grandparents did acknowledge some long-standing acquaintances among their social relationships. Family work in Sessions 9 and 10 therefore focused on how the grandparent's limited social engagement was impacting on their grandson and three other grandchildren. Also, sessions addressed the ways in which the family could increase its social interactions in order to provide opportunities to practice relationship skills. The family agreed to schedule one weekly activity that would require relationships with other people. Also, the grandparents enrolled their grandson in Cub Scouts, so that he would have the opportunity to practice relationship skills with peers and authority figures in a more structured setting. Finally, the session focused on teaching the skills needed to initiate and sustain peer relationships. Thus, the entire family role-played how to plan an activity with other children, how to call on the phone and ask them to come over, how to implement the activity, and how to let the other children know that the activity had been enjoyable. The family then practiced implementing this plan outside the session and reported back at subsequent sessions how this plan had succeeded and ways in which it required additional refinement.

Session 11: Adaptive Behavior Functioning

When 9-year-old Dale was brought for evaluation by his divorced father, the interview in the assessment phase indicated adaptive behavior deficits, such as lack of an age-appropriate repertoire of interpersonal relationship skills and failure to assume responsibility for chores around the house. As part of the assessment, the Survey Form of the Vineland Adaptive Behavior Scales was administered, with the father serving as the respondent.

Vineland scores were consistent with interview data in the socialization domain, indicating that Dale lagged behind his peers in acquiring peer relationship skills and in his ways of coping with frustration. Contrary to Dale's and his father's beliefs, however, the Vineland scores indicated that, in fact, his domestic daily living skills were age appropriate, and discussion regarding this latter domain permitted father and son to achieve a more realistic view of Dale's behavior in this domain. Because intelligence and adaptive behavior are correlated only at low IQ levels, the low Vineland socialization scores could be discussed with the family as attributable to some other cause, and the clinician connected these data with other indices of depression exhibited by Dale. Work in Session 11 then focused on helping father and son to understand better how delayed adaptive skill acquisition was related to depression, and a plan was designed targeting how Dale would be helped to practice these skills with the assistance of his father. At the same time, a major area of conflict between father and son was reduced, as age-appropriate expectations for chores were clarified and Dale's good efforts in this area were acknowledged by his father.

Sessions 12 and 13: Family Functioning

Assessment of the family of 7-year-old Oscar revealed both structural and communication difficulties. The father had experienced an injury resulting in a chronic pain condition necessitating extensive medical care and frequent, unplanned visits to health care facilities. Because of his medical condition, he was unable to perform many of the behaviors associated with his paternal role, such as helping his son with homework, engaging in athletic activities with him, and participating in disciplinary acts. In her attempts to cope with her husband's medical difficulties, the mother began to feel that she needed to be strong and keep the family together. She did so by assuming increasing responsibility for parenting tasks, which was both condoned and resented by the father. As a result, the father felt worthless and disconnected from his family, feelings he was unable to articulate. The mother's growing parental burdens engendered resentment in her, paralleling the feelings experienced by her husband. Therefore, the family's functioning was characterized by a structural imbalance in which the mother had assumed and was delegated enormous responsibility for parenting, and the father increasingly had become disenfranchised. The resultant tension, resentment, and anger were not verbalized, but were felt by Oscar, who had limited language for labeling these feelings and for talking about his experience of family life.

Work in the family sessions, therefore, focused on articulating the family status and facilitating family members' ability to talk about their sadness and fear about the father's medical condition. Such discussion provided validation for Oscar's feelings, and provided him with words to describe his sadness, anger, and fear about his father's disability and increasing unavailability to him. The work further focused on helping the family identify ways that the father could participate in parenting his son. This intervention resulted in a structural shift between the parents that reduced marital tension, which in turn helped to alleviate the dysphoric affects engendered in Oscar.

CONCLUSIONS

Over the past two decades, two developments have impacted our thinking about childhood depression. The first of these developments is the realization that children are susceptible to depression: Earlier beliefs were that children did not possess the developmental and cognitive capacity to become depressed. The second development is the clinical experience and emerging research implicating family structural and interactive processes in the onset and maintenance of depression in children and adolescents. IFT, the treatment model presented here, reflects and extends both of these main streams of thinking. Because so much of the discussion here is based on preliminary research and theoretical extrapolation from more established work with adult populations, this chapter should be viewed as work in progress. Although there is reason to be increasingly confident about the efficacy of IFT, further research will permit refinement of IFT over the coming years.

The literature review reveals an emerging understanding of the complexities of the families of depressed children, and points to clear directions that should be taken to advance understanding of this field. Additional research is needed, for example, to shed further light on the unique and differentiating characteristics and interaction patterns of these families, including the sibling subsystem. One potentially fruitful approach is to examine applicability of conceptual and empirical models of the interpersonal functioning of depressed adults to depressed children and adolescents. Researchers pursuing this avenue must bring to bear a developmental appreciation of both the child and the family life cycle.

Clarification of the dynamics of families with depressed youth will permit better articulation of relevant treatment interventions. As an example, this chapter presents a model of interpersonal family therapy based on existing literature on the symptomatology and functional deficits observed in depressed youth and their families, as well as other authors' writings on family therapy for depressed individuals. Clinical experience and pilot research suggest that this model of family therapy for depressed youth helps reduce the child's depression and maladaptive family interaction patterns. Larger scale treatment outcome studies are needed to identify which family interventions, either alone or in combination with other modalities (e.g., individual or group therapy, pharmacotherapy), are most effective for which depressed youth and their families. It is a growing conviction that given the family's primacy in the lives of children and adolescents, the association between dysfunctional family interactional patterns and depression in youth, and the demonstrated efficacy of family therapy for a variety of childhood disorders, family therapy may prove the treatment of choice for many depressed children and adolescents.

REFERENCES

Achenbach, T. M. (1991a). *Manual for the Child Behavior Checklist/4-18 and 1991 Profile*. Burlington, VT: University of Vermont.

Achenbach, T. M. (1991b). *Manual for the Teacher's Report Form and 1991 Profile*. Burlington, VT: University of Vermont.

Achenbach, T. M. (1991c). *Manual for the Youth Self-Report and 1991 Profile*. Burlington, VT: University of Vermont.

Achenbach, T. M., & Edelbrock, C. (1983). *Manual for the Child Behavior Checklist and Revised Child Behavior Profile*. Burlington, VT: University of Vermont.

Achenbach, T. M., & Edelbrock, C. (1986). *Manual for the Teacher's Report for and Teacher Version of the Child Behavior Profile*. Burlington, VT: University of Vermont.

Achenbach, T. M., & Edelbrock, C. (1987). *Manual for the Youth Self-Report and Profile*. Burlington, VT: University of Vermont.

Achenbach, T. M., McConaughy, S. H., & Howell, C. T. (1987). Child/adolescent behavioral and emotional problems: Implications of cross-informant correlations for situational specificity. *Psychological Bulletin, 101,* 213–232.

Altmann, E. O., & Gotlib, I. H. (1988). The social behavior of depressed children: An observational study. *Journal of Abnormal Child Psychology, 16,* 29–44.

American Psychiatric Association. (1994). *Diagnostic and statistical manual of mental disorders* (4th ed.). Washington, DC: Author.

Angold, A. (1988). Childhood and adolescent depression: I. Epidemiological and aetiological aspects. *British Journal of Psychiatry, 152,* 601–617.

Angold, A., & Costello, E. (1992). Comorbidity in children and adolescents with depression. *Child and Adolescent Psychiatric Clinics of North America, 1,* 31–51.

Angold, A., Costello, E. J., Pickles, A., & Winder, F. (1987). *The development of a questionnaire for use in epidemiological studies of depression in children and adolescents.* London: Medical Research Council.

Armsden, G. C., McCauley, E., Greenberg, M. T., Burke, P. M., & Mitchell, J. R. (1990). Parent and peer attachment in early adolescent depression. *Journal of Abnormal Child Psychology, 18,* 683–697.

Arthur, J. A., Hops, H., & Biglan, A. (1982). *LIFE (Living in Familial Environments) coding system.* Unpublished manuscript, Oregon Research Institute.

Asher, S. R., & Wheeler, V. A. (1985). Children's loneliness: A comparison of rejected and neglected peer status. *Journal of Consulting and Clinical Psychology, 53,* 500–505.

Barrera, M., & Garrison-Jones, C. (1992). Family and peer social support as specific correlates of adolescent depressive symptoms. *Journal of Abnormal Child Psychology, 20,* 1–16.

Beach, S. R. H., & O'Leary, K. D. (1992). Treating depression in the context of marital discord: Outcome and predictors of response for marital therapy versus cognitive therapy. *Behavior Therapy, 23,* 507–528.

Beach, S. R. H., Sandeen, E. E., & O'Leary, K. D. (1990). *Depression in marriage: A model for etiology and treatment.* New York: Guilford.

Beardslee, W. R. (1990). Development of a preventive intervention for families in which parents have serious affective disorder. In G.I. Keitner (Ed.), *Depression and families: Impact and treatment* (pp. 101–120). Washington, DC: American Psychiatric Press.

Beardslee, W. R., Hoke, L., Wheelock, I., Rothberg, P. C., van de Velde, P., & Swatling, S. (1992). Initial findings on preventive intervention for families with parental affective disorders. *American Journal of Psychiatry, 149,* 1335–1340.

Beardslee, W. R., Salt, P., Porterfield, K., Rothberg, P. S., van de Velde, P., Swatling, S., Hoke, L., Moilanen, D. L., & Wheelock, I. (1993). Comparison of preventive interventions for families with parental affective disorder. *Journal of the American Academy of Child and Adolescent Psychiatry, 32,* 254–263.

Beck, A. T., Brown, G., Steer, R. A., Eidelson, J. I., & Riskind, J. H. (1987). Differentiating anxiety and depression: A test of the cognitive content-specificity hypothesis. *Journal of Abnormal Psychology, 96,* 179–183.

Beck, A. T., Rush, A. J., Shaw, B. F., & Emery, G. (1979). *Cognitive therapy of depression.* New York: Guilford.

Beck, A. T., Ward, C. H., Mendelson, M., Mock, J. E., & Erbaugh, J. (1961). An inventory for measuring depression. *Archives of General Psychiatry, 4,* 561–571.

Beck, A. T., Weissman, A., Lester, D., & Trexler, L. (1974). The measurement of pessimism: The hopelessness scale. *Journal of Consulting and Clinical Psychology, 42,* 861–865.

Bedrosian, R. C. (1988). Treating depression and suicidal wishes within the family context. In N. Epstein, S.E. Schlesinger, & W. Dryden (Eds.), *Cognitive-behavioral therapy with families* (pp. 292–324). New York: Brunner/Mazel.

Bell-Dolan, D. J., Reaven, N. M., & Peterson, L. (1993). Depression and social functioning: A multidimensional study of linkages. *Journal of Clinical Child Psychology, 22,* 306–315.

Berman, A. L., & Jobes, D. A. (1991). *Adolescent suicide: Assessment and intervention.* Washington, DC: American Psychological Press.

Bowlby, J. (1981). *Attachment and loss: Vol. 3. Sadness and depression.* Harmondsworth, Middlesex: Penguin.

Bowman, M. L. (1990). Coping efforts and marital satisfaction: Measuring marital coping and its correlates. *Journal of Consulting and Clinical Psychology, 54,* 463–474.

Brand, A. H., & Johnson, J. H. (1982). Note on reliability of the Life Events Checklist. *Psychological Reports, 50,* 1274.

Burt, C. E., Cohen, L. H., & Bjorck, J. (1988). Perceived family environment as a moderator of young adolescents' life stress adjustment. *American Journal of Community Psychology, 16,* 101–122.

Canino, I. A., & Spurlock, J. (1994). *Culturally diverse children and adolescents: Assessment, diagnosis, and treatment.* New York: Guilford.

Caplan, M., Weissberg, R. P., Bersoff, P. M., Ezekowitz, W., & Wells, M. L. (1986). *The middle school alternative solutions test (AST) scoring manual.* Unpublished manuscript, Yale University, New Haven, CT.

Chiariello, M. A., & Orvaschel, H. (1995). Patterns of parent–child communication: Relationship to depression. *Clinical Psychology Review, 15,* 395–407.

Cicchetti, D., & Schneider-Rosen, K. (1984). Toward a transactional model of childhood depression. In D. Cicchetti & K. Schneider-Rosen (Eds.), *Childhood depression* (pp. 5–27). San Francisco: Jossey-Bass.

Cicchetti, D., & Schneider-Rosen, K. (1986). An organizational approach to childhood depression. In M. Rutter, C. E. Izard, & P. B. Read, (Eds.). *Depression in young people: Developmental and clinical perspectives* (pp. 71–135). New York: Guilford.

Clarkin, J. F., Glick, I. D., Haas, G. L., Spencer, J. H., Lewis, A. B., Peyser, J., DeMane, N., Good-Ellis, M., Harris, E., & Lestelle, V. (1990). A randomized clinical trial of inpatient family intervention: V. Results for affective disorders. *Journal of Affective Disorders, 18,* 17–28.

Clarkin, J. F., Haas, G. L., & Glick, I. D. (Eds.) (1988). *Affective disorders and the family: Assessment and treatment.* New York: Guilford.

Coie, J. D., Dodge, K. A., & Coppotelli, H. (1982). Dimensions and types of social status: A cross-age perspective. *Developmental Psychology, 18,* 557–570.

Cole, P. M., & Kaslow, N. J. (1988). Interactional and cognitive strategies for affect regulation: A developmental perspective on childhood depression. In L. B. Alloy (Ed.), *Cognitive processes in depression* (pp. 310–343). New York: Guilford.

Compas, B. E., Grant, K. E., & Ey, S. (1994). Psychosocial stress and child and adolescent depression: Can we be more specific? In W. M. Reynolds & H. F. Johnston (Eds.), *Handbook of depression in children and adolescents* (pp. 509–523). New York: Plenum.

Connell, J. P. (1985). A new multidimensional measure of children's perceptions of control. *Child Development, 56,* 1018–1041.

Conners, K. C. (1990). *Conners' Rating Scales Manual.* North Tonawanda, NY: Multi-Health Systems.

Coyne, J. C. (1976). Toward an interactional description of depression. *Psychiatry, 39,* 28–40.

Coyne, J. C. (1984). Strategic therapy with married depressed persons: Initial agenda, themes, and interventions. *Journal of Marital and Family Therapy, 10,* 53–62.

Coyne, J. C. (1988). Strategic therapy. In J. F. Clarkin, G. L. Haas, & I. D. Glick (Eds.), *Affective disorders and the family: Assessment and treatment* (pp. 89–114). New York: Guilford.

Coyne, J. C., Downey, G., & Boergers, J. (1992). Depression in families: A systems perspective. In D. Cicchetti & S. L. Toth (Eds.), *Developmental perspectives on depression: Rochester Symposium on Developmental Psychopathology* (Vol. 4, pp. 211–250). Rochester, NY: University of Rochester.

Coyne, J. C., Schwoeri, L., & Sholevar, G. P. (1994). Treatment of depression within a family context. In G. P. Sholevar (Ed.), *The transmission of depression in families and children* (pp. 193–222). Northvale, NJ: Aronson.

Cummings, E. M., & Cicchetti, D. (1990). Toward a transactional model of relations between attachment and depression. In M. T. Greenberg, D. Cicchetti, & E. M. Cummings (Eds.), *Attachment in the preschool years: Theory, research, and intervention* (pp. 339–372). Chicago: University of Chicago Press.

Diamond, G. , & Siqueland, L. (1995). Family therapy for the treatment of depressed adolescents. *Psychotherapy, 32,* 77–90.

DiGiuseppe, R. (1986). Cognitive therapy for childhood depression. In A. Freeman, N. Epstein, & K.M. Simon (Eds.), *Depression in the family* (pp. 153–172). Binghamton, NY: Haworth.

Dodge, K. A., McClaskey, C., & Feldman, E. (1985). Situational approach to the assessment of social competence in children. *Journal of Consulting and Clinical Psychology, 53,* 344–353.

Downey, G., & Coyne, J. C. (1990). Children of depressed parents: An integrated review. *Psychological Bulletin, 108,* 50–76.

Dunn, J., & Brown, J. (1991). Relationships, talk about feelings, and the development of affect regulation in early childhood. In J. Garber & K. A. Dodge (Eds.), *The development of emotion regulation and dysregulation* (pp. 89–110). New York: Cambridge University Press.

Dunn, L., & Dunn, L. (1981). *Peabody Picture Vocabulary Test–Revised Manual.* Circle Pines, MN: American Guidance Service.

Epstein, N. B., Keitner, G. I., Bishop, D. S., & Miller, I. W. (1988). Combined use of pharmacological and family therapy. In J. F., Clarkin, G. L. Haas, & I. D. Glick (Eds.), *Affective disorders and the family* (pp. 153–172). New York: Guilford.

Falloon, I. R. H., Hole, V., Mulroy, L., Norris, L. J., & Pembleton, T. (1988). Behavioral family therapy. In J. F. Clarkin, G. L. Haas, & I. D. Glick (Eds.), *Affective disorders and the family: Assessment and treatment* (pp. 117–133). New York: Guilford.

Feldman, L. B. (1976). Depression and marital interaction. *Family Process, 15,* 389–395.

Feldman, S. S., Rubenstein, J. L., & Rubin, C. (1988). Depressive affect and restrain in early adolescents: Relationships with family structure, family process and friendship. *Journal of Early Adolescence, 8,* 279–296.

Fitts, W. H., & Roid, G. H. (1988). *Tennessee Self Concept Scale–Revised Manual.* Los Angeles: Western Psychological Services.

Fleming, J. E., & Offord, D. R. (1990). Epidemiology of childhood depressive disorders: A critical review. *Journal of the American Academy of Child and Adolescent Psychiatry, 29,* 571–580.

Foley, S. H., Rounsaville, B. J., Weissman, M. M., Sholomskas, D., & Chevron, E. (1989). Individual versus conjoint interpersonal psychotherapy for depressed patients with marital disputes. *International Journal for Psychiatry, 10,* 29–42.

Forehand, R. Brody, G., Slotkin, J., Fauber, R., McCombs, A., & Long, N. (1988). Young adolescents and maternal depression: Assessment, interrelations and family predictors. *Journal of Consulting and Clinical Psychology, 56,* 422–426.

Forman, S. G. (1993). *Coping skills interventions for children and adolescents.* San Francisco: Jossey-Bass.

Freeman, A., Epstein, N., & Simon, K. M. (Eds.). (1986). Depression in the family. *Journal of Psychotherapy and the Family, 2.*

Garber, J., & Dodge, K. A. (Eds.). (1991). *The development of emotion regulation and dysregulation.* New York: Cambridge University Press.

Garber, J., & Kashani, J. H. (1991). Development of the symptom of depression. In M. Lewis (Ed.), *Child and adolescent psychiatry: A comprehensive textbook* (pp. 293–310). Baltimore: Williams & Wilkins.

Garrison, C. Z., Schluchter, M. D., Schoenback, V. J., & Kaplan, B. K. (1989). Epidemiology of depressive symptoms in young adolescents. *Journal of Child and Adolescent Psychiatry, 28,* 343–351.

Goldstein, S., & Solnit, A. J. (1984). *Divorce and your child: Practical suggestions for parents.* New Haven, CT: Yale University Press.

Gollan, J., Gortner, J., & Jacobson, N. S. (1996). Partner relational problems and affective disorders. In F. Kaslow (Ed.), *The handbook of relational diagnosis and dysfunctional family patterns* (pp. 322–337). New York: Wiley.

Goodman, S. H., Gravitt, G. W., & Kaslow, N. J. (1995). Social problem solving: A moderator of the relation between negative life stress and depression symptoms in children. *Journal of Abnormal Child Psychology, 23,* 473–485.

Gotlib, I. H., & Colby, C. A. (1987). *Treatment of depression: An interpersonal systems approach.* New York: Pergamon.

Gotlib, I. H., & Hammen, C. L. (1992). *Psychological aspects of depression: Toward a cognitive-interpersonal integration.* Chichester, England: Wiley.

Hammen, C. (1991). Depression runs in families: *The social context of risk and resilience of children of depressed mothers.* New York: Springer-Verlag.

Handford, H. A., Mattison, R., Humphrey, F. J., & McLaughlin, R. E. (1986). Depressive syndrome in children entering a residential school subsequent to parent death, divorce, or separation. *Journal of the American Academy of Child Psychiatry, 25,* 409–414.

Harter, S. (1985). *Manual for the Self-Perception Profile for Children (Revision of the Perceived Competence Scale for Children).* Unpublished manuscript, University of Denver.

Hodges, K., McKnew, D., Cytryn, L., Stern, L., & Kline, J. (1982). The Child Assessment Schedule (CAS) diagnostic interview: A report on reliability and validity. *Journal of the American Academy of Child Psychiatry, 21,* 468–473.

Holder, D., & Anderson, C. M. (1990). Psychoeducational family intervention for depressed patients and their families. In G. I. Keitner (Ed.), *Depression and families: Impact and treatment* (pp. 157–184). Washington, DC: American Psychiatric Press.

Hollon, S. D., & Kendall, P. C. (1980). Cognitive self- statements in depression: Development of an Automatic Thoughts Questionnaire. *Cognitive Therapy and Research, 4,* 383–395.

Hopper, R. B., & Kirschenbaum, D. S. (1985). Social problem solving and social competence in preadolescents: Is inconsistency the hobgoblin of little minds? *Cognitive Therapy and Research, 9,* 685–701.

Hoyt, L. A., Cowen, E. L., Pedro-Carroll, J. L., & Alpert-Gillis, L. J. (1990). Anxiety and depression in young children of divorce. *Journal of Clinical Child Psychology, 19,* 26–32.

Izard, C. E., Dougherty, F. E., Bloxom, B. M., & Kotsch, W. E. (1974). *The differential emotions scale: A method for measuring the subjective experience of discrete emotions*. Unpublished manuscript, Vanderbilt University.

Jacobson, N. S., Dobson, K., Fruzzetti, A. E., Schmaling, K. B., & Salusky, S. (1991). Marital therapy as a treatment for depression. *Journal of Consulting and Clinical Psychology, 59*, 547–557.

Jacobson, N. S., Fruzetti, A. E., Dobson, K., Whisman, M., & Hops, H. (1993). Couple therapy as a treatment for depression: II. The effects of relationship quality and therapy on depressive relapse. *Journal of Consulting and Clinical Psychology, 61*, 516–519.

John, K., Gammon, D., Prusoff, B., & Warner, V. (1987). The Social Adjustment Inventory for Children and Adolescents (SAICA): Testing a new semi-structured interview. *Journal of the American Academy of Child and Adolescent Psychiatry, 26*, 898–911.

Johnson, J. H., & McCutcheon, S. M. (1980). Assessing life stress in older children and adolescents: Preliminary findings with the Life Events Checklist. In I. G. Sarason & C. D. Spielberger (Eds.), *Stress and anxiety* (Vol. 7, pp. 111–125). Washington, DC: Hemisphere.

Kaslow, F. W. (Ed.). (1996). *Handbook of relational diagnosis and dysfunctional family patterns*. New York: Wiley.

Kaslow, N. J., Brown, R. T., & Mee, L. (1994). Cognitive and behavioral correlates of childhood depression. In W. M. Reynolds & H. F. Johnston (Eds.), *Handbook of depression in children and adolescents* (pp. 97 – 121). New York: Plenum.

Kaslow, N. J., & Carter, A. S. (1991). Gender-sensitive object-relational family therapy with depressed women. *Journal of Family Psychology, 5*, 116–135.

Kaslow, N. J., Croft, S., & Hatcher, C. (in press). Depression and bipolar disorder in children and adolescents. In S. Netherton, C. E. Walker, & D. Holmes (Eds.), *Comprehensive textbook of child and adolescent disorders*. New York: Oxford University Press.

Kaslow, N. J., Deering, C. G., & Ash, P. (1996). Relational diagnosis of child and adolescent depression. In F. W. Kaslow (Ed.), *Handbook of relational diagnosis and dysfunctional family patterns* (pp. 171–185). New York: Wiley.

Kaslow, N. J., Deering, C. G., & Racusin, G. R. (1994). Depressed children and their families. *Clinical Psychology Review, 14*, 39–59.

Kaslow, N. J., & Racusin, G. R. (1988). Assessment and treatment of depressed children and their families. *Families Therapy Today, 3*, 1–5.

Kaslow, N. J., & Racusin, G. R. (1990a). Childhood depression: Current status and future directions. In A. S. Bellack, M. Hersen, & A. E. Kazdin (Eds.), *International handbook of behavior: Modification and therapy* (2nd ed., pp. 649–667). New York: Plenum.

Kaslow, N. J., & Racusin, G. R. (1990b). Family therapy or child therapy: An open or shut case. *Journal of Family Psychology, 3*, 273–289.

Kaslow, N. J., & Racusin, G. R. (1994). Family therapy for depression in young people. In W.M. Reynolds & H. F. Johnston (Eds.), *Handbook of depression in children and adolescents* (pp. 345–364). New York: Plenum.

Kaslow, N. J., Stark, K. D., Printz, B., Livingston, R., & Tsai, S. L. (1992). Cognitive Triad Inventory for Children: Development and relation to depression and anxiety. *Journal of Clinical Child Psychology, 21*, 339–347.

Kazdin, A. E. (1990). Evaluation of the automatic thoughts questionnaire: Negative cognitive processes and depression among children. *Psychological Assessment: A Journal of Consulting and Clinical Psychology, 2*, 73–79.

Kazdin, A. E., Moser, J., Colbus, D., & Bell, R. (1985). Depressive symptoms among physically abused and psychiatrically disturbed children. *Journal of Abnormal Psychology, 94*, 298–307.

Kazdin, A. E., Rogers, A., & Colbus, D. (1986). The hopelessness scale for children: Psychometric properties and concurrent validity. *Journal of Consulting and Clinical Psychology, 54*, 241–245.

Keitner, G. I., & Miller, I. W. (1990). Family functioning and major depression: An overview. *American Journal of Psychiatry, 147*, 1128–1137.

Kendall, P. C., Kortlander, E., Chansky, T. E., & Brady, E. U. (1992). Comorbidity of anxiety and depression in youth: Treatment implications. *Journal of Consulting and Clinical Psychology, 60*, 869–880.

Klerman, G. L., Weissman, M. M., Rounsaville, B. J., & Chevron, E. S.(1984). *Interpersonal psychotherapy of depression*. New York: Basic Books.

Kovacs, M. (1989). Affective disorder in children and adolescents. *American Psychologist, 44*, 209–215.

Kovacs, M., & Beck, A. T. (1977). An empirical-clinical approach toward a definition of childhood depression. In J. G. Schulterbrandt & A. Raskin (Eds.), *Depression in childhood: Diagnosis, treatment, and conceptual models* (pp. 1–25). New York: Raven.

Koverola, C., Pound, J., Heger, A., & Lytle, C. (1993). Relationship of child sexual abuse to depression. *Child Abuse and Neglect, 17,* 393–400.

Krementz, J. (1981). *How it feels when a parent dies.* New York: Knopf.

Kupersmidt, J. B., & Patterson, C. J. (1991). Childhood peer rejection, aggression, withdrawal, and perceived competence as predictors of self-reported behavior problems in preadolescents. *Journal of Abnormal Child Psychology, 19,* 427–449.

LaGreca, A. M., Dandes, S. K., Wick, P., Shaw, K., & Stone, W. (1988). Development of the Social Anxiety Scale for Children: Reliability and concurrent validity. *Journal of Clinical Child Psychiatry, 17,* 84–91.

Lang, M., & Tisher, M. (1978). *Children's Depression Inventory.* Victoria, Australia: Australian Council for Educational Research.

Lavoie, R. D. (1990). *The F.A.T. city learning disability workshop* [PBS video]. 1320 Braddock Place, Alexandria, VA 22314.

LeCroy, C. W. (1994a). *Handbook of child and adolescent treatment manuals.* New York: Lexington.

LeCroy, C. W. (1994b). Social skills training. In C. W. LeCroy (Ed.), *Handbook of child and adolescent treatment manuals* (pp. 126–169). New York: Lexington.

Lefkowitz, M. M., & Tesiny, E. P. (1980). Assessment of childhood depression. *Journal of Consulting and Clinical Psychology, 48,* 43–50.

Leitenberg, H., Yost, L. W., & Carroll-Wilson, M. (1986). Negative cognitive errors in children: Questionnaire development, normative data, and comparisons between children with and without self-reported symptoms of depression, low self-esteem, and evaluation anxiety. Journal of Consulting and Clinical Psychology, 54, 528–536.

Lewinsohn, P. M., Clarke, G. N., Hops, H., & Andrews, J.(1990). Cognitive-behavioral treatment for depressed adolescents. *Behavior Therapy, 21,* 385–401.

Locke, H., & Wallace, K. (1959). Short marital adjustment and prediction tests: Their reliability and validity. *Marriage and Family Living, 2,* 251–255.

Magana, A. B., Goldstein, M. J., Karno, M., Miklowitz, D., Jenkins, J., & Falloon, I. F. (1986). A brief method for assessing expressed emotion in relatives of schizophrenic patients. *Psychiatry Research, 17,* 203–212.

Masten, A. S., Morison, P., & Pellegrini, D. S. (1985). A revised class play method of peer assessment. *Developmental Psychology, 21,* 523–533.

Matson, J. L., Rotatori, A. F., & Helsel, W. J. (1983). Development of a rating scale to measure social skills in children: The Matson Evaluation of Social Skills with Youngsters (MESSY). *Behaviour Research and Therapy, 21,* 335–340.

McCauley, E., & Myers, K. (1992). Family interactions in mood-disordered youth. *Child and Adolescent Psychiatric Clinics of North America, 1,* 111–127.

McCubbin, H. I., Patterson, J. M., & Wilson, L. R. (1992). FILE: Family Inventory of Life Events and Changes. In D. Olson, H. McCubbin, H. Barnes, A. Larsen, M. Muxen, & M. Wilson (Eds.), *Family inventories* (rev. ed., pp. 83–120). St. Paul, MN: Family Social Science, University of Minnesota.

Minuchin, S. (1974). *Families and family therapy.* Cambridge, MA: Harvard University Press.

Minuchin, S., & Fishman, H. C. (1981). *Family therapy techniques.* Cambridge, MA.: Harvard University Press.

Moos, R. H., & Moos, B. S. (1981). *Family Environment Scale manual.* Palo Alto, CA: Consulting Psychological Press.

Moreau, D., Mufson, L., Weissman, M. M., & Klerman, G. L. (1991). Interpersonal psychotherapy for adolescent depression: Description of modification and preliminary application. *Journal of the American Academy of Child and Adolescent Psychiatry, 30,* 642–651.

Mufson, L., Moreau, D., Weissman, M. M., & Klerman, G. L. (1993). *Interpersonal psychotherapy for depressed adolescents.* New York: Guilford.

Norcross, J. C., & Goldfried, M. R. (Eds.). (1992). *Handbook of psychotherapy integration.* New York: Basic Books.

Nowicki, S. & Duke, M. P. (1994). Individual differences in the nonverbal communication of affect: The diagnostic analysis of nonverbal accuracy scale. *Journal of Nonverbal Behavior, 18,* 9–35.

Nowicki, S., & Strickland, B. R. (1973). A locus of control scale for children. *Journal of Consulting and Clinical Psychology, 40,* 148–154.

O'Leary, K. D., & Beach, S. R. H. (1990). Marital therapy: A viable treatment for depression and marital discord. *American Journal of Psychiatry, 147,* 183–186.

Olson, D. H., Larsen, A. S., & McCubbin, H. I. (1992). Family strengths. In D. Olson, H. McCubbin, H. Barnes, A. Larsen, M. Muxen, & M. Wilson (Eds.), *Family inventories* (rev. ed., pp. 56–70). St. Paul, MN: Family Social Science, University of Minnesota.

Olson, D. H., Portner, J., & Lavee, Y. (1985). FACES III. In D.H. Olson, H.I. McCubbin, H. Barnes, A. Larsen, M. Muxen, & M. Wilson (Eds.), *Family inventories* (pp. 1–42). St. Paul, MN: Family Social Science.

Orvaschel, H., & Puig-Antich, J. (1987). *Schedule for Affective Disorder and Schizophrenia for School-Age Children–Epidemiologic version.* Pittsburgh: Western Psychiatric Institute and Clinic.

Oster, G. D., & Caro, J. E. (1990). *Understanding and treating depressed adolescents and their families.* New York: Wiley.

Patterson, G., & Forgatch, M. (1990). Initiation and maintenance of process disrupting single-mother families. In G. R. Patterson (Ed.), *Depression and aggression in family interaction* (pp. 209–244). Hillsdale, NJ: Lawrence Erlbaum Associates.

Petersen, A. C., Sarigiani, P. A., & Kennedy, R. E. (1991). Adolescent depression: Why more girls? *Journal of Youth and Adolescence, 20,* 247–271.

Piers, E. V. (1969). Manual for the Piers-Harris children's self concept scale. Nashville: Counselor Recording and Tests.

Piers, E. V. (1984). *Revised Manual for the Children's Self-Concept Scale.* Los Angeles: Western Psychological Services.

Poznanski, E. O. (1982). The clinical phenomenology of childhood depression. *American Journal of Orthopsychiatry, 52,* 308 – 313.

Prince, S. E., & Jacobson, N. S. (1995). A review and evaluation of marital and family therapies for affective disorders. *Journal of Marital and Family Therapy, 21,* 377–401.

Puig-Antich, J., Goetz, D., Davies, M., Kaplan, T., Davies, S., Ostrow, L., Asnis, L., Twomey, J., Iyengar, S., & Ryan, N. (1989). A controlled family history study of prepubertal major depressive disorder. *Archives of General Psychiatry, 46,* 406–418.

Puig-Antich, J., Kaufman, J., Ryan, N. D., Williamson, D., Dahl, R. E., Lukens, E., Todak, G., Ambrosini, P., Rabinovich, H., & Nelson, B. (1993). The psychosocial functioning and family environment of depressed adolescents. *Journal of the American Academy of Child and Adolescent Psychiatry, 32,* 244–253.

Puig-Antich, J., Lukens, E., Davies, M., Goetz, D., Brennan-Quattrock, J., & Todak, G. (1985a). Psychosocial functioning in prepubertal major depressive disorder: I. Interpersonal relationships during the depressive episode. *Archives of General Psychiatry, 42,* 500–507.

Puig-Antich, J., Lukens, E., Davies, M., Goetz, D., Brennan-Quattrock, J., & Todak, G. (1985b). Psychosocial functioning in prepubertal major depressive disorder: II. Interpersonal relationships after sustained recovery from affective episode. *Archives of General Psychiatry, 42,* 511–517.

Puig-Antich, J., & Ryan, N. (1986). *Schedule for Affective Disorder and Schizophrenia for School-Age Children (6–18 years)–Kiddie–SADS (K–SADS).* Unpublished manuscript, Western Psychiatric Institute and Clinic, Pittsburgh.

Quay, H. C. (1983). A dimensional approach to behavior disorder: The Revised Behavior Problem Checklist. *School Psychology Review, 12,* 244–249.

Quay, H. C., & Peterson, D. R. (1987). *Manual for the Revised Behavior Problem Checklist.* Coral Gables, FL: University of Miami, Department of Psychology.

Racusin, G. R., & Kaslow, N. J. (1991). Assessment and treatment of childhood depression. In P. A. Keller & S. R. Heyman (Eds.), *Innovations in clinical practice: A sourcebook* (Vol. 10, pp. 223–243). Sarasota, FL: Professional Resource Exchange.

Racusin, G. R., & Kaslow, N. J. (1994). Child and family therapy combined: Indications and implications. *American Journal of Family Therapy, 22,* 237–246.

Radke-Yarrow, M., Cummings, E., Kuczynski, L., & Chapman, M. (1985). Patterns of attachment in 2- and 3-year-olds in normal families with parental depression. *Child Development, 56,* 884–893.

Rehm, L. P. (1977). A self control model of depression. *Behavior Therapy, 8,* 787–804.

Reynolds, C. R. & Richman, B. O. (1978). What I think and feel: A revised measure of children's manifest anxiety. *Journal of Abnormal Child Psychology, 6,* 271–280.

Robin, L. A., Bedway, M., & Gilroy, M. (1994). Problem-solving communication training. In C. W. LeCroy (Ed.), *Handbook of child and adolescent treatment manuals* (pp. 92–125). New York: Lexington.

Rotherman-Borus, M. J., Piacentini, J., Miller, S., Graae, F., & Castro-Blanco, D. (1994). Brief cognitive-behavioral treatment for adolescent suicide attempters and their families. *Journal of the American Academy of Child and Adolescent Psychiatry, 33,* 508–517.

Schrodt, G. R. (1992). Cognitive therapy of depression. In M. Shaffi & S. L. Shaffi (Eds.), *Clinical guide to depression in children and adolescents* (pp. 197–217). Washington, DC: American Psychiatric Press.

Seligman, M. P., Abramson, L. Y., Semmel, A., & von Baeyer, C. (1979). Depressive attributional style. *Journal of Abnormal Psychology, 88,* 242–247.

Seligman, M., & Darling, R. B. (1989). *Ordinary families, special children: A system approach to childhood disability.* New York: Guilford.

Seligman, M. P., Peterson, C., Kaslow, N. J., Tanenbaum, R. L., Alloy, L. B., & Abramson, L. Y. (1984). Attributional styles and depressive symptoms among children. *Journal of Abnormal Psychology, 93,* 235–238.

Seligman, M. P., Reivich, K., Jaycox, L., & Gillham, J. (1995). *The optimistic child: A revolutionary program that safeguards children against depression and builds lifelong resilience.* Boston: Houghton Mifflin.

Shaffi, M., & Shaffi, S. L. (Eds.) (1992). *Clinical guide to depression in children and adolescents.* Washington, DC: American Psychiatric Press.

Shapiro, J. P., Leifer, M., Martone, M. W., & Kassem, L. (1990). Multimethod assessment of depression in sexually abused girls. *Journal of Personality Assessment, 55,* 234–248.

Sholevar, G. P. (1994). *The transmission of depression in families and children: Assessment and intervention.* Northvale, NJ: Aronson.

Siepker, B. B., & Kandaras, C. S. (1985). *Group therapy with children and adolescents: A treatment manual.* New York: Human Sciences Press.

Singleton, L. C., & Asher, S. R. (1977). Peer preferences and social interaction among third-grade children in an integrated school district. *Journal of Educational Psychology, 69,* 330–336.

Skinner, H. A., Steinhauer, P. D., & Santa-Barbara, J. (1983). The family assessment measure. *Canadian Journal of Community Mental Health, 2,* 91–105.

Spanier, G. B. (1976). Measuring dyadic adjustment: New scales for assessing the quality of marriage and similar dyads. *Journal of Marriage and the Family, 38,* 15–28.

Sparrow, S., Balla, D., & Cicchetti, D. (1984). *The Vineland Adaptive Behavior Scales: Interview Edition, Survey Form.* Circle Pines: American Guidance Service.

Spitzer, R. L., Williams, J. W., Gibbon, M., & First, M. B. (1990). *Structured clinical interview for DSM–III–R Patient Version 1.0 (SCID–P).* Washington, DC: American Psychiatric Press.

Stark, K. D. (1990). *Childhood depression: School-based intervention.* New York: Guilford.

Stark, K.D., Humphrey, L. L., Crook, K., & Lewis, K. (1990). Perceived family environments of depressed and anxious children: Child's and maternal figure's perspective. *Journal of Abnormal Child Psychology, 18,* 527–547.

Stark, K. D., Humphrey, L. L., Laurent, J., Livingston, R., & Christopher, J. (1993). Cognitive, behavioral, and family factors in the differentiation of depressive and anxiety disorders during childhood. *Journal of Consulting and Clinical Psychology, 61,* 878–886.

Stark, K. D., Raffaelle, L., & Reysa, A. (1994b). The treatment of depressed children: A skills training approach to working with children and families. In C. W. LeCroy (Ed.), *Handbook of child and adolescent treatment manuals* (pp. 343–397). New York: Lexington.

Stark, K. D., Rouse, L. W., & Kurowski, C. (1994a). Psychological treatment approaches for depression in children. In W. M. Reynolds & H. F. Johnson (Eds.), *Handbook of depression in children and adolescents* (pp. 275–307). New York: Plenum.

Stark, K. D., Rouse, L. W., & Livingston, R. (1991). Treatment of depression during childhood and adolescence: Cognitive-behavioral procedures for the individual and family. In P. Kendall (Ed.), *Child and adolescent therapy* (pp. 165–206). New York: Guilford.

Strauss, C. C., Lahey, B. B., Frick, P., Frame, C. L., & Hynd, G. W. (1988). Peer social status of children with anxiety disorders. *Journal of Consulting and Clinical Psychology, 56,* 137–141.

Teichman, Y. (1986). Family therapy of depression. In, A. Freeman, N. Epstein, & K. M. Simon (Eds.), *Depression in the family* (pp. 9–39). New York: Haworth.

Teichman, Y., & Teichman, M. (1990). Interpersonal view of depression. *Journal of Family Psychology, 3,* 349–367.

Wallerstein, J. S., & Corbin, S. B. (1991). The child and the vicissitudes of divorce. In M. Lewis (Ed.), *Child and adolescent psychiatry: A comprehensive textbook* (pp. 1108–1117). Baltimore: Williams & Wilkins.

Waring, E. M., Chamberlaine, C. H., Carver, C. M., Stalker, C. A., & Schaeffer, B. (1995). A pilot study of marital therapy as a treatment for depression. *American Journal of Family Therapy, 23*, 3–10.

Warner, V., Weissman, M., Fendrich, M., Wickramaratne, P., & Moreau, D. (1992). The course of major depression in the offspring of depressed parents: Incidence, recurrence, and recovery. *Archives of General Psychiatry, 49*, 795–801.

Wechsler, D. (1981). *Manual for the Wechsler Adult Intelligence Scale-Revised*. San Antonio: The Psychological Corporation.

Wechsler, D. (1991). *Manual for the Wechsler Intelligence Scale for Children* (3rd ed.). San Antonio: The Psychological Corporation.

Weissman, M. M., & Bothwell, S. (1976). Assessment of social adjustment by patient self-report. *Archives of General Psychiatry, 33*, 1111–1115.

Weller, R., Weller, E., Fristad, M., & Bowes, J. (1991). Depressed in recently bereaved prepubertal children. *American Journal of Psychiatry, 148*, 1536–1540.

Wilkes, T. R., & Belsher, G. (1994). The final phases of cognitive therapy: Obstacles and aids to termination. In T. R. Wilkes, G. Belsher, A. J. Rush, & E. Frank (Eds.), *Cognitive therapy for depressed adolescents* (pp. 244–276). New York: Guilford.

Wilkes, T. R., Belsher, G., Rush, A. J., & Frank, E. (1994). *Cognitive therapy for depressed adolescents*. New York: Guilford.

Wirt, R. D., Lachar, D., Klinedinst, J. K., & Seat, P. D. (1990). *Multidimensional description of child personality. A manual for the Personality Inventory for Children. 1990 Edition*. Los Angeles: Western Psychological Services.

Woodcock, R. W., & Johnson, M. B. (1989). *Manual for the Woodcock-Johnson Tests of Achievement-Revised*. Allen, TX: DLM Teaching Resources.

Chapter 6

Child Sexual Abuse

David J. Hansen
Debra B. Hecht
Kristine T. Futa
University of Nebraska–Lincoln

Recent decades have brought widespread recognition of child sexual abuse, as well as the numerous problems and consequences associated with it (Briere, 1992; Browne & Finkelhor, 1986a; Damon & Card, 1992). Given the well-documented problems of sexual abuse, the lack of empirically validated treatments is surprising. Treatments have typically lacked a theoretical basis and evaluation has been minimal and poorly conducted (O'Donohue & Elliot, 1992).

A major problem is that empirically evaluated treatment protocols are not available. Even if a procedure is found to be effective, other sites cannot replicate the process. The need for standardized treatment protocols is well-established (Weisz, Weiss, & Donenberg, 1992), and the mental health field in general is striving for standardized, effective treatments that can be disseminated to practitioners (Chambless et al., 1996; Task Force on Promotion and Dissemination of Psychological Treatment Procedures, 1995). This emphasis is reflected in current federal priorities that fund research to develop and evaluate standardized treatment approaches.

This chapter presents a treatment protocol developed from a systematic review of the literature (Hecht, Futa, & Hansen, 1995) and evaluated in a clinical treatment setting (Futa, Hecht, & Hansen, 1996; Hecht, Futa, & Hansen, 1996). Assessment and intervention procedures are based on a three-factor model of the target areas impacted by sexual abuse: the individual or "self" (self-esteem, guilt, fears, etc.), relationships (peer, family), and sex (sexual knowledge, sexual abuse-specific knowledge). The limited research suggests that group treatment is the choice for abuse victims (Hiebert-Murphy, DeLuca, & Runtz, 1992) and inclusion of nonabusive parents in treatment is important for success (Damon & Waterman, 1986; Friedrich, Luecke, Beilke, & Place, 1992). This treatment protocol utilizes a parallel group format, with separate groups running simultaneously for the children and parents.

DESCRIPTION OF THE PROBLEM

Definitional Issues

Child sexual abuse, somewhat surprisingly, is difficult to define, and no criteria have been universally accepted (V. V. Wolfe & D. A. Wolfe, 1988). Most definitions of child sexual abuse consist of two main components: the specific sexual behaviors involved, and the ages of the victim and perpetrator (Browne & Finkelhor, 1986a; Faller, 1993; V. V. Wolfe & D. A. Wolfe, 1988). Sexual abuse tends to refer to a broad range of sexual behaviors. Noncontact offenses include behaviors, such as genital exposure, voyeurism, showing a child pornographic material, and inducing a child to undress or masturbate. Contact offenses include genital manipulation, digital or object penetration, penile penetration, and oral sex. Definitions emphasize sexual activity between children (e.g., under age 16) and older persons (generally defined as more than 5 years older than the child).

In addition to the age and sexual behavior components, another factor is usually considered when defining child sexual abuse: the relationship of the child and the perpetrator. If the perpetrator is a family member—including distant relations, in-laws, and step-relations—then abuse is considered intrafamilial or incestuous sexual abuse. If the perpetrator is an individual not related by marriage or blood, then abuse is considered extrafamilial. Most cases of abuse involve someone known to the family (V. V. Wolfe & D. A. Wolfe, 1988).

Estimates of Incidence and Prevalence

In recent reports from the states to the National Center on Child Abuse and Neglect (NCCAN, 1995, 1996), it has been estimated that between 1.9 to 2.3 children per 1,000 children were identified by Child Protective Services as sexually abused in the years from 1990 to 1994. A more scientific evaluation of incidence rates of abuse was conducted in the National Incidence Studies of child abuse and neglect, in which NCCAN (1988) surveyed a wide range of community professionals and agencies in a national probability sample of 29 counties. Many children identified as abused were not known to Child Protective Services. The 1986 data revealed that 2.5 children per 1,000 children were known to be sexually abused in the United States. Overall, estimates indicate that approximately 130,000 to 160,000 children nationwide are identified as victims of sexual abuse each year (NCCAN, 1988, 1995, 1996). These estimates of incidence are commonly believed to significantly underestimate the extent of the problem, because these numbers reflect only cases known to relevant agencies, and many instances of abuse are not identified or reported (Beutler, Williams, & Zetzer, 1994; Faller, 1993).

Estimates of the number of children sexually abused in the United States have increased greatly over the past several years. In the NCCAN National Incidence Studies, there was more than a 300% increase in sexual abuse from 1980 to 1986 (NCCAN, 1988). It is unclear whether such increases in estimates reflect an actual increase in incidence or are the result of increased identification and reporting due to growing public and professional awareness and concern.

Professionals estimate that between 1 in 3 and 1 in 4 women are sexually abused in some way during childhood (Faller, 1993). Rates for men are believed to be approximately 1 in 10, with some suggesting that it may be as many as 1 in 6 (Faller, 1993). It is often suggested that sexual abuse of males is more underreported than females, due to societal failure to view the behavior as abusive (e.g., sexual acts with an older female may be viewed by many, including the victim, as "experience" rather than abuse).

Consequences for Children

The possible psychological consequences of child sexual abuse are numerous and variable. Unfortunately, the research evidence is inconclusive, as many practical and methodological issues make it difficult to identify consequences of sexual abuse (Browne & Finkelhor, 1986a, 1986b; Faller, 1993; P. B. Mrazek & D. A. Mrazek, 1981; V. V. Wolfe & D. A. Wolfe, 1988). Researchers have used different definitions, focused on different outcome variables, used different methods and samples, used poor adjustment measures, overrelied on case material, and assumed causation from correlational findings. The research evidence is further limited by the fact that it is unclear whether symptoms in abused children are directly a result of the abuse or more globally a byproduct of family pathology and problems (Berliner, 1991). In addition, many variables may affect whether and how abuse has an impact, including factors such as the gender of the victim and perpetrator, type and severity of abuse, duration of and time since the abuse, family reaction and support following disclosure, and so on (Browne & Finkelhor, 1986a; Faller, 1993). Despite the complexity of the issue, the available research in the field is able to provide some insights as to the consequences of child sexual abuse.

Several studies have addressed consequences of child sexual abuse (see Browne & Finkelhor, 1986a, 1986b; Finkelhor, 1990; V. V. Wolfe & D. A. Wolfe, 1988, for detailed reviews). No one symptom or syndrome is found universally in all victims (Browne & Finkelhor, 1986a; Faller, 1993) and up to 50% may be asymptomatic (Beutler et al., 1994). Research has found sexual abuse to be associated with a number of internalizing behaviors, including anxiety (e.g., McClellan, Adams, Douglas, McCurry, & Storck, 1995), depression (e.g., Livingston, 1987; Wozencraft, Wagner, & Pelligrin, 1991), problems with self-esteem (e.g., Tong, Oates, & McDowell, 1987), suicidal ideation (e.g., McClellan et al., 1995; Wozencraft et al., 1991), sleep disturbances (e.g., McClellan et al., 1995; Wells, McCann, Adams, Voris, & Ensign, 1995), somatic complaints (e.g., Livingston, 1987), and fear of males (e.g., Wells et al., 1995).

Several studies have also noted the presence of externalizing problems, including self-abusive behaviors (e.g., McClellan et al., 1995), delinquency (e.g., Einbender & Friedrich, 1989), cruelty (e.g., Einbender & Friedrich, 1989; McClellan et al., 1995), and substance abuse problems (e.g., McClellan et al., 1995). In addition, problems with school performance (e.g., Einbender & Friedrich, 1989; Wells et al., 1995) and concentration (e.g., Wells et al., 1995), as well as problems with relationships and social competence (e.g., Einbender & Friedrich, 1989), are noted in the literature as a possible correlates of child sexual abuse.

Sexual behavior is another possible area of impact. Sexually abused children appear to know more about sex and are more interested and curious about sexual matters or genital regions (e.g., Friedrich & Reams, 1987; Wells et al., 1995). Heightened sexual activity, such as compulsive masturbation, precocious sexual play, overt sexual acting out toward adults and peers, even sexual victimizing of other children also appears to be related to a history of sexual abuse (e.g., McClellan et al., 1995; P. B. Mrazek & D. A. Mrazek, 1981). Another possible consequence of sexual abuse is self-consciousness about the child's own body (Wells et al., 1995).

Somewhat less is known about the long-term consequences of sexual abuse. Commonly identified long-term effects include anxiety, depression, self-destructive behavior, poor self-esteem, feelings of isolation, difficulty trusting others, substance abuse, patterns of revictimization, sexual dysfunction, and sexual deviance (Browne & Finkelhor, 1986a, 1986b; V. V. Wolfe & D. A. Wolfe, 1988). Although it is difficult to draw firm conclusions, it appears that abuse experiences involving father figures, genital contact, and force have the most serious consequences (Browne & Finkelhor, 1986a).

Importance of Parental Support

There is no one profile of a sexually abused child, and the extent of the impact of abuse varies from individual to individual. Research, however, indicates that parental support after disclosure may be a key factor in reducing impact of sexual abuse in the child, including maintaining school performance, activities, peer relations, and protection against serious mental health symptoms (Everson, Hunter, Runyon, Edelsohn, & Coulter, 1989; Spaccarelli, 1994). Poor family support, as evidenced by conflict and poor cohesion, is related to increased likelihood of internalizing and externalizing problems (Friedrich, Beilke, & Urquiza, 1987; Gold, Milan, Mayhall, & Johnson, 1994). Support may protect victims by assisting them in processing what happened to them in a less negative way and ensuring that they obtain needed services. For example, mothers' compliance with Child Protective Services (CPS) workers has been found to be one of the best predictors for lowered likelihood of suicidal ideation in children (Wozencraft et al., 1991).

It appears that parental support is a key factor in mediating the effects of child sexual abuse. It is important, however, to remember that the family members may be experiencing their own emotional distress in reaction to the child's victimization. When a child is victimized, it affects not only the abused child but the entire family system, and family members may need support for the feelings and stressors they are experiencing. Davies (1995) examined parental distress and ability to cope following disclosure of extrafamilial sexual abuse. Most parents felt they needed assistance dealing with the abuse, especially during the early postdisclosure stage. Problems experienced by parents following disclosure included increased strain for both parent–child and spousal relationships, depression, posttraumatic stress, and unresolved anger.

Families may not only need assistance in dealing with the aftermath of child sexual abuse, but it is also possible that parents may need assistance in adjusting to their own preexisting mental health issues that are uncovered once they enter the mental health arena. For example, maternal history of sexual abuse or maternal psychiatric symptoms may interact with the child's response to the sexual abuse (Friedrich & Reams, 1987). Family variables may interact with abuse-related variables in a manner that exacerbates or modifies the possible maladjustment noted in sexually abused children.

Conceptualizations About the Impact of Sex Abuse

Finkelhor (Browne & Finkelhor, 1986b; Finkelhor & Browne, 1985) proposed a well-known conceptualization that provides an understanding of the psychological impact of sexual abuse. The model proposes that sexual abuse may be analyzed in terms of four trauma causing factors, or "traumagenic dynamics": *traumatic sexualization, betrayal, powerlessness,* and *stigmatization.* Traumatic sexualization is the process where the child's sexuality is affected in a way that is developmentally inappropriate and interpersonally dysfunctional. Betrayal refers to the dynamic where a person on whom the child once depended caused harm. The child's trust and vulnerability are manipulated, expectations that others will provide protection are violated, and there is a lack of support and protection from caregivers. Powerlessness, or disempowerment, refers to the dynamic where the victim's will, desires, and sense of efficacy are compromised. The dynamic includes invasion of bodily territory; use of force or trickery to involve the child; the child's inability to believe the abuse occurred; and feelings of vulnerability, fear, and the inability to protect oneself. The final traumagenic dynamic is stigmatization. This refers to the negative feelings of guilt, shame, lowered self-esteem, and a sense of differentness from others. This traumagenic conceptualization of how sexual abuse impacts on the child is one of the most parsimonious and comprehensive models to date, yet it does experience criticism. For example, these dynamics have not been demonstrated to be consequences of abuse, the extent or presence of these dynamics varies considerably, and not all victims experience all dynamics (Conte, 1990).

Conte (1985, 1990) suggested that sexual abuse has first- and second-order sources of trauma or impact. *First-order* factors are the direct result of sexual abuse, such as the sexual behavior itself and actions by perpetrators to gain sexual access to the child and maintain silence (e.g., threat, force, bribes). *Second-order* factors result from processing first-order events. For example, threats or force may create fear, which may result in the development of abuse specific fears (e.g., fear of the perpetrator or the location where the abuse occurred) or more general fear (e.g., men).

Newberger and DeVos (1988) provided a transactional model, which identifies the process of interaction among three dimensions in the impact and recovery from sexual abuse: *social cognition, environmental sensitivity*, and *emotional-behavioral functioning*. The social cognition domain consists of the child's cognitive appraisal of the event. The child's beliefs about control and personal efficacy potentially influence the outcome of abuse. For example, the belief that victimization is one's own fault may contribute to poorer outcomes. The second domain, environmental sensitivity, suggests that the child lives in an environmental context that influences the child's psychological processes and functioning. Interactions with parents, relatives, friends, adults, community institutions (i.e., school, sports teams), legal and law enforcement institutions, and therapists may lessen or exacerbate the impact of abuse. The third domain consists of the child's emotional (e.g., distress, anxiety, depression) and behavioral functioning (e.g., aggression, somatization, sexualized behavior, achievement). Newberger and DeVos (1988) suggested that the domains are active and mutually influence one another, so that alterations in one domain change functioning in other domains.

ASSESSMENT METHODS

As previously noted, sexual abuse can impact on a variety of areas of child functioning, including internalizing, externalizing, and sexual behaviors. In addition, parental support of the child is important, yet the parents may experience significant distress themselves. Given these possibilities, a broad-based assessment is necessary.

The goals and focus of assessment when working with sexually abused children vary with regard to the phase of involvement. For example, prior to disclosure, assessment may involve examining for the possibility of sexual abuse. Following disclosure, assessment may focus on the child's adjustment, treatment needs and so forth. The latter is the focus of this chapter; this chapter does not address assessment to identify possible abuse (see Damon & Card, 1992, or Faller, 1993, for further information on identifying abuse). The procedures are intended for situations in which abuse has already been identified and documented, and treatment needs are being determined. It is likely, however, that in some cases that additional abuse will be identified. In these situations, it is important to contact Child Protective Services or the relevant law enforcement agency to make a report and allow an independent investigation. Details about the abusive acts and the child's adjustment are usually collected, as much as possible, from sources other than the child (e.g., CPS, parents).

Typically, formal assessments are conducted prior to treatment, halfway through treatment, immediately following treatment, and at short-term follow-up (e.g., 2 months). The following discussion of measures is divided into measures that utilize child report and those that rely on parent report. Brief discussion of the psychometric support for the measures, when available, is included.

Child Report Measures

Children's Impact of Traumatic Events Scale–Revised.   The Children's Impact of Traumatic Events Scale–Revised (CITES–R; V. V. Wolfe, Gentile, Michienzi, Sas, & D. A. Wolfe, 1991) is a structured interview that was designed to measure the impact of sexual abuse from the child's perspective, and is appropriate for children age 8 to 16. The CITES–R consists of 78 items with 11 subscales that cluster around four general areas. The scales related to PTSD include Intrusive Thoughts, Avoidance, Hyperarousal, and Sexual Anxiety. Those related to Social Reactions include Negative Reactions from Others and Social Support. Abuse Attributions consist of Self-Blame/Guilt, Empowerment, Vulnerability, and Dangerous World. The last global area deals with Eroticism. The content of the questions reflect the child's thoughts and feelings about what happened to them, rather than the actual events.

Fears Related to Victimization.   The Fears Related to Victimization scale (previously known as the Sexual Abuse Fear Evaluation, or SAFE; V. V. Wolfe & D. A. Wolfe, 1986) was developed as a subscale of the Fear Survey Schedule for Children–Revised (FSSC–R; Ollendick, 1983). The FSSC–R is an 80-item measure that lists situations that children (age 8 to 16) are asked to rate on a scale of how upsetting it is, using a 3-point scale from *none* to *a lot*. The Fears Related to Victimization scale includes 27 of the items of the FSSC–R that sexually abused children appear to find particularly distressing. Psychometric analysis has further divided these 27 items into two internally consistent factors: 11 items known as Sex-Associated Fears (e.g., talking or thinking about sex, watching people kiss on television), and 13 items labeled Personal Discomfort (e.g., saying "no" to an adult, telling on someone, mean looking people) (V. V. Wolfe, Gentile, & Klink, 1988).

Revised Children's Manifest Anxiety Scale.   The Revised Children's Manifest Anxiety Scale (RCMAS; Reynolds & Richmond, 1978) is a 37-item questionnaire that assesses general anxiety in children and adolescents (age 6 to 19). Twenty-eight items pertaining to physiological, subjective, and motoric symptoms of anxiety comprise the Total Anxiety score. These items are further divided into the subscales of Physiological Anxiety, Worry/Oversensitivity, and

Social Concerns/ Concentration. The remaining nine items are the Lie scale. The RCMAS has been shown to be internally consistent and reliable, and has normative information and clinical cut-offs based on age and sex.

Children's Depression Inventory.   The Children's Depression Inventory (CDI; Kovacs, 1992) is a 27-item measure that asks children and adolescents (age 7 to 17) to rate cognitive and somatic symptoms of depression. Respondents are asked to rate how they have felt in the past 2 weeks on a 3-point scale, with higher scores indicating higher severity. The CDI has six scores: Negative Mood, Anhedonia, Negative Self-Esteem, Interpersonal Problems, Ineffectiveness, and a Total Depression Score that includes items from all of the subscales. Adequate internal consistency has been demonstrated for all of the scales. The five subscales have been found to be moderately intercorrelated with each other, and each is highly correlated with the Total score. Norms are available for boys and girls separately, age 7 to 12 and 13 to 17.

Hopelessness Scale for Children.   The Hopelessness Scale for Children (Kazdin, Rodgers, & Colbus, 1986) includes 17 true–false items and can be used with children as young as 6 or 7 years old. A total hopelessness score is obtained. The Hopelessness Scale for Children was found to have excellent internal consistency and split-half reliability. Scores on this scale are positively correlated with depression scores from the Children's Depression Inventory and negatively correlated with self-esteem scores from the Coopersmith Self-Esteem Inventory.

Coopersmith Self-Esteem Inventory (SEI).   The Self-Esteem Inventory (Coopersmith, 1981) contains 58 items that measure children's attitudes about themselves in social, academic, family, and personal areas of experience. The SEI also contains a Lie scale. The concept of self-esteem, as it is measured by the SEI, refers to the children's approval or disapproval of themselves. Norms for this measure are available for children in the third through eighth grade. The SEI has good internal consistency and adequate construct and concurrent validity.

Parent Report Measures

Child Experiences Form.   The Child Experiences Form (CEF; Malinosky-Rummell, 1992) consists of questions about the occurrence of various types of interactions considered to exemplify sexual abuse (e.g., "Did anyone ever kiss or hug you in a sexual way when you did not want this?"). It was originally intended for adults to report on their own childhood experiences. This measure has been modified for this program: Parents respond for their children because it was felt that it would be too traumatic to ask the children these questions without an established therapeutic relationship and this information is necessary before treatment begins. In addition to describing the sexual act that occurred, there are questions about the identity (e.g., relationship to victim) and age of the perpetrator(s), the duration of the abuse, disclosure, and any legal or community response to the abuse that occurred.

Child Behavior Checklist.   The Child Behavior Checklist (CBCL; Achenbach, 1991) has versions designed for administration to the child, parents or caregivers, and teachers to assess for behavioral problems and the social competencies of the child. The parent report CBCL consists of 118 behavior problem items along with 20 social competence items designed to obtain information regarding the child's activities and interests, peer relationships, and school functioning. The CBCL contains Behavior Problem scales that vary according to the child's age and gender. These scales may include the following: Schizoid or Anxious, Depressed, Uncommunicative, Obsessive-Compulsive, Somatic Complaints, Social Withdrawal, Ineffective, Aggressive, and Delinquent. The CBCL also distinguishes between internalizing and externalizing profiles presented by the child. The Social Competencies scales consist of Activities, Social, and School. There is substantial evidence supporting the psychometric properties of the CBCL, including test–retest reliability; longer term stability; interrater agreement; and content-, construct-, and criterion-related validity (Achenbach, 1991).

Child Sexual Behavior Inventory.   The Child Sexual Behavior Inventory (CSBI; Friedrich et al., 1992) is a 35-item parent report inventory designed for the assessment of sexual behavior in children 2 to 12 years old. The CSBI assesses a variety of sexual behaviors relating to self-stimulation, sexual aggression, gender-role behavior, and personal boundary violations. Excellent internal consistency has been demonstrated for both a normative sample and a clinical sample of children with a history of sexual abuse. Four week test–retest correlations were adequate. Validity of the CSBI was supported by significant differences between the clinical and normative samples on the total score and a majority of the CSBI items.

Family Adaptability and Cohesion Evaluation Scales.   The Family Adaptability and Cohesion Evaluation Scale–III (FACES III; Olson, 1986) is a 20-item self-report measure to assess adaptability, cohesion, and family satisfaction. It is based on the Circumplex Model of marital and family systems, and focuses on the constructs of cohesion and adaptability. Family cohesion assesses the degree to which a family member feels bonded to other members, whereas adaptability assesses the flexibility of the family system in response to stress. The 20-item FACES III is taken twice, once for perceptions of the family system and once for an ideal description. It assesses the manner in which a family member perceives the family system and compares it to that family member's ideal family system to provide an estimate of satisfaction. Internal consistency was adequate for the cohesion and adaptability scales. Four- to five-week test–retest reliability for the cohesion and adaptability scales was also good. The cohesion and adaptability scales are orthogonal with minimal correlation between them. Cohesion, but not adaptability, had a significant relation with social desirability. Moderate correlation between family members was found for the cohesion and adaptability scales.

Family Crisis-Oriented Personal Evaluation Scales.   The Family Crisis-Oriented Personal Evaluation Scales (F–COPES; McCubbin, Larsen, & Olson, 1982; McCubbin, Olson, & Larsen, 1987) is a 30-item self-report measure used to assess effective problem-solving coping attitudes and behavior used by families in response to problems or difficulties. The F–COPES assesses two dimensions of family interaction, internal family strategies, and external family strategies. Internal family strategies are the ways that individual members deal with problems by using resources within the nuclear family system. External family strategies are the active behaviors the family uses to acquire resources outside of the nuclear family (i.e., church, extended family, friends, neighbors, community resources). The F–COPES yields a total score as well as scores for five subscales: Acquiring Social Support, Reframing, Seeking Spiritual

Support, Mobilizing Family to Acquire and Accept Help, and Passive Appraisal. Internal consistency and 4-week test–retest reliability of the total score and the five subscales was excellent. The F-COPES demonstrates good factorial validity and concurrent validity with other family measures.

Parenting Stress Index.   The Parenting Stress Index (PSI; Abidin, 1986) is a 120-item self-report index for the assessment of stress associated with parenting. The PSI was also designed to assist with the identification of dysfunctional parent–child relationships. The PSI consists of two domains, the Parent Domain and Child Domain, with subscales in each of the domains. The subscales within the Child Domain are Adaptability, Acceptability, Demandingness, Mood, Distractibility/Hyperactivity, and Reinforces Parent. The subscales within the Parent Domain are Depression, Attachment, Restrictions of Role, Sense of Competence, Social Isolation, Relation-ship with Spouse, and Parent Health. There is also an optional Life Stress Scale to assess the parent–child relationship in the context of other life stressors the family may be experiencing. Adequate internal consistency and reliability for the domains and subscales has been demonstrated. Evidence for the concurrent and construct validity of the PSI has been demonstrated.

Symptom Checklist–90–Revised.   The Symptom Checklist–90–Revised (SCL–90–R; Derogatis, 1994) is a 90-item self-report inventory designed to screen for a broad range of psychological symptom patterns. The SCL–90–R consists of nine primary symptom dimensions: Somatization, Obsessive-Compulsive, Interpersonal Sensitivity, Depression, Anxiety, Hostility, Phobic Anxiety, Paranoid Ideation, and Psychoticism. The SCL–90–R also provides three global scores, which include the Global Severity Index, Positive Symptom Distress Index, and Positive Symptom Total. The SCL–90–R has exhibited high levels of internal consistency and good 10-week test–retest reliability. The SCL–90–R has demonstrated convergent and discriminant validity with Minnesota Multiphasic Personality Inventory.

Additional Assessment Issues

Whether working with individuals or groups, one cannot underemphasize the importance of the clinical interview to identify treatment targets (e.g., whether this treatment protocol may be useful and appropriate) and evaluate child and parent motivation for treatment. In addition, clinical observation during treatment of the children and parents is important for evaluating their emotional reactions to the session content (e.g., whether they are distressed, angry, etc.). Careful observation of the children in particular (e.g., out of seat, making noises or other distractions, etc.) has been helpful to understand their reactions to session content and prevent problems and disruptions.

TREATMENT OVERVIEW

This treatment protocol for sexually abused children and their nonoffending parents was developed from a systematic review of the literature (Hecht et al., 1995) and the procedures have been evaluated in a clinical treatment setting (Futa et al., 1996; Hecht et al., 1996). This treatment program is referred to as Project SAFE, which stands for Sexual Abuse Family

Education. The clients have been primarily sexually abused female children, with their nonabus-ing parent(s) (primarily mothers). Children are referred by local agencies and have been evaluated for abuse by CPS or the police before participating.

As noted earlier, the protocol was designed to address three critical target areas impacted by sexual abuse: the individual or "self" (self-esteem, guilt, internalizing, etc.), relationships (social interactions and externalizing problems with peers and family), and sex (sexual knowl-edge and abuse). Because externalizing behaviors primarily occur in interactions with others (e.g., aggression, noncompliance), this chapter emphasizes and targets them as "relationship" issues.

Treatment procedures include education, skill building, problem solving, and support. Child and parent groups each meet for 90-minute sessions for approximately 12 weeks. Treatment characteristics (time frame, procedures, etc.) are based on prior research with sexual abuse victims and other children (e.g., Damon & Waterman, 1986; Deblinger, McLeer, & Henry, 1990; de Young & Corbin, 1994; Friedrich, 1990; Friedrich, Luecke, et al., 1992; Kitchur & Bell, 1989; Mandell & Damon, 1989; Wagner, Kilcrease-Fleming, Fowler, & Kazelskis, 1993). Length of 12 sessions for both parents and children allows enough time for group cohesion and resolution of issues that might arise (Friedrich, 1990). Sessions are usually videorecorded for supervision and evaluation of treatment integrity (i.e., these tapes are coded to ensure that the therapists adhered to the treatment protocol).

Groups are led by thoroughly trained master's level therapists. Use of cotherapists for each group helps with modeling of skills, dealing with problems that arise (e.g., a disruptive child), and observing client participation and reactions. Female therapists are generally used as services are provided primarily for girls, and female therapists are recommended for short-term therapies with sexually abused girls (Wagner et al., 1993).

The children's group generally contain five to eight children of the same sex, with no less than three children in a group. Research suggests that boys and girls experience different consequences of sexual abuse (Finkelhor, 1990) and clinical trials suggest these should be addressed within same-sex groups (Friedrich, Luecke, et al., 1992; Hiebert-Murphy et al., 1992). Children are usually between the age of 8 and 12, but the upper and lower limits are somewhat flexible. Other treatments have focused on this age group as well (e.g., Damon & Waterman, 1986; Kitchur & Bell, 1989; Mandell & Damon, 1989). The following are the exclusion criteria: severe child or parent psychopathology, unwillingness to talk about abuse or denial of abuse (child or parent), significantly impaired intellectual functioning (child or parent), and severe behavior problems (e.g., extreme noncompliance that would interfere with participation, sexual offending).

Treatment covers a broad range of topics using a variety of techniques, with several consistent procedures across sessions. Each children's group begins with "Circle Time" to review how their previous week went, including naming one good thing and one bad thing that happened. Snacks are utilized during group to help break up the intensity of the sessions and provide time for social interactions. The last structured group activity is also Circle Time, with the children or therapist naming one good thing that each group member did, which helps promote positive self-esteem (Corder, Haizlip, & DeBoer, 1990). A brief play time is the final activity. This helps end sessions on a good note and allows the lead therapist for the children to go to talk to the parents.

The parents' group sessions generally begin with a brief discussion of the child's behavior during the previous week. Then the content of the children sessions is reviewed and related issues for the parents are discussed. Problem solving is carried out to address problematic child behaviors that may occur during participation in treatment (e.g., reemergence of fearful or anxious behavior). At the end of the session, one of the child therapists comes in to discuss how the children reacted to that week's session and answer any questions the parents might have about the procedures. This has proven useful to provide needed reassurances to the parents about how their children are doing in treatment.

TREATMENT MODULE SUMMARIES

The following discussion describes the 10 treatment modules. Given space limitations, the following narrative only provides a general overview of each module. A detailed treatment manual is available from the authors on request. In most cases, each module can be considered a "session." However, that at times it is important to work on a module over two sessions. For example, it can be useful to cover Module 3, Sharing What Happened to Me–Part I, and Module 7, Learning to Cope with My Feelings, during two sessions. For groups of younger children (e.g., near or below 8 years old), or intellectually limited children, it may be useful to expand more of the modules across more than one session, whereas for groups of older or brighter children it may not be necessary.

Module 1: Welcome and Orientation

Goals. The first module is designed to introduce the purpose and intent of the group. Group rules are established and issues surrounding confidentiality are addressed. In addition, the process of building rapport and becoming a cohesive group is begun. Basic information about sexual abuse is provided to the parents.

Children's Group. The children are asked to explain why they are participating in this group. Therapists then explain that during these sessions the group will talk about feelings, the abuse and their feelings about it, how things have changed for them and their families, how to stop abuse from happening again, and general information about their bodies and sex. Confidentiality is explained to the children, and they are assured that although their parents will hear about the types of things they talk about, the therapists will not specifically repeat what they say to their parents. Group rules are then generated by the group members and written down on a large sheet for posting and future use. Aside from standard rules about respect, participation, and safety, other rules might be included, such as "It's O.K. to cry in group" and "If you don't want to answer a question, that's O.K., but you have to say why." Consequences for rule violations are also discussed. The children then discuss what it means to be a part of a group, as well as unique qualities about themselves that make them individuals. This serves to help members get to know each other.

Parents' Group. Parents are informed that this group provides support and education on how to better help their children process the abuse experience. An overview of the topics is provided, specifically talking about the communication skills and parenting skills the adults will learn. The importance of parental support in the children's therapy process is emphasized.

A group contract discussing attendance and confidentiality is signed by all group members to help facilitate group cohesion and to help with attendance. Parents are also provided with basic definitions and information about the prevalence and impact of sexual abuse. Parents are given the opportunity to discuss the changes that they would like to see in their children and families as a result of this group.

Module 2: Understanding and Recognizing Feelings

Goals.   This module addresses the identification of feelings, both in one's self and others. It addresses the differences in the range, intensity, and multidimensionality of feelings, as well as some of the possible causes and consequences of emotions. This section also addresses parental roles in helping children express their feelings. In addition, parents discuss which of their own feelings they feel are appropriate to express in front of their children, and become aware of some of the adaptive or maladaptive coping techniques they might be modeling.

Children's Group.   After Circle Time and a review of the rules, each child is given an envelope with various feeling faces. Everyone gets a chance to pick out an emotion and describe it (e.g., where in their body they feel it, possible causes and consequences of that feeling, the last time the child felt that way). The children then hear different stories designed to elicit an array of emotions and are asked to hold up the feeling face that represents how they would feel (e.g., "Your friend's puppy throws up all over your lap and then dies" might elicit disgust and sadness). Discussion focuses on the different emotions that children pick for the same story, and validates that individual differences in feelings do exist. To demonstrate the different intensities that emotions can have, signs with different emotions are placed on the floor, and the children are given different colored chips. They are asked to place on the signs the number of chips that represents how much they would feel that particular emotion in response to the story. A game of "emotional charades" is played, where the children act out the feeling they choose, and the discussion focuses on how emotions are recognized in others.

Parents' Group.   The parents group begins with a discussion of their children's behaviors the previous week and a summary of what the children are covering that day. Parents then discuss how their children express their feelings through their behavior, and at times, how the behavior might not seem to match the feeling. For example, a child who is feeling scared might act aggressively rather than withdrawn. Parents are then asked to talk about how the expression of feelings is encouraged or discouraged in their homes. Parents explore how they express their feelings and how their children respond. Adaptive coping skills are generated and discussed, such as seeking social support, exercising, engaging in relaxing activities, and so on.

Module 3: Sharing What Happened to Me–Part I

Goals.   This module attempts to address and reduce the feelings of isolation and stigmatization around the abuse through disclosure to the group. This process is meant to help the children and their parents identify their feelings regarding the telling of their stories, and to help the parents cope with their own feelings, as well as their children's feelings. Additionally, other people's reactions to the disclosure are discussed. It usually takes 2 (or even 3) weeks to complete this module. The children may become upset during this topic and extra breaks and play time might be necessary to reduce the anxiety.

Children's Group.   After Circle Time, the children engage in a discussion about the differences between "good" and "bad" secrets. Specifically, good secrets are described to be like "surprises" that are told later, and bad secrets are things you are never to tell, even though you do not think they are right. Sexual abuse is identified as a bad secret. Worksheets with cartoon figures are used to define the scope of what is considered sexual abuse (pornography, voyeurism, contact, etc.). The children are then read vignettes about a child who has been molested and has either tried to keep the secret or has told another friend or adult. The discussion focuses on reasons to tell or not tell and the associated feelings. Providing examples of other children's abuse experience is a less threatening way of leading up to the children's own disclosure, and shows they are not alone and many other children have also been abused. The children are then read the story "Promise Not to Tell" (Wachter, 1983) about a girl who tells about her experience with her stepfather and are given time to discuss their feelings about what happened in the story. The therapists then facilitate discussion of the feelings associated with telling about abuse, with questions such as "What will other's think about me when I tell them this happened?" The children are asked to share their own stories. A summary sheet (modified from one by deYoung & Corbin, 1994) with multiple-choice questions (e.g., regarding where the abuse took place, etc.) is used to provide a structured, nonthreatening format for providing information about their abuse. The children can either read their responses off the sheet or tell their story in their own way. Each disclosure should also include a description of who they told and their reaction. Discussions and questions should focus on feelings, and therapists should work toward normalizing these feelings and addressing any faulty assumptions or cognitions that the children may express.

Parents' Group.   The session begins with a discussion of their children's behaviors the previous week and a summary of the children's group topics for the day. The parents are informed that the children are going to be covering difficult material, they might be upset after the session, and problematic behaviors that may have previously gone away might temporarily reemerge (e.g., acting out, withdrawal). Parents are reminded that the goals of this module are to reduce the children's sense of secrecy and shame around the abuse, and one of the best ways to do this is to talk about what happened and hear that these things happened to other children also. Parents are reminded that they need to be supportive of their children and be available to talk about difficult topics. Parents are encouraged to send the message to their children that they are loved and appreciated. The parents then hear the story "Promise Not to Tell" (Wachter, 1983), process their feelings about it, and anticipate their children's reactions. Parents are asked to tell their children's story and are specifically asked to talk about how they found out, how they reacted, and their feelings about the abuse. Parents are also encouraged to talk about to whom they have disclosed and what that was like for them. Coping strategies to help parents deal with their own reactions are reviewed (e.g., relaxation strategies, seeking support, cognitive restructuring). Parents then discuss how they anticipate their children will feel and act as a result of this session, and techniques to handle these feelings and behaviors are discussed. Emotional expression and sharing with children are encouraged, and role plays are used to model this. Parents are also encouraged to go home and write a letter to their child about what they did right in response to the disclosure, and what they wish they had done, or wish they had done differently. This letter is not to be given to the children, but it often helps parents deal with some of the guilt.

Module 4: Sharing What Happened to Me–Part 2

Goals. This module focuses on the offender. General information about why offenders offend is provided with the intent of placing the blame for the abuse on the perpetrator. In addition, hearing about other children's experiences is thought to decrease the feelings of isolation and stigmatization that commonly occur in sexually abused children.

Children's Group. After Circle Time, the children are read "Jenny's Story" (Terkel & Rench, 1984). This story is about a girl who is molested by her father and eventually stops the abuse. It describes the family dynamics and shows that her father is having some problems. Questions about why the father acted as he did and what should happen to him are discussed. This discussion moves toward why adults and older children sometimes sexually abuse younger children. The therapists then role play some situations in which a "child" was molested by someone close to the family, and how the child was afraid but chose to tell about the abuse, and now feels guilty because that person was removed from the home. The "therapist" reassures the child that she did nothing wrong and was right to tell. Children are asked to talk about their feelings about their own offenders, and how these might have changed from before the abuse. The session ends with the children drawing about their feelings, giving them some time to wind down after such a difficult discussion. The children are given a homework assignment for the next week: a worksheet designed to identify the children's support network.

Parents' Group. Parents are asked how their children responded at home after last week's session and then provided with a summary of this week's group. Parents are given the opportunity to discuss their reactions to their children's disclosure, and specifically asked what they thought they did well and what they wished they had not done or had handled better. "Jenny's Story" (Terkel & Rench, 1984) is read and the group is asked for their reactions to the story. Their own feelings about the offender and how they might be different pre- and postabuse are discussed and processed. Parents are given support and ideas on how to be sensitive to their children's feelings surrounding the abuse, and how to deal with their own strong reactions of anger or guilt. Although some children might talk about their feelings, others might start acting out or withdrawing. Parents discuss how to handle these reactions, and how to reinforce positive expressions of emotions. Parents are informed that their children will receive a homework sheet on support networks, and are asked to help their children complete it.

Module 5: My Family

Goals. This module is designed to identify family strengths and sources of social support to help reduce feelings of isolation. The effects of disclosure on the family are discussed and processed in order to help improve family dynamics. Specific concerns when the offender was a family member or close family friend are also addressed.

Children's Group.   The children's homework assignment starts the discussion. Each child is asked to share who the important people in their lives are, and why those people are important. Children are asked to identify who on their homework sheet they would talk to if they were sad, angry, and so on, if that did not spontaneously emerge in the earlier discussion. The children are also specifically asked who on their sheet they would tell a big secret, such as their abuse. The children are asked to draw a family portrait and discuss their relationship with their family members. Special care should be taken to address current changes in the family, such as the offender or the child leaving the home. The group then discusses some of the changes that occur in families after abuse is disclosed, and examples are given such as parents being angry, children being angry at parents, or parents becoming overprotective and not allowing children to play with friends or go to the park.

Parents' Group.   Parents are reminded that this is the midway point of therapy. A brief review of topics covered to date is provided, as well as a preview of things to come. The focus of this session is to talk about the impact of the abuse on the family, and how relationships have changed. Issues of overprotectiveness are addressed, and the importance of allowing their children to have social interactions is emphasized. Family strengths and sources of social support for parents are identified and discussed.

Module 6: Understanding My Feelings About What Happened to Me

Goals.   This module is designed to assist the families in understanding their feelings surrounding the abuse and enhance positive self-image. Feelings such as anger, self-blame, guilt, shame, and stigmatization are targeted. The enhancement of child peer relationships is also targeted.

Children's Group.   After circle time, children play the Hat Game. A hat is filled with questions pertaining to issues such as self-image, stigmatization, guilt, shame, and self-blame. Examples of such questions include: "Has your body changed since the abuse? How?" "Have you felt like you could have stopped it?" "Do you think it was your fault?" The hat is passed from one person to the next and each child is asked to read and respond to the question selected. After the Hat Game, peer relations are addressed. The children are asked to identify a special friend and what makes that person a good friend. The discussion focuses on sharing feelings with friends and how their friends react (e.g., cheering them up, listening, etc.). More appropriate and less appropriate ways to show a friend that you like them are also discussed.

Parents' Group.   Parents are educated about possible feelings their children may be experiencing as they are dealing with recovery from sexual abuse (i.e., anger, betrayal, fear, sadness, shame, guilt, helplessness). It is also noted that parents may experience similar emotions. The stages of grief are discussed in the context of child sexual abuse (i.e., shock/denial, anger, guilt/depression, bargaining, acceptance). A parent's version of the Hat Game is incorporated into the session to address these feelings. Examples of questions in the hat include: "Do you ever feel like you are a bad parent?" "Do you ever feel like the abuse was your fault?" "Do you ever feel like your friends look at you differently now?" Other group members are also welcome to comment on each parent's responses to the questions. After the Hat Game, the parents focus on the development of their children's peer relationships, including the benefits of their children having friends and the ways they may help promote healthy friendships.

Module 7: Learning to Cope With My Feelings

Goals. The primary goal of this session is to identify ways family members may deal with their feelings in a healthy manner. The relation between how individuals and the manner in which they behave are discussed, and education about feelings of anxiety and depression is provided. Specific coping skills as problem solving, relaxation training, and other forms of stress reduction are addressed.

Children's Group. The children learn about the relation between their mood and the behaviors they exhibit with the help of a "relationship between feelings and behavior" worksheet. Examples of questions on the worksheet include: "I find a place to be alone when I feel _____." or "When I feel confused I _____." How to recognize feelings in terms of bodily sensations (e.g., muscle tension, nervousness) are also discussed. Problem-solving skills and relaxation training skills are learned as ways to cope with feelings.

Parents' Group. The parents' group is given the "relation between feelings and behavior" worksheet and asked to respond to each of the questions as it pertains to their child. The parents also identify the relation between feelings and behavior as it pertains to themselves. They are asked how they behave within the family system when they are experiencing various emotions (e.g., anger, happiness, guilt). The group generates a list of coping techniques they find useful when they are experiencing distress. Techniques described include problem-focused coping (e.g., problem solving, finding more information), tension reduction and relaxation techniques (e.g., exercise, engaging in pleasurable activities), and using social support systems (e.g., friends, family, church, mental health professionals).

Module 8: Learning About Our Bodies

Goals. This session concentrates on learning correct information about sex, increasing comfort with dialogue in the family about sex-related issues, learning the difference between "good" and "bad" touches, improving the children's self-image, and correcting incorrect self-perceptions about "damaged goods."

Children's Group. The discussion of differentiating "good" and "bad" touches begins by identification of the private places on the body. The children then distinguish between the different types of touches, and scenarios are presented, such as "Is it O.K. for your mom or dad to pat you on the bottom?" "How about a neighbor or a friend?" "When is it O.K. and when is it not O.K.?" The children then discuss whether they feel that their bodies have changed since they have experienced a "bad" touch (i.e., their abuse) to gain insight into their bodily self-image and self-perceptions. Sex education concentrates on the natural curiosity children have about the body and sex, how boy's and girl's bodies are different, masturbation, what is homosexuality, and dating and relationships. Children also discuss what they like about being a boy or a girl and gender roles. Children discuss if girls can do the things they labeled as boy roles and vice versa. Children are reminded that there are only two group sessions remaining and discuss their feelings regarding termination.

Parents' Group. The parents' group focuses on increasing the parents' ability and comfort in discussing sexuality and other sex issues with their children. It is noted that different families have different opinions on various sex-related issues (e.g., masturbation, contraception, homosexuality), thus increasing the importance of discussing these issues directly with their children. The parents then discuss how issues of sex and sexuality are discussed within the family. Questions such as "Who in the family usually discusses such issues with the children?" and "How comfortable do you feel about discussing sex with your child?" are posed to the parents. Parents identify strategies to facilitate their discussions of sex with their children (e.g., when, where, with whom, doing what activity). The parents then role play responses to children's questions. The session also includes discussion about their children's body image at their stage of development and how sexual abuse may affect body image. Ways to enhance their children's body image and self-esteem are identified.

Module 9: Standing Up for Your Rights

Goals. This section was designed to help empower the children and teach them how to appropriately assert themselves with the hope of preventing future abuse. It also serves to identify support networks, reinforcing the notion that the children have people to turn to if something happens to them.

Children's Group. The children are led in a discussion on how to say "no" when someone does something they do not like or makes them feel uncomfortable. Reasons why they might not say "no" are discussed, like threats of harm or loss of love or friendship. The children are then read the story "Just In Case" (Wachter, 1983) to illustrate that children can and do say "no" to adults. Role-play scenarios give the children the opportunity to practice saying "no," and the therapists and other group members can help give suggestions and model assertiveness and problem-solving skills. The topic then switches to "what if something bad happens again." The emphasis remains on who would the child tell. The final discussion is used to process issues surrounding the upcoming termination of the group.

Parents' Group. The parents hear the story "Just in Case" (Wachter, 1983) and some of the role-play scenarios in which the children are participating. Parents discuss how they can help enhance their children's support networks to ensure the children know there are people available who will listen to them. A brief overview of assertiveness training is presented and the parents discuss the difference between assertion, aggression, and defiance. Parents are encouraged to think about how they respond to their children's assertiveness (e.g., do they view it as defiance?). Prevention issues are also addressed. Parents are asked to generate ways of preventing future abuse, and therapists add any methods that are left out. Termination of treatment is also discussed, and alternative avenues of support for the families are explored.

Module 10: Good-bye

Goals.   This final section provides a summary of the group experience and discusses ways of maintaining gains and coping with separation.

Children's Group.   The children review the information covered over the past months in a game format. A "Jeopardy" type board is used with categories such as "Understanding and Recognizing Feelings," "Sharing What Happened," "Learning about Our Bodies," and so on. Children answer questions as if contestants on a game show and every child is able to win a prize. The children are then given the opportunity to say what they liked or disliked about the group, as well as what they learned. The discussion turns to what they will miss about the group and how they will cope without it (e.g., journals, friends, etc.). The parents and children then join together for a party to celebrate how hard everyone has worked and to help give some closure to the sessions.

Parents' Group.   The parents review some of the major themes of the group and discuss what they did and did not like about this therapy process. They are asked to focus on the changes that they have seen in their children and themselves. If necessary, referral sources are discussed. The parents then join the children for the party.

MAINTENANCE AND GENERALIZATION STRATEGIES

Use of relevant and effective treatment strategies is, of course, the most critical part of achieving lasting, generalized impact. In addition, a variety of techniques designed to promote maintenance and generalization has been incorporated into the treatment protocol.

Full involvement of the parents and children in treatment is essential for treatment success. Three types of treatment adherence are needed: attending sessions regularly, participating within sessions, and completing out-of-session assignments or tasks (e.g., using skills learned, etc.). Strategies to facilitate adherence include mailing reminder postcards so that they arrive the day before each group session, providing childcare for younger children who are not participating in treatment, contracting with parents and children to attend all session, and maintaining the attention of group members by keeping all members involved. Use of procedures that are acceptable to the clients (i.e., socially valid) facilitate continued participation in treatment. Parents and children have found the goals of treatment, the group approach, the education and skills training procedures, and the effects of participation acceptable.

Involvement of the parents in treatment is probably the most important strategy for enhancing maintenance and generalization. Several factors associated with parallel treatment of the parents are important for generalization, including the following:

1. Parents are the persons who are responsible for the health, well-being, and safety of the child, and are generally with the child more than any other adult. They are going to be most able to identify and address problems that may arise, both during and long after treatment .

2. The family, as well as the child victim, might have faulty attributions about the abuse and the child that need to be addressed (Berliner, 1991). For example, it can be very helpful to deal with the parents' expectations and anxiety about the impact of the abuse on their child.

Parents sometimes have extreme perspectives on the consequences of abuse (e.g., "My child has been damaged and will never fully recover from this.") Or the parents may hold very specific beliefs about the short- and long-term consequences of the abuse that may lead to self-fulfilling prophecies. For example, if it is believed the child will have a fear of males, behaviors may be mistakenly labeled as fearful, the child may be told that she is afraid of males, the child's expectations about herself and males may change over time, and this may eventually facilitate the development of a significant fear of males.

3. It is often found that the mothers have been sexually abused themselves and they need to work through their own trauma again so that they can be helpful to their children (Damon & Waterman, 1986). Involvement of the parents in therapy allows for the communication of this possibility to the parents, for screening for the presence of such problems, and for making necessary referrals for treatment.

4. The parent's need for treatment may go beyond dealing with their abuse history. Mothers and children often share common issues with respect to the abuse (e.g., guilt, shame, concerns about others' views, etc.) and it can be very useful to address them directly and simultaneously (Damon & Waterman, 1986). Parents are better able to deal with the child's feelings of guilt, shame, and so on, if they are learning (or have learned) to deal with such feelings.

5. There is often an impaired relationship between child victims and their mothers, especially in incest cases, and it is often unclear whether symptoms in these children are directly a result of the abuse or more globally a byproduct of family pathology (Berliner, 1991). Involvement of parents in treatment facilitates the identification and remediation of these issues, which should hopefully lead to more lasting and generalized effects.

6. Because intervention can produce fast and powerful results, it is useful to involve the parents and keep them up to date on the child's treatment so that they can respond better to changes at home and enhance the therapeutic process (Damon & Waterman, 1986).

The group format is also useful for enhancing the generalization of treatment. Group intervention may facilitate generalization through exposure to increased stimulus and response exemplars (Stokes & Osnes, 1989). For instance, there is increased exposure to the problems, strategies, and solutions of others; additional opportunity for modeling of appropriate behaviors and responses; opportunities to rehearse skills with more individuals; and extensive opportunity for feedback and reinforcement from group members as well as the therapist. The emotional support provided by the group has immediate effects that may ultimately facilitate generalization and maintenance by facilitating continued involvement of the parents and children in therapy.

Another strategy for enhancing generalization and maintenance is teaching general strategies for problem solving and coping (Stokes & Osnes, 1989). As parents and children, together or separately, encounter reoccurring or new problems posttreatment, they should be able to adapt the general strategies learned in group to these new situations.

PROBLEMS IN IMPLEMENTATION

Although the treatment procedures have been repeatedly revised and refined, there always are problems that will arise in implementing the intervention. The major issues are listed here:

1. Recruiting sufficient numbers of families to have homogeneous groups of three or more children (e.g., same gender, small age range) may be a challenge, depending on size of the community, the availability of other services, and so on.

2. Many parents do not have sufficient childcare resources and need to bring younger, nonabused children to the clinic during sessions. Providing childcare for younger children not involved in treatment is helpful to facilitate recruitment and ongoing participation of families.

3. Lack of transportation to sessions can be a problem for some families. Holding sessions in a facility near a bus route (or other mass transit) can be useful. Providing reimbursement for transportation expenses, or even providing transportation to families in need, can be even more valuable.

4. As noted previously, failure to attend sessions due to forgetting, other conflicts, and so forth, can happen. It can be useful to contract with parents and children to attend all sessions, including having everyone in group sign a contract. Other strategies include sending reminder postcards prior to each session and finding an opportune time to hold sessions (e.g., after school for children and work for most parents, yet not too late).

5. It can be difficult to have the group(s) run smoothly if families miss a session. Catching families up can be done by holding a separate session, such as asking the family to arrive early before the next group, or reviewing the prior session content in detail during the group session.

6. Participation of all members during sessions can be difficult to achieve. It has been valuable to establish group rules (e.g., arriving on time, not interrupting others, etc.) and to maintain attention within session by taking turns. To keep members sharing and participating, group members are told they must say something other than "I don't know" when asked.

7. Disruptive children can create significant problems. Sometimes the disruptiveness can occur because the content of the sessions upsets the youth; at other times, the disruptiveness may be merely the result of behavior problems. Having siblings in a group can cause additional difficulties because of the family dynamics (e.g., they may tease one another) or because of different reactions and perspectives on shared experiences (e.g., they may have been abused by the same offender). Use of cotherapists to lead groups is ideal for being able to handle disruptions (e.g., for time outs). Cotherapists are also useful for continuity in case of therapist illness.

8. Leaving sufficient time at the end of the session to allow time for winding down is critical, especially for the children. It is nice to have a snack and more general play or talk time to allow them to step away from the problems of sexual abuse and feel more like a kid.

9. A setting with sufficient space is needed, including two rooms large enough for groups. In addition, as the children's group can get rather loud (e.g., from disruptive children, or youthful exuberance), it is helpful to have the sessions in a location where the noise will not disrupt other clinical work.

10. Keeping the parents informed about the content of the children's sessions, the progress of the children, is valuable to alleviate parental anxiety about the children. Individual feedback to parents can also be useful, especially posttreatment.

CASE ILLUSTRATION

The treatment protocol was designed primarily for use in small groups, but it may be applied to families or even individuals. Application of the protocol with a family is described in the following illustration to allow a more specific and personal description of the issues and procedures.

The family was referred to the outpatient university-based clinic for treatment of sexual abuse issues by an in-home therapist from another agency, who conducted parent training and family interventions. Mr. and Mrs. P. have four children: Steve (age 9), Gary (age 8), Billy (age 6), and Brian (age 2). Mr. P. Also has a daughter, Karen (age 17), from a previous relationship. Mrs. P. does not work outside of the home and Mr. P. works as a construction worker.

Steve, Gary, and Billy were sexually abused by their half sister, Karen, when they were 5, 4, and 1 year old, respectively. Karen was 13 years old and was living in their home at the time. Abuse consisted of exposure, fondling, oral contact, and digital-anal penetration and lasted for a period of approximately 3 months. The older boys had some memories of this and remember talking to the authorities about the abuse. After disclosure, Mrs. P. recalls responding with shock, guilt, and especially anger. Mr. P. was also quite angry at that time.

Approximately 6 months prior to treatment, Steve, Gary, and Billy disclosed that they had been sexually abused by an older neighborhood boy, Sam (age 13). The boys previously viewed Sam as a friend. Abuse consisted of being exposed to sexually explicit material, exposure and fondling, watching others engaged in sexual acts, oral sex, and anal intercourse. Such abuse lasted for approximately 5 months. Mrs. P. recognized that the boys' behavior had changed around the time they initially disclosed the abuse. Steve began acting out more, Gary became more withdrawn, and Billy became more sensitive and cried more often.

Mr. and Mrs. P. arrived at the initial assessment session with their four boys. Mr. P. appeared very impatient and frustrated with the assessment procedures. Mrs. P. tried to engage him in the process and urged him to be patient. Mrs. P. was cooperative with the assessment, but asked many questions about the measures. The boys were quite active, and appeared to enjoy taking turns reading aloud and filling out the questionnaires. When assessment questions asked about certain sexual issues or fears, the boys appeared to be distressed and fearful: Steve tended to antagonize his brothers; Gary was anxious and afraid to walk down the hall where there were undergraduate students waiting for class; Billy became quiet and sought comfort from an adult.

Billy's self-report did not provide an accurate assessment, given that he did not appear to understand many of the measures. Overall, the child report measures suggested the boys were experiencing some anxieties and fears related to their victimization. Specifically, they reported difficulty sleeping, feeling uncomfortable around other people, having intrusive thoughts about the abuse, and low self-esteem. Gary reported many more symptoms and fears than either of his brothers. He reported clinical levels of depressive and anxious symptoms on the Children's Depression Inventory and the Revised Children's Manifest Anxiety Scale. Parental reports of the children's behavior on the Child Behavior Checklist also reflected that Gary had more severe problems than either of his brothers. Mr. and Mrs. P. reported that none of their children were currently acting out in a sexual manner.

After the initial assessment session, Mr. P. did not return until near the midpoint of treatment. He returned for one session, stating it was to show the boys the he "cared." As a possible explanation for his not returning, Mrs. P. reported that her husband avoids thinking about or discussing the issue of sexual abuse.

Mrs. P. reported feelings of self-blame and anger as her primary reactions to her children's abuse. She also expressed fears regarding sexual abuse affecting her children's development. Mrs. P. appeared protective of her children, as evidenced by her not being able to concentrate and feeling distressed when hearing her children crying or acting out behaviorally (e.g., yelling) in the adjacent therapy room. Mrs. P. appeared overwhelmed in dealing with daily stressors and managing her children.

Mrs. P. reported that initially the boys did not like coming to therapy and they often acted up when she was trying to get them ready to leave home. The boys, however, would generally happily enter the clinic, hug the therapist, and work well throughout the session. When they did act out in sessions, it appeared to be primarily a result of their interactions as siblings rather than distress over the subject matter. Time-out procedures were introduced, but were never really necessary after each boy had received one or two time-outs.

The boys' behavior in session did deteriorate when the issue of sexual abuse and secrets was brought up (Module 3). They became unmanageable and distracted, and were unable to complete the session. Steve got angry or defiant. Gary would either make distracting noises or become very withdrawn. Billy would often climb under his chair. The boys would respond to questions, however, and these behaviors were viewed as their reactions to upsetting session content. The boys' negative behaviors decreased as therapy continued, and they were able to participate in discussions about the abuse that lasted almost the entire session. Their in-home therapist reported they were better able to initiate discussions with her regarding their abuse, as well.

As discussion about sexual abuse disclosure continued, Mrs. P. verbalized increased feelings of anger, frustration, and helplessness. Mrs. P. and the family also missed many sessions during this phase of therapy due to either forgetting to attend session or illnesses in the family. When they did attend, Mrs. P. spent the first part of the session venting about stressful events in her life or her feeling angry and victimized by the police, the legal system, and society. At times she also expressed dissatisfaction over therapy due to her perception of the boys' increased acting out behavior and teasing one another at home and at school. Mrs. P. was angry that she and her family had to spend time and energy attending therapy while the perpetrators were currently free without consequences and changes in their lifestyles. Mrs. P.'s own history of child sexual abuse was discussed at this time in relation to her children's victimization.

Shortly after completion of the disclosure phase, Mrs. P. became more invested in the therapeutic process, as demonstrated by increased attendance and participation in sessions. She was better able to attend to the issues at hand and actively participated in discussions. She was particularly active in identifying coping strategies to assist her in dealing with stressors, as well as in identifying social support systems for her and her family. She also allowed herself to go out with a friend one night, an activity in which she rarely engaged. Mrs. P. actively participated in providing the therapists with insights and feedback regarding issues to address with the boys, as well as behavior management techniques that could be used by the therapists in the therapy sessions.

The boys all felt their family was supportive of them throughout this process. They were upset, to varying degrees, about the loss of their friend Sam. They all felt they could have stopped the abuse if they had just told Sam to stop. This was especially true for Steve, who felt like he was "dumb" because he let it happen. Steve, Gary, and Billy feared their friends would think they were "stupid" if they find out about the abuse. The boys seemed to respond very positively to stories and role plays that showed other children were abused and had some of the same feelings that they have. As therapy progressed, the boys began to spontaneously correct their own irrational beliefs.

By the end of treatment, the boys were better able to talk about sexual abuse and share their feelings about what happened, and had increased their knowledge and skills about how to protect themselves in the future. All three boys exhibited fewer behavior problems and Gary showed decreased anxiety and depressive symptoms. The boys had an improved understanding that the sex abuse was not their fault and were experiencing improved self-esteem. Communication improved between the mother and boys on issues related to sex and sexual abuse. Mrs. P. had seen positive changes in the boys behavior and reported fewer concerns about the impact of the abuse on her children's development. Mrs. P. seemed less distressed about her boys, and more optimistic about the boys' ability to deal with their abuse experiences and to respond effectively in possible abuse situations in the future. Mrs. P. and her sons evaluated the goals, procedures, and effects of treatment positively.

CONCLUSIONS

Child sexual abuse is a widespread problem with serious and varied consequences. Despite the increased attention to the problem in recent decades, there is still much to learn about providing effective treatment. This chapter describes a standardized treatment protocol, based on research and experience, and evaluated in a clinical treatment setting. A parallel group format for parents and children is used, with intervention procedures of education, skill building, problem solving, and support. Given space limitations, only brief summaries of the treatment modules are provided. A detailed treatment manual is available from the authors on request. Treatment was designed primarily for sexually abused children, age 8 to 12, and their nonabusive parents. It can be generalized to older and younger ages, as well as adapted for smaller groups, including siblings. Much of the protocol (e.g., the educational content and many of the activities) can be useful for work with individuals as well.

REFERENCES

Abidin, R. R. (1986). *Parenting Stress Index* (2nd ed.). Charlottesville, VA: Pediatric Psychology Press.

Achenbach, T. M. (1991). *Manual for the Child Behavior Checklist/4-18 and 1991 Profile*. Burlington: University of Vermont.

Berliner, L. (1991). Therapy with victimized children and their families. *New Directions for Mental Health Services*, *51*, 29–46.

Beutler, L. E., Williams, R. E., & Zetzer, H. A. (1994). Efficacy of treatment for victims of child sexual abuse. *The Future of Children*, *4*, 156–175

Briere, J. N. (1992). *Child abuse trauma: Theory and treatment of the lasting effects*. Newbury Park, CA: Sage.

Browne, A., & Finkelhor, D. (1986a). Impact of child sexual abuse: A review of the research. *Psychological Bulletin*, *99*, 66–77.

Browne, A., & Finkelhor, D. (1986b). Initial and long-term effects: A review of the research. In D. Finkelhor (Ed.), *A sourcebook on child sexual abuse* (pp. 143–179). Beverly Hills, CA: Sage.

Chambless, D. L., Sanderson, W. S., Shoham, V., Johnson, S. B., Pope, K. S., Crits-Christoph, P., Baker, M., Johnson, B., Woody, S. R., Sue, S., Buetler, L., Williams, D. A., & McCurry, S. (1996). An update on empirically validated therapies. *The Clinical Psychologist*, *49*(2), 5–18.

Conte, J. R. (1985). The effects of sexual abuse on children. A critique and suggestions for future research. *Victimology*, *10*, 110–130.

Conte, J. R. (1990). Victims of child sexual abuse. In R. T. Ammerman & M. Hersen (Eds.), *Treatment of family violence: A sourcebook* (pp. 50–76). New York: Wiley.

Corder, B. F., Haizlip, T., & DeBoer, P. (1990). A pilot study for a structured, time-limited therapy group for sexually abused pre-adolescent children. *Child Abuse and Neglect, 14*, 243–251.

Coopersmith, S. (1981). *Self-esteem inventories*. Palo Alto, CA: Consulting Psychologists Press.

Damon, L. L., & Card, J. A. (1992). Incest in young children. In R. T. Ammerman & M. Hersen (Eds.), *Assessment of family violence: A clinical and legal sourcebook* (pp. 148–172). New York: Wiley.

Damon, L., & Waterman, J. (1986). Parallel group treatment of children and their mothers. In K. MacFarlane & J. Waterman (Eds.), *Sexual abuse of young children* (pp. 244–298). New York: Guilford.

Davies, M. G. (1995). Parental distress and ability to cope following disclosure of extrafamilial sexual abuse. *Child Abuse and Neglect, 19*, 399–408.

Deblinger, E., McLeer, S. V., & Henry, D. (1990). Cognitive behavioral treatment for sexually abused children suffering post-traumatic stress: Preliminary findings. *Journal of the American Academy of Child and Adolescent Psychiatry, 29*, 747–752.

Derogatis, L. R. (1994). *SCL–90–R: Administration, scoring, and procedures manual* (3rd ed.). Towson, MD: Clinical Psychometric Research.

deYoung, M., & Corbin, B. A. (1994). Helping early adolescents tell: A guided exercise for trauma-focused sexual abuse treatment groups. *Child Welfare League of America, 73*, 141–154.

Einbender, A. J., & Friedrich, W. N. (1989). Psychological functioning and behavior of sexually abused girls. *Journal of Consulting and Clinical Psychology, 57*, 155–157.

Everson, M. D., Hunter, W. M., Runyon, D. K., Edelsohn, G. A., & Coulter, M. L. (1989). Maternal support following disclosure of incest. *American Journal of Orthopsychiatry, 59*, 197–207.

Faller, K. C. (1993). *Child sexual abuse: Intervention and treatment issues*. Washington, DC: U.S. Department of Health and Human Services.

Finkelhor, D. (1990). Early and long-term effects of child sexual abuse: An update. *Professional Psychology: Research and Practice, 21*, 325–330.

Finkelhor, D., & Browne, A. (1985). The traumatic impact of sexual abuse: A conceptualization. *American Journal of Orthopsychiatry, 55*, 530–541.

Friedrich, W. N. (1990). *Psychotherapy of sexually abused children and their families*. New York: Norton.

Friedrich, W. N., Beilke, R. L., & Urquiza, A. J. (1987). Children from sexually abusive families: A behavioral comparison. *Journal of Interpersonal Violence, 2*, 391–402.

Friedrich, W. N., Grambsch, P., Damon, L., Hewitt, S. K., Koverola, C., Lang, R. A., Wolfe, V., & Broughton, D. (1992). Child Sexual Behavior Inventory: Normative and clinical comparisons. *Psychological Assessment, 4*, 303–311.

Friedrich, W. N., Luecke, W. J., Beilke, R. L., Place, V. (1992). Psychotherapy outcome of sexually abused boys. *Journal of Interpersonal Violence, 7*, 396–409.

Friedrich, W. N., & Reams, R. A. (1987). Course of psychological symptoms in sexually abused young children. *Psychotherapy, 24*, 160–170.

Futa, K. T., Hecht, D. B., & Hansen, D. J. (1996, November). Working with sexually abused children and their nonoffending parents: A conceptualization and treatment. In J. R. Lutzker (Chair), *Child abuse and neglect: The cutting edge*. Symposium conducted at the meeting of the Association for the Advancement of Behavior Therapy, New York.

Gold, S. R., Milan, L. D., Mayall, A., & Johnson, A. E. (1994). A cross-validation study of the trauma symptom checklist. *Journal of Interpersonal Violence, 9*, 12–26.

Hecht, D. B., Futa, K. T., & Hansen, D. J. (1995, November). *A qualitative analysis of group therapy for sexually abused children and adolescents: How prior treatments can guide future interventions*. Paper presented at the Association for the Advancement of Behavior Therapy Convention, Washington, DC.

Hecht, D. B., Futa, K. T., & Hansen, D. J. (1996, November). *Group treatment for sexually abused children and their nonoffending parents: Development and initial evaluation of a standardized treatment protocol*. Paper presented at the Association for the Advancement of Behavior Therapy Convention, New York.

Hiebert-Murphy, D., DeLuca, R. V., & Runtz, M. (1992). Group treatment for sexually abused girls: Evaluating outcome. *Families in Society: The Journal of Contemporary Human Services, 73*, 205–213.

Kazdin, A. E., Rogers, A., & Colbus, D. (1986). The hopelessness scale for children: Psychometric characteristics and concurrent validity. *Journal of Consulting and Clinical Psychology, 54*, 241–245.

Kitchur, M., & Bell, R. (1989). Group psychotherapy with preadolescent sexual abuse victims: Literature review and description of an inner-city group. *International Journal of Group Psychotherapy, 39*, 285–310.

Kovacs, M. (1992). *Children's Depression Inventory*. Canada: Multi-Health Systems.

Livingston, R. (1987). Sexually and physically abused children. *Journal of the American Academy of Child and Adolescent Psychiatry, 26*, 413–415.

Malinosky-Rummell, R. R. (1992). *Relationship of childhood physical abuse with college women's self-reported interpersonal behavior and ratings of assertiveness, passiveness, and aggressiveness in heterosexual interactions.* Unpublished doctoral dissertation, West Virginia University, Morgantown.

Mandell, J. G., & Damon, L. (1989). *Group treatment for sexually abused children.* New York: Guilford.

McCubbin, H. I., Larsen, A. S., Olson, D. H. (1982). F–COPES: Family coping strategies. In D. H. Olson, H. I. McCubbin, H. Barnes., A. Larsen, M. Muxen, & M. Wilson (Eds.), *Family inventories: Inventories used in a national survey of families across the family life cycle* (pp. 101–119). St. Paul: University of Minnesota.

McCubbin, H. I., Olson, D. H., & Larsen, A. S. (1987). F–COPES: Family Crisis Oriented Personal Evaluation Scales. In H. I. McCubbin & A. I. Thompson (Eds.), *Family assessment inventories for research and practice* (pp. 259–270). Madison: University of Wisconsin.

McClellan, J., Adams, J., Douglas, D., McCurry, C., & Storck, M. (1995). Clinical characteristics related to severity of sexual abuse: A study of seriously mentally ill youth. *Child Abuse and Neglect, 19*, 1245–1254.

Mrazek, P. B., & Mrazek, D. A. (1981). The effects of child sexual abuse: Methodological considerations. In P. B. Mrazek & C. H. Kempe (Eds.), *Sexually abused children and their families* (pp. 236–245). New York: Pergamon.

National Center on Child Abuse and Neglect (1988). *Study of national incidence and prevalence of child abuse and neglect: 1986.* Washington, DC: U.S. Department of Health and Human Services.

National Center on Child Abuse and Neglect (1995). *Child maltreatment 1993: Reports from the States to the National Center on Child Abuse and Neglect.* Washington, DC: U.S. Department of Health and Human Services.

National Center on Child Abuse and Neglect. (1996). *Child maltreatment 1994: Reports from the States to the National Center on Child Abuse and Neglect.* Washington, DC: U.S. Department of Health and Human Services.

Newberger, C. M., & De Vos, E. (1988). Abuse and victimization: A life-span developmental perspective. *American Journal of Orthopsychiatry, 58*, 505–511.

O'Donohue, W. T., & Elliot, A. N. (1992). Treatment of the sexually abused child: A review. *Journal of Clinical Child Psychology, 21*, 218–228.

Ollendick, T. H. (1983). Reliability and validity of the revised fear survey schedule for children (FSSC–R). *Behaviour Research and Therapy, 21*, 685–692.

Olson, D. H. (1986). Circumplex Model VII: Validation studies and FACES III. *Family Process, 25*, 337–350.

Reynolds, C. R., & Richmond, B. O. (1978). What I think and feel: A revised measure of children's manifest anxiety. *Journal of Abnormal Child Psychology, 6*, 271–280.

Spaccarelli, S. (1994). Stress, appraisal, and coping in child sexual abuse: A theoretical and empirical review. *Psychological Bulletin, 116*, 340–362.

Stokes, T. F., & Osnes, P. G. (1989). An operant pursuit of generalization. *Behavior Therapy, 20*, 337–355.

Task Force on Promotion and Dissemination of Psychological Procedures. (1995). Training in and dissemination of empirically-validated psychological treatments: Report and recommendations. *The Clinical Psychologist, 48* (1), 3–23.

Terkel, S. N., & Rench, J. E. (1984). *Feeling safe, feeling strong: How to avoid sexual abuse and what to do if it happens to you.* Minneapolis: Lerner Publications.

Tong, L., Oates, K., & McDowell, M. (1987). Personality development following sexual abuse. *Child Abuse and Neglect, 11*, 371–383.

Wachter, O. (1983). *No more secrets for me.* Boston: Little, Brown.

Wagner, W. G., Kilcrease-Fleming, D., Fowler, W. E., & Kazelskis, R. (1993). Brief-term counseling with sexually abused girls: The impact of sex of counselor on clients' therapeutic involvement, self-concept, and depression. *Journal of Counseling Psychology, 40*, 490–500.

Weisz, J. R., Weiss, B., & Donenberg, G. R. (1992). The lab versus the clinic: Effects of child and adolescent psychotherapy. *American Psychologist, 47*, 1578–1585.

Wells, R. D., McCann, J., Adams, J., Voris, J., & Ensign, J. (1995). Emotional, behavioral, and physical symptoms reported by parents of sexually abused, nonabused, and allegedly abused prepubescent females. *Child Abuse and Neglect, 19*, 155–163.

Wolfe, V. V., Gentile, C., & Klink, A. (1988). *Psychometric properties of the sexual abuse fear evaluation (SAFE).* Unpublished manuscript, University of Western Ontario, London, Ontario.

Wolfe, V. V., Gentile, C., Michienzi, T., Sas, L., & Wolfe, D. A. (1991). The Children's Impact of Traumatic Events Scale: A measure of post-sexual-abuse PTSD symptoms. *Behavioral Assessment, 13,* 359–383.

Wolfe, V. V., & Wolfe, D. A. (1986). *The Sexual Abuse Fear Evaluation (SAFE): A subscale for the Fear Survey Schedule for Children–Revised.* Unpublished questionnaire, Children's Hospital of Western Ontario, London, Ontario.

Wolfe, V. V., & Wolfe, D. A. (1988). The sexually abused child. In E. J. Mash & L. G. Terdal (Eds.), *Behavioral assessment of childhood disorders* (2nd ed., pp. 670–714). New York: Guilford.

Wozencraft, T., Wagner, W., & Pelligrin, A. (1991). Depression and suicidal ideation in sexually abused children. *Child Abuse and Neglect, 15,* 505–511.

Chapter 7

Childhood Obesity

Lucene Wisniewski
Marsha D. Marcus
University of Pittsburgh Medical Center

DESCRIPTION OF PEDIATRIC OBESITY

There is an alarmingly high prevalence of obesity in children and adolescents in the United States and these rates are increasing. Between 1976 and 1980, prevalence of pediatric obesity was estimated to be 17% (McDowell, Engel, Massey, & Maurer, 1981), and more recent data suggest that approximately 22% of individuals between 6 and 17 years old are overweight (Troiano, Flegal, Kuczmarski, Campbell, & Johnson, 1995). Thus, the rate of obesity in young people has dramatically increased, especially over the past 10 years (Troiano et al., 1995). The increased prevalence of childhood obesity is of concern due to its relation with obesity-related morbidity, long-term psychosocial consequences, and adult overweight. Most importantly, in contrast to the poor outcome of obesity in adults, *efficacious* treatments have been developed for overweight children (e.g., Epstein, Valoski, Wing, & McCurley, 1990, 1994).

Contrary to previous beliefs, pediatric obesity is related to considerable morbidity across the lifespan. Greater overweight is associated with higher blood pressure, even in children as young as 5 and 6 years old (Gutin et al., 1990), and adolescent obesity predicts adverse health effects in adulthood (Must, Jacques, Dallal, Bajema, & Dietz, 1992). Moreover, increased mortality due to cardiovascular disease has been found in the adult relatives of persistently obese children (Burns, Moll, & Lauer, 1992). Such a relation between childhood obesity and family mortality appears to be especially strong if the obese child also has elevated blood pressure.

The obese child suffers both short- and long-term psychosocial consequences related to weight status. Specifically, obese children have been found to be the victims of social stigmatization (Counts, Jones, Frame, Jarvie, & Strauss, 1986; Goodman, Richardson, Dornbusch, & Hastorf, 1963; Strauss, Smith, Frame, & Forehand, 1985), and themselves endorse negative stereotypes of obese individuals (Counts et al., 1986). It is not surprising, then, that a recent review of the literature found the self-esteem of obese children to be poorer than that of their nonobese peers (French, Story, & Perry, 1995). The psychosocial consequences of pediatric obesity are not limited to childhood. Research has shown that adult women who were overweight as adolescents, when compared to normal weight peers, had completed fewer years of school, were less likely to be married, had lower household income, and had higher rates of household poverty (Gortmaker, Must, Perrin, Sobol, & Dietz, 1993). Males who were overweight as adolescents were less likely to be married than nonoverweight men (Gortmaker et al., 1993).

Children do not "outgrow" their obesity, because many obese children remain obese (Webber, Freedman, & Cresanta, 1986), and childhood weight is related to adult weight (Guo, Roche, Chumlea, Siervogel, & Gardner, 1994). Children who have a family history of overweight may be at particular risk for adult obesity as the relation between childhood and adult obesity is especially strong if at least one parent is obese (Charney, Goodman, McBride, Lyon, & Pratt, 1976).

Despite compelling evidence of psychosocial and medical morbidity related to pediatric obesity, its treatment remains controversial. Some have argued that it is not judicious to treat overweight in children (Mallick, 1983), warning that dieting may negatively affect growth and contribute to the development of eating disorders. Although there are some data indicating a decrease in growth rate during moderate calorie restriction (Dietz & Hartung, 1985), most studies have demonstrated that moderate calorie restriction does not affect long-term growth (Epstein, McCurley, Valoski, & Wing, 1990; Epstein, Valoski, & McCurley, 1993; Epstein, Wing, Koeske, & Valoski, 1986). Further, although stringent calorie restriction may be inadvisable, available data suggest that moderate dieting in normal weight adolescents is not associated with eating disorder symptoms (Neumark-Sztainer, Butler, & Palti, 1995). Also, there is no evidence that moderate decreases in intake and increases in activity enhance the risk of disordered eating in obese children (Epstein, Valoski, et al., 1994).

Given the consequences of pediatric obesity, and that most children will not outgrow their obesity, an aggressive approach to treating childhood obesity must be considered to reduce the probability of a lifelong struggle with weight. Fortunately, safe and effective weight control programs have been designed for the treatment of moderately obese children. In some behavioral, family-based, treatment programs, weight losses have been maintained for up to 5 (Epstein, McCurley, Wing, & Valoski, 1990) and 10 years posttreatment (Epstein, Valoski, et al., 1990,1994). These long-term successes are even more striking in light of the poor outcome found in the treatment of adult obesity (National Institutes of Health, 1992).

This chapter provides the information necessary to conduct a full assessment of obesity and obesity-related behaviors in children as well as the practical and theoretical information essential for the provision of treatment. This chapter also discusses issues relating to the provision of treatment to minority children, children who are severely obese, and children who may have psychiatric difficulties. Finally, a case study is included detailing typical difficulties encountered in the implementation of this treatment.

ASSESSMENT METHODS

As is discussed in greater detail, a behavior change program designed to target pediatric obesity must focus on modifying eating and exercise-related behaviors. The assessment of obesity, eating, and exercise is therefore critical to ensure an adequate behavioral analysis and to monitor change.

Defining Obesity in Children

There is no globally accepted definition of obesity for the pediatric population. In adults, the definition of obesity is governed by actuarial estimates of the relation between given weights for height and morbidity and mortality (e.g., Metropolitan Life Insurance Company, 1983). As there are currently few data that correlate childhood obesity and mortality rates, a statistical definition has been adopted. For example, childhood overweight may be defined as body weight at or above the 85th percentile compared to the *statistically normative values* for other children of the same age, height, and gender. A statistical definition of obesity has implications for prevalence estimates, because at any given time only 15% of children can be considered obese. Furthermore, the statistical boundary for obesity may fluctuate depending on the assessment measure used, as some have recommended that scores at or above the 95th percentile of body mass index (BMI) indicate obesity (Hammer, Kraemer, Wilson, Ritter, & Dornbusch, 1991).

Although the term *obesity* generally refers to an excess of *body fat*, there is no direct method of assessing body fat in living people. Overweight therefore usually is indexed in terms of weight. Overweight is used as an estimate of body fat based on the assumption that variations in weight for a given height are predominantly due to differences in body fat (Flegal, 1993). Consequently, for a definition of obesity to be considered adequate, it must be related to an individual's degree of body fat.

Assessment of Obesity

The assessment of body weight in and of itself is quite simple, as a well calibrated, reliable scale is the only equipment necessary to determine a child's weight. However, weight alone does not impart a complete clinical picture, and it is important to consider the height, age, and gender of the child as well. For example, the fact that a new patient weighs 110 lb provides little information about this child's weight status. Different conclusions will be drawn if the 110-lb child is an 8-year-old girl measuring 49 inches than if the child is a 12-year-old boy measuring 62 inches. The determination of obesity involves calculations that consider height, age, and gender.

Body weight is the most commonly used and easily available measurement for the assessment of pediatric obesity. Height and weight data from the National Health and Nutrition Examination Survey (NHANES; Hamill et al., 1979) have been used to develop growth charts based on the measurements of a large sample of U.S. children. Weights falling at or above the 85th percentile on these charts are considered to reflect obesity. By following these charts, an individual's percentage overweight can be determined using the following equation: [(real weight − ideal weight)/ideal weight] x 100, where "ideal" refers to weights at the 50th percentile for children of the same age, height, and gender as the index child.

An individual's weight alone may not provide a complete clinical picture, as weight and height charts do not consider body build or body fatness. The body mass index (BMI), which approximates the linear relation between height and weight (Weill, 1977), is another widely used measure of obesity in both children and adults, and has been significantly correlated both with subcutaneous and total body fatness (Duerenberg, Weststrate, & Seidell, 1991; Roche, Siervogel, Chumlea, & Webb, 1981). BMI is easy to use, as it is readily computed from measured height and weight [BMI = weight (kg)/height $(m)^2$]. As can be seen in Table 7.1, normative BMI scores vary as a function of age and gender (Must, Dallal, & Dietz, 1991). This table may be used as a reference to evaluate obesity in children and adolescents.

Measurement of skinfold thickness has been used to approximate body fat on the basis of the established correlations between skinfolds at specific sites and total body fat (Durnin & Womersley, 1974). However, without adequate training in the use of this technique, the information obtained can be unreliable, especially in obese individuals (Forbes, 1964).

Finally, although there are other, more sophisticated ways to assess obesity in children (e.g., underwater weighing, electrical impedance), for practical clinical purposes it has been suggested that weight and BMI give adequate estimates of obesity (Wardle, 1995). Highly accurate assessment of a child's obesity is not necessary, as most children who seek treatment for weight control will be significantly overweight and therefore easy to detect. Indeed, there is a significant correlation between the visual assessment of obesity and tricep skinfold thickness beyond the 85th percentile (Rauh & Scvhumsky,1969).

Assessment of Eating

Commonly used research assessments of eating include the 24-hour recall, 3-day food record, and food frequency questionnaires (see Crawford, Obarzanek, Morrison, & Sabry, 1994, for a discussion of these methods). For clinical purposes, however, daily self-monitoring of eating and drinking behavior is sufficient. It is important to be aware, however, that many individuals (Klesges, Eck, & Ray, 1995), particularly those who are overweight (Lichtman et al., 1992), underreport dietary intake.

When assessing eating behavior, the child is asked to report the what, where, when, and how much of daily intake. The particulars of this method are discussed further in the self-monitoring section of this chapter and an example is shown in Fig. 7.1. During the

TABLE 7.1
50th, 85th, 95th Percentiles of Body Mass Index for Children Age 6–18

Age	Males Percentiles			Females Percentiles		
	50th	85th	95th	50th	85th	95th
6	14.54	16.64	18.02	14.31	16.17	17.49
7	15.07	17.37	19.19	14.98	17.17	18.93
8	15.62	18.11	20.33	15.66	18.18	20.36
9	16.17	18.85	21.47	16.33	19.19	21.78
10	16.72	19.60	22.60	17.00	20.19	23.20
11	17.28	20.35	23.73	17.67	21.18	24.59
12	17.87	21.12	24.89	18.35	22.17	25.95
13	18.53	21.93	25.93	18.95	23.08	27.07
14	19.22	22.77	26.93	19.32	23.88	27.97
15	19.92	23.63	27.76	19.69	24.29	28.51
16	20.63	24.45	28.53	20.09	24.74	29.10
17	21.12	25.28	29.32	20.36	25.23	29.72
18	21.45	25.92	30.02	20.57	25.23	29.72

Note. From Must, Dallall, & Dietz (1991). Copyright 1991 by American Society for Clinical Nutrition. Adapted by permission.

Time	Food and Drink	Amount	Calories	Location
7:15	Skim milk	1/2c.	40	home/kitchen
	Cheerios	3/4c.	80	
	Orange juice(frozen, unsweetened)	1/2c.	40	
	Rye bread toast (plain)	2 slices	160	
noon	Chicken breast	1 ounce	100	school/cafeteria
	Wheat bread	2 slices	160	
	Mustard	2 tsp.	0	
	Lettuce	1/2c.	5	
	Tomato (medium)	1/2	10	
	Apple (small)	1	40	
	Skim Milk	1/2c.	40	
6:00	Turkey breast (broiled)	3 ounces	150	home/kitchen
	Green beans (steamed, plain)	1/4c.	10	
	Baked potato (plain)	1	80	
	Salad (tossed)	1 c.	20	
	Lite Dressing	1 tbsp.	30	
	Skim milk	1/2c.	40	
9:00	Graham crackers	3	80	home/kitchen
	Skim milk	1/2c.	40	
		Total Calories	1125	

FIG. 7.1. Example of dietary self-monitoring.

assessment period, which may last from 1 to 2 weeks, the child is directed not to change eating behavior. It is important for the children to describe their typical eating behavior during this time before changes are implemented.

An initial evaluation of an obese child who presents for weight management may also include an evaluation of a child's eating disorder symptoms. The Children's version of the Eating Attitudes Test (ChEAT) (Maloney, McGuire, & Daniels, 1988) is a psychometrically sound scale designed to assess a variety of attitudes and behaviors associated with disordered eating. This self-report questionnaire may be used in conjunction with an interview to detect eating disorder symptoms. As is discussed later in this chapter, this aspect of the evaluation may be particularly important in the assessment of severely overweight children and adolescents (Wisniewski, 1995). Children who self-report significant eating disorder symptomology should be referred for a more complete psychological assessment prior to initiation of weight management.

Assessment of Activity

Researchers use indirect calorimetry, double-labeled water, single plane (e.g., Caltrac) or triaxial accelerometers (e.g., Tritrac) to assess *energy expenditure,* that is, calories expended in physical activity (see Schoeller & Racette, 1990, for a review of these techniques). In the clinical setting, however, self-report in the form of an exercise diary is likely to be the most practical technique for measuring energy expenditure (Wardle, 1995). Participants can keep a daily record of the date, time, and duration of the activity, as well as whether they enjoyed the activity. This method is also discussed in detail in the self-monitoring section of this chapter. It should be noted that estimates of energy expenditure do not provide information about physical fitness (i.e., the ability of the body to function at an optimal level). For a more comprehensive discussion of fitness see Shephard (1994).

Pretreatment Issues

Before beginning treatment, all participants should be evaluated by a physician to rule out contraindications for moderate calorie restriction and increases in exercise. Not all children and families who present for obesity treatment will be able to benefit from treatment. Some issues that may potentially interfere with treatment include a parent's willingness and ability to be involved in treatment, a parent's eating disorder symptoms, as well as the child's age. These issues should be evaluated as part of an initial assessment.

Parent's Involvement in Treatment.   Most behavioral weight control programs for children acknowledge that the successful treatment of childhood overweight necessitates changes in the parent's eating and exercise behaviors as well as the child's. Parent's involvement in treatment is essential, as the adults largely determine the types of foods served in the home, how food is prepared, as well as influence what types of activities children participate in. In many pediatric weight control programs, parents are asked to engage in treatment along with their children. Specifically, parents and children are expected to monitor eating and exercise, to make better food choices, and to participate in exercise. Treatment outcome studies have demonstrated that actively involving a parent in treatment improves long-term outcome (Epstein, Nudelman, & Wing, 1987). Involving parents in treatment may have benefits for other family members as well, because parental involvement has been shown to have a positive influence on the weight of other, nontreated members of the family (Epstein et al.,1987).

The model of parental involvement in childhood obesity treatment is considered to be the gold standard. However, for a variety of reasons, parental inclusion in treatment is not always possible. The benefit of treating a child if the parent or guardian is unable or unwilling to participate is therefore unclear. Although the efficacy of treatment with and without parental involvement has been evaluated (e.g., Brownell, Kelman, & Stunkard, 1983), these were randomized, controlled outcome studies in which all families initially agreed to participate in treatment. It is easy to imagine that the study families were different from families in which the parent/guardian were unable or unwilling to participate in treatment. These data cannot inform all decisions with respect to treatment. It is probably not judicious to treat a very young obese child without a parent or guardian, as young children have little control over their own intake and activity. Older children, especially adolescents, may have more ability to control these factors, making treatment success more likely. In general, the decision to treat a child without a parent or guardian is a clinical one and must be decided on a case-by-case basis.

Treatment may not be recommended for all who desire it, as some families may not benefit from treatment. For example, family conflict has been associated with poor dietary habits (Kinter, Boss, & Johnson, 1981) and attrition from a weight control program (Kirschenbaum, Harris, & Tomarken, 1984), and both parent and child psychological problems have been shown to deleteriously affect weight loss and weight maintenance (Epstein, Wisniewski, & Weng, 1994). Therefore, an assessment of family cohesion as well as psychological problems will provide a more complete clinical picture and allow the family and the therapist to decide whether weight control treatment is indicated.

Finally, it is important to note that the successful treatment outcome programs described in the literature have been developed for use with middle-class families who have emotional and economic resources, as well as parents who are able and willing to be actively involved in treatment. It is as yet unclear how these treatments will fare with children and families with different characteristics.

Parental Eating Problems. Because obesity runs in families (Garn & Clark, 1976), it is not surprising that some parents of obese children struggle with their own eating difficulties (Wisniewski, 1995; Wisniewski, Wren, & Marcus, 1996). In some cases, a parent's eating difficulties may indicate the need for further treatment as they may not be sufficiently addressed by a family-based weight control program. It is therefore recommended that the therapist evaluate the parent's eating habits and attitudes during assessment and make appropriate referrals when necessary.

Age of Child. The age at which one should consider actively treating an overweight child is debatable. Treatment has been shown to be effective for children as young as age 5 (Epstein, Wing, Penner, & Kress, 1985). Most empirical studies, however, have focused on 8- to 12-year-old children, and there have been no studies of the treatment of overweight children younger than age 5. There may, however, be an indication to treat obese children who are younger than 5 if they are seriously overweight, and/or have a family history of severe overweight. However, the treatment of very young children necessitates close monitoring by a pediatrician and a nutritionist.

TREATMENT

Once an adequate assessment has been conducted, the appropriate treatment modality must be chosen. In the research setting, the behavioral treatment of pediatric obesity is traditionally conducted in a group format, as group treatment is more time- and cost-efficient. The treatment program outlined here has been designed to accommodate either a group or an individual format, because there may be situations in which treating the individual is more judicious or practical.

The mode and timing of the provision of didactic treatment information must also be considered, as individual children and families will be able to understand and master concepts and change behavior at different rates. In fact, a childhood obesity treatment program designed to consider individual differences in the learning rates of diet, exercise, and behavior modification techniques was shown to produce greater weight losses than a program that provided information on a fixed schedule (Epstein, McKenzie, Valoski, Klein, & Wing, 1994). Therefore, the rate at which individual children are able to master the recording of all aspects of diet and exercise behaviors differs and this must be taken into consideration.

Session Structure

In successful research programs, the child and parents have typically been seen together at the beginning of the session to review the week's progress and to address family issues. After this, the child and parents have been seen separately to discuss relevant issues and for the provision of didactic information. This session structure may be optimal, as it allows for the therapist to address both family and individual issues; however, it is also time consuming. A therapist must therefore weigh the benefits of this model considering time constraints, family dynamics, and developmental level of the child.

In any event, every therapy session should begin with the recording of the participant's weight on the therapist's scale. The therapist should review the participant's progress over the previous week and engage in problem solving around any difficult situations that may have arisen. Next, after the homework or behavioral goal from the previous week is reviewed, the didactic information for the current week should be provided and new homework assigned. Sessions generally last between 60 and 90 minutes. This information is summarized in Fig. 7.2.

Treatment Length

Research-based pediatric weight loss programs usually have continued for approximately 4 to 6 months. Though some programs may offer posttreatment meetings, the most common method is to end treatment completely. Use of a finite treatment model has been successful for some populations (e.g., Epstein, Valoski, et al., 1990), but may not be adequate for all patients. A paradigm that conceptualizes obesity as a chronic problem may benefit many patients. Using a model consistent with the treatment of diabetes mellitus, children who were in control of their weight would be seen by a therapist only periodically (e.g., once every 6 weeks). If and when a child begins to regain weight, more regular treatment would be indicated.

Role of the Therapist

The primary goal of the behavior therapist attempting to treat pediatric obesity is to facilitate behavior change by conducting an adequate functional behavior analysis and teaching strategies to change eating and exercise behavior. This goal is best accomplished within the context of a strong, nonjudgmental therapeutic relationship, as it is imperative that the child and family feel comfortable revealing all aspects of their eating and exercise behaviors.

```
**************************************************
         1. Record weight of all family members
   2. Review self-monitoring & homework from previous week
            3. Present didactic information
               4. Assign new homework
**************************************************
```

FIG. 7.2. Typical session structure.

A therapist desiring to treat pediatric obesity also should be aware of cultural and religious factors that may influence dietary and activity choices (e.g., eating vegetarian; keeping Kosher). It is imperative that therapists convey to the family that a behavior change program to modify eating- and exercise-related behaviors is not a *diet* program, per se, but a lifestyle change program. The term *diet* implies that an individual will make changes for a time-limited period, whereas *lifestyle* change suggests changes that are more enduring.

TREATMENT COMPONENTS

The essential elements of any effective weight control program are diet, exercise, and behavior modification. This section reviews the theoretical and practical material necessary for a behavior therapist to conduct pediatric weight control treatment.

Diet

The treatment of overweight may be different from the treatment of other childhood disorders in that there is a great deal of didactic information for the therapist to understand and the child and family to learn. It is important for therapists to become familiar with the information here as they will be relied on to not only to teach the information to the participants, but also to dispel the weight control myths that the child or family may already hold. Although in this culture children may have beliefs about dieting (Wardle & Beales, 1986), it cannot be assumed that these beliefs are accurate. It is therefore important to demystify the process of weight control for overweight children and their families. Finally, new information on weight control issues is proliferating and clinicians working in this area must make a commitment to staying abreast of the research literature. For example, several years ago the research literature and popular press were warning the weight conscious public of the effect "yo-yo dieting" on cardiovascular risk factors, morbidity and mortality, and future weight loss efforts (e.g., Brody, 1992; Brownell & Rodin, 1994). Most recently, however, the National Task Force on the Prevention and Treatment of Obesity (1994) declared that there was no compelling evidence for these claims.

Energy Balance. People who are neither gaining nor losing weight are believed to be in a state of energy balance. That is, they are consuming and expending the same amount of energy in calories. Individuals are believed to be in a state of positive energy balance when taking in more energy than expending, and as a result, gain weight. The converse is also true. People who are losing weight are believed to be in a state of negative energy balance, where they are taking in less energy than they are expending. In order to alter energy balance, changes must be made in either intake, expenditure, or both.

A pound is comprised of approximately 3,500 calories. Therefore, in order for an individual to lose 1 lb, a negative energy balance that equals or exceeds 3,500 calories must be achieved through decreasing energy intake (calories) and/or increasing energy expenditure (activity). Although either decreased energy intake or increased energy expenditure can be utilized to achieve a negative energy balance, the combination of diet and exercise is encouraged. For example, an individual might decrease daily intake by 300 calories and increase daily exercise by 200 calories in order to lose 1 lb per week.

It has been recommended that the optimal diet for treating obese children should be sufficiently balanced to promote growth, modestly restrictive to promote weight loss, and adequately structured to promote adherence (Epstein & Wing, 1987). A child should never be advised to consume fewer than 1,000 calories/day, because it may be difficult to consume a nutritionally balanced diet on fewer calories. Further, it is especially important that growing children consume a diet that is high in calcium and iron, and vitamin supplements should be unnecessary if the child is eating a balanced diet. It is therefore recommended that children receive consultation from a dietitian during treatment.

In adults, fat restriction is a standard component of a reduced calorie diet. There have been concerns about prescribing low fat diets for children, as it is feared they may be deficient in total calories and may have a negative effect on growth (Kaplan & Toshima, 1992; Mauer, 1991). The committee on Nutrition of the American Academy of Pediatrics has recommended an average daily intake of 30% of total calories from fat (American Academy of Pediatrics Committee on Nutrition, 1992). Recent data have indicated that children consuming a diet providing 28% of calories from fat maintained adequate growth and nutritional adequacy over a 3-year period (DISC Collaborative Research Group, 1995). Thus, although severe fat restriction is not encouraged, moderating fat intake to 30% of calories from fat is appropriate for children.

Calorie and Weight Goals.   When setting a calorie limit for overweight children it is important to consider the child's reported initial intake and to suggest a moderate calorie decrease. An average daily caloric intake can be estimated from several days of baseline food and beverage recording. A calorie restriction goal may be set based on the daily average. Ideally, the calorie goal should reflect a decease of 500 calories from baseline in order to promote a weekly weight loss of 1 lb. Take for example, a 10-year-old, female child who weighs 150 lb, who self-reports an average of 1,800 calories a day. A 500 calorie-per-day decrease, or a daily goal of 1,300 calories can be safely recommended.

Given that a particular child is overweight, calorie goals are necessary to promote safe and effective weight losses. Setting target weight goals for children is more difficult. The first complicating issue is the concept of "normal" weight. As already stated, the normal weights for a given height, age, and gender are derived statistically, and thus are somewhat arbitrary. A weight goal at the 50th percentile may not be reasonable for all children, especially those with a strong family history of overweight. Target weights should be goals that a child can maintain over time. The second complicating factor in setting a child's target weight is that the target will increase with age and with growth. Helping a child to stop gaining weight, may therefore be an adequate goal, depending on the child's degree of obesity.

Given these limitations, it may be most appropriate to set target weights successively in 5-lb increments rather than choosing a child's statistically average weight. For example, if on assessment a child weighs 150 lb, an initial goal of 145 lb would be set. When the 145-lb goal has been successfully met and maintained, a new goal of 140 lb can be established. This method of setting decreasing goal weights may be used until a reasonable body weight is achieved, that is, a weight that can be maintained over time and is associated with improved appearance and health parameters (for discussion, see Foster & Kendall, 1994).

Exercise

There are data to suggest that the dramatic increase in childhood overweight reported earlier is not fully explained by increases in intake (McDowell et al., 1994). Thus, decreased exercise or increased sedentary behavior may contribute to overweight in children. It is therefore necessary to articulate to families the importance of exercise is weight loss and maintenance. The addition of an exercise component to pediatric weight control treatment has been shown to enhance weight loss compared to diet alone (Epstein et al., 1985). It may be especially difficult, however, to motivate obese children to exercise because they reliably have been shown to choose being sedentary over being active (Epstein, Smith, Vara, & Rodefer, 1991).

Exercise recommended to children and their families to promote weight loss and maintenance should be of sufficient duration and consistency to maximize caloric expenditure. Aerobic activities that may be encouraged include walking, running, bicycling, swimming, ball playing (e.g., basketball, football), or aerobics. Weight lifting or calisthenics, however, are not aerobic activities and therefore should not be the primary exercise prescribed for weight loss. These activities promote strength and flexibility and may be used in conjunction with an aerobic activity. Many treatment programs recommend that children walk for exercise because walking is almost always available, needs no special equipment or skills, and is easy to do. Specifically, individuals may be asked to exercise for at least 20 minutes, 3 to 5 times per week. It is important to consider the risks of injury and noncompliance when making an exercise prescription, especially considering the individual's initial activity level.

In addition to prescribed aerobic exercise, it is recommended that children increase the time they spend engaging in lifestyle activities. Lifestyle activities are those that can be easily incorporated into a person's daily routine and may be viewed simply as taking the opportunity to be more active. Some examples of lifestyle activity include walking up stairs instead of taking the elevator, walking to and from school, walking around or playing during lunch or recess, or parking a few streets away from a destination. Benefits of lifestyle exercise include increased energy expenditure, and possibly decreased intake, as it is difficult to eat while being active.

In the past several years, researchers and clinicians interested in increasing exercise in obese children have been turning their attention toward sedentary behaviors. Sedentary behaviors are believed to compete with being active and may even promote poor eating habits. For children, a behavior that strongly competes with being active is television watching. In fact, 70% of high school students reported spending at least 1 hour watching television each school day (Heath, Pratt, Warren, & Kann, 1994). These data are compelling, as the prevalence of obesity has been found to increase by 2% for each additional hour of television watched (Dietz & Gortmaker, 1985). Television watching also appears to affect fitness, with lower fitness associated with heavy television viewing (Tucker, 1986). Similarly, television appears to have an influence on eating, as it has been found to promote poor eating habits (Jeffrey, McLellarn, & Fox, 1982) and stimulate eating, especially in obese individuals (Falciglia & Gussow, 1980). Decreasing access to an obese child's available sedentary behaviors may actually promote activity and weight loss (Epstein et al., 1995), suggesting that specifically targeting sedentary behaviors for change may be a vital component to include in pediatric weight control programs.

Behavior Modification

Providing individuals with information about diet and exercise is often not enough to produce long-term changes in weight (Epstein, Wing, Steranchak, Dickson, & Michelson, 1980). Participants will often tell us: "I know *what* to do, I just can't get myself to *do* it". It is in this situation that the role of the behaviorally trained professional becomes paramount. Behavior modification techniques have been designed to directly and indirectly affect eating and exercising behavior, and these techniques are taught to children and families in order to facilitate behavior change. Research has demonstrated that addition of behavior modification techniques improves weight loss compared to diet and exercise information alone (Epstein et al., 1980). Some of the behavior modification techniques commonly used in the treatment of overweight children are described here.

Self-monitoring

Self-monitoring, or recording of all eating and exercise behavior, is the cornerstone of any behavioral weight control program. In a pediatric behavioral weight control program, the self-monitoring of diet, activity, and weight is critical. Self-monitoring is beneficial as it helps the therapist and the child to become more aware of behavior patterns and to determine where changes need to occur. Self-monitoring also provides the necessary information on which individuals can evaluate their progress.

Self-monitoring of Diet.   On a daily basis, children and parents are asked to record everything they eat and drink. They record the record the date and time that food is eaten as well as the type of food, the amount eaten, how the food was prepared (e.g., baked, fried), and the food's caloric value. Patients can be advised to buy a book of calorie counts at any major bookstore. Figure 7.1 provides an example of dietary self-monitoring.

Self-monitoring of Activity.   Self-monitoring of aerobic activity should include the date and time during which the child engaged in the activity, a description of the activity (e.g., running, walking), and the duration (e.g., 20 minutes). A record of how much the exercise was enjoyed may be included, and may provide important information to the clinician. Lifestyle activity may also be recorded by participants in order to track the progress of the type of activity (e.g., how many flights of stairs climbed).

Self-monitoring of Weight.   Participants are directed to weigh themselves at the same time daily, in order to establish weighing as a habit and also to limit the influence of normal daily variations in weight. Participants should weigh themselves on wakening or just before bed, wearing similar clothing each time. Weights may be graphed on a chart in order to monitor progress. Changes in weight may be correlated with data obtained from the self-monitoring of diet and exercise. It is important for both therapist and participant to remember, however, that weight change is not the only indicator of success and that changes in behavior are critical.

Stimulus Control

Stimulus control techniques are strategies to help participants self-manage environmental cues. The objective is to increase cues for behaviors congruent with weight loss and decrease cues congruent with weight gain. Families can be asked to remove high fat foods and snacks from the house, for example, as seeing these foods may prompt eating. Families may also be asked to replace high fat snacks with easily available low calorie snacks (e.g., fruits and vegetables) and to refrain from skipping meals, as the internal cue of intense hunger may lead to overeating. Within the meal itself, stimulus control techniques that may be employed include eating only in one room, using smaller plates, not serving food family style, preparing less food at each meal, and eating more slowly.

Shaping/Goal Setting

The notion of taking gradual steps and setting realistic goals in changing eating and exercise behaviors is germane to pediatric weight control programs, because behavior change is an incremental process. Goals should initially be set so that the participant is likely to succeed and the changed behavior is reinforced. These goals can gradually increase in difficulty with the child's developing success. For example, if a child is eating 10 cookies every day, an initial goal might be to limit cookies to 8 per day. Once the child has succeeded in decreasing intake to 8 cookies/day, new goals may be made in stepwise increments. Even though the desired long-term goal would be to decrease cookie intake to a much lower level (e.g., 1 per day), this initial goal is more likely to be reached.

Developing Alternatives to Overeating and Inactivity

When the behavior change goal is to reduce the frequency of a behavior, simply helping to decrease the behavior may not be sufficient. A new, more adaptive behavior in place of the old may better help to maintain behavior change. Children and families can be helped to find behaviors that will substitute for eating/overeating and inactivity. It is important to find substitutes that are equally or more enjoyable than the behavior in which the individual currently engages. A behavioral analysis may be used to evaluate the behaviors that would benefit from substitution. For example, self-monitoring records and discussion have indicated that Sue asks her mother for more to eat immediately after dinner. If a further evaluation suggests that this behavior is a result of boredom rather than hunger, some behavioral alternatives to eating after dinner when bored might be offered. For example, she could be encouraged to play a board game, go for a walk, call a friend, or go outside.

Contracting

Contracts are explicit agreements that specify contingencies for behavior change. Contracts are useful to motivate children, but they also function to engage the family with each other. Contracts for specific behavior changes should be used on a regular basis. Contracts are best employed as negotiations between parent and child, but a therapist–child contract may have utility. Wording in the contract should be very specific and expectations for behavioral goals and rewards made clear.

Planning Ahead

The ability to plan in advance the content of meals and time for exercise is an important skill for those who wish to achieve weight control. Planning ahead, however, may be a difficult concept for some children, depending on their developmental level. Families are asked to plan meals ahead of time, taking into consideration the overall calorie goal and daily events. Planning meals helps children learn that they need to consider the calorie content of a specific meal with respect to their daily goal. For example, if children know that they are going to a birthday party at night, they may choose to plan to eat less at lunch or dinner or to omit a snack so that they can have a piece of birthday cake and not exceed their calorie limit. With respect to exercise, participants are encouraged to plan regular days and times for their activity and to anticipate any obstacles that might impede engaging in exercise.

Assertiveness

Children often find themselves the object of others' need to feed. It is important to teach children how to effectively and appropriately say "No, thank you" to well-meaning friends and relatives who offer high calorie foods or unplanned snacks. A child can learn to say "No, thank you, I am not hungry" or "No, thank you, I am trying to eat less." Role play may be used with children around specific situations in which they have difficulty declining offered food (e.g., grandma's house during the holidays, birthday parties at school).

Parent Training

The behavior modification techniques described here are successful in helping participants lose weight if they are used and if they are used as directed. Treatment programs that promote parental involvement rely on parents to reinforce treatment recommendations during the days between appointments. However, it is easy to assume that parents are proficient in implementing treatment plans without evaluating whether or not they possess the necessary skills. It is therefore essential to teach parents the principles of behavior change, permitting them to learn how to effect change in their children. Parent training added to weight control treatment results in better long-term weight losses (Israel, Stolmaker, & Andrian, 1985). Parents may be taught the general principles of behavior change with respect to all behaviors, not just eating and exercise behaviors. Generalization of knowledge allows the parents to use behavior change principles to change any behavior. The emphasis on changing a child's behavior should be on positive reinforcement through increased attention, praise, token economy, point system, or contracting rather than punishment or response cost. The interested reader is referred to Barkley (1987) for a discussion of parent training.

Relapse Prevention

Use of relapse prevention strategies has become standard in behavior modification programs. Relapse prevention strategies are designed to prevent occurrence of a relapse once behavior change has been initiated and to prevent initial lapses in behavior from escalating to a full relapse. Although a full discussion of the relapse prevention model is beyond the scope of this chapter, the interested reader is directed to Marlatt and Gordon (1985).

Specifically, with respect to the treatment of pediatric obesity, participants may be taught to identify, anticipate, and expect lapses and high-risk situations. Cognitive-behavioral strategies are taught to help individuals cope with these incidents as well as to moderate their reaction to them. For example, if Mary had several days of overeating, under-exercising, failing to self-monitor, and consequently gains weight, she may conclude "I am failing this program; I should give up because I will never lose weight." Using the relapse prevention model, Mary may be taught that everyone experiences lapses and her negative thinking could lead to a relapse. Alternative, constructive thoughts as well as a "re-start" plan may be explored.

In this example, Mary can be helped to examine her negative thought and to counter it with "Everyone has lapses, I can get back on track and lose weight by using my re-start plan." A restart plan might include initiating all self-monitoring (e.g., diet, exercise, weight) and setting achievable calorie and exercise goals.

TREATMENT OUTLINE

Weeks 1 to 3

During Weeks 1 to 3, the therapist provides an orientation to the program, helps participants develop reliable self-monitoring skills, and establishes the therapeutic relationship. The therapist should also use these initial sessions to conduct the behavioral analysis of the patient's current eating and exercise behaviors. By the end of these sessions, several initial behavioral goals with respect to eating and exercise should be negotiated.

Training in self-monitoring techniques is provided and parents are taught how to best help their child record accurately. It is important early on to discuss with parents how to interact around the self-monitoring, as negative evaluation for eating and exercise behavior may result in child resistance or dishonesty.

Adherence to the treatment recommendations described in this chapter should result in weight losses of approximately 1 to 2 lb per week. Although a small initial weight loss (1–2 lb) over the first three sessions may be anticipated, patients and therapists alike should be aware that the 1–2 lb weekly weight losses are not expected until calorie restriction becomes a focus of treatment. Clear expectations for weight loss should therefore be conveyed early in treatment.

Weeks 4 to 8

During Weeks 4 through 8, a calorie limit and weekly exercise goal are set for each participant. Participants are instructed about behavioral techniques, such as contracting, stimulus control, assertiveness, shaping/goal setting, and meal planning. Use of data from the self-monitoring sheets during these sessions is imperative. These data provide important information about behavior change, especially how behavior affects weight change.

Weeks 9 to 11

During weeks 9 to 11 parents are provided with parent management training in order to help them effectively implement the behavior change strategies recommended for weight loss. During these sessions, parents are also taught to model appropriate eating and exercise behavior and to refrain from encouraging eating as a way to cope with emotion. Children may be taught strategies to cope with peer teasing, to increase self-acceptance, and to engage in noneating behaviors when upset, bored, or stressed.

Weeks 12 to 14

During Weeks 12 to 14, special topics such as sneak eating, the use of food as a reinforcer, and self-acceptance/self-esteem issues may be discussed, depending on the family's needs. If the family is doing well, these sessions may be shorter in duration (30–45 min). If the family is struggling in treatment at this point, these sessions may also be used to further reinforce topics from earlier sessions.

Weeks 15 to 16

During the final weeks of the program, relapse prevention strategies and termination issues should be discussed in depth. Each participant should write up a relapse prevention plan. Patients, fearful of relapse, may request booster sessions after treatment ends, though research evidence has found the utility of these sessions to be equivocal (e.g., Perri, McAdoo, Spevak, & Newlin, 1984). A planned period without treatment may therefore be helpful to entrain self-management skills.

OTHER POPULATIONS

The treatment described previously was developed based on the available published research literature. As noted, however, available findings have generally been derived from the study of Caucasian, upper-middle-class, moderately overweight children without significant psychological difficulties. Effectiveness of this treatment with other obese populations is unknown, and there is unfortunately little guidance for therapists who would like to treat them. Until empirical evidence shows otherwise, it is recommended that therapists use the treatment techniques described here when treating obese minority children, severely obese children, and children with psychological problems. These techniques have been found to be safe and effective, and may be tailored to meet the needs of the individual children.

Minority Children

High rates of overweight have been identified in several minority populations, including African-American women, Native Americans, and Mexican Americans (see Kumanyika, 1994, for a review). Recent epidemiological data have shown great increases in the prevalence of overweight in African-American youth in particular (Troiano et al., 1995). It has been suggested that effective treatments designed for one population are not necessarily appropriate for another cultural group, because weight-related attitudes and behaviors are influenced by culture (Kumanyika, 1994). With few exceptions (e.g., Wadden et al., 1990), empirically evaluated treatments have not been developed specifically for minority children.

Treatment programs should be adapted to incorporate the cultural norms and eating and activity patterns of the population to be treated. For example, African Americans have been found to eat a large proportion of fried and high fat food (Patterson, Harlan, Block, & Kahle, 1995), suggesting that these foods in particular, rather than a decrease in calories alone, need to be targeted for change. In addition, African-American females have been found to be satisfied with their body shape at heavier weights than their Caucasian counterparts (Harris, Walters, & Waschull, 1991), although obesity-related conditions such as hypertension, heart disease, and stroke are found to occur in higher rates in African Americans than in Caucasians (Kumanyika, 1990). These data suggest that it may be more appropriate for weight control treatment to focus on the medical risk rather than the body dissatisfaction associated with obesity when treating African-American girls.

Severely Obese Children

Little is known about severe pediatric obesity (BMI $\geq$ 37) or its treatment, as the empirical treatment literature has focused predominantly on the moderately obese child. A review of the literature found few descriptions of treatments for these youngsters (e.g., Boeck et al., 1993; Suskind et al., 1993), and no published controlled outcome trials. Available data have suggested that severely obese children and adolescents who present for weight control may have special treatment needs, as there are higher rates of psychiatric and medical comorbidity (Wisniewski, 1995; Wisniewski, Marcus, & Wren, 1994) as well as eating disordered thoughts and behaviors (Wisniewski, 1995) in this population. Treatment of this population should therefore include a multidisciplinary approach (e.g., psychology, psychiatry, pediatrics, endocrinology) in order to ensure that all treatment needs are addressed.

Children With Psychopathology

Little is known about psychological problems in moderately overweight children who present for weight loss treatment. Although higher rates of psychological problems have been found in obese adults who seek treatment compared to community samples (Black, Goldstein, & Mason, 1992; Goldsmith et al., 1992), there are no such data pertaining to children. Overweight itself may not predispose children to psychological difficulties, as we have found that child psychopathology among applicants to a pediatric weight control program was related to parental distress rather than the child's obesity (Epstein, Klein, & Wisniewski, 1994). If they do exist, however, psychiatric problems in overweight children or their parents may influence treatment. It has been shown that subclinical psychological problems in parents and children can negatively influence the child's weight control both during and after treatment (Epstein, Wisniewski, et al., 1994). In addition, children who developed psychological problems after a treatment program were found to be less successful in long-term weight control (Epstein, Wisniewski, et al., 1994).

Comorbid psychopathology does not necessarily preclude treatment. In fact, in the adult literature, behavioral obesity treatment reliably has been found to decrease depressive symptoms (Wing, Epstein, & Marcus, 1984). In children, a careful screening of psychopathology may aid in anticipating the child's strength's and weaknesses during treatment. Children who suffer from attention deficit hyperactivity disorder (ADHD), for example, may have problems with impulsive eating. Anxious children may have difficulty self-monitoring, if they interpret their overeating behavior as imperfect. There are clearly some situations, however, in which obesity treatment should be precluded by the treatment of the psychopathology (e.g., when there is evidence of suicidality). Thus, it is recommended that the initial assessment include an evaluation of social and psychological functioning.

CASE ILLUSTRATION

Lisa A. was a 12-year-old Caucasian female child who presented for weight loss treatment with her mother, Mrs. A. Lisa had been referred by her pediatrician, who was concerned about her increasing degree of overweight given that she had a significant family history of obesity (both parents were approximately 50% over their ideal weight). At the time of assessment Lisa weighed 95 lb, and measured 53 inches. At this weight, given height, age, and gender, Lisa was considered to be 40% above statistically normative weight. At presentation, mother reported that Lisa had been gaining excess weight steadily since approximately age 8. Lisa currently lives with her mother and 15-year-old brother Joe, as her parents were divorced when she was 9 years old. Joe reportedly did not currently have a weight problem. Mrs A. also stated her own goal to lose 25 lb during the program.

As the next group treatment cycle would not begin for several months, Lisa and her mother were offered and accepted individual treatment. On referral, Lisa's pediatrician reported that she was in good health and gave his written permission for Lisa to engage in moderate calorie restriction and exercise in a supervised weight loss program. Lisa was seen for a total of 20 sessions over 7 months. These sessions were held weekly for 16 weeks, biweekly for 2 weeks, and then 2 monthly sessions

During assessment, no eating disorder symptoms or other psychological problems were reported. A 7-day self-monitoring record indicated that Lisa ate an average of 1,200 calories/day, engaged in no regular physical activity, and spent approximately 3 hours a day watching television. Although Lisa ate sweets occasionally, she frequently chose the school provided lunch which included high calorie meats and vegetables (e.g., fried chicken, french fries, creamed corn), and often ate dinner at a fast food restaurant. In particular, the time between returning home from school (3 p.m.) until Mrs A. arrived home from work (5:15 p.m.) appeared to be a particularly difficult time for Lisa. She spent most of this time watching television and eating high calorie snack foods (e.g., potato chips and dip).

Treatment began successfully, with both Lisa and Mrs. A. complying with self-monitoring instructions and losing weight (Lisa 3 lb and Mom 5 lb). By Week 4, however, inconsistent self-monitoring became an issue in treatment. Lisa reported that she was often "too busy" to record her eating and activity and that it "took too long." After further evaluating this problem, it became clear that mother also felt that she was "too busy" to record and that nightly progress meetings had ceased. Problem-solving strategies were used to identify and alter variables that were interfering with recording (e.g., waiting too long after a meal; making negative statements about recording). Lisa was asked to record her lunch during the session and she was timed with a stopwatch. Lisa was able to realize that recording her intake took only a few minutes each time. In addition, Mrs. A. was encouraged to provide a positive role model for recording and her own ambivalence about behavior change were explored. In this session, Mrs. A's desire to help Lisa succeed in the program was reinforced. By Session 7, both Lisa and Mrs. A. were recording regularly.

Engaging Lisa in exercise was somewhat more challenging. Not only did Lisa reportedly "hate" to exercise, her favorite extracurricular activity was watching television. After an unsuccessful attempt to increase Lisa's exercise through positive reinforcement, a different approach was attempted. Lisa and her mother wrote contingency contracts focusing on decreasing sedentary activity, in particular television watching. As a result of the decrease in television watching, especially after school, Lisa became more active with friends in the neighborhood, was eating less after school, and by the end of treatment had begun to use the exercise bicycle that had been collecting dust in her basement.

Some other issues emerged during treatment. Lisa's brother, Joe, a growing adolescent boy, ate large portions. Lisa often felt deprived if her mother attempted to give her smaller portions than Joe. She was provided with some education about the nutritional needs of boys and girls and older and younger people. Mrs. A. was helped to set limits and not feel as if she was "starving" her daughter.

Another problem was that Lisa and Joe spent weekends with their father who did not cook. They spent the weekend eating out at fast food restaurants. Lisa would follow the lifestyle change program during the week, but had difficulty keeping within her calorie limit on the weekend. Mr. A. was invited to attend several sessions in order receive education about the program. Lisa was taught assertiveness skills and time was spent examining fast food menus and choosing more healthy meals.

Toward the end of treatment, Lisa and Mrs. A. became concerned that they would not be able to control their eating without the "threat" of being weighed in on a weekly basis. At this time, sessions were faded to biweekly and then monthly. At the same time, Lisa was encouraged to develop her own relapse prevention plan. She decided that if she gained more than 3 lb she would begin to self-monitor her eating and activity.

At the end of 16 weeks, Lisa had lost 15 lb and maintained that weight loss over the 20 weeks of treatment. Mrs. A. lost 20 lb by Week 16, but had regained 6 lb by the end of treatment.

CONCLUSIONS

The rate of pediatric obesity is high and appears to be rising. Moreover, the psychosocial and physiological sequelae of pediatric obesity suggest that treatment is imperative. Fortunately, efficacious family-based, behavioral weight control programs have been developed to treat overweight children and their families. It is important for a therapist who is attempting to provide pediatric weight control treatment to have a strong background in behavior modification as well as a knowledge about diet and exercise. The behavior therapist's goal in this treatment is to facilitate behavior change by conducting an adequate functional behavior analysis and teach appropriate strategies to alter eating and exercise behaviors. Treatment programs may be provided within a group or individual format and continue for 12 to16 weeks. The program outlined in this chapter originated from the relevant empirical treatments conducted with relatively homogenous populations (i.e., Caucasian, moderately overweight, without psychiatric comorbidity); the effectiveness of this treatment with other populations is as yet unknown.

REFERENCES

American Academy of Pediatrics, Committee on Nutrition. (1992). Statement on cholesterol. *Pediatrics, 90,* 469–472.

Barkley, R. A. (1987). *Defiant children: A clinician's manual for parent training.* New York: Guilford.

Black, D. W., Goldstein, R. B., & Mason, E. E. (1992). Prevalence of mental disorder in 88 morbidly obese bariatric clinic patients. *American Journal of Psychiatry, 149,* 227–234.

Boeck, M., Lubin, K., Loy, I., Kaasparian, D., Grebin, B., & Lombardi, N. (1993). Initial experience with long-term inpatient treatment for morbidly obese children in a rehabilitation facility. *Annals of the New York Academy of Sciences, 699*, 257–259.

Brody, J. E. (1992, November 23). For most trying to lose weight, dieting only makes things worse. *New York Times*, p. A1.

Brownell, K. D., Kelman, J. H., & Stunkard, A. J. (1983). Treatment of obese children with and without their mothers: Changes in weight and blood pressure. *Pediatrics, 71*, 515–523.

Brownell, K. D., & Rodin, J. (1994). Medical, metabolic, and psychological effects on weight cycling. *Archives of Internal Medicine, 154*, 1325–1330.

Burns, T. L., Moll, P. P., & Lauer, R. M. (1992). Increased familial cardiovascular mortality in obese school children: The Muscatine Ponderosity Family Study. *Pediatrics, 89*, 262–268.

Charney, E., Goodman, H. C., McBride, M., Lyon, B., & Pratt, R. (1976). Childhood antecedents of adult obesity. Do chubby infants become obese adults? *New England Journal of Medicine, 295*, 6–9.

Counts, C. R., Jones, C., Frame, C. L., Jarvie, G. J., & Strauss, C. C. (1986). The perception of obesity by normal-weight versus obese school-age children. *Child Psychiatry and Human Development, 17*, 113–120.

Crawford, P., Obarzanek, E., Morrison, J., & Sabry, Z. I. (1994). Comparative advantage of 3-day food records over 24-hour recall and 5-day food frequency validated by observation of 9- and 10-year-old girls. *Journal of the American Dietetic Association, 94*, 626–630.

Dietz, W. H., & Gortmaker, S. L. (1985). Do we fatten our children at the television set? Obesity and television viewing in children and adolescents. *Pediatrics, 75*, 807–812.

Dietz, W. H., & Hartung, R. (1985). Changes in height velocity of obese preadolescents during weight reduction. *American Journal of Diseases in Children, 139*, 705.

DISC Collaborative Research Group. (1995). Efficacy and safety of lowering dietary intake of fat and cholesterol in children with elevated low-density lipoprotein cholesterol. *Journal of the American Medical Association, 237*, 1429–1435.

Duerenberg, P., Westrate, J. A., & Seidell, J. C. (1991). Body mass index as a measure of body fatness: Age- and sex-specific prediction formulas. *British Journal of Nutrition, 65*, 105–114.

Durnin, J. A., & Womersley, J. (1974). Body fat assessed from total body density and its estimation from skinfold thickness: Measurements on 481 men and women aged from 16 to 72 years. *British Journal of Nutrition, 32*, 77–97.

Epstein, L. H., Klein, K. R., & Wisniewski, L. (1994). Child and parent factors that influence psychological problems in obese children. *International Journal of Eating Disorders, 15*, 151–158.

Epstein, L. H., McCurley, J., Valoski, A., & Wing, R. R. (1990). Growth in obese children treated for obesity. *American Journal of Diseases of Children, 144*, 1360–1364.

Epstein, L. H., McCurley, J., Wing, R. R., & Valoski, A. (1990). Five-year follow-up of family-based behavioral treatments for childhood obesity. *Journal of Consulting and Clinical Psychology, 58*, 661–664.

Epstein, L. H., McKenzie, S. J., Valoski, A., Klein, K. R., & Wing, R. R. (1994). Effects of mastery criteria and contingent reinforcement for family-based child weight control. *Addictive Behaviors, 19*, 135–145.

Epstein, L. H., Nudelman, S., & Wing, R. R. (1987). Long-term effects of family-based treatment for obesity on nontreated family members. *Behavior Therapy, 2*, 147–152.

Epstein, L. H., Smith, J. A., Vara, L. S., & Rodefer, J. S. (1991). Behavioral economic analysis of activity of choice in obese children. *Health Psychology, 10*, 311–316.

Epstein, L. H., Valoski, A., & McCurley, J. (1993). The effect of weight loss by obese children on long-term growth. *American Journal of Diseases of Children, 147*, 1076–1080.

Epstein, L. H., Valoski, A. M., Vara, L. S., McCurley, J., Wisniewski, L., Kalarchian, M. A., Klein, K. R., & Shrager, L. R. (1995). Effects of decreasing sedentary behavior and increasing activity on weight change in obese children. *Health Psychology, 14*, 109–115.

Epstein, L. H., Valoski, A., Wing, R. R., & McCurley, J. (1990). Ten-year follow-up of behavioral, family-based treatment for obese children. *Journal of the American Medical Association, 264*, 2519–2523.

Epstein, L. H., Valoski, A., Wing, R. R., & McCurley, J. (1994). Ten-year outcomes of behavioral family-based treatment for childhood obesity. *Health Psychology, 13*, 373–383.

Epstein, L. H., & Wing, R. R. (1987). Behavioral treatment of childhood obesity. *Psychological Bulletin, 101*, 331–342.

Epstein, L. H., Wing, R. R., Koeske, R., & Valoski, A. (1986). Effect of parent weight on weight loss in obese children. *Journal of Consulting and Clinical Psychology, 54,* 400–401.

Epstein, L. H., Wing, R. R., Penner, B. C., & Kress, M. J. (1985). Effect of diet and controlled exercise on weight loss in obese children. *Journal of Pediatrics, 107,* 358–361.

Epstein, L. H., Wing, R. R., Steranchak, L., Dickson, B., & Michelson, J. (1980). Comparison of family-based behavior modification and nutrition education for childhood obesity. *Journal of Pediatric Psychology, 5,* 25–36.

Epstein, L. H., Wisniewski, L., & Weng, R. (1994). Child and parent psychological problems influence child weight control. *Obesity Research, 2,* 509–515.

Falciglia, G. A., & Gussow, J. D. (1980). Television commercials and eating behavior of obese and normal-weight women. *Journal of Nutrition Education, 12,* 196–199.

Flegal, K. M. (1993). Defining obesity in children and adolescents: Epidemiologic approaches. *Critical Review of Food Science Nutrition, 33,* 307–312.

Forbes, G. B. (1964). Lean body mass and fat in obese children. *Pediatrics, 34,* 308–314.

Foster, G. D., & Kendall, P. C. (1994). The realistic treatment of obesity: Changing the scales of success. *Clinical Psychology Review, 14,* 701–736.

French. S. A., Story, M., & Perry, C. L. (1995). Self-esteem and obesity in children and adolescents: A literature review. *Obesity Research, 3,* 479–490.

Garn, S. M., & Clark, D. C. (1976). Trends in fatness anad the origins of obesity. *Pediatrics, 57,* 433–456.

Goldsmith, S. J., Anger-Friedfeld, K., Beren, S., Rudolph, D., Boeck, M., & Aronne, L. (1992). Psychiatric illness in patients presenting for obesity treatment. *International Journal of Eating Disorders, 12,* 63–71.

Goodman, N., Richardson, S. A., Dornbusch, S. M., & Hastorf, A. H. (1963). Variant reactions to physical disabilities. *American Sociological Review, 28,* 429–435.

Gortmaker, S. L., Must, A., Perrin, J. M., Sobol, A. M., & Dietz, W. H. (1993). Social and economic consequences of overweight in adolescence and young adulthood. *New England Journal of Medicine, 329,* 1008–1012.

Guo, S., Roche, A. F., Chumlea, W. C., Siervogel, R. M., & Gardner, J. D. (1994). The predictive value of childhood body mass index values for adult overweight. *American Journal of Clinical Nutrition, 59,* 810–819.

Gutin, B., Basch, C., Shea, S., Contento, I., DeLozier, M., Rips, J., Irigoyen, M., & Zybert, P. (1990). Blood pressure, fitness, and fatness in 5- and 6-year-old children. *Journal of the American Medical Association, 264,* 1123–1127.

Hamill, P. V. V., Drizd, T. A., Johnson, C. L., Reed, R. B., Roche, A. F., & Moore, W. M. (1979). Physical growth: National Center for Health Statistics percentiles. *American Journal of Clinical Nutrition, 32,* 607–629.

Hammer, L. D., Kraemer, H. C., Wilson, D. M., Ritter, P. L., & Dornbusch, S. M. (1991). Standardized percentile curves of body-mass index for children and adolescents. *American Journal of Diseases of Children, 145,* 259–263.

Harris, M., Walters, L. C., & Waschull, S. (1991). Gender and ethnic differences in obesity-related behaviors and attitudes in a college sample. *Journal of Applied Social Psychology, 21,* 1545–1566.

Heath G. W., Pratt, M., Warren, C. W., & Kann, L. (1994). Physical activity patterns in American high school students. Results from the 1990 Youth Risk Behavior Survey. *Archives of Pediatric Adolescent Medicine, 148,* 1131–1136.

Israel, A. C., Stolmaker, L., & Andrian, C. A. G. (1985). The effects of training in parents in general child management skills on a behavioral weight loss program for children. *Behavior Therapy, 16,* 169–180.

Jeffery, D. B., McLellarn, R. W., & Fox, D. T. (1982). The development of children's eating habits: The role of television commercials. *Health Education Quarterly, 9,* 78–93.

Kaplan, R. M., & Toshima, M. T. (1992). Does a reduced fat diet cause retardation in child growth? *Preventive Medicine, 21,* 33–52.

Kinter, M., Boss, P. G., & Johnson, N. (1981). The relationship between dysfunctional family environments and family member food intake. *Journal of Marriage and the Family, 43,* 633–641.

Kirschenbaum, D. S., Harris, E. S., & Tomarken, A. J. (1984). Effects of parental involvement in behavioral weight loss therapy for preadolescents. *Behavior Therapy, 15,* 485–500.

Klesges, R. C., Eck, L. H., & Ray, J. W. (1995). Who underreports dietary intake in a dietary recall? Evidence from the Second National Health and Nutrition Examination Survey. *Journal of Consulting and Clinical Psychology, 63,* 438–444.

Kumanyika, S. K. (1990). Diet and chronic disease issues for minority populations. *Journal of Nutrition Education, 22,* 89–96.

Kumanyika, S. K. (1994). Obesity in minority populaitons: An epidemiologic assessment. *Obesity Research, 2,* 166–182.

Lichtman, S. W., Pisarska, K., Bremen, E. R., Pestone, M., Dowling, H., Offenbacher, E., Weisel, H., Heshka, S., Matthews, D. E., & Heymsfield, S. B. (1992). Discrepancy between self-reported and actual caloric intake and exercise in obese subjects. *New England Journal of Medicine, 327,* 1893–1898.

Mallick, M. J. (1983). Health hazards of obesity and weight control in children: A review of the literature. *American Journal of Public Health, 73,* 78–82.

Maloney, M. J., McGuire, J. B., & Daniels, S. R. (1988). Reliability testing of a children's version of the Eating Attitude Test. *Journal of the American Academy of Child and Adolescent Psychiatry, 27,* 541–543.

Marlatt, G. A., & Gordon, J. R. (Eds.). (1985). *Relapse prevention.* New York: Guilford.

Mauer, A. M. (1991). Should there be intervention to alter serum lipids in children? *Annual Review of Nutrition, 11,* 375–391.

McDowell, A., Engel, A., Massey, J., & Maurer, K. (1981). Plan and operation of the second National Health and Nutrition Examination Survey, United States, 1971–1973. *Vital Health Statistics, 1.*

McDowell, M. A., Briefel, R. R., Alaimo, K., Bischof, A. M., Caughman, C. R., Carroll, M. D., Loria, C. M., & Johnson, C. L. (1994). *Energy and macronutirent intakes of persons ages 2 months and over in the United States: Third National Health and Nutrition Examination Survey, Phase 1, 1988-1991.* Advance data from vital and health statistics, No. 255. Hyattsville, MD.: National Center for Health Statistics.

Metropolitan Life Insurance Company. (1983). 1983 Metropolitan Height and Weight Tables. *Statistical Bulletin.*

Must, A., Dallal, G. E., & Dietz, W. H. (1991). Reference data for obesity: 85th and 95th percentiles of body mass index (wt/ht^2) and triceps skinfold thickness. *American Journal of Clinical Nutrition, 53,* 839–846.

Must, A., Jaques, P. F., Dallal, G. E., Bajema, C. J., Dietz, W. H. (1992). Long-term morbidity and mortality of overweight adolescents: A followup of the Harvard Growth Study of 1922–35. *New England Journal of Medicine, 327,* 1350–1355.

National Institutes of Health. (1992). NIH Technology Assessment Conference on Methods for Voluntary Weight Loss and Control. *Annals of Internal Medicine, 116,* 942–949.

National Task Force on the Prevention and Treatment of Obesity. (1994). Weight cycling. *Journal of the American Medical Association, 272,* 1196–1202.

Neumark-Sztainer, D., Butler, R., & Palti, H. (1995). Dieting and binge eating: Which dieters are at risk? *Journal of the American Dietetic Association, 95,* 586–589.

Patterson, B. H., Harlan, L. C., Block, G., & Kahle, L. (1995). Food choices of Whites, Blacks, and Hispanics: Data from the 1987 National Health Interview Survey. *Nutrition and Cancer, 23,* 105–119.

Perri, M. G., McAdoo, W. G., Spevak, P. A., & Newlin, D. B. (1984). Effect of multicomponent maintenance program on long-term weight loss. *Journal of Consulting and Clinical Psychology, 52,* 480–481.

Rauh, J. L., & Schumsky, D. A. (1969). Relative accuracy of visual assessment of juvenile obesity. *Journal of the American Dietetic Association, 55,* 459–464.

Roche, A. F., Siervogel, F. M., Chumlea, W. C., & Webb, P. (1981). Grading body fatness from limited anthropometric data. *American Journal of Clinical Nutrition, 34,* 2831–2838.

Schoeller, D. A., & Racette, S. B. (1990). A review of field techniques for the assessment of energy expenditure. *Journal of Nutrition, 120,* 1492–1495.

Shephard, R. T., (1994). *Aerobic fitness and health.* Champaign, IL: Human Kinetics.

Strauss, C. C., Smith, K., Frame, C., & Forehand, R. (1985). Personal and interpersonal characteristics associated with childhood obesity. *Journal of Pediatric Psychology, 10,* 337–343.

Suskind, R. M., Sothern, M. S., Farris, R. P., von Almen, T. K., Schumacher, H., Carlise, L., Vargas, A., Escobar, O., Loftin, M., Fuchs, G., Brown, R., & Udall, J. N. (1993). Recent advances in the treatment of childhood obesity. *Annals of the New York Academy of Sciences, 699,* 181–199.

Troiano, R. P., Flegal, K. M., Kuczmarski, R. J., Campbell, S. M., & Johnson, C. L. (1995). Overweight prevalence and trends for children and adolescents. *Archives of Pediatric and Adolescent Medicine, 149,* 1085–1091.

Tucker, L. A. (1986). The relationship of television viewing to physical fitness and obesity. *Adolescence, 21,* 797–806.

Wadden, T. A., Stunkard, A. J., Rich, L., Rubin, C. J., Sweidel, G., & McKinney, S. (1990). Obesity in Black adolescent girls: A controlled clinical trial of treatment by diet, behavior modification, and parental support. *Pediatrics, 85,* 345–352.

Wardle, J. (1995). The assessment of obesity: Theoretical background and practical advice. *Behavior Research Therapy,*
33, 107–117.

Wardle, J., & Beales, S. (1986). Restraint, body image and food attitudes in children from 12 to 18 years. *Appetite, 7,*
209–217.

Webber, L. S., &Freedman, D. S., Cresanta, J. L. (1986). Tracking of cardiovascular disease rick factor variables in
school age children. In G. S. Berenson (Ed.), *Causation of cardiovascular risk factors in children: Perspectives on*
cardiovascular risk factors in early life. New York: Raven.

Weill, W. B. (1977). Current controversies in childhood obesity. *Journal of Pediatrics, 91,* 175–187.

Wing, R., Epstein, L., & Marcus, M. (1984). Mood changes in behavioral weight loss programs. *Psychosomatic*
Research, 28, 189–196.

Wisniewski, L. (1995). Group treatment of morbidly obese pre-pubescent children. In F. Wren (Chair), *Childhood*
obesity: Psychopharmacology, group treatment, co-morbidity, and epidemiology. Symposium conducted at the
meeting of the American Academy of Child and Adolescent Psychiatry, New Orleans.

Wisniewski, L., Marcus, M., & Wren, F. (1994, November). *Demographic characteristics and psychiatric and medical*
comorbidity in morbidly obese adolescents. Paper presented at the annual meeting of the Association for the
Advancement of Behavior Therapy, San Diego.

Wisniewski, L., Wren, F., & Marcus, M. (1996, March). *Medical and psychiatric comorbidity in severely obese children*
and adolescents presenting for weight loss. Paper presented as the annual meeting of the Society for Behavioral
Medicine, Washington, DC.

Chapter 8

Child Witnesses of Interparental Violence: Child and Family Treatment

Melissa K. Runyon
University of Miami School of Medicine

Isandy Basilio
Nova Southeastern University

Vincent B. Van Hasselt
Nova Southeastern University

Michel Hersen
Pacific University

Recent epidemiological research indicates that a woman is battered by her partner every 8 seconds (Straus & Gelles, 1986; Straus, Gelles, & Steinmetz, 1980). Further, it is estimated that forms of marital violence, including hitting, beating, and threatening with weapons, are experienced by more than 1.8 million women each year (Straus, 1977; Straus et al., 1980; Straus & Gelles, 1986). Moreover, there is a consensus that this number is probably a gross underestimate, given that many cases of marital violence are not reported. Until recently, family violence treatment focused on the battered woman and the male batterer, but directed a modicum of attention to the potential effects on the estimated 3.3 million children witnessing interparental violence (Carlson, 1984; Silvern & Kaersvang, 1989). For example, investigations conducted over the past decade suggest that children experience a number of problems associated with witnessing conjugal violence. Some of these difficulties include aggression (Jouriles, Pfiffner, & O'Leary, 1988), anxiety-withdrawal (Forsstrom-Cohen & Rosenbaum, 1985), motor excess (Jouriles et al., 1988; Jouriles, Murphy, & O'Leary, 1989), social problem-solving deficiencies (Rosenberg, 1987), conduct disorder (Jouriles et al., 1989), and personality disorders (Fantuzzo et al., 1991; Jouriles et al., 1989). Illustrative is a study conducted by Hughes (1988) demonstrating that children who witness interparental violence evince higher levels of anxiety and lower levels of self-esteem than a nonwitness comparison group. In another investigation, female child witnesses reported higher levels of anxiety, depression, and aggression relative to nonwitness counterparts (Forsstrom-Cohen & Rosenbaum, 1985).

Results of other investigative efforts (Jaffe, Wolfe, Wilson, & Zak, 1986a; Silvern & Kaersvang, 1989) reveal that many child witnesses exhibit adjustment difficulties similar to those of physically and sexually abused children. Specifically, these children may experience posttraumatic stress symptoms, such as nightmares, intrusive thoughts, recurring memories of violence, hypersensitivity, and anxiety. Additionally, children witnessing interparental violence, when compared to children from nonviolent homes, endorsed more depressive symptoms on the Children's Depression Inventory (Christopolous et al., 1987; Hughes, 1988) and displayed lower levels of empathy and sensitivity toward others (Hinchey & Gavalek, 1982; Rosenberg, 1987). Further, Rosenberg (1987) reported that child witnesses tended to use more passive or aggressive strategies for solving interpersonal problems.

Jaffe, Wilson, and Wolfe (1986b) garnered data indicative of gender differences in the effects of witnessing conjugal violence: Female witnesses experienced more internalizing behavior problems (e.g., anxiety, dependency needs, perfectionism, depression, irritability) and social dysfunction. Male counterparts tended to exhibit both internalizing and externalizing disorders (e.g., aggression and adjustment problems). Overall, children from violent families had significantly more behavioral difficulties than children from nonviolent homes. Several studies (Hershorn & Rosenbaum, 1985; Hughes & Barad, 1983; Porter & O'Leary, 1980; Rosenbaum & O'Leary, 1981; Wolfe, Zak, Wilson, & Jaffe, 1986) have replicated these findings.

Researchers have suggested that, in addition to gender, the effects of witnessing interparental violence are mediated by age (Hughes & Barad, 1983; Jaffe, Wolfe, & Wilson, 1990). For example, Hughes and Barad (1983) found that preschool-age child witnesses reported lower levels of self-competence than older child witnesses and nonwitness comparisons. And investigators have identified various symptoms that child witnesses exhibit depending on age. In particular, infants often exhibit impaired physical health, poor sleeping habits, and excessive crying, whereas preschoolers tend to have more fears, irritability, and somatic complaints (Jaffe et al., 1990). Further, older children and adolescents are generally aggressive, oppositional, and display conduct problems.

Another factor mitigating the effects of witnessing violence is parenting style (Hershorn & Rosenbaum, 1985; Jouriles et al., 1988). When examining children who witness interparental violence, parents who reported less punitive childrearing strategies had offspring with fewer behavioral problems than more punitive parents. Further, Green (1983) identified three parenting styles associated with reported posttraumatic symptomalogy and child behavioral disturbance. The first style, "harsh and punitive childrearing," is related to presence of conduct disorder, poor impulse control, and increased aggression toward others. "Scapegoating" appears to correspond with poor self-concept and depression in children. Finally, "maternal deprivation and abandonment" is associated with a lack of basic trust, low frustration tolerance, and separation anxiety. As becomes evident, the relation between parenting style and child behavioral disturbance is crucial in the design of treatment strategies.

Beyond the deleterious emotional and behavioral effects characterizing many children witnessing interparental violence, there is an increased risk for physical harm. Roy (1988) suggested that child witnesses are likely to be physically injured (either directly or indirectly) during violent episodes. Indeed, children may be hit or pushed when attempting to intervene; or they may be inadvertently injured by objects thrown by parents during a domestic dispute. Consequently, interventions must provide children with a personal safety plan to decrease the likelihood of physical injury.

Although research supports the relation between witnessing conjugal violence and negative psychological sequelae in children, few interventions have been developed that are specifically geared toward this population. The few extant programs suggest that group treatment is the most widely used modality for treating child witnesses (Alessi & Hearn, 1984; Grusznski, Brink, & Edelson, 1988; Hughes, 1982; Jaffe, Wilson, & Wolfe, 1986b; Jaffe, Wolfe, &

Wilson, 1990; Patterson, 1993; Peled & Davis, 1992). Although there has been little empirical validation of the efficacy of group interventions implemented to date, Jaffe et al. (1986b) provided promising preliminary results. These investigators examined the effectiveness of 10 group sessions for child witnesses residing in a shelter. Group treatment focused on identifying feelings, dealing with anger, acquisition of safety skills, determining and utilizing social supports, improving self-concept, examining feelings of responsibility for family violence, coping with instability in the family environment, and exploring gender stereotypes. Following treatment, there was an increase in children's ability to respond to emergency situations skillfully, and to identify positive aspects of themselves. A second study revealed significant improvements in overall social and emotional adjustment, and school behavior as a function of group participation (Jaffe, Wilson, & Wolfe, 1986b).

Other evaluations of group therapy for child witnesses have yielded improved social skills and fewer physical complaints (Cassady, Allen, Lyon, & McGeehan, 1987), as well as increased self-esteem and nonviolent conflict resolution skills (Grusznski et al., 1988). Unfortunately, the heuristic value of the aforementioned protocols is unclear due to the failure to include no-treatment control conditions.

There is a general agreement among professionals in the area that posttrauma healing is facilitated when children feel supported by peers who have had similar experiences (Galante & Foa, 1986; Lystad, 1985; Terr, 1989; Weinberg, 1990; Yule & Williams, 1990). This provides further evidence for the utility of group treatment with child witnesses. In addition, group treatment provides children with opportunities for socialization, feedback regarding socially desired behavior, and role playing of appropriate peer interactions.

The purpose of this manual is to provide a detailed description of a group treatment strategy designed for child witnesses and their families receiving services at the Parent and Child Training (PACT) Project of the Interpersonal Violence Program (IVP) at Nova Southeastern University. PACT consists of two components: Child Treatment Program (CTP) and Parent Treatment Program (PTP). CTP involves educating children about interparental violence, identification and expression of feelings, ensuring safety of family members, and teaching children a variety of anger management and social problem-solving skills. PTP consists of information concerning emotional and behavioral effects of interparental violence on child witnesses, child behavior management strategies, and alternative methods of conflict resolution (e.g., anger management strategies). Fifteen CTP and 15 PTP sessions are conducted concurrently. Sessions 6, 12, and 18 involve both children and parents and provide an opportunity for parents to practice management skills with the child and to receive performance feedback from staff. The purpose of this chapter is to outline the assessment process, describe the PACT treatment components, and discuss general problems in implementation of the program.

ASSESSMENT

Children and their families participating in IVP are administered a standard assessment battery to determine their level of social and emotional adjustment, ascertain behavioral deficits and excesses, identify appropriate treatment targets, and examine treatment outcome. Assessment involves administration of a variety of instruments to children, parents, and teachers. Where possible, both parents complete the parent packet to allow for interparental comparisons. This may provide information on whether the child's problems are being exaggerated or minimized by one parent. In addition, multiple sources of information may also provide a clearer picture of the child's functioning. However, many of the families referred to PACT are separated or divorced; therefore, the assessment must rely on one parent's report.

Children are administered the measures listed in Table 8.1, with the exception of the Child Impact of Traumatic Events Scale–Revised (CITES–R). The CITES–R is administered only to those children where there is suspicion of sexual abuse.

Child Measures

Schedule for Affective Disorders and Schizophrenia for Children (Present Episode) (K–SADS– P).   The K–SADS–P (Puig-Antich & Chambers, 1986) is a semistructured psychiatric interview, administered to children age 6 to 18 and their parents. This instrument assesses current episodes of child psychopathology. The interview covers *DSM–III* symtomatology for the following psychiatric disorders: Major Depression, Dysthymia, Mania, Hypomania, Bipolar Disorder, Schizoaffective Disorder, Schizophrenia, Schizophreniform Disorder, Brief Reactive Psychosis, Paranoid Disorder, Schizotypal Personality Disorder, Attention Deficit Disorder, Conduct Disorder, Overanxious Disorder, Separation Anxiety Disorder, Phobia, Obsessive Compulsive Disorder, Depersonalization Disorder, Panic Disorder, Anorexia Nervosa, Bulimia, Alcohol and Substance Abuse, and Posttraumatic Stress Disorder. Severity of symptoms is evaluated on a scale from 0 (*no information*) to 6 (*severe*), or 1 to 4 depending on the particular symptom being addressed. Symptom severity is assessed over two time periods: the last week, and the last episode or last year, whichever is the shortest. The interrater and test–retest reliability of the K–SADS–P has been shown to be acceptable ($r = .83$ and $r = .83$, respectively) (Apter, Orvaschel, Laseg, Moses, & Tyano, 1989).

Children's Depression Inventory (CDI).   The CDI (Kovacs & Beck, 1983) contains 27 items that assess mood, pessimism, appetite loss, suicidality, and other depressive symptomatology in children and adolescents age 8 to 17. A summative score ranging from 0 to 54, reflecting the severity of the child's depression, is derived from children's responses. Cutoff scores representing clinical levels of depression vary across gender and age groups. However, the mean cut-off score for a sample of 705 males and females ranging from 7 to 13 years of age is 9.65 with a standard deviation of 7.3 (Finch, Saylor, & Edwards, 1985). Smucker, W. E. Craighead, L. W. Craighead, and Green (1986) examined the psychometric properties of the CDI and determined that the coefficient alpha index of reliability was .84 for males and .87 for females.

TABLE 8.1

Interpersonal Violence Program Child Assessment Packet

Schedule for Affective Disorders and Schizophrenia for Children (K–SADS–P)
Children's Depression Inventory (CDI)
Revised Children's Manifest Anxiety Scale (RCMAS)
Children's Inventory of Anger (CIA)
Harter Self-Perception Profile
Child version—age 11 years and below
Personal Data Form (PDF)
Family Environment Scale–Revised (FES–R)
Child version—age 7 to 11
Children's Impact of Traumatic Events Scale–Revised (CITES–R)

Revised–Children's Manifest Anxiety Scale (RCMAS).   The RCMAS (Reynolds & Richmond, 1985) consists of 37 items that evaluate level of anxiety among children and adolescents. In addition to a summative score of general anxiety (TOT) ranging from 0 to 37, items are divided into four subscales: Physiological Anxiety (PA), Worry and Oversensitivity (WO), Social Anxiety (CA), and a Lie Scale (LIE). Examples of RCMAS items are: "I worry about what other people will think about me," and "I have trouble making up my mind." Cutoff scores vary across age groups; however, the overall mean scores on each subscale for a normative sample of 4,972 were PA: Mean = 4.10, WO: Mean = 4.81, CA: Mean = 2.80, LIE: Mean = 3.03, and TOT: Mean = 11.70 (see Reynolds & Richmond, 1978).

The Children's Inventory of Anger (CIA).   The CIA (Nelson, Hart, & Finch, 1993) is a 71-item self-report instrument that assesses anger in children age 7 and above. Scenarios are presented in which children are likely to become angry and the examinee indicates their perceived level of anger if they were placed in the particular situation. Sample items are: "On the playground a boy/girl younger than you pushes you down," and "You convince your mother to let you ride your bike and then you find that it has a flat tire." Split-half reliability coefficients ranged from .83 to .95 for a nonclinical sample (Finch, Saylor, & Nelson, 1983) and from .93 to .96 for a psychiatric sample (Mayhall, Nelson, Politano, & Wendall, 1986). Test–retest reliability is acceptable for both clinical populations (r = .82) (Montgomery, Nelson, & Finch, 1979) and nonclinical populations (r = .63 to .90) (Finch, Saylor, & Nelson, 1987).

Harter Perceived Self Competence Scale for Children–Revised (PSCS–R).   The child version of the PSCS–R (Harter, 1985) is a 36-item inventory that examines the perceived competence level of children age 7 to 11. Sample items of the child version include: "Some kids would rather play outdoors in their spare time, but other kids would rather watch T.V.," and "Some kids find it hard to make friends, but other kids find it's pretty easy to make friends." Harter (1985) provided normative data for both males and females Grades 3 through 8.

Personal Data Form (PDF).   The PDF (Emery & O'Leary, 1982) is a 38-item self-report inventory that determines the child's level of perceived conflict and acceptance in the home, peer group, and school. Items are scored on a 3-point scale: *not true* (0), *sometimes true* (1), *true* (2). The authors found that the scale correlates highly with the parents' report of conflict (Emery & O'Leary, 1982).

Children's Version Family Environment Scale (CVFES).   The CVFES (Pino, Simmons, & Slawinoski, 1984) consists of 30 items assessing perceptions of the family environment of young children age 5 to 11. Children are shown pictures of family interactions and asked to select the one that looks most like their own family. This instrument measures 10 areas related to the family environment, including cohesion, expressiveness, conflict, independence, achievement-orientation, intellectual-cultural orientation, active-recreational orientation, moral-religious emphasis, organization, and control. Subscale scores are obtained by summing the numbers corresponding to each item endorsed. A normative sample consisted of 158 nonclinical children, Grades 1 through 6, from diverse socioeconomic and ethnic groups. The test–retest administration to the normative sample over a 4-week interval yielded good reliability (r = .80).

The Children's Impact of Traumatic Events Scale–R (CITES–R).   The CITES–R (V. V. Wolfe, Gentile, Michienski, Sas, & D. A. Wolfe, 1991) is administered only to those children who are suspected to be victims of sexual abuse. Guidelines for suspicion include a reported history of sexual abuse, endorsement of two or more possible sexual assault indicators (see Table 8.2) (Grimm & Montgomery, 1985), or endorsement of five or more critical items (see Table 8.3) on the Child Sexual Behavior Inventory (Friedrich, 1990). The instrument contains 54 items that assess the impact of abuse from the child's perspective. It consists of 11 subscales that load on four dimensions: posttraumatic symptoms (intrusive thoughts, avoidance, hyperarousal, and sexual anxiety), social reactions (negative reactions from others and social support), abuse attributions (self-blame and guilt, empowerment, vulnerability, and dangerous world), and eroticism. Examples of a CITES–R items are "I try not to think about what happened," and "I think of what happened to me even when I don't want to."

Parent Measures

All parent(s) or guardian(s) complete the PACT Parent Assessment Packet (see Table 8.4) to assess family environment, parental stress and psychopathology, and parental perception of the child's behavioral and emotional functioning.

Medical/Developmental History Form.   This form elicits specific information regarding medical problems; developmental delays; and educational, developmental, family, and social history.

TABLE 8.2
Sexual Assault Indicators (Grimm & Montgomery, 1985)

Increase in physical complaints (i.e., headaches, nausea, etc.)
Nightmares and difficulty sleeping
Bed-wetting
Painful defecation
Unexplained gagging
Change in appetite
Excessive masturbation
Sexual experimentation that is not developmentally appropriate
Exhibiting explicit knowledge of the sex act, precocious sex play, and developmentally unusual sexual behavior or language
Increase in aggressive or inappropriate touching of peers
Extreme reluctance to being examined by a doctor (i.e., tantrum)
Vaginal or urethral discharge or pain
Oral, anal, or genital venereal disease
A sudden unexplained change in behavior such as clinging, whining, excessive fear of being touched, fear of going home or to a babysitter or relatives
Regression to infantile behavior
Excessive acting out behavior
Depression

Note: From Grimm & Montgomery, 1985. If two or more of these symptoms are reported, sexual abuse is suspected and the CITES–R is administered to the client.

TABLE 8.3

Critical Items on the CSBI

Touches other people's private parts
Overly aggressive (females)
Extremely passive (males)
Tries to undress others
French kisses
Touches women's breasts
Touches sex parts in public
Touches sex parts in private
Asks to view explicit television
Shows sex parts to adults
Attempts to view pictures of nude people
Talks about wanting to be the opposite sex
Imitates sex behavior with dolls
Rubs body against people or furniture
Asks others to engage in sex
Masturbates with hand
Inserts objects into vagina or anus
Puts mouth on sex parts
Imitates intercourse
Very interested in the opposite sex
Shows sex parts to children
Hugs adults he or she does not know well
Masturbates with object
Uses words to describe sex acts
Talks about sex acts

Note: **From Friedrich et al., 1992. If five or more of the above critical items are endorsed for the child, sexual abuse is suspected and the CITES–R is administered.**

TABLE 8.4

Interparental Violence Program Parent Assessment Packet

Schedule for Affective Disorders and Schizophrenia for Children (K–SADS–P)
Beck Depression Inventory (BDI)
Beck Anxiety Inventory (BAI)
Beck Hopelessness Scale (BHS)
Parenting Stress Index (PSI)
Locke–Wallace Marital Adjustment Test
Life Experiences Survey (LES)
Child Abuse Potential Inventory (CAP)
Knowledge of Behavioral Principles as Applied to Children (KBPAC)
Family Environment Scale–Revised (FES-R)
Children's Sexual Behavior Inventory (CSBI)
Harter Perception Profile
Quay–Revised Behavior Problem Checklist (RBPC)
Eyberg Child Behavior Inventory
Medical/Developmental History Form

Beck Depression Inventory (BDI).   The BDI (Beck, Ward, Mendelsohn, Mock, & Erbaugh, 1961) is the most frequently employed measure of depressive symptomatology in adults. Individuals endorse items reflecting intensity of depressive symptoms, which yields a summative score reflecting the severity of depression. Scores between 11 to 17 suggest mild depression, those from 18 to 29 reflect moderate depression, and scores of 30 or more indicate severe depression.

Beck Hopelessness Scale (BHS).   The BHS (Beck, Weissman, Lester, & Trexler, 1974) is a 20-item self-report instrument assessing negative expectancies and pessimism about the future, which are strongly correlated with depression and suicidality. Items are answered in a true–false format. Sample questions include "I look forward to the future with hope and enthusiasm," and "I might as well give up because I can't make things better for myself." An overall score is obtained by summing the numbers corresponding to the given response. A score of nine or above is of clinical significance. The authors report high internal consistency (r = .93) for the instrument (Beck et al., 1974).

Beck Anxiety Inventory (BAI).   The BAI (Beck & Steer, 1990) is a 21-item self-report anxiety symptom inventory. Items are rated using a 4-point scale ranging from 0 (*not at all*) to 3 (*severely, I could barely stand it*). The Total Score ranges from 0 to 63 and is the sum of the numbers 0 to 3 corresponding to endorsed items. Scores from 0 to 9 reflect normal levels of anxiety, scores from 10 to 18 represent mild anxiety, scores from 19 to 29 indicate moderate anxiety, scores above 30 suggest severe anxiety. Beck and Steer (1990) reported BAI test–retest and alpha coefficients of .75 and .92, respectively.

Parenting Stress Index (PSI).   The PSI (Abidin, 1986) is a 101-item parent report measure that assesses the degree to which a parent perceives parenting as difficult. Respondents rate problems on a 5-point scale (*strongly agree* to *strongly disagree*). A sample item is "When my child wants something, my child usually keeps trying to get it." Scores are determined separately for child and parent domains. The former measures perceived adaptability, acceptability, demandingness, mood, distractibility, and whether or not the child reinforces the parent. Depression, attachment, restrictions of role, sense of competence, social isolation, relationship with spouse, and parent health scales comprise the parent domain. An obtained stress score greater than 122.7 on the parent domain is clinically significant.

Locke–Wallace Marital Adjustment Scale (LWMAS).   The LWMAS (Locke & Wallace, 1959) is a 15-item instrument that assesses marital adjustment by asking respondents to indicate the degree to which they concur on a particular issue. The first item, a general index of marital happiness, is given extra weight in scoring. Items 2 through 15 are assessed on a 6-point scale (0 = *always disagree*, 5 = *always agree*). Examples of LWMAS items are "Handling family finances," and "Sex relations." The range of this measure is 2 to 158 with scores over 100 reflecting relationship problems. The authors reported good internal consistency (r = .90) and discriminant validity (i.e., adjusted vs. maladjusted couples).

Life Experiences Survey (LES).   The LES (Sarason, Johnson, & Siegal, 1978) asks parents to indicate positive and negative changes experienced in their family during the past year. Respondents rate level of stress associated with reported changes on a 7-point scale ranging from extremely negative (–3) to extremely positive (+3). A negative change score is obtained by summing the impact ratings of events reported as negative; a positive change score is derived from those events experienced as positive. A total change score is based on the sum of the impact ratings of both positive and negative events. A clinically significant total score is greater than 15.97 for males and 16.61 for females.

The Child Abuse Potential Inventory (CAP).   The CAP (Milner, 1986) is a 116-item self-report measure designed to identify parents who engage in abusive behavior toward their child. Parents indicate whether they agree or disagree with statements reflecting child problems, unhappiness, loneliness, negative self-concept, and other behavioral and personality domains. Cutoff scores are used to predict whether the parent is at high risk for being abusive. Examples of a CAP items are "Children should never be bad," and "I always try to check on my child when it's crying." Milner (1986) reported that the instrument measures six main constructs: distress, rigidity, unhappiness, problems with others, problems with one's child and one's self, and problems with one's family. The CAP has been found to have high discriminant validity (Milner, 1986).

The Knowledge of Behavioral Principles as Applied to Children (KBPAC).   The 50-item KBPAC (O'Dell, Tarler-Benlolo, & Flynn, 1979) taps the parents' understanding of basic child management skills. It includes a brief description of problematic parent–child situations, followed by four possible responses for example: "A baby often screams for several minutes and gets parents' attention. Which of the following is probably the best way for the parents to reduce the screaming? (a) If there is nothing wrong with the child, ignore his screaming even though the first few times he screams even louder; (b) Ignore all noises and sounds the child makes; (c) Babies usually have good reasons for screaming; (d) none of the above." Advantages of the KBPAC include good reliability and validity, utilization of problematic situations associated with abusive behavior, presentation of behavioral principles to parents in layman's terms, and identification of specific problem areas that subsequently can be targeted in treatment (O'Dell et al., 1979).

Family Environment Scale–Revised (FES–R).   The FES–R (R. H. Moos & B. S. Moos, 1986) consists of 90 items assessing perceptions of the family environment of adolescent children and adults age 12 and above. The instrument measures 10 areas related to the family environment including cohesion, expressiveness, conflict, independence, achievement-orientation, intellectual-cultural orientation, active-recreational orientation, moral-religious emphasis, organization, and control. Examples of FES–R items are "Family members almost always rely on themselves when a problem comes up," and "Family members really help and support one another." The authors reported acceptable test–retest reliability coefficients ranging from .68 for the Independence subscale to .86 for the Cohesion subscale. Also, mean score cutoffs are provided based on the data obtained from a nonclinical population.

Children's Sexual Behavior Inventory (CSBI).   The CSBI (Friedrich et al., 1992) is a 106-item checklist completed by parents that assesses various aspects of sexual behavior: self-stimulation, sexual aggression, gender-role behavior, and personal boundary violations in children age 2 to 12. Parents rate the frequency of the behaviors on a 4-point scale ranging from *never* to *at least once a week.* Example of a CSBI items are, "Masturbates with object," and "Imitates the act of sexual intercourse."

Harter Perceived Self-Competence Scale for Children–Revised (PSCS–R, Teacher Form). The child version of the PSCS–R (Teacher Form) (Harter, 1985) is a 16-item inventory that examines the parent or teacher's perception of children's behavior age 7 to 11. Sample items of the child version include: "This child is really good at his/her schoolwork," or "This child can't do the schoolwork assigned," and "This child finds it hard to make friends," or "For this child it's pretty easy."

Quay Revised Behavior Problem Checklist (RBPC).   The RBPC (Quay & Peterson, 1983) is an 89-item checklist that asks parents to rate the severity of their child's problem behavior on a 3-point scale (0 = *no problem*, 1 = *mild problem*, and 3 = *severe problem*). The instrument assesses the domains of conduct disorder, socialized aggression, attention problems, anxiety and withdrawal, psychotic behavior, and motor excess. Quay (1983) established mean scores suggestive of clinical behavior disturbance for both a clinical and nonclinical population. Quay and Petersen (1983) presented extensive reliability (mean test–retest reliability across subscales of .67, mean interrater reliability across subscales of .64) and discriminative validity data.

The Eyberg Child Behavior Inventory (ECBI).   The ECBI (Eyberg & Ross, 1978) lists 36 disruptive behaviors for which the parent indicates on a 7-point scale (1 = *never*, 7 = *always*) how often the child exhibits each response. A problem scale also assesses whether or not the parent perceives the behavior as undesirable (1 = *yes*, 0 = *no*). Burns and Patterson (1991) demonstrated that the items loaded on three factors: oppositional defiant disorder, attention deficit hyperactivity disorder, and conduct disorder. Sample items include "gets angry," and "fails to finish tasks." If the sum of the intensity scores is greater than 127, significant behavioral disturbance is suggested (Robinson, Eyberg, & Ross, 1980); a problem score of greater than 11 is clinically significant. Adequate split-half reliability, internal consistency, and test–retest reliability have been demonstrated for this instrument (Robinson et al., 1980). Additionally, scores on the ECBI have discriminated between conduct-disordered and nonclinical children (Webster-Stratton, 1985).

PACT PROCEDURE

Following completion of the assessment battery, an initial intake evaluation is scheduled. When contacting the parents or guardian for this appointment, they are is asked to bring toys for children so that the child is occupied while Parent Measures are being completed.

For children under 6, an interview is conducted with the parent or guardian. This 30- to 60-minute unstructured interview provides background information and relevant social, medical, developmental, and family history. The K–SADS–P (Puig-Antich & Chambers, 1986) (described earlier) is administered to the guardian to determine diagnostic symptomatology. Further, a brief unstructured interview also is conducted with the child if the child is 6 years or older in order to obtain a history of the presenting problems.

Referral Criteria

Children are eligible for group treatment at PACT if they are between the age of 6 and 9, exhibit some form of emotional or social dysfunction, have one or both parents concurrently receiving treatment in the Family Violence Project (FVP) of the Interpersonal Violence Program, and have witnessed some form of violence (i.e., emotional, physical, or sexual) in the home. PACT offers group treatment for children who have witnessed interparental violence. If it is determined from the assessment that a child exhibits suicide or homicide potential, psychosis, or extreme aggression that may place other children at risk, individual therapy or inpatient treatment is recommended. A child with a history of physical or sexual abuse may also be referred for individual psychotherapy. Also, every effort is made to accommodate the special needs of physically challenged children in individual treatment (i.e., an interpreter for the hearing disabled). However, an appropriate referral to an outside agency is made if the program is unable to meet the child's specific needs.

CHILD TREATMENT PROGRAM

Six is the recommended group size for preschool and elementary school-age children participating in the Child Treatment Program (CTP). Sessions should not exceed 90 minutes, including a 15-minute refreshment break. Two cofacilitators are used for modeling and role playing of trained skills and to provide performance feedback to group members.

Session 1: Introduction

The goals of Session 1 are to introduce children to the purpose of the group, establish ground rules for the group, build rapport and cohesiveness among group members, and evaluate and monitor group behavior.

Group Introductions.   Co-facilitators introduce themselves to the children: "Children, please sit down in a circle. Hello, I'm _____, and I'm _____, and we are going to be meeting with you each week at this time. We are looking forward to getting to know all of you and have each of you tell us your name, so let's start with you (points to first child)." Children state their name and then group leaders clarify names. "Okay, we want to make sure we know your names, because sometimes we have a hard time remembering names.... And if any of you forget someone else's name in the group that's okay, but please be polite by asking that person's name." The cofacilitator then goes around the circle repeating each child's name: "Hello, Johnny, Hello, Sue, we're happy to have each of you here."
"We are going to have 18 meetings in this room at the same time each week." The cofacilitator introduces a poster with 18 boxes labeled meeting 1 through 18. "Can you count to 18? Count along with us." Cofacilitators count the number of boxes. "That's the number

of times we're going to meet and when we get to the last box, that is our last meeting together. Each of you will be given an opportunity to check off a box on this poster when each meeting ends. Your mother/father/parents are going to join us during three of these meetings. Each meeting lasts for 1 hour and 30 minutes. That's about as long as it takes to watch three cartoons. During the last 15 minutes of each group, you may play with the toys and have the snack that your parent prepared."

Rationale. "You are here because your mother/father/parents said that they have a problem with fighting at home. For many children, seeing parents fight can be scary, confusing, and sad. It's okay for you to feel this way and for you to talk about your feelings. It's not okay for your parents to hurt one another or to hurt you, and if anything like that happens at your house, you can tell us. During the meetings, we are going to talk about your feelings and your families, and learn things to help you feel better. It's important that you understand that your parent's fighting is not your fault and that the group is to help you feel better about yourselves and to make sure you don't get hurt. Do you have any questions?"

Group Rules. "We need to establish group rules, so that each of us gets a chance to talk and feel that other group members are listening. First, everything we say in here is private. What you say is just between us unless you tell me that you are going to hurt yourselves, hurt someone else, or that someone else is hurting you. We have to tell someone else if these things are happening to make sure that you are safe. For example, if you tell me that someone like your mother/father is hitting you, I have to tell. If you tell me that someone has touched your private parts, I have to tell. You haven't done anything wrong, but I have to tell to make sure you are safe. It is not okay for these things to happen to you. Do you understand?"

"Second, there is no talking outside of this room about what other group members have said. Remember, what others say in the group is private." Rules are listed on the chalkboard.

1. No hitting; hitting is not okay because someone could get hurt. The number one rule is that you can't do anything that may hurt yourself or someone else.
2. No interrupting; we talk one at a time.
3. Everyone gets a chance to talk.
4. We sit quietly and listen when another group member is talking.
5. No name calling; name calling can make others feel bad about themselves.
   "Do you have any questions about any of the rules?"

Following the opportunity for questions, cofacilitators review the rules and model both appropriate and inappropriate behaviors. For example, one facilitator says, "I'm going to sit quietly and listen to _____ while he/she is talking." As the other facilitator talks, the listener sits quietly and makes eye contact. Afterward, the listener states, "I sat quietly and looked at _____ while he/she was talking." Next, both facilitators begin talking simultaneously and the children are asked if that is appropriate behavior. When children respond "no," these individuals are asked what they would have done differently.

"At the end of each session while eating our snack, we are going to decide if you were able to follow the rules." The cofacilitator presents a chart with each observable rule listed (see Table 8.5). "For each one you follow, you can place a check on the list. If you have a check for three rules, you earn a star for that day. You are a group winner for that day, because you

TABLE 8.5

Monitoring and Evaluation Chart for Group Behavior

1. No hitting
2. Talking one at a time
3. Sitting quietly and listening
4. No name calling
5. Participated in group
GROUP WINNER!!!!!!!

took turns talking, sat quietly listening to other group members, and participated during group. That's great! If you have a star for 10 meetings, you can trade the stars for a reward during the last meeting."

Group Task. Eighteen group behavior monitoring charts are placed in a packet that the children personalize by writing their name and drawing a picture on the cover. Personalizing the evaluation packet provides children with a sense of belonging to the group, and opportunities to share and build rapport with group members. Also, the exercise allows cofacilitators to observe peer interactions among group members and to praise prosocial behavior.

Crayons and evaluation packets are distributed to child dyads. Children are given 15 minutes to decorate the evaluation cover with their name and to draw their favorite activity. After completing the drawings, children are asked to describe the picture to their partner: "Describe your picture to your partner, and partners listen carefully."

"Now we are going to tell the group about our partner's picture." The cofacilitators begin by stating: "This is _____ 's picture and he/she likes to _____." While presenting the picture to the group, a description is provided. The leaders then offer praise for the behavior. For example, "You did a wonderful job drawing the picture; it's beautiful." After the cofacilitators model the presentation, each pair is given an opportunity to share pictures. The leaders praise the children for drawing behavior as well as for positive peer interactions (e.g., listening to what partner said about picture, presenting partner's picture).

Socialization Activity. Fifteen minutes is allotted for unstructured play, snack time, and behavioral monitoring and evaluation. While the children participate in unstructured activities, cofacilitators review desired behaviors for group participation with each child. For example, "(child's name), did you sit quietly and listen today?" If the child and cofacilitators agree, the child is allowed to place a check on the chart. Positive reinforcement for desirable behavior is provided: "That's right you were a model group member. You sat quietly and listened. That's wonderful!" When there is a discrepancy, the child is informed of undesirable behavior and encouraged that he/she is capable of performing the desired response. For example, "(child's name) do you remember when you ran over to the chalkboard and talked about your teacher while _____ was talking? You were not sitting quietly, so you don't earn a check. I bet that you can earn that check by sitting quietly and listening next week." The child is given a star to put on the chart only if the rules were followed.

Session 2: Effects of Witnessing Violence

The goals of Session 2 are to review group rules, define abuse and violence, provide an understanding that violence is not appropriate, provide education regarding the effects of witnessing interparental violence, and monitor and evaluate group behavior.

Reviewing Group Rules.   A poster presentation of the rules is briefly reviewed.

Introduction.   Descriptions of other treatment programs for child witnesses include an educational component for defining abuse and increasing children's understanding of the behavioral and emotional effects of witnessing interparental violence (Alessi & Hearn, 1984; Grusznski et al., 1988; Hughes, 1982; Jaffe, Wilson, & Wolfe 1986b; Peled & Davis, 1992). The purpose of the educational component described here is to provide children with an understanding of violence and abuse, educate children that the use of violence is inappropriate, and normalize ambivalent feelings that may be experienced by child witnesses.

Rationale.   "Today, we are going to talk about what abuse and violence means. Many children are hurt at home or see other people get hurt and they don't know that it's not okay for this to happen."

Defining Abuse.   "Abuse/violence is any behavior that one person does to another that physically hurts the person or hurts their feelings. If a person is called a bad name and their feelings are hurt, that person is being abused. It is abusive if we kick or punch someone." Each group member is asked: "What does abuse mean to you (child's name)?"

Appropriate responses are praised by the cofacilitators. In addition, successive approximations of desired responses are verbally reinforced (e.g., "That's right, abuse is when you hurt someone either by hitting them or calling them names—very good").

Types of Abuse.   After defining abuse, the three types of abuse are presented on the chalkboard. "There are three types of abuse: feeling (psychological) abuse, physical abuse, and sexual abuse. *Feeling abuse* is when we call someone a name or threaten to hurt them. Calling someone stupid or saying we will hit someone if they do not pick up the toy is feeling abuse."

Each child is asked to provide an example of feeling abuse. Feedback is provided to reinforce appropriate responses.

Example 1:
Cofacilitator: "(child's name), What is feeling abuse?"
        Child: "Calling someone a bad name."
Cofacilitator: "That's right. It is calling someone a bad name, but what would be a bad name?"
        Child: "Stupid weenie."
Cofacilitator: "Stupid weenie is a great example of feeling abuse. You did a great job!"

Example 2:

Cofacilitator:	"(Child's name), What is feeling abuse?"
Child:	"If I kick you."
Cofacilitator:	"Kicking me is a great example of physical abuse, but it is not feeling abuse. Feeling abuse is calling someone a name or threatening to hurt them. Try again. What is feeling abuse?"
Child:	"Dummy."
CoFacilitator:	"Telling a person he/she is dumb is feeling abuse. You worked really hard to think of that answer. Good job."

Physical and sexual abuse are defined, examples are presented and elicited, and feedback is provided to facilitate learning.

"*Physical abuse* is any aggressive behavior that hurts someone. Hitting, biting, and pushing is physical abuse. A person's body is private and that person has the right to protect it. *Sexual abuse* is touching someone in a place he or she doesn't want to be touched. Touching private parts or having someone talk about your private parts is sexual abuse. It is not okay for these things to happen to you or your family members and you should tell us or someone else who can help you if this happens. Abuse does not happen in everybody's home, but if it happens in your home, you need to tell."

Effects of Witnessing Interparental Violence.   The educational component emphasizes how child witnesses feel and react to interparental violence. The presentation is purposely geared toward other children, because it is too early in the group process to ask children to share family secrets. Requesting specific information about interparental violence at this stage may result in an increased attrition rate, interference with rapport building, and a decrease in group participation. This section establishes commonalities about problem areas among group members and prepares children to discuss domestic violence in the next session.

"Many children see their dads hit their mothers. Kids love both mom and dad, so this is confusing. They may feel angry that dad hits mom and they may try to protect mom. They may be afraid that dad is going to hurt them or mom. Other times, kids may laugh, play, and have fun with dad. Kids can become even more confused and wonder how dad can be both loving and mean. Many kids blame themselves for the fighting, but the fighting is not the child's or the mother's fault. Dad is the one hitting and he is responsible for his behavior. Kids often feel angry with mom for staying with dad. Many kids who see dad hit mom feel this way and its okay. Sometimes kids feel better if they talk about dad hitting mom. It is often hard to talk about. Kids sometimes think about dad hitting mom so much that they can't pay attention in school. They can become so angry that they have difficulty controlling their tempers and take it out on others by hitting and saying mean things. Other kids feel confused and extremely sad. Many kids who see dad hitting mom feel this way. If any of you have similar feelings, there are things you can learn during the group that can help you feel better."

Socialization Activity.   Children participate in unstructured play, snack time, and behavioral monitoring and evaluation during the last 15 minutes of the session. At the end of group, parents are asked to bring an audiotape for their children the following week.

Session 3: Violence in Your Family

The stated goals of Session 3 are to review group rules, encourage children to share the violence experienced in the family, review types of abuse, introduce a relaxation exercise to decrease anxiety associated with discussing interparental violence, and monitor and evaluate group behavior.

Reviewing Group Rules.   A poster presentation of the rules is briefly reviewed.

Introduction.   Treatment programs emphasize the importance of encouraging children to discuss interparental violence they have witnessed and their associated feelings (Alessi & Hearn, 1984; Grusznski et al., 1988; Hughes, 1982; Jaffe, Wilson, & Wolfe, 1986b; Peled & Davis; 1992). Researchers have suggested that children's drawings and stories about the drawings can be utilized to assist children in understanding their reactions to traumatic experiences (Lipovsky, 1992; Pynoos & Eth, 1986). The procedure implemented to elicit specific information concerning violence in the family is adapted from a trauma workbook by Deaton and Johnson (1991). This strategy allows children to discuss feelings and thoughts associated with the family drawing.

Obtaining Information About Family.   "Today we are going to talk about your family. Let's start by drawing a picture of our families. Everyone please draw a picture of your family including all members that live in your house." Drawing supplies are distributed to group members. Initially, cofacilitators model how to share the family drawing for children. The following inquiries are made about each child's family drawing:

"Tell us who is in your drawing."
"What are you and your other family members doing?"
"How are you feeling?"
"How is your _____ (mother, father, sister, brother, grandmother) feeling?"
"What are you thinking about?"
"What are other family members thinking about?"
"Do you wish you were there or somewhere else? Why?"

After each child shares the family drawing, group members are asked, "Is there anything else you would like to know about another member's picture?" The cofacilitator may inquire further depending on the child's responses to initial questions; empathy and support are provided.

Children are reinforced for their effort, group participation, and drawing abilities: "Thank you for sharing your family pictures with the group. We really appreciate it, because sometimes it's hard to talk about our families, especially if things happen in our families that cause us pain and sadness. You worked hard drawing beautiful pictures. You chose so many bright colors for your pictures. That's excellent! (*child's name*), I really liked how you helped _____ hold up her/his picture. Thanks for asking _____ about his/her picture; that shows you're interested. (Each child is given a specific compliment for appropriate behavior.) You all did a wonderful job of sitting quietly and listening to the other group members."

Types of Abuse/Violence.   "The last time you were here, we talked about abuse and violence. What are the three types of abuse?" Children are given time to respond. Feedback is
given to reinforce appropriate responses and to correct inappropriate answers. The cofacilitator offers prompts if children have difficulty generating specific types of abuse (i.e., feeling,
physical, and sexual abuse). Similar guidelines are followed for eliciting examples of the
three forms of abuse.

Violence in the Home.   "Your mom/parents have stated that they have a problem with
fighting in the home. Tell us what kind of abuse you see them use (feeling, physical, or sexual
abuse) when they fight at home." Examples of prompts that may be used include: "Does your
dad hit your mother? Does your dad kick your mother? If your dad does these things, he is
using physical abuse during fights. Does your dad yell at your mom? Do you think it hurts
mom's feelings when he calls her stupid? Dad is using feeling abuse when he calls your mom
stupid. Have you ever seen your dad touch your mom in private places when she says no? If
dad did, then he was using sexual abuse. Draw a picture of the worst fight your parents have
ever had. Include who was fighting and what happened during the fight."
    Upon completion of the drawing, the following inquiries are made:

"Who causes the fights in your family?"
"Who else causes the fights?"
"What does each person do to cause the fight?"
"When there is a fight, what are you afraid will happen, to you, to mom, to dad, or to
    anyone else?"
"Where did you go or what did you do during the worst fight?"
"What do you remember about the worst fight?" Prompts may be offered (i.e., breaking of
    objects, hitting, screaming, crying).
"How did you feel during the worst fight?" "If its hard to say, draw a picture of the way
    you felt."

Empathy, validation of feelings, and support are provided for children's responses to these
questions. If discussing the drawing is highly anxiety provoking, questioning is discontinued.

Rationale for Relaxation Training.   Questions about violence in the family are likely to
increase anxiety level. Therefore, relaxation skills training is introduced as an effective method
to reduce tension and to improve self-control. "Many kids feel scared when they talk about
fighting at home. You just talked about the scary things that happen in your home. We are going
to listen to music and stretch our bodies to help us think less about these scary things. You can
do this at home when you feel fearful." Cofacilitators instruct children to observe as they model
relaxation skills during the introduction; however, children are asked to lie on mats and close
their eyes in subsequent training sessions.

Relaxation Training Exercise.   Although the utility of progressive muscle relaxation has not
been demonstrated empirically for this specific population, it has been effective in reducing
the physiological responses to feared stimuli in children (Laxer, Quarter, Kooman, & Walker,
1969; Laxer & Walker, 1970; Van Hasselt, Hersen, Bellack, Rosenblum, & Lamparski, 1979).

Morris and Kratochwill (1983) presented a muscle relaxation sequence that requires 20 to 25 minutes to implement. The currently employed script is modified to include fantasy, as recommended by Koeppen (1974) to help maintain the child's attention and interest.

For example, "Pretend you're a big blowfish; take a deep breath and hold it for about 10 seconds. Hold it in like a big round blowfish. Now, let it out and watch the air bubbles float up through the water. Raise both of your hands about halfway above the couch, pretend that you are reaching for a colorful rainbow, and breathe normally. Drop your hands and relax."

Socialization Activity. Children participate in unstructured play, snack time, and behavioral monitoring and evaluation during the last 15 minutes of the group.

Session 4: Personal Safety Planning and Anxiety Management Training

The stated goals of Session 4 are to review group rules, develop a personal safety plan to reduce risk for physical harm, practice relaxation to decrease anxiety level, and monitor and evaluate group behavior.

Reviewing Group Rules. A poster presentation of the rules is briefly reviewed.

Introduction. As pointed out previously by several clinicians and researchers (Grusznski et al., 1988; Hughes, 1982; Ragg & Webb, 1992; Roy, 1988), children are at risk for physical harm during violent episodes between parents. Consequently, children are taught to identify anger cues that signal violent episodes, and safely remove themselves from dangerous situations. The safety plan is also introduced during the parenting group to prevent the parent from punishing the child for leaving the home during a violent episode.

Rationale. "Last time, we talked about dads hitting or yelling at moms. When this happens it can be scary for you, because you and your mom could get hurt. You are going to learn to tell when your dad is getting mad, so that you can leave the house and get help for you and your mother. You are going to learn to keep yourself safe."

Identifying Anger Cues. A story is used to introduce anger cues and safety skills to young children:

> One afternoon, Steve and Becky were eating a snack after school. They heard their father slam the door as he entered the house. Steve and Becky became scared, because they knew what had happened before when dad came home and slammed the door. Dad came into the kitchen and asked where's dinner. His face was red and his voice was loud. He pounded the table with his hand when mom said that he hadn't called to tell her he was coming home early and that dinner was not prepared. Steve and Becky looked at each other; they knew dad was mad. Steve and Becky immediately got up from the table and went into the family room to use the phone. Steve stood watch at the door for dad, while Becky picked up the phone, dialed 911 and said, "My brother, my mom, and I are in trouble. My dad is going to hurt mom. Please come to 210 Maple Avenue." Steve and Becky walked quietly out the door and went to Mrs. Smith's house. The police come to their house to help. Becky, Steve, mom, and dad are safe.

The children are asked, "In the story, how did Steve and Becky know that dad was angry?"

Children are provided with prompts, positive reinforcement, and feedback to facilitate acquisition of anger cues. Examples are provided if children are unable to identify cues (e.g., slamming doors, pounding fist, red face, loud voice): "Kelly, that's right; they knew dad was angry because his face was red. Good job, you listened carefully to the story." "John, you're right; they knew dad was angry, because of his face. What about dad's face showed he was angry?" "That's a good answer; his face was red." "At home, how do/did (dad no longer in home) you know dad was angry/mad?"

The cofacilitator may coach children for additional cues: "Show us how your dad looks when he gets angry; How does he sound? What does he do?" Cofacilitators suggest additional anger cues to children including raising voice, clinching teeth, wrinkling forehead, squinting eyes, saying "nasty" things to others, making fists, pounding table or wall with fists, punching wall, and throwing objects. Only facial expressions that are associated with anger are initially modeled for children. Modeling aggressive actions could be anxiety evoking for the child. Verbal praise is provided for appropriate responses, and children are coached to provide further answers.

Developing the Safety Plan.   "We are going to make a plan, like the one Becky and John used in the story, that will get you out of the house and protect you and your mom when dad is mad." Children and cofacilitators are divided into two groups of four. The name and address of each child is written on a 5 X 7 index card. Answers to the following questions are written on the card for each child: "What are some things you have done to protect yourself?" "What other things can you do to protect yourself?" Prompting is used to help children generate ideas. "Who are some of the people you trust and could go to or call for help?" (e.g., police, relative, neighbor, teacher). Names and phone numbers of identified helpers are listed. "Each one of you are going to go through your safety plan next week."

Relaxation Training Exercise.   Progressive deep muscle relaxation skills are rehearsed using a muscle relaxation sequence described by Morris and Kratochwill (1983). The currently employed script is modified to include fantasy, as recommended by Koeppen (1974) to help maintain the child's attention and interest.

For example, "Pretend you're a turtle; take a deep breath and hold it for about 10 seconds. Now, like the turtle stretch your head out of the shell and blow it out. Raise both of your hands about halfway above the couch, pretend that you are reaching for a colorful rainbow, and breathe normally. Drop your hands and relax."

To reduce tension, children are instructed to practice the exercise biweekly for 30 minutes per session at home. After the session, tapes are presented to parents along with an explanation of how relaxation benefits the child, and how they can help their child complete the homework assignment. Parents are also asked to record the frequency and duration of exercises throughout the week.

Rationale for Parents.   "As you may already know, many children who witness violence in the home experience intense fears and anxiety. Your child has learned a relaxation technique that has been shown to be effective in reducing these. Encourage your child to practice relaxing at least twice a week for 30 minutes. You can help your child learn to relax by recording the frequency and duration of exercises on the Relaxation Training Monitoring Form (see Table 8.6).

TABLE 8.6

Relaxation Training Monitoring Form

Day of the Week that Relaxation Training was Practiced	How Long Did You Practice Relaxation Training?	How Did You Feel Afterward?
1.		
2.		
3.		
4.		
5.		
6.		
7.		

Socialization Activity.   Children participate in unstructured play, snack time, and behavioral monitoring and evaluation during the last 15 minutes of the group.

Session 5: Behavior Rehearsal of Safety Plan

The stated goals of Session 5 are to review group rules, rehearse personal safety plans, and monitor and evaluate group behavior.

Reviewing Group Rules.   A poster presentation of the rules is briefly reviewed.

Rationale.   "Today you are going to practice your safety plans to make sure you know what to do at home when your dad or someone else is angry. Before you practice, we are going to show you how."

Modeling of Safety Plan for Children.   Cofacilitators provide a running narrative of behavior while modeling a safety plan for the children:

First facilitator while looking at doll: "Why don't you have dinner ready? I'm starved, the least you could do is have something for me to eat."

Second facilitator: "Dad's raising his voice and pointing at mom. He's angry. I'm going into the bedroom, picking up the phone, and dialing 911. Please come to 210 Maple Avenue; my dad is going to hurt my mom. I hang the phone up and walk quietly out the back door to Mrs. Jones' house to wait for the police."

For younger children, the scenario can involve going to neighbor's house and asking the neighbor to call the police. Children are asked to identify anger cues and safety precautions. Prompting, positive reinforcement, and performance feedback are provided to facilitate learning.

Behavioral Rehearsal of Safety Plan.   Each group member is given an opportunity to rehearse the personal safety plan, with the exception of multiple siblings who initiate plans as a group. A scenario describing a family argument is introduced to the child. Group participation is encouraged when the children are asked to identify anger cues in the scenario. After identifying cues, the children are asked at what point they would initiate the safety plan. The plan developed during the previous session is reviewed with the children.

For example, "Last week you said you would go into the bedroom, dial 911, ask for them to come to your house, walk quietly out the backdoor, and go to Janie's house to wait for the police. Okay, you said you would leave when dad started raising his voice. Go ahead and show us what you would do. Good; you're picking up the phone and dialing 911."

The cofacilitator role plays the scenario with the child:

Cofacilitator:	"Hello this is the 911 emergency operator."
Child:	"Please help us. My mom and dad are fighting."
Cofacilitator:	"Where do you live?"
Child:	"210 Maple Avenue."
Cofacilitator:	"Are you going to stay in the house?"
Child:	"No, I'm going to Janie's house."
Cofacilitator:	"The police will come to help your mom. Go ahead and leave the house."

Prompting the child is necessary to shape safe behavior:

"(Child's name), you called for help. What do you do next? Good; you're walking out the door. What are you going to do when you get to Janie's? That's great. You tell her parent(s) that your mom and dad are fighting and that you called for help. Quick thinking; you stay with them until the police arrive." Prompting, positive reinforcement, and performance feedback are provided to facilitate learning and to shape the child's behavior.

Socialization Activity.   Children participate in unstructured play, snack time, and behavioral monitoring and evaluation during the last 15 minutes of the group.

Homework.   Children are instructed to continue listening to the "feeling good" tape at least twice a week. Parents are asked to encourage children to comply and to monitor progress.

Session 6: Implementation and Observation of Child Behavior Management Skills

The stated goals of Session 6 are to introduce children's group rules to parents, provide a rationale to group members for the integration of this session, rehearse attending to and praising the child's behavior, and practice personal safety plans.

Reviewing Group Rules.   A brief explanation of children's group rules and the behavioral monitoring system is provided to parents.

Introduction.   Begin group by establishing and building rapport with parents and their children by providing group introductions and positive reinforcement for appropriate implementation of child management skills and safety plans. The four cofacilitators introduce themselves to the families at this time and provide the following rationale for integration of children and parents into the group.

"Hello, our names are _____, _____, _____, and _____. We are meeting together today in order to practice and rehearse some of the skills that you have learned over the past few weeks. Then, we will rehearse the personal safety plan that you and your child has developed. In addition, we will practice the skills of attending and praising your child while they play with these toys."

Behavioral Rehearsal of Attending and Praising. Group cofacilitators present the following rationale for the use of attends and praise: "We would like to rehearse the skills for reinforcing your child while he/she plays with the toys. This will be done so that you can 'catch your child being good.' Pair off with your child and we will provide feedback on how you are doing with these skills. Please remember to maintain eye-contact, get down on your child's level, use a normal tone of voice, attend to your child's play activity, and provide descriptive praise. Are there any questions?" Each of the cofacilitators provides descriptive praise, and coaches parents in their use of attends and positive reinforcement. The following prompts can be used:

> *Prompt 1*: "You're really doing a great job at describing what Johnny's doing. Show him how much you enjoy how he's playing by giving him a pat on the shoulder. Look at how happy your child looked when you did that."
>
> *Prompt 2*: "You're really trying and doing well attending to your child. You're sitting close and looking at him at his level. You're using a pleasant tone of voice and you're smiling while he plays. You're doing an excellent job."
>
> *Prompt 3*: "You're doing a great job of looking at your child and using a pleasant voice. How about describing in detail the activity he's doing while he's drawing that picture. For example, you're picking up the yellow crayon and look at the bright sun you just drew."

After providing parents with verbal praise and performance feedback, cofacilitators ask parents and children to return to their chairs. Any questions, comments, or concerns should be addressed at this point.

Implementing Personal Safety Plans. This treatment component is omitted from a session if children are placed at increased risk for physical harm due to a parent's disapproval of the procedure (e.g., a father who becomes increasingly aggressive in the home because he does not want his child to participate in treatment).

Rationale. "Many children who live in homes where violence occurs are at risk for physical harm. Parents may not intentionally harm the child; however, the child may be injured while attempting to intervene. Your child has outlined a plan for maintaining personal safety in the home. We know that you don't want to see your child injured. We'd like for you to help us teach your child how to use the plan at home and to communicate to him/her that you approve of his/her actions for maintaining safety. First, he/she is going to identify cues that represent anger and then your child is going to remove himself/herself from the dangerous situation. Do you have any questions?"

Behavioral Rehearsal. Cofacilitators role play a situation involving escalating parental anger. Parents are coached to prompt and reinforce children for identifying anger cues. Praise is given to parents for desired interactions with the child. Each child is given an opportunity to rehearse the personal safety plan.

For example, "Last week you said you would go into the bedroom, dial 911, ask for them to come to your house, walk quietly out the back door, and go to Janie's house to wait for the police. Okay, you said you would leave when dad started raising his voice. Go ahead and show us what you would do. Good; you're picking up the phone and dialing 911."

The cofacilitator role plays the scenario with the child:

Cofacilitator:	"Hello this is the 911 emergency operator."
Child:	"Please help us. My mom and dad are fighting."
Cofacilitator:	"Where do you live?"
Child:	"1137 Walnut Avenue."
Cofacilitator:	"Are you going to stay in the house?"
Child:	"No, I'm going to Janie's house."
Cofacilitator:	"The police will come to help your mom. Go ahead and leave the house."

Prompting the child is necessary to shape safe behavior:

"(Child's name), you called for help. What do you do next? Good; you're walking out the door. What are you going to do when you get to Janie's? That's great. You tell her parent(s) that your mom and dad are fighting and that you called for help. Quick thinking; you stay with them until the police arrive." Cofacilitators and parents provide prompts, positive reinforcement, and performance feedback to the child for appropriate responding.

Rationale. Cofacilitators present the following rationale for practicing the parent's personal safety plan: "Today we are going to practice the safety plans that your parents have also made for increasing safety in your home. We are going to begin by providing several examples in which you all can identify the early cues of anger; then we will practice how you are to remove yourself from a dangerous situation. Do you have any questions?

Behavioral Rehearsal. Cofacilitators role play a situation involving escalating anger. Parents are coached to prompt and reinforce children for identifying anger cues. Praise is given to parents for desired interactions with the child. Parents are given an opportunity to rehearse the personal safety plan with their children.

Group members role play a scenerio in which they implement the personal safety plan and contact the social support resources that they have identified. First, a scenerio involving a family argument is described. Then, parents are asked to identify possible anger cues based on the scenerio. After identifying anger cues, parents are asked to initiate the personal safety plan with their child and to contact outside support. The following example can be used: "Your partner arrives home and begins to scream at you about the lack of money in your account to pay the monthly bills. You stated in your safety plan that the first thing you would do if he engaged in such behavior is to take your children and leave the situation and go into your bedroom. The second step would be to call your family and let them know you are having an argument and that you are coming over to stay with them. You tell your children about your safety concerns and ask them to leave quietly through the back door of the house."

Parents are prompted with the following questions: "What should you do next? When is the best time to leave the situation?" Cofacilitators provide parents and children with prompts, positive reinforcement, and performance feedback for the effective implementation of their personal safety plan.

Homework. The parent and child are provided copies of their personal safety plans recorded in the Personal Safety Plan Monitoring Form (see Table 8.7) and are asked to rehearse the plan at least six times (at least once a week) at home before the next parent–child session. Parents are also reminded to bring completed relaxation recording forms for children the following week and to bring in blank tapes for recording the progressive muscle relaxation procedure that parents are learning.

Socialization Activity. Children and parents participate in unstructured play and snack time during the last 15 minutes of the group. Parents are given the opportunity to practice positive interactions with their child by reviewing the group behavior chart and by providing praise and rewards (stars) for appropriate behavior.

Session 7: Identification of Feelings

The stated goals of Session 7 are to review group rules, teach children to identify feeling states, review homework and practice relaxation, and monitor and evaluate behavior.

Reviewing Group Rules. A poster presentation of the rules is briefly reviewed.

Homework Review. Children are asked to briefly describe what happened when they rehearsed the safety plan with their parents. Group members use "brain-storming," a technique whereby group participants generate all possible solutions in order to resolve problems in implementing the plan. Cofacilitators provide positive reinforcement and performance feedback for respones.

Rationale. "Many children have a hard time saying how they feel. This week you are going to learn about feelings, because talking about feelings can help you feel happier and let others know what you want and need."

Identifying Feelings and Emotions. Children are shown pictures of facial expressions (i.e., happy, sad, angry, surprised) and asked to identify the associated emotion. After identifying the emotion reflected by the expression, children are asked to identify a specific time when they experienced the emotion. For example:

TABLE 8.7

Personal Safety Plan Monitoring Form

Contact Person	Phone Number	Number of Times You Practiced at Home?	Evaluate Results
1.			
2.			
3.			
4.			

Cofacilitator:	"That's right John, that's an angry face. Tell us about a time when you felt angry."
John:	"I had an angry face when my friend broke my SEGA."
Cofacilitator:	"I would probably feel angry if someone broke my toy."

Cofacilitators provide positive reinforcement for the child's effort and the expression of feelings, and offer empathy and support to the child when personal feelings are shared. The group is supported and praised for expression of personal feelings: "Sometimes it's hard to express feelings. Thank you for sharing your feelings with us."

Homework Review. "Let's talk about the 'feeling good' tapes you have been listening to over the past few weeks." Crayons and feeling sheets are distributed to group members. Exercise recording forms (see Table 8.6) are reviewed and each child is asked if using the tapes was beneficial. For example: "(Child's name), we see that you listened to your 'feeling good tape' twice this week. Please color the face on the sheet that shows how you felt before you listened to the 'feeling good' tape. Now take the second sheet and color the face that shows how you felt after listening to the tape."

An emphasis is placed on mood improvement reported by the child following the relaxation exercise. For example: "That's wonderful; you were able to use your 'feeling good' tape when you felt scared to help yourself feel better."

Relaxation Training Exercise. Relaxation skills training is initiated using the description provided in Session 3. The following rationale is provided: "Some of you stated that you felt better after listening to the 'feeling good' tape. It's okay if you didn't feel better. That just means that you may need to practice relaxing. Let's practice now."

The currently employed script as described in Session 3 is modified to include fantasy, as recommended by Koeppen (1974) to help maintain the child's attention and interest.

For example, "Pretend you're a big blowfish; take a deep breath and hold it for about 10 seconds. Hold it in like a big round blowfish. Now, let it out and watch the air bubbles float up through the water. Raise both of your hands about halfway above the couch, pretend that you are reaching for a colorful rainbow, and breathe normally. Drop your hands and relax."

Homework. Children are instructed to continue practicing relaxation skills at home. Parents are asked to help children complete the "Feeling Sheets" before and after listening to the audiotape. The following explanation is provided to parents: "You have been helping your child learn to relax to reduce their anxiety. You can further help by monitoring your child's feelings. Before relaxing, ask your child to color the face associated with the present feeling. Ask your child to color the face that represents the way he/she is feeling after the exercise. Return the sheets to us each week along with the relaxation recording form."

Socialization Activity. Children participate in unstructured play, snack time, and behavioral monitoring and evaluation during the last 15 minutes of the group.

Session 8: Review of Safety Plans and Anxiety Management Techniques

The stated goals of Session 8 are to review group rules and review personal safety plans, learn alternative relaxation techniques to decrease anxiety level, and monitor and evaluate group behavior.

Reviewing Group Rules.   A poster presentation of the rules is briefly reviewed.

Reviewing Safety Plan.   The procedure described in Session 5 is used for reviewing safety plans. Children are instructed to rehearse individual safety plans independently.

For example, "Last week you said you would go into the bedroom, dial 911, ask for them to come to your house, walk quietly out the backdoor, and go to Janie's house to wait for the police. Okay, you said you would leave when dad started raising his voice. Go ahead and show us what you would do. Good; you're picking up the phone and dialing 911."

The cofacilitator role plays the scenario with the child:

Cofacilitator:	"Hello this is the 911 emergency operator."
Child:	"Please help us. My mom and dad are fighting."
Cofacilitator:	"Where do you live?"
Child:	"210 Maple Avenue."
Cofacilitator:	"Are you going to stay in the house?"
Child:	"No, I'm going to Janie's house."
Cofacilitator:	"The police will come to help your mom. Go ahead and leave the house."

Prompting the child is necessary to shape safe behavior: "(Child's name), you called for help. What do you do next? Good; you're walking out the door. What are you going to do when you get to Janie's? That's great. You tell her parent(s) that your mom and dad are fighting and that you called for help. Quick thinking; you stay with them until the police arrive." Cofacilitators and parents provide prompts, positive reinforcement, and performance feedback to the child for appropriate responding.

Behavioral rehearsal, prompting, positive reinforcement, and performance feedback are used to facilitate learning and to shape safe behavior. If children have implemented the safety plan at home, then they may be asked to describe what occurred and to demonstrate how the situation was handled. The children's feelings and actions are validated via support and empathy. Additionally, the recurrence of violence in the home has important implications for treatment. Potential risk for the children must be assessed and must be immediately addressed with the parent.

Homework Review.   Homework is reviewed by examining "Feeling Sheets" and Relaxation Recording Forms (see Table 8.6) following the procedure used in Session 7.

For example: "(Child's name), we see that you listened to your 'feeling good tape' twice this week. Please color the face on the sheet that shows how you felt before you listened to the 'feeling good' tape. Now take the second sheet and color the face that shows how you felt after listening to the tape."

Alternative Relaxation Skills.   According to Morris and Kratochwill (1983), most children become skilled in relaxation after three training sessions. Alternative techniques for relaxing are introduced for those children who have not achieved high levels of relaxation by this session.

Various alternative relaxation techniques have been suggested. Hendricks and Willis (1975) proposed a musical stretching exercise that is outlined by Peled and Davis (1992):

> Let's all begin walking slowly around the room, getting the feeling of our bodies in motion. Feel the way we move, the way our feet contact the floor. As you walk, begin to raise your arms, stretching as high as you can on each step…feeling yourself stretch from your toes to your fingers (pause one minute). And now, with each slow step, stretch from side to side, bending like a tree in the wind (pause 30 seconds). And now, bend forward, and walk with your arms hanging loosely almost to the floor (pause 30 seconds). And now, take slow, giant steps, stretching your legs (pause 30 seconds). And now, once more, stretch up to reach to the sky (pause 10 seconds). And now, stand still and feel good. (pp. 3|25–3|26)

Imagery and fantasy is added to further engage children. "Raise your arms as high as you can, as if you are reaching for the rainbow. Pretend that you can touch the rainbow if you stretch just a little further. Stretch, you're almost there. You are going to touch the beautiful rainbow."

Imagery and fantasy alone can be used with children to induce relaxation (Lipovsky, 1992). Ask group members to describe a safe place where they can go. Prompt children for specific details about the place. The therapist may embellish details in order to make the image more vivid (e.g., a fantasy candyland, toyland, floating through the clouds on balloons). As the scenario is developed, group members must concur that the scene is both relaxing and safe. The cofacilitator begins with deep breathing exercises and then introduces the imagery. Children are instructed to use imagery to relax.

Socialization Activity.   Children participate in unstructured play, snack time, and behavioral monitoring and evaluation during the last 15 minutes of the group.

Session 9: Esteem Building

The stated goals of Session 9 are to review group rules, improve self-concept, and learn to give and receive compliments.

Reviewing Group Rules

A poster presentation of the rules is briefly reviewed.

Self-Esteem Building   Investigations of the effects of witnessing interparental violence have revealed that child witnesses exhibit lower levels of self-esteem compared to nonwitnesses (Hughes, 1988; Hughes & Barad, 1983). Therefore, an esteem-building exercise is used to increase children's self-concept. Moser's (1991) *Don't Feed the Monster on Tuesdays!* helps children understand the importance of self-worth and provides practical self-talk strategies for children to evaluate and strengthen self-esteem.

Moser (1991) is read to the children. Children are asked to identify negative self-talk and methods for challenging negative thoughts. An explanation of the "monster" is provided to the children: "The monster is not real. The monster is the bad things we think and say about ourselves. For example, when we tell ourselves we are ugly or that we can't do something."

The following questions are used for discussion:

"What did the book call how we feel about ourselves?"

"How did the children in the book feed the monster?"

"What negative things did they think that made them feel badly about themselves?"

"How did they stop feeding the monster and start having positive thoughts about themselves?"

"Have you ever fed your monster?"

"What kinds of negative things do you say to yourself?"

"What positive things do you say to yourself to help you feel better about yourself."

Children are asked to identify positive self-traits: "Let's say one thing that we like about ourselves. I'll start. I'm smart and I work hard."

Each child is given an opportunity to make one positive self-statement. If the child has difficulty generating ideas, cofacilitators and other group members may provide prompts (e.g., "Johnny, you are a nice person. I really like the way you treat others by asking them if you can help"). Cofacilitators reinforce positive comments generated by group members (e.g., "Jill, I agree. You do have pretty green eyes. That's wonderful that you were able to tell us something that you liked about yourself").

Giving and Receiving Compliments

Rationale.   "Now that we have talked about things that we like about ourselves, let's practice giving and receiving compliments. Many kids have trouble giving and receiving compliments. Today, you are going to learn to give and receive compliments which can make you feel better about yourselves and make others feel good at the same time."

Defining Compliments.   "A compliment is saying something nice to someone about something they did or said or saying something that you like about them, for example: "You look good today in that blue dress," "You are a good friend," or "You did a good job drawing the picture."

Modeling Compliments.   The cofacilitator models giving a compliment for the children. The scenario includes giving the compliment, making eye contact with the person, smiling at the person, and stating the compliment in a pleasant voice tone. Then, the cofacilitator provides a narrative about the components included in the compliment.

Accepting Compliments.   When someone gives you a compliment, you can accept it by saying thanks; ignore the person and pretend you did not hear it; tell them they did not mean it; brag and say, "You already knew it," or immediately return the compliment. Children are asked to indicate how they would respond. If they choose an inappropriate response, they are asked how they would feel if someone responded to them in that manner. They are then asked how they would want others to respond. Prompting and positive reinforcement are used to facilitate learning.

Role Playing.   Cofacilitators role play giving and receiving compliments for the children. They review specific components involved in complimenting (e.g., voice tone, eye contact).

Then, children are asked to give each group member a compliment. Prompting, positive reinforcement, and performance feedback are provided to shape desired behaviors.

Socialization Activity.   Children participate in unstructured play, snack time, and behavioral monitoring and evaluation during the last 15 minutes of the group.

Session 10: Introduction of Assertive Behavior

The stated goals of Session 10 are to review group rules, demonstrate that anger is an appropriate feeling state, teach the difference between aggressive, passive, and assertive responses, and rehearse assertive behavior.

Reviewing Group Rules.   A poster presentation of the rules are briefly reviewed.

Introduction.   Assertiveness training has been effective for increasing assertive responses, reducing aggressive behavior, and improving self-concept in children and adolescents (Bornstein, Bellack, & Hersen, 1977; Huey & Rank, 1984; Tanner & Holliman, 1988; Van Hasselt, Hersen, Whitehill, & Bellack, 1979). Although the utility of assertion training for treating child witnesses has yet to be empirically determined, Rosenberg (1987) reported that children witnessing interparental violence tend to use passive or aggressive stategies for resolving interpersonal problems.

Therefore, the potential value of assertion training is suggested to reduce aggressive behaviors and to increase assertive responses in this population.

Rationale.   "Many children either act aggressively to get what they need, or feel left out because they don't ask for what they need at all. Today, you are going to learn how to ask for what you need in a way that doesn't hurt somone else."

Several books are available to introduce assertion to children (Palmer, 1977; Waters, 1980). It is recommended that Palmer (1977) *The Mouse, the Monster, and Me* be used because passive, assertive, and aggressive responses are defined and assertive responses are demonstrated.

Defining Assertive, Aggressive, and Passive Behavior.   Palmer's book describes the "passive mouse" and the "assertive monster." For example:

> This book is not really about mice, or monsters. It is about you, however....and how you sometimes act like a mouse or like a monster. And it is about how you can act less like a monster or less like a mouse and...be more like you. Mice can be nice. And people who act like our friend mouse are sometimes so nice that they allow themselves to be walked on by other people. And sometimes...mice get squashed. Some words people use to describe this kind of mouse are shy, timid, afraid, and unassertive. (pp. 6–7)

Part I (Palmer, 1977) defines aggressive and passive behavior for children. After reading Part I, the following questions are posed for discussion:

"How does the monster act?"

"How does the mouse act? And what happens when the mouse is passive?"

"Have you ever been aggressive and acted like the monster?"

"Have you ever been passive like the mouse?"

"How did you feel when this happened?"

Prompting, positive reinforcement, and performance feedback are provided to shape desired responses. If children describe negative feelings associated with acts of aggression and passivity, emphasis is placed on those feelings and how learning to assertively ask for what they need can help them feel better about themselves.

Part II focuses on personal strengths and power. Power is defined as "the ability to be in charge of your own life" (Palmer, 1977, p. 15). Assertive behavior is defined as follows: "When you make choices and decisions for yourself, you are being assertive. Assertive may be a new word for you. Being assertive just means you are letting…yourself and others know what you want, not in a pushy way like monsters do, or in a scared way like mice do, but in an honest way, just being you" (p. 19).

Parts III and IV introduce rights and making assertive requests. Parts V, VI, and VII focus on learning to say no, accepting criticism, and giving compliments. The latter section is briefly reviewed because giving and receiving compliments were introduced in Session 9.

Modeling Assertive Behavior. A situation is presented to the children in which one child is playing with "play dough" and another wants to play. Cofacilitators model three responses an aggressive response where one grabs the play dough out of the other's hands, an assertive response where one asks, "May I please have some play dough; I want to play," and a passive response where one just sits and watches the other play. Children are then asked to identify the best response. Advantages of the assertive response are discussed (e.g., "You got what you need without hurting someone else," "You made eye contact," "You used a calm tone of voice"). Following the discussion, children are divided into groups of two and asked to role play the situation. Cofacilitators provide children with prompts, positive reinforcement, and performance feedback to facilitate learning of assertive behavior.

Socialization Activity. Children participate in unstructured play, snack time, and behavioral monitoring and evaluation during the last 15 minutes of the group.

Session 11: Assertive Behavior and Anger Management Training

The stated goals of Session 11 are to review group rules, rehearse assertive requests, identify anger cues, introduce anger management techniques, and practice relaxation exercise.

Reviewing Group Rules. A poster presentation of the rules is briefly reviewed.

Practicing Assertive Requests. Cofacilitators model assertive requests for the group. Group members are arranged in dyads and presented with a situation that requires making an assertive request. Each individual in the dyad is asked to practice the request. Cofacilitators provide positive reinforcement and performance feedback to shape appropriate assertive behavior (e.g., "You got what you need without hurting someone else," "You made eye contact," "You used a calm tone of voice when you asked John for the toy").

Introduction.   In his book, *Don't Pop Your Cork on Mondays*, Moser (1988) discussed anger-provoking and stressful situations, different responses to stress, and stress management techniques.

Rationale.   "We are going to talk about ways you can remain calm, so you don't lose your temper. First, you are going to learn when you are angry. If you can tell that you're getting angry, you can stop the anger. This may keep you from getting into trouble or hurting someone else."

Identifying Anger Triggers and Cues.   Anger triggers (antecedents) and cues are introduced with the story. The following questions are raised for discussion:

"What are the different ways that people respond to stress?"
"What did the book say were some causes for losing your temper?"
"How did the book say people know when they are getting angry?"
"What are some things the book suggested you could do to stay calm and not blow
   your stack?"

Children are asked to identify situations in which they are likely to lose their temper. These situations are used to model anger control strategies. Next, children identify personal anger cues.
   "You have learned how to tell when your dad is angry. How do you know when you are angry when (identified situation) occurs. How do you feel?" Prompts may be provided to children. For example: "Just before you lost your temper, does your heart start beating faster? Do you clench your fists? Do you grit your teeth? Do you feel hot?" Positive reinforcement and performance feedback are employed to help children learn to identify anger cues.

Anger Management Skills.   Children are presented the following anger control strategies physical exercise (e.g., jump rope, play ball), progressive muscle relaxation, deep breathing exercises, visual imagery, counting backward to 20, and calming self-talk.

Modeling Anger Management Skills.   Cofacilitators model anger management skills, with the exception of progressive muscle relaxation, which was previously introduced. For example: "Joe, you said that you get angry when your parents don't listen to you and then you break things around the house to get their attention. You also said that you knew you were getting angry when your heart started pounding faster."
   During the role play of the identified situation, the cofacilitator models anger control skills: "I'm tugging on mom's shirt. Mom, you're not listening. (Mom): Go away. Mom, listen to me. My heart begins pounding. I'm tightly clenching mom's shirt. I let go of the shirt and I go into my room. 20, 19, 18, 17,…1. I take a few deep breaths and go talk to mom. Mom, can we please talk?"

Cofacilitators review the anger triggers and cues, and discuss how anger was reduced in the scenario.

Role Playing. Group dyads are instructed to implement anger management skills in the previously described anger-provoking situation. Cofacilitators provide prompts, positive reinforcement, and performance feedback to shape appropriate responses.

Homework. Children are instructed to implement the anger-management strategy of their choice at home or school in the following week when confronted with anger-provoking situations.

Relaxation Training Exercise. "Previously, you learned relaxation skills for managing anger. Let's practice relaxing. Stand up and stretch. Reach for the sky like a tree growing toward the bright sunlight. Let you arms drop to your sides and dangle like a weeping willow. Drop your shoulders. Notice how your arms feel light and dangly." Deep breathing may be integrated with imagery.

Socialization Activity. Children participate in unstructured play, snack time, and behavioral monitoring and evaluation during the last 15 minutes of the group.

Session 12: Application of Child Behavior Management Skills

The stated goals of Session 12 are to review children's group rules, and review child-management procedures (attends, rewards, ignoring, and time-out).

Review Group Rules. The children's group rules are briefly reviewed.

Behavioral Rehearsal of Child Management Skills. Co-facilitators present the following rationale for the use of attends and praising. "We would like to begin by rehearsing the skills of reinforcing your child while they play with these toys. You will pair off with your child and we will provide feedback on how you are doing with these skills. Please remember to maintain eye-contact, place yourselves at your child's level, use a normal voice tone, attend to your child's play activity, and provide lots of praise. Are there any questions?" Cofacilitators provide descriptive praise and coach parents in their use of attends and positive reinforcement.

A brief review is provided for the use of ignoring and time-out procedures introduced in PTP Sessions 3, 5, and 7. For example, parents are instructed to continue playing with their child until an undesired behavior occurs. Following the undesired response, parents are asked to use ignoring procedures. Children and their parents are praised for their collective efforts and coached in the appropriate use of the technique. Several guidelines in the use of ignoring skills are emphasized to the parents: briefly remove all attention from your child, refuse to argue, scold, or talk; turn your head and avoid eye contact; do not show anger (or any other emotion) in your manner or gestures; be certain your child's behavior does not result in a material reward; and provide attention *when and only when* your child's negative behavior ceases.

Then, time-out is rehearsed. The following rationale is provided: "We are going to practice time-out so that we can identify any difficulties you may be having in implementing the technique at home." Children are informed that, "Although you've done nothing wrong to be placed in time-out during this session, we are going to practice time-out to make sure you and your parents understand the procedure."

The following sequence of steps utilized during the time-out procedure are exemplified to parents: Provide a specific command to your children for the behavior that you would like them to engage in. If your children comply within 5 seconds after a command is given, attend and praise their compliant behavior. If your children do not comply with your command within 5 seconds, provide a warning.... Wait another 5 seconds.... If your children do not comply within this time, provide another command that states that you intend to place them in time-out for the specified length of time (the children remains in time-out for a duration of 1-minute for each year of their age).... At this time, take your children's hand and manually guide them to the time-out area that you have preselected. And, when children have completed time-out, return them to the original situation that caused them to be in time-out and repeat the command with which you wish your children to comply.

The following prompts can be used:

Prompt 1: "You're doing a great job; you described in a neutral tone of voice the specific behavior in which you wanted Johnny to engage. You provided a warning after waiting 5 seconds, and he followed your command and picked up the toy. Show him how much you enjoyed his compliance by giving him a pat on the shoulder. Look at how happy your child looked when you did that."

Prompt 2: "You're really trying and doing well with the time-out procedure. You're sitting close and looking at him at his level, you're using a neutral tone of voice when you told him to go to time out. You provided a warning; and after the warning, you waited another 5 seconds. Then, you placed him in the time-out chair. How long should Bobby remain in time-out? You're doing an excellent job."

After each parent has been provided with performance feedback and praise, the cofacilitators ask parents and children to return to their chairs. Any questions, comments, or concerns are addressed.

Homework.   The parent and child are given copies of the personal safety plan and asked to rehearse the plan once at home before the next session and to record results in the Personal Safety Plan Monitoring Form (see Table 8.7). Parents continue to practice attending, active ignoring, and time-out, and to continue implementing the reward system throughout the following week. Parents are asked to record results in Practice Attending, Reinforcing, and Ignoring your Child Monitoring Form (see Table 8.8), and the Time-Out Monitoring Form (see Table 8.9).

Socialization Activity.   Children and parents participate in unstructured play and snack time during the last 15 minutes of the group. Parents are again given the opportunity to monitor and reward the child's desired behavior.

TABLE 8.8

Practice Attending, Reinforcing, and Ignoring Your Child Monitoring Form

Specific Behaviors Used in PARC and Ignoring	Type Of Reinforcer	Day	Time	Total # Of Times Used
1.				
2.				
3.				
4.				
5.				
6.				

TABLE 8.9

Time-Out Monitoring Form

Behavior That Resulted in Time-out	When Did the Behavior Occur?	Steps You Used in Time-out Procedure	How Long Was Your Child in Time-out?	Any Problems Occur?
1.				
2.				
3.				
4.				
5.				
6.				

Session 13: Anger Management Training

The stated goals of Session 13 are to review group rules, rehearse personal safety plans and rehearse assertive requests, and review anger management techniques.

Reviewing Group Rules.   A poster presentation of the rules is briefly reviewed.

Behavior Rehearsal of Safety Plan.   The children's personal safety plans are rehearsed.

For example, "Last week you said you would go into the bedroom, dial 911, ask for them to come to your house, walk quietly out the backdoor, and go to Janie's house to wait for the police. Okay, you said you would leave when dad started raising his voice. Go ahead and show us what you would do. Good; you're picking up the phone and dialing 911."

The cofacilitator role plays the scenario with the child:

Cofacilitator:	"Hello this is the 911 emergency operator."
Child:	"Please help us. My mom and dad are fighting."
Cofacilitator:	"Where do you live?"
Child:	"1137 Walnut Avenue."
Cofacilitator:	"Are you going to stay in the house?"
Child:	"No, I'm going to Janie's house."
Cofacilitator:	"The police will come to help your mom. Go ahead and leave the house."

Prompting the child is necessary to shape safe behavior: "(Child's name), you called for help. What do you do next? Good; you're walking out the door. What are you going to do when you get to Janie's? That's great. You tell her parent(s) that your mom and dad are fighting and that you called for help. Quick thinking; you stay with them until the police arrive." Cofacilitators and parents provide prompts, positive reinforcement, and performance feedback to the child for appropriate responding.

Behavioral rehearsal, prompting, positive reinforcement, and performance feedback are used to facilitate learning and to shape safe behavior.

Role-Playing.   Assertive requests are first modeled by cofacilitators. Then, group members are divided into dyads. Each dyad is presented a scenario requiring an assertive request (e.g., "You come home and find that your younger sister has taken your favorite SEGA game from your room. What do you do?"). Cofacilitators utilize prompts, positive reinforcement, and performance feedback to shape assertive behavior.

Review of Anger Management Skills.   Children are asked to identify anger management techniques. Cofacilitators model anger management skills, with the exception of progressive muscle relaxation, which was previously introduced. For example: "Joe, you said that you get angry when your parents don't listen to you and then you break things around the house to get their attention. You also said that you knew you were getting angry when your heart started pounding faster."

During the role play of the identified situation, the cofacilitator models anger control skills: "I'm tugging on mom's shirt. Mom, you're not listening. (Mom): Go away. Mom, listen to me. My heart begins pounding. I'm tightly clenching mom's shirt. I let go of the shirt and I go into my room. 20, 19, 18, 17,…1. I take a few deep breaths and go talk to mom. Mom, can we please talk?"

Cofacilitators review the anger triggers and cues, and discuss how anger was reduced in the scenario.

Group members describe how they implemented the skills at home or school.

Socialization Activity.   Children participate in unstructured play, snack time, and behavioral monitoring and evaluation during the last 15 minutes of the group.

Session 14: Social Problem-Solving

The stated goals of Session 14 are to review group rules, and teach social problem-solving skills.

Reviewing Group Rules.   A poster presentation of the rules is briefly reviewed.

Introduction.   Social problem-solving skills training is a behavioral intervention that has been applied to ameliorate interpersonal skills deficits in withdrawn, isolated, and aggressive children (Michelson, Sugai, Wood, & Kazdin, 1983; Ollendick, 1982; Van Hasselt & Christ, 1994). In addition, investigators have demonstrated that child witnesses tend to use passive or aggressive strategies for solving interpersonal difficulties (Rosenberg, 1987). Therefore, the proposed treatment model trains children to employ assertive and nonimpulsive problem-solving methods.

Rationale.   "Many children have a hard time solving problems and behaving and talking with other people. You are going to learn ways to solve problems that get you what you want. You are also going to learn to behave and talk with other people in a way that makes both you and them feel good."

Definition of Social Problem-Solving Skills.   "Problem-solving skills are the five steps you take to solve a problem. These steps are to: (1) identify the problem, (2) identify the goal, (3) generate possible solutions, (4) choose the best solution, and (5) give self-reinforcement."

Problem-Solving Steps.   Problem-solving steps are explained to group members and presented on the chalkboard:

> *Step one* is to stop and think of the problem. This gives you a chance to think of what the problem really is. *Step two* is to identify the goal. Ask yourself what you want to happen and what you would like to do. *Step three* is to come up with ways of solving the problem and to determine possible consequences. List four ways of solving the problem and a likely consequence. A "consequence" refers to what might happen as a result of your trying to solve a problem. For example, if you hit someone to get your toy back, the consequence may be that you get hit back. *Step four* is to choose the best solution for the problem. After choosing the solution, ask yourself if it worked. Did you get what you wanted? Then in *Step five*, tell yourself what a good job you did in solving the problem.

Role Playing.   Cofacilitators describe a problem situation to the group. They attempt to resolve the problem via the aforementioned problem-solving steps. The decision-making process and most effective solution(s) are discussed. The group is then asked to role play the situation:

"You have been waiting to play 'Super Mario Brothers' at the arcade for an hour and another child runs in front of you and grabs the machine."

"What is the problem in this situation? It's not fair that he jumped in front of me and that I won't get to play."

"What do you want to happen? I want to play the game before I have to go home."

"What are ways to solve the problem and what are the possible consequences?"

Possible solutions: (1) push him out of the way, (2) do nothing, (3) assertively tell him that I was waiting, and/or (4) tell the arcade owner.

Possible consequences: (1) he may hit me back or I might hurt him, (2) I don't get to play the game, (3) he may move out of the way, ignore me, or threaten to hit me, (4) someone else may be in line when I return; the owner might tell him to let me play first.

"What is the best way to solve the problem or to get what you want?" Children role play assertively requesting that the child let him play first (Solution 4). Prompting is used to help children generate possible solutions. Positive reinforcement and performance feedback are provided to shape effective problem-solving behaviors. Children are also encouraged to employ self-reinforcement for selecting the best responses (e.g., positive self-talk).

Socialization Activity.   Children participate in unstructured play and snack time, and behavioral monitoring and evaluation during the last 15 minutes of the group.

Session 15: Review of Problem-Solving Steps and Introduction of Role-Taking Skills

The stated goals of Session 15 are to review group rules, review problem-solving steps, and intoduce role-taking skills.

Reviewing Group Rules. A poster presentation of the rules is briefly reviewed.

Problem-Solving Steps. The five problem-solving steps are reviewed:

Step one is to stop and think of the problem. This gives you a chance to think of what the problem really is. *Step two* is to identify the goal. Ask yourself what you want to happen and what you would like to do. *Step three* is to come up with ways of solving the problem and to determine possible consequences. List four ways of solving the problem and a likely consequence. A 'consequence' refers to what might happen as a result of your trying to solve a problem. For example, if you hit someone to get your toy back, the consequence may be that you get hit back. *Step four* is to choose the best solution for the problem. After choosing the solution, ask yourself if it worked. Did you get what you wanted? Then in *Step five*, tell yourself what a good job you did in solving the problem.

Group members are presented a problem situation and asked to generate effective solutions as a group. Positive reinforcement and performance feedback are provided to shape desired problem-solving behavior.

Rationale. "Previously, you learned to identify and label feelings. Today, you are going to learn to walk in someone else's shoes. That is, you are going to learn how to identify what others are feeling."

Understanding the Feelings and Perspectives of Others (Role Taking). Children are asked to identify how they can tell when a person is sad, happy, angry, assertive, and scared. Prompts are used to help children describe verbal and nonverbal cues associated with each feeling. After children describe feeling cues, cofacilitators describe affect-laden situations and model behavior associated with feelings. Facial expressions, tone of voice, and body posture are emphasized (e.g., sad—brows pulled down, mouth curved downward, gazes directed at floor, tearful, speaks softly).

Dyads are asked to role play a situation portraying one of the aforementioned emotions. Other group members are asked the following questions regarding the role play encounter:

"What is the person feeling?"
"What is it about the voice and body that tells you they feel this way?"
"What do you think the person is thinking?"
"What do you think this person is like?"

Prompts are used to help group members identify appropriate responses. Positive reinforcement and performance feedback are provided to facilitate skills acquisition.

Knowing When to Assert Yourself. Cofacilitators model a situation where a parent is talking on the phone. Group members are asked whether this is the best time to make an assertive request. Additionally, they are asked to determine an appropriate time for making requests (e.g., ask mom to talk while she is relaxing in the living room). Cofacilitators model a situation involving parents arguing. Children are then asked if this is the time to be assertive. Prompts are used to generate reasons (e.g., dad might get angrier and hit mom, dad might hit me, mom and I might get hurt) why this is not the best time to be assertive.

Other examples of problematic situations include when parents demand that the child do something, when gang members at school steal the child's belongings, and any situation where assertive behavior increases the child's risk of harm.

Socialization Activity.   Children participate in unstructured play and snack time, and behavioral monitoring and evaluation during the last 15 minutes of the group.

Session 16: Skills Integration

The stated goals of Session 16 are to review group rules, and integrate assertion, social problem-solving, and anger management skills.

Reviewing Group Rules.   A poster presentation of the rules is briefly reviewed.

Skills Integration.   Cofacilitators role play a situation for group members that integrates use of previously trained skills. The following are examples of scenarios presented to the children:

Scenario 1: "You are on the playground and a child older than you steals your lunch."

Group members are instructed to use anger management strategies to calm themselves (e.g., deep breathing, calming self-statements) when their lunch is stolen.

Scenario 2: "You have a class geography project due tomorrow and you don't have the colored pencils necessary to complete the map."

Then, group members are instructed to use the five problem-solving steps to solve the art supply problem:

Step one is to stop and think of the problem. This gives you a chance to think of what the problem really is. *Step two* is to identify the goal. Ask yourself what you want to happen and what you would like to do. *Step three* is to come up with ways of solving the problem and to determine possible consequences. List four ways of solving the problem and a likely consequence. A "consequence" refers to what might happen as a result of your trying to solve a problem. For example, if you do not complete the project, the consequence may be that you earn an F in the Geography course. *Step four* is to choose the best solution for the problem. After choosing the solution, ask yourself if it worked. Did you get what you wanted? Then in *Step five*, tell yourself what a good job you did in solving the problem.

An effective solution might be to ask the parent to take them to the store to buy the colored pencil: "Group members go into the kitchen to ask mom to take them to the store. She is cooking dinner, the roast burns, she burns her hand on the stove, and curses loudly." Group members are asked to identify how mom is feeling. Then, they are asked if this is appropriate time to make a request. They identify an appropriate time to ask at which point they are asked to practice assertively requesting that mom take them to the store.

Cofacilitators briefly review each skill before they are implemented by group members. Prompting is used to help children generate desired responses. Positive reinforcement and performance feedback is provided to strengthen desired behaviors.

Socialization Activity   Children participate in unstructured play and snack time, and behavioral monitoring and evaluation during the last 15 minutes of the group.

Session 17: Group Evaluation and Termination

The stated goals of Session 17 are to review group rules, help children cope with termination of treatment, and encourage children to increase their personal support system.

Reviewing Group Rules.   A poster presentation of the rules is briefly reviewed.

Treatment Review.   Cofacilitators briefly summarize the course of treatment. Children are provided feedback and praise for specific behavior changes that have occurred. Children are instructed to draw a picture of themselves and the other group members. Each child is asked to describe what the people in the picture are doing. After describing picture, the children are asked to discuss what they have learned during the group.

Discussion of Termination.   "This is our last meeting together, but we will meet next week with your parents. During the group, you have shared a lot of things about yourselves and have developed new friends. It's not easy to say good-bye to friends. Let's take this time to say good-bye. You may want to add your new friends' addresses and telephone numbers to your safety cards, so you have someone to talk to when you feel scared or happy. We added our names and telephone number to your list, so you can call if you need help. Remember, if you feel scared, you have us and many others you can call for help."

Socialization Activity.   Children participate in unstructured play and snack time, and behavioral monitoring and evaluation during the last 30 minutes of the group. Safety cards are distributed and cofacilitators assist children in recording names, addresses, and phone numbers of group members.

Session 18: Rehearsal of Child Behavior Management Techniques

The stated goals of Session 18 are to review children's group rules, rehearse child management procedures, and answer questions and address problems that arise.

Rationale.   "Today is the last session that we will have together and we are going to practice all of the child management strategies that we have learned." Parents are instructed to engage in an unstructured play activity with their child. They are asked to implement the skills of attending, praising, and ignoring their child during play. If a child engages in an undesired behavior (e.g., taking a toy away from another child), the parent is instructed to use time-out.

The following sequence of steps utilized during the time-out procedure are emphasized to parents: Provide a specific command to children for the behavior that you would like them to engage in. If children comply within 5 seconds after a command is given, then attend and praise their compliant behavior. If children do not comply with the command within 5 seconds, provide a warning—wait another 5 seconds.... If children do not comply within this time, then provide another command that states that you intend to place children in time-out for the specified length of time (the children remain in time-out for a duration of 1-minute for each year of their age). At this time, take children's hand and manually guide them to the time-out area that you have preselected. When your children have completed time-out, return them to the original situation that caused them to be in time-out and repeat the command with which you wish your child to comply. Cofacilitators provide positive reinforcement and performance feedback to children and parents for the accurate implementation of skills.

Following the unstructured play activity, any questions, concerns, or problems that have arisen in skills implementation are addressed. Then, parents and children are provided feedback concerning: cooperation during the program, performance during exercises and role plays, and observable changes in behavior. Children and parents are praised for their cooperation and efforts in acquiring and implementing the various techniques.

Socialization Activity.   Group members are given the opportunity to socialize and say "good-byes" during the last 30 minutes of the group. Parents are asked to practice monitoring and rewarding the child's behavior. Each child who has earned 10 stars over the course of treatment is given a tangible reward (e.g., small stuffed toy, coloring book).

PARENT TRAINING PROGRAM

The Parent Training Program (PTP) consists of 18 treatment sessions. Fifteen of these sessions focus on information concerning emotional and behavioral effects of interparental violence on children, safety planning, child behavior management, and alternative conflict resolution strategies. Sessions 6, 12, and 18 include both children and parents. These sessions provide an opportunity for implementation and practice of strategies trained in group meetings. PTP sessions do not exceed 90 minutes. The recommended group size is 8 to 10 members. As with the CTP, two cofacilitators are employed to model procedures and provide performance feedback.

Session I: Introduction

The stated goals of Session 1 are to introduce parents to the child management program, establish group rules and discuss confidentiality issues, and define abuse and violence.

Introduction.   Research examining child witnesses of interparental violence indicates that a less punitive parenting style is a mediating factor in the effects of witnessing violence in the home (Hershorn & Rosenbaum, 1985; Jouriles et al., 1988). The purpose of PTP is to teach parents alternate strategies to mitigate the effects of witnessing violence on their children. This is accomplished by providing parents with information about emotional and behavioral effects of interparental violence on children, development of a safety plan, child behavioral management (e.g., positive reinforcement, extinction, and behavioral contracting), and alternate methods of conflict resolution (e.g., anger management skills, progressive muscle relaxation, and problem-solving strategies).

Introduction.   There is a focus on establishment of rapport and empathy with parents related to their current child-related difficulties. Cofacilitators introduce themselves to parents: "Hello, my name is _____, and I'm _____. We would like to begin group by having each of you introduce yourselves." Each parent is provided an opportunity to state his or her name. "Treatment will consist of 18 group sessions; 15 of these sessions involve learning, modeling, role playing, feedback and homework assignments on topics covered in each session. Three of these sessions will be spent practicing, role playing, and carrying out the skills that you are learning *with your child.* "

Issues of Confidentiality.   "Your participation in the group is encouraged and, as such, the confidentiality of group members is of utmost importance. You are asked not to disclose information related to other group members. Limitations to confidentiality are: reports of, feelings, or acts of self-harm or harm toward others; neglect, physical, or sexual abuse of a child (18 years of age or younger) or an elder. Our state laws require immediate reporting of these incidents to the state agency handling these problems. Failure to report consitutes a felony in our state."

Group Rules.   "At this time, I would like to present the following rules that we will follow to make the group process run smoothly":

1. Courtesy is vital to group process; therefore, only one person speaks at a time (no side conversations).
2. The focus is on sharing positive interactions (no blaming, arguing, finger-pointing).
3. Attendance and active participation is crucial; if travel arrangements are necessary, you are encouraged to car pool together.
4. Please ask for clarification if something is not clear.
5. Homework assignments must be completed prior to group meetings.

Rationale.   "The purpose of the Parent Training Program (PTP) is to provide education and alternative methods of resolving conflicts that may arise with your children. PTP is designed to teach you that your child is highly influenced by you as a parent and that most of your child's behavior is learned through daily interactions with him or her, as well as caretakers, peers, and teachers. Previous research has clearly shown that a combination of both parent and child interventions is the most effective way of generating positive change in your child's behavior. By using the various child behavior management strategies that we will cover, you will learn strategies for improving your child's behavior. The goal of these interventions is to understand your child's behavior and to increase positive interactions with your child."

Overview of PTP.   "At this time, we would like to provide an overview of the techniques that we will be covering. *First*, you will learn about the behavioral and emotional effects of violence in the home on children. *Second*, we will teach you management procedures to help you deal more effectively with your child's behavior. *Third*, you will learn ways to control your anger and cope with stress. *Fourth*, we will cover methods for enhancing communication with your child and for solving child-related problems. And *finally*, we will discuss ways to help you increase the support system outside of the home."

The topic of violence is introduced by asking parents the following questions: "What are some reasons that violence occurs in families? Why does violence occur in your family?" Several examples are elicited from group members and they are praised for their contributions to the discussion.

Then, the "intergenerational transmission of violence" hypothesis is presented:

> There have been several theories that attempt to explain the origins of family violence. The explanation that has received most attention and support in recent years is called the "intergenerational transmission of violence" theory. According to this theory, most parents use violence as a way of resolving problems because they themselves witnessed their parents using violence for dealing with conflicts. Further, most parents involved in domestic violence report that they: (1) were emotionally and physically abused during their own childhoods, and/or (2) have never learned nonviolent ways of handling stress or conflict. Common reasons parents give for witnessing or being the victim of violent acts by a careprovider include: "That's just the way things were; if chores weren't done, mom or dad would whip us;" "Dad would come home drunk and get angry; there was no apparent reason for being hit." "Have any of you had similar experiences occur in your childhood?"

Cofacilitators respond reflectively and empathically and positively reinforce group discussion. If parents report that they have not experienced violence in their family of origin then a cofacilitator states: "That's right, not all people who use violence grew up in violent families;" or "Not all people who witness violence in their family use violence, but many use violence as a way of resolving conflict."

"Our program emphasizes breaking the cycle of violence in your family and implementing alternative strategies of communicating and managing your child. Despite the best intentions of parents in shielding their children from witnessing violence, studies have shown that children are, nevertheless, aware of such acts occurring in the home. For example, one investigation found that children listened to arguments and more serious violence between their parents as they remained in their bedrooms, while their mothers believed that they slept through these incidents (Rosenberg & Rossman, 1990). As a result, it is possible that your child may also have witnessed or heard violence and conflict between you and your partner."

Defining Abuse.   "Abuse is any behavior that one person does to another that physically hurts the person or their feelings." Each group member is asked: "What does abuse mean to you (parent's name)?"

Types of Abuse.   Definitions of physical, sexual, and emotional abuse are provided: *Physical abuse* is any behavior that results in personal injury, injury to animals, or property destruction. Examples of physical abuse include: hitting, kicking, slapping, or throwing objects. *Emotional abuse* occurs when someone engages in verbal behavior that is threatening or intimidating toward another person, or coerces them into doing something against their will. Examples of emotional abuse are: isolating someone from contact with others, making verbal threats to injure someone, insulting someone, and controlling another person's behavior. *Sexual abuse* involves engaging in sexual behavior against someone's will. Examples of sexual abuse include: fondling, forcing someone to expose bodily parts, and vaginal or anal penetration. Group members are asked to generate examples of each form of abuse. Cofacilitators reinforce group discussion and provide feedback.

After defining and generating examples of the three types of abuse, parents are told: "These forms of abuse are an ineffective means of communicating your needs to others. You and your children will be taught about the negative impact that these behaviors have on you and your child. In addition, you are learning strategies to decrease these behaviors and to produce more positive outcomes for you and your family. This group will provide you with an opportunity to learn more effective strategies to deal with your child in order to produce more positive outcomes for everyone. Do you have any questions?"

Session 2: Effects of Witnessing Interparental Violence

The stated goals of Session 2 are to review group rules, review types of abuse, educate parents about the emotional and behavioral sequelae of witnessing interparental violence on children, and examine current child management strategies.

Review.   "We are going to begin today by reviewing: (1) group rules, and (2) types of abuse that were discussed during our last session." The group rules are described to parents.

Definitions of physical, sexual, and emotional abuse are provided: *Physical abuse* is any behavior that results in personal injury, injury to animals, or property destruction. Examples of physical abuse include: hitting, kicking, slapping, or throwing objects. *Emotional abuse* occurs when someone engages in verbal behavior that is: threatening or intimidating another person, or coerces them into doing something against their will. Examples of emotional abuse are: isolating someone from contact with others, making verbal threats to injure someone, insulting someone, and controlling another person's behavior. *Sexual abuse* involves engaging in sexual behavior against someone's will. Examples of sexual abuse include: fondling, forcing someone to expose bodily parts, and vaginal or anal penetration.

Introduction.   Research has shown that children who have witnessed interparental violence have an increased risk for developing behavioral, emotional, social, physical, and cognitive difficulties (Alessi & Hearn, 1984; Jaffe, Wolfe, Wilson, & Zak 1986a; Wallerstein, 1983; Wallerstein & Kelly, 1980). Therefore, PTP will provide information to parents concerning the deleterious effects of witnessing violence in the home.

Effects of Witnessing Interparental Violence: An Overview.   "The effects of witnessing interparental violence on children are varied. For example, it has been shown that these children may exhibit aggression, nightmares, intrusive thoughts, anxiety, withdrawal, depression, and irritability. Younger children (toddlers and preschoolers) are, by definition, more limited in their ability to think and talk, and are most likely to experience somatic complaints (e.g., stomach problems, crying, irritability, upsetting dreams), and to regress to earlier stages of functioning (e.g., wetting their beds). What problems have you observed in your own children?" Parents are prompted and reinforced for generating examples of their child's behavioral difficulties.

"Children who have witnessed violence in the family may also find it difficult to handle frightening external events (e.g., physical danger to you or your child) or negative internal events, such as the overwhelming emotions they feel (e.g., anxiety, fear, confusion, anger) during and after violent episodes. Such children often fear that their mother will be hurt or that father will be taken out of home as a result of such violence. They see the person that they love and care for being loving at one point and hurting at another. This sends conflictual messages to children about the use of violence as a way of resolving problems because they are limited in their understanding of what is going on between their parents; also, they may feel responsible for the violence."

"Research also suggests that social problem-solving abilities are affected in children who witness interparental violence. Specifically, children tend to exhibit either aggressive or passive means of solving interpersonal problems. Examples of *aggressive* strategies children may use to problem-solve include: (a) forcefully taking away another child's toy, (b) fighting or hitting others, or (c) threatening to harm someone. Some *passive* strategies children may use to solve interpersonal problems are: (a) walking away from another child who is using bullying tactics, (b) wishing for something to change without letting others know, or (c) waiting for another person to resolve an issue. We have just decribed various aggressive or passive strategies that children may use to solve interpersonal problems. Have you observed your child use any of these approaches to solve interpersonal problems?"

Current Behavior Management Practices.   "Let's discuss the current strategies that you use to manage your child's undesirable behavior." The following examples are provided:

Example 1

Cofacilitator:	"(*Parent's name*), you stated that Sarah wets the bed and you identified this as a problem. How do you respond when Sarah wets the bed?"
Parent:	"I get up and change the sheets, put her pajamas in the laundry, and often let her sleep in my bed."
Cofacilitator:	"What does Sarah do?"
Parent:	"She goes to sleep and continues to wet the bed."
Cofacilitator:	"It sounds like changing the sheets, putting the pajamas in the laundry, and letting Sarah sleep in your bed has not been effective for stopping bedwetting. Some problems require a more structured and systematic approach than others. Our group will cover alternative parenting strategies that have proven effective with these kinds of problems."

Example 2

Cofacilitator:	"(*Parent's name*), you have mentioned that you have been having trouble with Anthony because he does not listen to you when you tell him to do something. What would you like to have happen instead?
Parent:	"I want Anthony to listen to me. I have had trouble getting Anthony to stop yelling when I tell him to do something. The other day I told him to stop watching TV and come to the dinner table and eat dinner when it was served, but he didn't listen to me and he continued to watch TV."

Cofacilitator:	"So you would like Anthony to eat dinner when you serve it. How do you respond when Anthony does not listen to you when you want him to eat dinner?"
Parent:	"I end up yelling at him a few times to come to dinner, generally I give up yelling and take dinner to him on the couch."
Cofacilitator:	"So it sounds like when Anthony is noncompliant with your command to eat dinner, yelling at him and subsequently giving up and taking dinner to him on the couch has not been effective in getting Anthony to eat dinner when it is served at the table. You will be learning several techniques over the next few sessions that will help you to reduce Anthony's noncompliant behavior."

Ask each parent to generate an example of an undesirable behavior that has proven difficult to change. Provide prompting, verbal praise, and feedback to reinforce parents for their contribution to the group discussion.

Homework. "Your first homework assignment involves monitoring your child's undesirable behavior. It is important to identify problem behaviors before we focus on decreasing that behavior. What we would like you to do for our next session is to record undesirable behaviors that your child engages in this week, how often the behavior occurs during the week, and how you handled the situation using the Target Behavior Monitoring Form (see Table 8.10)."

Session 3: Introduction of Behavioral Principles

The stated goals of Session 3 are to review the behavioral and emotional effects of witnessing interparental violence on children, define basic behavioral principles, and practice attending and reinforcing.

Homework Review. "We are going to begin today by reviewing the behavioral and emotional effects of witnessing interparental violence on children, and homework assigned during the last session related to monitoring and recording your child's undesirable behavior."

TABLE 8.10

Target Behavior Monitoring Form

1. Describe your target behavior in observable terms:

_____

_____

2. Provide a daily report, as follows:

Day	How Often Did the Behavior Occur Today?	What Did You Do About the Behavior?
1.		
2.		
3.		
4.		
5.		
6.		
7.		

Parents are asked to generate examples of the effects of witnessing interparental violence on children (e.g., aggression, intrusive thoughts, irritability, somatic complaints, fear, confusion, anger).

In addition, the Target Behavior Monitoring Form completed by each parent is reviewed. Noncompliance is addressed via the following explanation: "Homework is a vital part of monitoring the progress that is occurring in your interactions with your child. Observing your child and monitoring his or her behavior is important to provide significant behavioral changes. You are strongly encouraged to comply with homework assignments so that you can talk about your experiences during the group."

Cofacilitators provide the following prompt to parents: "*(Parent's name)*, I see that you have identified fighting with brothers, forgetting to pick up toys, and noncompliance with bedtime as problem areas with your child. You have done a very good job of identifying these behaviors." Praise and performance feedback are provided for their efforts and completion of homework assignments. "We would like you to continue to monitor your child's behavior. In future groups, the focus will be on changing these difficulties."

Introduction.   Components of the child management program (positive reinforcement, extinction, time-out, and behavioral contracting), although not yet directly examined with parents of child witnesses of interparental violence, have been empirically validated as effective treatment approaches with punitive families (Clark, 1985; Cohn & Daro, 1987; Forehand & McMahon, 1981; Kelly, 1983; Trickett, & Kuczynski, 1986; D. A. Wolfe, Edwards, Manion, & Kaverola, 1988; D. A. Wolfe, Kaufman, Aragona, & Sandler, 1981). Research suggests that child witnesses exhibit behavioral problems similar to those children who have been abused (e.g., aggression, anxiety, irritability) (Jaffe et al., 1986b). Therefore, the present model incorporates treatment strategies that have proven efficacious with punitive parents.

Rationale.   "The purpose of parent training is to teach you better ways to manage your child's behavior. In order to do this, it is important to begin teaching your child what behavior it is that you like. During this session, you are going to be learning skills that will help you interact better with your child and to change his or her behavior."

Defining Behavior.   "Behavior is anything that your child does that can be observed. Examples of behaviors include: smiling, reading a book, and yelling. When telling your child to perform a desired behavior, be sure to: define the behavior, specify who performs the behavior, and explain when and where it is to occur. For example, "Sally ran out into the street yesterday." Provide the following prompts to parent to develop an understanding of defining the behavior: "What was the behavior?" "Who performed the behavior?" "When did the behavior occur?"

"What we would like you to do now is to share an example of a behavior that your child frequently exhibits."

Cofacilitators provide the following prompts for child management errors described by parents when providing examples of behavior:

Prompt 1: Describing When a Behavior Is "Not" Occurring. For example: "He didn't make his bed," or "She yelled at me." Parents are informed that for every problem behavior there is a positive counterpart response that they would like their child to perform. In this example, the positive behaviors are "to make his bed" or "to speak in a normal voice tone."

Prompt 2: *Describing a Series of Behaviors.* When parents describe a series of behaviors, for example, "cleaning up after themselves," ask them to define the discrete behaviors that comprise "cleaning up after themselves" until parents can provide an operational definition with concrete examples.

Example 1:

Cofacilitator:	"What specific behavior do you want your child to engage in that means cleaning up after himself?"
Parent:	"I want him to clean up the toys."
Cofacilitator:	"That's good. Cleaning up his toys is a specific behavior. When would you like him to clean up his toys?"
Parent:	"After he's done playing with them."
Cofacilitator:	"That is excellent! You stated the exact behavior that you want your child to engage in, which was to "clean up his toys" and you also stated when the behavior was to occur, "after he is finished playing with them."

Prompt 3: *Labeling Emotions Rather Than Defining Behavior.* Parents are asked to identify the specific responses that previously have been attributed to an "emotional" state.

Example 2:

Cofacilitator:	"You mentioned that Monica gets angry. What happens just before you notice that Monica is angry?"
Parent:	"I tell her that she can't watch TV until she washes the dishes."
Cofacilitator:	"So what is the desired behavior you want her to perform?"
Parent:	"I want her to wash the dishes."
Cofacilitator:	"You identified the specific behavior of washing the dishes and you would like Monica to do them before she watches TV. Good job."

Defining Reinforcers and Punishers. "Certain events that occur following behaviors (consequences) either increase or decrease the frequency of the behavior. There are two types of consequences that follow a behavior: reinforcers or punishers. *Reinforcers* are events that follow behaviors that *increase* their frequency of occurrence in the future. *Punishers* are events that follow behaviors which *decrease* their frequency of occurrence in the future."

Cofacilitators provide the following examples of consequences that are reinforcing or punishing.

Example 1: Your child came home after school and promptly finished his homework and you told him, "What a great job you did with your homework." We know that your praise is reinforcing if your child does his homework promptly after school the next day.

Example 2: Your child has a temper tantrum everytime you are on the phone talking to someone. He continues to yell until you give him the cookie that he wanted. Your giving him the cookie is reinforcing to him if he has temper tantrums in the future when you're on the phone. He knows that if he has tantrums, you will give in and give him the cookie (the reinforcer). The temper tantrum is reinforced because it gets him what he wants.

Example 3: Your child wishes to tell you the exciting news of his good grades on his report card. However, you continue to read the newspaper and yell out, "When's dinner ready?" The consequence of ignoring your child is punishing if he does not attempt to show you future report cards.

Example 4: Your child yells at you for not giving her the toy. You ignore her yelling and pretend to continue working until she stops yelling. The consequence of ignoring her is likely to be punishing if, in the future, episodes of yelling for toys decreases. She has learned that yelling does not get her what she wants (the toys).

"Now that you have heard several examples, we would like you to provide examples of reinforcers and punishers that you use with your children."

Practice Attending and Reinforcing your Child (PARC).   A cofacilitator presents the following rationale for the PARC procedure: "The strategy that you will be learning in this session is called Practicing Attending and Reinforcing your Child, or 'PARC.' The primary objective of this procedure is to apply the behavioral principles that we've just learned in order to increase your child's desired behavior. This goal is accomplished by providing positive attention/reinforcement after the desired behavior occurs, while ignoring your child by withholding that attention when your child engages in undesirable behavior."

"This procedure is sometimes difficult because problem behaviors are usually more obvious to you than the positive responses you would like to strengthen. You may inadvertently attend to undesirable behaviors in an attempt to decrease them. However, even if you yell at your child to stop whining, this provides him attention which may actually increase his or her whining. An increase in undesirable behavior occurs because your attention is one of the most important reinforcers for your child. Various research programs have utilized this technique with families much like your own and have found it to be an effective method of increasing positive behaviors in children. With the positive attention you provide to your child, you will also increase the quality of time spent with your child. Are there any questions?"

Attending and Reinforcing Skills.   "When your child's behavior is followed by something reinforcing, such as your attention, he/she will act that way in the future to gain your attention. Therefore, paying attention to your child's positive behavior immediately and frequently will increase the rate of the behavior. One method for increasing desired behaviors is 'attending.' Attends are verbal descriptions or running commentaries of your child's appropriate activity, in which you describe aloud exactly what your child is doing. An example of attends is simply describing overt (observable) behavior. For example: 'Your're placing the pieces of the puzzle together. Good job!' or, 'You're placing the blocks on top of each other; Great!' Another type of attends involves emphasizing a prosocial behavior. For example: 'You're sharing your toys so nicely with your friend. That's great.'"

Cofacilitators model attending skills to parents. One cofacilitator assumes the role of the parent and the other enacts the role of the child. Several points in the use of attending are pointed out to the parents: attend to child at his or her level (e.g., by sitting on the floor and look directly at the child), exhibit positive facial expressions, use a pleasant voice tone, employ physical contact (e.g., pat on back), and incidental learning.

Modeling Exercise.

Example 1:

Cofacilitator 1:	(begins drawing with crayons and paper on the floor)
Cofacilitator 2:	(also sits down on the floor and attends to the behavior) "Look at how you are taking the blue crayon and drawing a big blue sky. Now, you're taking the yellow crayon and look at how bright that sun your drawing looks. You're drawing so quietly and nicely."
Cofacilitator 2:	"See how I used descriptive praise and described what he/she was doing that I liked. I praised him/her for sitting nicely and quietly. I got down on his/her level, made eye contact, smiled, and spoke in a pleasant tone of voice."

The following rationale is provided to parents for the attending skill of incidental learning: "Incidental learning is another form of attending to your child's desired behavior. Incidental learning requires that you attend to your child's prosocial behavior, while at the same time, providing questions and prompts designed to teach your child about the activity in which he or she is engaged." Cofacilitators model the use of incidental learning.

Example 2:

Cofacilitator 2:	"We are going to elaborate on the use of incidental learning from the example that we just provided."
Cofacilitator 1:	(continues drawing with crayons and paper on the floor)
Cofacilitator 2:	(also sits down on the floor and attends to the behavior) "Look at how you are taking the blue crayon and drawing a big blue sky. Now, you're taking the yellow crayon and look at how bright that sun your drawing looks. You're drawing so quietly and nicely. Do you know what happens to the big blue sky when night time comes along?"
Cofacilitator 1:	"Gee, I guess the sky becomes dark and a bunch of stars are in the sky."
Cofacilitator 2:	"You are right! The sky does become dark and the stars do come out at night. Can you draw those stars."
Cofacilitator 1:	(begins drawing)
Cofacilitator 2:	"Do you remember when we looked at the pictures of the Big Dipper the other day?"
Cofacilitator 1:	"Yea, the Big Dipper looks like a big giant spoon."
Cofacilitator 2:	"Do you remember what happens to the Big Dipper?"
Cofacilitator 1:	"It shoots out of the sky."
Co-facilitator 2:	"That's right, you've really done a great job drawing the stars and you also remembered what happens to the Big Dipper. That's wonderful."

Parents are asked to identify the important aspects that were included in the attending examples. Parents are provided with prompting, performance feedback, and praise for their participation in generating examples of attending skills. Cofacilitators ask parents to divide into dyads and instruct one parent to engage in the child's favorite playtime activity while the other parent role plays "attending" to the behavior. Cofacilitators observe, coach, and narrate appropriate use of attends; provide descriptive praise; and provide performance feedback throughout the interaction to facilitate learning.

Homework.   Parents are asked to continue monitoring their child's undesirable behavior using the Target Behavior Monitoring Form (see Table 8.10). In addition, the following rationale for attending skills homework is provided: "Homework for the next 2 weeks is to engage in an activity with your child that he/she enjoys. Set aside 15 minutes per day in which you and your child spend time playing one of your child's preferred activities. During this time, you are to practice the skills covered in this session. Practice the use of attends and rewards when your child is displaying desired behavior that you would like to see increased. Also, record your activity using the Practice Attending and Reinforcing your Child (PARC) Monitoring Form (see Table 8.11). Record specific behaviors that you attended to and reinforced. In addition, record the day, time, activity, and total frequency that you utilized these techniques during the week."

Session 4: Personal Safety Planning

The stated goals of Session 4 are to introduce child's personal safety plan, develop a personal safety plan to reduce risk of physical harm to family members, and discuss social support building.

Rationale.   An explanation of the child's safety plan is provided to parents. "Your child will be taught in group to identify early signs of anger in your family (e.g., hearing you and your partner beginning to raise your voices during an argument, hearing objects being thrown in the home). To ensure the safety of all family members in your home, your child will learn to seek outside assistance when these episodes occur. They will be taught to walk to or call a friend, relative, or neighbor for help. In addition, your child will be taught to call the police when a violent episode takes place. It is very important that you support your child in his/her efforts to stop the violence, because safety for all family members is the primary concern. Do you have any questions or concerns that you would like to discuss about your child's safety plan? You are going to develop a personal plan for promoting safety as well."

Introduction.   Victims of violence often lack social support and/or are isolated from family and friends (Jaffe et al., 1990). As a result, they subject themselves and their children to the harmful effects of violence due to the perceived unavailability of alternative resources. Therefore, one of the aims of PTP is to help parents establish social support networks, and to utilize these resources to reduce risk of potential harm to themselves and their children.

TABLE 8.11

Practice Attending and Reinforcing Your Child (PARC) Monitoring Form

Specific Behaviors in Which You Used PARC	Type of Reinforcer	Day	Time	Total # of Times You Used PARC
1.				
2.				
3.				
4.				
5.				
6.				

Rationale. "The focus of this session is to expand available social resources outside of your immediate family to help you and your child remain safe. Social support-building involves seeking or receiving the help of others to protect your child and you. As when we developed your child's safety plan in the previous session, we are going to generate a safety plan that can be used when you suspect that a violent episode is eminent."

"The *first* step in developing a safety plan is to learn to *identify anger cues.* Examples of anger cues that signal a violent episode include: your partner's voice gets louder, your partner engages in physical or threatening gestures, or your partner throws objects. The next step is to determine available resources. Personal strategies that can be used when you suspect a violent episode might occur include: asking others (e.g., friends, family members, or neighbors) for help, leaving a threatening situation, hiding or disguising your place of residence, and having your children ask for assistance outside the home. *Informal* sources of help include: notifying family members, in-laws, neighbors, or friends about the abuse. You can ask them if you may call and seek their help if violence occurs. *Formal* sources of help consist of: calling police, obtaining a restraining order, going to a shelter, contacting lawyers or clergy, or attending women's support group. Social service agencies can also be utilized to provide immediate assistance (e.g., welfare, food stamps, crisis nurseries for children at risk for abuse, housing, and transportation services)."

Parents are asked to generate examples of personal strategies, informal, and formal help sources that they can use for their own personal safety plan. Parents then write down on an index card the names and contact numbers of such social supports. They are instructed to carry the card with them at all times.

Behavior Rehearsal of Safety Plan. Group members role play a scenerio in which they implement the personal safety plan and contact the social support resources that they have identified. First, a scenerio involving a family argument is described. Then, parents are asked to identify possible anger cues based on the scenerio. After identifying anger cues, parents are asked to initiate the personal safety plan and to contact their outside support. The following example can be used: "Your partner arrives home and begins to scream at you about the lack of money in your account to pay the monthly bills. You stated in your safety plan that the first thing you would do if he engaged in such behavior is to take your children and leave the situation and go into your bedroom. The second step would be to call your family and let them know you are having an argument and that you will be coming over to stay with them. You tell your children about your safety concerns and ask them to leave quietly through the back door of the house."

Parents are prompted with the following questions: "What should you do next? When is the best time to leave the situation?" Parents are provided with positive reinforcement and performance feedback for their efforts.

Homework. "Practice your own and your child's safety plan at home with the children for the next 2 weeks. When practicing your personal safety plan, inform your child of the purpose of the safety plan. It is presented as a method to insure the safety of all family members. Contact family, friends, or neighbors about the plan and arrange with them, in advance, to use their support when you have safety concerns. Monitor and record the results in the Personal Safety Plan Monitoring Form (see Table 8.7) and bring them with you during the next session.

In addition, you are to practice your child's personal safety plan at home with your child. First, role play the personal safety plan with your child. Begin by recognizing anger cues and then practice with your child what they would say if they were to call family, friends, neighbors, or the police. Then, practice how you and your child would leave the home during a violent episode. Note any difficulties in implementing the plan, and monitor the frequency of your home practice."

Reminder to Parents. "The cofacilitators for your child's group have asked us to tell you to pick up your child's relaxation training tape at the end of this session. Your children will be listening to the relaxation tapes as part of their homework assignment. We will also cover relaxation methods in a later session to help you develop alternative methods of coping with stress."

Session 5: Review of Personal Safety Plan and PARC

The stated goals of Session 5 are to review safety plans and basic behavioral principles, practice attending and reinforcing, introduce extinction/ignoring, and provide rationale for the integrated session.

Safety Plan Review. The procedure presented in the previous session is used for reviewing personal safety plans and social support building. Parents form dyads to rehearse individual safety plans. Role playing, prompting, positive reinforcement, and performance feedback are employed to consolidate skill acquisition. If parents have implemented the safety plan at home, they are asked to describe the episode to the group, demonstrate how the situation was handled, and discuss the outcome (i.e., success or problems in implementation).

"Last week you were asked to practice your own, as well as your child's personal safety plan at home. We would like to review how you implemented these." Cofacilitators ask group members to role play the parent's personal safety plan. Performance feedback and positive reinforcement are provided for their efforts. "We will also have an opportunity next week to practice both your own and your child's personal safety plans to ensure that you have learned how to carry them out effectively."

Homework Review. "We are also going to review basic behavioral principles (e.g., behavior and consequences) and homework assigned on the use of PARC procedures." Provide the following definition of behavior: "Behavior is anything that your child does that can be observed. Examples of behaviors include: smiling, reading a book, and yelling. When telling your child to perform a desired behavior, be sure to define the behavior, specify who performs the behavior, and explain when and where it is to occur. What we would like you to do now is to share an example of a behavior that your child frequently exhibits." Provide the following prompts to parent to develop an understanding of defining the behavior: "What was the behavior?" "Who performed the behavior?" "When did the behavior occur?"

Provide the following definition of consequences (i.e., reinforcers and punishers): "Certain events that occur following behaviors (i.e., consequences) either increase or decrease the frequency of the behavior. There are two types of consequences that follow a behavior: reinforcers or punishers. *Reinforcers* are events that follow behaviors that *increase* their frequency of occurrence in the future. *Punishers* are events which follow behaviors that *decrease* their frequency of occurrence in the future. Now we would like you to provide examples of reinforcers and punishers that you use with your children."

The following rationale for a review of the homework on the use of attending skills is provided: "For homework, you were asked to practice the use of attends and rewards when your child displayed a desired behavior, and record these results in the Practice Attending and Reinforcing your Child (PARC) Monitoring Form (see Table 8.11). We would like to review the specific behaviors that you attended to and reinforced, as well as the day, time, activity, and total frequency that you utilized these techniques during the week." Prompting, positive reinforcement, and performance feedback are provided to facilitate skill acquisition.

Types of Reinforcers.   "In addition to attending, there are other types of reinforcers that increase the child's rate of positive behavior. These include social and nonsocial reinforcers. Examples of social reinforcers are:

1. *Physical rewards:* smiles, hugs, pats, kisses, pleasant eye contact and voice tone, and parental attention.
2. *Verbal rewards*: statements of praise and appreciation (e.g., "Thank you for picking up the toys," "Your room looks great and you did such a good job cleaning it");
3. *Activity rewards:* special activities with your child (e.g., playing a game, reading your child a story).

Nonsocial rewards are particulary effective when you are trying to teach your child a new behavior. These include money, stars, points, and toys. Cofacilitators ask parents to repeat the types of reinforcers and to provide examples they have or would like to use with their child. In addition, the following rationale for use of reinforcers is given to parents:

"There are several guidelines that you should follow when you are rewarding your child for desired behaviors. First, praise is more effective in strengthening your child's desirable behavior if you *praise the behavior* rather than the child. Focus on the specific behavior that you would like to see increased so that your child is aware of what you liked. For example, you have just arrived home and recognize that your child has cleaned her room. It is important to praise her behavior by saying something like: 'Oh, Sally you did a wonderful job cleaning your room; look at how neatly you stacked your clothing in the closet,' rather than simply stating, 'Sally, you are a good girl.' With the latter statement, Sally may not recognize what she did that was good. Second, rewards should be specific and immediately follow desirable behavior. Third, rewards should be used *every time* the behavior occurs, especially when the child is first learning a new response. Also, consistency is very important. What do you think happens if you reward your child for engaging in a desired behavior once and not the second time it occurs? You are not likely to see an increase in the desired behavior because your child may be confused about what was reinforced. Finally, after your child has learned the behavior, you can gradually reward less often."

Introduction of Extinction/Ignoring.   "Another skill that can be used along with attending and rewarding your child's appropriate behavior is ignoring. *Ignoring* involves briefly not paying attention to your child when he/she is engaging in an undesired response. Behavior often tends to decrease when it does not receive attention. Guidelines you can use when ignoring undersirable behavior include: briefly remove all attention from your child; refuse to argue, scold or talk; turn your head and avoid eye contact; do not show anger (or any other emotion) in your manner or gestures; be certain your child's behavior does not result in a material reward, and provide attention *when and only when* your child's negative behavior ceases. Ignoring can be applied to weaken the following behaviors: whining and fussing, pouting and sulking, loud crying intended to manipulate parents, complaining, insistent begging and demanding, mild temper tantrums. However, if your child's undesirable behavior is a danger to him/herself or others, or involves the destruction of property, other behavioral strategies (to be presented later) will be necessary."

Cofacilitators model use of attending, reinforcing, and ignoring. One cofacilitator plays the role of the parent and the other enacts the role of the child:

Cofacilitator 1:	(begins playing with a puzzle on the floor)
Cofacilitator 2:	(sits down next to the cofacilitator on the floor and attends to the behavior) "Look at how well you are putting those pieces of the puzzle together; you're making the face on the clown complete. You're putting the puzzle together so nicely."
Cofacilitator 1:	(begins throwing the pieces of the puzzle on the floor)
Cofacilitator 2:	(sits down next to the cofacilitator on the floor and withdraws her attention by eliminating eye contact and verbal interaction with the co-facilitator)
Cofacilitator 1:	(resumes putting the pieces of the puzzle together)
Cofacilitator 2:	(looks back at the cofacilitator and begins attending to her appropriate behavior) "Look, you put all of the pieces together and you have really done a great job!"

Cofacilitators ask parents to form dyads. One of the parents in the dyad is instructed to engage in the child's favorite playtime activity while the other practices use of attends, reinforcing positive activity, and ignoring. Cofacilitators observe, coach, and narrate appropriate use of attends and provide descriptive praise. They also provide performance feedback throughout the interaction.

Rationale for Integrated Session.   Cofacilitators provide the following rationale for the child's attendance next session: "You have all been putting considerable effort into learning the procedures that we have been covering during the past few sessions. We would like to help with any difficulties you may have in implementing the skills of attending, rewarding, ignoring, and also practice the personal safety plans generated by you and your child. It is also important to remind your children about attending the next session with you because they might forget during the week."

Homework.   Parents are asked to continue monitoring and record their child's undesirable behavior using the Target Behavior Monitoring Form (see Table 8.10). Target behaviors identified by parents. In addition, the following rationale for attending skills homework is provided: "Homework for this week is to engage in an activity with your child that he/she enjoys. Set aside 15 minutes per day in which you and your child spend time playing one of your child's preferred activities. During this time, you are to practice the skills covered during the present and the last session. Practice use of attends and other social reinforcers when your child is displaying prosocial behavior that you would like to see increase, and use of ignoring when your child is engaging in inappropriate behavior. Also, recording of your activity is to be carried out using the Practice Attending, Reinforcing, and Ignoring your Child Monitoring Form (see Table 8). Record specific behaviors that you attended to, reinforced, and ignored. In addition, record the day, time, activity, and frequency with which you employed these techniques during the week."

Session 6: Integrated Parent and Child Treatment

As noted earlier, Session 6 is an integrated session that includes both children and parents. This session provides an opportunity for implementation and practice of strategies trained in previous group meetings. The stated goals for Session 6 are to practice attending to, reinforcing, and ignoring child's behavior, and rehearse parent and child personal safety plans (refer to Session 6 in CTP).

Session 7: Time-Out

The stated goals of Session 7 are to review homework, provide instruction in the use of effective commands, and present the time-out procedure.

Homework Review. Review homework (assigned in Session 4, 5, and 6) for use of attends, rewards, and ignoring. Provide praise and performance feedback to parents for their efforts and completion of homework assignments.

Rationale. "Now that we have covered methods for increasing appropriate behavior, let's discuss a strategy that increases your child's compliance with your requests. *Time-out* is a mild, but effective punishment, designed to decrease your child's negative responses. Time-out is an especially useful procedure for you to learn because it can be employed without resorting to coercive methods of child behavior management. In addition, time-out can be applied when you find yourself becoming angry in dealing with your child's misbehavior. By using this procedure, you also can be a rational and non-aggressive model for your child."

The following definition of time-out is provided: "Time-out means removing your child from access to reinforcement. Time-out can be used with children between the age of 2 and 12 years of age. For time-out to work effectively, you must precisely follow the steps we will present. Time-out should be used if your child: engages in behavior that is harmful to himself or to others (e.g., hits another child), and/or destroys property (e.g., throws a toy, breaks a valued object). In addition, time-out should be implemented if your child does not comply with a command that you have given him/her after one time-out warning. Do you have any questions?"

Appropriate Commands. "When using time-out, it is important to give your child clear and direct commands. Commands consist of stating specifically what you want your child to do and when you want it done. When giving a command to your child, be sure to say it using the least amount of words necessary (between 2 to 10 words), say it in a normal tone of voice, and maintain eye contact by getting down to your child's eye level. Examples of appropriate commands are: "Sally, please put your toys away in the toy box now!" and "Brian, please brush your teeth now!" Notice, how I used all of the components we just talked about when delivering these commands: I put myself at the child's level, I looked right at the child, and I used a pleasant but firm tone of voice."

Each parent is asked to generate examples of child commands. Praise and performance feedback are provided for their efforts.

Inappropriate Commands. There are several common mistakes that are made when delivering a command to children:

1. Giving a *series of commands* in the same sequence (e.g., "Johnny, make your bed, pick up your toys, and then clean your room"). This is too much for them to remember. Therefore, they are less likely to comply. It is important to be specific and state one command at a time.
2. Giving vague commands (e.g., "Be careful"). We cannot assume that children know that "Be careful" means not to walk out into the middle of the street. Be specific and tell your children, "Don't walk out into the middle of the street."
3. Phrasing commands in the form of a question (e.g., "Would you like to take your bath now?"). Commands are directives that you want children to follow, so beware of asking them to perform a behavior because children may respond by saying "No."
4. Using "Let's" commands, which suggest that parents will provide help (e.g., "Let's clean up your room"). Do not state a command this way if you have no intention of helping your child.

"Do any of these examples remind you of interactions that you have had with your child(ren)? What could you have done differently in these situations? What should occur after a command is given?" Cofacilitators deliver performance feedback and provide praise to parents when they appropriately use commands.

Time-Out Steps. "Now that you understand how to give commands, let's discuss the important steps to follow when using time-out with your child":

Step 1: Provide a specific command to children (e.g., "Susan, please pick up your toys and put them in the toy box").

Step 2: If child comply within 5 seconds after a command is given, attend and praise their compliant behavior. Verbal praise for compliance should be provided *frequently* and *immediately* (e.g., "Thank you, Susan, for picking up your toys and putting them in the toy box like I asked you to, you did a fine job").

Step 3: If children do not comply with your command within 5 seconds, provide a warning: "Susan, please pick up your toys and put them in your toy box now or you will go to time-out for 7 minutes" (the child remains in time-out for a duration of 1-minute for each year of their age). Wait another 5 seconds (count to yourself, not out loud). If children do not comply within this time, give the following command in a calm but firm voice (not lecturing, scolding, or arguing): "Susan, because you did not pick up your toys, you are now going to time-out for

7 minutes." At this time, take the child's hand and manually guide him/her to the time-out area that you have preselected (preferably a chair facing the wall).

Step 4: Release from time-out is contingent on children staying in the time-out chair for the total amount of time and spending at least the last 30 seconds of time-out quietly. If children are not quiet for the last 30 seconds of time-out, they are required to remain in time-out until they remain quiet for at least the last 30 seconds. For example, if your 7-year-old child has been yelling for 6 minutes and 30 seconds, but remains quite for at least 30 seconds, he/she can be released from time-out. If children have been quiet throughout most of time-out but yell during the last 30 seconds, they should remain in time-out until they are silent for 30 seconds.

Step 5: If children are resistant to going to time-out, physically assist them by picking them up and placing them in the time-out area (do not utilize excessive force when placing your child in time-out). If children attempt to leave the time-out area before the alotted time interval elapses, physically assist them to remain in the chair. You can physically confine children to remain in the time-out chair with minimal force by standing in back of the time-out chair and resting your arms against their shoulders and cuffing their forearms (cofacilitator demonstrates the appropriate way to confine a child in the time-out chair). If children attempt to slide off the chair, place your hands under their armpits and raise them onto the chair.

Step 6: When children have completed time-out, return them to the original situation that caused them to be in time-out and repeat the command with which you wish them to comply: "Susan please, pick up your toys now!" If children comply, praise them (e.g., "Thank you Susan for putting your toys in the toybox"). If children fail to comply, repeat the time-out procedure.

Cofacilitators model the appropriate use of commands and time-out:

Cofacilitator 1: "Susan, please pick up your toys and put them in the toy box."

Cofacilitator 2: "No! I don't want to."

Cofacilitator 1: (waits 5 seconds and provides warning)"Susan, please pick up your toys and put them in the toy box or you will go to time-out for . . ." (Cofacilitator tells parents that Susan is 6 years old and asks how long she should be placed in time-out; answer: 6 minutes.)

Cofacilitator 2: "No, I'm not going to; you're a meany."

Cofacilitator 1: (waits another 5 seconds)"Susan, because you did not pick up your toys, you are going to time-out for 6 minutes." (Cofacilitator manually guides the other cofacilitator to the time-out chair.)

Cofacilitator 2: After being placed in time-out chair, the child attempts to leave the chair. Cofacilitator 1 models the appropriate way to confine a child in the time-out chair, standing behind the chair and resting arms against the cofaciltator's shoulders and cuffing forearms.

Cofacilitator 1: Asks parents the following questions: (a) "Susan has been in the time-out chair for 5:30 seconds, but she has been wiggling and talking during this time; Should she be released from time-out? (b) "Susan has been in the time-out chair for 5:30 seconds, but she was wiggling and talking for the first 5:30 seconds; however, for the last 30 seconds she has been quiet, should she be released from time-out?" (c) "Susan has been in the time-out chair for 5:30 seconds, but she was quiet for the first 5:30 seconds; however, for the last 30 seconds she has been wiggling and talking. Should she be released from time-out?" How much longer should she remain in time-out?"

Cofacilitator 1: Releases from time-out and returns the other cofacilitator to where the toys are and provides the following directive: "Susan, please, pick up your toys now."

Cofacilitator 2: (complies with the directive and begins placing toys in the toy box).
Cofacilitator 1: "Thank you, Susan, for putting your toys in the toy box."

Following the demonstration, parents are divided into dyads. They are asked to role play a time-out scenerio (one parent assumes the role of the child and the other assumes the role of the parent). Cofacilitators observe, coach, and narrate appropriate use of time-out and provide descriptive praise. They also provide performance feedback throughout the role play to facilitate skill acquisition.

"Follow these important rules when trying time-out at home: First, select a time-out area in your home. Choose a place away from toys, people, windows, TV's, radios, or anything else that your child likes. The child's bedroom or bathroom are not good places for time-out. The bedroom contains things that he likes, and bathrooms may contain unsafe substances that may potentially harm your child. The best place to conduct time-out is at the end of a hallway. A small chair should be placed in the time-out area so that your child can be reminded that this is the time-out area in case misbehavior occurs. Second, you need to pinpoint the undesired behavior that you would like to change (e.g., child cleans up toys after he has played with them). Now, identify one behavior that your child engages in that you would like to eliminate. For homework, you will be implementing the time-out procedure to reduce the rate of this undesired behavior."

"Third, you need to explain to your child the rationale for using time-out. Sit down with your child and explain that you love and care for him or her and that is why you are going to begin a procedure that will help him or her stop a behavior that has been causing a problem. Explain this using a calm voice tone without scolding your child. Also, tell your child the specific behavior that will lead to time-out and mention that everytime the behavior occurs, he or she will be placed in time-out. Explain how long time-out will last and how he or she will know when it is over. Explain that if the child is quiet and behaves, he or she can come out as soon as the time is up. If the child argues, leaves time-out, yells, kicks the door, and so on, the time will be increased until he or she is quiet. If the child makes a mess, he or she will be expected to clean it up. Practice time-out with your child so that he or she is aware of the punishing consequence of the procedure."

"Finally, once you have explained the use of time-out to your child, begin implementing the procedure the *next time* the behavior occurs and *everytime* thereafter. Remember, do not debate or argue with your child; this only delays the use of time-out and reinforces their argumentativeness.

Homework. "For homework, explain the time-out procedure to your child. State that you will implement it the next time the undesirable behavior occurs. Then, use the time-out procedure when the targeted behavior occurs at home. Record the behavior, indicating when it occured, and the steps you used in carrying out the procedure in using Time-Out Monitoring Form (see Table 8.9). Do not begin time-out if you do not have time to spend with your child. When you first actually use the technique, your child may strongly protest. However, if you follow through with time-out, the negative behavior will eventually decrease. Further, this will save you time and anguish in the long run." In addition, the parents are instructed to continue monitoring the child's undesirable behavior on the Target Behavior Monitoring Form (see Table 8.10).

Session 8: Behavior Rehearsal of Child Management Skills

The stated goals of Session 8 are to review attends, reinforcers, ignoring, and time-out homework.

Review. "During this group, we want to review the child behavioral management skills that we have covered previously." Cofacilitators model attending, reinforcing, and ignoring skills to parents. One cofacilitator assumes the role of the parent and the other enacts the role of the child. Several points in the use of attending and reinforcing positive activity are pointed out to the parents: attend to children at level (e.g., by sitting on the floor and look directly at the child), exhibit positive facial expressions, use a pleasant voice tone, employ physical contact (e.g., pat on back), and incidental learning.

Several guidelines in the use of ignoring skills are emphasized to the parents: briefly remove all attention from your child; refuse to argue, scold, or talk; turn your head and avoid eye contact; do not show anger (or any other emotion) in your manner or gestures; be certain your child's behavior does not result in a material reward; and provide attention *when and only when* your child's negative behavior ceases.

Cofacilitators ask parents to divide into dyads and instruct one parent to engage in the child's favorite playtime activity while the other parent role plays "attending," "reinforcing positive activity," and "ignoring" the behavior. Cofacilitators observe, coach, narrate appropriate use of attends; provide descriptive praise; and provide performance feedback throughout the interaction to facilitate learning. Any difficulties that parents have in implementing these procedures are discussed.

Then, time-out homework is reviewed. Parents are divided into dyads and are asked to role play a time-out scenerio (one parent assumes the role of the child and the other assumes the role of the parent). Cofacilitators observe, coach, provide feedback, and narrate appropriate use of time-out and provide descriptive praise.

Homework. Parents are instructed to continue monitoring of PARC, ignoring, and time-out use. In addition, the parents are instructed to continue monitoring the child's undesirable behavior on the Target Behavior Monitoring Form (see Table 8.10).

Session 9: Reward System

The stated goals of Session 9 are to review homework, and introduce the reward system.

Homework Review. Review homework (assigned in Sessions 3, 5 and 7) for use of PARC, ignoring, and time-out procedures. Praise and performance feedback are provided to parents for their efforts and completion of homework assignments.

Introduction of the Reward System. "Today we would like to focus on how to develop a reward system for your child. We have emphasized in the past that it is important to provide your child with both social and nonsocial reinforcers or rewards. Social reinforcers are physical (e.g., smiles, hugs, pats, kisses, pleasant voice tone), verbal (e.g., praise), or activities (e.g., playing a game, reading your child a story). Nonsocial reinforcers consist of things such as money, toys, points, or stars.

During your interactions with your child, you have probably noticed that it can be difficult to reinforce him or her as often as you would like. With the reward system that we are going to develop, we want your child to experience positive consequences for reaching a desired goal. We mentioned previously that it is important for you to *immediately reinforce* your child whenever a desired behavior occurs. However, daily demands sometimes make this difficult for you to carry out. The reward system provides the child with reinforcement for appropriate behavior when you are unable to offer more immediate tangible positive consequences."

Definition of Reward System. "A reward system helps motivate your child to improve his or her behavior. It is designed to reinforce adaptive or prosocial desired behavior. The reward system provides a way for your child to earn tokens, points, check marks, happy faces, or stars. After a certain number of these are accumulated, they can be exchanged for a particular reward that your child likes (e.g., activities, privileges, toys). Your child learns that there are positive consequences and thus, has incentive to repeat the desired behavior that earned a chosen reward."

Steps in Developing a Reward System. "There are several steps that are important to follow when you are developing a reward system for your child. First, you need to focus on one or more positive behaviors whose frequency you would like to increase. Identify a target behavior that you can observe and count and describe it in a positive rather than a negative way (e.g., 'clean bedroom' instead of 'stop having a messy bedroom'). Avoid the use of vague labels such as lazy or unmotivated. Then using the Target Behavior Monitoring Form (see Table 8.10) choose four positive behaviors that you would like to increase."

If parents are unable to provide examples, prompt by saying: "Some behaviors that other parents would like to see their children engage in include: completing homework before playing, putting toys away when they finish playing, getting to bed on time, and getting up in the morning and being dressed after being called only once."

"The second step involves developing a point-reward calender on which you: write down the targeted behaviors from the monitoring chart that you have identified earlier (one per line), indicate the time when you will check to determine whether or not the behavior has occurred, and record the amount of points that your child might earn for that behavior." Cofacilitators provide a calender model for parents (see Table 8.12). "You may ask your child to help in designing the calender; this provides an opportunity to engage in a positive activity with your child. This is also an excellent time to praise your child for engaging in a desired behavior. Once you have developed the calender, display it in a place where it is easily seen by both you and your child. Most parents find that hanging the calender on the refrigerator door helps remind them to reward their children."

"Next, you need to generate a list of small nonsocial rewards, privileges, and other incentives for your child. We like to call this list a Reinforcer Menu." Cofacilitators show parents a sample Reinforcer Menu (see Table 8.13). "Ask your children what rewards they would like to receive after they have earned their points. After you and your children determine possible rewards, decide how many points each reward will 'cost.' Examples of possible rewards include: watching TV for 10 minutes (2 stars), new toy (10 stars), play time (5 stars), or having a special dessert (10 stars). Then, you and your child will monitor and record the points earned and spent. When your child earns a star, allow him/her to record it on the calender and provide

TABLE 8.12

Reward Calendar

Target Behavior	Points	Mon	Tue	Wed	Thur	Fri	Sat	Sun
1.								
2.								
3.								
4.								

TABLE 8.13

Reinforcer Menu

Menu Item	Amount of Points Needed to Earn Item
1.	
2.	
3.	
4.	

praise for his/her good behavior. Praising the specific behavior that your child performed to earn the star is very important (e.g., 'Here is a star for picking up your toys and putting them in the toybox'). After your child has earned the alotted number of points (stars, stickers, etc.) for a particular behavior, he or she can exchange the points for a reward on the Reinforcer Menu. Your child should be reinforced immediately with the reward because he/she will learn that engaging in the desired behavior will be followed by a (social or nonsocial) reward. This will increase the rate of the desired behavior. However, if the child does not perform the behavior he or she will not earn the social or nonsocial reinforcers listed on the Reinforcer Menu. Remember, your child has been performing these behaviors for a long time and we can't expect his or her behavior to change overnight."

Homework. "For homework this week you are to develop a reward system. Ask your child to participate in the activity with you. Be sure to include all of the points that we covered during this session and follow the example that we provided. Remember the following steps: *explain the identified target behaviors* that you would like your child to perform, use the target behavior monitoring chart and *design a calender* (see Table 8.12) that specifies the number of points your child will earn for performing each behavior, *develop a menu of reinforcers* (see Table 8.13), and *use the reward system* everytime the behavior occurs during the week. Please bring the Target Behavior Monitoring Form (see Table 8.10), Reward Calendar, and Reinforcer Menu with you to the next session.

Session 10: Anxiety Management Training

The stated goals of Session 10 are to review reinforcement and reward system, and introduce progressive muscle relaxation.

Homework Review. Cofacilitators present the following description and give each parent the opportunity to describe the Reward Calendar and Reinforcer Menu that they have developed. Parents are asked to provide one example in which the child earned points for emitting the desired behavior during the week. The following prompts are provided to help parents describe the desired behavior:

Prompt 1: "Let's see, Sammy took out the garabage on Monday, Wednesday, and Saturday without being told; and look here, he earned three points and was able to stay up and watch TV for 30 minutes."

Prompt 2: "Jackie picked up her toys after she finished playing with them and put them in the toy box; that earned her 5 stars toward an item on the Reinforcer Menu. You must be real proud of her. Have you told Jackie how proud you are of her for picking up the toys?"

Prompt 3: "Bobby cleaned his room this week and earned four checks on the calender. "Have you thought about what reward you'd like to get for him?"

Review at least one example of each of the Reward Calendars and provide verbal praise to parents for completing the homework assignment.

Rationale for Relaxation Training.   "There are several procedures that you can use to cope with stressful situations. For example, simply take a few slow deep breaths and hold your breath and then exhale. This helps you reduce tension and maintain a controlled response to stress-provoking situations. In addition, it will allow you to shift your attention from the stressful situation and provide a brief interruption before you begin to react to the event. How do you usually react to a situation when you are stressed or angry? Do you think clearly when you feel this way?" A progressive muscle relaxation procedure adapted from Bernstein and Carlson (1993) is introduced at this point: "There is another useful technique that is called progressive muscle relaxation. It has been shown to be effective for managing stress, and it is most useful when you detect the early signs of anger or tension. There are several physical signs of stress or anger (e.g., muscle tension, rigid posture, clenched fists)." The following prompts are provided to help parents identify stress and anger cues: "How do you know when you are getting angry?" "What happens to your body?" "How do you feel?" "How do you react?" "When you first notice these signs, you can use progressive muscle relaxation (PMR)."

"PMR consists of learning to tense and then relax various muscle groups throughout the body. At the same time, close and careful attention is directed to feelings associated with both tension and relaxation. You are also encouraged to recognize and pinpoint tension and relaxation as they appear in everyday situations. In PMR, we want you to eventually achieve rapid and significant tension reduction. The way to accomplish this is to tense each of the muscle groups that we will cover and then release that tension. In doing this, you will notice the difference between a state of tension and a state of relaxation." A cofacilitator then works with participants in a group format to carry out PMR. Each parent also is provided audiotaped intructions for the PMR procedure.

Homework.   Parents are asked to review and practice their personal safety plan, reinforcer system, PARC, and time-out procedures. In addition, they are intructed to practice PMR using the audiotape at least three times over the following week. Parents are also asked to continue monitoring and record their child's undesirable behavior using the Target Behavior Monitoring Form (see Table 8.10).

Session 11: Anger Management Training

The stated goals of Session 11 are to review personal safety plan, educate parents about effects of modeling aggressive behavior on children, introduce anger control strategies, and rehearse PMR.

Homework Review.   Parents are instructed to review the child management skills presented in prior sessions. Also a review of the parent's personal safety plan is conducted in this session.

"During this group, we want to review the child behavioral management skills that we have covered previously." Cofacilitators ask parents to divide into dyads and instruct one parent to engage in his/her child's favorite playtime activity while the other parent role plays "attending," "reinforcing positive activity," and "ignoring" the behavior, as well as implementing the time-out procedure.

Several points in the use of attending and reinforcing positive activity are pointed out to the parents: attend to children at their level (e.g., by sitting on the floor and look directly at the child), exhibit positive facial expressions, use a pleasant voice tone, employ physical contact (e.g., pat on back), and incidental learning. Several guidelines in the use of ignoring skills are emphasized to the parents: briefly remove all attention from your children; refuse to argue, scold, or talk; turn your head and avoid eye contact; do not show anger (or any other emotion) in your manner or gestures; be certain your child's behavior does not result in a material reward; and provide attention *when and only when* children's negative behavior ceases.

The following sequence of steps utilized during the time-out procedure are exemplified to parents: Provide a specific command to children for the behavior that you would like them to engage in. If children comply within 5 seconds after a command is given, attend and praise their compliant behavior. If children do not comply with your command within 5 seconds, provide a warning—wait another 5 seconds…. If children do not comply within this time, provide another command. At this time, take children's hand and manually guide them to the time-out area that you have preselected. And, when children have completed time-out, return them to the original situation that caused them to be in time-out and repeat the command with which you wish them to comply.

Cofacilitators observe, coach, and narrate appropriate use of attends, reinforcement, ignore, and time-out procedures; provide descriptive praise; and provide performance feedback throughout the interaction to facilitate learning. Any difficulties that parents have in implementing these procedures are discussed.

Parents are instructed to form dyads to rehearse the implementation of personal safety plans and social support building. Role playing, prompting, positive reinforcement, and performance feedback are employed to consolidate skill acquisition. If parents have implemented the safety plan at home, they are asked to describe the episode to the group, demonstrate how the situation was handled, and discuss the outcome (i.e., success or problems in implementation).

Introduction.   Each year, 13 million couples engage in physically assaultive behaviors (e.g., shoving, hitting, kicking, throwing objects). Further, over 2 million children display similar violent tendencies toward their siblings or peers (Straus et al., 1980). By now it is known that exposure to angry and aggressive models clearly increases the likelihood that children will also resolve conflicts in a similar manner (Patterson, 1986). Evidence also has been accumulated supporting the utility of stress management procedures for parents in families characterized by domestic violence (Egan, 1983; Golden & Consorte, 1982; Twentyman, Rohrbeck, & Amish, 1984). Specifically, anger management techniques appear to have value in training nonviolent alternatives to conflict resolution.

Rationale.   "Parents of young children are very vulnerable to stressful situations. For example, child behavior problems, employment, and financial concerns can be frustrating for parents. The factors that most often lead to punitive behavior toward children include: negative emotional states (e.g., anger, depression), hypersensitivity to a child's misbehavior, and limited resources for solving problems. Further, children who witness their parents using violent means of resolving conflict may model use of these methods to reduce their own stress. The goal of this session is to review techniques that will assist you in controlling your feelings of anger or frustration. We will focus on identifying anger cues, implementing anger control strategies, and maintaining control of impulses and anger in conflict and stressful situations."

Identification of Anger Cues.   "In learning to manage anger and stress, it is helpful to determine how you currently deal with conflicts. 'What are some specific examples of situations in which you have lost your temper? When did your child perform an undesirable behavior that upset you? What happened right before you became angry?'" If parents are unable to generate examples, the following examples are provided: "Situations that other parents have reported as evoking anger are: Johnny breaks your favorite vase when he was told not to play with it, Samantha does not get ready in the morning when you need to take her to school, or Brian frequently fights with other children and is sent home from school." Anger antecedents are further assessed by asking: "How do you know when you're angry? What was your reaction when your child performed an undesired behavior? What would your reactions be to the following situations: Johnny jumped in the pool when you told him not to, Samantha did not do her homework and you get a notice from school that she is failing in her classes; Brian arrives 2 hours late for dinner."

Consequences of anger are examined with the following questions: "What happens to you or to others around you when you lose your temper?" Using the examples provided, state the following consequences: "When Johnny jumped into the pool, I picked him up and shook him and told him never to do it again. When I found out that Samantha had not been keeping up with her homework and was failing her classes, I yelled at her. When Brian got home late, I spanked him."

Parents are asked to provide examples of anger-provoking situations and to role play the identification of antecedants, behaviors, and consequences. The following examples can be used: You arrive home and find out that your child has written on the wall with crayons, Johnny has broken your favorite vase, you arrive home and find both your children fighting over who is going to watch TV, and you observe your child hit another child over a toy.

Rehearsal of PMR.   At the end of this session, parents are asked to rehearse the PMR procedure. The following rationale is provided to the parents: "As noted in prior sessions, PMR consists of learning to tense and then relax various muscle groups throughout the body. In PMR, we want you to eventually achieve rapid and significant tension reduction. The way to accomplish this is to tense each of the muscle groups that we will cover and then release that tension. In doing this, you will notice the difference between a state of tension and a state of relaxtion." A cofacilitator then works with participants in a group format to carry out PMR.

Homework.   Parents are instructed to review their personal safety plan, practice PMR, and continue monitoring PARC, ignoring, time-out, and the reward system. In addition, parents are asked to record the antecedants, behaviors, and consequences of any anger-provoking episodes using the Anger Monitoring Form (see Table 8.14). Parents are also asked to continue monitoring and record their child's undesirable behavior using the Target Behavior Monitoring Form (see Table 8.10).

Session 12: Application of Child Behavior Management Skills

As noted earlier, Session 12 is an integrated session that includes both children and parents. This session provides an opportunity for implementation and practice of child management strategies trained in previous sessions. The stated goals of Session 12 are to review children's group rules, practice the parent's personal safety, and review and rehearse child management procedures (i.e., attends, rewards, ignoring, and time-out; refer to Integrated Session 12 in CTP).

Session 13: Anger Management Training

The stated goals of Session 13 are to review homework, identify anger triggers, introduce anger control strategies, and rehearse PMR.

Review homework.   Homework on anger antecedants, behaviors, and consequences is reviewed.

"During the last session we identified antecedants, behaviors, and consequences of anger-provoking situations. We are going to be reviewing your responses to the Anger-Monitoring Form" (see Table 8.14). Parents are provided the following prompts to assess for anger antecedants, behaviors, and consequences: "What are some specific examples of situations in which you have lost your temper? When did your child perform an undesirable behavior that upset you? What happened right before you became angry?" Anger antecedants are further assessed by asking: "How do you know when you're angry? What was your reaction when your child performed an undesired behavior?" Consequences of anger are examined with the following questions: "What happens to you or to others around you when you lose your temper?" Performance feedback and positive reinforcement are provided for their efforts.

Identification of Anger Triggers.   "Anger may be triggered by a variety of situations or events. However, the earlier you can identify anger-provoking triggers, the easier it will be to control your anger. Triggers to anger can be verbal (e.g., someone is unpleasant or threatening

TABLE 8.14

Anger Monitoring Form

Anger Provoking Situation	What Happened Before You Noticed You Were Getting Angry?	What Did You Do About the Situation?	What Happened Afterward?
1.			
2.			
3.			

toward you) or nonverbal (e.g., when someone is hitting or striking at you)." Parents are asked to provide examples of verbal and nonverbal anger triggers that they have experienced.

"Anger also may be triggered when a person makes incorrect judgments about situational events (e.g., 'Sally never seems to do what she is told; however, she often may not remember what it was that she was supposed to do, or she may not yet have learned what to do in a particular situation'). In addition, negative thoughts or self-statements can lead to feelings of anger (e.g., 'that kid never listens to me')." Parents are asked to provide examples of incorrect appraisals and negative self-statements that have made them feel angry.

Introduction of Self-Instruction.
"You have just identified several anger triggers and anger-related self-statements that can produce angry feelings. You have learned that it is not only the event itself that can provoke angry feelings, but how you think about and interpret these events. Today, we will discuss alternative self-statements that will help you manage your thoughts so that you can bring your anger under control. Self-statements are things that you say to yourself that guide your behavior or can remind you to do certain things. There are several reminders that you can use in anger-provoking situations that can help you remain calm. Examples of alternative self-statements that you can use when you first begin to recognize that you are angry are the following:

"I can manage this situation."
"I know how to regulate my anger."
"Stay calm and continue to relax."
"Don't assume or jump to conclusions."
"My muscles are starting to feel tight, it's time to relax and slow things down."

Cofacilitators role play an anger-provoking situation and model appropriate use of self-statements to remain calm. The following example can be used: "You arrive home and notice that your child has broken your favorite vase despite the fact that he has been told not to touch the vase or play with his ball in the living room. You begin having negative thoughts (e.g., he's such a bad kid; he's going to get the worst beating he's ever had) and you find yourself getting angrier. At this time you start by saying to yourself, "I can handle this situation without blowing my cool; calm down and take a few deep breaths."

Parents are asked to provide examples of anger-provoking situations. Then, they are instructed to role play these situations using alternative self-statements. Cofacilitators provide praise and performance feedback to parents for their efforts.

Introduction of Thinking Ahead.
"Thinking ahead is another anger-control strategy that you can use when you're feeling angry as a result of a conflict. Thinking ahead involves use of self-instructions or reminders before engaging in a behavior that is likely to produce negative consequences (e.g., 'If I scream at my child, then he will learn aggressive ways of handling conflict')." Parents are asked to identify anger-provoking examples and to role play these situations using thinking ahead strategies.

Homework.
Parents are instructed to continue monitoring PARC, ignoring, time-out, and the reward system, and to practice PMR at home as needed. In addition, they are asked to

identify anger triggers, responses, and consequences that occur throughout the week. Further, they are instructed to implement anger-control strategies (e.g., self-instruction, identification of negative consequences, thinking ahead procedures) whenever possible, and to record results using the Anger-Control Monitoring Form (see Table 8.15). Parents are also asked to continue monitoring and record their child's undesirable behavior using the Target Behavior Monitoring Form (see Table 8.10).

Session 14: Anger Management Review

The stated goals of Session 14 are to review homework on responses and consequences to anger triggers, and implementation of anger-control strategies.

Homework Review. Homework is reviewed and anger triggers, responses, and consequences to anger-provoking situations are discussed. In addition, anger control strategies (self-instruction, identification of negative consequences, and thinking ahead) are reviewed.

Homework. Parents are also asked to monitor use of child management procedures (PARC, ignoring, time-out, and reward system), and identify anger triggers and the utilization of anger control strategies. They are asked to record when and how skills were implemented in the Anger-Control Monitoring Form (see Table 8.15). Parents are also asked to continue monitoring and record their child's undesirable behavior using the Target Behavior Monitoring Form (see Table 8.10).

Session 15: Problem-Solving Strategies

The stated goals of Session 15 are to review homework, and introduce problem-solving strategies.

Homework Review. Homework is reviewed and identification of anger triggers, responses, and consequences to anger-provoking situations, as well as use of anger control strategies are discussed.

Introduction. Problem-solving skills are important to help people solve interpersonal difficulties in a rational nonviolent manner. These skills consist of five steps designed to establish effective conflict resolution. The five steps are: Clearly and specifically define a problem, generate as many solutions to the problem as possible, identify the pros and cons for each of the solutions, rank order the solutions from worst to least effective, evaluate the

TABLE 8.15

Anger-Control Monitoring Form

Anger-Trigger	Response	Consequence	Anger-Control Strategy Utilized (Self-Instruction, Identification of Negative Consequences, Thinking Ahead, PMR)
1.			
2.			
3.			

effectiveness of the solution in solving the problem, and use self-reinforcement for solving the problem, or selecting another alternative solution if the first one was ineffective. The aim of problem-solving training is to provide parents with alternative methods of resolving conflicts. Problem-solving approaches have proven effective in remediating problem-solving deficits in punitive parents (Jacobson, 1977; D. A. Wolfe, Sandler, & Kaufman, 1981).

Rationale. "Anger interferes with our ability to effectivly solve conflictual situations. In this session, we will cover problem-solving strategies that will help you to cope with frustrating or anger-provoking sevents. However, in order to implement the approach you must first be able to recognize when you are angry. Begin by noticing the physical cues of anger (e.g., getting a warm feeling in your body, clenching your fists or teeth). Stop, and take a few deep breaths and then exhale. This helps to reduce tension and maintain a controlled response to stress-provoking situations. Problem solving involves several steps. First, you need to clearly and specifically define a problem. A adequate definition of the problem includes antecedents and cues. The second step is to generate as many solutions to the problem as possible. The third step involves identifying the pros and cons for each of the solutions. In the fourth step, solutions are rank ordered. The fifth step is to evaluate the effectiveness of the solution in solving the problem. And the final step consists of self-reinforcement for solving the problem, or selecting another alternative solution if the first one was ineffective." Parents are asked to role play problem-solving strategies:

Cofacilitator:	"What is the problem?"
Parent:	"Mark continually stays up late at night and does not get up in the morning on time and misses the school bus."
Cofacilitator:	"What can you do about the problem? Generate as many solutions to the problem as you possibly can."
Parent:	"Get Mark to sleep on time; set up an alarm clock by his bed; not take him to school if he misses the bus; or not allow him to watch TV late at night."
Cofacilitator:	"Rank order the solutions to the problem from what you consider to be the most to the least effective solution. Then begin with what you have selected as the best solution and use the others if necessary, until the problem is solved."
Parent:	"First, I would not allow Mark to watch TV late at night and he would get to go to bed on time; then I would set up an alarm by his bed."
Cofacilitator:	"That was great; you came up with all of those solutions and ranked ordered them. Remember to give yourself credit for coming up with the best solution to the problem."

Ask parents to think of additional examples in which they can use problem-solving strategies.

Homework. Parents are instructed to continue to employ and monitor the use of child management and anger-control strategies at home. In addition, they are asked to record the use of problem solving over the past week and to record results on the Problem-Solving Monitoring Form (see Table 8.16). Parents are also asked to continue monitoring and record their child's undesirable behavior using the Target Behavior Monitoring Form (see Table 8.10).

TABLE 8.16

Problem-Solving Monitoring Form

Define Problem	Generate 3 Solutions	Pros & Cons of Each Solution	Rank Order Solutions	Effectiveness of Each Solution	Self-Reinforce or Select Another Alternative
1.					
2.					
3.					

Sessions 16: Integration of Skills

The stated goals of Sessions 16 are to review child management procedures, anger-control skills, and problem-solving strategies.

Rationale.   "In this session we will review child management, anger-control procedures, and problem-solving strategies that we have covered in previous sessions."

Behavioral Rehearsal.   The following example is provided to parents practice previously trained skills:

Cofacilitator: "We are going to begin by providing an example and go through a step-by-step analysis of how to approach this problem situation. Imagine that you find that your child has hit a peer with a toy truck. What would be the first step in dealing with this scenerio?"

Parent: "I would probably find myself getting angry with my child for hitting the other one."

Cofacilitator: "Good, so you're beginning to identify early anger cues. What would you do?"

Parent: "Remove myself from the situation, practice deep breathing exercises, and tell myself to keep my cool."

Cofacilitator: "That's great! You are implementing anger-control strategies. What would you do next?"

Parent: "I would ask myself what is the problem in this situation? The problem is that my child is hitting another child."

Cofacilitator: "So you're generating a definition of the problem; what steps do you need to implement to generate a solution?"

Parent: "I would generate as many possible solutions to this problem, pick the pros and cons, rank order the solutions, and select the one that I think is best."

Cofacilitator: "That's right; so in this example, what would you do?"

Parent: "I would remove the child from the situation and probably have him or her take a time-out."

Cofacilitator: "Excellent! You remembered the situations that we stated would result in a child being sent to time-out. In this example the child's behavior of hitting the other child is a danger to others. You did a wonderful job."

Cofacilitators ask parents to generate other examples; cofacilitators provide positive reinforcement, coaching, and performance feedback for appropriate implementation of procedures.

Homework.   Parents are instructed to continue to implement and monitor the use of child management, anger-control, and problem-solving skills at home. Parents are also asked to continue monitoring and record their child's undesirable behavior using the Target Behavior Monitoring Form (see Table 8.10).

Session 17: Termination

The stated goals of Session 17 are to review homework, evaluate changes that parents have made in the management of their children, discuss termination, and encourage parents to establish a social support network.

Homework Review.   A final review is provided on monitoring and identifying anger triggers and use of anger control techniques, use of child management strategies, and application of problem-solving approaches. In addition, parents are reminded that the next session is an integrated session with their child. The child management skills of attending, rewarding, ignoring, and time-out are rehearsed.

Rationale.   "This is going to be our final parent group meeting. Next week we will meet with both you and your child for our final PACT session together." Cofacilitators provide parents with positive feedback regarding their cooperation with the program, performance during exercises and role plays, completion of homework assignments, and observable changes in behavior. Positive reinforcement is provided for their efforts in implementing newly acquired skills over the course of the group and to encourage them to continue these efforts in the future. Parents are encouraged to further establish social support with other group members by having them exchange phone numbers and write them on their personal safety cards. Group members are asked to give their own personal farewells to each other and to staff.

Homework.   Parents are asked to continue monitoring and record their child's undesirable behavior using the Target Behavior Monitoring Form (see Table 8.10).

Session 18: Child Management Skills Review and Termination

As noted earlier, Session 18 is an integrated session that includes both children and parents. This session provides an opportunity for implementation and practice of child management strategies trained in previous sessions. The stated goals of Session 18 are to review group rules, rehearse child management procedures, answer questions and address problems that arise, and have parents reward child for program completion (refer to Integrated Session 18 in CTP).

PROBLEMS IN IMPLEMENTATION AND LIMITATIONS

Various difficulties may arise when implementing the treatment approach with parents and their children. For example, if a child's participation in a group topic increases the risk of further violence, that specific topic is not addressed. Specifically, if developing and practicing a personal safety plan places the child at risk for harm, because the parent disapproves of the child's participation in that particular exercise the child would not be asked to rehearse that safety plan at home. Additionally, crisis situations are addressed immediately and structured procedures are suspended. Depending on the type of crisis, resolution may occur within the group process. However, knowledge of physical and sexual abuse directed to the child or mother is dealt with on an individual basis. For example, the parent and child meet with the therapist and an appropriate report to a state agency is conducted, and/or a referral to a shelter is made to assure the safety of all family members. In such cases, once the initial crisis has been resolved and the child or mother are no longer at risk for physical harm, treatment recommendations are reconsidered and consultation and/or appropriate referrals to another Interpersonal Violence specialty program are made to ensure that the specific issue is properly addressed.

The delay of structured procedures may interfere with execution of the treatment program. Delay of structured procedures may occur because children and parents learn at different rates. Therefore, presentation of a particular topic may be more time consuming than estimated. For example, children who have been exposed to physical and sexual abuse prevention programs at school are likely to learn abuse prevention strategies more quickly than children who have not been exposed to such information. In addition, in cases where child management procedures are inadequately implemented, further explanation and instruction are warranted to ensure skill acquisition (i.e., parents often implement the time-out procedure incorrectly). Acquisition of parenting skills is imperative to produce behavioral change that increase the client's motivation to comply with the treatment protocol. For example, parents who actively apply behavioral management strategies that result in a decrease in children's undesired behavior are likely to comply with future assignments. Further, clients who become relaxed while practicing relaxation exercises are likely to continue using this anxiety-reducing techniques and to comply with techniques presented on subsequent sessions. Noncompliance with homework assignments and inactive implementation of procedures taught during group may further interfere with the efficacy of treatment. Additional delays in treatment may arise depending on the child's attentiveness. For example, young children may become restless, resulting in periodic breaks during the session.

Furthermore, the varying developmental levels of children limit the number of clients who can be served in the group format. Subsequently, the age range of children in a group is restricted (i.e., 5–8, 9–11, 12–14, 15–17).

The stressful nature of the family environment for this particular population may also interfere with treatment progress. For example, a parent and child involved in legal proceedings (i.e., custody hearings, obtaining a restraining order) and other stressful situations may result in interference with their ability to follow through with homework assignments and to attend group sessions. Inconsistent group attendance results in obtaining insufficient knowledge of the skills (i.e., behavior management techniques, anger management strategies, relaxation training) covered during that session and the subsequent sessions, in light of the cumulative nature of treatment program.

In addition to problems in implementation, there are various limitations to the group treatment approach. The treatment program may not be effective for clients functioning at lower intellectual levels. For example, a parent or child, whose level of intellectual functioning is in the mentally retarded range would have difficulty processing information presented and implementing targeted skills (i.e., behavior management techniques, anger management strategies, relaxation training, problem-solving skills).

As noted earlier, the group treatment would not be advantageous for children presenting with severe behavior difficulties. Specifically, children who evince extreme aggression may disrupt group and place other members at risk; therefore, requiring more intensive individual treatment at the Interpersonal Violence Program (IVP) focusing on reducing aggressive behavior.

Another constraining factor is that the group approach is time limited. Depending on the severity of the targeted problem areas, clients may require continued treatment following the 18 group sessions. Treatment addresses numerous issues, personal safety skills, esteem, aggressive behavior, and poor problem-solving abilities that can be identified in children who witness interparental violence. However, given the time-limited focus of this treatment, the child may require long-term intervention to ameliorate the psychological and behavioral sequelae of witnessing violence.

REFERENCES

Abidin, R. R. (1986). *Parenting stress manual* (2nd ed.). Charlottesville, VA: Pediatric Psychology Press.

Alessi, J. J., & Hearn, K. (1984). Group treatment of children in shelters for battered women. In A. R. Roberts (Ed.), *Battered women and their families* (pp. 49–61). New York: Springer.

Apter, A., Orvaschel, H., Laseg, M., Moses, T., & Tyano, S. (1989). Psychometric properties of the K–SADS–P in an Israeli adolescent inpatient unit. *Journal of the American Academy of Child and Adolescent Psychiatry, 28*, 61–65.

Beck, A. T., & Steer, R. A. (1990). *The Beck Anxiety Inventory manual.* New York: The Psychological Corporation.

Beck, A. T., Ward, C. H., Mendelsohn, M., Mock, J., & Erbaugh, J. (1961). An inventory for measuring depression. *Archives of General Psychiatry, 4*, 561–571.

Beck, A. T., Weissman, A., Lester, D., & Trexler, L. (1974). The measurement of pessimism:The hopelessness scale. *Journal of Consulting and Clinical Psychology, 42*, 861–865.

Bernstein, D. A., & Carlson, C. R. (1993). Progressive relaxation: Abbreviated methods. In P. M. Lehrer & R. L. Woolfolk (Eds.), *Principles and practice of stress management* (2nd ed., pp. 53–88). New York: Guilford.

Bornstein, M. R., Bellack, A. S., & Hersen, M. (1977). Social-skills training for assertive children: A multiple-baseline analysis. *Journal of Applied Behavior Analysis, 10*, 183–195.

Burns, G. L., & Patterson, D. R. (1991). Factor structure of the Eyberg Child Behavior Inventory. *Journal of Clinical Child Psychology, 20*, 439–444.

Carlson, B. E. (1984). Children's observations of interpersonal violence. In A. R. Roberts (Ed.), *Battered women and their families* (pp. 147–166). New York: Springer.

Carlson, B. E. (1987). Observation of spouse abuse: What happens to the children. *Journal of Interpersonal Violence, 2*, 278–291.

Cassady, L. B., Allen, E. L., Lyon, E. & McGeehan, D. (1987, July). *The child-focused intervention program: Treatment and program evaluation for children in a battered women's shelter.* Paper presented at the Third National Family Violence Researcher Conference, Durham, NH.

Christopoulos, C., Cohn, D. A., Shaw, D. S., Joyce, S., Sullivan-Hanson, J., Kraft, S. P., & Emery, R. E. (1987). Children of abused women: Adjustment at time of shelter residence. *Journal of Marriage and the Family, 49*, 611–619.

Clark, L. (1985). *SOS help for parents: A practical guide for handling common everyday behavior problems.* Bowling Green, KY: Parent's Press.

Cohn, A.H., & Daro, D. (1987). Is treatment too late: What ten years or evaluative research tells us. *Child Abuse and Neglect, 11*, 433–442.

Davis, L. V., & Carlson, B. E. (1987). Observation of spouse abuse: What happens to the children. *Journal of Interpersonal Violence, 2*, 278–291.

Deaton, W., & Johnson, K. (1991). *Living with my family: A Hunter House trauma workbook.* Claremont, CA: Hunter House.

Egan, K. (1983). Stress management and child management with abusive parents. *Journal of Clinical Child Psychology*, *12*, 292–299.

Emery, R. E., & O'Leary, K. D. (1982). Children's perceptions of marital discord and behavior problems of boys and girls. *Journal of Abnormal Psychology*, *10*, 11–24.

Eyberg, S., & Ross, A. W. (1978). Assessment of child behavior problems: The validation of a new inventory. *Journal of Clinical Child Psychology*, *7*, 113–116.

Fantuzzo, J. W., DePaola, L. M., Lambert, L., Martino, T., Anderson, G., & Sutton, S. (1991). Effects of interparental violence on the psychological adjustment and competencies of young children. *Journal of Consulting and Clinical Psychology*, *59*, 258–265.

Finch, A. J., Saylor, C. F., & Edwards, G. I. (1985). Children's depression inventory: Sex and grade norms for normal children. *Journal of Consulting and Clinical Psychology*, *13*, 424–425.

Finch, A. J., Saylor, C. F., & Nelson, W. M. (1983, August). *The children's inventory of anger: A self-report measure.* Paper presented at the convention of The American Psychological Association, Anaheim, CA.

Finch, A. J., Saylor, C. F., & Nelson, W. M. (1987). Assessment of anger in children. In R. J. Prinz (Ed.), *Advances in behavioral assessment of children and families*, (Vol.3). Greenwich, CT: JAI Press.

Forehand, R.L., & McMahon, R.J. (1981). *Helping the noncompliant child: A clinician's guide to parent training.* New York: Guilford.

Forsstrom-Cohen, B., & Rosenbaum, A. (1985). The effects of parental marital violence on young adults: An exploratory investigation. *Journal of Marriage and Family*, *47*, 467–471.

Friedrich, W. N. (1990). *Psychotherapy of sexually aroused children and their families.* New York: Norton.

Friedrich, W, N., Grambsch, P., Damon, L., & Green, A. (1983). Dimension of psychological trauma in abused children. *Journal of the American Academy of Child Psychiatry*, *22*, 231–237.

Friedrich, W. N., Grambsch, P., Daomon, L., Hewitt, S. K., Koveroia, C., Lang, R. A., Wolfe, V., & Broughton, D. (1992). Child sexual behavior inventory: Normative and clinical comparisons. *Psychological Assessment, 4*, 303–311.

Galante, R., & Foa, D. (1986). An epidemiological study of psychic trauma and treatment effectiveness for children after a natural disaster. *Journal of the American Academy of Child Psychiatry*, *25*, 357–363.

Golden, W.L., & Consorte, J. (1982). Training mildly retarded individuals to control their anger through the use of cognitive behavior therapy techniques. *Journal of Contemporary Psychotherapy*, *13*, 182–187.

Green, A. H. (1983). The abused child and adolescent. In C. J. Kesterbaum & D. T. Williams (Eds.), *Handbook of clinical assessment of children and adolescents* (Vol. II, pp. 843–863). New York: New York University Press.

Grimm, C., & Montgomery, B. (1985). *T is for Touching: A sexual abuse prevention program for children ages 3–6.* Fargo, ND: Red Flag Green Flag Resources, Rape and Abuse Crisis Center.

Grusznski, R. J., Brink, J. C., & Edelson, J. L. (1988). Support and education groups for children of battered women. *Child Welfare*, *142*, 431–444.

Harter, S. (1985). *Manual for the self-perception profile for children-revised.* Unpublished manuscript, University of Denver.

Hendricks, G., & Willis, R. (1975). *The centering book: Awareness activities for children and adults to relax the body and mind.* Englewood Cliffs, NJ: Prentice Hall.

Hershorn, M., & Rosenbaum, A. (1985). Children of marital violence: A closer look at the unintended victims. *American Journal of Orthopsychiatry*, *55*, 260–266.

Hinchey, F. S., & Gavelek, J. R. (1982). Empathic responding in children of battered women. *Child Abuse and Neglect*, *6*, 395–401.

Hughes, H. M. (1982). Brief interventions with children in a battered women's shelter: A model preventive program. *Family Relations*, *31*, 495–502.

Hughes, H. M. (1988). Psychological and behavioral correlates of family violence in child witnesses and victims. *American Journal of Orthopsychiatry*, *58*, 77–89.

Hughes, H. M., & Barad, S. J. (1983). Psychological functioning of children in a battered women's shelter: A preliminary investigation. *American Journal of Orthopsychiatry*, *53*, 525–531.

Huey, W. C., & Rank, R. C. (1984). Effects of counselor and peer-led groups' assertive training on Black adolescent aggression. *Journal of Counseling Psychology*, *31*, 95–98.

Jacobson, N.S. (1977). Problem solving and contingency contracting in the treatment of marital discord. *Journal of Consulting and Clinical Psychology*, *45*, 92–100.

Jaffe, P., Wilson, S., & Wolfe, D. A. (1986a, August). *Impact of group counseling for child witnesses to wife battering*. Paper presented as part of the Symposium on Children in Shelters for Battered Women, at the annual meeting of the American Psychological Association, Washington, DC.

Jaffe, P., Wilson, S., & Wolfe, D.A. (1986b). Promoting changes in attitudes and understanding of conflict resolution among child witnesses of family violence. *Canadian Journal of Behavioral Science, 18*, 356–366.

Jaffe, P., Wolfe, D. A., & Wilson, S. (1990). *Children of battered women*. Newbury Park, CA: Sage.

Jaffe, P., Wolfe, D., Wilson, S. K., & Zak, L. (1986a). Family violence and child adjustment: A comparative analysis of girls' and boys' behavioral symptoms. *American Journal of Psychiatry, 143*, 74–77.

Jaffe, P., Wolfe, D. A., Wilson, M. A., & Zak, L. (1986b). Similarities in behavioral and social maladjustment among child victims and witnesses to family violence. *American Journal of Orthopsychiatry, 56*, 142–146.

Jouriles, E.N., Murphy, C. M., & O'Leary, K. D. (1989). Interspousal aggression, marital discord, and child problems. *Journal of Consulting and Clinical Psychology, 57*, 453–455.

Jouriles, E. N., Pfiffner, L. J., & O'Leary, S. G. (1988). Marital conflict, parenting, and toddler conduct problems. *Journal of Abnormal Child Psychology, 16*, 197–206.

Kelly, J.A. (1983). *Treating child-abusive families: Interventions based on skills training principles*. New York: Plenum.

Koeppen, A. S. (1974). Relaxation training for children. *Journals of Elementary School Guidance and Counseling, 9*, 14–21.

Kovacs, M., & Beck, A. (1983). *The Children's Depression Inventory: A self-rating depression scale for school-aged youngsters*. Unpublished manuscript, Western Psychiatric Institute and Clinic, Pittsburgh.

Laxer, R. M., Quarter, J., Kooman, A., & Walker, K. (1969). Systematic desensitization and relaxation of high test anxious secondary school students. *Journal of Counseling Psychology, 16*, 446–451.

Laxer, R. M., & Walker, K. (1970). Counterconditioning vs. relaxation in the desensitization of test anxiety. *Journal of Counseling Anxiety, 17*, 431–436.

Lipovsky, J. A. (1992). Assessment and treatment of post-traumatic stress disorder in child survivors of sexual assault. In D. W. Foy (Ed.), *Treating PTSD: Cognitive-behavioral strategies*. New York: Guilford.

Locke, H. J., & Wallace K. M. (1959). Short marital-adjustment and prediction tests: Their reliability and validity. *Marriage and Family Living, 21*, 251–255.

Lystad, M. (1985). Innovative mental health services for child disaster victims. *Children Today, 12*, 13–17.

Mayhall, C. A., Nelson, W. M., Politano, P. M., & Wendall, N. H. (1986, March). *Psychiatric investigations of the children's inventory of anger with emotionally disturbed children*. Paper presented at the 32nd annual meeting of the Southeastern Psychological Association, Orlando, FL.

Michelson, L., Sugai, D. P., Wood, R. P., & Kazdin, A. E. (1983). *Social skills training and assessment with children*. New York: Plenum.

Milner, J. S. (1986). *The child abuse potential inventory: Manual* (2nd ed.). Webster, NC: PSYTEC.

Montgomery, L. E., Nelson, W. M., & Finch, A. J. (1979, March). *Anger in children: Preliminary investigations of anger-evoking stimuli in children*. Paper presented at the annual meeting of the Southeastern Psychological Association, New Orleans.

Moos, R. H., & Moos, B. S. (1986). *Family environment scale manual* (2nd ed.). Palo Alto, CA: Consulting Psychologists Press.

Morris, R. J., & Kratochwill, T. R. (1983). *Treating children's fears and phobias: A behavioral approach*. Elmsford, NY: Pergamon.

Moser, A. (1988). *Don't pop your cork on Mondays: The children's anti-stress book*. Kansas City, MO: Landmark Editions.

Moser, A. (1991). *Don't feed the monster on Tuesday: The children's self-esteem book*. Kansas City, MO: Landmark Editions.

Nelson, W. M., Hart, K. J., & Finch, A. J. (1993). Anger in children: A cognitive-behavioral view of the assessment-therapy connection. *Journal of Rational-Emotive & Cognitive-Behavior Therapy, 11*, 135–150.

O'Dell, S. L., Tarler-Benlolo, L., & Flynn, J. M. (1979). An instrument to measure knowledge of behavioral principles as applied to children. *Journal of Behavior Therapy and Experimental Psychiatry, 10*, 29–34.

Ollendick, T. H. (1982). *The social competence project*. Unpublished manuscript, Virginia Polytechnic Institute and State University, Blacksburg.

Palmer, P. (1977). *The mouse, the monster and me*. San Luis Obispo, CA: Impact Publishers.

Patterson, G. (1986). Performance models for antisocial boys. *American Psychologist, 41*, 432–444.

Patterson, S. (1993). *I wish the hitting would stop: A workbook for children living in violent homes.* Fargo, ND: Red Flag Green Flag Resources.

Peled, E., & Davis, D. (1992). *Groupwork with child witnesses of domestic violence: A practitioner's manual.* Minneapolis, MN: Domestic Abuse Project.

Pino, C. J., Simmons, N., & Slawinoski, M. J. (1984). *The children's version of the family environment scale manual.* New York: Slosson Educational Publications, Inc.

Porter, B., & O'Leary, K. (1980). Marital discord and childhood behavior problems. *Journal of Abnormal Child Psychology, 8,* 287–295.

Puig-Antich, J., & Chambers, W. J. (1986). *Kiddie-Schedule for affective disorders and schizophrenia–Present episode.* Pittsburgh: Western Psychiatric Institute and Clinic.

Pynoos, R. S., & Eth, S. (1986). Witness to violence: The child interview. *Journal of the American Academy of Child & Adolescent Psychiatry, 25,* 306–319.

Quay, H. (1983). A dimensional approach to behavior disorder: The revised behavior problem checklist. *School Psychology Review, 12,* 244–249.

Quay, H. C., & Peterson, D. R. (1983). *Interim manual for the revised behavior problem checklist.* Unpublished manuscript, University of Miami.

Ragg, D. M., & Webb, C. (1992). Group treatment for the preschool child witness of spouse abuse. *Journal of Child and Youth Care, 7,* 1–19.

Reynolds, C. R., & Richmond, B. O. (1978). What I think and feel: A revised measure of children's manifest anxiety. *Journal of Abnormal Child Psychology, 6,* 271–280.

Reynolds, C. R., & Richmond, B. O. (1985). *Revised–Children's Manifest Anxiety Scale manual.* Los Angeles: Western Psychological Services.

Robinson, E. A., Eyberg, S. M., & Ross, A. W. (1980). The standardization of an inventory of child conduct problem behaviors. *Journal of Clinical Child Psychology,9,* 22–29.

Rosenbaum, A., & O'Leary, K. D. (1981). Children: The unintended victims of marital violence. *American Journal of Orthopsychiatry, 51,* 692–699.

Rosenberg, M. S. (1987). Children of battered women: The effects of witnessing violence on their social problem-solving abilities. *The Behavior Therapist, 10,* 85–89.

Rosenberg, M. S., & Rossman, B. B. (1990). The child witness to marital violence. In R. T. Ammerman & M. Hersen (Eds.), *Treatment of family violence: A sourcebook* (pp. 183–207). New York: Wiley.

Roy, M. (1988). *Children in the crossfire: Violence in the home-How does it affect our children.* Deerfield Beach, FL: Health Communications.

Sarason, I. G., Johnson, J. H., & Siegal, J. M. (1978). Assessing the impact of life changes: Development of the life experiences survey. *Journal of Consulting and Clinical Psychology, 46,* 932–946.

Silvern, L., & Kaersvang, L. (1989). The traumatized children of violent marriages. *Child Welfare, 143,* 421–436.

Smucker, M. R., Craighead, W. E., Craighead, L. W., & Green, B. J. (1986). Normative and reliability data for the Children's Depression Inventory. *Journal of Abnormal Child Psychology, 14,* 25–39.

Straus, M. A. (1977). Wife-beating: How common and why? *Victimology, 2,* 443–458.

Straus, M. A., & Gelles, R. J. (1986). Societal change and change in family violence from 1975 to 1985 as revealed by two national surveys. *Journal of Marriage and the Family, 48,* 465– 479.

Straus, M. A., Gelles, R. J., & Steinmetz, S. K. (1980). *Behind closed doors: Violence in the American family.* Garden City, NY: Doubleday.

Tanner, V. L., & Holliman, W. B. (1988). Effectiveness of assertiveness in modifying aggressive behaviors of young children. *Psychological Reports, 62,* 39–46.

Terr, L. (1989). Treating psychic trauma in children: A preliminary discussion. *Journal of Traumatic Stress, 2,* 2–20.

Trickett, P.K., & Kuczynski, L. (1986). Children's misbehaviors and parental discipline strategies in abusive and nonabusive families. *Developmental Psychology, 22,* 115–123.

Twentyman, C., Rohrbeck, C., & Amish, P. (1984). A cognitive-behavioral model of child abuse. In S. Saunders (Ed.), *Violent individuals and families: A practitioner's handbook.* Springfield, IL: Thomas.

Van Hasselt, V. B., & Christ, M. A. (1994). *Social-problem solving skills training for adolescents.* Unpublished manuscript, Nova Southeastern University, Fort Lauderdale, FL.

Van Hasselt, V. B., Hersen, M. Bellack, A. S., Rosenblum, N., & Lamparski, D. (1979). Tripartite assessment of the effects of systematic desensitization in a multiphosic child: An experimental analysis. *Journal of Behavioral Therapy and Experimental Psychiatry, 10,* 51–56.

Van Hasselt, V. B, Hersen, M., Whitehill, M. B., & Bellack, A. S. (1979). Social skill assessment and training for children: An evaluative review. *Behaviour Research and Therapy, 17*, 413–437.

Wallerstein, J. S., & Kelly, J.B. (1980). *Surviving the breakup: How children cope with divorce*. New York: Basic Books.

Waters, V. (1980). *Rational stories for children*. New York: Institute for Rational Emotive Therapy.

Webster-Stratton, C. (1985). Mother perceptions and mother–child interactions: Comparison of a clinic referred and a non-clinic group. *Journal of Clinical Child Psychology, 14*, 334–339.

Weinberg, R. B. (1990). Serving large numbers of adolescent victim-survivors: Group interventions following trauma at school. *Professional Psychology: Research and Practice, 21*, 271–278.

Wolfe, D. A., Edwards, B., Manion, I., & Kaverola, C. (1988). Early intervention for parents at risk of child abuse and neglect: A preliminary investigation. *Journal of Consulting and Clinical Psychology, 56*, 40–47.

Wolfe, D.A., Kaufman, K., Aragona, J., & Sandler, J. (1981). *The child management program for abusive parents*. Winter Park, FL: Anna.

Wolfe, D.A., Sandler, J., & Kaufman, K. (1981). A competency-based parent training program for child abusers. *Journal of Consulting and Clinical Psychology, 49*, 633–640.

Wolfe, D. A., Zak, L., Wilson, S., & Jaffe, P. (1986). Child witnesses to violence between parents: Critical issues in behavioral and social adjustment. *Journal of Abnormal Child Psychology, 14*, 95–104.

Wolfe, V. V., & Gentile, C., Michienski, T., Sas, T., Wolfe, D. A. (1991). The children's impact of traumatic events scale: A measure of post-sexual-abuse PTSD symptoms. *Behavioral Assessment, 13*, 359–383.

Yule, W., & Williams, R. M. (1990). Post-traumatic stress reactions in children. *Journal of Traumatic Stress, 3*, 279–295.

Chapter 9

An Ecobehavioral Approach to Child Maltreatment

Brad Donohue
Nova Southeastern University

Elissa R. Miller
Nova Southeastern University

Vincent B. Van Hasselt
Nova Southeastern University

Michel Hersen
Pacific University

DESCRIPTION OF THE PROBLEM

Child neglect and abuse is a complex multifactorial problem with many contributing and interdependent variables (see Briere, Berliner, Bulkley, Jenny, & Reid, 1996). The number of reported cases of child maltreatment has increased markedly over the past decade. Indeed, approximately 3 million children were reportedly maltreated in the United States in 1993 (Curtis, Boyd, Liepold, & Petit, 1995), and child maltreatment is often associated with significant psychopathology. For instance, parents of maltreated children are often immature, easily annoyed, demonstrate inadequate knowledge of child development, have poor child management skills (Wolfe, 1985), are at risk to abuse illicit substances (Chaffin, Kelleher, & Hollenberg, 1996), and experience high rates of marital conflict and abuse (Stark & Flitcraft, 1988). Moreover, these psychopathologies reciprocally interact with the behaviors of their maltreated children. Relative to nonabused children, abused children are aggressive, demonstrate poor social skills (Fantuzzo, 1990), are poorly engaged in familial relationships, are disruptive, and demonstrate fears and anxieties (see Donohue, Ammerman, & Zelis, 1997). Therefore, investigators have underscored the heuristic value of examining and treating the family as a unit rather than targeting a "problem child" or "abusive parent" (Lutzker, 1990). In this light, the behavioral interventions are the treatment of choice for child abuse and neglect, as these standardized interventions emphasize functional assessment and are easily tailored to fit individual needs (Donohue et al., 1997). Indeed, cognitive-behavioral interventions are consistently more effective than other therapy modalities in the treatment of child maltreatment. These interventions have included child management skills training (e.g., Brunk, Henggeler, & Whelan, 1987; Egan, 1983), stress management and problem-solving skills training (e.g., Gaudin, Wodarski, Arkinson, & Avery, 1990; Schinke et al., 1986; Whiteman, Fanshel, & Grundy, 1987), or a combination of these interventions (e.g., Kolko, 1996). Uncontrolled studies have demonstrated improvements in home cleanliness and reductions in home hazards via identification of home stressors, installation of home safety equipment, and cleanliness training (see Tertinger, Greene, & Lutzker, 1984). Intervention appears to be augmented if it is administered in situ (i.e., the setting where the difficulties take place; Kolko, 1996). When treatment occurs in the natural environment, and data are obtained on a range of relevant family variables, the approach transcends the usual unidimensional intervention to yield systematic and programmed maintenance effects across problematic areas and settings.

This chapter provides a detailed description of Project SAFE, a broad-spectrum cognitive-behavioral program for families characterized by some form of child physical abuse/neglect, or at high risk for child maltreatment. Treatment components are designed to improve family relationships, home safety hazards, stress, anger, child management skills, and communication. The program consists of 3 assessment sessions and 16 sessions of treatment (90 minutes duration). Intervention is ideally implemented in the home. Follow-up sessions are held 1, 3, and 6 months post-treatment, and treatment "booster" sessions are scheduled as needed.

Assessment

A team of two clinicians perform the initial intake evaluation conducted in the family's home. One clinician administers a structured intake interview to the target child, while the other clinician conducts a structured interview with the caregiver(s). The interview assesses relevant social, medical, developmental, and family history in addition to obtaining a history of the presenting problem. During the next session, the following assessment battery is orally administered to child victims and their caregivers to examine behavioral deficits and excesses, ascertain their level of social and emotional adjustment, and identify appropriate treatment targets.

Child Measures

Children's Depression Inventory (CDI).   The CDI (Kovacs & Beck, 1983) is a 27-item self-report questionnaire. This measure assesses mood, pessimism, appetite loss, suicidality, and other depressive symptomatology in children and adolescents ages 8 to 17. A summative score, ranging from 0 to 54 with higher scores indicating greater severity of depression, is derived from children's responses. The clinical cut-off score is 9.7 (Finch, Saylor, & Edwards, 1985). Smucker, Craighead, Craighead, and Green (1986) found the reliability of this measure to be adequate.

Revised–Children's Manifest Anxiety Scale (RCMAS).   The RCMAS (Reynolds & Richmond, 1985) consists of 37 items that evaluate level of anxiety among children and adolescents. In addition to a score that reflects an attempt to present oneself favorably (lie scale), scores may be derived for General Anxiety, Physiological Anxiety, Worry and Oversensitivity, and Social Anxiety.

Fear Survey Schedule for Children–Revised (FSSCR).   The FSSC–R (Ollendick, 1983) consists of 80 items that evaluate fears in children and adolescents. Scores may be derived for Total Fear, Fear of Failure and Criticism, Fear of the Unknown, Fear of Injury and Small

Animals, Fear of Danger and Death, and Medical Fears. The Fear of Failure and Criticism and Fear of the Unknown subscales are particularly relevant to maltreated populations. Cut-off scores are available elsewhere (see Ollendick, King, & Frary, 1989).

The Children's Version Family Environment Scale (CVFES).   The CVFES (Pino, Simons, & Slawinowski, 1984) consists of 30 items assessing perceptions of the family environment of young children (5 to 11 years).The CVFES measures 10 areas related to the family environment (i.e., cohesion, expressiveness, conflict, independence, achievement-orientation, intellectual-cultural orientation, active-recreational orientation, moral-religious emphasis, organization, control). Reliability of this measure is adequate (Pino, Simons, & Slawinowski, 1984).

Family Environment Scale–Revised (FES–R).   The FES–R (Moos & Moos, 1986) consists of 90 items assessing perceptions of the family environment of adolescent children and adults (older than 11 years). The FESR measures 10 domains of the family environment (i.e., cohesion, expressiveness, conflict, independence, achievement-orientation, intellectual-cultural orienta-tion, active-recreational orientation, moral-religious emphasis, organization, control). Test–re-test reliability is good, and cut- off scores are available (see Moos & Moos, 1986).

The Youth Satisfaction Scale–Revised (YSS–R).   The YSS–R (Donohue, Van Hasselt, War-shal, Hersen, & Schoenwald, 1996) is a 10-item self-report measure that assesses happiness of children (6 to 17 years) with their caregivers in 10 domains of the relationships. Items are rated on a 0–100 scale of happiness. Scores may be obtained for Overall Happiness, Communication, Chores, Friends, Curfew, Discipline, Dress, Rewards, School Performance, and Home Conduct Rules. Psychometric properties of the original scale were not ascertained (Besalel & Azrin, 1981). However, the YSS–R has demonstrated adequate internal reliability (Chronbach's alpha = .80) and concurrent validity in a population of maltreated children and adolescents (Donohue et al., 1996).

The Children's Impact of Traumatic Event Scale–Revised (CITES–R).   The   CITES–R (Wolfe et al., 1991) is administered only to those children suspected to be victims of sexual abuse. The CITES–R consists of 54 items that assess the impact of abuse from the child's perspective (i.e., posttraumatic symptoms, social reactions, abuse attributions, eroticism).

Caregiver Measures

Beck Depression Inventory (BDI).   The BDI (Beck, Ward, Mendelsohn, Mock, & Erbaugh, 1961) is a self-report measure consisting of 21 items that reflect intensity of depressive symptoms. Scores between 11 to 17 suggest mild depression, 18 to 29 reflect moderate depression, and scores of 30 or more indicate severe depression.

Parenting Stress Index Short Form (PSISF).   The PSISF (Abidin, 1990) is a self-report meas-ure of stress in the parent–child system. Thirty-six items assess the degree to which parents perceive parenting as difficult. Scores are determined separately for child, parent, and parent–child domains. The child domain assesses perceived adaptability, demandingness, mood, and child's level of distractibility and activity. Child acceptability, child reinforces parent, and parental attachment comprise the parent–child dysfunctional interaction domain. The parent domain measures depression, restriction of role, social isolation, and relationship with spouse. An obtained stress score greater than or equal to 36 on Parental Distress is clinically significant.

The Child Abuse Potential Inventory (CAPI).   The CAPI (Milner, 1986) is a 116-item self-report measure that may be used to identify parents who engage in abusive behavior toward their children. Parents indicate whether they agree or disagree with statements reflecting child problems, unhappiness, loneliness, negative self-concept, and other behavioral and personality domains. Cut-off scores are used to predict whether the parent is at high risk for being abusive. The CAPI measures six main constructs (i.e., distress, rigidity, unhappiness, problems with others, problems with one's child and one's self, problems with one's family). Discriminant validity of the CAPI has been demonstrated (Milner, 1986).

The Eyberg Child Behavior Inventory (ECBI).   The ECBI intensity scale (Eyberg & Ross, 1978) lists 36 disruptive behaviors for which the parent indicates on a 7-point scale (1 = *never*, 7 = *always*) how often the child exhibits each behavior. Additionally, a problem scale assesses whether or not the parent perceives the behavior as problematic (1 = *yes*, 0 = *no*).

Family Environment Scale–Revised (FES–R).   The FES–R (Moos & Moos, 1986) consists of 90 items assessing perceptions of the family environment of adolescent children and adults (greater than 11 years). Ten areas of the family's environment are assessed (i.e., cohesion, expressiveness, conflict, independence, achievement-orientation, intellectual-cultural orientation, active-recreational orientation, moral-religious emphasis, organization, control). Reliability of the FES–R is adequate, and cut-off scores are available elsewhere (Moos & Moos, 1986).

Parent Satisfaction Scale–Revised (PSS–R).   The PSS–R (Donohue et al., 1996) is a 10-item self-report measure assessing happiness of caregivers with their children in 10 domains of the relationship. Items are rated on a 0–100 scale of happiness. Scores may be obtained for Overall Happiness, Communication, Chores, Friends, Curfew, Discipline, Dress, Rewards, School Performance, and Home Conduct Rules. Although psychometric properties of the original scale were not ascertained (Besalel & Azrin, 1981), the PSS–R has demonstrated excellent internal reliability (Chronbach's alpha = .91) and concurrent validity in a population of caregivers of maltreated children (Donohue et al., 1996).

Children's Sexual Behavior Inventory (CSBI).   The CSBI (Friedrich et al., 1992) is a 106-item checklist that is completed by parents. The CSBI may be used to assess sexual behaviors of children suspected of sexual abuse (i.e., self-stimulation, sexual aggression, gender-role behavior, personal boundary violations).

Teacher Measures

The Sutter Eyberg Student Behavior Inventory (SESBI).   The SESBI Intensity scale (Eyberg & Ross, 1978) includes 36 disruptive behaviors for which the teacher indicates on a 7-point scale how often the child exhibits each behavior (1 = *never*, 7 = *always*). A problem scale assesses whether or not the teacher perceives these behaviors as problematic.

DEVELOPMENT OF STANDARDIZED TREATMENT PROGRAM

Review of Literature.   Development of this treatment program followed a number of discrete, ongoing, empirical phases. The first phase involved a review of the literature to determine victim and perpetrator symptomology due to the various forms of child maltreatment, and to identify efficacious psychological interventions to remediate these problems. Based on this review, a number of empirically derived treatment procedures were modified to comprehensively address environmental hazards and neglect, anger control, behavioral child management, family relationships, skill deficits relevant to child care (e.g., toileting, self-hygiene), and lack of motivation for therapy.

Writing the Initial Treatment Manual.   The next step in developing the standardized treatment program consisted of writing a treatment manual for each intervention. These manuals were intended to be clear and simple so that clinicians could follow them as a guide during sessions. Each manual included a brief overview and rationale of the treatment method and specific steps for treatment implementation.

Evaluating the Treatment Manual in Training Sessions.   Training sessions were conducted after each treatment manual was written. During initial training sessions, a training coordinator modeled the role of the therapist and clinicians experienced in the treatment of maltreated children took turns modeling the role of their patients. When problems were encountered with the manual during these interactions the group performed problem solving until a solution was derived. After the training session, the coordinator modified the manual to include these solutions and distributed this revised manual to all program clinicians with instructions to be prepared for its implementation during the next training session. During this next session, all clinicians took turns modeling the role of a therapist, and the training coordinator modeled a compliant patient. Again, if problems were experienced with the manual, or if possible improvements became apparent, the group utilized problem solving to derive solutions, and the manual was again revised. For each treatment manual, training sessions were conducted until the manual appeared to be worthy of implementation.

Evaluating the Treatment Manual in Vivo.   The last stage of development involved an evaluation of each treatment manual in vivo. Specifically, the revised manual was given to all clinicians to utilize with their cases. Each clinician was given instructions to administer treatment as the manual described and subsequently report to the training coordinator any difficulties of treatment implementation, including suggestions to improve the manual. The problem was then addressed in a training meeting where all program clinicians generated solutions that were subsequently incorporated into the manual.

This highly standardized manner of revision took full advantage of clinicians' experiences in the home; however, the process was extremely time consuming. Indeed, for approximately 1 year manuals were continuously revised as new problems were experienced in the homes. Many manuals appeared to be intuitively quite sound on paper but were ineffective in practice, and were therefore eliminated from protocol. Thus, each of the interventions presented in this chapter have undergone dozens of revisions, and are currently being evaluated in a large scale treatment outcome study.

Implementation of Treatment Protocol

Establishing Rapport.   Families that have been reported to Child Protective Services may not desire counseling, and often proclaim that "the system" has unjustly put their family "through the mill." This is to some extent true, but regardless, family members are characteristically guarded as the first session begins. It is therefore extremely important that clinicians establish themselves as generalized reinforcers early in therapy. When entering the home, clinicians are instructed to immediately begin complimenting family members with pleasant affect (e.g., "Your home is beautiful." "Wow! You sure do have a great hand shake." "What beautiful children."). After a brief overview of the project, the family is asked to describe their thoughts about having to participate in therapy. Caregiver concerns (e.g., "I don't like the way I've been treated by my caseworker." "You should try to take care of these kids, they don't listen to anyone.") are consequenced with empathetic statements (e.g., "I can see you've been through a lot." "These types of situations can be very demanding for parents."). Caregivers often initially believe that clinicians do not think they are good parents. Therefore, clinicians descriptively praise any desired parenting practices or expressions of affection (e.g., "It's wonderful to hear that you reward your son for doing his homework; so many parents forget rewards these days." "I really like how you're letting your son sit on your lap, he really loves you."). When children express their concerns (e.g., "My grandma never lets me go out." "School is too tough.") they are also provided a high degree of empathy (e.g., "It's common for kids your age to want more freedom." "You're not kidding, school is tough."). Moreover, when children perform desired behaviors they are provided generous amounts of descriptive praise (e.g., "Thanks for getting the door for me, you're going to make a lot of friends that way."). Praise is also noncontingently administered (e.g., "What a good kid!"). Empathy and praise are provided throughout therapy, particularly when motivation is wanting.

Improving Motivation.   Good rapport with the family is a necessary precursor for treatment motivation. However, other methods may also be utilized. For example, the roleplay is paramount to this program, and noncompliance to roleplaying is initially quite common. Many subtle techniques may enhance compliance to this technique (i.e., instructing patient to perform a role-play rather than asking the patient to "give it a try," excusing nonparticipants, concurrent modeling and prompting during the family member's rehearsal, avoiding laughter when modeling). Threatening to tell probation officers or child protective caseworkers of noncompliance is typically ineffective, and often hurts rapport. Conversely, however, caregivers may be told that their hard work will be reflected in a monthly letter to their probation officer, judge, and so on. Noncompliance to homework assignments is common, and often due to the clinician's lack of enforcement. If an assignment is not performed, and the clinician says, "That's okay, don't worry about it," then the family member will do just that. To avoid this dilemma, clinicians blame noncompliance to homework on some extraneous variable (e.g., holidays, rough week at work), and then instruct the noncompliant family member to take a few minutes to perform the recording process in retrospect to the best of his/her ability. If noncompliance to homework is a result of illiteracy, a literate family member is assigned to assist in secretarial duties for the illiterate family member. In addition to praise, a material reward may be established for this duty. Illiterate persons may also utilize pictures to represent behaviors when recording therapy assignments.

Decreasing No-Shows.   Twenty-four hour reminder calls, telephone calls to the family 30 minutes prior to scheduled sessions to verify the appointment, and immediately informing Child Protective Services caseworkers or judges when no-shows occur (if court mandated for treatment) will likely reduce no-shows for scheduled sessions. In addition, because the interventions are standardized, if a clinician is unable to attend a scheduled session, another clinician may be scheduled.

Enhancing Safety of Clinicians.   In order to enhance the safety of clinicians when they travel to destitute crime-infested neighborhoods, clinicians may perform therapy in pairs whenever possible, and schedule appointments so that the sessions terminate prior to dusk. In addition, whenever possible, clinicians travel to homes in the same car (ideally in male/female dyads).

Brief Overview of the Treatment Program

Cognitive-behavioral intervention consists of sixteen 90-minute home-based sessions. Additional booster sessions may be scheduled when necessary. Ideally, two clinicians perform therapy concurrently with all family members living in the home. However, because interventions are robust, one clinician may implement most interventions with select family constellations.

Treatment protocol consists of 10 interventions that are implemented sequentially and cumulatively. Thus, after an intervention is implemented for the first time, it is reviewed during all subsequent sessions. Each intervention is described in a treatment manual that contains a brief overview, sample rationale, and specific steps for implementation. Some manuals contain a section depicting solutions to common problems that often occur during implementation of treatment. Manuals are structured such that one caretaker (custodian) and one target child are targeted per intervention. However, additional caretakers, significant others, and children may be included, and interventions may be omitted or modified whenever appropriate. The complete package of interventions includes the following:

Intervention	*Targets of Intervention*
Communication Guidelines (page 286)	communication, compliance to session protocol
I've Got a Great Family (page 288)	communication, relationship enhancement
Consequence Review (page 290)	motivation to use nonaversive disciplines
Home Safety and Beautification (page 296)	home hazards and neglect
Social Skills to Obstruct Peril (page 305)	interpersonal safety skills
SAFE Point System (page 309)	child/adolescent misconduct
Catching My Child Being Good (page 320)	child management, relationship enhancement
Identification/Escape From At-Risk Situations (page 324)	prevention of abusive interaction
Positive Practice (page 336)	child management
ICARE (page 342)	child management, prevention of abusive interaction, stress management

COMMUNICATION GUIDELINES

I. Brief Overview

A1. Families of maltreated children often violate many prosocial communication practices with one another during treatment sessions (e.g., brothers yell at sisters, parents interrupt children). Of course, this makes it difficult to administer therapy. The present guidelines are designed to interrupt detrimental communication patterns and obtain commitments to practice more benign ways of familial interaction.

II. Presenting Guidelines

A. Brief rationale.
    1. Provide a brief rationale for communication guidelines that includes the following:
        a. Guidelines will be reviewed to improve positive communication.
        b. Guidelines apply to all members.
        c. Family members will be instructed to correct all guidelines that are broken.
        d. Other families have reported success using these guidelines.
            For example: "We will have to cover a lot of material in the upcoming treatment sessions. Therefore, before we begin I would like to review some guidelines that are designed to increase positive communication during our sessions. These guidelines will apply to all family members. Other families have reported that these guidelines are extremely helpful."
B. Taking turns when communicating, instead of interrupting.
    1. Tell the family that the first guideline is to take turns when talking, instead of interrupting.
    2. If necessary, provide an example of compliance and noncompliance with the guideline.
        For example: "An example of someone breaking this guideline would be if a person started talking while someone else was talking. A family member would be taking turns if the speaker was allowed to finish talking before feedback was attempted."
    3. Ask the family why it is important to take turns communicating ideas without interruptions.
        a. Praise any statements that suggest it is important to avoid interruptions.
        b. The following prompts may be used to elicit comments that suggest it is important to take turns:
            1. Would misunderstandings occur?
            2. Do people get annoyed when they are interrupted?
    4. If the assessment reveals that interruptions have been a problem for the family, then instruct each family member to roleplay a situation in which one family member waits until another family member is done speaking before making a comment.
        For example: "Johnny, I'm about to instruct your mom to start talking. Wait until she pauses for a few seconds, and then ask her if you can go to the movies this weekend."

5. Obtain a commitment from each family member to attempt to avoid interruptions.
6. Provide descriptive praise, suggestions to improve performance, and/or modeling to demonstrate skills, whenever necessary.
7. The remaining communication guidelines should be presented much like the first guideline:
   a. State the guideline.
   b. If necessary, provide an example of compliance and noncompliance to the guideline.
   c. Ask the family why it is important to follow the guideline presented.
   d. Praise statements that suggest it is important to follow the guideline.
   e. Provide prompts, if necessary, to elicit statements that suggest the guideline is important.
   f. If the assessment reveals that the family may have a difficulty complying with the guideline, instruct each member to role-play a situation involving compliance with the guideline.
   g. Provide descriptive praise, suggestions to improve performance, and/or modeling to demonstrate skills, when necessary.
   h. Obtain a commitment from each family member to follow the guideline.
8. Communication guidelines include:
   a. Avoid the word "no" when asked to do something. Instead agree to do some part of the request (i.e., compromise).
   b. Be sincere.
   c. Never roll eyes back or use sarcasm.
   d. No swearing or belittling comments.
   e. Keep hands to self, except when showing signs of affection (e.g., hugs, kisses).
   f. Avoid absolutist statements (e.g., should, must, have to).
   g. Let family members speak for themselves.
   h. Stay focused and answer questions briefly and specifically.
   i. Do not speak for more than 1 minute without requesting feedback.
   j. Speak in a soft and audible tone.

III. Maintenance of Guidelines

A. Teaching the family what to do when family members are noncompliant to guidelines during future therapy sessions.
   1. After reviewing the guidelines, and obtaining a commitment from each family member to comply with each of these guidelines, tell the family that when guidelines are violated, the clinician will instruct the noncompliant family member to immediately correct the violation.
   2. When family members violate guidelines in future sessions, the clinician should immediately terminate the response, and instruct the perpetrator to correct the violation. (It may be necessary to model the correct response, particularly in beginning sessions.)
      For example: "Hold on! Remember the guideline about speaking softly. Please restate your comment softly."

I'VE GOT A GREAT FAMILY

I. Brief Overview

A1. Belittling, disparaging, and contemptuous comments (e.g., "My brother is a jerk. He doesn't do anything right.") are common in families of abused children. Derogatory statements typically contribute to aversive relationships and exacerbate problems related to poor self-esteem. The I've Got a Great Family procedure attempts to teach family members to increase the frequency and quality of complimentary statements in the target child's family.

II. Presenting the Procedure

A. Provide rationale.
  1. State a brief rationale for I've Got a Great Family that includes the following:
     a. Research has shown that families who state positive things to one another are prone to have pleasant relationships.
     b. The family will learn to increase the frequency and quality of positive statements to one another.
     c. Families have reported great success with this procedure.
        For example: "Studies have found that families who say good things to each other have positive relationships. The procedure you are about to learn is called I've Got a Great Family. This procedure will help your family say positive things to each other more often. Families have reported great success with this procedure, and I think you all will do especially well because there is a lot of love in this family."
B. Positive Statement Exchange.
  1. Give each literate family member a copy of Things I Like About My Family (see Table 9.1).
  2. In the top row of the form, list the names of each family member (one family member per column).
     a. The clinician may assist illiterate family members with reading and writing when needed.

TABLE 9.1

Things I Like About My Family

Family Member 1	Family Member 2	Family Member 3	Family Member 4	Family Member 5	Family Member 6

3. Instruct each family member to complete the additional rows with things that are liked about each family member.
   a. In order to prevent one family member from receiving more positive statements than another, the first row should be completed before advancing to the second row, and so on.

      For example: "I want you to all fill in one positive statement for each family member in the first row. When you are done recording one positive statement for each family member I want you to go to the second row and fill in one positive statement for each family member. Then do the rest of the rows in a similar manner."

4. While family members complete their lists, the clinician may utilize the following prompts to increase responding:
   a. "You are all writing a lot of positive things about each other."
   b. "Remember, positive qualities can include doing chores, signs of affection, types of things that are done well."

5. After completing the lists for approximately 10 minutes, the clinician should instruct family members to take turns complimenting each other using the items recorded in their lists, according to the following guidelines.
   a. Instruct the caregiver to state a positive statement about each member in the family (from the first row).
   b. Instruct family members to respond to the caregiver's compliments by saying, "Thank you, I think you're (positive statement about the caregiver that is listed in first row)."
   c. This process should continue such that each family member is provided an opportunity to tell all other family members a positive statement that is listed in their first row (e.g., family members 1 and 2 exchange positive statements about each other, then family members 1 and 3, 1 and 4, 2 and 3, 2 and 4, 3 and 4).
   d. When the second row is complete, positive statements should be distributed for the second row in a similar manner, then third row, fourth row, and so on.
   e. The process of taking turns should continue until no positive statements remain.
   f. Praise family members for making positive statements, and then prompt recipients to disclose what they liked about the positive things that were stated to them.

      For example: "Okay, let's begin. Mrs. Jones, tell Johnny something that you like about him from your first row. And Johnny, I want you to respond by telling your mother 'Thank you.' Then tell your mother something that you like about her from your first row. (caregiver and child exchange positive statements) Mrs. Jones, that was a beautiful compliment. Wasn't that great how Johnny returned your compliment by smiling and telling you that he loved you? Johnny, what did you like about what your mother said? (child responds) Yeah, she sure did have a great big smile. Mrs. Jones, tell Mr. Jones something that you like about him from your first row. Mr. Jones, respond with a thank you and tell your wife something you like about her from your list. (caregiver's exchange positive statements) Oh, that's wonderful! Mrs. Jones gets up a half hour early so that she can make you breakfast, and you worked overtime for her last week so that she could get that watch she wanted. Mr. Jones, what positive things were going through your head as she stated that nice thing to you?"

TABLE 9.2

I've Got a Great Family

Family Member	Monday	Tuesday	Wednesday	Thursday	Friday	Saturday	Sunday

C. Assigning Homework.
  1. Tell the family that it will be necessary to practice stating positive statements between sessions.
  2. Give each family member a copy of the I've Got a Great Family recording form (see Table 9.2).
  3. Instruct each family member to write the names of all other family members in the left column.
     a. It may be necessary for adults to read and write responses.
  4. Tell the family that at least one positive statement should be stated to each family member per week, and subsequently recorded in the I've Got a Great Family recording form.
  5. Elicit a reinforcer that caregivers may provide children each day for completion of homework and/or a reward for the most positive statements, and then get a commitment from each family member to perform the homework.
  6. Remind the family that a statement of appreciation and/or a positive statement should be reciprocated.
D. Reviewing Homework.
  1. Ask family members to take turns telling the clinician positive statements that were provided since last session.
     a. Praise efforts to provide positive statements.
     b. Elicit positive feelings from family members regarding their statements.
        For example: "How did that feel when Johnny told you that he loved you?"
  2. Provide each family member with a copy of I've Got a Great Family recording form, and assign at least one positive statement per week per family member for homework.

CONSEQUENCE REVIEW

I. Brief Overview

A1. Caregivers of maltreated children frequently engage in actions associated with child abuse (e.g., poor parenting practices). Of course, a great percentage of these caregivers do not consider these actions to be problematic or in need of intervention. Thus, the Consequence Review procedure was developed to motivate caregivers to avoid these deleterious actions and seek out alternative behavioral patterns. In this procedure, caregivers are prompted to provide their own negative consequences of child abuse. Importantly, caregivers are prompted to review negative aspects of these consequences in great detail.

II. General Guidelines for Clinicians

A. The clinician should not impose his/her values as to the wrongfulness of behaviors associated with child abuse; instead unpleasant consequences of abuse will be elicited from the caregiver.
  1. Demonstrate neutral affect, except when instructed to provide empathy for unpleasant consequences, or praise nonabusive behavior.
  2. Avoid the word *abuse*, unless the caregiver uses this word. Instead, specifically describe the abusive behavior (e.g., hitting with stick instead of physical abuse).

III. Treatment Implementation

A. Rationale.
  1. State a brief rationale for Consequence Review that includes the following:
     a. Awareness of the referral agent's concern regarding the specific abusive behavior(s) identified.
     b. Current interest in perpetrator's concerns regarding reported incident(s).
     c. To appreciate perpetrator's concerns, his/her unpleasant consequences will be recorded.
        For example: "I have been informed about the concerns that your Child Protective Service caseworker has regarding your hitting Johnny with the stick. However, at this time I am most interested in learning about your thoughts regarding this incident. To help me better appreciate the concerns that you may be experiencing, I will write down some of the unpleasant consequences that you have experienced since the time you hit him with the stick."
B. Obtain a 0 to 100 rating of overall unpleasantness.
  1. Ask the caregiver to rate, on a scale of 0 to 100, how unpleasant it would be for him/her if the reported abusive behavior(s) was to continue (0 = *not unpleasant at all*, 100 = *the most unpleasant incident ever* experienced by the caregiver).
        For example: "Mary, on a scale of 0 to 100, with a 0 being equal to *not unpleasant at all*, and 100 being equal to *the most unpleasant incident that you have ever experienced*, how unpleasant would it be for you if you continued to hit Johnny with sticks?"
  2. Place this rating at the bottom of the Consequence Review Summary Worksheet, labeled Preliminary Overall Rating of Unpleasantness (see Table 9.3).
C. Elicit initial unpleasant consequences of abusive behavior from the caregiver.
  1. Ask the caregiver to disclose unpleasant consequences for the behavior(s) that was identified to be abusive.
        For example: "What do you consider to be unpleasant consequences about hitting Johnny with sticks?"

TABLE 9.3

Consequence Review Summary Worksheet

Initial Unpleasant Consequences	Prompted Consequences	Final Ratings	Unpleasant Consequence Ranking	Rating of Ranked Consequence
			1)	
			2)	
			3)	
			4)	
			5)	
			6)	
			7)	
			8)	

Preliminary Overall Rating of Unpleasantness: _____.

Final Overall Rating of Unpleasantness: _____.

    a. Do not prompt the client for consequences. If the client does not understand, or is unable to provide consequences, rephrase the question.

    b. The caregiver may provide several consequences that are not related, or are distantly related.

        For example: I probably would get a divorce, I get upset, being arrested, my family/friends would think I was abusive, I might hurt my child, I might have to take my child to the hospital.

        1. Each unrelated consequence should be recorded in separate a row in the Initial Consequences column of the Consequence Review Summary Worksheet.

    c. The caregiver may list consequences that are interrelated, according to some general theme.

        For example: being arrested, being raped in prison, bad food in prison.

        1. Interrelated consequences should be recorded in the same row.

    d. The caregiver may list a series of consequences that follow a logical sequence of order.

        For example: He'll get taken away, and I'll be sad because I won't have someone to talk with at night.

        1. Consequences that follow a logical sequence of order should be placed in the same row.

  2. After each initial consequence is stated, the clinician should prompt additional consequences by stating, with very neutral affect, "Anything else."

D. Prompt additional unpleasant consequences (prompted consequences).
1. Ask what is unpleasant/upsetting about each of the initial consequences, and prompt additional unpleasant consequences.
   a. Clinician prompts include:
      1. What is so bad about (initial consequence)?
      2. Is it unpleasant for you to (initial consequence)?
      3. Why is it upsetting for you to (initial consequence)?
   b. An example vignette for the caregiver's response "I get upset when I have to hit my kid" is as follows:

   Caregiver: "I get upset when I have to hit my kid."
   Clinician: "What do you get upset about?"
   Caregiver: "Lots of things. Like, I must be a bad parent."
   Clinician: "Why is that upsetting to you?"
   Caregiver: "I don't know, I just don't feel good about myself."
   Clinician: "Is it distressing for you to have these thoughts?"
   Caregiver: "Very distressing."
   Clinician: "So another consequence would be distressing thoughts that you might be a bad parent."

2. For each consequence that is elicited, prompt the caregiver for additional problems with the unpleasant consequences.
   For example: "So, you would have distressing thoughts that you were a bad parent. Would it be upsetting if other people thought you were a bad parent for hitting Johnny with sticks?"
3. Other prompts include:
   a. Jail.
      1. Is it possible that you might go to jail if (abusive behavior) continues?
      2. What would be unpleasant about having to go to jail?
   b. Caregiver's feelings.
      1. Do you get upset when (abusive behavior) occurs?
      2. Does it upset *you* when your child gets upset?
      3. What type of feelings do you experience when (abusive behavior) occurs?
   c. Child's feelings.
      1. How does your child feel when (abusive behavior) occurs?
      2. How would it affect you negatively if your child fears you?
   d. Relationship with spouse.
      1. Do you and your spouse disagree in any ways with (abusive behavior)?
      2. Has (abusive behavior) caused problems in your marriage?
   e. Life changes.
      1. Is it possible that your child may be removed from your home because of (abusive behavior)? If so, would this be upsetting to you?
      2. Do you feel that this incident has been an invasion of your privacy, or an inconvenience?
      3. Has anyone that you know (e.g., people at work, child's school, friend's, neighbors) said anything upsetting/annoying to you about (abusive behavior)? If so, what don't you like about what these people stated?

f. Injury.
    1. What type of injuries might occur?
    2. How would these injuries affect you?
4. Consequences that are prompted should be recorded in the Prompted Consequences column of the Consequence Review Summary Worksheet in the row corresponding to its initial consequence.
    a. For example: The prompted consequences "I would have medical expenses" and "my child could get an infection" would be recorded in the same row as the initial consequence "I might hurt my child."

E. Obtain ratings.
    1. Each Initial Consequence will perhaps have several Prompted Consequences in its row.
    2. State the Initial Consequence for each row followed by the Prompted Consequences that belong to that row.
    3. Ask the caregiver to rate each row of consequences for unpleasantness (0 to 100; i.e., each row of initial and prompted consequences will be rated once collectively).

> For example: "You have told me a lot more about the consequences that I originally asked you to rate for unpleasantness. I'd like you to rate how unpleasant each of these consequences is for you. However, before you rate these consequences I will repeat all the unpleasant things that you told me about each consequence. Zero equals not unpleasant to you at all, and 100 equals the most unpleasant incident that you have experienced. The first unpleasant consequence that you told me about was the possibility of hurting your child. You stated that other unpleasantries might occur from this, including infection and medical expenses. How would you rate this group of consequences from 0 to 100?"

    4. Record each rating in the Ratings column.

F. Based on the ratings, rank each row of unpleasant consequences.
    1. Rank the rows such that higher rated consequences have lower rankings.
       For example:

Ranking	Rating	Unpleasant Consequence
1	100	—getting arrested beat-up or raped boring hard time getting a job later
2	100	—my child might get hurt medical expenses risk of infection
3	95	—getting divorced miss my spouse no security loss of income
4	90	—thoughts "I'm a bad parent" anxiety loss of confidence
5	80	—people would think I was abusive embarrassment

7	70	—I might get upset headache makes me do things I wouldn't normally do
8	40	—medical expenses takes away from family income
9	15	—risk of infection child could get seriously sick guilt

2. Repeat the consequences in the order for which they are ranked, and ask the caregiver if the rankings are correct.
   a. Change the order of the rankings, if necessary.
3. Place these ranked consequences in the Unpleasant Consequence Ranking column of the Consequence Review Summary worksheet.
   a. The highest ranked consequence should be listed at the top of the column, and consequences should progressively become less unpleasant.
4. If many consequences are elicited, only the top 3 or 4 ranked consequences should be listed to save time.

G. What to do with Rating of Ranked Consequence column.
1. Record the rating that corresponds to each Ranked Unpleasant Consequence in the Rating of Ranked Consequence column.

H. Obtain final *overall* rating of unpleasantness.
1. Ask the caregiver to again rate, on a scale of 0 to 100, how unpleasant it would be for him/her if (abusive behavior) were to continue (0 = *not unpleasant at all*, 100 = *most unpleasant incident ever experienced*).
2. Place this rating at the bottom of the Consequence Review Summary Worksheet, next to the Preliminary Overall Rating of Unpleasantness.

IV. Review Unpleasant Consequences

A. Empathize.
1. Empathize with the caregiver regarding how unpleasant these consequences must be for him/her, and reinforce the idea that the caregiver has a right to feel this way.
   a. Nonverbal distress should be demonstrated by the clinician when reviewing the unpleasantness of the caregiver's consequences (e.g., sullen facial expression, soft tone, slow rate of speech).
      For example: "Well, I now have a better understanding of some of the stressors that you've been having to deal with at home. I agree that these consequences are very unpleasant, and most people would feel the same way."

B. Stress great likelihood that these consequences will occur if abusive behavior continues.
1. Repeat several of the top-ranked consequences, and reinforce the idea that there is a high probability that these unpleasant consequences will occur if the reported abusive behaviors continue.
      For example: "You stated that you would probably have to go to jail if you hit your child with your hand or any other objects. Based on what I have seen with the court system, I totally agree with you. I can appreciate how terribly

upsetting and stressful it is to be forced to go to jail. I'm going to do the best I can to help you to learn alternative disciplining methods. I know jail isn't meant for you. I would hate to see you have to go there."

C. Comparing Preliminary and Final Overall Unpleasantness Ratings.

    1. If the Final Overall Rating of Unpleasantness is greater than the Preliminary Overall Rating of Unpleasantness, instruct the caregiver to explain why this is so. Then reinforce any ideas that indicate that the caregiver is more aware of these unpleasant consequences.

    2. If the Preliminary Overall Rating is greater than the Final Overall Rating, then do not compare these ratings

D. Future reviews.

    1. Consequence reviews should be performed whenever resistance or lack of motivation occurs in therapy.

    2. Consequence reviews should include the top ranked unpleasant consequences only (i.e., rankings 1 to 3).

    3. Do the following when performing a consequence review:

       a. State the three top ranked consequences, one row at a time.

       b. After each row of consequences is stated, ask the caregiver why it was originally thought to be unpleasant.

          For example: "Mr. Jones you originally said that you were most upset with the possibility that you would have to go to jail if you were caught hitting Johnny with sticks. Why is this consequence so unpleasant to you?"

       c. Tell the caregiver that these consequences are likely to occur if (abusive behavior) occurs.

          For example: "That's right, if you continue to hit Johnny with sticks you said that you will probably go to jail, and knowing the system like I do I would have to agree that you probably would go to jail."

       d. Empathize with the caregiver regarding the undesirability of these consequences.

          For example: "I think it would be devastating if you had to go to jail, and I see here that you stated that you would probably not get a good job after jail, that would be unfortunate for your whole family."

       e. Prompt the caregiver to respond to the unpleasantness of these consequences.

          For example: "How would you feel if you lost custody of your child?"

       f. Empathize with the caregiver regarding the undesirability of these consequences.

SAFE AND FRIENDLY ENVIRONMENT (SAFE)

I. Home Safety and Beautification

A. Brief overview of home safety and beautification.

    1. Households of children that have been maltreated are often not safe environments, particularly for toddlers. Moreover, family members are often unaware of potential home hazards that may harm their children (e.g., access to medications, toxins, electrical outlets, insufficient nutrition). Relatedly, these homes are frequently messy (e.g., unmade beds, dirty dishes) and contain broken household items (e.g., air

conditioners, locks), and encouragement and assistance for maintaining a clean home are often absent. Caregivers are often not aware of their tenant rights to have household items replaced or repaired, and/or do not have appropriate assertiveness skills to request home improvements from their landlords. Toys, pictures on bedroom walls, or other basic stimulating props are frequently absent from the homes of maltreated children because caregivers are restricting these objects as punishment, do not think these things are important, or cannot afford such possessions. Effective social stimulation is also warranted, as maltreated children are habitually deficient in social skills that influence their safety and well-being (e.g., conflict resolution, denying sexual advances and offers to leave with strangers). The Safe and Friendly Environment (SAFE) intervention may be utilized to enhance home safety, stimulation within the home, home beautification, and social skills that may prevent danger from others.

Home safety and beautification involves a tour of the home to descriptively praise family members for their efforts to prevent home hazards and maintain a clean, stimulating and beautiful home for children. To accomplish this task, clinicians utilize the Home Safety and Beautification form (see Table 9.4). The first 9 items on this form are pertinent to home hazards, Item 10 pertains to home cleanliness and beautification, and Items 11 to 15 consist of home props that facilitate personal and social growth for children.

B. Delineation of home safety and beautification items.
 1. Item 1: Toxins.

Examples.   Children eating medications that are left on kitchen or bathroom counters in nonchildproof containers. Young children drinking cleaning detergents left under kitchen and bathroom sinks. Children drinking pesticide or paint left on garage floors or closets. Adolescents drinking toxic amounts of alcohol left in kitchen cabinets. Children getting ill from illicit drugs found in dresser drawers of their caregivers. Babies eating paint chips on walls or ceilings.

Solutions.   Install safety latches on cabinets or drawers that contain toxins. Restrict toxins to child-proof containers. Place toxins in inconspicuous areas that are inaccessible to at-risk children (e.g., garage shelf, locked box). Instruct at-risk children to draw frown faces (or anything that represents danger) on containers that contain toxins. Scrape paint chips off ceilings and walls. Remove flammable toxins from heat sources.

Special considerations.   The family should be taught to implement the most convenient solution possible for each hazard (e.g., toxins may be left in cabinets if safety latches are installed or children are able to demonstrate that toxins are harmful). It may be necessary to provide nonmotivated caregivers with safety latches, and assist with installation of safety latches during home tours.

 2. Item 2: Electrical hazards.

Examples.   Young children sticking metal objects into electrical appliances (e.g., toasters) or electrical outlets that do not have plugs, cover plates, or switch plates. Touching exposed wires (e.g., spliced stereo wires). Hair dryers and radios falling into bath tubs. Cutting fingers on electric can openers or electric saws.

TABLE 9.4

Home Safety and Beautification Form

Safe, Clean, and Stimulating Items	Kitchen	Bathrm	Dining	Closet	Bedrm	Bedrm		Total
1. Toxins (medications, cleaning detergents, paint, pesticides, alcohol, etc. are in child-proof containers, out of reach, locked up, protected by safety latches)								
2. Electrical hazards (wires are covered with electrical tape, outlets have cover plates and plugs, electrical appliances are out of reach)								
3. Sharp objects (knives, sharp tools, etc. are out of reach, sharp corners are padded, no exposed nails)								
4. Heavy objects (irons, iron pans, tools, etc. are out of reach; shelves & furniture secure)								
5. Small objects (coins, super balls, crayons, etc. are not in reach of small children)								
6. Weapons (guns, combat knives, brass knuckles, numb chucks, explosives, etc. are absent, securely locked, or disengaged)								
7. Home access (door and window locks are present and working, windows and doors are secure, exterior lights are bright)								
8. Adequate temperature control (vents, heaters and airconditioners work; doors and windows are sealed, fans are present)								
9. Adequate food (enough, 4 food groups are present, limited sweets, not spoiled)								
10. Cleanliness (beds are made, clean floors and children, items are where they belong)								
11. Household items (toys, furniture, rugs, appliances, light bulbs, etc. work and are not excessively worn)								
12. Adequate toys (enough, developmentally appropriate, complete, working)								
13. Adequate children's books (enough, developmentally appropriate, not worn)								
14. Adequate clothing (enough, fits, clean, in style)								
15. Adequate decor (wall decorations, appropriate pictures, painted walls)								

Family Name: _____   Date: _____

Solutions.   Cover all exposed electric wires with electrical tape (tape may be painted to blend into background walls). In the homes of young or developmentally delayed children, insert safety plugs or night lights into electrical outlets. Put cover plates on all electric outlets. Place switch plates on all electrical switches. Put electrical appliances in inconspicuous places that young or developmentally delayed children cannot reach. Remove electrical appliances from areas that contain water (baths, sinks, pools).

Special considerations.   It is highly recommended that electricians or landlords be instructed to perform all electrical work when electricity may be live. It may be necessary to teach caregivers assertion skills specific to requesting electrical service from their landlords.

3. Item 3: Sharp objects.

Examples. Children getting cut by knives that were left on kitchen counters. Children cutting heads on sharp coffee table corners while playing. Poking eye on protruding curtain rods. Children cutting their mouths on razors that were left on bathroom counters or bathtubs. Stepping or bumping into nails that stick out of basement or garage walls or floors.

Solutions. Place sharp objects in areas that are inaccessible to at-risk children (e.g., place knives in back of kitchen counter. Put new razors in medicine cabinets. Wrap old razors in electrical tape and throw away). Tape cloth or cardboard on sharp corners (e.g., table corners). Replace sharp objects with rounded pieces (e.g., sharp curtain rods may be replaced with window blinds). Use a hammer to remove protruding nails. Teach children to pick up glass with a paper towel or avoid broken glass.

4. Item 4: Heavy objects.

Examples. Young children pull chords, wires, and ropes that connect to heavy objects (e.g., iron, tools). Children pull handles of iron pans that extend over the floor when being used for cooking. Unfastened storage shelves fall on children who attempt to remove objects from the shelves.

Solutions. Place heavy objects that are connected to chords, wires, and ropes in places that are inaccessible to children. When pans are on the stove, move pan handles towards the wall. Securely fasten heavy shelves against the wall with nails. Dismantle or remove heavy objects that may fall and cause injury (e.g., throw away a flimsy television stand and put the television on the floor until it is replaced).

5. Item 5: Small objects.

Examples. Pennies, rubber balls, screws, erasers, toys that have small pieces that are broken, and may be swallowed by small children.

Solutions. Keep small objects away from infants and young toddlers.

6. Item 6: Weapons.

Examples. Children and adolescents shooting themselves with guns that were not locked in metal containers, children stabbing themselves with swords that were used for decoration, adolescents seriously injuring others in gang fights using brass knuckles or high-powered rifles that were stored in their room, shooting family members in the night due to mistaken identity, children being injured from explosives (e.g., firecrackers). Weapons hanging on walls for decorations.

Solutions. Remove weapons (e.g., guns, brass knuckles, swords, combat knives, explosives) from the home. Dismantle/disengage guns that the caregiver refuses to remove from the home (assuming possession of firearm is legal). Lock all weapons in a metal box that is inaccessible to children and adolescents.

Special considerations.   This is an extremely delicate topic, as caregivers may be vehement about keeping weapons for their personal safety.

7. Item 7: Home access.

Examples.   Homes that have broken windows or doors. Doors or windows that have broken or insufficient locks. Homes with insufficient exterior lights, and/or no alarm system. Homes that have all windows either barred or "boarded" to prevent robbery (causing a potential fire hazard).

Solutions.   Replace, add, or secure broken or absent windows and doors (windows may be "boarded" provided there are numerous alternative escape routes in the event of fire). Replace, repair, or add locks, exterior lights, or alarm systems when these are absent, broken, or insufficient.

Special considerations.   Most families cannot afford alarm systems. However, locks may be inexpensively purchased from hardware stores, garage sales, flee markets, auctions, Salvation Army, and so on. When renting apartments or homes, state laws may require landlords to repair or replace damaged locks, doors, or windows that threaten the welfare of the family. It may be necessary to teach caregivers assertion skills specific to requesting service from their landlords.

8. Item 8: Adequate temperature control.

Examples.   Nonworking vents, fans, and air conditioners, poorly sealed windows and doors in tropical climates during summer. Doors and windows that are not sealed, lack of hot water, and heaters that do not work, in polar climates during winter.

Solutions.   Temperature is too hot: clean vents, buy fans, seal windows and doors from warm drafts, teach caregiver to assertively request landlord to fix or install air conditioner. Temperature is too cold: buy portable heaters, buy blankets, seal windows and doors from cold drafts, tape plastic over windows, teach caregiver to assertively request landlord to fix heater.

Special considerations.   Often these families are not able to afford heating and cooling. In these cases, county resources should be informed of the hazardous conditions. Electric companies may be called to request emergency assistance. Cooling and heating equipment may be purchased inexpensively from the Salvation Army, garage sales, auctions, and flee markets. It may be necessary to teach caregivers assertion skills specific to requesting adequate temperature control from their landlords.

9. Item 9: Adequate food.

Examples. It is very common to see children who have unlimited access to candies, cookies and other nonnutritious foods that are kept on kitchen counters or tables. Indeed, obese children are sometimes allowed to eat whenever and whatever they want. Perhaps even more frequently, rations from all four major food groups (fruits and vegetables, meat and poultry, breads and cereal, milk) may not be found in kitchens. In fact, caregivers often ask their children to fix their own lunches and dinners, which often results in unbalanced meals. Children sometimes get sick from eating spoiled foods.

Solutions. Hide or eliminate candies and other foods with high amounts of sugar, teach the caregiver to prepare meals that include each of the four major food groups. Check kitchen cupboards to make sure all food groups are present. Teach family members to serve appropriate caloric amounts (calorie books are available at most grocery stores). Inspect refrigerators for spoiled foods.

Special considerations. Although the kitchen may be examined to see if foods are spoiled or to see if ample rations of the four major food groups are present, it will be necessary to ask the family about the type and amount of foods eaten. If the family cannot afford adequate foods, then food stamps may be requested at state welfare services.

10. Item 10: Cleanliness.

Examples. Clogged toilets, unbathed children, children with dirty diapers, unswept floors, clothes on the floor, unmade beds, many roaches or other insects, dirty dishes in sinks and around the house, used toothpaste on the bathroom sink, mildew stains on shower curtains; no tooth-brushes, toothpaste, soap, shampoo, and so on.

Solutions. Set up contingency contracts for performance of chores and other cleaning behaviors. Encourage parents to descriptively praise children for their performance of chores and other cleaning behaviors. Encourage family members to flush toilets, wash dishes, do laundry, bathe, clean bathrooms, make beds, vacuum, sweep, change dirty diapers, and brush their teeth. Encourage caregivers to buy toothbrushes, cleaning detergents, and brooms. Teach caregivers to assertively request insect pesticides from landlords.

11. Item 11: Household items.

Examples. Badly stained and worn carpets, sofas, and recliners; broken chairs, drawers, refrigerators, stoves, washing machines, closet doors, beds; holes in walls.

Solutions. Repair or replace broken items, whenever possible (e.g., use hammer and nail to fix broken drawer, fix hole in wall or put a picture in front of the hole). Assertively request landlord to repair or replace broken or worn appliances (e.g., refrigerators), rugs, and damaged property (e.g., holes in walls).

Special Concerns. When caregivers cannot repair broken or worn items, and new replacements are too costly, used replacements may be inexpensively purchased at garage sales, the Salvation Army, and flea markets. Relatives may also be sources from which to obtain used replacements.

12. Item 12: Adequate toys.

Examples.   Deflated balls, toys that are developmentally inappropriate (e.g., a 9-year-old riding a tricycle). Bikes with flat tires. No batteries for battery-operated toys. Board games with missing parts. Toys are absent. Family members do not know how to play organized games.

Solutions.   Encourage/teach caregivers to play games that do not require toys (e.g., tag, hide and go seek, Simon says, football, basketball). Fix broken or incomplete toys or board games (e.g., blow up deflated balls, make fake money for board games). Teach/encourage caregivers to buy age-appropriate toys as rewards for desired behaviors. Buy batteries for battery operated toys.

13. Item 13: Adequate children books.

Examples.   No books. Books that are not age appropriate. Books that are excessively worn or broken.

Solutions.   Encourage caregivers to read to their younger children. Encourage caregivers to help children write or draw their own books. Encourage caregivers to buy new or used books that are age-appropriate. Used books may be purchased very inexpensively at the Salvation Army, garage sales, and flea markets; new books may be solicited from established book stores (i.e., charitable donations). Books may also be borrowed from relatives and libraries or obtained from local charities (e.g., United Way, churches).

14. Item 14: Adequate clothing.

Examples.   Less than three outfits. Clothes do not fit, or are out of style. Clothes are dirty. Clothes are inappropriate (e.g., an adolescent girl wearing a "see-through" blouse, concert shirts with satanic symbols).

Solutions.   Encourage caregivers to take children clothes shopping (new or used) and allow older children to select their own clothes as rewards for performance of desired behaviors. Encourage caregivers to wash laundry at least once per week. Encourage/teach older children to wash laundry, and wear appropriate clothing. Encourage children to borrow or trade clothes with relatives, peers, or friends.

15. Item 15: Adequate decor.

Examples.   Lack of wall decorations (e.g., family pictures, posters). Inappropriate pictures from the wall (e.g., nude pictures on bedroom ceilings and walls, satanic pictures). Outdated wallpaper, and ceilings that need to be painted.

Solutions.   Encourage family members to put decorations on the wall (e.g., good report cards, posters, family pictures). Encourage family members to remove inappropriate pictures on the wall. Encourage family members to tear off out-dated wall paper and paint their home, when necessary. Encourage family members to grow plants in their home.

C. Presenting a rationale for home safety and beautification to the family.
   1. Provide a brief rationale for home safety and beautification that includes the following:
      a. The average household contains many potential hazards that are overlooked by family members.
      b. Hazards are situations in which someone may get hurt.
      c. Home accidents are a leading cause of death and injury for children.
      d. Home safety and beautification may enhance pride and self-esteem in the family.
      e. With the caregiver's permission, the clinician and entire family will tour the home to praise efforts to have a safe, stimulating, and beautiful home, and to identify methods to further improve home safety, stimulation, and beautification.
      f. Room(s) may be excluded from the tour if the caregiver wishes, although it is recommended that all rooms be examined.
         For example: "The average American home contains many potential hazards that family members are not aware of. Hazards, as you may know, are situations that lead to someone getting hurt. In fact, home accidents are one of the leading causes of death and injury for children. Safe, stimulating, and clean homes lead to pride and raise self-esteem. Therefore, with your permission we will go through different rooms of your home and point out things that you have done to make your home safe, stimulating, and beautiful. We will also identify other ways to further improve the safety and beauty of your home. If you like we can skip one or more rooms in your house. However, I highly recommend that we tour all rooms. Many families have reported great satisfaction with this procedure, and I think it will be particularly effective with your family because you all have a great deal of pride in your own performance."
D. Motivating family members for home safety and beautification.
   1. To enhance motivation, perform the following:
      a. Ask the family why it would be important to perform safety and beautification tours of the home.
      b. Praise family members for responses that suggest it is important to perform these tours.
      c. Ask caregiver if there are any rooms in the house that should be "off-limits."
      d. Ask caregiver if the safety tour should be implemented immediately or during the next session, and then implement the procedure accordingly (caregivers typically choose the next session so that the house may be cleaned).
         For example: "Why would it be important to perform home safety and beautification tours? (Caregiver's response) That's exactly right. Your family will be safer. Are there any rooms that you would like to omit from these tours? (caregiver's response) I think it's wonderful that you want to tour the whole house. You obviously have a lot of pride in your home. Would you prefer to start the tours today or next week? (caregiver's response) Great, we'll start next week."

E. Home safety and beautification tours.
    1. Complete the Home Safety and Beautification form (see Table 9.4), according to the following guidelines:
        a. Record the family name and date at the bottom of the Home Safety and Beautification form.
        b. Record all rooms, closets, and storage areas of the home that are not already listed in the upper row (e.g., additional bedrooms, garage, living room, study).
        c. Do not include rooms that the caregiver wants to have excluded from the tours.
            For example: "Here is a copy of the Home Safety and Home Beautification form. I will record the date and name of your family at the bottom. I also need to record all rooms, including storage areas and closets. I already have the kitchen, bathroom, dining area, closet, and two bedrooms listed. What other rooms, storage areas, and closets did I miss?"
    2. For each room, perform the following for each safe, clean, and stimulating item listed in the Home Safety Beautification form.
        a. Descriptively praise family members for preventing possible hazards, being clean, or providing children with a stimulating home environment.
            For example: "This bedroom is beautiful. I really like how you put your medications on top of your dresser in a child-proof container. There certainly are no cleaning detergents, paints, or other dangerous toxins left out in this room. Johnny, you must really be proud of your father."
        b. For each room record a check mark (or smiley face) for items that are safe, clean, or stimulating.
            For example: "I'll put a big smiley face in the bedroom column for Toxins."
        c. When hazards, messes, or lack of stimulation are identified, ask family members what is deleterious, but only after the family is descriptively praised for something that was done correctly for that same item.
            For example: "Putting the dresser in front of the electrical outlet is an excellent idea because Johnny can't put a metal object in the outlet and electrocute himself. What is dangerous about this outlet?"
        d. Descriptively praise family members for identifying deleterious circumstances.
            For example: "I agree, Mr. Jones. It would be very easy for your son to stick his finger in this electrical outlet."
        e. Ask the family how they can remedy possible hazards, messes, or lack of stimulation.
            For example: "How can you prevent this outlet from being dangerous?"
            1. If a family member suggests an appropriate method, provide descriptive praise, and then help the caregiver implement the suggested method.
                For example: "Putting a cover plate on this outlet sounds great. Let's put this night stand in front of the outlet until you buy a cover plate. You can buy a green one to match your wall for about 50 cents."
            2. If family members do not suggest an appropriate method, praise effort, and then provide a solution. Then ask the caregiver if s/he approves of this method, or can think of a better solution.

For example: "So you tried a cover plate, but it didn't fit because the outlet is broken. You certainly are trying to make your home safer. Well, let's get the landlord to turn off the power and put electrical tape around the wires. Until then we can move this night stand over a little bit so that Johnny can't get to it. If this isn't okay, can you think of something better?"

      a) If the caregiver accepts the clinician's solution, help the family members implement the solution.

      b) If the caregiver does not accept the clinician's suggestion, provide another suggestion until one is accepted or a family member states a method that is appropriate. Then help the family implement the solution.

  f. If a hazard, mess, or lack of stimulation is unable to be corrected immediately, instruct family members to perform behaviors that approximate elimination of deleterious circumstances, and/or make arrangements to eliminate deleterious circumstances.

For example: "I'm so glad that you want to get Johnny more toys at garage sales this weekend. Let's look at the paper to find some garage sales in your area that are selling toys."

3. Prior to exiting each room, ask the family if they can identify additional potential hazards, messes, or lack of stimulating props. If so, descriptively praise family members for their input, and then attempt to initiate amelioration of additional concerns.

For example: "Wow! Mr. Jones, I didn't even notice the cracked window. You really are on top of things. I think replacing the window is an excellent idea. Let's call the landlord after our tour and ask him to fix the window."

F. Monitoring progress.

1. After each tour, record the total number of check marks or smiley faces for each item in the last column, labeled "Total."

2. Reinforce treatment progress.

For example: "This is great! You were able to go from three smiley faces during the first week for no sharp objects to nine smiley faces for each of the last 7 weeks. That's a perfect score, as you have nine rooms in your home. This family has a lot to be proud of."

3. Point out deficient items in the home that require particular attention, and attempt to arrange contingency management, if necessary.

For example: "We need to pay special attention to cleanliness. Your family is not getting smiley faces because the beds are not made. Dad, could you think of anything that Johnny might be able to receive for making his bed, at least until he develops this good habit?"

4. Future tours may decrease in frequency, as the home becomes safe, beautiful, and stimulating.

III. Social Skills To Obstruct Peril (SSTOP)

A. Brief overview of Social Skills To Obstruct Peril (SSTOP).

1. Maltreated children are habitually deficient in social skills that maintain their safety and welfare. SSTOP is a social skills training approach that teaches victims of child abuse to respond to interpersonal situations in their home environments that may lead to danger. The first three skills (i.e., appropriate response to being teased, appropriate response to an aggressive threat, appropriate response to having a possession taken without asking) may be utilized with peers and siblings, and the fourth skill (i.e., appropriate response to an offer to leave with a stranger) is pertinent to strangers. Clinicians teach each skill via role-playing at-risk situations that are generated with the target child. The skills are applicable to all children and adolescents, although clinicians must be sensitive to developmental norms. The Social Skills To Obstruct Peril form may be utilized to monitor progress (see Table 9.5).

B. Item 1: Appropriate response to being teased.

   1. Provide a brief rationale that includes the following:

      a. Sometimes teasing leads to sad feelings and physical confrontations that result in injury.

      b. An example in which teasing led to injury (examples should be age-appropriate).

      c. The child will be taught to respond to teasing.

> For example: "Kids sometimes say mean things to each other. This is too bad because teasing makes people angry and upset, and may even lead to someone getting hurt. For example, the other day I saw a child punch his older sister in the eye after she called him stupid, and then he wasn't allowed to go to the movies that night. I also know a child who pushed his friend off a porch after his friend kept singing liar, liar, pants on fire. The child who was pushed cut his leg, and the other boy was not allowed to play outside for a whole week. I'm going to teach you how to deal with other kids when they tease you so that you don't ever get hurt like the children I just mentioned. I think you're going to learn quickly because you're smart."

   2. Ask the child to disclose a situation in which s/he was teased, including what was said, and how the target child responded.

      a. If the child is unable to provide a situation in which s/he was teased, ask the child to disclose a situation in which someone else was teased, including what was said, and how the child responded.

TABLE 9.5

Social Skills To Obstruct Peril (SSTOP)

Target Social Skill	Brief Description of Situation Modeled	Smiley Face (if Appropriate Skill Is Demonstrated)
1) Appropriate response to being teased (ignore, nonaggressive attempt to terminate teasing, avoids swears or belittling comments)		
2) Appropriate response to threats of aggression (nonaggressive attempt to terminate/punish assaultive behavior, avoids swears or belittling comments)		
3) Appropriate response to stealing (nonaggressive attempt to get stolen property back, avoids swears or belittling comments)		
4) Appropriate response to an offer to leave with stranger		

Family Name:_____

Date: _____

b. If the child is unable to provide a situation in which someone else was teased, ask the child to disclose a hypothetical situation.

> For example: "What could a girl say to a boy that would be mean?"

3. Descriptively praise any responses that would likely resolve the problem of being teased.

> For example: "I think that you did a great job in telling the teacher that Joe was calling you a weakling. I especially like how you warned him that you would tell the teacher if he didn't stop."

4. Instruct the child to attempt to respond in the same situation. The clinician will model the role of the teasing child.

> For example: "Let's pretend to do what you just told me about. I'll pretend like I'm Joe calling you a weakling, and you be yourself."

5. After the roleplay, descriptively praise any responses that would likely resolve the problem of being teased.

> For example: "I thought you did a marvelous job. When I called you a weakling the first time, you started to walk away. I kept calling you weakling, and you went to tell the teacher what I was doing so that she could help solve the problem."

6. Ask the target child and caregiver what they liked about the target child's performance, and then suggest behaviors that might further improve the child's performance, modeling whenever necessary.

> For example: "What did you all like about the way Johnny responded to being teased that time? (caregiver's response) I also thought he kept his cool and didn't swear at me. Johnny, the next time we try this I want you to try and solve the problem with the teaser before telling your teacher. Give him a warning. You could even tell him that he probably didn't mean to make you upset but that if he continues you will have to tell the teacher. Here, let me show you what I mean."

7. Instruct the target child to role play the same situation, utilizing the clinician's suggestions.

> For example: "Let's try that situation again, and this time I want you to give me a warning just like the one I did."

8. After the role play, descriptively praise any responses that would likely resolve the problem of being teased, and risk of danger.

> For example: "That was so much better. You told me that you didn't want to, but if I kept teasing you, then you would have to tell the teacher. Your face was like a robot when I was teasing you. That was great."

9. When the situation is appropriately performed by the child, the clinician should record a smiley face in the Social Skills to Obstruct Peril monitoring form, including a brief description of the situation.

10. In the remaining therapy sessions, the target child should practice how to respond to teasing following the following guidelines.
    a. Extent of practice should occur as needed.
    b. Each situation role-played should be generated by the child.
    c. Each situation should include a different perpetrator (i.e., peers, siblings).

      d. The clinician should provide hypothetical situations whenever the child is unable to do so.

C. Item 2: Appropriate response to an aggressive threat.

  1. Provide a brief rationale that includes the following:

      a. Injury may result in consequent aggressive threats.

      b. An example in which an aggressive threat led to injury.

      c. The child will be taught to effectively respond to threats of aggression.

> For example: "Children sometimes get hurt after other kids threaten to hurt them. For example, I remember a time when a neighborhood bully said he was going to punch a smaller boy. This got the smaller boy angry, and he called the bully a jerk. The bully got upset and gave the smaller boy a bloody nose. In this situation, the boy could have done things that may have stopped the bully from hitting him. I'm going to teach you things that may be done when someone threatens you. I think you're going to learn quickly because you're very smart."

  2. The procedures depicted in steps "B2" to "B10" (i.e., teaching child to respond to teasing) should be utilized to teach the target child to appropriately respond to aggressive threats.

D. Item 3: Appropriate response to having a possession taken without asking.

  1. Provide a brief rationale that includes the following:

      a. Injury may result when things are taken without permission.

      b. An example in which taking a possession without asking led to injury.

      c. The child will be taught to effectively respond to children who take possessions without asking.

> For example: "Sometimes children get hurt when things are taken without asking the owner for permission. For example, last week a boy punched his neighbor in the arm for taking his radio. She then kicked him in the knee, and he had to go to the doctor's office. The next skill will help you react to people when they take something that is yours without asking you for permission. I think you're going to do this one really good, because you're good at keeping your cool."

  2. The procedures depicted in steps "B2" to "B10" (i.e., teaching child to respond to teasing) should be utilized to teach the target child to appropriately respond to having a possession taken without asking.

E. Item 4: Appropriate response to a stranger's offer.

  1. Provide a rationale that includes the following:

      a. A stranger is someone that is not known by the target child or his/her caregivers (stated to young children only).

      b. Harm may result when children accept offers to go places, or accept things from strangers.

      c. An example in which accepting an offer from a stranger led to harm (the example should reflect age of child).

      d. The child will be taught to effectively respond to offers from strangers.

> For example. "A stranger is someone that you or your parents don't know very well. Most people that children or their parents don't know are nice, but sometimes they are not. Sometimes kids get hurt if they accept offers to go

places or do things with strangers. Some strangers try to get children to go into their cars or places where nobody lives so that they can take the children away from their families, or make them do things they don't want to do. Sometimes strangers even give children candy and other things that make them sick. I'm going to teach when strangers are probably not nice, and what to do when strangers offer you things, or ask you to do things with them."

2. The procedures depicted in steps "B2" to "B10" (i.e., teaching child to respond to teasing) should be utilized to teach the target child to appropriately respond to a strangers offer.

SAFE POINT SYSTEM

I. Brief Overview

A1. Many children who have been victims of child abuse engage in delinquent behavior. The following point system may be utilized with children who are experiencing problems with their conduct, and who are at least 10 years of age. The point system is designed to teach caregivers to consistently reward their children for completion of prosocial behaviors that are incompatible with delinquent behaviors. Briefly, the child receives points for engaging in these behaviors, and these points may then be exchanged for reinforcers.

II. Brief Rationale

A. Provide a brief rationale for the point system that includes the following:
   1. The caregiver and youth have expressed a dissatisfaction with the reinforcers they receive from one another.
   2. The youth will earn points for performing behaviors desired by the caregiver.
   3. The caregiver will provide selected reinforcers to the youth in exchange for these points.
   4. Efficacy of the point system.

> For example: "You have both told me that you are dissatisfied with the reinforcement that you receive from one another. The procedure you are about to learn is called the point system. Your child will be given points for doing things that you would like him to do. He will then be able to exchange these points for things that he wants and you are able to provide. Studies indicate that this procedure is extremely effective in enhancing family relationships in situations similar to your own. Do you have any questions?"

III. Interview with Caregiver

A. Adolescent List of Benefits.
   1. Hand the youth the Adolescent List of Benefits form (see Table 9.6).
   2. Instruct the youth to go to the waiting room and complete the following:

TABLE 9.6

List of Benefits

Suggested List of Benefits	Rating (0 to 100)	How Often Could Caregiver Provide These (Daily, Weekly, Monthly)
1. Use of the car for ___hours	>_____	>_____
2. ___Money for shopping spree (i. e., clothes etc.)	>_____	>_____
3. Paid school lunch	>_____	>_____
4. Prepared favorite dessert	>_____	>_____
5. Invite for sleepover/friend	>_____	>_____
6. Nondrug/alcohol party at home	>_____	>_____
7. Buy a pet	>_____	>_____
8. Wash laundry	>_____	>_____
9. Caregiver bakes a cake or cookies	>_____	>_____
10. Provided transportation to a desired place within ___ miles	>_____	>_____
11. Scuba, sport, or fitness club membership	>_____	>_____
12. Sleep overnight at approved friend's house	>_____	>_____
13. Trip to ___with family	>_____	>_____
14. Caregivers do _____chore	>_____	>_____
15. ____ minutes of long distance on phone	>_____	>_____
16. One month phone payments for own phone	>_____	>_____
17. Eat out at a favorite restaurant	>_____	>_____
18. Presents (i. e., c.d.'s, etc.)	>_____	>_____
19. Privacy time	>_____	>_____
20. To _____.	>_____	>_____

Additional Benefits	Rating (0 to 100)	How Often Could Caregiver Provide These (Daily, Weekly, Monthly)
1. _____	>_____	>_____
2. _____	>_____	>_____
3. _____	>_____	>_____
4. _____	>_____	>_____
5. _____	>_____	>_____

    a. Check all items that s/he would like to receive, or receive more often.

    b. Next to each desired reinforcer, rate (on a scale of 0 to 100) how important it is to receive the chosen reinforcers (0 = *completely unrewarding*, 100 = *completely rewarding*).

    c. Tell the youth to add to the list any privileges or benefits that were not listed, and to rate these items on the same 0 to 100 scale.

B. Review target behaviors with caregiver.

    1. After the youth is excused, refer the caregiver to an uncompleted copy of the Point System Recording Sheet (see Table 9.7).

    2. Tell the caregiver that all listed behaviors (far left column) have been associated with nondelinquent, drug-free behavior and as such they will become the main targeted behaviors in therapy.

    3. Refer to Item 1, and tell the caregiver that the youth will earn a check for attending all scheduled classes at school, then perform the following guidelines:

        a. Record all current subjects for which the youth is enrolled in school, and the dates for the upcoming week, in the Attendance Sheet (see Table 9.8).

TABLE 9.7

SAFE Point System Recording Sheet

Date	M	T	W	T	F	S	S	M	T	W	T	F	S	S
1. Attended all classes at school for the day (earn a ✔)														
2. No signs of drug use (earn a ✔)														
3. 15 min with caregiver/day (earn a ✔)														
4. Caregiver informed of whereabouts at all times. (earn a ✔)														
5. On time for curfew (earn a ✔)														
6. ___Mins. of homework (1 pt.)														
7. Good test or quiz (1–4 pts.)														
8. Good report card grade (7–28 pt.)														
9. Introduce friend to caregiver (3 min. conversation) (1 pt.)														
10. Counseling (3 pt.)														
11. 5 min. Review of Day (1 pt.)														
12. (pt.)														
13. (pt.)														
14. (pt.)														
15. (pt.)														
16. (pt.)														
17. (pt.)														
18. (pt.)														
19. (pt.)														
20. Planning Day (1 pt.)														
Daily point total														
Less points exchanged for rewards														
Cumulative total of points earned														

TABLE 9.8

Attendance Sheet

Course	Mon.	Tues.	Wed.	Thurs.	Fri.

This student is trying to improve his/her attendance. If this student attended your class for the day, please sign your name in the box corresponding to the course that you teach, and the day of attendance, including any comments you feel are noteworthy.

b. Tell caregiver that validation of school attendance will consist of having each teacher sign the Attendance Sheet on a daily basis. Teacher(s) will give the signed copy to the youth, which will then be given to the caregiver during the point review later that evening.

c. If the form is lost, the youth will not earn a check for the day that it is lost. However, until a new form is obtained, the youth may construct his/her own form to record teacher signatures for classes attended.

d. The caregiver should call the school once per week to validate the authenticity of signatures.

e. If the youth is not attending school, inform the caregiver that the youth will be given a check for completion of one of the following:

    1. _ hours of employment (validated with pay stub).

    2. Completion of an employment application (must be copied for validation).

    3. Completion of work around the house (job duties to be determined by caregiver).

f. If the youth is not attending school due to weekends, summer vacation, or holidays, the youth should earn an check for the day without attending school.

4. Refer to Item 2, and tell the caregiver that the youth will earn a check for being drug and alcohol free for the day, and then review the following guidelines:

a. Signs of drug use may include finding drug items in the youth's room or in his/her possession (e.g., drugs, roach clips), or physical signs of intoxication (e.g., red eyes, slurred speech, unsteadiness).

b. Model the previous drug signs for caregiver (if necessary).

c. Ask the caregiver if any signs of drug use were omitted, and provide feedback for accuracy of responding.

5. Refer to Item 3, and tell the caregiver that the youth will earn a check for spending more than 15 minutes per day with the caregiver, and then review the following guidelines:

a. It is important to reward this behavior because it will provide opportunities to practice communication skills.

b. More time with the youth will provide opportunities to inquire about the youth's day, and learn more about the youth.

c. Instruct the caregiver to talk about things that interest the youth during these times.

6. Refer to Item 4, and tell the caregiver that the youth will earn a check for disclosing his/her whereabouts throughout the day when outside the home, then review the following guidelines:

a. The youth must tell the caregiver where s/he will be during the evening *before* "going out."

b. If plans change, the youth must call the caregiver to ask if it would be possible to change plans.

c. Caregivers must be given the telephone numbers of all destinations, in case of emergency.

d. The caregivers should randomly call, or visit, the youth at least two times per week to verify the youth's whereabouts (automatic "call back" may also be used if the caregiver has this telephone accessory).

e. The caregivers should listen for signs of intoxication during the phone calls. If intoxication is suspected, perform the following:
1. Ask the youth where s/he is located, and make arrangements to have the youth come home (e.g., taxi, sober friend, caregiver).
2. Do not criticize the youth for drinking/drug use. Instead, the caregiver should provide discipline during the next day.

7. Refer to Item 5, tell the caregiver that the youth will earn a check for being on time for curfew, then perform the following guidelines:
a. Ask the caregiver to disclose the youth's curfew time, and then record this time next to Item 5.
b. If there is no curfew, the clinician should ask the caregiver to record a curfew time for each of the 7 nights per week.
c. The clinician may have to problem solve appropriate curfew times based on the history of the youth.
1. If the youth later disagrees with this curfew time, a time should be mutually determined via compromise.

8. Tell the caregiver that if the youth performs any of these first five behaviors prior to curfew, s/he will receive a check mark in the box corresponding to the targeted behavior that was performed and the day that it occurred. The youth will also be given 1 point, and an opportunity to earn additional points for that day. Thus, the youth must perform these five behaviors in order to earn points for the day.

9. Refer the caregiver to Item 6, and ask how many minutes of homework the child performs each day on average, then review the following guidelines with the caregiver.
a. If the child is doing no homework presently, write 15 minutes next to Item 6 on the recording sheet. Explain to the caregiver that the child will earn 1 point for each 15 minutes of homework completion.
b. If the child is performing homework presently, fill in the daily average next to Item 6 on the recording sheet.
c. If the caregiver wants more homework to be performed in order to earn 1 point, explain that it is necessary to start with an amount that will assure success, and gradually increase the required time as the youth becomes more responsible.
d. The student must perform the following guidelines to receive a point for homework:
1. The caregiver must have opportunities to inquire as to any difficulties the youth might be having with homework, and to verify that the child is on task.
2. Ideally, the youth should study in a room with no distractions (e.g., no television, no radio, no company). However, it may be necessary to include these incentives initially, and gradually fade them out.

10. Refer to Item 7, and tell the caregiver that the youth will earn points for improving test or quiz grades, then perform the following:
a. Record in the Point Values for Tests and Quizzes Chart (see Table 9.9) all courses at school for which the youth is currently enrolled.
b. For each course, record the point values that would be obtained for an "A," "B," "C," and "D" according to the following guidelines.

TABLE 9.9
Point Values for Tests and Quizzes Chart

Courses	A	B	C	D

1. One point will be earned for each test or quiz that is one letter grade above the most recent report card grade for that subject (e.g., A child who received an "F" in math for the last report card would be given one point for obtaining a "D" on a quiz or test in math).
2. Similarly, two points will be earned for tests or quizzes that are two letter grades above the most recent report card grade for that subject.
3. Three points for tests or quizzes that are three letter grades above the last report card grade for that subject.
4. Four points for tests or quizzes that are four letter grades above the last report card grade.

   c. Tell the caregiver that for each test or quiz that is brought home in the future, the youth will earn the amount of points listed in the Point Values for Tests and Quizzes chart for that subject.

   d. Quiz the caregiver on a few hypothetical quiz grades to determine if the caregiver knows how many points should be provided.

11. Refer to Item 8, and tell the caregiver that the child will earn more points for improved report card grades, then perform the following:

   a. Record all courses at school for which the child is currently enrolled in the Point Values for Report Card Grades chart.

   b. For each course, record the point values that would be obtained for an "A," "B," "C," and "D" in the Point Values for Report Card Grades chart, according to the following guidelines.

      1. The youth will receive 7 points for each report card grade that is one letter grade above the last report card grade for that subject (e.g., The youth would receive 7 points for obtaining a "D" in Math on a report card if an "F" was earned for the most recent report card).

      2. Fourteen points will be given for report card grades that are two letter grades above the most recent report card.

3. Twenty-one points will be earned for report card grades that are three letter grades above the most recent report card.

4. Twenty-eight points will be earned for report cards that are four letter grades above the most recent report card.

c. Tell the caregiver that for each report card grade that is brought home in the future, the child will earn the amount of points listed in the table for that subject.

d. Quiz the caregiver on a few hypothetical report card grades to determine if the caregiver knows how many points should be provided.

For example: "How many points would Johnny receive if he brought home a "B" in math on his next report card?"

12. Refer to Item 9, and tell the caregiver that the youth will receive one point for introducing a friend to the caregiver, and then tell the caregiver the following:

a. This will provide an opportunity to descriptively praise the youth's friends that appear to be "good influences."

b. It is likely that many of the youth's friends will be delinquent and/or substance abusers initially. When these persons are introduced it will be important to descriptively praise their positive qualities and ignore their negative qualities (e.g., If a friend uses drugs and is truant from school but works full-time, the youth could be praised for being a hard worker).

c. If the caregiver is critical to these persons, the youth may surreptitiously spend time with the undesired friend, and thus be unsupervised.

13. Refer to Item 10, and tell the caregiver that the youth will receive points for attending therapy sessions because this will help make therapy a reinforcer.

a. 3 points will be earned for active participation and compliance throughout session.

b. Two points will be earned or satisfactory participation, and compliance throughout most of the session.

c. One point will be earned for attendance, albeit poor participation.

14. Refer to Item 11, and tell the caregiver that the youth will earn 1 point for reviewing his or her day at the end of the night for at least 4 minutes.

a. Briefly explain that the review should praise the youth for time spent with "safe" associations (e.g., drug and delinquent-free individuals and activities), and to assist with problem-solving for time spent with "at-risk" associations (e.g., drug-using and delinquent individuals and activities).

15. Refer to Item 12 and 19, and tell the caregiver that the youth will receive points for performance of eight target behaviors (e.g., chores, day without swears) the caregiver would like the youth to perform more often. Then perform the following:

a. Ask for eight primary behaviors that the caregiver would like the youth to perform more often, and record each of these responses next to Items 12 to 19.

b. Behaviors should be observable, and specific.

c. In general, the number of points given for performance of these behaviors will depend on how often these behaviors are desired.

1. Behaviors that are desired on a daily basis = 1 point (e.g., washing dishes).

2. Behaviors that are desired on a weekly basis = 7 points (e.g., washing the laundry).

3. Behaviors that are desired on a monthly basis = 28 points (e.g., tuning up the car).

16. Refer to Item 20, and tell the caregiver that the youth will be given 1 point for performing the Daily Planner (see Table 9.10) because this will allow the caregiver to reinforce prosocial desires. Then explain the following guidelines:

   a. In order to earn this point the youth must have scheduled his/her day with nondelinquent, prosocial activities during the preceding day or night.

   b. Plans should be recorded in the the Daily Planner.

   c. Each hour of the day must have an activity scheduled in order to receive the point.

   d. Plans that change should be discussed with the caregiver during the point review.

C. Obtain all reinforcers the caregiver is capable of providing the youth.

   1. Go to the room where the youth is completing the List of Benefits, and briefly answer any questions the youth may have.

   2. Obtain the list from the youth, and go back to where the caregiver is waiting.

   3. Refer the caregiver to the List of Benefits and ask the caregiver how often s/he could provide the reinforcers that were listed by the youth (i.e., daily, weekly, monthly) if the youth were a "perfect child."

      a. If the caregiver states that it is not possible to provide a reinforcer that is listed, tell the caregiver to compromise the reinforcer so that the youth would be able to receive some part/aspect of the reinforcer.

         For example: If the caregiver stated that the youth could not use the car during the night, the caregiver could be asked if the youth could use the car during other times.

TABLE 9.10

Daily Planner

Time	Monday	Tuesday	Wednesday	Thursday	Friday	Saturday	Sunday
6–7 a.m.							
7–8 a.m.							
8–9 a.m.							
9–10 a.m.							
10–11 a.m.							
11–12 p.m.							
12–1 p.m.							
1–2 p.m.							
2–3 p.m.							
3–4 p.m.							
4–5 p.m.							
5–6 p.m.							
6–7 p.m.							
7–8 p.m.							
8–9 p.m.							
9–10 p.m.							
10–11 p.m.							
11–12 p.m.							
12–1 a.m.							
1–2 a.m.							
2–3 a.m.							
3–4 a.m.							
4–5 a.m.							
5–6 a.m.							

4. Next to each selected reinforcer in the List of Benefits, record how often the caregiver could provide the reinforcer.

> For example: mother does laundry = weekly; use of car for 2 hours = daily; supervised overnight party with clean friends = monthly.

5. Additional reinforcers may be obtained in the following manner:
   a. Ask the caregiver if there are any things that were not listed that the youth would enjoy.
   b. Ask the caregiver what the youth enjoys doing that could be made contingent on desired behavior.
   c. Ask the caregiver what the youth complains about, and then convert these responses to reinforcers (e.g., complains about no privacy when on telephone = private phone line for youth).

IV. Interview With Youth

A. Excuse the caregiver, and visit the youth individually so that point values may be assigned.
   1. Review guidelines for targeted behaviors with the youth.
   2. Provide the following rationale:

> For example: "I know that performance of these behaviors will require effort on your part, so I would like to have your caregiver reward these efforts. What I would like to do now is find out more specifically what some of the things are that you enjoy so that I can work out an exchange system that will fairly reward your efforts for performance of the behaviors I just showed you."

   3. Refer to the List of Benefits, and record in the Reinforcement Menu (see Table 9.11) all reinforcers that the youth had marked as 100, and the caregiver stated s/he could provide, utilizing the following guidelines.

TABLE 9.11
Reinforcement Menu

Daily Benefits

1) _____exchange 1 point;	2) _____exchange 1 point
3) _____exchange 1 point;	4) _____exchange 1 point
5) _____exchange 1 point;	6) _____exchange 1 point

Weekly Benefits

1) _____exchange 7 point;	2) _____exchange 7 point
3) _____exchange 7 point;	4) _____exchange 7 point
5) _____exchange 7 point;	6) _____exchange 7 point

Monthly Benefits

1) _____exchange 28 point;	2) _____exchange 28 point
3) _____exchange 28 point;	4) _____exchange 28 point
5) _____exchange 28 point;	6) _____exchange 28 point

Other Benefits

1) _____exchange __ point;	2) _____exchange __ point
3) _____exchange __ point;	4) _____exchange __ point
5) _____exchange __ point;	6) _____exchange __ point

*This contract is in effect from _____ to _____. It will be dropped, extended, or renegotiated _____. Each night at _____ time, we will get together and record earned points for the day, according to the point values agreed upon on the other side of this document. If this chart is not presented to the caregiver by _____p.m. each night, no points will be earned for the day. Privileges will be provided at this time by the caregiver.

Caregiver: _____ Youth: _____

    a. All reinforcers that the caregiver stated could be given on a daily basis should be recorded as "Daily Reinforcers."

    b. All reinforcers that the caregiver stated could be given on a weekly basis should be recorded as "Weekly Reinforcers."

    c. All reinforcers that the caregiver stated could be given on a monthly basis should be recorded as "Monthly Reinforcers."

4. For any reinforcers that were given a score of 60 to 99 by the youth, and the caregiver stated s/he could provide, ask the youth if there is anything that would make this reinforcer a "100."

    a. Any reinforcers that are changed in this manner must be approved by the caregiver before being implemented into the system.

    b. If the youth does not modify the reinforcer, the reinforcer should be added to the Reinforcement Menu, as is.

5. Verbally state all reinforcers that the caregiver said s/he was capable of providing but were not originally listed by the youth (or any reinforcers that were compromised by the caregiver) and perform the following for each reinforcer:

    a. Ask the youth how important it is to receive the reinforcer on a scale of 0 to 100 (100 = *completely rewarding*, 0 = *completely unrewarding*).

    b. Any reinforcers that = 100 should be recorded in the Reinforcement Menu according to the frequency that the caregiver stated s/he could provide the reinforcer (e.g., daily, weekly, or monthly).

    c. For all reinforcers with a score of 60 to 99, ask the youth if there is anything that could make this reinforcer a 100.

        1. Any reinforcers that are enhanced in this manner must be approved by the caregiver before being recorded in the Reinforcement Menu.

        2. Unmodified reinforcers should be recorded in the Reinforcement Menu, as is.

V. The Point Value Exchange

A. Explain contingency exchange to the caregiver and youth.

1. Bring the caregiver back into the room.

2. Tell the youth and caregiver the following:

    a. All reinforcers that the caregiver said s/he could provide on a daily basis will require the exchange of one point.

        1. These reinforcers should be listed in the Daily Benefits section of the Reinforcement Menu.

    b. All reinforcers that the caregiver had said s/he could provide on a weekly basis will require the exchange of 7 points.

        1. These reinforcers should be listed in the Weekly Benefits section of the Reinforcement Menu.

    c. All reinforcers that the caregiver said s/he could provide on a monthly basis will require the exchange of 28 points.

        1. These reinforcers should be listed in the Monthly Benefits section of the Reinforcement Menu.

3. Any reinforcers that the caregiver said s/he could provide at a frequency different from 1 day, 1 week, or 1 month, may be negotiated and added in one of the blank spaces provided at the end of the Reinforcement Menu.
4. Ask the caregiver how much money s/he is able to give the youth each month, if the youth were a perfect child.
   a. Divide the amount of money possible by the amount of days in the month (e.g., if 30 days in the month and $30.00 possible: 30/$30.00 = $1.00).
   b. The result will be the amount of money equal to 1 point (round this amount to the nearest .50 cents to make math easier).
   c. The youth should not be given money directly, if possible. Rather, the amount of money earned should be recorded. When the child wishes to spend the money, the caregiver may buy the child the desired item. This will reduce unaccounted money that may be used for deviant purposes (e.g., drugs).
   d. If it is inconvenient for the caregiver to buy the product, the youth may be given the money directly. However, a receipt should be provided to prove that the product was bought.
   e. Any unaccounted for money will result in a loss of points for the lost amount (e.g., If $5.00 is unaccounted for [no receipt], then the youth will lose 5 points).

VI. Roleplaying the Point System

A. Clinician modeling.
   1. Assuming the role of the caregiver, the clinician should model the role of the caregiver during a point exchange for a hypothetical day.
      a. Refer the caregiver and youth to the SAFE Point System Recording Sheet, and in response to a hypothetical day, begin informing the youth why s/he did or did not receive a check (or point) for each targeted behavior.
      b. Descriptively praise the youth's efforts (whether or not a response was correctly performed).
   2. Add the appropriate number of points earned for the day (if any) to the Daily Point Total row corresponding to the appropriate day.
   3. The clinician should hand the Reinforcement Menu to the youth and ask if there is anything that s/he would like to exchange for the earned points (if points were earned).
   4. Any points that were not exchanged for reinforcers should be transferred to the Cumulative Total of Points Earned row for the day of review.
   5. If no points were earned, the clinician should provide encouragement for the next day.
B. Caregiver and youth rehearse the point exchange.
   1. Instruct the caregiver and youth to role play the day that was just modeled, while the clinician provides descriptive praise and feedback for correct responding.
   2. Instruct the caregiver and youth to role play the present day.
   3. If the caregiver and youth have difficulties with the point exchange (the math in particular), the clinician should instruct the caregiver and youth to practice the point exchange for several hypothetical days.

VII. Review of Point System in Subsequent Sessions

A. Review the previous week
  1. All sessions should begin by reviewing the math in the recording form.
  2. Descriptively praise for accuracy of recording, and completion of targeted behaviors.
  3. Validate that the chosen reinforcers were provided to the youth.
  4. Validate that the caregiver monitored the youth's behavior.
  5. Validate that no reinforcers from the menu were provided noncontingently (e.g., without exchange of points).
  6. Modify the point system (e.g., adding rewards, increasing curfew time) via negotiation between the caregiver and the youth, whenever necessary.
  7. The clinician should instruct the caregiver and youth to role-play targeted behaviors when possible (e.g., "Pretend like your brother is a new friend and introduce me to your mother.").
      a. Of course, the clinician should teach the caregiver and youth skills related to the target behaviors (e.g., how to properly introduce a friend to caregiver).

CATCHING MY CHILD BEING GOOD

I. Brief Overview

A1. It is often necessary to teach caregivers of abused children non-aversive child management procedures. In this endeavor, most behavior clinicians initially teach parents to reinforce their children when desired behaviors occur, and ignore their children when undesired behaviors occur. The Catching My Child Being Good procedure is a standardized method to accomplish this task via instruction, roleplaying, feedback, and therapy assignments.

II. Teaching the Caregiver to Reinforce
Desired Behaviors and Ignore Undesired Behaviors

A. Brief rationale.
  1. Provide a brief rationale that includes the following:
      a. Children often engage in undesired behaviors.
      b. Catching My Child Being Good is an effective disciplinary procedure.
      c. The caregiver will learn to reinforce desired behaviors and ignore undesired behaviors.
      d. Ignoring is not appropriate if the child is destroying property or if someone is at-risk to be hurt.
          For example: "As you know children routinely engage in undesired behaviors. The procedure you are about to learn is called Catching My Child Being Good, and this procedure will help you to reinforce your child when he is performing desired behaviors and ignore him when he is performing undesired behaviors. Of course, you would not ignore him when property is being damaged or he is a threat to hurt himself or others. Later, we will review other disciplines that may be used in these situations. Parents have reported great results with this procedure, and I feel that this procedure will be particularly useful with Johnny because your attention is so important to him."

B. Teaching the caregiver to reinforce desired behavior (target children should not be present).
   1. Instruct the caregiver to list several of the target child's favorite interactive playtime home activities (e.g., playing catch, dolls, blocks, tinker toys, trucks, interactive board games, coloring, talking about music).
   2. Select an activity that is likely to facilitate interaction between the child and caregiver.
   3. Tell the caregiver to pretend as if s/he is the target child engaged in the chosen activity, and utilize instruction and modeling to demonstrate each of the following behaviors:
      a. *Attends*: verbal description of desired behavior.
         For example: "You're moving the car into the garage."
      b. *Descriptive praise*: telling children exactly what they did that was liked.
         For example: "I love how you are driving the car carefully so that no one gets hurt."
      c. *Immediate reinforcement*
      d. *Pleasant affect*: laughing, smiling.
      e. *Tactile reinforcement*: pat on head or back, feeling a child's arm when making a muscle, tickling (be specific as to what is appropriate), hugging, cuddling, bouncing.
      f. *Pleasant tone*: soft, pleasant, conversational tone of voice.
      g. *Incidental teaching*: when the child spontaneously shows interest in something, tell the child something about the object.
         For example: "Yes, that's a boat. Boats sail on the water. Pretend like this is water and sail your boat."
      h. *Ask questions*
         For example: "Do you know where frogs swim?"
      i. *Avoid criticism*
         For example: "It does look a lot like a horse, but that animal is a zebra because it has black stripes."
   4. As the previous techniques are modeled during the roleplay with the caregiver, the clinician should continuously provide descriptive feedback.
         For example: "Mrs. Jones, I love how you are moving the car on all four of its wheels. You are such a good driver. What color is your truck? (caregiver answers "orange") It looks like orange, but this color is yellow. Notice how I told you exactly what I liked about how you were playing with the truck. I asked you what color your truck was, and when you gave me the wrong answer I told you that you were close before I gave you the correct answer. Why was that a good idea? (caregiver's response) Exactly, I want you to learn your colors, and I also didn't want you to feel bad about telling me the wrong answer. So I wasn't critical."
   5. Instruct the caregiver to practice these skills while the clinician pretends to be the child. The clinician should perform the following during the role-play:
      a. Prompt the caregiver to perform specific skills when appropriate.
         For example: "Pat my back while you tell me how great I'm parking my car."
      b. Praise effort.
         For example: "That was a great first try at something that is extremely difficult to learn."

   c. Descriptively praise correct responding.

      For example: "Wow, you really are a fast learner. That's wonderful how you are making eye contact, and have a wonderful smile on your face."

   d. Always descriptively praise before suggesting behavioral change.

      For example: "I really like how you told me that I was doing a nice job with my car. Tell me what exactly I'm doing with the car that you like and that will be a perfect example of descriptive praise."

   e. Model correct responding.

      For example: "It is very important to let me know that you approve of how I'm playing. See how I have a big smile on my face as I tell you that you are moving the car slowly and carefully around the building."

C. Teaching the caregiver to ignore undesired behavior.

  1. Tell the caregiver that it is best to ignore undesired behavior unless the target child:

    a. Is performing, or has performed, a behavior that is harmful to self or others.

    b. Is destroying, or has destroyed, property.

  2. Tell the caregiver that s/he will be taught to use other techniques to discipline the above exceptions.

  3. Instruct the caregiver to assume the role of his/her child in a play interaction, and instruct the caregiver to perform an undesired behavior that typically occurs at home that may be ignored (e.g., sticking out tongue, swearing, throwing objects).

      For example: "Pretend to be Johnny playing with a train, and start doing an undesired behavior that he does when he plays with trains."

  4. During the roleplay, the clinician should ignore undesired behavior utilizing the following guidelines:

    a. Immediately look away.

    b. Face should be emotionless.

    c. Do not talk to the child.

    d. Do not touch the child.

  5. Instruct the caregiver to roleplay ignoring skills while the clinician models the role of a child performing several undesired behaviors that may be ignored.

    a. The clinician should perform the following feedback during the roleplay, when appropriate:

      1. Prompt the caregiver to perform specific skills.

         For example: "As soon as I say that you are a jerk I want you to turn your head and ignore everything I say."

      2. Praise effort.

         For example: "Nice try."

      3. Descriptively praise correct responding.

         For example: "I like how you turned your head completely around, I couldn't even see your face at all."

      4. Provide suggestions to improve performance.

         For example: "I thought you did a marvelous job in turning your head away from me, but remember not to talk to me. That would give me attention for an undesired behavior."

      5. Model correct responding.

For example: "Watch how I turn my entire back and play with this toy as soon as he calls me a jerk."

D. In vivo play interaction with caregiver and target child.
   1. Instruct the caregiver to ask the target child to choose a favorite play activity.
   2. Instruct the caregiver to engage the child in the selected game, and practice Catching My Child Being Good.
   3. Descriptively praise appropriate responding and offer suggestions to further improve performance.

   For example: "You're doing a great job telling him exactly what you like. Ask him some questions about what he's doing, and then try to tell him interesting things about what he says."

   4. In each future session instruct the caregiver and child to perfom at least 10 minutes of in vivo play interaction until most techniques are performed correctly without prompting.

E. Therapy assignment.
   1. Give the caregiver a copy of Catching My Child Being Good (see Table 9.12).
   2. Tell the caregiver that it will be necessary to practice reinforcing the target child's desired behaviors each day.
   3. Ask the caregiver to disclose two 15-minute time periods that are convenient to practice catching the target child being good and record these times in the Catching My Child Being Good recording form.
   4. Tell the caregiver to record the following information after each home practice session:
      a. Time the activity is performed.
      b. Activity performed.

      For example: playing with blocks, playing with cars, listening to music, dancing.

TABLE 9.12

Catching My Child Being Good

	Mon.	Tues.	Wed.	Thurs.	Fri.	Sat.	Sun.
Time:							
Activity:							
How Did I Catch My Child Being Good?							
Time:							
Activity:							
How Did I Catch My Child Being Good?							

     c. Brief description of outstanding methods used to catch the target child being good. For example: called him smart, patted him on the back of his head.

  5. Instruct the caregiver to practice the recording process by recording the in vivo play interaction that was just performed in session with the child.

  6. Provide praise for correct recording, and make suggestions to improve recording.

F. Review of homework in subsequent sessions.

  1. Ask the caregiver to describe several interactions from the preceding week. If the homework sheet is incomplete, instruct the caregiver to retrospectively complete the responses.

  2. Provide descriptive praise for all desired behaviors.

     For example: "That's really great how you were able to play the entire game without telling him what to do. I like how you went outside to play catch with him. That must have made him very happy, and you sound like you got a lot out of it, too. Tell me more about the positive things that happened."

  3. Provide solutions to help the caregiver with problems that may have been encountered during homework performance.

     For example: "I think it may help to talk more about your son's interests, and wait until he asks about an interest of yours."

  4. After reviewing homework for Catching My Child Being Good, assign the same homework for the upcoming weeks, or at least until the caregiver is able to establish these skills in the home.

III. The HEARD Procedure

A. Helping caregivers listen to the concerns of their children.

  1. Teaching caregivers to listen to the concerns or interests of their victimized children is difficult as these caregivers have a tendency to provide advice prematurely. The HEARD procedure may be utilized to encourage and support children in solving their own problems.

  2. The HEARD procedure consists of the following steps:

     a. H = Hear all the things the child wants to report (i.e., nod head up and down, maintain eye-contact).

     b. E = Empathize with the child (e.g., "I'm really sorry to hear that. You sound really frustrated.").

     c. A = Alternatives should be elicited from the child (e.g., "What do you think would help to solve this problem?").

     d. R = Review consequences of each alternative (e.g., "What might happen if you do the first thing you thought might work?")

     e. D = Decide on a solution (e.g., "Which one do you want to choose?").

IDENTIFICATION AND ESCAPE FROM AT-RISK SITUATIONS

I. Brief Overview

A1. Victims and perpetrators of child maltreatment frequently do not recognize cues that may indicate when abusive behaviors are forthcoming. In addition, once abuse occurs, children may engage in behaviors that put them at risk to be more severely mistreated. Hence, the purpose of this procedure is to teach children to identify early precursors of abuse, and safely escape from abusive situations. Similarly, a section is dedicated to teaching perpetrators to identify cues that put them at-risk to perform abusive behavior, and engage in behaviors that eradicate abusive interaction. Extreme caution should be exercised when implementing this procedure. Indeed, perpetrators should be thoroughly assessed prior to their involvement in this procedure.

II. Initial Interview With Perpetrator and Significant Other

A. Rationale for treatment.
1. Without the target child being in the room, provide the perpetrator and significant other (if available) with a rationale for treatment that includes the following:
   a. Family members often do not recognize cues that place children at-risk to be physically abused.
   b. The perpetrator will be taught to identify early precursors of abuse and prevent abusive behavior.
   c. Target children will be taught to identify, and escape from, situations that put them at risk to be harmed.
   d. The clinician will rely on the significant other and perpetrator for assistance.
      For example: "Family members often do not recognize things that lead to someone getting hurt. Mr. Jones, the procedure you are about to learn will help you to recognize situations or cues that place you at risk to hurt Johnny. In addition, you will be taught to use techniques to help calm you when Johnny does things that upset you. Johnny will be taught to recognize, prevent, and safely get away from situations that indicate you are likely to hurt him. I will rely on both of you to help me teach Johnny these skills. I feel that these techniques will be especially effective with you, Mr. Jones, because there is a lot of love in this family, and you stated that you don't want anger to get the best of you again."
2. Ask why it would be important for the target child to recognize cues that typically lead to abusive behavior.
   For example: "Tell me why you think it is important for Johnny to recognize things (cues) that usually happen before you lose your temper and use excessive physical punishment."
3. Provide praise for any statements that suggest it is important for the child to recognize cues of violence.
   For example: "You're absolutely right. If the school teacher notices any bruises, she is obligated to tell protective services and you might lose custody of your child."
4. Ask why it may be important for the target child to withdraw from the perpetrator when these cues occur.
   For example: "Why might it be important for Johnny to get away from you when he notices these cues?"
5. Praise statements that suggest it is important to withdraw from the perpetrator when these cues occur.

For example: "You're exactly right. If Johnny doesn't recognize your anger, and remains in your presence, you may actually get more angry and do something you'll regret."

B. Obtaining commitments from the perpetrator and significant other.

   1. Tell the perpetrator and significant other that the escape component may include:

      a. The child going to a safe place (e.g., public locations, a friend or relative's house).

      b. The child calling 911.

> For example: "I will be teaching Johnny to quietly walk away from Mr. Jones when he is at risk to be harmed. Usually, he will walk to another room in the house, or to the yard to play. If he or someone else is in immediate danger, he will be taught to walk to a friend or relative's house. If necessary, as a last resort he will be taught to call 911 at first safe opportunity so that a nonemotionally involved professional may help to sort out things."

   2. Obtain a commitment from the perpetrator and significant other that they will assist with escape routes.

> For example: "Mr. and Mrs. Jones, I would like you both to help Johnny to safely avoid Mr. Jones when at risk cues occur. Can I count on you both to assist me with this plan?"

   3. If the perpetrator does not want to assist, perform the following:

      a. Empathize with any concerns the perpetrator may have, and/or attempt to resolve concern.

      b. Explain that other perpetrators have initially experienced similar concerns but have later expressed satisfaction.

      c. Tell the perpetrator to state two or three negative consequences that might result from abusive behavior, and provide empathy after each consequence is disclosed.

> For example: "I see your point. It would be embarrassing to have the police come to your home. Many caregivers have stated that they do not want the police to know about their private business. However, these same persons have reported satisfaction after receiving this treatment. Remember, Johnny will be instructed to call 911, or go to a friend or relative's house, only if all other techniques have failed. Earlier in therapy you told me several negative consequences that might occur if you hit Johnny. Tell me about one of these consequences. (caregiver's response) That's right, Mr. Jones. You love your child so much. It would terrible for you if protective services removed Johnny from your home. What other things would happen if you hit Johnny? (caregiver's response) Unfortunately that is also true. You probably would have to go to jail. Jails are a terrible place to stay, and as you mentioned, you might get raped. I don't want to see that happen to you."

   4. If the perpetrator continues to express a desire to avoid participation, the clinician should state that it is hoped that the perpetrator will change his/her mind, but until that time the clinician will work with the target child and significant other alone (Elicit perpetrator's permission in doing so, if appropriate). Then excuse the perpetrator from the room, and do not include the perpetrator in this procedure.

> For example: "I understand your concern, Mr. Jones. I hope you decide to change your mind and participate in this aspect of the program. Until that time, I will have to work with Johnny and Mrs. Jones. Do you mind if I ask your son and wife to practice things they can do in these situations?"

C. Elicit precursors of abuse-associated behavior from the perpetrator and significant other.
1. Provide a rationale for the at-risk list that includes the following:
   a. At-risk cues often precede excessive physical punishment (harm).
   b. A list of common at-risk cues will be read although some may not apply.
   c. The perpetrator, child, or both, may be responsible for the occurrence of these cues. However, the task is to learn how to eliminate these interactions, not to find fault.

   > For example: "I'm about to read some things that often occur before parents lose their tempers and/or hit their children. I will call these things at-risk cues because when they happen children are at risk to be harmed. These cues may have been performed by Mr. Jones, Johnny, or both of you. However, I don't want to spend our time pointing fingers. Instead, I want to identify the cues that do apply to your family so that we may learn how to eliminate risk if these situations occur."

2. For each cue in the Common At-Risk Cues column of the At-Risk Cues form (see Table 9.13), ask if the cue has occurred in the home, and if so, circle each endorsed cue that was, or had potential to be, associated with violence.
   a. The clinician should utilize information gathered in the assessment to make cues applicable.
   b. The clinician should generalize cues to broader contexts whenever possible.

TABLE 9.13

Common At-Risk Cues

Common At-Risk Cues	At-Risk Situations
a. Kicking or hitting walls/objects	_____
b. Drinking or drugging	_____
c. Throwing/breaking objects	_____
d. Arguments	_____
e. Hitting others	_____
f. Threats	_____
g. Screaming	_____
h. Swearing	_____
i. Derogatory (bad) statements	_____
j. Not doing what is asked	_____
Other At-Risk Cues	_____
1.	_____
2.	_____
3.	_____
4.	_____
5.	_____
6.	_____

For example: "The first cue is hitting or kicking a wall or object. This is a common cue, and I know that Johnny punched a hole in the door about a year ago. Have any walls, doors, or other objects been kicked or hit by you, your wife, or your children?"

3. After all cues are reviewed in the list, ask if there are any cues that were not listed, and if so, record these cues in the Other At-Risk Cues column.

4. For each endorsed cue, ask for a brief description of a recent situation in which the cue occurred.

> For example: "Very briefly, tell me about the most recent situation in which a wall or object was hit in this home."

5. Record an abbreviated description of each situation in the At-Risk Situations column corresponding to the respective cue (just enough information to recognize the situation later in the session).

> For example: Dad, kick TV, mad Johnny didn't lower it

6. Praise the perpetrator and significant other for their effort, and then excuse them from the room and visit the target child individually.

> For example: "You were both wonderful in helping me identify at-risk cues. I would now like to speak with Johnny to teach him about the things we talked about earlier."

III. Initial Interview With the Target Child

A. Provide a rationale for treatment.

1. Without the significant other or perpetrator in the room, provide a treatment rationale to the child that includes:

   a. A statement that the perpetrator wants help in decreasing excessive physical punishment (harmful behaviors).

   b. A statement that removes blame from the child.

   c. A statement that the child will be taught to remain safe and/or safely retreat from the perpetrator during at risk situations.

   > For example: "Your daddy told me that he gets angry sometimes, and does things that he regrets, like throwing things at you, and punching you. Your daddy realizes that these things hurt you very much, and he wants me to help him so that this doesn't happen anymore. It's not your fault that he does these things, but until your daddy is better, I will teach you to safely get away from him or be safe when he is first starting to get angry or upset. Other children have said that this helps them a lot, and I think you're going to do great."

B. Elicit precursors of physical abuse from the child.

1. Tell the target child that a number of cues will be read that put the child in danger.

   > For example: "I'm going to read you a bunch of things that may lead to danger. We'll call these at-risk cues because when they happen you are at-risk to be hurt by your father."

2. For each endorsed at-risk cue in the Common At-Risk Cues column, read the cue to the child and utilize its corresponding situation to teach the child that this cue may signal danger.

For example: "Your daddy said that when he punches or kicks things he is really upset. He told me about a time when he kicked the TV because you didn't turn it down. If he kicks the TV, or any other object, he is angry and more likely to do something that he will regret, like hit you."

3. For each cue that *was not* endorsed by the perpetrator or significant other, ask the child if the cue ever occurred.

For example: "Have you ever seen your dad drink alcohol or use drugs?"

    a. If so, circle the cue, and ask the child to briefly describe a recent situation involving the at-risk cue.

    b. Record an abbreviated description of the situation (just enough information to recognize the situation later in the session) in the At-Risk Situations column corresponding to the cue, if the cue was associated, or could have been associated with violence.

For example: Came home wobbling, tripped on toy, eyes red, talked funny.

    c. Inform the child that this cue places the child at risk to be abused utilizing its corresponding situation.

For example: "You can tell your dad is drinking because he doesn't walk straight, his eyes get red, and he talks funny. When you see this happen you are more likely to get hurt because he pushed you over the couch last week when he was drunk and he may do that again."

    d. Praise the child for identifying the situation.

For example: "I'm glad you were able to tell me about the time he pushed you over the couch."

4. After all cues are reviewed with the child, ask the child to disclose other at-risk cues that were not listed.

For example: "Are there any other things that have happened before your father has hurt you, or tried to hurt you?"

    a. Record each new cues in the "Other Risks" column.

    b. For each new cue, obtain a recent situation in which the cue had preceded abusive behavior, and record the situation in the "At-Risk Situations" column corresponding to the at-risk cue.

    c. Inform the child that this cue places the child at-risk to be abused utilizing its corresponding situation.

    d. Praise the child for disclosing the situation.

IV. Interview With Significant Other, Perpetrator, and Child

A. Praise commitments to perform the treatment procedure.

1. Bring the significant other, perpetrator, and child into the same room.
2. Praise the perpetrator for wanting to help the child recognize, and safely retreat from, at-risk cues.
3. Praise the significant other for wanting to help the clinician teach the child to retreat from at-risk cues.
4. Prompt the perpetrator to tell the child why it is important to safely retreat from the perpetrator when these situations occur.

5. Praise the perpetrator for any responses that indicate the importance of a safe retreat (provide prompts if the perpetrator is unable to provide these responses).
6. Instruct the perpetrator to leave the room with the secondary clinician to practice behaviors that will decrease risk.
    a. If a secondary clinician is not available, the clinician should work with the child and significant other first.
7. Instruct the significant other and child to remain in the room with the primary clinician to practice behaviors that decrease danger in at-risk situations.

V. Interview With Perpetrator

A. Teach the perpetrator what to do when at-risk cues occur.
    1. Ask the perpetrator why it would be important to immediately attempt to terminate anger after recognizing an at-risk cue.
        a. Praise the perpetrator for statements that suggest anger should be eliminated after recognition of an at-risk cue.
        b. Provide prompts to suggest that anger should be eliminated after recognizing at-risk cues, whenever necessary.
    2. Read the first at-risk cue and situation, and then ask what negative consequences occurred after this cue.
        For example: "Mr. Jones, the first at-risk cue is kicking or hitting objects or walls. This happened when you kicked the TV when Johnny didn't turn it down. What negative consequences occurred after this cue?"
            a. Provide empathy for statements that reflect negative consequences.
                For example: "I'm sorry you felt so bad that you made your son cry. I can see that you must have been very upset after this happened."
            b. Provide prompts that suggest negative consequences, whenever necessary.
                For example: "You're wife must have felt terrible."
    3. Ask what might have decreased the perpetrator's anger after the at-risk cue was recognized in the first situation.
        For example: "What could you have done to decrease your anger when Johnny didn't turn down the TV?"
            a. Provide descriptive praise for statements that are likely to decrease anger.
                For example: "Relaxation is so important, and breathing slow and deep is a great way to get relaxed."
            b. Provide prompts that are likely to decrease anger.
                For example: "Some people say that they can become relaxed by thinking of relaxing words or statements, or by thinking about relaxing scenes."
    4. Instruct the perpetrator to rehearse an attempt to decrease anger in response to the first at-risk situation (the clinician should model the role of the target child).

For example: "Mr. Jones, pretend like you just got home from work and Johnny is listening to the TV too loud. You feel yourself starting to get angry after he doesn't turn it down when you ask. You kick the TV and suddenly realize this is an at-risk cue. Show me how you would decrease your anger in this situation. I'll be Johnny."

5. Ask the perpetrator what s/he liked about the roleplay.
6. Provide praise, feedback, problem solving, and/or modeling to facilitate effectiveness in decreasing anger.
    a. Clinicians may utilize the following techniques to assist with anger reduction: thought stopping, self-instructional training, cue-controlled relaxation, and time outs.
7. Ask what could have been done to resolve the first situation after anger was eliminated.
    a. Praise the perpetrator for stating behaviors that are likely to resolve the situation.
    b. Provide prompts that are likely to decrease risk in the situation.
        For example: "If he left the room it may be easier for you to avoid following him. Remember, his consequence is that he is not able to watch TV. You may get angry if you follow him, and he is already being punished by not being able to watch TV for an hour."
8. Instruct the perpetrator to roleplay an attempt to resolve the situation in response to the first at-risk situation (the clinician should model the role of the target child).
        For example: "Mr. Jones, pretend like you're in the same situation. You just finished your relaxation exercises and you are not angry. Show me how you would resolve this situation. I'll pretend like I'm Johnny walking out of the room."
9. Ask what was liked about the roleplay.
10. Provide praise, feedback, problem solving, and/or modeling to facilitate effectiveness in resolving the situation.
    a. Clinician may utilize the following techniques to assist with resolution: walking away, child management techniques (e.g., positive practice, overcorrection), ignoring undesired behaviors, letting the child walk away.
11. Repeat Steps 2 through 10 for remaining at-risk situations.
12. The number of at-risk situations roleplayed per future session will vary according to need, motivation, and rate of learning. However, in general, one situation per session is typical.

VI. Interview With Child and Significant Other (Perpetrator Not Present)

A. Teach the child what to do when at-risk cues occur.
    1. Tell the significant other and child that they will be taught to decrease danger when at-risk cues occur.
    2. Ask the significant other where the child could go when danger occurs (e.g., relative's home, friend's home, store).
    3. Ask the significant other to provide the child with numbers for these safe places.

a. If the significant other does not know the numbers at that time, the numbers may be given to the child later.

b. The significant other should help the child memorize the numbers as soon as possible.

4. In response to the first at-risk cue and situation, roleplay an escape in which the significant other models the perpetrator allowing the clinician to walk quietly and inconspicuously to another room that has easy access to an outside door or open window and does not contain potential weapons (e.g., knives, rods).

> For example: "The first at-risk cue is kicking or hitting walls/objects. You told me that your daddy kicked the TV because you didn't turn it down when he asked. The first thing to do when your daddy hits something like the TV is to quietly walk to another room when he is not talking to you. The room should have an open window or door that leads outside so that you can get away from your daddy in case he gets more angry. It is important to make sure that the room does not have any weapons, like knives or hammers. Can you tell me some things that could be used as a weapon? (child's response) That's right, bats could be used as weapons. What rooms could you go to if your daddy raised his voice in the living room? (child's response) The back porch sounds like a great place to go because it has an outside door, and there is nothing there that can be used as a weapon. Let's pretend like we're in the living room. Your mommy will pretend like she is your daddy kicking the TV, and I'll pretend like I'm you walking to the porch quietly. Notice how your mom has just kicked the TV, and I'm not saying anything. I'm walking to the porch, and I'm looking at the ground."

5. In response to the first at-risk cue and situation, instruct the child to perform an escape while the significant other roleplays a non-intrusive perpetrator.

> For example: "Johnny, you try to do exactly what I just did. Mrs. Jones, don't say or do anything as he walks away."

6. Praise the child for behaviors that place him at decreased risk to be abused.

7. Provide prompts that place the child at decreased risk to be abused.

> For example: "Is there another room that you could go to that has a large window or door that leads to outside? The bathroom doesn't allow you to get away from your dad in case he gets more angry."

8. In response to the first at-risk cue and situation, roleplay an escape in which the significant other models an intrusive perpetrator (i.e., angrily follow the clinician, physically inhibit the clinician from walking away, tells clinician not to leave). In response to the intrusive behavior, the clinician should remain still, say nothing, and comply with the perpetrator (as appropriate). As soon as the perpetrator walks away or shifts attention to something else (e.g., makes a phone call), the clinician should model a retreat to a safe place (e.g., close friend or relative's house).

> For example: "Let's pretend that your daddy tells you that you can't walk away from him, grabs you, or follows you. During these times don't move or say anything, and do as he says as long as he doesn't ask you to hurt yourself or someone else. As soon as he walks away or starts paying attention to something else, like the phone, your mother, or the television, you should go to your grandmother's house. Can you think of any things that he might pay

attention to which would allow you to safely retreat? (child's response) Yes, if he started to make coffee that would be a perfect time to quietly walk to the safe place. Now I'll pretend like I'm walking away from your daddy after he kicked the TV. Your mommy will pretend to be your daddy telling me I can't go. At first I'll just stand here saying nothing. As your mom goes to get coffee, I'll walk away to the back porch. I won't walk over to your grandmother's house now, because we're just practicing, but I would if this was really happening with your father."

9. In response to the first at-risk cue and situation, instruct the child to perform an escape while the significant other roleplays an intrusive perpetrator.

For example: "Johnny, I'll pretend to kick the TV and you quietly walk away. When I tell you that you can't go, you try to remain quiet and stand still. When I go to get coffee, you quietly walk to the back porch and then to your grandma's house."

10. Praise the child for performance of behaviors that place him/her at decreased risk to be abused.

11. Provide prompts that teach the child to engage in behaviors that reduce risk to be abused.

For example: "Don't forget that I have to be paying attention to something else before you try to walk to the porch. That time I was still talking to you."

12. Inform the child that if no children or significant others are present in the home with the perpetrator after the child escapes, the child should phone the significant other and explain what had happened.

   a. Make sure the child knows how to reach the significant other. If the child is unable to contact the significant other, the child should tell the safe person what circumstances led to the child's retreat from home, and ask the safe person to attempt to contact the significant other.

For example: "Johnny, if no one is home with your father, when you get to your grandmother's house you should try to phone your mother and explain what happened. Mrs. Jones, if you aren't home at night, where could you be reached? (caregiver's response) Johnny, do you know the phone number for your mother's work? (child's response) Great! If you can't get a hold of your mother, you should tell your grandmother everything that happened, and ask her to try to get a hold of your mother."

13. The clinician should model a phone call to inform the significant other of what happened prior to the escape.

For example: "Let's pretend like I just walked to grandma's house. The first thing I'm going to do is call you, Mrs. Jones. I'll tell you exactly what happened. Mrs. Jones, you just act like yourself. Mom, I walked to Grandma's house because Daddy kicked the TV, and told me that I had to stay there while he was yelling at me. I walked away when he went to the bathroom. I didn't tell him I was walking away. He's the only one at home."

14. Instruct the child to practice making a phone in which the significant other is notified of what happened prior to the escape.

15. Praise the child for accurate responding, and prompt the child to correct inaccurate statements, and add relevant information.

For example: "You did a beautiful job in telling your mother that he kicked the TV and told you not to leave the room when you tried to leave. Tell her what happened before he kicked the TV."

16. Tell the child that if the significant other or children are present with the angry perpetrator after the child escapes from the home, the target child should call 911 at first safe opportunity.

   a. The child should memorize his/her address so that s/he can give this to the police. The child should be informed that s/he may have to wait a long time, but should not hang up.

      For example: "Johnny, if you walk to a safe place, and your mommy or brother is home with your daddy. I want you to call 911 and tell them what happened. Johnny, what is your address? (child's response). Exactly right. When you call 911 you may have to wait a long time, but don't hang up."

17. A 911 roleplay should be performed for the first at-risk cue and situation, including praise for accurate responding and prompts to correct inaccurate responses.

18. Repeat Steps 4 through 17 for another at-risk situation.

19. The number of at-risk situations roleplayed per future session will vary according to need, attention span of child, motivation, and rate of learning. However, in general, one to two situations per session is typical.

B. Teach the significant other what to do when at-risk cues occur (child should be present).

1. Tell the significant other that s/he may help the child to safely retreat from at-risk situations by signaling the child to exit to another room when at-risk cues are first identified (e.g., raising one finger), and if at-risk situations exacerbate, signaling the child to go to a safe place at earliest safe opportunity (e.g., raising two fingers).

2. Instruct the significant other to tell the child what signal s/he will use to:

   a. Signal the child to go to another room.

   b. Signal the child to go to a safe place.

3. Tell the significant other that after the child has gone to the safe place, the significant other should, at earliest safe opportunity, meet the child at the safe place.

4. Tell the significant other that s/he and the child should remain at the safe place until a session has been scheduled with a program clinician, or other mental health professional (i.e., crisis clinician) to assist with risk assessment.

5. Provide the significant other with a list of telephone numbers for several local shelters.

6. Instruct the significant other to place a bag of clothes, toiletries, money, and a set of keys to the house and car in a car and/or safe place to be used during emergency situations.

   a. The bag should be placed in a safe place and/or car.

7. Instruct the significant other and child to place several quarters outside the home in an inconspicuous location so that the child may use a pay phone during emergency situations.

VII. Special Problems and Concerns

A. Two or more children in the home are at-risk to be abused.

    1. When two or more children in the home are at-risk for abuse in the family (e.g., siblings), the oldest child in the family should be identified as the target child.
       a. During escape training, children older than 5 years of age should be present with the target child so that they may learn to perform the escape routes.
       b. When appropriate, the oldest child and/or significant other should be instructed to escort children younger than 5 years (or with severe intellectual deficits) to safe locations when at risk cues occur.
B. Children are at-risk for sexual abuse.
    1. The escape procedure for children at-risk for sexual abuse will be largely the same as it is for physical abuse. However, the Additional At-Risk Cues recording form (see Table 9.14) should be administered prior to the At-Risk Cues recording form.
C. The significant other is/has been abusive.
    1. When the significant other is/has been abusive to the child, a non-abusing adult relative or friend (or older adolescent sibling) should perform the role of the significant other.
    2. If no one is available to perform the role of significant other, the child must learn the procedure by him/herself.
D. The significant other is at risk to be abused.
    1. When significant others are at risk to be abused by the perpetrator, s/he should be encouraged to identify at risk cues, and subsequently practice escape routes similar to those of the child.
E. The perpetrator is unavailable for treatment, but does have contact with the victim, or is expected to have contact with the victim.
    1. Perpetrators often visit their victims, or have intentions of visiting their victims, and are unavailable for treatment (e.g., jail, treatment refusal, court mandates no contact with victim).
    2. When these situations arise, the child and significant other should roleplay escape routes as a method of prevention.

TABLE 9.14

Additional At-Risk Cues

Common At-Risk Cues	At-Risk Situations
a. Seeing two or more people naked together	_____
b. Seeing someone undress	_____
c. Seeing someone sit with legs spread	_____
d. Being touched in private spots	_____
e. Seeing naked pictures in magazines/TV	_____
f. Being asked to play doctor	_____
g. Being asked to take off clothing	_____
h. Being asked to touch private parts	_____
i. Being asked to take a shower/bath while someone watches or gets in	_____
Other Risks	_____
1. _____	_____
2. _____	_____
3. _____	_____

POSITIVE PRACTICE

I. Brief Overview

A1. Maltreated children are often unable to perform desired behaviors due to insufficient and inconsistent learning and/or physical or intellectual limitations. Moreover, caregivers are often unaware of these limitations and erroneously assume that their children know how, or should know how, to perform behaviors that have not adequately been learned. Lofty expectations may cause frustration and upset for both the child and the caregiver, which may in turn exacerbate the learning process. Positive practice is a disciplinary method that may be utilized to nonaversively punish undesired behaviors by having children practice target behaviors in an environment that fosters acceptance, patience, and support. This procedure is applicable to all ages, and is especially effective for maltreated children.

II. Treatment Implementation

A. Brief rationale.
    1. Provide a rationale for positive practice that includes the following:
        a. Children often perform undesired behaviors due to insufficient learning and/or developmental limitations.
        b. Provide an example of an extrinsic circumstance that may have influenced the target child to perform an undesired behavior.
        c. The caregiver will learn to instruct the target child to practice desired behaviors when undesired behaviors are performed by the target child.
        d. Provide an example of positive practice.
            For example: "Children often do behaviors that are undesired because they haven't learned, or don't have the ability, to do the right thing consistently. For example, Johnny ran into the street the other day without looking both ways, even though you've told him to look both ways many times before. He probably was in a rush to visit his friends and is too young to appreciate the importance of looking both ways before crossing the road. The procedure you are about to learn is called positive practice. Positive practice is a discipline that focuses on teaching children to practice desired behaviors after they perform actions that are not desired. For example, after Johnny forgot to look both ways before crossing the street, he could be instructed to practice looking both ways several times prior to crossing the street. Positive practice has been very effective with other families, and I think your teaching skills will be a great benefit. Do you have any questions?"
B. Teaching the caregiver when positive practice is applicable.
    1. Present several examples in which positive practice is applicable. After stating each example tell the caregiver why positive practice is applicable, including what specific behaviors need to be practiced.
            For example: "I am going to provide you with several examples in which positive practice may be used as an effective discipline, and then I'll explain why positive practice is appropriate. For example, if Johnny dropped a model

airplane, positive practice would be great because he didn't mean to drop the plane. He just needs to learn how to handle the plane carefully. Maybe he could be instructed to carefully place a plane on the table several times. If he wet his bed, positive practice would be an appropriate discipline because he needs to learn how to monitor his bladder and retain fluids by practicing to go to the bathroom at night. He could practice getting up from his bed and going to the toilet several times. Positive practice may also be used if he takes a candy bar from another child. He needs to learn how to ask permission. He could practice asking for the candy bar several times. He could also be instructed to practice asking for other things so that he is likely to remember this practice next time he wants something. Positive practice can even be used to improve performance in sporting events. For example, children may strike out a lot because they haven't learned to swing the bat correctly. In this example, the child could practice swinging at pitched balls.

2. Provide several examples in which positive practice is applicable and after each example is depicted perform the following:
   a. Ask the caregiver why positive practice is applicable.
   b. Ask the caregiver what behavior(s) need to be practiced.
   c. Descriptively praise correct responding.
   d. Provide prompts whenever necessary to elicit correct responding.
      For example: "Children often forget to call home to ask permission to stay out later. Why would positive practice be a good discipline for this undesired behavior? (caregiver responds) I agree. He hasn't learned to consistently ask for permission to stay out late. Forgetting is best consequenced with positive practice. What behaviors would have to be learned? (caregiver responds) That's a good point. Buying a watch would definitely be helpful. And what would the child need to practice with his watch? (caregiver responds) You really are a natural at positive practice. Pretending to call you a few times before his curfew would be a perfect way to practice being aware of the time."

3. Instruct the caregiver to provide at least three situations in which positive practice is applicable, and for each situation ask the caregiver to indicate why positive practice is applicable and what behaviors need to be practiced. Then perform the following:
   a. Descriptively praise the caregiver for statements that indicate positive practice is appropriate.
   b. Descriptively praise the caregiver for stating what behavior(s) need to be learned.
   c. Provide prompts whenever necessary to elicit correct responding.
      For example: "Tell me a situation in which it would be appropriate to use positive practice. (caregiver responds) That's wonderful how you realize that Johnny probably spilled his soup because he didn't realize it was too hot to hold. I like how you stated that positive practice is appropriate because he hadn't learned to check the soup to make sure it was not hot. You really have a good grasp of this procedure. What behaviors would he have to practice? (caregiver responds). Practicing to look for steam, and holding the mug by the handle is a perfect solution. Tell me another situation in which it would be appropriate to use positive practice. (caregiver responds) I agree that positive practice would be great to use when he jumps in the lake without

permission, but think hard. Even if you know that he did it intentionally, you could still make him practice doing something. What can he practice to teach him to remember not to jump in the lake? (caregiver respond) Exactly, he could practice asking you permission to jump in the lake. He could even practice going to different parts of the camp ground, and running to you from these locations to ask your permission."

4. Demonstrate to the caregiver that children often make excuses for their performance of undesired behaviors (e.g., "I got distracted"), and by assuming children are telling the truth in these situations the caregiver is provided with an opportunity to use positive practice.

For example: "Children often make excuses to explain why they performed undesired behaviors. For example, Johnny might say that because he was playing basketball, he forgot to walk the dog. When excuses are made it is best to agree, even if you think he's making it up. You can then instruct him to practice behaviors that would prevent the undesired behavior in the future. For example, he could practice walking the dog several times prior to playing basketball during the next day. You could also instruct him to run home from the basketball court a couple of times so that he could practice telling you that he had to walk the dog. Thus, he is more likely to remember to walk the dog in the future. If the basketball court is too far away, he could pretend like he's telling his basketball friends that he has to go home several times. You could even instruct him to practice handling objections that he's likely to hear from his friends."

5. Ask the caregiver why s/he thinks it would be important to agree with the target child when s/he makes excuses for his/her undesired behaviors, and then reinforce any responses that suggest it is important to agree.

a. If the caregiver expresses concern that acceptance of excuses may reinforce excuse behavior, tell the caregiver that the child is being consequenced for making excuses by having to practice behaviors that would help prevent the undesired behavior in the future.

C. Teaching the caregiver the specific steps of positive practice.

1. Tell the caregiver that after positive practice is determined to be applicable, the caregiver should state the desired behavior.

For example: "Mr. Jones, after you determine that positive practice is an appropriate discipline, you will state the desired behavior. In other words, the behavior that you would have liked him to do in that situation. For example, a desired behavior for slamming the door to loud might be to practice closing the door softly."

2. Tell the caregiver that the next step is to tell the child that performance of the desired behavior is difficult so that the child is more receptive to practicing the desired behavior.

For example: "The next step is to tell the child that the desired behavior is difficult. So, for example, I might say, Johnny with all the activity in our house over the holidays it is easy to get distracted and forget to shut the door softly."

3. Inform the caregiver that the next instruction will be to briefly explain to the child why it is important to practice the desired behavior using a calm voice with neutral affect and without criticism.

For example: "The next step is to briefly tell the child why it is important to practice the desired behavior. It is important to avoid a lecture, so I recommend that you do this in less than a few sentences. For example, Johnny, it's important that you practice shutting the door softly so that you don't wake up the baby, or give me a headache. Notice how my voice was calm and my face was neutral, without a frown or smile."

4. Instruct the caregiver to roleplay the positive practice procedure (previous three steps), and provide descriptive praise for correct responding (prompt when necessary to elicit correct responding).

For example: "Tell me what you would say to Johnny if he slammed the door. Do the same things I just did as best you can. (caregiver responds) Excellent! You told me why it was important to practice shutting the door softly in a calm tone of voice. You also did a fine job in avoiding critical comments. What could you tell me to make me realize that you think shutting the door softly is difficult?"

5. Tell the caregiver that the child should then be instructed to practice the desired behavior, according to the following guidelines:

   a. Duration of practice (i.e., time of practice, number of practice trials) is determined according to the following two criteria:

      1. *Seriousness* (i.e., dangerous or troublesome undesired behaviors require more practice).

      2. *Frequency* (i.e., frequently performed undesired behaviors require more practice).

   b. Practice should be pleasant for the child.

   c. When the child is hesitant, hands should be used to gently guide the child into correct responding.

   d. Encouragement should be provided when the child is performing the correct behavior.

   e. Whenever possible, positive practice should be performed "immediately" after the undesired behavior is performed.

   For example: "Mr. Jones, the last step is to instruct the child to practice the desired behavior. The number of times the child practices the desired behavior, or the length of time the child practices, should be determined by seriousness and frequency. Undesired behaviors that are more serious, or that occur frequently, should be practiced more than less serious behaviors or behaviors that don't occur that often. It is important that the practice is pleasant for the child. Remember that children learn best when they are not upset. If Johnny has difficulty in his practice you should use your hands to gently guide him whenever appropriate. For example, if he was making a model airplane, you could guide his hands when he was putting small pieces together. Always provide encouragement and praise throughout practice, and perform practice immediately after recognizing the undesired behavior, whenever possible."

   f. Ask for the caregiver's understanding of the guidelines, and then provide descriptive praise for correct responding (provide prompts to elicit correct responding, when necessary).

6. The clinician should model the previous guidelines (Step 5) for an undesired behavior that is appropriate for positive practice.

For example: "Watch how I use my hands to teach you how to hold this coffee mug that you kept dropping. If you dropped the mug for the first time, and it was plastic and couldn't break, the frequency and seriousness are not severe, so I would probably only make you practice passing the cup from hand to hand for a few seconds. I would also have you do it right after you dropped the mug, if possible. You're doing great moving the mug back and forth in your hands. Notice how my face is pleasant. That's it, you really are doing a great job passing it back and forth carefully."

7. Instruct the caregiver to roleplay the previous guidelines for an undesired behavior appropriate for positive practice, and then provide descriptive praise, instruction, and modeling when appropriate.

D. Utilizing applicable situations to practice the implementation of positive practice.

1. Ask the caregiver to roleplay positive practice for the following behaviors (practice should approximate the behaviors listed after each respective undesired behavior):

   a. Dropping a passed football: Practice catching a football.
   b. Dropping an object: Practice moving similar objects to different locations.
   c. Slamming door: Practice opening and shutting a door.
   d. Yelling: Speak several sentences using a soft tone of voice.
   e. Swearing: State several compliments about the person to whom the swear was directed.
   f. Stealing: Practice offering to share possessions with the victim, and politely asking the victim for other possessions.
   g. Being late for curfew due to forgetting the time: Practice coming home at specified times.
   h. Bed-wetting: Practice getting out of bed and going to the bathroom.

2. After each role play, descriptively praise the caregiver for correct responding, and explain and/or model how to correctly administer positive practice when the caregiver is incorrect.

3. If the caregiver continues to have difficulties identifying desired and undesired behaviors, it may be necessary to review the principles of reinforcement and punishment (see Catching My Child Being Good procedure).

E. Assigning homework.

1. Provide the caregiver with a copy of the Positive Practice Recording Sheet (see Table 9.15), and then instruct the caregiver to perform the following behaviors for homework:

   a. Positive practice should be attempted at home whenever appropriate.
   b. One positive practice per day may be recorded in the Positive Practice Worksheet. (The desired behavior and number of trials should be recorded in the column corresponding to the day the positive practice was performed.)
   c. Record one hypothetical positive practice to demonstrate the recording process.

2. Instruct the caregiver to record a hypothetical positive practice for the present day, and then provide descriptive praise for correct responding (provide prompts to elicit correct responding, when necessary).

3. Provide the caregiver with a copy of the Positive Practice Worksheet (see Table 9.16) to assist with implementation of this procedure in the home.

TABLE 9.15

Positive Practice Recording Sheet

Positive Practice	Mon.	Tues.	Wed.	Thurs.	Fri.	Sat.	Sun.
Desired Behavior Practiced							
Number of Times Practiced							

TABLE 9.16

Positive Practice Worksheet

1. Identify the specific undesired behavior that was performed.
2. Identify the desired specific behavior.
3. Tell the child "WHY" practice will be needed.
   Tips: –Use a calm, even–toned voice without anger.
       –Whenever possible, do the positive practice immediately.
4. Instruct the child to practice the desired behavior
   Tips: –If the undesired behavior is not a serious one, or occurs infrequently, then a short duration of
       practice may be sufficient.
       –Practice should not be unpleasant for the child.
       –Use your hands to guide the child when the child seems hesitant to perform practice.
       –Provide praise when the child is performing the correct behavior.
       –Explain how to perform the desired behavior when the child is hesitant.
5. If the child refuses to do positive practice, perform the time out procedure.

Examples of Positive Practice:
bed–wetting–Practice getting out of bed and going to the bathroom several times.
repeatedly dropping glass objects–Practice moving glass objects to different locations.
slamming door–Practice opening and shutting door several times.
yelling–Speak several sentences using a soft tone of voice.
swearing–State several compliments about the person at whom the swear was directed.
stealing–Practice asking for similar objects in an appropriate manner.
dropping a passed football–Practice catching a football several times.
being late for curfew–Write phone numbers of all friends to contact in the future, and describe how to inform caregivers of
    whereabouts in various situations using another phone in the house.

F. Reviewing homework in future sessions.
   1. Praise homework compliance, even if incomplete.
   2. If homework is incomplete, instruct the caregiver to perform homework in retrospect.
   3. Instruct the caregiver to disclose several desired behaviors that were practiced since
      last contact, and after each positive practice is disclosed perform the following:
      a. Descriptively praise the caregiver for correct responding.
      b. Provide prompts to elicit correct responding.
      c. Provide instruction and modeling to teach correct responding.

For example: "Tell me some of the desired behaviors that you had Johnny practice this week. (caregiver responds) I like how you had him practice waiting for you to stop talking before he asked if he could go outside to play. How was your voice and facial expression? (caregiver responds) I like how you were looking me in the eye. Watch how I smile a little as I talk."

G. Solutions to commonly experienced problems.

    1. The caregiver is too punitive (e.g., assigns excessive practice, frowns).

        a. Caregivers should be immediately reminded that positive practice is an attempt to teach desired behaviors, and children learn best when teaching is pleasant.

        b. Model pleasant and appropriate use of positive practice.

        c. Instruct caregiver to role play pleasant administration of the procedure.

    2. The child refuses to perform positive practice.

        a. Noncompliance to positive practice usually occurs when the caregiver is too aversive and/or not implementing all steps. Therefore, assure that the caregiver is implementing positive practice correctly (i.e., more roleplaying).

        b. Tell the caregiver to assist the child in performance of the desired behavior and fade out this assistance as the child initiates practice.

            For example: "It's hard to vacuum without hitting the table. Let me show you how to move it slowly (caregiver puts his hand next to the child's hand and begins to move the vacuum, fading out manual guidance as the child initiates movement of the sweeper)."

        c. Teach the caregiver to wait 5 seconds after initiating the instruction to practice the desired behavior. If the child does not initiate the practice, the caregiver should tell the child that a valued reinforcer will be withheld if practice is not initiated. If the child remains noncompliant, the caregiver should tell the child that the reinforcer will be withheld for the specified duration.

            For example: "If you don't practice asking me if you can turn up your stereo, I will have to restrict you from listening to your stereo for the rest of the evening. (child does not initiate practice, and caregiver turns off stereo). If you change your mind, let me know. I will let you listen to the stereo as soon as you're done practicing."

ICARE

I. Brief Overview Of ICARE

A1. When physical abuse occurs it almost always occurs consequent to the perpetrator's perception that the victim has performed an undesired behavior. Although the motives for child abusive behavior vary, negative emotional states (e.g., upset, anger, frustration) are activated (or exacerbated) at first recognition of the undesired behavior and generally intensify with the passage of time. Of course, negative emotional states interfere with rational thinking, and may contribute to ineffective methods of discipline. The ICARE procedure may be utilized to help perpetrators of child abuse, and caregivers of child abuse victims, terminate negative emotional arousal and select appropriate disciplines when their children perform undesired behavior.

II. Pre-ICARE Training

A. Reviewing explanations for undesired behaviors that remove blame from the child.
    1. Provide a rationale that suggests children are not fully accountable for their undesired behaviors, and that the caregiver will review possible explanations that influence the target child to perform undesired behaviors that are not necessarily the target child's fault.

> For example: "Some people have a tendency to hold children fully accountable for their undesired behaviors. People who point fingers do not realize that children are exposed to many situations in today's society that influence them to perform undesired behaviors. I would like to review explanations that you feel may explain why Johnny engages in undesired behaviors that are not necessarily his fault."

    2. Refer caregiver to the Possible Explanation Form (see Table 9.17).
      a. For each possible explanation (item), review the following:
        1. In three or four sentences explain why other caregivers believe that the item response influences their children to perform undesired behaviors.
        2. Ask the caregiver how the response may influence the target child to perform undesired behaviors.
        3. Reinforce caregiver statements that remove blame from the child.
        4. Write a brief summary of the caregiver's explanation in the Personalized Possible Explanation column.
        5. When all possible explanations are finished, ask the caregiver if s/he can think of any explanations that were not listed. If so, perform the preceding guidelines for these explanations (i.e., Steps 1 to 4).

> For example "Here is a list of possible explanations that other caregivers believe influence their children to perform undesired behaviors. The first explanation is seeing violence, sex, or crime on TV. Television often has violent scenes in which the criminal is not punished for violent or delinquent crimes such as murder, rape, or theft. In fact, many programs show the bad guy laughing and getting away with crime. Sometimes children see other kids getting lots of money or status for selling drugs. These parents state that it isn't the fault of their children that these programs are not censored. How might television influence Johnny to perform undesired behaviors. (caregiver's response) Yea, that sounds terrible. It's so confusing for children to see drug dealers give children money to watch for the police, and drug dealers definitely try to get children to do these types of things. I'll summarize your explanation as influence of drug dealers on TV."

    3. Instruct the caregiver to rate each Personalized Possible Explanation on a scale of 0 to 100 (0 = *does not explain why my child misbehaves at all*, 100 = *completely explains why my child misbehaves*).
      a. Record these ratings in the 0 to 100 Rating column.
    4. After all personalized explanations are recorded, recite the top three rated personalized possible explanations, and ask the caregiver if these are the three greatest influences.

TABLE 9.17

Possible Explanation Form

Possible Explanations From Other Caregivers	Personalized Explanations	0–100 Rating
1. Violence or sex seen on TV, or in person		
2. Exposure to bad influences		
3. Divorce/separation of someone close		
4. Inconsistent discipline		
5. Harsh punishments		
6. Drugs or alcohol		
7. Has not learned to pay attention		
8. A rough life		
9. Being teased		
10. Has not learned how to do the desired behavior consistently		
11. Exposure to delinquent friends		
12. Being poor		
13. Emotional at the time		
14. Confusion		
15. Part of development/growing up		
16. Death of a loved one		
17. Being sexually abused		
18. A recent move or transition		
19. Mentally/emotionally handicapped or learning disabled		

For example: "You said the influence of drug dealers, delinquent friends, and your ex-husband are the three greatest influences that you feel contribute to his performance of undesired behaviors. Is that correct?"

5. Circle the top three rated personalized possible explanations in the Possible Explanations form.

B. Test the ability of possible explanation rehearsal to eliminate anger.

1. Ask the caregiver to disclose a recent situation (scene) in which his/her child performed an undesired behavior that led to the caregiver being upset or angry.

2. Tell the caregiver that in a minute s/he will be instructed to perform the following:

a. Imagine the scene, beginning immediately at first recognition of the undesired behavior.

b. Raise a finger when anger is about 50 on a 0 to 100 scale of anger/upset (100 = *highest intensity of anger/upset, 0 = no anger/upset experienced*).

c. Immediately after the caregiver indicates that anger is at 50, the clinician should continuously state the caregiver's three highest rated Personalized Possible Explanations until the caregiver indicates that anger is at 0 by raising a finger. (The clinician should validate that no anger/upset is present immediately after the finger is raised.).

d. Record the time it takes the anger to decrease from 50 to 0.

For example: "Tell me a recent undesired behavior that Johnny performed that made you feel angry or upset. (caregiver's response) In a moment I am going to ask you to shut your eyes and imagine that situation. I want you to imagine the situation just before he yells at you, when you were not at all angry. We'll call this 0% anger. When you are about half as angry as you ended up in that situation, about 50% angry, I want you to raise your finger.

I will then state some of the Possible Explanations that you mentioned. I want you to think about these explanations while you imagine the scene. If your anger goes back to 0%, I want you to raise your finger again. What is your understanding of what I want you to do? (caregiver's response) Good. Shut your eyes and let's begin. (caregiver raises finger for 1st time) Johnny was raised in a poor area with delinquents everywhere. His father tells him all kinds of crap when he's drunk. Drug dealers influence him to do negative things. (caregiver raises finger for second time) Are you experiencing any anger?" (If no, record the time. If yes, instruct the caregiver to reenter the scene and continue as described until the anger is 0.)

C. Test the ability of consequence rehearsal to eliminate anger.
   1. Another trial should be performed exactly as described. However, during this trial the clinician will repeatedly state the three highest rated negative consequences for abusive behavior elicited from the Consequence Review procedure.

   > For example: "We're going to do one more trial. However, when you indicate that you are 50% angry, I am going to repeatedly state your three most aversive consequences associated with hitting Johnny. Begin imagining the same situation, and let me know when you are 50% angry. (caregiver raises finger for the first time) If you hit Johnny you will probably go to jail and may get raped. He will be sad, and he may resent you later. Your wife will be upset, and you will probably get into arguments. (caregiver raises finger for the 2nd time) Are you experiencing any anger?" (If no, record time. If yes, instruct the caregiver to reenter the scene and continue as described).

D. Choosing to use possible explanation rehearsal or consequence rehearsal to reduce anger/upset.
   1. Review the two rehearsals (trials) with the caregiver, including the following:
      a. Reveal the times to the caregiver.
      b. Ask the caregiver which trial was more effective in eliminating anger/upset.
      c. Praise the caregiver for being able to reduce anger using the most effective method.
      d. Ask the caregiver which method would probably help decrease anger/upset the most at home.

      > 1. For example: "Well, I see that my stating possible explanations helped you to reduce anger to 0 in 30 seconds, whereas my stating negative consequences reduced anger to 0 in 45 seconds. I think it's great that you were able to eliminate anger from 50% using both methods so quickly. Which method do you feel was most effective in reducing your anger? (caregiver's response) I agree, you really seem to be able to identify with the possible explanations. Which method do you feel will help you most in eliminating anger/upset at home?"

   2. The selected method (possible explanation or negative consequence) will be utilized in the ICARE procedure after Thought Stopping is performed (described later).

E. Rating the progression of anger.
   1. Tell the caregiver that s/he will now learn to rate the progression of anger/upset.
   2. Teach the caregiver about the progression of anger utilizing the following:
      a. Anger/upset may be present prior to the child's undesired behavior, but it is not focused on the child until the child performs an undesired behavior.

   b. On first awareness of an undesired behavior, the anger is barely present, if at all.
   c. Anger/upset progressively becomes more intense as negative thoughts are imagined.
   d. It becomes more difficult to terminate anger/upset as negative thoughts are stated.
       For example: "Sometimes people are angry before their children do undesired behaviors. For example, a mother may be mad at her boss, but this anger does not become focused on her child until the child does a behavior that she does not like. As soon as the child does the undesired behavior, anger is barely present, if at all. However, as she continues to think negatively about the child or situation, anger gets worse, and it becomes harder to stop being angry. Sometimes anger progresses quite fast, as you probably know."
3. Tell the caregiver that anger will be identified according to the following scale:
       0 = No anger present.
       1 to 5 = First awareness of the undesired behavior.
       6 to 10 = First negative thought.
       11 to 20 = A few negative thoughts are stated.
       100 = Most anger ever experienced.
4. Provide an example in which anger progresses from a 0 (no anger) to about 10 to 20 (a few derogatory thoughts are stated) for a situation in which a child does an undesired behavior.
   a. For example: "I would like to provide you with an example of how anger might progress from 0 to 20. For example, if a child draws on the wall with crayons, a 0 might be me walking into the room and seeing the child on the bed. A 5 might be seeing the wall with crayon marks for the first time, before thinking about it. Anger might increase to a 10 after the first negative thought, such as I can never leave this kid alone. Anger is likely to increase to about a 20 after a few negative thoughts are made. For example, he does nothing but get into trouble, this is going to take me a couple of hours to wash off. I'm about to explode."
5. Instruct the caregiver to describe three situations in which anger progressed from 0 to 20 on the aforementioned scale, and praise the caregiver for closely approximating the scale when describing his/her thoughts that were experienced.
   a. For the first and second situation it is easiest to ask the caregiver when the anger was a 0, 2–5, 10, 15, and 20 while s/he describes the situation.
       For example: "Describe a recent situation in which Johnny performed an undesired behavior that got you angry. While describing this situation, I want you to tell me what you said to yourself when the anger was about a 0, 2 to 5, 10, 15, and 20. (caregiver's response) That's real close, but remember a 2 to 5 occurs when the undesired behavior is first recognized. In your example, just seeing Johnny punch Kate might be a 5. At that time you haven't had any thoughts, you just recognized that he did a behavior. What might be a 10? (caregiver's response) Exactly, just saying, "Johnny is messing up again," will increase your anger to about a 10. What might you say to yourself at about the 20 level? (caregiver's response) Perfect, you said about three negative things about Johnny."

III. ICARE Training

A. Brief rationale.

1. Provide a brief rationale for ICARE that includes the following:
   a. Children engage in undesired behaviors that get caregivers angry/upset.
   b. The ICARE procedure is a technique that may be utilized to stop angry thoughts early, help the caregiver relax, and nonemotionally identify and implement the most effective discipline.
   c. The ICARE procedure has been tremendously effective for other caregivers.
   d. The ICARE procedure is expected to be especially effective with this caregiver.

      For example: "You've told me that Johnny engages in undesired behaviors that get you angry. Anger interferes with the ability to clearly think about effective disciplines. The procedure you are about to learn is called ICARE. This procedure will help you to stop angry thoughts early, and then help you to relax during these situations. You will then be taught to nonemotionally identify the most appropriate discipline, and attempt this discipline with no anger. This procedure has been very effective with other caregivers, and I suspect it will be especially effective with you. Do you have any questions?"

2. Tell the caregiver that ICARE consists of several techniques, and that each technique will be practiced individually, and later roleplayed in sequence.

   For example: "You are about to learn a series of techniques that you may use to prevent anger from occurring when you discipline your child's undesired behaviors. Each of these techniques will be taught one at a time. I will model each technique, and then I will give you an opportunity to perform the technique. I'll provide prompts when you need help."

B. Teaching the caregiver to use thought stopping.
   1. Tell the caregiver that the ideal time to terminate anger is a "2 to 5" on the anger scale (i.e., First awareness of the undesired behavior.).
   2. Tell the caregiver that firmly stating "Stop" as soon as the undesired behavior is recognized will help to terminate thoughts associated with anger.
   3. Model the termination of anger using thought stopping after an undesired behavior is first recognized during an imagined scene.

      For example: "Watch how I yell stop when I pretend to recognize an undesired behavior. I'm walking into the kitchen. I look up and see that Johnny didn't wash the dishes. Stop!"
   4. Instruct the caregiver to practice the termination of anger using thought stopping when the undesired behavior is first recognized during an imagined scene (the caregiver should "think out loud" for this and all subsequent roleplays).

      For example: "Imagine that you are walking into the house and you see that Johnny forgot to take out the trash. Describe yourself going into the house, and forcefully state 'stop' out loud as soon as you notice that the garbage has not been taken out."
   5. Praise the caregiver for terminating anger at first recognition of the undesired behavior, and stating "stop" forcefully.

      For example: Caregiver's response: "I'm in the living room vacuuming the rug and I hear Johnny and his friend yelling when I told them to play quietly. Stop!" Clinician's Response: "That's great how you stated stop immediately after you recognized the undesired behavior. You didn't even allow yourself to think about the undesired behavior. You also stated stop forcefully. I could tell you really meant it."

6. If the caregiver does not yell stop immediately after recognizing the undesired behavior, the clinician should immediately prompt the caregiver to yell stop.

>For example: Caregiver's response: "I'm in the living room vacuuming the rug and I hear Johnny and his friend yelling when I told him to play quietly. What am I going to do with this kid? I've had it!"

>Clinician interrupts: "Yell stop, now! You can solve the problem later."

C. Negative consequence or possible explanation rehearsal.

1. Tell the caregiver that after stop is stated it will be necessary to imagine two or three top-rated negative consequences or 2 or 3 top-rated possible explanations. (The method of rehearsal utilized will depend on which one the caregiver selected from earlier trials.)

>For example: "You found that your anger was reduced when you said 2 or 3 possible explanations that explained how Johnny may have been influenced by things that were possibly out of his control. I think you said Johnny was raised in a poor area with delinquents everywhere, and his father and drug dealers are particularly bad influences. So after stating 'stop' you would state these things."

2. Model negative consequence or possible explanation rehearsal.

   a. If negative consequence rehearsal was selected by the caregiver during Pre-ICARE Training, the following should be modeled:

      1. "I can't get angry. If I get angry I might lose control and (two or three negative consequences) might occur. I just need to take my time and discipline this undesired behavior."

         >For example : "I can't get angry, if I do I might have to go to jail and get raped, and my wife and kid will be upset. I just need to take my time and discipline this undesired behavior."

   b. If possible explanation rehearsal was selected by the caregiver during Pre-Icare Training, the following should be modeled:

      1. "It isn't all his fault. S/he has (2 to 3 possible explanations). I just need to take my time and discipline this undesired behavior."

         >For example : "It isn't all his fault. Johnny has been raised with delinquents in a bad neighborhood, and his father and drug dealers are very bad influences. I just need to take my time and discipline this undesired behavior."

3. Instruct the caregiver to perform negative consequence or possible explanation rehearsal.

4. Reinforce the caregiver for correct responding, and provide prompts to elicit correct responding, when necessary.

   >For example: "That was fantastic how you said it wasn't all his fault, and then you mentioned a couple of reasons that could explain why Johnny engaged in the undesired behavior."

D. Cue-controlled relaxation.

1. Tell the caregiver that the next step involves elimination of all bodily signs of tension.

   >For example: "The next step is to make sure all muscles in your body are relaxed, and if not to try to get them relaxed."

2. Instruct the caregiver to perform a muscle review with the clinician in which s/he tense (5 seconds) and relax (5 seconds) the following muscles, one muscle at a time:
   a. Forehead
   b. Nose (scrunch nose, then relax)
   c. Lips (pucker lips, then relax)
   d. Neck
   e. Shoulders (hunch shoulders towards ears, then drop)
   f. Biceps (make a muscle, then drop arm)
   g. Forearms
   h. Fists (squeeze, then let fingers dangle)
   i. Lungs (hold breath, then slowly exhale)
   j. Thighs (press knee caps together, then let legs rest)
   k. Calves (press toes to floor, then relax feet on floor)
3. It is important to check for injuries, particularly back injuries, and contact lenses prior to performing this exercise.
4. While tensing and relaxing these muscles, tell the caregiver to concentrate on the contrast between tension and relaxation.

> For example: "Do you wear contacts or have any injuries? (caregivers response) Okay! I want you to practice tensing and relaxing the major muscles in your body. We'll start with your head and work down to your toes. I want you to tense and then relax each muscle for 5 seconds. I'll do the muscle review with you so that you can see how I tense and relax these muscles. Let's start with the forehead. Tighten your forehead by scrunching it up and causing wrinkles like I'm doing. Great, hold it. Feel the tension. Okay, release the tension. That's it. Concentrate on the relaxed feelings, particularly your forehead. Calm, comfortable, warm feelings in your forehead. Now let's scrunch up our noses." (and so on)

5. After the tensing and relaxing muscle review, ask the caregiver if any muscles get particularly tense during anger provoking situations.
6. Tell the caregiver that after s/he performs negative consequence rehearsal (or possible explanation rehearsal), a muscle review should be performed that *does not* include the tension component, and includes the following:
   a. Attempt to relax all muscles that are tense, although all muscles should be reviewed to make sure they are relaxed.
   b. Relaxing cue words (e.g., relax, calm, soothing) should be imagined while the caregiver focuses on tense muscles during the review.

> For example: "When you try this at home do not tense your muscles. Just concentrate on relaxing each muscle, while stating relaxing words. If the muscle is already relaxed, go to the next muscle."

7. Model the muscle relaxation review without tension phase.

> For example: "Watch how I do the relaxation exercise. Okay, here I go. My forehead feels relaxed, my nose and mouth are comfortable. My neck is tight. I'm focusing on bringing relaxation into my neck. It feels so good resting peacefully on my shoulders. My shoulders are relaxed and I'm breathing comfortably. My arms are gently hanging limp."

8. Instruct the caregiver to perform a the muscle relaxation review without the tension phase.

> For example: "Now you do the muscle relaxation review without the tension phase. Just like I did."

9. Descriptively praise the caregiver for correct responding, and provide prompts to elicit correct responding, whenever necessary.

E. State the undesired behavior.

1. Tell the caregiver that before discipline is attempted the undesired behavior should be stated in objective behavioral terms, without emotion and in less than one or two sentences.

> For example: "Before you discipline Johnny, it is important to state what the undesired behavior is in objective terms without emotional content. Let me provide you with some examples of what I mean. I asked him to take out the garbage by 7 a.m. on Thursday, and he didn't. He pushed Kate on the floor. He didn't complete his math assignment Wednesday night. He called his teacher a bad name in math class today. He didn't go into his bed when I asked him to go to bed."

2. Ask the caregiver to briefly state at least three undesired behaviors that have evoked anger in the past, and then descriptively praise correct responding and provide prompts to elicit correct responding whenever necessary.

> For example: "Tell me some undesired behaviors that Johnny has done that have made you angry in the past. (caregiver's response) Add the time that he didn't wash the dishes, and your description will be perfect. (caregiver's response) Let's do some more examples."

F. State the desired behavior.

1. Provide at least three examples of converting undesired behaviors into desired behaviors.

> For example: "If the undesired behavior was that he didn't take out the garbage by 7 p.m. Thursday, then the desired behavior would be to take out the garbage by 7 p.m. on Thursdays. Let me give you a couple more examples."

2. Provide the caregiver with several undesired behaviors that are commonly performed by children, and ask the caregiver to transform these undesired behaviors into desired behaviors.

   a. Review examples until the caregiver is able to clearly convert at least three undesired behaviors into desired behaviors. Utilize descriptive praise and feedback whenever necessary.

G. Review positive alternatives to discipline undesired behavior.

1. Tell the caregiver that the undesired behavior must then be punished using positive practice, ignoring, loss of privileges, or other disciplinary methods.

2. Tell the caregiver that it is important to think of several disciplines that may be used, and then think about the pros and cons of these disciplines and select the best discipline. Then provide an example of this process.

> For example: "The secret in picking the best discipline is to think of several disciplines, and then evaluate the pros and cons of each one before selecting one. For example, if I had to discipline a child for sticking his tongue out at

me, I could use positive practice or ignoring. Positive practice is best used when children have not learned to perform the desired behavior, and ignoring is best used when children are not a threat to hurt themselves or someone else, or destroy property. Positive practice is a good discipline because it teaches children what to do, and I do want him to learn to say hello with his tongue in his mouth. However, I'm in a rush to leave, and I don't have much time to perform the practice. Ignoring wouldn't take that much time, and he would be consequenced by my lack of talking to him. I think I will choose to ignore him."

3. Instruct the caregiver to state several disciplines that may be utilized for an undesired behavior. The caregiver should be instructed to select one after evaluating the pros and cons of each.

4. Descriptively praise correct responding, and provide prompts to elicit correct responding.

For example: "I really like how you generated three disciplines that are all great for use with children. I especially liked how you thought about the pros and cons for each discipline before choosing positive practice. You said that you would use positive practice because he hasn't stolen before, and it's likely that he just hasn't learned that it is important not to take money from your purse without asking. Just like you said, I think you could have restricted his ice cream for a week, but you didn't because you thought positive practice would teach him what to do."

H. Imagine doing selected discipine.

1. Inform the caregiver that next step involves imagining successful implementation of the selected discipline, and then model this component step.

For example: "The next step involves imagining yourself doing the discipline with Johnny. It is important to imagine yourself implementing the discipline perfectly, and imagining your son responding favorably. If I was imagining myself ignoring Johnny when he made faces at me, it might sound something like this: Johnny is whining so I walk into the kitchen. He follows me, but I keep on looking away. I'm reading the soup can to find out how much water to add. He gets tired and walks away."

2. Instruct the caregiver to imagine successful implementation of the chosen discipline, and provide descriptive praise and feedback for correct responding.

I. Self-reinforcement.

1. Tell the caregiver that after the discipline is implemented (or during), it is important to state several things that were good about the implementation of the chosen discipline.

For example: "After you discipline Johnny, or while you are disciplining him, it will be important to state things that were good about the discipline that you implemented. For example, I might say things like I really like the discipline I chose. Ignoring him made me feel calm and in control, and he didn't get any attention."

2. Instruct the caregiver to state several positive statements about the the chosen discipline.

3. Descriptively praise the caregiver for any statements that are positive, and provide prompts to elicit correct responding.

J. Practicing the ICARE procedure in its entirety.
  1. Model the entire ICARE procedure in sequence and without interruption utilizing a situation in which the child engaged in an undesired behavior that elicited anger.

    For example: "Now that you know all the steps, I'm going to put the whole thing together. I will pretend that Johnny just stuck his tongue out at me. I'm imagining that Johnny is walking in the room. I say hello to him and he sticks his tongue out at me. Stop! I shouldn't get angry. Johnny has been raised in a bad area with delinquents who influence him. I just need to take my time and discipline this behavior. I feel relaxed. My forehead, nose, lips, neck, shoulders and arms are relaxed. I'm taking a deep breath of comfort, and I'm exhaling relaxation. My legs are tense. I better concentrate on my thighs. I can feel them releasing tension and getting more and more relaxed. My calf muscles are relaxed completely. The undesired behavior is that Johnny just stuck his tongue at me. The desired behavior is that he keep his tongue in his mouth and talk to me nicely. Let me just think of some disciplines for this undesired behavior. If I yelled at him he would not learn how to keep his tongue in his mouth and he could get upset. However, I know he wouldn't like that. If I didn't let him use the TV he would learn that he will get a negative consequence for sticking his tongue out, but this doesn't teach him what to do. If I ignore him he would not be getting attention for sticking his tongue out, and he wouldn't get upset, but he wouldn't learn what to do. A good thing about ignoring is that I'm in a rush, and this discipline is fast. I think I'll ignore him because sticking his tongue out isn't hurting anyone or damaging property, and he will learn that it has no effect on me. He sticks out his tongue at me but I just turn my head and walk away. After a few seconds he comes over to me and says he's sorry. I really like how I found a discipline that I can do quickly and without providing him attention for the undesired behavior."

  2. Give the caregiver a copy of the ICARE Recording Form (Table 9.18) and tell the caregiver that performance on each practice trial will be recorded in the columns next to the items that are listed in the far left column. Also, tell the caregiver that some of the responses will be scored on a 0 to 100 scale and other responses require a brief description.

    For example: "Here is a copy of the ICARE Recording Form. As you can see, in the left column there are a number of items. When practice trials are performed, like the one I just did, we will both rate how effective the person was in performing these items. Some of the responses will be scored on a 0 to 100 scale, while other responses require a brief description."

  3. The clinician should demonstrate the evaluation and recording process by rating the clinician's practice trial.

    For example : "Let me show you how to rate a practice trial. I'll use the scene I just modeled. I would rate my Pre-Rating of Anger at about a 3 because I was able to yell stop as soon as I recognized that Johnny stuck his tongue out at me. My stop was stated very firmly, and forcefully. I would give my stop an intensity rating of a 90. I stated my three highest rated possible explanations. However, I didn't state them quickly, and my facial expression could have reflected a little less anger. I would rate my possible explanation rehearsal a 75. I would rate my relaxation about 90 because I was very

TABLE 9.18

ICARE Recording Form

Items	Date	Date	Date	Date	Date	Date	Date	Date
Pre-rating of anger (0–100 rating of anger)								
Stop (0–100 intensity rating)								
Negative consequences (or possible explanations) (0–100 rating of negativity; or 0–100 explanatory)								
Relaxation (0–100 rating of relaxation)								
Undesired behavior (What was it?)								
Desired behavior (What was it?)								
Discipline selected (e.g., time out, correction, positive practice, overcorrection, verbal or written contract, ignoring, loss of privilege, etc.)								
Implementation of discipline								
Self-reinforcement								
Post-rating of anger (0–100 rating)								

relaxed. I took my time reviewing all of my muscles, and was able to do this review in about 10 seconds. The undesired behavior was that he stuck his tongue at me. The desired behavior was that he keep his tongue in his mouth and talk to me calmly. The discipline chosen was to ignore. I would say that my imagined rehearsal was short but to the point, about a 90 rating. I liked this discipline because I am consequencing the undesired behavior by not letting him get any attention. I would rate my post anger at a 0 because I am not at all angry. I liked that I found a quick discipline that consequences his behavior in a way that doesn't give him any reinforcement."

4. Instruct the caregiver to provide his/her evaluation, and descriptively praise correct responding and consistency with the clinician's evaluation. Also, provide prompts to elicit correct responding and consistencies.

5. Instruct the caregiver to roleplay the entire ICARE procedure for another situation. While performing the ICARE procedure, the ICARE recording form may be utilized as a guide to prompt correct responding, and the clinician should perform the following during the caregiver's performance.

   a. Provide praise and encouragement throughout the caregiver's ICARE performance.

   b. Whenever the caregiver hesitates the clinician should prompt or model the correct response.

6. Provide praise for successful completion of the trial, and then instruct the caregiver to evaluate his/her performance according to the items on the ICARE Recording Form. (The clinician should also evaluate the caregiver's performance utilizing a separate recording form.)

   For example: "That was a great first trial. Before we review your trial and record how you thought you did on the ICARE Recording Form. I'll record how I thought you did on this form."

7. Instruct the caregiver to disclose his/her responses to the items, one at a time from top to bottom. After each response is disclosed, perform the following:

   a. Descriptively praise correct responding.

b. Disclose the clinician's response for the item, and praise consistency with the clinician's evaluation of performance.

c. Provide prompts to elicit correct responding, when necessary.

> For example: "Tell me how you rated your intensity. (caregivers response) Twenty sounds about right, because you said three or four things about Johnny that were negative. Twenty is not much different from my rating. I gave you a 30. How could you have brought your score down lower? (caregiver responds) I agree. If you said less things about the undesired behavior, you could catch yourself before it got out of control by saying stop strongly. How did you rate your stop?" (and so on)

8. Instruct the caregiver to perform more trials utilizing the aforementioned guidelines.

K. Homework.

1. Provide the caregiver with a blank ICARE Recording Form.

2. Assign the caregiver to practice at least one ICARE trial at home per day for undesired behaviors that have happened in the past, and record the caregiver's evaluation of each trial in the ICARE Recording Form.

3. Do not assign the caregiver to attempt the ICARE procedure in vivo.

> For example: "I want you to practice at least one ICARE trial at home per day in a quiet room in your house. Imagine situations in which Johnny has performed undesired behaviors in the past. For each trial, record your performance evaluation in the ICARE Recording Form. We'll go over this form next time we meet."

L. Reviewing homework in subsequent sessions.

1. The ICARE Recording Form should be reviewed each session, and should consist of the following:

a. Instruct the caregiver to disclose his/her responses for several of the trials.

b. Descriptively praise caregiver for attempting homework and correct responding.

c. Provide prompts to elicit correct responding, whenever necessary.

> For example: "Tell me how you rated your performance for one of the trials that you performed since I saw you last. (caregiver's response) That's great how you attempted your homework. It seems like you stopped your anger right after he threw the ball in the pool. That's terrific. How could you have increased your intensity? (caregiver's response) Squeezing your hands as you say stop to yourself seems like a real winner. I'm particularly impressed with your decision to use positive practice. Why did you think that discipline would be most effective? (caregiver's response) I think many caregivers wouldn't have thought about teaching him what to do as a discipline. Way to go, and I guess your hard work paid off as you said that your post-anger rating was 0. Tell me about the second trial you did?" (and so on)

2. Instruct the caregiver to perform several trials, and after each trial provide feedback according to the guidelines (prompts may be utilized during performance, whenever necessary).

CONCLUDING COMMENTS

Less than a decade ago, empirically derived prescriptive treatments, such as the one reviewed in this chapter, were primarily utilized in treatment outcome studies. Indeed, the recent introduction of prescriptive psychological treatments to the private sector has been marked by resistance and uncertainty. Many treatment providers are concerned that standardized clinical methods are unable to address multifaceted and multidimentional clinical problems. Of course, standardized approaches are limited in this respect. However, contemporary demands have necessitated that psychological treatment providers go beyond the commonly accepted practice of determining and utilizing treatment methods based solely on "clinical lore" or their interpretation of procedures depicted in treatment outcome studies. Moreover, standardized empirically supported therapies are becoming increasingly comprehensive and sophisticated. For instance, this manual includes 10 therapies that incorporate several treatment components to address multiple problems evinced by the victim and his/her family. Relatedly, in developing these interventions we found that inexperienced clinicians who adhered to treatment protocol demonstrated much greater success with their families than did those experienced clinicians who did not closely adhere to their treatment manuals. As expected, experienced clinicians who demonstrated treatment protocol adherence were most effective. Thus, we highly recommend that this manual not be used as a replacement for clinical supervision and staff training, but rather as a guide to enhance intervention.

REFERENCES

Abidin, R. (1990). Parenting Stress Index. Charlottesville, VA: Pediatric Psychology Press.

Beck, A. T., Ward, C. H., Mendelsohn, M., Mock, J., & Erbaugh, J. (1961). An inventory for measuring depression. *Archives of General Psychiatry, 4*, 561–571.

Besalel, V. A. & Azrin, N. H. (1981). The reduction of parent–youth problems by reciprocity counseling. *Behaviour Research and Therapy, 19*, 297–301.

Briere, J., Berliner, L., Bulkey, J. A., Jenny, C., & Reid, T. (Eds.). (1996). *The APSAC handbook on child maltreatment.* Thousand Oakes, CA: Sage.

Brunk, M., Henggeler, S. W., & Whelan, J. P. (1987). Comparison of multisystemic therapy and parent training in the brief treatment of child abuse and neglect. *Journal of Consulting and Clinical Psychology, 55,* 171–178.

Chaffin, M., Kelleher, K., & Hollenberg, J. (1996). Onset of physical abuse and neglect: Psychiatric, substance abuse, and social risk factors from prospective community data. *Child Abuse and Neglect, 20,* 191–203.

Curtis, P. A., Boyd, J. D., Liepold, M., & Petit, M. (1995). *Child abuse and neglect: A look at the states.* Washington, DC: Child Welfare League of America.

Donohue, B., Ammerman, R. T., & Zelis, C. (1997). Child physical abuse and neglect. In T. S. Watson & F. M. Gresham (Eds.), *Child behavior therapy: Ecological consideration in assessment, treatment, and evaluation.* New York: Plenum.

Donohue, B., Van Hasselt, V. B., Warshal, S., Hersen, M., & Schoenwald, D. (1996, November). Relationship satisfaction among victims of and perpetrators of child maltreatment: Is it reciprocal? In J. R. Lutzker (Chair), *Child abuse and neglect: The cutting edge.* Symposium conducted at the Association for the Advancement of Behavior Therapy, New York.

Egan, K. (1983). Stress management and child management with abusive parents. *Journal of Clinical Child Psychology, 12,* 292–299.

Eyberg, S., & Ross, A. W. (1978). Assessment of child behavior problems: The validation of a new inventory. *Journal of Clinical Child Psychology, 7,* 113–116.

Fantuzzo, J. W. (1990). Behavioral treatment of the victims of child abuse and neglect. *Behavior Modification, 14,* 316–339.

Finch, A. J., Saylor, C. F., & Edwards, G. I. (1985). Children's depression inventory: Sex and grade norms for normal children. *Journal of Consulting and Clinical Psychology, 13*, 424–425.

Friedrich, W. N., Grambsch, P., Damon, L., Koverola, C., Wolfe, V., Hewitt, S. K., Lang, R. A., & Broughton, D. (1992). Child Sexual Behavior Inventory: Normative and clinical comparisons. *Psychological Assessment, 3*, 303–311.

Gaudin, J. M., Jr., Wodarski, J. S., Arkinson, M. K., & Avery, L. S. (1990). Remedying child neglect: Effectiveness of social network interventions. *Journal of Applied Social Sciences, 15*, 97–123.

Kolko, D. J. (1996). Clinical monitoring of treatment course in child physical abuse: Psychometric characteristics and treatment comparisons. *Child Abuse and Neglect, 20*, 23–43.

Kovacs, M., & Beck, A. (1983). *The Children's Depression Inventory: A self-rating depression scale for school-aged youngsters*. Unpublished manuscript, Western Psychiatric Institute and Clinic, Pittsburgh.

Lutzker, J. R. (1990). Behavioral treatment of child neglect. *Behavior Modification, 14*, 301–315.

Milner, J. S. (1986). *The Child Abuse Potential Inventory: Manual* (2nd ed.). Webster, NC: PSYTEC.

Moos, R. H., & Moos, B. S. (1986). *Family Environment Scale manual* (2nd ed.). California: Consulting Psychologists Press.

Ollendick, T. H. (1983). Reliability and validity of the Revised Fear Survey for Children (FSSCR). *Behavior Research and Therapy, 21*, 685–692.

Ollendick, T. H., King, N. J., & Frary, R. B. (1989). Fears in children and adolescents: Reliability and generalizability across gender, age, and nationality. *Behaviour Research and Therapy, 27*, 19–26.

Pino, C. J., Simmons, N., & Slawinoski, M. J. (1984). *The children's version of the Family Environment Scale manual*. New York: Slosson Educational Publications.

Reynolds, C. R., & Richmond, B. O. (1978). What I think and feel: A revised measure of children's manifest anxiety. *Journal of Abnormal Child Psychology, 6*, 271–280.

Reynolds, C. R., & Richmond, B. O. (1985). *Revised–Children's Manifest Anxiety Scale manual*. California: Western Psychological Services.

Robinson, E. A., Eyberg, S. M., & Ross, A. W. (1980). The standardization of an inventory of child conduct problem behaviors. *Journal of Clinical Child Psychology, 9*, 22–29.

Schinke, S. P., Schilling, R. F., Kirham, M. A., Gilchrist, L. D., Barth, R. P., & Blythe B. J. (1986). Stress management skills for parents. *Journal of Child and Adolescent Psychotherapy, 3*, 293–298.

Smucker, M. R., Craighead, W. E., Craighead, L. W., & Green, B. J. (1986). Normative and reliability data for the Children's Depression Inventory. *Journal of Abnormal Child Psychology, 14*, 25–39.

Stark, E. & Flitcraft, A. (1988). Women and children at risk: A feminist perspective on child abuse. *International Journal of Health Services, 18*, 97–118.

Tertinger, D. A., Greene, B. F., & Lutzker, J. R. (1984). Home safety: Development and validation of one component of an ecobehavioral treatment program for abused and neglected children. *Journal of Applied Behavior Analysis, 17*, 159–174.

Whiteman, M., Fanshel, D., & Grundy, J. F. (1987). Cognitive-behavioral interventions aimed at anger of parents at risk of child abuse. *Social Work, 32*, 469–474.

Wolfe, D. (1985). Child-abusive parents: An empirical review and analysis. *Psychological Bulletin, 97*, 462–482.

Wolfe, V. V., Gentile, C., Michienski, T., Sas, T., & Wolfe, D. A. (1991). The children's impact of traumatic events scale: A measure of post-sexual-abuse PTSD symptoms. *Behavioral Assessment, 13*, 359–383.

Part III

Treatment of Adolescent Disorders and Problems

Chapter 10

Application of the Teaching-Family Model to Children and Adolescents With Conduct Disorder

---

Kathryn A. Kirigin
Montrose M. Wolf
University of Kansas

This chapter describes the essentials of the Teaching-Family Model system as applied in a small family-style residential group home setting. The treatment model began in 1967 in Lawrence, Kansas, with the establishment of Achievement Place for Boys. Since then, the program has been refined, replicated, and disseminated nationally. The Teaching-Family Model now includes an integrated system of staff selection and training, specific behavioral treatment strategies, and routine quality control procedures. It is this system of service delivery as applied to problem adolescents that has provided the foundation for our research efforts. Based on nearly 30 years of research experience with the model's application to children and adolescents with severe behavior problems, the model can best be described as one that emphasizes changing conduct rather than curing disorder.

DESCRIPTION OF CONDUCT DISORDERS

Conduct disorder is a psychiatric diagnostic category used to classify the behavior of children or teenagers who engage in multiproblem behavior over an extended period of time. According to the *DSM–IV* (American Psychiatric Association, 1994), "The essential feature of Conduct Disorder is a repetitive and persistent pattern of behavior in which the basic rights of others or major age-appropriate societal norms or rules are violated (Criterion A). These behaviors fall into four main groupings: aggressive conduct that causes or threatens physical harm to other people or animals (Criteria A1–A7), nonaggressive conduct that causes property loss or damage (Criteria A8–A9), deceitfulness or theft (Criteria A10–A12), and serious violations of rules (Criteria A13–A15)" (p. 85). At least three characteristics must have been present during the past 12 months with at least one present during the past 6 months. The problem behaviors are usually evident across settings such as home, school, and community, and cause "clinically significant impairment in social, academic, or occupational functioning (Criterion B)" (p. 85). Onset of conduct disorders can be in childhood or in adolescence.

Other characteristics that have been associated with conduct disorder include lack of empathy or concern for the feelings, wishes, and well-being of others; frequent misperception of the intentions of others; lack of appropriate remorse or guilt; blaming others; poor self-esteem; poor frustration tolerance; irritability, temper outbursts, and recklessness; higher accident rates; early onset of sexual behavior; drinking, smoking, and use of illegal substances; and low intelligence (leading to poor academic performance in school).

DESCRIPTION OF THE YOUTH SERVED IN
TEACHING-FAMILY GROUP HOMES

In 1967, when Achievement Place for Boys began admitting youths, all were adjudicated by the juvenile court for problems such as destruction of property, theft, ungovernable behavior, truancy, school failure, and running away from home. The problems typically crossed home, school, and community settings. Of the first 30 boys admitted to Achievement Place, 30% were diagnosed with adolescent adjustment reaction, 20% as unsocialized aggressive, 17% with childhood schizophrenia, 10% as psychopathic personality, and 7% as psychotic personality. According to juvenile court records, 57% had committed some type of felony and 40% had a history of drug abuse. According to school records, 80% were labeled as school behavior problems, and 53% were characterized as emotionally disturbed (E. L. Phillips, E. A. Phillips, Fixsen, & Wolf, 1974). Although some of the diagnostic categories have changed over the years, the presenting problems have remained quite similar. Recent diagnoses of children and adolescents served in Teaching-Family programs cover the full range of disorders listed in the *DSM–IV*. Regardless of the psychiatric diagnoses, all of the residents admitted to the Teaching-Family programs have exhibited many of the problems that make up the diagnostic category of Conduct Disorder.

Although there is no reporting mechanism in place to estimate the prevalence of diagnostic labels assigned to youth in Teaching-Family residential programs, diagnostic information from Boys Town, which uses the Teaching-Family Model, is informative. Since 1994, over 500 Boys Town residents have completed the Diagnostic Interview Scale for Children (DISC–R). Results show that 40% of the boys and 40% of the girls at Boys Town met the criteria for a diagnosis of conduct disorder (Almquist, personal communication, April 1996).

A BRIEF DESCRIPTION OF THE TEACHING-FAMILY MODEL

The Achievement Place (Teaching-Family) Model is a residential treatment approach originally developed to provide an alternative to institutionalization for adolescent boys characterized as delinquent or at risk for delinquency ("predelinquent"). The model began as a set of behavioral treatments applied by a husband–wife team (teaching-parents) to correct problem behaviors of the six to eight children who resided with them in a family-style group home setting. In the early days of the program, the most conspicuous behavioral treatment was the token economy or motivation system (E. L. Phillips, E. A. Phillips, Fixsen, & Wolf, 1972). The token system offered structure by spelling out consequences for both appropriate and inappropriate behavior (E. L. Phillips, 1968). Later, a self-government system was added that provided the youth with the opportunity to have input into the treatment program procedures and goals (Fixsen, E. L. Phillips, & Wolf, 1973; E. L. Phillips, E.A. Phillips, Wolf, & Fixsen, 1973). Next was the explication of specific skill-teaching strategies for correcting problem behavior (Kirigin et al., 1975). The final step in program development was the recognition of the importance of relationship development between teaching-parent and youth in promoting positive behavioral change (Solnick, Braukmann, Bedlington, Kirigin, & Wolf, 1981; Willner, Braukmann, Kirigin, Fixsen, E. L. Phillips, & Wolf, 1977).

From the beginning, the program was designed so it could be replicated in other communities. Over time, despite encountering problems in attempts to replicate and disseminate treatment strategies, a conceptualization of the essential elements of the model evolved. Today, the Teaching-Family Model involves a complex system of care driven by the direct care staff (the teaching-parents), supported by knowledgeable trainers and evaluators, with all members of the system accountable for their contribution to the system (Wolf, Kirigin, Fixsen, Blase, & Braukmann, 1995). To implement the model fully within the context of a group home setting serving six to eight youths requires about a year of ongoing training and support services provided by qualified Teaching-Family training sites. Currently, there are 27 agencies throughout the country certified by the Teaching-Family Association to provide Teaching-Family services.

Over the years, considerable effort has been devoted to describing the treatment procedures, training protocols, and evaluation technology that comprise the Teaching-Family Model. To date, there are at least three published handbooks that describe the procedural elements of the Teaching-Family Model (Boys Town Family Home Program: Training Manual, 1986; E. L. Phillips, E. A. Phillips, Fixsen, & Wolf, 1972, 1974), a two-volume staff training manual (Braukmann & Blase, 1979), and a manual for consultation (Boys Town Family Home Program: Consultation Manual, 1990). Replication of both the treatment methods and the program outcomes has been documented in scores of published articles, including one by Wolf, Kirigin, Fixsen, Blase, and Braukmann (1995) describing the development of the model, and another by Kirigin (1996) focusing on the application of the model to children and adolescents with severe problem behaviors. Condensing volumes of procedural descriptions, training protocols, and evaluation methods to a 50- to 100-page manual is a daunting task. But it also provides the opportunity to present current thinking about a treatment model that continues to evolve. Before describing the treatment and training procedures, we consider some key features of the Teaching-Family Model.

THE ESSENTIAL ELEMENTS OF THE TEACHING-FAMILY MODEL

The Teaching-Family Model is an integrated system that includes program goals, treatment methods applied within a specific environmental context, and reciprocal feedback systems to ensure the youths are receiving optimal care and are progressing toward their individual treatment goals. Elements of the Teaching-Family Model have been outlined in detail by the Teaching-Family Association (Teaching-Family Association Newsletter, 1990) and Wolf et al. (1995). The key elements of the model are illustrated in Table 10.1.

TABLE 10.1

The Elements of the Teaching-Family Model

Program Goals
1. Humane intervention procedures
2. Effective treatment of behavior problems
3. Responsive to the program consumers
4. Replicable
5. Cost-effective treatment

Treatment Program Environment
1. Live-in direct care married couple (teaching-parents)
2. Family-style living
3. Maximum of eight residents
4. Full time teaching-parent assistant (at minimum)
5. Proximity to and accessibility to family, school, and community settings

Treatment Program Components
1. Skill-teaching systems (descriptive praise, preventive, and corrective teaching)
2. Procedures to encourage the development of mutually rewarding relationships between teaching-parents and residents
3. Individualized motivation systems that emphasize personal responsibility
4. Self-government systems which empower residents to make treatment and life decisions
5. Integration of treatment procedures to promote optimal outcomes

Program Support Services for Teaching-Parents
1. Initial preservice orientation and skill training workshop
2. Routine phone and in-home consultation
3. Regular inservice skill training to promote continued skill development
4. Annual consumer evaluation to obtain feedback about the strengths and weaknesses of program implementation from program consumers including the youth, their parents and teachers, and other relevant stakeholders
5. Training-site consumer evaluation that gives teaching-parents the opportunity to assess the overall quality of the training and support services

There is no such thing as a free-standing autonomous Teaching-Family group home. All bona fide teaching-family group homes are affiliated with a training site or center that has been certified by the Teaching-Family Association as capable of providing the full complement of training, consultation, and evaluation services needed to sustain a Teaching-Family Model treatment program. A training site typically consists of administrative staff, trainers, consultants, and program evaluators. A site can serve as few as four group homes or as many as 100. Most training sites serve group homes that are in close proximity (within a 2-hour drive) to their administrative offices to facilitate program training, support, and evaluation services.

Within the first 30 days of their employment as teaching-parents, all couples participate in a preservice workshop providing from 50 to 100 hours of instruction in the basic elements of the Teaching-Family Model. Focus of the initial training workshop is to provide orientation to the philosophy and technology of treatment, and to provide couples with the basic teaching, motivation, and relationship development skills they will need to implement the treatment program (Braukmann, Kirigin Ramp, Tigner, & Wolf, 1984). Once the preservice workshop is completed and teaching-parents return to their group homes to apply the model, serious learning of the model commences. To facilitate the learning process, each couple works with a training consultant experienced in the treatment model. The consultant is available to a couple to answer questions about procedures and to provide support and feedback to ensure correct application of the treatment elements. With new couples, a consultant may be in daily phone contact, and will visit at least weekly. As the couples' skills develop, consultation contacts are adjusted accordingly, but include no less than monthly in-home visits to observe teaching-parents as they apply the program components, and to review the treatment plan for each youth. Phone consultation continues to be available on an "as needed" basis.

Teaching-parent and support staff accountability is a hallmark of the Teaching-Family Model. Accountability is based on consumer-driven feedback systems. Teaching-parents receive feedback both from consultants and youth and from related "consumer" groups involved with the youth's care. The support staff, consisting of trainers, consultants, and evaluators, receives feedback on the quality of their services from the teaching parents as well as agencies (boards of directors and social service referral entities) they serve. It is consumer feedback that determines whether teaching-parents achieve certification status indicating mastery of the Teaching-Family Model; it is consumer feedback that determines whether a training site achieves certification as a Teaching-Family training site.

ASSESSMENT METHODS

Regardless of the presence of diagnosis or label, all youths are referred to Teaching-Family programs because they have experienced problems in their schools, homes, and communities. In the state of Kansas, all group home referrals are processed through the juvenile court system, either as adjudicated offenders or as children in need of care. For many, their problems have origins in childhood and most have experienced other types of intervention prior to their placement in group home settings. There are, however, limits to the kind of youth who can be served in Teaching-Family homes. For example, most Teaching-Family group homes refuse to accept youths whose behavior presents a danger to teaching-parents or their children, or to other youths in the home.

There are no standardized behavioral assessment protocols in place for Teaching-Family youth. Identification of the referring problem or problems that precipitate a youth's placement generally comes from information contained in the social case histories and related admission material, supplemented by interviews with the youths, their parents, and relevant social service staff. From these materials and sources, teaching-parents attempt to translate the information into behaviorally specific antecedent conditions and overt, observable behaviors that constitute the major presenting problems. In general, the problems are defined in the broadest sense as any behavior that is perceived as harmful to others, is disturbing or disruptive, or produces negative outcomes for the youth.

Once the youth is in placement, behavioral assessment is an ongoing activity carried out by the teaching-parents and support staff (consultants) who observe the youth's behavior firsthand as they interact with the staff, peers, parents, and others. These direct observations are supplemented by youth self-report; by secondhand observations of other professionals such as teachers, social workers, and therapists who regularly interact with the youth; and by ongoing contacts with the youth's parents or guardians. The goal of the varied and multiple-sources assessment strategy is to pinpoint the problem behaviors that preclude the youth's successful functioning in family, school, or community settings. Conduct assessment in the group home is a daily activity that covers such routine behaviors as greeting and departure skills, asking permission, accepting criticism, following instructions (compliance), accepting the answer "no," reporting whereabouts, asking for help, cooperation, keeping commitments, accepting responsibility, rational problem solving, personal hygiene, and general housekeeping tasks.

Problem assessment sets the occasion for creating a behavioral treatment plan that defines socially acceptable alternatives for each of the identified problem behaviors. For example, a youth who displays passive aggressive behavior in response to criticism from an adult will learn the skills of accepting feedback as well as those of disagreeing appropriately. The treatment planning process is facilitated by the availability of a skill curriculum (Dowd & Tierney, 1992) and related resource material that have extended the original set of social, self-care, and academic skills contained in the revised edition of the *Teaching-Family Handbook* (E. L. Phillips et al., 1974).

TREATMENT COMPONENTS

Treatment procedures focus on developing appropriate conduct as a means of addressing the disorder. Regardless of the presenting problems, when a youth first enters the treatment program, teaching-parents begin to teach five basic social skills: following instructions, accepting criticism, asking permission, reporting whereabouts, and basic social pleasantries (acknowledging the presence of another person, greeting and departure skills). The behavioral steps for each skill are illustrated in Table 10.2. Other basic social skills taught during the first few weeks include accepting compliments, accepting positive points, accepting point fines, and accepting the answer "no." Without these basic skills, especially those pertaining to following instructions and accepting criticism, learning of more difficult and complex skills is precluded. Most youths learn these basic skills during the first few weeks in the program. Learning is facilitated by 20 to 30 interactions with the teaching-parents each day with specific focus on one or two "target" skills.

TABLE 10.2

Basic Social Skills and Definitions

Following Instructions
  1. Maintain eye contact (facial expression should be neutral or positive).
  2. Say okay.
  3. Get started within 5 seconds.
  4. Check back when the task is complete.

Accepting Criticism
  1. Maintain eye contact (facial expression should be neutral).
  2. Acknowledge the feedback by saying okay (neutral voice tone).
  3. Make a statement of correction.
  4. Ask for feedback as to the adequacy of correction (e.g., Is that better?).

Requesting Permission
  1. Maintain eye contact.
  2. Phrase the request in the form of a question.
  3. Don't argue if the answer is no.

Greeting Skills (meeting a person for the first time)
  1. Stand up and approach the guest.
  2. Maintain eye contact.
  3. Extend your hand and give a firm handshake.
  4. In a clear voice, state your name (e.g., Hi, my name is Mike.)
  5. Give a follow-up statement such as, "It's nice to meet you."

Skill Teaching Procedures

The skill teaching element of the teaching-family treatment is an essential feature of the Teaching-Family Model. The skill shaping process is an arduous task that requires patience and planning. The process is guided by the treatment plan, which identifies and defines the long-term target skills as well as the specific behaviors that will contribute to achievement of the goals. At any one time, a youth will have two to three target skills. Strategies for teaching specific behavioral skills rely on the principles of learning and behavior shaping. Each social skill is defined as a series of observable steps. To teach these skills, teaching-strategies that emphasize positive feedback and reinforcement using the principles of behavior shaping have been developed. For teaching-parents, to implement effective behavior shaping requires a clear definition of the behavioral steps that comprise each skill, the ability to observe those behaviors in the youth's repertoire that most closely approximate the steps needed for the skill, and selective attention to appropriate behavior. Being able to sustain eye contact with an adult, for example, is a behavior many youths lack. Eye contact is also a component of many of the basic skills taught in Teaching-Family programs. For a youth who looks down or away when interacting with teaching-parents, praise and point consequences are awarded initially for any glances at the teaching-parents. Once glancing behavior has increased, teaching-parents selectively reward longer and longer gazes until natural sustained eye contact is achieved. The skill shaping process may require days or even months, depending on the youth's entry skills and the complexity of the skill being taught.

Complex social skills development is also promoted using modeling principles Modeling of the desired behavior by the teaching-parents and other youths appears to facilitate the learning process for many youths. By having the teaching-parents model the same type of skills they expect the youths to demonstrate as they interact with the youths and other program consumers, the teaching-parents emphasize the functional value of the skill for all family members.

Before each target is set, teaching-parents discuss the specific behavioral criteria with the youth. The skill steps are described and/or demonstrated. The teaching-parent then offers a rationale that will explain, in terms that the youth can understand, the value of the skill to the youth and how successful acquisition will lead to the achievement of the targeted treatment goal. In general, rationales are descriptions of the natural positive consequences, either personal or social, that the youth is likely to experience when performing the skill. The point of this phase of skill acquisition is to get the youth to agree on the skill definition, to be able to name the skill steps, and to make a commitment to acquiring the skill. To facilitate a youth's acquisition of skill steps, some teaching-parents utilize peer tutoring, whereas others post the skill steps or use study sessions where youths earn points for being able to identify the steps for important target skills. Usually this phase can be accomplished in a few brief sessions.

Once the youth can verbalize steps to the particular skill (e.g., following instructions), the next phase involves structured practice of the skill in controlled, behavioral rehearsal situations using a preventive teaching interaction strategy (E. L. Phillips et al., 1974) shown in Table 10.3. Interactions in this phase of skill acquisition usually occur in a neutral setting and begin in the absence of any presenting problem. To initiate a preventive teaching interaction, the teaching-parents will begin by reiterating the skill steps and the rationales followed by a skill rehearsal exercise that provides the youth with a hypothetical situation in which to demonstrate the skill. A general rule of thumb is that there be at least two skill rehearsals each day for each target behavior identified.

TABLE 10.3
Preventive Teaching Interaction

1. *Introduce the skill to be taught.* For example, "Billy, today we are going to work on learning how to follow instructions."

2. *Describe the specific behavioral steps that comprise the skill.* For example, "Billy, there are four steps to following instructions in our home. The first is to look at the person who is giving the instruction, while keeping a pleasant or neutral facial expression. Second, say 'Okay.' Third, you need to get started on the task immediately (that is within 5 secs.). And fourth, be sure to check back with the teaching-parent when the task is completed."

3. *Provide a rationale that specifies the value of this skill for the youth.* For example, "Billy, learning to follow instructions without arguing will help you with your teachers, your coaches, and your parents, as well as here at Achievement Place."

4. *Avoid lecturing the youth.* That is, try to make the teaching more of an interaction and less of a lecture by seeking acknowledgment from the youth as you describe the skill steps or the rationale. For example, asking youths if they understand the skill steps or the rationale is a good way to keep them engaged in the interaction.

5. *Have the youth verbalize the steps to the skill.* "Bill, can you name the four steps?" (Generally point consequences would be awarded for each step named.)

6. *Have the youth practice the steps to the skill.* "All right, Billy, let's pretend that it's dinner time, and you're watching TV. I'm going to ask you to turn off the TV. Now can you remember the steps to following instructions? (Again, the youth is often asked to repeat the new skill steps before practice). Okay great, you've got the steps down. Now let's practice. Billy, would you please turn off the TV and come to dinner?"

7. *Provide feedback and points for those steps that the youth displayed correctly.* Praise the youth for those skills done correctly. For example, "Billy, you did a great job looking at me, saying okay, and getting started within 5 seconds. That's three of the four steps to instruction following. You've just earned 100 points for each of the three steps you practiced correctly." Then, describe those skills that still need to be mastered. "Next time, you need to add 'checking back' once you've completed the instruction and you'll have all the steps down."

Once the youth reliably can demonstrate the skill in preventive teaching interactions, the prompts to name the skills are gradually faded. To move from displaying the skill in a neutral setting to the real situations that occur in the group home context, the teaching-parents employ a delayed practice strategy (E. L. Phillips et al., 1974). When the youth has mastered the skill in a practice situation, the teaching-parents inform the youth that they will seek them out in the next 10 to 15 minutes and give them the opportunity to demonstrate it. Situations usually are contrived and simplified to increase likelihood of successful performance of the skill. For example, with instruction following, after the 10-minute interval has passed, the teaching-parent seeks out a youth and asks him to follow a simple instruction (e.g., sit down, or to retrieve a point card, or to turn on the stereo). The point here is to give "practice" instructions than can be completed quickly. Such delayed practice continues until the interval between the prompt and the practice is at least 24 hours. For the first few delayed practices, the teaching-parent may prompt the youths to name the skills before displaying them. The goal, however, is to get the youths to display the skill in planned behavior rehearsal sessions without immediate prompts or reminders of the necessary skill steps.

Once the youths have mastered the target skill through delayed practice, the next challenge is to teach them to display the skill under real conditions using real situations. For example, a teaching-parent might have a real request to make of a youth. Again, rather than just make it and see what happens, teaching-parents will first prompt the youth to let him/her know what skills are expected. For example, the teaching-parent might begin by letting a youth know that he/she is going to be receiving a real, not a practice, instruction that needs to be followed. The teaching-parent may prompt the youth to verbalize the steps that make up the skill before presenting the real situation. Once the youth names the skills, the teaching parents will provide the real instruction. If the youth performs all of the steps to "instruction following," praise and points are provided along with a rationale that emphasizes how the skill will help them succeed in everyday interactions with other people. If youths do not demonstrate all of the steps, a corrective teaching-interaction strategy is applied as illustrated in Table 10.4.

In general, corrective teaching is not employed to deal with a problem behavior, until the alternative skill has been introduced using preventive teaching. Corrective teaching occurs in response to the youth's imperfect use of a skill, or failure to display it. The steps to corrective teaching are similar to those used in preventive teaching, with the addition of a description of the inappropriate behavior observed and point consequences for the inappropriate behavior. The remainder of a corrective teaching interaction focuses on describing and practicing the appropriate behavior.

Once a youth can accept corrective feedback from the teaching-parents, the next step is to teach the youth to use skills with other people such as teachers, parents, and peers. To promote skill generalization, a preventive teaching strategy is again employed with multiple practice sessions before the youth is asked to demonstrate the skill with the new person or setting. The process of skill generalization is illustrated in Table 10.5.

Relationship Development

One component of the model believed to be essential to effective skill teaching and treatment is the quality of the relationship between the teaching-parents and their youth (Bedlington, Kirigin, Wolf, Brown, & Tigner, 1979). There is evidence that youth ratings of satisfaction with the fairness, concern, and pleasantness of the teaching-parents is correlated with program effectiveness in reducing deviant behavior (Kirigin, Braukmann, Atwater, & Wolf, 1982). Over the years, there have been countless examples of highly rated couples as well as those receiving low youth satisfaction ratings. Part of what is known about preferred teaching-parent behaviors has been gleaned by observing natural contrasts in teaching-parent behavior associated with these differential ratings.

TABLE 10.4

Corrective Teaching-Interaction

1. *Begin the interaction with recognition of the youth's effort or progress in learning the skill or some type of statement of empathy for the difficulty involved in learning the skill.* For example, "Bill, I know it can be tough to learn new things and I know you've been working hard. When I asked you to empty the trash in the family room, I noticed that you looked at me, you said okay right away. You seem to have those steps down. Great!"

2. *Describe the inappropriate behavior observed.* "Bill, you forgot to check back and when I went to look for you I noticed that the trash basket was still full."

3. *Provide point consequences for the inappropriate behavior.* "Billy, you've earned a negative 1,000 points for not following instructions."

4. *Describe the appropriate behavior or acceptable alternative to the inappropriate behavior.* "Billy, when someone asks you to do something, you need not only look at him or her and say okay, like you did when I asked you to take out the trash. You also need to get right to the task and check back with the person to let them know you've done the job. Does that make sense?"

5. *Provide a rationale to the youth specifying some of the immediate natural consequences the behavior will gain for the youth.* "When you can do all the steps to instruction following, people are more likely not to nag you and they'll also be more likely to do what you ask them to do."

6. *Avoid lecturing by periodically requesting acknowledgment from the youth.*

7. *Have the youth practice the desired behavior with the opportunity to re-earn up to one half the value of the points lost.* "Billy, let's practice the four steps to instruction following. (Do you remember what the four steps are?) Okay, would you please empty the trash in the familyroom?"

8. *Provide feedback on the practice and positive point consequences up to one half of the value lost for the inappropriate behavior.* "Billy, you did a terrific job of using each of the steps to instruction following. Great work on getting started and checking back to let me know you'd finished the job. For practicing this skill with me, you've just earned 500 points."

9. *Provide general praise for cooperation, attention, and effort in learning skills to correct the problem.* "Excellent job of learning how to follow instructions."

TABLE 10.5

Corrective Teaching-Interaction

---

1. *Describe skill that has been mastered and the new setting to which it needs to be applied.* For example, "Billy, you've been doing a terrific job of accepting negative feedback from the teaching-parents. The next thing you need to learn is how to use those same skills when the feedback comes from peers."

2. *Review the specific behavioral steps that comprise the skill.* For example, "Billy, there are four steps to accepting negative feedback. The first is to look at the person who is giving the feedback, while keeping a pleasant or neutral facial expression. Second, say 'Okay'. Third, make a statement of change or request specifics steps needed to correct the problem. Fourth, demonstrate the change."

3. *Provide a rationale that specifies the value of generalizing this skill for the youth or ask the youth to supply one.* For example, "Being skilled at accepting negative feedback from your peers without getting defensive or arguing will get you more respect and will help avoid fights and bad feelings."

4. *Avoid lecturing the youth.* That is, try to make the teaching more of an interaction and less of a lecture by seeking acknowledgment or input from the youth as you describe the skill steps or the rationale.

5. *Have the youth verbalize the skill steps they will employ.*

6. *Have the youth practice the steps to the skill.* To facilitate generalization, it is important to describe the setting conditions. For example, "Tonight at family conference, your roommate is going to give you some negative feedback about your borrowing his shirt and returning it with a big stain. Now let's pretend I'm Joey and I say 'Bill, I don't mind lending you my clothes, but I don't appreciate getting my shirt back with a big spot on it.'"

7. *Provide feedback and points for those steps that the youth displayed.* "Bill, you did a terrific job of maintaining a neutral expression on your face, good eye contact, and saying you were sorry. You've earned 300 points for those steps. Now you need to add a step which is what you can do to fix the situation. How about offering to wash the shirt? If you can add in that last step you will earn 500 points next time we practice. Let's work on this skill again in about 30 minutes."

From research and observation, some notions have been garnered about factors that seem to help promote positive relationship development. According to Willner et al. (1977), youths identified pleasant voice tone, offers to help, joking, positive feedback, fairness, point giving, explanations of how or what to do, explanations of why (rationale-giving), concern, enthusiasm, politeness, getting right to the point, and smiling as desirable teaching-parent qualities. Many of these behaviors such as offers to help, behavioral specificity, positive feedback, and rationales are incorporated into teaching-strategies Other qualities such as showing concern, joking, politeness, and enthusiasm are referred to as *quality components*. These are elements that seem to enhance the value of the teaching interactions. Additional qualities that appear to contribute to positive teaching-parent youth relationships are similar to the qualities of effective teachers and counselors: empathic listening, accepting of cultural differences, being nonjudgmental.

Accordingly, teaching-parent effectiveness seems directly tied to the *reinforcing value* that the teaching-parent has for a youth (Solnick, Braukmann, Bedlington, Kirigin, & Wolf, 1981). It can be further speculated that such reinforcing value is related to the teaching-parent's verbal and nonverbal interactions with the youths and their ability to mediate other important reinforcers. Teaching-parents enhance their reinforcing value with preventive teaching to help the youths avoid problems and with the use of a corrective teaching strategy when problems occur. In both cases, the emphasis is on positive teaching process (one that emphasizes praise, encouragement, and support) as well as positive outcomes for the youth (points earned, recognition, and skill acquisition). With corrective teaching addressing a problem behavior, there is the concurrent opportunity to re-earn a proportion of lost points by practicing the appropriate skill, thus ending the interaction with point earnings, praise, and encouragement.

Relationship development begins at the time a prospective youth is interviewed as a candidate for a teaching-family program. It is a process of learning about the youth and of learning from the youth. As with any parent–child relationship, teaching-parent–youth relationships are authority based. Early in the relationship, it is the teaching-parents, as authority figures, who define appropriate and inappropriate behavior, who set and enforce the rules. As youths acquire skill proficiency, greater authority is delegated to the youths, but teaching-parents are forever authority figures.

Teaching-parents begin to develop a relationship with the youths by defining their role as a skill-teacher. As skill-teachers, teaching-parents need to convince the youths by word and by deed that they are not in the punishment business, that is, to provide negative consequences for a youth's adjudicated misbehaviors Rather, teaching-parents begin by defining their role as a teaching role. In a teaching capacity, their goal is not to take away behaviors or skills that the youth already has, but to provide opportunities to expand the youth's skill repertoire to increase chances for success in a broad range of settings. The key is to create an environment that sets youths up for success, rather than one that capitalizes on their failures. Once the teaching role is defined, it is up to the teaching-parents to demonstrate the role in practice.

During the youth's first few days and weeks in the program, the emphasis is on preventive teaching interactions and descriptive praise for observed appropriate behaviors in order to promote relationship development. Fortunately, the task of positive teaching is made easier by what teaching-parents often refer to as the "honeymoon period" when a youth first enters the program. During the honeymoon, a youth is likely to display his "best" skills while checking out the dynamics of the group home treatment environment. The honeymoon may only last a few hours or it may continue for several days. Regardless of its length, it is important for teaching-parents to capitalize on whatever positive behaviors the youths are displaying and to focus on preventive teaching that will optimize their likely success. Generally, it is during the first 2 weeks in a Teaching-Family program that the foundation is laid for complex skill development by teaching youths to follow instructions and to accept critical feedback, including point losses and corrective teaching.

Preventive teaching is critical to relationship development because it sets the youth up for success and creates an opportunity for the youth to display skills that earn points and praise from the teaching-parents. To optimize the success of preventive teaching, it should be carried out in close proximity to the actual opportunity to perform the skill. For example, teaching the steps to greeting visitors to the home just before a guest is scheduled to arrive increases likelihood of successful performance of greeting skills.

When approximations to the skill are then observed, descriptive praise and points are used to reinforce the youth's demonstration of the behaviors. Descriptive effective praise in the Teaching-Family Model includes the following components: (a) a positive statement that describes the appropriate behavior(s); (b) linking the behavior(s) to the skill taught in the preventive teaching session; (c) providing a reason specifying the natural consequences or the value of the skill to the youth; and (d) providing point consequences for displaying the behaviors.

Use of praise combined with youth-centered rationales concurrent with the presentation of points are essential features of all of the Teaching-Family Model relationship development strategies. It is through the process of social reinforcers associated with tangible point consequences that the reinforcing value of the teaching-parents is enhanced.

Relationship development is a time-consuming process of learning about each youth as a person. It is about the process of discovering likes and dislikes, strengths and weaknesses, thoughts and feelings. It is a process that requires a personal commitment of time and energy. In order to incorporate youth-centered rationales, it is essential to know what the youth values and what his reinforcers are. This learning process can only be accomplished by interacting with the youth, by observing them and talking with them, and by taking a genuine interest in their lives.

Relationships imply connections, common experiences, and reciprocity. It is a bidirectional process where teaching-parent behavior has an impact on the behavior of the youths and vice versa. Knowing how to connect with children and adolescents means knowing how to talk with them in a language they can understand, knowing how to have fun with them, and teaching them how to be fun to be around. Knowing how to communicate with youths and how to get the point across effectively can be acquired with experience. Learning to talk with youths involves sensitivity to their concerns, responsiveness to their feedback, acceptance of their criticism, and an openness to change.

Motivation System

Effective teaching requires effective individualized motivation. Motivation for youths in teaching-family homes initially comes in the form of points provided as consequences that gain a youth access to desired privileges, activities, and other reinforcers. Youths earn points for desirable behavior and lose points for inappropriate or undesirable behavior. The motivation system, in and of itself, is not seen as a direct teaching tool. Rather, it provides a practical and convenient means to reinforce desired behavior and to discourage inappropriate behavior with tangible consequences. To facilitate skill teaching, point earnings are accompanied by statements of descriptive praise, identifying the particular behavior as well as a reiteration of the reasons the behavior will benefit the youth in the immediate future. The delivery of negative consequences (point losses) simply sets the occasion for teaching youths the appropriate alternative that will help avoid future point losses. With most interactions involving a loss of points, youths are provided the opportunity to re-earn up to one half of the lost points by practicing the desired alternative. This procedure, known as positive correction, ensures that there is some response cost for the inappropriate behavior, while keeping the focus of the interaction on skill acquisition that will help avoid future point losses.

The motivation system also extends to environments away from the group home using strategies of home-based reinforcement that were developed initially to deal with school behavior problems (Bailey, Wolf, & E. L. Phillips, 1970) and later extended to work environments (Ayala, Minkin, E. L. Phillips, Fixsen, & Wolf, 1973) and home settings (Turnbough, Brown, E. L. Phillips, Fixsen, & Wolf, 1974). With home-based reinforcement, the youths carry a note that requires teachers, parents, or employers to check a "yes" or "no" in response to a series of questions about the youth's behavior in their setting. Points are earned or lost in the group home based on the feedback on the note. Again, point losses set the occasion for a discussion and practice of alternative skills.

The motivation system is constructed as a series of systems that begins with maximum structure and supervision that is gradually lessened over time as the youth acquires skills and demonstrates proficiency. Youths who enter teaching-family programs begin on a daily system, advance to a weekly point system, and finally go to a merit system where points are replaced by social and tangible consequences that operate in many family environments.

The Daily System. The motivation system begins with exaggerated structure and close supervision by teaching-parents. Youths are required to earn a "daily difference" (calculated by subtracting point losses from point earnings) of 10,000 points, which are used to purchase privileges for the following day. The purpose of the daily system is to "hook" youths on the points and to teach them the basic social skills outlined in Table 10.2 that will permit them to advance to the weekly system. The youths on a daily system are expected to be within visual contact of the teaching-parents at all times, except when they are in their rooms or the bathrooms. To maintain use of privileges during the day, a youth is required to keep a positive point balance (more positive points earned than points lost). If a negative balance is achieved at any time during the day, there is an immediate loss of access to privileges. This "zero balance" rule helps insure that youths are continuously motivated to engage in point-earning behaviors. Generally, youths on a daily system will have 20 to 30 interactions with the teaching-parent staff. Each interaction will be worth from 500 to 1,000 points, with values determined by the importance of the behavior as well as its difficulty. About half of the interactions should focus on preventive skill teaching of the basic skills, with the remainder focused on descriptive praise, including points and rationales for observed displays of the basic skills.

To maintain a positive and preventive teaching focus for a youth on the daily point system, teaching parents are expected to maintain a positive-to-negative interaction ratio of no less than 4:1. That is, for every one negative interaction, there should be at least four positive interactions, most of which pertain in some way to correcting the problem behavior evident in the negative interaction. So, for example, when a youth experiences a point loss for failing to give eye contact when following an instruction, at least one or two of the subsequent corrective interactions should involve effective praise and points for any noted display of eye contact, emphasizing its value as an important component of instruction following. In the absence of such an opportunity, a preventive teaching interaction should be used. Here it is important to remember that it is the teaching-parents' behavior that often sets the occasion for the youth to display the skills practiced in preventive teaching. If sustained eye contact is the goal, multiple opportunities must be provided that can be observed directly and that produce feedback in the form of points and praise for skill improvement.

Occasionally, a youth on a daily system may fail to earn the 10,000-point daily difference needed to purchase privileges for the next day. To avoid complete loss of motivation when a serious problem occurs, the youth is given the opportunity to make-up the privileges by earning twice the daily difference. At the point in the day at which the "make-up daily difference" is achieved, the youth has access to privileges.

Youths are required to stay on a daily point system until they earn a minimum number of points, which varies between 300,000 and 600,000. During the daily system, which generally requires 2 weeks to a month to accomplish, the youth should have learned the relationship between point earning activities and privileges should be earning privileges at least 80% of the time. The youth should also know and be able to demonstrate the five basic social skills (without prompting) in a structured skill-rehearsal.

The Weekly System.   Once the youth have met criterion on the daily system, they advance to the weekly system. With the weekly system, the youth experiences a reduction in the structure and direct supervision along with a corresponding increase in the types of privileges that can be purchased on a weekly basis. On a weekly system, the number of point interactions generally will average between 8 and 10 per youth per day, with a positive-to-negative interaction ratio that lies between 8:1 and 4:1. The weekly system, which has been characterized as the "workhorse" of the motivation system, is used to continue to refine the "basic skills" and to build those skills that are directly tied to the treatment plan and to a youth's completion of the program.

On a weekly system, the youth is required to earn a 5,000-point daily difference to purchase the basic privilege package of television, phone, stereo, and unsupervised time. Extra points can be used to negotiate for special privileges such as playing video games or going to a friend's house or to a movie or dance. Extra points can also be used to purchase bonds, which are used to advance to the final phase of the motivation system, the Merit System.

As with the daily system, failure to achieve sufficient points to purchase privileges does not mean full loss of privileges for the following week. A make-up system, which requires the youth to earn twice the 5,000-point daily difference, is available once weekly. For example, a youth on a weekly make-up, would have access to privileges each day only after having earned 10,000 points.

The Merit System.   There are two conditions that are necessary for moving on to the merit system. First, the youth must have purchased at least 100 bonds, which are available as part of the privilege system for them on the weekly system. Second, youth must have mastered the skills identified on their treatment plan. The merit system provides a test of the youth's ability to maintain appropriate behavior under more normalized conditions, without point consequences, and by negotiating privileges based on their behavior. The youth no longer carry a point card. Instead, they receive feedback from the teaching-parents and the other residents regarding their social, academic, and self-care behaviors.

Of particular importance during the merit system review is the youth's ability to accept positive as well as negative feedback from both teaching-parents and peers. Appropriate behavior is rewarded with social reinforcers such as praise and attention. Inappropriate behavior produces demerits, whose value is set by the severity and importance of the problem behavior. Behaviors that are not a problem for the youth are given a low demerit value of 1 or 2. Those directly related to the youth's treatment plan, or that would place the youth at risk in the community, school, or family, are given higher demerit values. For example, for a youth who never had problems with peers, failure to accept feedback from a peer may result in only 1 demerit. For the same youth with a history of problems accepting feedback from adults, failure to display the skill of accepting criticism could earn as many as 3 to 5 demerits.

To complete the merit system, a youth can accumulate no more than 10 demerits each week for 4 consecutive weeks. The intent here, albeit arbitrary, is to provide a youth with an opportunity to maintain skills under much less structure and scrutiny. With youths who have an average length of stay of about a year, over 80% of their experience will have been with the point system. The process of weaning youths from the structure and possible dependence on a point system has not been investigated in any systematic way. It is known, however, that the merit system rarely is mastered on a youth's first attempt. Rather, it takes several attempts for most youths to learn to function with less structure and reduced feedback.

Self-Government

The self-government system is an important element of the Teaching-Family system of behavior change. It provides the youths with the skills and opportunities to be active participants rather than passive recipients of the treatment program. In the context of family conference, youth learn how to participate in group discussion, to give constructive criticism and compliments, to problem solve, and to develop effective decision-making skills. At family conferences, which typically occur each day, youths learn the basic skills needed to participate in group discussion and to solve personal as well as family living problems. The problem-solving model is based on a SODAS system that includes specification of the problem (S), development of options for addressing the problem (O), discussing the disadvantages (D) and the advantages (A) for each proposed option, and developing a plan for solving (S) the problem. The intent of the family conference is to empower the youths by giving them the skills to solve their own problems.

Teaching youths the prerequisite family-conference skills requires a carefully individualized plan for each resident. The basic rules of family conference include the ability to sit still, maintaining eye contact with the speaker, active listening, hand raising to be recognized, offering opinions, and voting on issues. Once these skills are mastered, the more complex skills of giving feedback to peers, accepting feedback from peers, peer confrontation, and peer reporting can be addressed. The family conference also provides a testing ground for generalization of the skills to a peer group situation. For example, once a youth has learned the skill of accepting feedback from the teaching-parents and other adults, family conference provides the mechanism for extending that skill into the peer group. Family conference can be used as a vehicle for furnishing the youths with the tools to learn problem-solving skills, to suggest rule changes, to decide on appropriate consequences for infractions, and to discuss treatment issues common to the group. Family conference also provides the opportunity for group teaching about issues or skills that apply to all of the residents. For example, dealing with name calling at school is an issue that affects many youths. Rather than teach each youth individually a specific conflict avoidance skill, family conference can provide a more efficient means to introduce the skill to all of the youths. Having family meetings can also provide the opportunity for youths to generate rationales for acquiring or using the skills, which in many cases can be much more effective and credible than those provided by teaching-parents.

STAFFING AND ADMINISTERING TEACHING-FAMILY PROGRAMS

To operate a successful teaching-family home requires both the direct care staff (the teaching-parents and teaching-parent assistants) and a support staff consisting of trainers, consultants, and evaluators. Of these staff, it is the teaching-parents who carry out the most essential role as group home program directors and implementers of the treatment model.

There are no standardized personnel inventories, job interview protocols, or aptitude tests that allow teaching-parent recruiters to predict which couples will be successful in applying the Teaching-Family Model. Having some experience with parenthood is often seen as a desirable characteristic because parents have some awareness of the realities and constraints that come with living with children.

A national survey of Teaching-Parent couples (B.A. Graham, G. G. Graham, Kirigin, & Wolf, 1995) offered the following portrait of the couples. Approximately 60% have one or more children, up to a maximum of three. Of the remaining 40%, half reported having been married for less than 1 year prior to accepting the group home position. Teaching parents range in age between 21 and 60 with a mean age of about 33.5 years. Over 75% of the respondents noted some college experience, with the majority having received a bachelor's degree.

According to information from the Teaching-Family Association (formerly the National Teaching-Family Association), which monitors all Teaching-Family programs throughout North America, the average tenure for teaching-parents is about 2 years (Teaching-Family Association Publications Committee, 1993). Fewer than 10% stay less than 1 year and an equal percentage remain on the job for 5 or more years. Teaching-parents are assisted by at least one and often two full-time teaching-parent alternates or associates, who provide supplementary services and weekend relief for the teaching-parents.

Having a high tolerance for the stress of parenting created by day-to-day living with six or eight seriously challenging youth, as well as the demands of working with their social workers, probation officers, school teachers, and parents, cannot be underestimated as important to teaching-parent survival, if not success. Perhaps the most important prerequisite for the job appears to be a genuine concern for children, coupled with a commitment to positive skill teaching. One critical characteristic of successful teaching-parents appears to be their ability to model the same skills they are attempting to teach. Another quality of successful teaching-parents appears to be their personal commitment to learning and receptivity to feedback, which seem essential for mastery of the model procedures.

Personnel who serve the teaching-parents as trainers, consultants, and evaluators typically are drawn from the ranks of former teaching-parents or teaching-parent assistants who have demonstrated competence in implementing the Teaching-Family Model. Specific training protocols for training trainers, consultants, and evaluators vary considerably across the country, but in general, most involve skill training and ongoing supervision and feedback from staff who demonstrated proficiency as support staff. In addition, the support staff receive formal evaluations, at least annually but often more frequently, from their teaching-parent consumers who are the recipients of the training and support service.

RECIPROCAL SYSTEMS FEEDBACK TO ASSESS MODEL IMPLEMENTATION

Complete and accurate implementation of the Teaching-Family Model is a complex endeavor that involves multiple systems consisting of the direct care staff (the teaching-parents), the training site staff (workshop trainers, consultants, evaluators, and site director), and the Teaching-Family Association. An important factor in the evaluation of the treatment model and its survival over a 30-year period is the model's commitment to routine and systematic feedback from the consumers. Over the years, our concept of consumers has been extended beyond the original formulation, which included the only the consumers of the treatment services. Today, the need for feedback at all levels of service delivery is recognized and the feedback system now includes those persons and agencies who are recipients of the training, consultation, and evaluation services.

The Teaching-Parent Evaluation System

After the teaching-parents have been in their home for about 6 months, a complete consumer feedback evaluation and in-home evaluation is conducted by their site evaluators. The evaluator administers private confidential questionnaires to each youth in the home. The questionnaire includes a series of questions about the fairness, concern, pleasantness, and effectiveness of the teaching-parents. In addition to the youths, the consumer evaluation questionnaires are sent to everyone who has any responsibility for the youths, including the school teachers and counselors, juvenile court personnel, social welfare officials, members of the group home board of directors, parents, and the youths. These consumers receive mailed questionnaires that ask about their satisfaction with the effectiveness of the program, the cooperation and communication of the teaching-parent staff, and the quality of the treatment environment.

In addition to the consumer ratings, evaluation of the teaching parents includes an in-home assessment conducted by two members of their training site. The in-home evaluation is used to assess the teaching-parents skills in implementing the teaching strategies, the motivation system, relationship development, and self-government system. Evaluators also review program records including youth treatment plans and progress reports and they evaluate the physical condition of the home.

The in-home evaluation is a very important part of the quality control system. It provides the training staff with feedback about the implementation process. By directly observing skills of the teaching-parents and the social skills of the youths, the in-home evaluation helps protect against incomplete training or misapplication of the treatment procedures. By detecting imperfect application of the teaching interaction components or noting target skills that are developmentally inappropriate or unnatural, evaluators provide important program quality safeguard.

A written consumer evaluation report, summarizing results of the consumer evaluation and the professional in-home evaluation is distributed to the teaching-parents, the consultant, and the site administrators within 1 month of the evaluator's visit. The consultant uses such feedback to identify teaching-parent strengths and to develop plans for correcting detected problems. For example, school teachers may report that teaching-parents never communicate with them or help with the youths' school problems. The consultant's task is to help teaching-parents develop a plan for routine contact with teachers, to encourage its implementation, and to monitor the outcome.

After a year in the home, the teaching-parents undergo a certification evaluation. Again, all of the consumers receive mailed questionnaires or are interviewed by phone. A complete in-home professional evaluation is conducted including interviews with all youths. If the teaching-parents achieve criteria ratings, average scores of at least 6 on a 7-point scale for each question in each consumer area, they are certified. If they do not meet these criteria, they receive help from their consultant to develop corrective plans and are given a reasonable time frame to work on the problem areas; and another evaluation is conducted after the appropriate period. Generally, the teaching-parents complete the retake evaluations by meeting all criteria. Once certified, teaching-parents must continue to meet criteria on *annual* consumer evaluations and in-home professional evaluations to maintain their certification. If they don't achieve criterion in an area, their consultant helps them develop solutions and then reevaluations are conducted.

Site Staff Evaluation System

At the training site level of service delivery, performance of trainers, consultants, and evaluators is reviewed by the site director. All teaching-parents provide routine feedback about their training, consultation, and evaluation experiences. After each section of the initial training workshop, they complete questionnaires rating the quality and the usefulness of the presentation and the skills of the trainer. Teaching-parents also provide regular evaluation of consultation, including the availability of the consultant, clarity of advice, usefulness of feedback, and responsiveness to their program needs. In addition, the performance of the teaching-parents, as assessed by the consumer evaluation, provides information on the consultant's skill in helping teaching-parents master the Teaching-Family Model procedures. Feedback on trainer and consultant behavior is reviewed by the site director. As with teaching-parent evaluations, evaluations of training and consultation staff help identify strengths and pinpoint weaknesses. Identified weaknesses in training or consultation set the occasion for a corrective action plan, which can be monitored with repeated administration of the evaluation.

A unique feature of this feedback system is its reciprocal nature. Site staff routinely provide informal and formal feedback to the teaching-parents on the quality of program implementation. Teaching-parents also routinely provide informal and formal feedback to the site trainers, evaluators, and consultants about their satisfaction with the training and support services provided.

MANAGING TEACHING-FAMILY MODEL IMPLEMENTATION AT THE NATIONAL LEVEL

In 1977, the Teaching-Family Association (TFA) was formed with the specific purpose of safeguarding the quality of the Teaching-Family Model implemented at the regional training site. Each year, every TFA regional training site must submit a report to their designated subcommittee of TFA's Certification Committee, made up of three members who rotate off every 2 or 3 years. The report includes information about each of the annual consumer evaluations of the teaching-parents, an annual consumer evaluation of site services, a roster of site staff and their qualifications, and staff and teaching-parent turnover.

Every 3 years, at least two members of the subcommittee visit the site. Before they visit, the TFA national office mails out a complete set of questionnaires to the site's consumers and to the teaching-parents. Consumers and teaching-parents are asked to rate the quality of site services and to give specific suggestions for improving them. This feedback is summarized by staff at the national Teaching-Family Association office and distributed to the onsite reviewers prior to their visit. The onsite review includes visits to a sample of group homes and interviews with selected residents. The subcommittee members also gather firsthand information from the boards of directors, the community agencies, the site administrators, the training, consultation, and evaluation staff, and the teaching-parents. Agency records are checked for data about adherence to TFA policies and standards. Informal reliability checks are run to see if the data gathered onsite are different from the data reported in the previous annual reports.

Each year at the TFA annual meeting a report about each training site is prepared by the respective subcommittee and is distributed and discussed at the certification committee meeting, which is made up of representatives from the sites. Each site's strengths are listed and the site's problems are described. Solutions to any problems noted by the site's subcommittee are proposed. Finally, the certification committee votes by secret ballot on whether to certify each site. The certification committee meeting includes full, although confidential, disclosure of problems and discussion of solutions for each site. This important specification of behavior, monitoring, and skill-teaching function at the national level is an essential element of quality program implementation. Final action on certifying sites takes place at the meeting of the council of representatives at the annual TFA convention.

The council is made up of equal numbers of certified teaching-parent practitioners and "individual" representatives. Individual representatives consist of administrators, consultants, evaluators, researchers, and other non-teaching-parent members of the sites. Each regional training site selects a teaching-parent and an individual representative to serve on the council. The council meeting is presided over by the President who is elected for a 2-year term by all the members of TFA. The council conducts the routine business of the organization, develops policy, and has the final say about certification of sites. With few exceptions, the council typically has accepted the recommendations made by the certification committee regarding certification of the sites.

CONCLUSION

Changing the behavior of conduct disordered children and adolescents is labor intensive and long term. Post-treatment follow-up outcomes on youths who entered their Teaching-Family programs at an average age of 15 and remained for about 8 months suggest the durability of social skill training (Ramp, Gibson, & Wolf, 1990; Youngbauer, 1986) but a lack of an enduring effect on criminal behavior once the youths exit the treatment program. Unfortunately there is insufficient data to determine possible differential program impact on children who entered at a younger age and stayed longer. It is known that Teaching-Family programs in Kansas, as well as those evaluated as part of a Boys Town Follow-up Study (Oswalt & Daly, 1991), have produced consistent during-treatment effects. In both cases, Teaching-Family residents showed improvements in social skills (Youngbauer, 1986), grades and school attendance (Conrad, 1988) exceeding those of youths in non-Teaching-Family homes. Teaching-Family participants were also less likely to have formal contact with the juvenile justice system, self-report fewer delinquent acts, consume fewer drugs, and were less likely to run away from the treatment program than non-Teaching-Family comparison youths (Kirigin Ramp, Wolf, & Braukmann, 1990). Youths in Teaching-Family homes also rate their treatment experience more favorably than comparison youths (Kirigin & Wolf, 1994).

The Teaching-Family Model system of treatment is complex and behavior change during treatment is achieved only with effort. Relationships between teaching-parents and their residents are not developed overnight. Skill teaching requires consistency of definition and countless opportunities for repetition. The importance of consistent, supportive, enduring environments to address the needs of children and adolescents with serious problem behaviors has remained unchanged for the past 10 years (Wolf, Braukmann, & Kirigin Ramp, 1987) Experience with the Teaching-Family Model suggests that there is no such thing as a quick fix or "cure" for problem behaviors that have been developed and refined over a 14- or 15-year history. Behavior shaping of alternative, more adaptive skill repertoires takes a long time and it is a very stressful undertaking for the teaching-parents who pursue live-in child-care as their chosen profession (B. A. Graham et al., 1995).

Unfortunately, in recent years there has been a social service movement away from long-term treatment to short-term confinement. The family preservation movement has shifted emphasis from out-of-home placement to in-home family-based intervention. Within the past year as managed care, borrowed from health services, is extended into the social service sphere, the length of time in placement has being cut back severely. In Kansas, for example, 6-month group home-placements are now the norm. Although this shift makes sense from a cost perspective, there is little evidence to support its long-term efficacy in treating conduct-disordered youth. Given the failure of longer term treatment to achieve enduring outcomes, it is difficult to conclude that less treatment would be better.

From this perspective, the problem with effective treatment for conduct disordered children and adolescents does not rest with the treatment per se, but with our conceptualization of the problem as a set of symptoms that can be cured. A more comprehensive, long-term approach is clearly called for. With the Teaching-Family model, a replicable, consumer-preferred system of care has been created that produces demonstrable effects while the system is in place. Given the tenuous future of long-term group home treatment in a cost-conscious managed care environment, there appears to be increasing need to explore other less expensive placement alternatives. In recent years, we have seen an adaptation of the Teaching-Family Model system of care to in-home family services and to therapeutic foster care. Both hold potential for less restrictive, more normalized, longer term treatment that may hold the key to producing more lasting effects.

ACKNOWLEDGMENTS

We appreciate the valuable and careful editing skills of Carol Warren as a reviewer of earlier drafts. We also wish to thank all of the countless Teaching-Family Model practitioners, in Kansas and throughout the country, who have contributed in ways large and small to the system we have described.

The research described herein was supported by Grant MH20030 from the Center for Antisocial and Violent Behavior, National Institute of Mental Health, the Department of Human Development, and the Bureau of Child Research of the University of Kansas.

REFERENCES

American Psychiatric Association. (1994). *Diagnostic and statistical manual of mental disorders* (4th ed.). Washington, DC: Author.

Ayala, H. E., Minkin, N., Phillips, E. L., Fixsen, D. L., & Wolf, M. M. (1973, September). *Achievement place: The training and analysis of vocational behavior.* Paper presented at the meeting of the American Psychological Association, Montreal.

Bailey, J. S., Wolf, M. M., & Phillips, E. L. (1970). Home-based reinforcement and the modification of pre-delinquents' classroom behavior. *Journal of Applied Behavior Analysis, 3,* 223–233.

Bedlington, M. M., Kirigin, K. A., Wolf, M. M., Brown, W. G., & Tigner, D. M. (1979). Relationship development. In C. J. Braukmann & K. A. Blase (Eds.), *Teaching-parent training manual* (Vol. 1, pp. 73–96). Lawrence: The University of Kansas Printing Service.

Boys Town Family Home Program: Consultation Manual. (1990). Boys Town, NE: Father Flanagan's Boys Home.

Boys Town Family Home Program: Training Manual. (1986) Boys Town, NE: Father Flanagan's Boys Home.

Braukmann, C. J., Bedlington, M. M., Belden, B. D., Braukmann, P. D., Husted J. J., Kirigin Ramp, K. A., & Wolf, M. M. (1985). The effects of community-based group-home treatment programs for male juvenile offenders on the use and abuse of drugs and alcohol. *American Journal of Drug and Alcohol Abuse, 11,* 249–278.

Braukmann, C. J., & Blase, K. B. (Eds.). (1979). *Teaching-parent training manuals* (2 vols.). Lawrence: University of Kansas Printing Service.

Braukmann, C. J., Kirigin Ramp, K. A., Tigner, D. M., & Wolf, M. M. (1984). The teaching-family approach to training group home parents: Training procedures, validation research, and outcome findings. In R. Dangle & R. Polster (Eds.), *Behavioral parent training: Issues in research and practice* (pp.144–161). New York: Guilford.

Conrad, B. J. (1988). *The use of self-reported and official grades in evaluating teaching-family program effectiveness.* Unpublished master's thesis, University of Kansas, Lawrence.

Dowd, T., & Tierney, J. (Eds.). (1992). *Teaching social skills to youth: A curriculum for child-care providers.* Boys Town, NE: Boys Town Press

Fixsen, D. L., Phillips, E. L., & Wolf, M. M. (1973). Experiments in self government with predelinquents. *Journal of Applied Behavior Analysis, 6*, 31–47.

Graham, B. A, Graham, G. G., Kirigin, K. A., & Wolf, M. M. (1995, October). *Findings of a national survey of teaching-parents: Job satisfaction and burnout.* Paper presented at the annual Teaching-Family Association Meeting, Banff, Alberta, Canada.

Kirigin, K. A. (1996). Achievement place teaching-family model for group home treatment of children with severe behavior problems. In M. Roberts (Ed.), *Model treatment programs in clinical psychology.* Mahwah, NJ: Lawrence Erlbaum Associates.

Kirigin, K. A., Ayala, H. E., Braukmann, C. J., Brown, W. G., Minkin, N., Fixsen, D. L., Phillips, E. L., & Wolf, M. M. (1975). Training teaching-parents: An evaluation and analysis of workshop training procedures. In E. A. Ramp & G. Semb (Eds.), *Behavior analysis: Areas of research and application* (pp. 161–174). Englewood Cliffs, NJ: Prentice-Hall.

Kirigin, K. A., Braukmann, C. J., Atwater, J., & Wolf, M. M. (1982). An evaluation of Teaching-Family (Achievement Place) group homes for juvenile offenders. *Journal of Applied Behavior Analysis, 15*, 1–16

Kirigin, K. A., & Wolf, M. M. (1994, April). A follow-up evaluation of Teaching-Family Model participants.: Implications for treatment technology. In R.W. Force (Chair), *Various strategies for evaluating therapeutic effectiveness in treatment programs.* A symposium presented at the Southwestern Psychological Association Meeting, Tulsa, OK.

Kirigin Ramp, K. A., Wolf, M. M., & Braukmann, C. J. (1990, September). *More follow-up data from young adulthood of the kids we have treated.* Paper presented in a meeting of the National Teaching-Family Association, Salt Lake City, UT.

Oswalt, G., & Daly, D. L. (1991, October). *Long-term effects of the Boys Town Family-Home Program.* Paper presented at the meeting of the National Teaching-Family Association, Omaha, NB.

Phillips, E. L. (1968). Achievement Place: Token reinforcement procedures in a home-style rehabilitation setting for pre-delinquent boys. *Journal of Applied Behavior Analysis, 1*, 213–223.

Phillips, E. L., Phillips, E. A., Fixsen, D. L., & Wolf, M. M. (1972). *The teaching-family handbook.* Lawrence: University of Kansas Printing Service.

Phillips, E. L., Phillips, E. A., Fixsen, D. L., & Wolf, M. M. (1974). *The teaching-family handbook* (2nd ed.). Lawrence: University of Kansas Printing Service.

Phillips, E. L., Phillips, E. A., Wolf, M. M., & Fixsen, D. L. (1973). Achievement Place: Development of the elected manager system. *Journal of Applied Behavior Analysis, 6*, 541–561.

Ramp, K. K., Gibson, D. M., & Wolf, M. M. (1990, October). *The long term effects of Teaching-Family model group home treatment.* Paper presented at the 13th Annual meeting of the National Teaching-Family Association, Snowbird, UT.

Solnick, J. V., Braukmann, C. J., Bedlington, M. M., Kirigin, K. A., & Wolf, M. M. (1981). Parent–youth interaction and delinquency in group homes. *Journal of Abnormal Child Psychology, 9*, 107–119.

Solnick, J. V., Braukmann, C. J., Belden, B. D., Kirigin, K. A., & Wolf, M. M. (1981, September). *Group-home interactions and their relationship to drug use and delinquency.* Paper presented at the meeting of the American Psychological Association, Los Angeles.

Teaching-Family Association Publications Committee. (1993, October). *Annual report.* Presented at the TFA annual meeting, San Antonio, TX.

Teaching-Family Association Newsletter (1990, Spring). *Elements of the teaching-family model.* Ashville, NC: National Teaching-Family Association.

Timbers, G. D., Fixsen, D. L., Phillips, E. L., & Wolf, M. M. (1973, September) *Teaching Family homes: Community based, family-style treatment programs for adolescents with severe behavior problems.* Montreal: American Psychological Association.

Timbers, G. D., Timbers, B. L., Fixsen, D. L., Phillips, E. L., & Wolf, M. M. (1973a, September) *Achievement Place for pre-delinquent girls: Modification of inappropriate emotional behaviors with token reinforcement and instructional procedures*. Paper presented at the meeting of the American Psychological Association, Montreal.

Turnbough, P. D., Brown, W. G., Fixsen, D. L., Phillips, E. L., & Wolf, M. M. (1974). Monitoring youths' and parents behavior in the natural home. In *Achievement place: Phase II* (Vol.2). Final Report for Grant #MH 20030 from the Center for Studies in Crime and Deliquency, National Institute of Mental Health.

Werner, J. S., Minkin, N., Minkin, B. L., Fixsen, D. L., Phillips, E. L., & Wolf, M. M. (1975). Intervention package: Analysis to prepare juvenile delinquents for encounters with police officers. *Criminal Justice and Behavior, 2,* 55–83.

Willner, A. G., Braukmann, C. J., Kirigin, K. A., Fixsen, D. L., Phillips, E. L., & Wolf, M. M. (1977). The training and validation of youth-preferred social behaviors of child-care personnel. *Journal of Applied Behavior Analysis, 10,* 219–230.

Wolf, M. M., Braukmann, C. J., & Kirigin Ramp, K. A. (1987). Serious delinquent behavior as part of a significantly handicapping condition: Cures and supportive environments. *Journal of Applied Behavior Analysis, 20,* 347–359.

Wolf, M. M., Kirigin, K. A., Fixsen, D. L., Blase, K. A., & Braukmann, C. J. (1995). The teaching-family model: A case study in data-based program development and refinement (and dragon wrestling). *Journal of Organizational Behavior Management, 15,* 11–6.

Youngbauer, J. A. (1986). *Social skills & delinquency: Are they related?* Unpublished master's thesis, University of Kansas.

Chapter 11

Substance Abuse

Mark G. Myers
University of California, San Diego
Eric F. Wagner
Nova Southeastern University
Sandra A. Brown
San Diego Veterans Affairs Medical Center
University of California, San Diego

DESCRIPTION OF THE DISORDER

By definition, substance abuse refers to a pathological involvement with alcohol and/or drugs. Presence of adolescent substance abuse is largely determined by consequences of substance involvement on functioning across life domains, with the extent of involvement (i.e., quantity and frequency of use) representing a less important indicator. Problematic substance involvement by youth is most often expressed in difficulties with interpersonal relationships, increased family conflict, deterioration of academic functioning, greater levels of negative affect (e.g., depression, anxiety), and involvement in various delinquent behaviors (e.g., truancy, theft, property destruction). Adolescent substance abuse is diverse by nature, leading to difficulties in determining the direction of causality. For some teens, increased substance involvement may occur in response to difficulties (e.g., stressful life events, other psychiatric disorders), and may eventually exacerbate the original problem. For youth who have experienced few objective life difficulties, increased involvement with alcohol and other drugs may precipitate deterioration in psychosocial functioning (e.g., school problems, withdrawal and isolation, legal problems). Alternately, substance abuse may be embedded within a variety of deviant behaviors and attitudes representing a "problem behavior" syndrome (R. Jessor & S. L. Jessor, 1977).

The nature of adolescent substance abuse must always be considered in the developmental context of adolescence. In particular, adolescence is a period marked by increased experimentation and involvement with substances, such that teen alcohol and drug use can be characterized as normative behaviors (e.g., Johnston, 1995; Shedler & Block, 1990). Although adolescent alcohol and drug involvement has generated considerable concern, youth alcohol problems have not been found to strongly predict adult alcohol dependence (e.g., Blane, 1976; Newcomb &

Bentler, 1988). However, adolescent drug abuse is associated with various negative conse-quences during early adulthood, such as problematic social relationships as well as physical and psychological difficulties (Newcomb & Bentler, 1988). Relatively little is currently known about outcomes for adolescents treated for substance abuse. Recent information from longitudinal studies of clinical course following treatment for adolescent substance abuse reveals that adolescents return to alcohol and drug use following treatment at rates comparable to those for adults (Brown, Myers, Mott, & Vik, 1994; Brown, Vik, & Creamer, 1989). In addition, these adolescents display continued problems with alcohol and drugs and high rates of antisocial behaviors that persist into early adulthood (Brown, 1993; Stewart, 1994). Thus, available empirical evidence demonstrates that adolescent substance abuse does not necessarily portend similar problems in adulthood. Yet, teens treated for substance abuse evidence continued difficulties following treatment.

Definitions of Adolescent Substance Abuse

Assessment and treatment of adolescent substance abuse is hampered by problems of definition. Diagnostic criteria for adolescent substance abuse and dependence are the same as those originally developed for adults. To date, little research has focused on reaching a valid definition of adolescent substance abuse, and few studies have examined the reliability and validity of current classification systems when applied to adolescents (Bukstein & Kaminer, 1994). The *Diagnostic and Statistical Manual of Mental Disorders* (4th ed., *DSM–IV*; American Psychiatric Association, 1994) defined psychoactive substance dependence as persistent self-administration of a substance that results in physiological dependence and compulsive drug-taking behavior. A *DSM–IV* diagnosis for substance dependence requires evidence of at least three of seven criteria within a 12-month period. The first two criteria describe physical consequences of substance use, tolerance and withdrawal. The remaining five criteria focus on preoccupation with substance use, involvement in obtaining the substance, failed efforts to control use, and impaired psychosocial functioning consequent to substance use.

In addition to substance dependence, the *DSM–IV* provides a diagnosis of psychoactive substance abuse, a milder form of problematic substance involvement that produces negative consequences, yet does not meet dependence criteria. The diagnosis of substance abuse involves a pattern of maladaptive substance use leading to clinically significant impairment or distress, and requires that one of four symptoms be evident within a 12-month period. This diagnosis rests on the negative consequences from substance involvement, and does not consider symptoms of physical dependence (i.e., tolerance and withdrawal).

Although *DSM–III–R* and *DSM–IV* criteria are often used with adolescents, several of the existing criteria may not be appropriate for adolescents (Stewart & Brown, 1995; Martin, Kaczynski, Maisto, Bukstein, & Moss, 1995). For example, adolescent substance abusers typically do not experience consequences (such as medical complications and a progression of the disorder) that correspond with an extended history of involvement such as commonly found for adults (Blum, 1987; Brown, Mott, & Stewart, 1992; Kaminer, 1994). A recent investigation (Martin et al., 1995) provided support for the *DSM–IV* definition of alcohol dependence when applied to adolescents. However, presentation for tolerance, withdrawal, and medical problems was found to differ between adults and adolescents. Moreover, the diagnosis of alcohol abuse was found to have little reliability when applied to adolescent drinkers. Investigations of this type highlight the need for adolescent specific diagnostic criteria.

ASSESSMENT

A good assessment forms the foundation for successful intervention with adolescent substance abusers. Although substance abusing teens share problems with alcohol and/or other drug use, they differ vastly from one another in the types and frequency of substances used, the actual and anticipated effects and consequences of use, the contexts and settings in which use occurs, and the factors that contribute to or accompany substance use involvement (Henly & Winters, 1989). A therapist's capacity to tailor an intervention to the particular needs of an adolescent client, which is believed to be essential for treatment success, derives directly from data collected in the initial assessment. The approach is to perform as comprehensive an assessment as possible, within the practical limitations of a clinical setting, using standardized and empirically validated assessment measures. Typically, this involves administration of both self-report questionnaires and semistructured interviews designed specifically for use with substance abusing adolescents. A good assessment derives from sound theory, and the approach recommended here adheres to a theoretical orientation in which substance use problems are conceptualized as resulting from interactions among biological, psychological, and social factors (see Donovan & Marlatt, 1988). Consistent with this biobehavioral conceptualization, experts in the evaluation of adolescent substance abuse have advocated a multidimensional approach to clinical assessment. Tarter, Ott, and Mezzich (1991) argued that the ideal adolescent substance abuse assessment should include evaluation of each of the following domains: the substance use behavior itself; the type and severity of psychiatric morbidity that may be present, and whether it preceded or developed after the substance use disorder; cognition, with specific attention to neuropsychological functioning; family functioning, organization, and interactional patterns; social skills; vocational adjustment; recreation and leisure activities; personality; school adjustment; peer affiliation; legal status; and physical health. Evaluation of similar domains has also been recommended by Tapert, Stewart, and Brown (in press); Winters (1990); Kaminer (1994); and others.

A biobehavioral conceptualization of adolescent substance abuse implies the need for broad-spectrum assessment (Donovan, 1988). Broad-spectrum assessment means that assessment data should include teens' self-reports (via self-monitoring, clinical interview, and/or structured reporting forms), significant others' reports (e.g., parents, teachers), psychometric testing, direct observation of the adolescent's behavior, and biological measures (e.g., urine toxicology screening). Although it is recommend that clinicians strive to achieve broad-spectrum assessment whenever possible, reports of the adolescents and their parents are often the only data available to the clinician. Such data can provide sufficient information for a valid assessment, but only when collected and utilized in a judicious manner. At a minimum, assessment of substance abusing teens should include the following four components: providing the adolescents and their family members with a rationale for the assessment procedure; interviewing the adolescents and family members about the presenting problem; administration to the adolescents of one or more standardized measures of domains of functioning potentially affected by substance use; and providing a feedback session with the adolescents and family members concerning results of the evaluation. In addition, performing a urine toxicology screen for presence of drugs may be a useful adjunct to verbal reports of substance use.

A good assessment also involves careful consideration of the purpose(s) underlying the evaluation. These may include any, several, or all of the following: to screen for problems; to establish a diagnosis; to establish eligibility and appropriateness for treatment; to understand the individual more comprehensively; to determine which form of treatment, if any, is most appropriate; to provide pretreatment scores that later can be compared with status on these same dimensions after treatment in order to assess and document improvement; and/or to build motivation (defined as the probability that a person will enter into, continue, and adhere to a specific change strategy) and strengthen commitment for change (Miller & Rollnick, 1991; Skinner, 1987). The purpose(s) behind an assessment needs to be clear to all individuals involved (including clinicians, adolescents, and their parents) prior to initiating the evaluation. Providing a rationale for assessment decreases the likelihood of misunderstandings among the clinician, the adolescent, and family members and can help to increase compliance with both the assessment itself and subsequent treatment recommendations.

Actual assessment begins with a brief open-ended interview with the adolescent and parents as to the presenting problem. Topics of discussion should include perception by the adolescent and family members' of the chronicity, severity, and origins of the substance use problem, as well as correlates/consequences of substance involvement. The clinician should be forewarned that adolescent and parent descriptions of presenting problems are often contradictory. When this occurs, it is recommended that clinicians openly acknowledge any contradictions that emerge without siding with adolescents or their parents. The clinician should also keep in mind that parents may request a meeting without the adolescent present, and decisions about whether to agree to such a meeting should be based on whether the clinician views it as necessary and potentially helpful. As a matter of course, confidentiality issues should be carefully considered and discussed before meeting with parents alone. Similarly, adolescents may also request an individual meeting with the clinician, which can be accomplished during the actual testing session. Again, confidentiality must be considered and discussed before meeting alone with an adolescent.

The next step in assessment is administration of standardized measures of domains related to the presenting problem. It is important to indicate that a urine sample will be requested, if this is the case, before commencing with the initial assessment, as this may motivate more honest reporting by the adolescent and serve to confirm self-reported use. The psychometric assessment of substance abusing individuals, including adolescents, typically involves one of two approaches (Donovan, 1988). *Sequential evaluation* begins with a substance screen; in the event that the screening suggests problems, it is followed with a basic substance use assessment (e.g., types of drugs used, frequency and recency of use), and progresses to specialized assessment (e.g., neuropsychological evaluation) when indicated. This approach is appropriate when it is unknown whether the adolescent has been involved with substances. The second approach, *clinical hypothesis testing*, involves generating several hypotheses about the presenting problem (i.e., substance abuse) that cut across biological, psychological, and social domains, and then examining each in turn. The latter approach is desirable when it is relatively certain prior to assessment that the adolescent is experiencing substance-related difficulties.

Until quite recently, there has been an absence of reliable and valid instruments for assessing adolescent substance abuse. As a result, many adolescent substance abuse treatment facilities have come to rely on clinical judgment or locally developed assessment measures (Owen & Nyberg, 1983). However, standardized and empirically validated assessment measures developed specifically for the assessment of adolescent substance abusers should be adopted. Such measures are now widely available (see the Center for Substance Abuse Treatment's (CSAT) *Treatment Improvement Protocol Series: Screening and Assessment of Alcohol- and Other Drug-Abusing Adolescents*, 1993) and possess several advantages over more traditional approaches. Features that commend use of standardized measures include provision of a benchmark against which clinical decisions can be compared and validated (e.g., normative comparison data, cutoff scores that indicate problems), immunity to rater bias and inconsistencies (i.e., objectivity), and a common language (e.g., definitions of problem use and domains of functioning) that facilitates improved communication within the field (Henly & Winters, 1989).

Several standardized and empirically validated adolescent substance abuse assessment instruments exist that are recommended for use in clinical settings. A particularly good screening measure is the Personal Experience Screening Questionnaire (PESQ; Winters, 1991), a 40-item self-report inventory designed to identify adolescents in need of a comprehensive drug abuse assessment. The PESQ includes a problem severity scale, two response distortion scales, and a supplemental information section providing data about the respondent's psychosocial status and drug use history. For more detailed assessment of substance involvement, the Customary Drinking and Drug Use Record (CDDR) is a structured interview that provides comprehensive quantitative data regarding consumption, consequences, and dependency and withdrawal symptoms associated with use of a variety of substances (Brown et al., 1989; Brown et al., in press). The CDDR evaluates current and lifetime use of beer, wine, and liquor and seven illicit substances (marijuana, amphetamines, cocaine, hallucinogens, inhalants, opiates, and barbiturates), as well as current use of cigarettes. For a comprehensive multidimensional self-report evaluation, the Drug Use Screening Inventory (DUSI; Tarter, 1990) is useful. The DUSI is a self-report measure that profiles substance use involvement in conjunction with the severity of impairment in nine domains of everyday functioning (e.g., school adjustment, social skills, family functioning). A unique aspect of the DUSI is an explicit attempt to link assessment findings to treatment; the DUSI produces a needs assessment, domain severity scores, and a diagnostic summary designed to facilitate the development of a treatment plan. For clinicians seeking a semistructured interview measure, the Teen Addiction Severity Index (T–ASI; Kaminer, Bukstein, & Tarter, 1991; Kaminer, Wagner, Plummer, & Seifer, 1993) should be considered. The T–ASI is an age-adapted version of the widely used Addiction Severity Index (McLellan, Luborsky, Woody, & O'Brien, 1980) and evaluates seven domains, including substance use, school, employment, family, peer/social, legal, and psychiatric disturbance. For a description of additional assessment instruments appropriate for adolescent substance abusers, consult CSAT's *Treatment Improvement Protocol Series: Screening and Assessment of Alcohol- and Other Drug-Abusing Adolescents* (1993).

There are no standardized and empirically validated assessment instruments designed specifically for parents of substance abusing adolescents. However, several instruments have been developed for collecting assessment data from parents and families of teens demonstrating adjustment difficulties. It is useful to include such instruments in assessment batteries. One good self-report measure of family strengths and weaknesses is the Family Assessment Measure (FAM–III; Skinner, Steinhauser, & Santo-Barbara, 1983). This self-report questionnaire, which can be completed by a parent and adolescent in approximately 45 minutes, yields scores on three scales: general overall family health, dyadic relations within the family, and respondents' perception of their functioning in the family. A briefer self-report measure of family functioning is the Adolescent–Parent Communication Form (Olson, Barnes, Larson, Muxen, & Wilson, 1982), which evaluates content and process issues related to family communication and can be completed in approximately 20 minutes by each parent and the adolescent. Additionally, parent forms of standardized psychiatric diagnostic interviews can yield important information on a substance abusing adolescent's psychiatric status. One of the more prominent of these instruments is the Diagnostic Interview Schedule for Children (DISC; Costello, Edelbrock, Dulcan, Kalas, & Klaric, 1984, 1987), which is valuable for data collection from parents of substance abusing youth.

Feedback to the adolescent and family members about results of a substance use assessment is a critical determinant of compliance with treatment recommendations. Miller and Rollnick (1991) described a particularly useful approach for providing substance abuse assessment feedback. They emphasized that personalized feedback can be persuasive input for convincing clients of the need to make changes in their personal conduct. This perspective is valid and the approach is immensely helpful in working with adolescents and their families. The following recommendations may be offered to clinicians providing personalized motivational feedback to adolescents and their families: Avoid trying to prove things to adolescents and their families; describe each assessment result along with information necessary to understand what it means, in full detail; avoid a confrontational "scare tactic" tone; solicit and reflect reactions by the adolescents and their family to the assessment information; remain open to feedback from the adolescents and their family; be prepared to deal with strong affective reactions; and, conclude the feedback session with summary of what was discussed, including: (a) the risks and problems that were identified in the assessment; (b) client reactions to the feedback, underscoring statements reflecting a willingness and interest in making positive changes; and (c) an invitation for the adolescent and family members to append or correct the summary.

TREATMENT

Overview

Substance abusing adolescents typically present with a variety of problems, including concurrent psychiatric disorders and family difficulties. Because of the complexity of presentation, it is often desirable to engage the teen in a program of treatment incorporating various components determined by the particular needs of each adolescent. However, rather than provide a description of multiple treatment components, this chapter focuses specifically on a cognitive-behavioral based skills training intervention for adolescent substance abuse. The intervention described herein is designed to be flexible and, as such, can be utilized as the primary treatment or incorporated as a component of a more comprehensive program. The training program outlined here, which focuses on skills deficits common to teen substance abusers, is presented as an individual focused intervention, but is readily applicable to groups.

Gender Issues

Substance abuse has traditionally been viewed as a predominantly male problem; however, recent years have seen increases in rates of substance abuse among females, in particular among adolescent girls (e.g., Johnston, 1994). Although less is known about features of substance abuse in girls than in boys, clinicians must be alert to gender-specific considerations. For example, evidence suggests that females treated for substance abuse have frequently experienced sexual abuse, a much less common phenomenon for males (e.g., Wallen, 1992).

Conversely,whereas antisocial behaviors are typical of substance abusing boys, these are less common for girls, and when present are often consequent to their substance involvement (Brown et al., 1996). In addition, female substance abusers display more depressive symptomatology than do males (Wilcox & Yates, 1993). Thus, clinicians should be alert to potential gender differences in clinical presentation when assessing for substance abuse and related problems. Sexual issues may arise in the course of intervention with female adolescents and must be treated with particular sensitivity, recognizing that teen girls may be uncomfortable discussing these concerns in the presence of males (a particular concern in mixed-gender group settings). It is also possible that circumstances presenting high risk for relapse differ for girls and boys. For example, the greater presence of depressive symptoms suggests that negative affect may represent a greater relapse risk for girls. Finally, gender differences in interactional styles must be considered when addressing topics such as refusal skills and assertiveness. In all, successful intervention with adolescent girls will require that the clinician be sensitive and alert to these gender issues.

Tobacco Use

Traditional definitions of abstinence from psychoactive substances have typically excluded use of tobacco products. However, tobacco use is highly prevalent among substance abusing teens and has been shown to have negative health consequences for this population (Myers & Brown, 1994). In addition, recent evidence suggests tobacco is the leading cause of death for individuals treated for alcohol problems (Hurt et al., 1996), highlighting the importance of addressing this issue. Unfortunately, there is little information available at this time as to effective treatment of adolescent tobacco use. There is the added difficulty that the recovery community typically condones and models cigarette use. Nonetheless, it is important that the clinician label nicotine as an addictive substance and assess motivation for tobacco-use behavior change. It is strongly recommended that the clinician encourage and support efforts at smoking cessation by the adolescent, and provide assistance to the extent possible (e.g., by giving the adolescent quit smoking materials such as those produced by the American Lung Association and identifying community resources for adolescent smoking cessation).

Background and Rationale

A cognitive-behavioral perspective recognizes the multiple factors that influence the development of alcohol and drug use problems, but focuses on the role of learned behaviors, cognitions or beliefs, and environmental forces. Specifically, alcohol and drug use behaviors are believed to originate from modeling by family members, peers, and society (Abrams & Niaura, 1987). Research demonstrates that beliefs about the influence or effects of substances initially develop during childhood as the individual observes the use of alcohol and drugs across family, peer, and sociocultural contexts (Christiansen, Goldman, & Inn, 1982; Goldman, Brown, & Christiansen, 1987). Beliefs about effects expected from alcohol and drug use are found to predict later involvement (Christiansen, Roehling, Smith, & Goldman, 1989). Thus, teens may initiate alcohol and drug use because they expect various positive consequences, such as tension or stress reduction, social facilitation, or expect pleasure from the "high." Experimentation with alcohol and drugs during adolescence is generally a normal part of teen development

(Shedler & Block, 1989). However, such experimentation may progress to problem use for vulnerable teens, in particular those who have poor or limited personal resources for managing negative affect, who experience difficulties engaging peers or resisting peer pressures for substance use, or who have difficulty experiencing positive feelings without alcohol and drug use (e.g., Bentler, 1992; Pandina & Schuele, 1983). In addition, adolescents who affiliate with deviant peers who model substance use, whose parents abuse alcohol and/or drugs, and who live in environments that provide greater access to substances of abuse are at higher risk for substance-related problems.

Skills-based interventions for treatment of substance abuse (e.g., Monti, Abrams, Kadden, & Cooney, 1989) have thus emerged in response to the deficits or vulnerabilities associated with substance abuse. The premise of this approach is that for treatment to be effective, substance abusing individuals must acquire and practice skills for managing situations and circumstances associated with substance use and learn how to experience reinforcement in the absence of alcohol and drug use. Similarly, coping skills are considered an important part of relapse prevention, as conceptualized within the cognitive behavioral model of relapse (Marlatt & Gordon, 1985). In Marlatt's model, relapse is defined as the process of a return to problematic alcohol and drug use rather than as a discrete event. Thus, relapse is considered to be a gradual process in which a single occurrence of alcohol or drug use (a slip) is considered a mistake and a learning opportunity rather than a failure signaling a return to prior levels of problematic substance involvement. The cognitive behavioral model of relapse identifies as high risk for relapse those situations in which an individual previously used alcohol or drugs, and that tax or exceed the available coping resources. The probability of relapse in a high-risk situation is thus seen related to the extent to which substances were previously used (and perceived as effective) to manage similar circumstances, anticipated outcomes of substance use, availability of effective coping strategies, and the individual's belief in their ability to successfully cope with the situation (self-efficacy). Investigations of outcome following treatment for teen substance abuse provide support for the role of coping in relapse and demonstrate the importance of strategies for managing temptations to use alcohol and/or drugs (e.g., Myers & Brown, 1990a, 1990b, 1996; Myers, Brown, & Mott, 1993). In particular, strategies for managing situations involving social pressure to use and awareness of negative consequences from substance use predict better treatment outcome for teen substance abusers (Myers & Brown, 1996). Consistent with this theoretical perspective and available research findings, the intervention outlined here concentrates on identifying the role alcohol and drug use occupy in the life of the adolescent, and focuses on identifying strategies and techniques by which to alter previous substance use behaviors.

Finally, in planning maintenance of behavior change, information as to the clinical course following treatment for adolescent substance abuse must be considered. Extensive research examining addictive behaviors has demonstrated that although interventions often succeed in producing initial cessation, the goal of extended abstinence from substance use is elusive. Whereas this conclusion is based primarily on evidence from adult addiction treatment, it is also supported by recent data from studies of outcome following treatment for adolescent alcohol and drug abuse (e.g., Brown, 1993; Brown, Myers, Mott, & Vik, 1994; Brown, Vik, & Creamer, 1989). Adolescents evidence high rates of relapse in the initial months following treatment (Brown, Mott, & Myers, 1990), with the first 6 months representing the period of greatest risk (Brown, 1993). However, following initial relapse, many adolescents succeed in reducing their substance involvement. For example, approximately one third of teens who relapse within the first 6 months demonstrate abstinence or limited, nonproblematic use when assessed again at 1 year posttreatment (Brown, 1993). Thus, continued intervention following treatment may be important to maintaining treatment gains.

COGNITIVE-BEHAVIORAL SKILLS TRAINING

Description of the skills training intervention consists of the following sections: an overview of session structure, description of three core sessions, followed by cognitive behavioral skill training modules grouped into sessions focused on interpersonal skills, skills for managing negative emotions, and relapse prevention. The following intervention is presented in an individual therapy format, but is easily adapted to groups.

Overview of Session Structure

Cognitive behavioral interventions are designed to be structured, such that each session contains similar elements and proceeds in a similar sequence. Each session begins with a review and discussion of previous material and homework assignments. Next, new material is introduced and discussed, then time is set aside for practice of new skills (i.e., role plays), and finally new homework is negotiated and detailed.

It is important to elicit feedback from the teen as to perceived helpfulness and relevance of previous materials and assignments. Also, one must assess the extent to which material was comprehended and assignments followed in order to identify barriers to performance. This approach will assist in tailoring the intervention to match the pace and ability of each adolescent as well as increasing motivation for intervention activities.

A rationale must always precede introduction of new material. The rationale provided should be consistent with the functional analysis framework of the intervention and will be enhanced by the therapist and adolescent providing examples relevant to the teen's personal experiences. It is helpful to provide handouts that outline each topic and provide examples relevant to homework assignments. Avoid extended lectures, because this may tax the adolescent's attention; instead, attempt to engage and involve the teen. When introducing new skills, role plays should be utilized to assist in acquiring skills. Generally, it is helpful to first have the therapist model the skill, and then involve the teen in a role play.

Homework assignments are an important part of treatment because these provide an opportunity for practicing skills introduced during sessions. When presenting homework, it is important to provide a rationale for each assignment and involve the teen in deciding the nature and extent of the assignment. Homework may involve "school-like" tasks, so anticipate problems with compliance by limiting the extent of assignments (be sensitive to teens perception of the workload), selecting in collaboration with the teen those experiences most likely to be successfully executed, and identifying potential barriers to completion (e.g., scheduling "homework" times).

Core Sessions

Cognitive-behavioral skills training interventions are designed to be flexible and adaptable to the individual needs of a given teen. As such, skill training modules can be introduced in a sequence matched to the negotiated goals of treatment. However, the first three sessions are usually conducted in the order outlined here so as to engage the teen in the treatment process, set goals for treatment, introduce the functional analysis approach, and identify areas for intervention.

Motivational Enhancement.   Because of the frequent difficulty of engaging individuals in treatment for substance abuse, motivation for changing addictive behaviors has recently received significant attention (e.g., Miller & Rollnick, 1991). Motivation is best conceptualized as a fluctuating state, and as such efforts must be made to monitor and maintain motivation for change. In attempting to procure adolescent participation and compliance with the intervention, it is particularly important to take steps to increase motivation and reduce resistance. Issues with authority are a common characteristic of adolescents in general, and are particularly evident among substance abusing adolescents. Thus, it is critically important to involve the teen in the process of making treatment decisions and setting goals: The greater the adolescent's sense of ownership and partnership in the treatment process, the more compliance and motivation will be improved and resistance will be diminished.

A useful approach to facilitating motivation and compliance is a client-treatment matching approach (Hester & Miller, 1988). An important principle of the client-treatment matching approach is that interventions matching the client's cognitive style are associated with better outcomes. Because adolescents vary in their level of cognitive development, this is a particularly important factor in treatment selection. Also important to promoting motivation and commitment is an approach that provides the teen with choices as to the content of the intervention. Providing choices and employing a collaborative rather than authoritarian approach may also function to reduce teen resistance to treatment. Although skills training forms the core of the intervention outlined herein, teens respond more positively when choices as to specific domains to be addressed and regarding which particular techniques and strategies are learned. Further, the teen can be offered choices for other elements of treatment (e.g., family therapy, therapy focused on other problem areas, etc.) pertinent to their personal situation and motivation for change.

Drawing from the client matching guidelines (e.g., Babor et al., 1991; Miller, 1989), the following are factors to consider in tailoring an intervention to the particular needs of an adolescent client:

Severity of substance involvement.
Other concurrent psychopathology.
Quality of support systems: home, family relationships, community resources, school, and peer relationships.
Severity of deviant or antisocial behaviors.
Personal characteristics: Aggression, impulsivity, self-esteem.
Social skills and functioning.
Physical health.
Academic status.

The process of client-treatment matching is based on information from a comprehensive assessment as already outlined, and includes negotiating the goals of treatment, selecting the level or intensity of intervention (e.g., inpatient vs. outpatient, frequency of sessions), choice of intervention (e.g., family therapy, group therapy, individual therapy, etc.), plans for maintaining behavior change (i.e., identifying and implementing supports for a drug-free lifestyle), and posttreatment assessment and followup (Miller, 1989).

When developing adolescent treatment goals, all the identified problem domains should be addressed rather than focusing exclusively on substance abuse. Findings from the assessment may contradict goals held by the teen, thus giving rise to resistance. If problems perceived by parents and the clinician differ from those identified by the teen, a functional assessment and motivational approach may be particularly important. One motivational strategy for reducing adolescent opposition to treatment goals involves testing goals or concerns identified by the adolescent. This approach involves agreeing to work toward a behavior change goal (that may not be directly related to substance use) identified by the adolescent. If the trial succeeds, the teen may be more open to continued intervention. On the other hand, failure to achieve the teen's self-identified goal will provide evidence for the validity of other concerns identified during the assessment.

As with many adolescent problems, family relations may be a particularly important area to address when treating adolescent substance abuse. The role of the family in outcome following treatment for adolescents substance abuse is highlighted by recent research showing that reestablishment of positive family relations, particularly by younger teens, appears to significantly facilitate successful treatment outcome (Brown, 1993; Stewart & Brown, 1993). In addition, reductions in teen substance use following treatment slowly lead to better family functioning (Stewart & Brown, 1993). The need for a family-based intervention should be determined based on assessment of family functioning as previously recommended. Although a discussion of family interventions is beyond the scope of the present chapter, empirical support exists for effectiveness of family intervention approaches in treating adolescent substance abuse (see Liddle & Dakof, 1995, for a review).

Introduction to the Behavior Chain/Functional Analysis.   Prior to embarking on the skills training modules, the adolescent client is introduced to the concept of a *functional analysis* of alcohol and drug use (McCrady, Dean, Dubreuil, & Swanson, 1985), which forms the framework for the intervention. A functional analysis is consistent with a skills training approach in that it serves to identify the functions served by alcohol and drug use (i.e., why do you use?). The rationale for choosing this approach centers on alcohol and drug use as a learned behavior that can be "unlearned." The functional analysis provides a tool for identifying reasons for someone's alcohol and drug use, and therefore can help suggest areas to be targeted for learning methods for coping or managing circumstances previously associated with use. After providing the rationale for the functional analysis, introduce the behavior chain as the tool used in functional analysis. It is best to draw out the behavior chain (consisting of triggers, thoughts, feelings, behavior, and consequences—positive and negative) on a flipchart or board and define each element (see Fig. 11.1).

Discussion of the behavior chain begins by introducing "antecedents" to behavior: triggers, thoughts, and feelings. The *trigger* is something that increases likelihood of substance use. A situation, event, place, or person can constitute a trigger (being at a party; offers of alcohol

Trigger → Thought → Feeling → Behavior → Consequences

Positive   Negative

FIG. 11.1. The behavior chain.

and/or drugs; an argument with friends or family). It is helpful to elicit examples of triggers from the teen at this point.

Although *thoughts* follow next in the behavior chain, it may be easier to first introduce the *feelings* component of the chain, because most teens are not familiar with the idea that thoughts lead to feelings. Elicit from the teen the kind of feelings associated with the triggers you have listed (e.g., anger and frustration may follow from an argument; urges or craving may result from being around alcohol and drugs). Once feelings are listed, the concept that thoughts lead to feelings is discussed. In discussing the role of thoughts clarify that people are often unaware of their thoughts in relation to feelings because they occur very quickly and may be "automatic" (e.g., Beck, Rush, Shaw, & Emery, 1979). At this point, using one of the triggers as an example, ask the adolescent to list some thoughts that may lead to the previously identified feelings (e.g., thoughts in response to an argument may be "it's not fair that they're mad at me, I didn't do anything wrong," or "I hate being treated that way"). Be prepared to provide examples of the type of thinking that may result from a given situation, because some adolescents may have difficulty with this task at first. Clarify that thoughts in reaction to a trigger can be positive or negative. It is important to ascertain that the link between trigger, thoughts, and feelings is clearly understood. To this end, go through several more examples representing a range of different triggers, thoughts, and feelings.

After introducing the antecedents, next discussed is the "behavior" link in the chain. The behavior of alcohol or drug use is always noted in order to emphasize how triggers may result in use. (Later, the behavior link of the chain is used to identify behaviors that can replace alcohol and drugs.) Next, move to the consequences part of the chain, beginning with positive consequences. Focusing on the behavior of alcohol and drug use, elicit the positive consequences or "goodies" that result from use in response to various triggers (e.g., use in response to an argument may lead to relief from anger and frustration, use in response to an urge in the face of an offer may facilitate socializing or getting along with others in the situation). It is important to acknowledge the positive consequences of use in order to highlight how alcohol and drug use is learned and reinforced, and also to maintain credibility in the face of skeptical adolescents who have been inundated with the message that "drugs are bad."

Once the positives have been listed, turn to the negative consequences that are most proximal to each particular substance use trigger. For example, using in response to the anger after an argument may provide temporary relief, but the same bad feelings return later, and by burying or "stuffing" the feelings the issues that led to conflict may never be addressed so nothing changes. Negative consequences of using in the face of temptation may prevent someone from having healthy rewarding interactions with others and can perpetuate the cycle of addiction. Have the teen generate as many consequences as possible and elaborate on the negative consequences to the extent possible, including the long-term costs of alcohol and drug abuse (e.g., difficulties establishing healthy relationships as a result of not having learned or used skills for managing conflict and arguments). Keep in mind that adolescents are generally more influenced by proximal rather than long-term consequences of their behavior. A focus on the balance between positive and negative consequences is useful to assess and provide motivation for change (i.e., on balance, does the good outweigh the bad?). Attention to this issue is important throughout the intervention because motivation for change tends to wax and wane. Keeping a record of the negatives can be an effective way of providing a concrete reminder for the reasons for change. It is the teen's perception of consequences that is important, in particular, the view that alcohol and drug use is "bad" must not be imposed by the clinician.

Once introduction to the behavior chain is completed, point out that this tool identifies several points or "links" that can be acted on to break the chain that leads to alcohol and drug use: avoiding or altering certain triggers can serve to disrupt the chain; acting to alter or reconsider perceptions or thoughts in response to a trigger can effectively avert the feelings that may motivate use; and finally, alternative behaviors or strategies can be learned in order to manage the feelings that formerly led to alcohol or drug use. An emphasis on optimism and the feasibility of this approach is valuable in motivating and engaging the teen. In addition, highlight that this approach allows for a variety of strategies and tools from which the teen will be able to choose those that best match their needs and abilities. Examples should be provided for how acting on the different links in the chain can change the behavior of alcohol and drug use. The purpose here is to illustrate how the behavior chain will be used throughout treatment to help identify new skills, strategies, and behaviors so the adolescent has the opportunity to change the old using behaviors.

Identifying Domains Influenced by Adolescent Alcohol and Drug Use.   Before embarking on the skills training modules, it is necessary to identify specific areas to be addressed. Because involving the adolescent in treatment decisions may serve to increase commitment and motivation, identifying specific areas for intervention must be done in collaboration with the teen. It is helpful to provide a "menu" of domains to work on and have the teen select areas of priority. A helpful adjunct in this task is to have the teen complete the adolescent version of the Inventory of Drug Taking Situations (IDTS; Annis & Graham, 1985). This 50-item self-report questionnaire includes situations from eight domains including conflict, social pressure, pleasant social situations, positive and negative emotions, physical discomfort, testing personal control, and urges. Responses are intended to be specific to a particular substance, and because teens tend to be polysubstance users it may be useful to complete the measure for the most frequently used substances. Do not assume that drug-taking situations will be identical across substances. Each item of the IDTS is scored on a 4-point scale from *never* used in this situation to *almost always* used in this situation. The questionnaire is scored to provide a profile of use across the eight areas, and can help in identifying areas to be targeted for intervention by focusing on circumstances associated with frequent use. The goal for this session is to produce a prioritized list, agreed to by the teen, of areas (or triggers) to be addressed. Having agreed on initial areas for intervention, assign the teen to complete behavior chains relevant to the first area selected to be addressed.

COGNITIVE-BEHAVIORAL SKILLS TRAINING MODULES

The following topics represent components typically included in a skills training intervention for substance abusing teens. Selection and sequencing of the actual components included in a course of treatment will depend on the areas identified for intervention from the functional analysis. Additional ingredients can be added if other problem areas arise or become apparent during the course of treatment. Note that the amount of time devoted to a given topic is determined by the needs and abilities of each teen. For convenience, skill modules are grouped into three domains: interpersonal skills, managing negative emotions, and relapse prevention.

Interpersonal Skills

Assertiveness.   The assertive skills component is generally introduced first because assertive behavior is relevant to other topic areas, particularly those involving interpersonal issues. The adolescent's level of ability will determine the pace of assertiveness training. It is important to provide information in manageable quantities and practice skills frequently. The rationale for learning assertiveness skills centers on how these can improve relationships with other people. Having good relationships can decrease the experience of negative emotions and thus diminish the risk of alcohol and drug use.

Begin with a discussion of assertiveness. Elicit the teen's definition and understanding of the concept, then refine the definition (if necessary), provide examples and discuss the following:

1. Assertive people: respect their own rights and rights of other people.
2. Passive people: respect others' rights but not their own.
3. Aggressive people: respect their own rights but not the rights of other people.

Next outline and discuss the rights to which each individual is entitled. It is helpful to provide a list of these rights and ask the teen to provide examples of violations of rights for each. Assist the teens in identifying personal examples where their rights were violated or where they violated others' rights based on information gathered from the assessment and prior interactions with the adolescent. Every person has the following rights:

1. Individuals have the right to make their own decisions.
2. Individuals have the right to their own feelings.
3. Individuals have the right to have their own thoughts, beliefs, and opinions.
4. Individuals have the right to express their own thoughts, beliefs, and opinions.
5. Individuals have the right to say no or yes in response to requests.
6. Individuals have the right to be healthy and safe and to not be abused (physically, emotionally, or sexually).

After introducing assertiveness and personal rights, identify examples of passive and/or aggressive behavior by the teen. Have the teen prioritize the identified problems with assertiveness and work through a few using the behavior chain to demonstrate the negative consequences of passive and/or aggressive behavior.

Next, discuss the following guidelines for behaving assertively, focusing on those pertinent to the behavior chains previously completed:

1. We can only control our own behavior, not that of others. You can ask others to change, but they have the right to refuse.
2. Know what you want to get out of a particular situation or circumstance.
3. Communicate clearly and specifically what it is you want.
4. Pay attention to your body language; don't adopt a passive or aggressive posture.
5. The timing of attempts at assertive behavior is important. In particular, make sure you are calm and composed when making a request or having a discussion with someone.

6. It is important to use "I" statements, and avoid words such as "you," "should," and "never."
7. Criticize the *behavior* you do not like rather than the *person*.
8. To provide constructive criticism, use the "sandwich" technique: First say something positive about the issue/person, then give criticism, and then end with something positive.
9. Be prepared to compromise. Plan ahead what it is that you're willing (and unwilling) to negotiate.

After discussion of the assertive guidelines, return to the behavior chains and rework them substituting assertive for passive or aggressive behaviors. Focus on the different short- and long-term consequences that result from assertive behavior. Next engage the teen in a role play of assertive behaviors, practicing a personal situation until the teen demonstrates improved performance and confidence. For example, issues surrounding sexual behavior may be particularly pertinent to this population because substance use often accompanies adolescent sexual behavior, and is associated with risky (i.e., unprotected) intercourse. For boys, issues of assertiveness may involve accepting refusals from a potential partner or taking responsibility for practicing "safe" sex. For girls, learning to say no effectively when pressured to engage in sexual behaviors may be particularly important.

Homework. Practice of assertiveness skills is critical, and it is particularly important to have success experiences. To this end, initial assignments should consist of relatively nonthreatening situations in which success is highly likely. Suggest that the teen complete behavior chains for triggers relevant to assertive behaviors drawn from their daily experiences. If parents are involved, encourage them to be supportive of the teen's attempts at assertiveness.

Giving and Receiving Criticism, Expressing Feelings. For this topic, ask teens to generate examples of situations where they have had difficulty giving or accepting criticism or expressing feelings (positive or negative). Most substance abusing teens have experienced considerable criticism prior to treatment entry, although it is not uncommon for youth to have difficulty articulating the circumstances. If the teen has difficulty generating examples, you can refer to the IDTS interpersonal conflict items to see which were endorsed as common use situations. For the identified examples, complete the behavior chain and then focus on how the antecedents and behavior in the situation might be changed to get a more positive outcome. Referring to the guidelines for assertive behavior, have the teen generate strategies for more effective behaviors. After discussion of the behavior chain and alternative behaviors, role play new behaviors in session until improvement is observed. Examples do not necessarily have to be related to substance use but should be concrete descriptions relevant to the topic. For instance, criticism from parents and family members over perceived failure to change problem behaviors may persist during and following treatment, and as such may be particularly salient.

Homework. Help the teen select a nonthreatening situation in which to practice the skills reviewed. Emphasize the value of planning prior to the situation (i.e., What is the goal? What responses will be most effective?). Suggest that the teen complete behavior chains for situations involving the expression of criticism and other feelings from their daily experiences.

Dealing with Conflict (Anger and Frustration).   From the list of identified trigger situations, have the teen identify and select situations in which they have had difficulty managing conflicts (arguments, fights), preferably a recent event or occurrence. It is useful to distinguish between and focus on both conflicts with family versus conflicts with friends and peers. Family-based conflict may carry over from events or behaviors associated with prior substance abuse (e.g., failure to fulfill responsibilities at home, noncompliance with restrictions), and peer conflict may arise in the context of attempts at behavior change (e.g., lack of peer support for efforts at abstinence, rejection or ridicule by substance using peers). Complete the behavior chain for the trigger(s), filling in the actual antecedents and behaviors that resulted in anger and/or frustration. Next, focus on the "links" in the chain that can be altered to avoid the negative outcomes experienced in the past. Identify thoughts (perceptions and beliefs about what occurred in the situation) and behaviors that were previously not effective in managing conflict before working on new more adaptive behaviors. Referring to the assertive behavior guidelines, have the teen generate alternative thoughts and behaviors in response to the trigger situation(s). After completing the behavior chain and outlining the consequences from the alternative responses, role play the new behaviors.

Homework.   Assist the teen in selecting a conflict situation that occurs frequently but is relatively minor for initial practice. One approach is to begin by identifying a recent conflict situation that was not resolved and have the teen address this particular issue (after practicing in session). Have the teen identify other conflicts—in particular, anticipated conflicts—that can be worked on in future sessions.

Managing Negative Emotions

This module focuses on teaching skills and strategies for managing common feelings of adolescence (such as depression, anxiety, and anger), which increase in frequency and intensity with puberty and substance involvement. This is a particularly important area to address because although adolescent relapse to alcohol and drug use occurs primarily in situations involving social pressure, relapse situations are frequently preceded by brief or protracted states of negative affect. Discuss with the adolescent that negative emotions are a normal part of everyday life and may arise even in situations in which the teen has responded or behaved appropriately. Teens may need assistance in specifying, labeling, and discriminating between feelings. Because negative emotions arise in a variety of contexts, it is helpful to provide a menu of strategies that will permit the teen to select the skills most relevant to their trigger situations and personal style. Based on the teens' list of triggers and your experience with them, select approaches relevant to managing feelings such as anxiety and tension, anger, and depression and boredom. Use the behavior chain to identify the factors (e.g., thoughts, behaviors) that may contribute to and exacerbate the emotions. It is beyond the scope of this chapter to outline mood management strategies in detail. Table 11.1 provides a brief guide to cognitive and behavioral mood management interventions. For specific details, refer to Burns (1989) for cognitive mood management approaches, and Clarke, Lewinsohn, and Hops (1990), which outlines interventions focused on increasing pleasant activities and changing negative thinking.

TABLE 11.1

Strategies for Managing Negative Emotions

Strategy	Depression	Anxiety	Anger
Cognitive restructuring	X	X	X
Negative and positive thinking	X	X	
Identifying thought distortions/testing assumptions	X	X	X
Relaxation training (e.g., progressive muscle relaxation)		X	X
Pleasant activities	X		X
Physical activities	X	X	X

Choice of strategies for managing negative emotions should be based on the type of triggers and/or affective states commonly experienced, and the level of cognitive sophistication of the adolescent (e.g., some teens may respond better to more concrete behavioral strategies than those involving abstract thought). Offering both cognitive and behavioral strategies can assist the process of selecting skills appropriate and acceptable to the teen. Further, it is important to assess the extent to which the adolescent client holds beliefs in the effectiveness of alcohol and/or drug use as means for managing negative affect. Similarly, it is important to assess the adolescent's perceptions of alternate strategies for accomplishing mood management, and their confidence, or self-efficacy, for being able to successfully carry out these strategies. Providing new means for managing affect, building confidence in the utility of these strategies, and enhancing self-efficacy for executing the behaviors is critical in countering beliefs regarding the effectiveness of substance use for ameliorating unpleasant mood states.

Having selected a particular negative emotion and corresponding trigger situations, use the behavior chain to outline the factors that may contribute to and exacerbate the emotions. Illustrate on the behavior chain how the selected mood management strategies can act to alter the consequences (e.g., because relaxation is the opposite of tension, progressive muscle relaxation is a skill that can help you feel less stressed and anxious and therefore you'll be less likely to use alcohol/drugs to calm yourself; developing activities that you enjoy can help you feel better when you're down and this way help you avoid using to get rid of depression; learning to think differently about situations that make you upset can reduce bad feelings and help you feel more in control). A clear understanding of how mood management strategies can improve unpleasant feelings is essential to motivate the teen to follow through and attempt these strategies. In-session practice and rehearsal should be targeted to improving compliance.

Homework. With the teen, identify upcoming or ongoing situations likely to engender negative emotions and prescribe techniques for practice. Again, it is important to select less stressful or threatening circumstances. Daily mood rating (e.g., daily rating of anxiety level on a 1 to 10 scale) may help to identify specific emotions to be targeted, can help to increase affect discrimination and labeling skills, and also serves to provide feedback for the effectiveness of mood management strategies.

Relapse Prevention

Rationale/High-Risk Situations. Discussion of relapse prevention begins with a definition of relapse and description of relapse as a process rather than an event (Marlatt & Gordon, 1985). An important point to make is that a single occasion of use (a slip or lapse) does not mean a return to abuse and dependence. How one reacts to an initial lapse will play a large role in what happens next. The most important thing is to view a lapse as a learning experience rather than focus on failure. The message is that resolution of alcohol and drug problems requires persistence and setbacks are to be anticipated. Discuss with the teen the likelihood of experiencing guilt and a sense of failure in the face of a lapse, and that this experience can serve as an opportunity to assess for difficulties and learn to avoid future lapses. Raising the possibility of a lapse is intended to raise awareness of relapse risks and allow planning for such an event, however it must be emphasized to the teen that discussing this issue does not imply permission to use. Be sure to elicit the teen's opinions and feedback regarding relapse and its definition.

Because substance abusing adolescents are typically involved with multiple substances, it is important to identify substance-specific issues. For example, motivations for use may vary by substance (e.g., teens may use stimulants to feel up or high, and use alcohol to "take the edge off" or manage feelings of anxiety). In addition, different substances may be perceived differently by adolescents. In particular, high prevalence of adolescent alcohol and marijuana use may result in perceptions of these as safe and acceptable substances, whereas other illicit drugs (amphetamines, cocaine, hallucinogens, etc.) may be seen as more risky. It is important to evaluate and assess such perceptions because these may influence relapse risk.

After discussion of relapse, introduce the concept of high-risk situations and the role of coping. Introduction of high-risk situations should be fairly straightforward, because many of the triggers discussed in previous sessions represent high-risk situations. As defined by Marlatt and Gordon (1985), situations formerly associated with alcohol and/or drug use or situations that may increase the likelihood of a return to use are considered high-risk situations. Although certain situations commonly represent a relapse risk (e.g., being at a party where alcohol and/or drugs are present), teens must also identify their unique risk situations in order to be prepared and avoid lapses. In addition, high-risk situations should be assessed in relation to the various substances with which the teens have been involved. For example, there may be situations associated with concurrent use of alcohol and other drugs (e.g., social situations), and others may be more specific (e.g., use of stimulants in the face of negative affect). The Inventory of Drug Taking Situations is helpful in identifying substance specific versus concurrent use situations. The rationale for skills training in relapse prevention centers on the notion that coping skills are necessary tools to reduce the likelihood of relapse in high-risk situations. It is helpful to elicit from the adolescent strategies and behaviors that have proven helpful in maintaining abstinence and reducing relapse. Success experiences are particularly important for enhancing self-efficacy (belief in one's ability to successfully carry out the behaviors) and building confidence in ability to successfully avoid relapse.

Following discussion of relapse prevention and high-risk situations, begin the process of identifying personal high-risk situations. Keep in mind that teens often underestimate the difficulty of coping successfully with relapse risk situations. In fact, it has been found that those teens who return to an abusive pattern of substance use are the most likely to characterize high-risk situations as easy to manage (Myers & Brown, 1990a). Therefore, it is important to provide examples of common high-risk situations and emphasize the risk involved. Examples of common adolescent high-risk situations include social situations, social pressure, and familial conflict. Although the role of negative affect has been discussed in detail, it is important to recognize that positive affect may represent an important trigger for relapse. It is important to assess the extent to which positive affect served to precipitate use in the past (using when celebrating, using when feeling good in order to feel even better). In addition, the Drug Taking Confidence Questionnaire (DTCQ; Annis & Graham, 1985) provides examples and suggestions of situations that may be difficult for the teen. This questionnaire accompanies the IDTS, consists of the same 50 items containing situation descriptions, and requires the respondent to rate their confidence in ability to resist the urge to use in each situation on a scale from 0 to 100 (*not at all confident* to *very confident*). Thus, responses to the DTCQ can help the adolescent identify situations that may be particularly difficult to manage successfully. Keep in mind that situations commonly associated with use in the past, as well as less frequent situations involving negative affect or unexpected opportunities for use, may all present risk for relapse. Previous results of functional analysis work will provide examples of the range of situations that may represent an increased risk for alcohol and/or drug use. For personal high-risk situations identified by the teen, assess perceived risk of relapse and ability to cope for each. Have the teen discuss in some detail why a particular situation may or may not be difficult and how they would manage the circumstances. It is important to provide feedback as to the likely accuracy of these perceptions and highlight the importance of being prepared for the unexpected.

Homework. Ask the teen to generate a list of situations likely to present a risk for relapse currently and in the future. In collaboration with the teen assign a number of situations for which a behavior chain will be completed, including alternatives to alcohol and/or drug use and coping strategies for avoiding relapse.

Coping with High-Risk Situations. Once a variety of high-risk situations has been identified, establish which are likely to pose the greatest risk. Consider the following factors in determining the extent of risk from a given situation: Has the teen successfully managed this type of situation without using? How often does the teen encounter this risk? Are the skills required to manage a situation an area of weakness for the teen? Does the teen have low self-efficacy for managing the situation? Does the teen underestimate the difficulty of managing the situation? Review upcoming events with a goal of identifying any situations that may fall into this category of particularly risky situations. Utilize the behavior chain to assess each identified situation, focusing on the antecedents, alternative behaviors, and means for managing the affective consequences of each situation.

For identified high-risk situations, planning and rehearsal are essential. Highlight the importance of having a coping strategy in mind before encountering a high-risk situation—there often is not time to think when the event occurs and affective reactions may be more intense than anticipated (e.g., anxiety at being confronted with alcohol or drugs, craving, or urges). Work with the teen to plan and rehearse various coping alternatives. Emphasize the importance of being prepared for the unexpected and accurate appraisal of potentially difficult situations. In order to anticipate and identify barriers to coping, engage the teen in a detailed discussion of how the plan will be carried out, what the consequences might be, how the teen and others may react, and self-efficacy for carrying out the plan. Finally, make a plan in the case of a slip. As mentioned earlier, it is important not to imply that a slip is permitted, however the therapist must recognize that such an event is highly likely. A concrete plan, with clear and simple steps to be followed may help diminish the likelihood of a protracted relapse in the case of a slip. It may help to enlist the teen to write and sign a "relapse recovery plan" contract for the teen to sign. This consists of a written plan of steps to follow in the case of a lapse.

The contract specifies that the teen agrees to follow the prescribed steps as soon as possible following an instance of alcohol or drug use. Also, make sure the teen carries a list of several names and phone numbers of individuals that will provide support for abstinence in a high-risk situation. Steps to include for managing a lapse may include calling the therapist, calling a sober friend, going to a support group meeting, getting rid of any remaining drugs or alcohol, reading a scripted paragraph to increase motivation for avoiding continued use (e.g., previously experienced negative consequences from use; gains made during treatment; benefits obtained from not using alcohol and drugs).

Homework.   Have the teen generate coping plans for different types of high-risk situations. After in-session practice of new behaviors, assign practice outside of the therapeutic setting. Have the teen practice skills initially in situations presenting minimal risk, very gradually entering more difficult circumstances. A primary goal of homework in this phase of treatment is to establish self-efficacy for avoiding relapse. The strategy of avoiding high-risk situations is useful early in treatment, but is unlikely to be effective over the long term. To help assure success experiences identify one or more support persons who can accompany the teen in relapse risk situations. The support person can be a nonusing peer, a parent, respected older youth or the therapist (if appropriate). Ultimately, the goal is to have the teens attribute their success and improvement to their own efforts and abilities. To this end, the use of avoidance and support persons should be faded out (judiciously) toward the end of treatment. The major recommendation here is practice through role plays, so there are several easily retrieved responses in the teen's repertoire.

Refusal Skills.   Because adolescents commonly relapse in social situations when confronted with pressure to use, discussion of refusal skills is particularly important. The importance of the peer group during adolescence, and the powerful role of peers in modeling and reinforcing alcohol and drug use behaviors highlight the importance of addressing these issues. Keep in mind that experimentation with substances is a normative adolescent behavior, and the prevalence of alcohol and drug use increases throughout adolescence. Thus, abstinence from alcohol and drug use represents a behavior that is contrary to that modeled in the adolescent's environment and represents a particularly significant challenge. Discussion and rehearsal of assertive skills may be particularly helpful in the context of refusal. In addition to behavioral skills, it is important to explore the teen's perception of what it means to them to refuse offers of drug use. The effect of alcohol and drug refusal on perceived acceptance and evaluation by others may be potent forces in influencing the likelihood of refusal (e.g., "my friends will reject me if I don't use"; "I won't fit in if I'm abstinent"; "I can't be comfortable with others if I'm not using"). Extended discussion of beliefs and attitudes surrounding this issue is particularly important in order to identify misperceptions or irrational beliefs held by the adolescent. Generating a list of irrational beliefs related to peer acceptance/rejection related to substance use will provide material for testing the accuracy of these thoughts using cognitive strategies for examining and correcting irrational thoughts, and may be effective in countering the forces of social influence. For example, fears of rejection by using peers can be addressed by having the teen examine these relationships: What is important about this friendship? How do you define a good friendship? How would you treat a friend who wanted to stop using? What things do you share with your friends other than using alcohol and drugs? It is important to provoke the adolescent to think through these issues without being pushed in a certain direction (e.g., refrain from suggesting that "true" friends would be supportive regardless of substance use) because this might elicit resistance. This topic will be particularly difficult for adolescents who cannot identify nonusing friends, and these issues may need to be linked to discussion of making new friends and identifying nonusing social supports. In such cases, validation of the fears concerned and expressed by the teen will be important. In addition, social skills training and plans for meeting new friends will need to be covered in session.

Homework.   For identified concerns regarding peer acceptance/attitudes, have the teen work on any related irrational thoughts by working to generate alternative, more accurate perceptions for each. The teen can also be asked to develop ideas for testing their beliefs (hypothesis testing) in relation to such concerns (e.g., how could you find out whether your friends really do look down on people who don't use?). In addition, identified strategies to manage peer pressure for use (whether perceived or actual) should be rehearsed and a specific plan generated. Select peer situations for practicing refusal skills. Initial practice may involve testing hypotheses about peer perceptions by having the teen ask friends about their attitudes toward nonusing peers in a generic (rather than personal) context. With time, progressively more difficult situations should be identified, responses practiced in session, and then refusal skills attempted in actual situations. As with coping in high-risk situations, it will be important to identify supports to accompany the teen in such situations to reinforce and facilitate success in refusal.

Goal Setting/Alternative Activities.   Substance abusing teens often have a sense that they will not enjoy life in the absence of drugs and alcohol. In fact, substances have become an integral part of their reinforcement network. To this end, an important part of relapse prevention is identifying and developing reinforcing activities that take place in nonsubstance using environments. Rewarding and enjoyable pursuits can help in enhancing self-esteem, developing a sense of autonomy, altering self-image, and providing a nonusing peer group. Involvement in alternative activities has been found to accompany successful resolution of substance abuse problems for some teens (Brown, 1993), and is particularly critical for teens not routinely participating in structured abstinence-focused groups (e.g., community-based support groups, AA, NA, etc.).

Teens in treatment have usually been abusing alcohol and drugs for a year or longer and tend to have few hobbies or extracurricular interests. Therefore, it is useful to set aside time for goal setting, or identifying potential areas of interest. A starting point is to find out in which, if any, activities the teen was involved in prior to the onset of substance use. In identifying potential areas of interest, it is also helpful to present a variety of domains (hobbies, recreational activities, sports, social activities, jobs) and explore the possibilities within each. The goal setting/activity planning can be approached systematically. First, in order to identify potential activities, it is helpful to provide menus or lists. Next, have the teen rank identified activities according to personal interest and importance. Help the teen come up with specific ideas for different types or domains of activities. Once specific activities are identified, discuss and plan how each will be pursued. It is important to anticipate barriers and make concrete, simple plans to facilitate compliance by the teen. First, the teen should identify a few long-term goals (e.g., have a job by the end of the year; become a proficient guitar player). Then, specific short-term plans should be developed for each goal (e.g., join one group in the next month, learn to play two songs on the guitar, identify a potential place of employment in the next month, etc.). The plans must be carefully constructed so as to anticipate possible barriers and ensure success so as to reinforce self-efficacy. It may be useful to have the teen keep a chart in which the short-term steps for each goal are identified, and then check off as these are accomplished. This format provides reinforcement by providing concrete evidence of progress toward the selected goals.

MAINTENANCE OF BEHAVIOR CHANGE

Continued contact following completion of the intervention plays an important role in maintenance of behavior change for adolescent substance abusers. Contact with the teen during the high risk for relapse initial posttreatment period and prompt reaction to lapses may serve to bolster successful resolution of alcohol and drug problems. Several pathways have been identified to successful outcome following adolescent substance abuse treatment; thus it is important to maintain a flexible approach to clinical intervention with adolescents following treatment. Of particular importance is therapist support for adolescent-initiated activities that assist in their abstinence, even if these vary from activities traditionally identified or recommended by treatment programs.

Available information on the course of adolescent alcohol and drug use following addiction treatment suggests means by which to improve the probability of successful outcome following treatment. Efforts at relapse prevention should continue throughout the initial 6 months posttreatment. This can be accomplished by scheduling follow-up visits and phone calls, gradually decreasing the frequency of interaction. Follow-up contacts will allow for assessment of maintenance of behavior change, allow for addressing problems that may have arisen, provide opportunities to reward self-change and maintenance efforts, assess and develop plans for new relapse risk situations that may be emerging, and evaluate whether new clinical symptoms may have appeared (e.g., anxiety, depression).

Another useful approach to maintaining behavior change is prompt attention to lapse and relapse episodes. It is important to keep in mind that adolescents differ from adults in that they often lapse on substances that were not previously their "drug of choice," and as many as one quarter of initial use episodes do not progress to full blown relapse. Thus, prompt attention to lapses may function to interrupt a return to earlier problematic patterns of drug and/or alcohol use. As previously mentioned, lapse episodes are considered an opportunity for learning rather than a failure. It is important to discuss these experiences in a nonjudgmental fashion and return to the functional analysis to provide perspective on the role and influence of substance use in their life. This opportunity should also be used to highlight the nature of relapse risk situations and the importance of vigilance, preparation, and motivation. A rapid response to lapse episodes can help mitigate the feelings of guilt and failure that commonly accompany relapse, and instill hope for future success.

Finally, providing support for nontraditional efforts at maintaining abstinence can help improve outcome for teens. Affiliation with traditional support systems for abstinence (AA/NA, recovery support groups) is found to be a strong predictor of long-term abstinence for youth. However, a significant portion of teens does not become affiliated with traditional 12-step efforts but achieve long-term abstinence by utilizing alternative supports or efforts that are equally effective (Brown, 1993). For example, some younger teens who are not involved in recovery organizations are able to maintain abstinence through increased involvement with the family and family efforts to restructure activities and communication. Therefore, in situations where a relatively supportive intact family unit exists, intervention aimed at improving family interactions and communication may result in adequate support for continued abstinence. Another nontraditional avenue for success is that of early individuation by older teens. These adolescents often have rampant alcohol or drug abuse in their families, and although not involved in the recovery community are able to support abstinence by gaining independence from their family. Such teens typically become involved in activities that provide drug-free environments (e.g., work, extracurricular activities, hobbies) and enhance self-reliance and self-esteem. Although relatively few teens with extended abstinence are found to utilize these alternative avenues, these strategies provide important alternatives for teens who do not become involved with abstinence-focused support groups.

PROBLEMS IN IMPLEMENTATION

There are several unique issues that arise in the treatment of youth who abuse alcohol and other substances. One of the most difficult issues in treating adolescent substance abuse is that of alcohol and drug involvement during the course of treatment. This issue is discussed in detail later. In addition, other issues that may lead to difficulties and suggested strategies that may diffuse resistance and enhance compliance are highlighted. Some of these are reiterated in the following discussion and bear particular attention by the clinician.

Substance Use During the Course of Treatment

For youth, it is assumed that the goal of treatment is abstinence from psychoactive substances. To this end, issues of continued use, lapse, and relapse must be addressed and agreed on at the outset of intervention. This is often difficult for teens as they may view only one substance as a problem and perceive use of other psychoactive substances as nonproblematic. Once an initial goal for treatment has been agreed on, it is important to decide on means by which substance use will be monitored, and the consequences of continued use or lapses. Monitoring of substance use can be accomplished through self-report by the adolescent, parent report, and urine toxicology screening. An obvious advantage of urine screening is the objective nature of biochemical measurement. In addition, urine screens may serve as a deterrent to use and facilitate honest reporting by the teen. In discussing urine screens with the adolescent client, this should be presented as a standard procedure that is required of all individuals treated for substance abuse. It is important to explain reasons for using urine screens, and to emphasize that the issue is one of accountability not trust. If adolescents have agreed to a goal of abstinence, they are responsible for working toward that goal and being forthcoming about lapses during the course of treatment. In addition, this procedure can also be justified as a means for protecting the adolescents from the dangers inherent in continued drug use.

Urine screens can be administered routinely, at random intervals, or at the clinician's discretion. Random screens may be more effective in detecting use because savvy drug users can plan around them. However, random screening is more difficult to implement in the context of a set treatment schedule (i.e., weekly sessions), and may be interpreted by the adolescent as an expectation that they will lapse, and lie about their use. Thus, regular screening (whether weekly, or less often) may be perceived as less intrusive than random drug testing. In the case that less frequent drug testing is deemed appropriate, clinicians should reserve the right to ask for a urine sample if they have reason to believe the adolescent is continuing alcohol and drug use. This can be presented as an option that will only be employed if clinicians feel it necessary and justified. Examples should be provided of circumstances under which this may occur (e.g., behavioral signs of withdrawal, unusual mood changes, reports of unusual behavior by family members), with an emphasis that the reasons for such a decision will be fully discussed with the adolescent if the issue should arise. Factors to be considered in choosing to implement urine screens include the financial cost of the procedure and its impact on the therapeutic relationship and process. This issue must be discussed with the adolescent and family members to clarify who will have access to the results and what are appropriate and inappropriate reactions by the parents or family (e.g., parents should be discouraged from punitive responses to a positive screen, but rather encouraged to discuss the event in a supportive manner and communicate their feelings in an appropriate fashion). Finally, clean urine screens should be interpreted as progress, and reinforced by discussion of gains made by the teen.

One important provision is that the adolescent not appear to sessions intoxicated. This should be agreed to up front, with the understanding that no useful work can be accomplished if the adolescent is under the influence during sessions. In the event that this does occur, the clinician is responsible for assessing the situation and taking appropriate action (e.g., Is the adolescent in any imminent danger? Can this person be sent home safely?). In addition, a makeup session should be scheduled as soon as possible to process the event.

With abstinence as the goal of treatment, it is reasonable to make explicit the expectation that the adolescent not use alcohol or drugs during the course of treatment. The reality of treatment, particularly in an outpatient setting, is that absolute abstinence during its course is often difficult to achieve. Additionally, lapse experiences during the course of treatment can result in useful learning experiences and lead to fruitful discussion. However, continued use may also indicate that treatment is not effective. Thus, the clinician must make explicit the consequences of use episodes. In general, it is effective to define abstinence as the goal of treatment with the understanding that lapses may occur but must be discussed openly and honestly in order for treatment to continue. In addition, repeated noncompliance and a pattern of use that does not diminish or show improvement with time may indicate a need to seek a more intensive treatment approach.

Compliance with Treatment

Several developmental factors will influence adolescent compliance with treatment. As discussed previously, motivation for change is a critical issue and must be assessed and addressed throughout. Adolescence is a period of life during which a critical task is the transition into and learning of adult roles and responsibilities. Yet, although expected to behave in an adult manner, adolescents typically have little control over events in their lives and often feel powerless or helpless. It is important to pay particular attention to this issue in setting goals and choosing the form of intervention. To this end, engaging the adolescent in collaborative decision making is particularly important to reduce resistance and enhance compliance (i.e., the adolescent should be provided with a sense of ownership over the goals and course of treatment).

Environmental considerations are also important for compliance. Attention should be given to the life context of the adolescent: What is the nature of the family environment, school, and community? To the extent that substance use is not readily modeled and reinforced in the environment and access to substances is limited, compliance should be better. On the other hand, adolescents who are frequently exposed to substance use at home and/or school, and who live in communities that have few resources for supporting recreation and drug-free activities can be expected to have more difficulty maintaining abstinence. Therefore, the choice of intensity of intervention (i.e., outpatient vs. residential treatment) should incorporate consideration of the adolescent's life context.

Another concern has to do with intervention content and learning. Adolescents in general present with a range of neurocognitive abilities, and many adolescents with substance use problems also evidence attentional difficulties. Thus, it is critical to tailor the information imparted to the cognitive level and abilities of the individual adolescent. Information should be imparted in manageable portions and at a level of language matched to the teen's level of comprehension. Session content should focus on concrete examples rather than abstract constructs. A failure to do so will result in frustration by the adolescent, which will decrease their motivation and compliance. In addition, techniques developed with and for adults are often inappropriate for adolescents. It is important that the clinician be sensitive to this and not make assumptions as to appropriateness of materials for adolescents. In determining whether a particular technique will work, the adolescents should be consulted as to whether it is acceptable, whether it makes sense, and how comfortable they feel with it. Feedback should be elicited in a manner that allows the adolescent to provide input without feeling that their intelligence or ability is being questioned.

Compliance with assignments is often problematic because any tasks that appear school-like are likely to be met with resistance. To the extent possible, tasks should focus on activities and behaviors rather than reading and writing. In addition to involving the teen in selecting assignments, it is often helpful to begin work during the session in order to identify a priori any potential obstacles or difficulties. Weekly review of assignments is critical to enhancing compliance. In particular, it is helpful to solicit feedback from the adolescent as to how helpful the task was and what would make it more useful rather than how much they liked or disliked it. This information can be used to modify future assignments and for problem solving around resistance and barriers to compliance.

Compliance and success with the selected course of treatment as well as environmental considerations should be used to determine the need for changes in intensity of intervention. For example, continued substance use and poor compliance should be taken as evidence for the need to increase treatment intensity. This may be accomplished through more frequent meetings or change from an outpatient to residential setting. Conversely, rapid improvement and good compliance may indicate that less intensive treatment may yield success. In either case, it is important to involve the adolescent in the decision to make any changes in the course of treatment.

CASE ILLUSTRATION

Noah was a 17-year-old biracial male with a 2-year history of polysubstance abuse, including marijuana, alcohol, and LSD. He was admitted for treatment to an inpatient psychiatric program for adolescents. Presenting symptoms included increased energy, grandiosity, euphoria, decreased need for sleep, and increased psychomotor activity. He received an intake diagnosis of Bipolar Disorder, Manic Episode.

The unit routinely screened for substance abuse at intake using the Personal Experience Screening Questionnaire (PESQ; Winters, 1991), and Noah scored above PESQ problem severity cut-off criteria (for age and gender) indicating the need for additional substance abuse evaluation. PESQ validity scale scores indicated no reason to suspect false or careless responding, so a more comprehensive substance abuse evaluation was conducted. Noah was interviewed by his primary therapist in the psychiatric program using the Teen Addiction Severity Index (T–ASI; Kaminer et al., 1991; Kaminer et al., 1993), and results indicated polysubstance involvement severe enough to warrant an additional diagnosis of polysubstance abuse. During the month prior to hospitalization, Noah reported using marijuana frequently, smoking cigarettes daily, drinking alcohol once, using LSD once, and smoking opium once. He had started using marijuana, alcohol, and LSD at age 15, and smoking cigarettes and using opium (only once) at age 17. Other noteworthy findings from the T–ASI concerned Noah's legal, family, academic, and psychiatric functioning. During the past year, he had been arrested twice while intoxicated, had experienced increasing difficulties getting along with his family members, had demonstrated a marked decline in academic performance (he had been enrolled in a school for the "gifted"), and had at least two manic episodes and possibly a third, each of which was accompanied by a dramatic increase in his substance use.

Despite the assessment findings, Noah was initially hesitant to view his substance use (or his manic episodes) as problematic in any way. Rather than address his substance use directly, the first few sessions were devoted to discussing aspects of Noah's life that he did find bothersome (i.e., "rolling with the resistance"). Noah acknowledged that his trouble with the police and his trouble with his mother were problems, particularly because these difficulties precipitated his hospitalization. In the first session, he expressed anger at authority figures for not tolerating his "uniqueness and individuality." After some discussion and reflection, Noah admitted that his behavior under the influence of substances had at times been extreme (e.g., exposing his genitalia in a family-oriented restaurant), and he agreed to spend future sessions considering whether his use of alcohol and other drugs might occasionally cause difficulties.

Noah was introduced to the concept of functional analysis in the next session. As is typical of teenagers, he quickly grasped the fundamentals of constructing a behavior chain. Among the triggers he reported was experiencing a rising mood, which the therapist noted is one of the cardinal symptoms experienced by people entering a manic episode. Noah remained skeptical about the notion that his mood elevations might be a problem, but observed that these periods were indeed distinct from his "normal, everyday existence." This offered an opportunity to discuss Noah's thoughts in response to episodes of rising mood. His thoughts included: "I can do anything," "Everybody's starting to notice me," and "I'm invincible." When asked how this type of thinking made him feel, Noah offered "great," "really creative," "excited," and "energetic." Other trigger– thought–feeling chains were discussed, but the chain beginning with rising mood remained the most compelling to Noah and the therapist. The remainder of the session was spent finishing the behavior chain, with particular attention to the consequences of using substances in response to rising mood. Positive consequences included "feeling really high and psychedelic," "laughing a lot," and "experiencing new things." Noah initially stated only one negative consequence, "feeling a little bit out of control." With gentle prodding from the therapist, Noah expanded the list to "getting arrested," "fighting with my mother," and "embarrassing myself" (specific to the occasion on which he exposed himself). He also noted that using substances in response to rising mood typically resulted in cognitive and mood changes, which might be both a positive and negative consequence.

The next session was spent primarily discussing whether Noah had truly experienced manic episodes. He described several extreme incidents that had occurred while he was experiencing periods of elevated mood (e.g., going to the blackboard in calculus class and filling the board with random pictographs while delivering an extended monologue about the history of the world), each of which he labeled as spontaneous and bizarre. He also noted that he had much difficulty concentrating during these periods and this had wreaked havoc on his school performance and chances of going to a good college. Grudgingly, Noah admitted that his life might be better if he had more control over these episodes. He concluded that: "I guess I do have manic episodes after all." The remainder of the session was spent employing a functional analysis approach to understanding Noah's episodes of mania. Among the most important triggers he identified was "taking lots of drugs."

Once Noah had arrived at the conclusion that he had experienced manic episodes in the past, he sought out as much information as was available to him about the disorder. This led to increased compliance with doctor's orders concerning a maintenance prescription of lithium carbonate. Subsequent sessions were spent teaching skills and strategies for identifying and managing mood lability. Specific attention was given to distinguishing between everyday mood swings and the beginnings of an episode of affective illness. Noah relied on his list of triggers for understanding the difference between the two and for developing strategies to avoid using drugs in response to elevated mood.

The final sessions were devoted to relapse prevention and goal setting. Noah identified people and places that were high risk, and generated an impressive array of strategies for managing situations in which he might experience temptations to use substances. Some of these strategies were clearly impractical, and the therapist pointed this out. Noah received this criticism well and offered several more practical alternatives. The distinction between a lapse and a relapse was also discussed, both in regard to episodes of substance use and mania. Plans for developing and maintaining social resources were discussed in the context of attending community-based abstinence support groups and becoming involved with new, nonusing friends at school. Finally, Noah described his short- and long-term goals (e.g., passing calculus, performing in the school play, going to a good college), and argued convincingly that a return to his previous patterns of alcohol and other drug use would interfere with the achievement of these objectives.

Noah was discharged from the hospital and was seen on an outpatient basis for weekly sessions for 1 month, and again a month later. These sessions were spent bolstering earlier gains and discussing Noah's successes and setbacks in response to life's challenges. Generally, he reported doing well and had made significant strides toward achieving his short-term goals. Both his substance use and mood problems seemed well in check, though he admitted to twice using marijuana since discharge. In both cases, the antecedents for use were discussed, and strategies for managing similar high-risk situations were developed. Noah ended treatment appearing well on his way toward achieving his long-term objectives.

CONCLUSIONS

This chapter has focused on the practical application of cognitive and behavioral intervention strategies for youth with alcohol and/or other drug problems. This chapter has highlighted the importance of utilizing well-standardized instruments and procedures in assessment and intervention with adolescents. Further, developmental factors dictate both special clinical approaches and issues with this population of substance abusers. Even more than with adults, motivational enhancement efforts play a key role in accurate assessment of adolescent substance involvement and successful progression through the therapeutic process. Cognitive and behavioral intervention strategies are well suited to youth who need to develop the skills and behavioral repertoires necessary to sustain the major lifestyle changes that support abstention. When coupled with therapist efforts to minimize environmental risks and enhance abstention focused social resources, cognitive and behavioral strategies facilitate a framework of understanding wherein teens learn they have choices with regard to their behavior. Additionally, sensitive utilization of cognitive and behavioral intervention strategies, and in particular behavioral rehearsal, creates learning opportunities for identification and engagement of the uncomfortable affect that often dominates transitions during puberty and accompanies negative consequences of substance involvement that persist long after use abates. Finally, recommendations are made that can provide sufficient constraints and consequences to allow adolescents alcohol- and drug-free periods necessary for skill development and refinement. Cognitive and behavioral efforts coupled with persistent support (e.g., booster sessions, follow up phone calls) over a 6-month period may not only aid remission of the substance abuse problem but foster resolution of other difficulties that emerge during adolescence.

REFERENCES

Abrams, D. B., & Niaura, R. S. (1987). Social learning theory. In H. T. Blane & K. E. Leonard (Eds.), *Psychological theories of drinking and alcoholism* (pp.131–172). New York: Guilford.

American Psychiatric Association. (1994). *Diagnostic and statistical manual of mental disorders* (4th ed.). Washington, DC: American Psychiatric Association.

Annis, H. M., & Graham, J. M. (1985a). *Drug Taking Confidence Questionnaire*. Toronto: Addiction Research Foundation.

Annis, H. M., & Graham, J. M. (1985b). *Inventory of drug taking situations*. Toronto: Addiction Research Foundation.

Babor, T. F., del Boca, F. K., McLaney, M. A., & Jacobi, B. (1991). Just say Y.E.S.: Matching adolescents to appropriate interventions for alcohol and other drug-related problems. Special focus: Alcohol and youth. *Alcohol Health & Research World, 15,* 77–86.

Beck, A. T., Rush, A. J., Shaw, B. F., & Emery, G. (1979). *Cognitive therapy of depression*. New York: Guildford.

Bentler, P. M. (1992). Etiologies and consequences of adolescent drug use: Implications for prevention. *Journal of Addictive Diseases, 11,* 47–61.

Blane, H. (1976). Middle-aged alcoholics and young drinkers. In H. Blane & M. Chafetz (Eds.), *Youth, alcohol, and social policy* (pp. 5–38). New York: Plenum.

Blum, R. W. (1987). Adolescent substance abuse: Diagnostic and treatment issues. *Pediatric Clinics of North America, 34,* 523–537.

Brown, S. A. (1993). Recovery patterns in adolescent substance abuse. In J. S. Baer, G. A. Marlatt, & R. J. McMahon (Eds.). *Addictive behaviors across the lifespan: Prevention, treatment and policy issues* (pp. 161–183). Beverly Hills, CA: Sage.

Brown, S. A., Gleghorn, A., Schuckit, M., Myers, M. G., & Mott, M. A. (1996). Conduct disorder among adolescent substance abusers. *Journal of Studies on Alcohol, 57,* 314–324.

Brown, S. A., Mott, M. A., & Myers, M.G. (1990). Adolescent drug and alcohol treatment outcome. In R. R. Watson (Ed.), *Prevention and treatment of drug and alcohol abuse* (pp. 373–403). Totowa, NJ: Humana Press.

Brown, S. A., Mott, M. A., & Stewart, M. A. (1992). Adolescent alcohol and drug abuse. In C. E. Walker & M. C. Roberts (Eds.), *Handbook of clinical child psychology* (2nd ed., pp. 677–693). New York: Wiley.

Brown, S. A., Myers, M. G., Lippke, L. F., Stewart, D. G., Tapert, S. F., & Vik, P. W. (in press). Psychometric evaluation of the Customary Drinking and Drug Use Record (CDDR): A measure of adolescent alcohol and drug involvement. *Journal of Studies on Alcohol.*

Brown, S. A., Myers, M. G., Mott, M. A., & Vik, P. (1994) Correlates of successful outcome following treatment for adolescent substance abuse. *Journal of Applied and Preventive Psychology, 3*, 61–73.

Brown, S. A., Vik, P. W., & Creamer, V. A. (1989). Characteristics of relapse following adolescent substance abuse treatment. *Addictive Behaviors, 14*, 291–300.

Bukstein, O., & Kaminer, Y. (1994). The nosology of adolescent substance abuse. *The American Journal of Addictions, 3*, 1–13.

Burns, D. D. (1989). *The feeling good handbook: Using the new mood therapy in everyday life.* New York: William Morrow.

Center for Substance Abuse Treatment. (1993). *Treatment improvement protocol series: Screening and assessment of alcohol- and other drug-abusing adolescents.* Department of Health and Human Services, publication # (SMA) 93–2009. Rockville, MD: USDHHS.

Christiansen, B. A., Goldman, M. S., & Inn, A. (1982). Development of alcohol-related expectancies in adolescents: Separating pharmacological from social-learning influences. *Journal of Consulting and Clinical Psychology, 50*, 336–344.

Christiansen, B. A., Roehling, P. V., Smith, G. T., & Goldman, M. S. (1989). Using alcohol expectancies to predict adolescent drinking behavior after one year. *Journal of Consulting and Clinical Psychology, 57*, 93–99.

Clarke, G., Lewinsohn, P., & Hops, H. (1990). *Leader's manual for adolescent groups: Adolescent coping with depression course.* Eugene, OR: Castalia Publishing.

Costello, A. J., Edelbrock, C., Dulcan, M. K., Kalas, R., & Klaric, S. (1984). Development and testing of the NIMH Diagnostic Interview Schedule for Children on a clinical population: Final report (Contract No. RFP–DB–81–0027). Rockville, MD: Center for Epidemiologic studies, National Institute for Mental Health.

Costello, A. J., Edelbrock, C., Dulcan, M. K., Kalas, R., & Klaric, S. (1987). *Diagnostic Interview Schedule for Children (DISC).* Pittsburgh, PA: Western Psychiatric Institute and Clinic, School of Medicine, University of Pittsburgh.

Donovan, D. M. (1988). Assessment of addictive behaviors: Implications of an emerging biopsychosocial model. In D. M. Donovan & G. A. Marlatt (Eds.), *Assessment of addictive behaviors* (pp. 3–48). New York: Guilford.

Donovan, D. M., & Marlatt, G. A. (1988). *Assessment of addictive behaviors.* New York: Guilford.

Goldman, M. S., Brown, S. A., & Christiansen, B. A. (1987). Expectancy theory: Thinking about drinking. In H. T. Blane & K. E. Leonard (Eds.), *Psychological theories of drinking and alcoholism* (pp.173–220). New York: Guilford.

Henly, G. A., & Winters, K. C. (1989). Development of psychosocial scales for the assessment of adolescents involved with alcohol and drugs. *International Journal of the Addictions, 24*, 973–1001.

Hester, R. K., & Miller, W. R. (1988). Empirical guidelines for optimal client-treatment matching. In E. R. Rahdert & J. Grabowski (Eds.), National Institute on Drug Abuse Research Monograph 77, *Adolescent drug abuse: Analyses of treatment research* (DHHS Publication No. (ADM88–1523). Washington, DC: U.S. Government Printing Office.

Hurt, R. D., Offord, K. P., Croghan, I. T., Gomez-Dahl, L., Kottke, T. E., Morse, R. M., & Melton, L. J. (1996). Mortality following inpatient addictions treatment: Role of tobacco use in a community-based cohort. *Journal of the American Medical Association, 275*, 1097–1103.

Jessor, R., & Jessor, S. L. (1977). *Problem behavior and psychosocial devleopment: A longitudinal study of youth.* New York: Academic Press.

Johnston, L. D. (1994). *National survey results on drug use from the Monitoring the Future Study, 1975–1993* (DHHS Publication No. ADM 94–3809). Washington, DC: U.S. Government Printing Office.

Johnston, L. D. (1995). *Drug use rises again in 1995 among American teens.* University of Michigan Press Release.

Kaminer, Y. (1994). *Adolescent substance abuse: A comprehensive guide to theory and practice.* New York: Plenum.

Kaminer, Y., Bukstein, O. G., & Tarter, R. E. (1991). The Teen Addiction Severity Index (T–ASI): Rationale and reliability. *International Journal of Addictions, 26*, 219–226.

Kaminer, Y., Wagner, E., Plummer, B. & Seifer, R. (1993). Validation of the Teen Addiction Severity Index (T–ASI). *American Journal on Addictions, 2*, 250–254.

Liddle, H. A., & Dakof, G. A. (1995). Family-based treatment for adolescent drug use: State of the science. In E. Rahdert et al. (Eds.). *Adolescent drug abuse: Clinical assessment and therapeutic interventions* (DHHS Publication No. ADM 95–3908). Washington, DC: U.S. Government Printing Office.

Marlatt, G. A., & Gordon, J. R. (1985). *Relapse prevention: Maintenance strategies in the treatment of addictive behaviors*. New York: Guilford.

Martin, C. S., Kaczynski, N. A., Maisto, S. A., Bukstein, O. M., & Moss, H. B. (1995). Patterns of *DSM–IV* Alcohol Abuse and Dependence Symptoms in Adolescent Drinkers. *Journal of Studies on Alcohol, 56*, 672–680.

McCrady, B. S., Dean, L., Dubreuil, E., & Swanson, S. (1985). The problem drinkers' project: A programmatic application of social-learning based treatment. In G. A. Marlatt & J. R. Gordon (Eds.), *Relapse prevention: Maintenance strategies in the treatment of addictive behaviors* (pp. 245–298). New York: Guilford.

McLellan, A. T., Luborsky, L., Woody, G. E., & O'Brien, C. P. (1980). An improved diagnostic evaluation instrument for substance abuse patients. *Journal of Nervous and Mental Disease, 40*, 620–625.

Miller, W. R. (1989). Matching individuals with interventions. In R. K. Hester & W. R. Miller (Eds.), *Handbook of alcoholism treatment approaches* (pp. 261–272). New York: Pergamon.

Miller, W. R., & Rollnick, S. (Eds.). (1991). *Motivational interviewing: Preparing people to change addictive behavior*. New York: Guilford.

Monti, P. M., Abrams, D. B., Kadden, R. M., & Cooney, N. L. (1989). *Treating alcohol dependence*. New York: Guilford.

Myers, M. G., & Brown, S. A. (1990a). Coping and appraisal in relapse risk situations among substance abusing adolescents following treatment. *Journal of Adolescent Chemical Dependency, 1*, 95–116.

Myers, M. G., & Brown, S. A. (1990b). Coping responses and relapse among adolescent substance abusers. *Journal of Substance Abuse, 2*, 177–190.

Myers, M. G., & Brown, S. A. (1994). Smoking and health in substance abusing adolescents: A two year followup. *Pediatrics, 93*, 561–566.

Myers, M. G., & Brown, S. A. (1996). The Adolescent Relapse Coping Questionnaire: Psychometric validation. *Journal of Studies on Alcohol, 57*, 40–46.

Myers, M. G., Brown, S. A., & Mott, M. A. (1993). Coping as a predictor of adolescent substance abuse treatment outcome. *Journal of Substance Abuse, 5*, 15–29.

Newcomb, M. D., & Bentler, P. M. (1988). *Consequences of adolescent drug use*. Newbury Park, CA: Sage.

Olsen, H. I, Barnes, H., Larson, A., Muxen, M., & Wilson, M. (1982). *Family inventories: Inventories used in a national survey of families across the family life cycle*. St. Paul, MN: Family Social Science, University of Minnesota.

Owen, P., & Nyberg, L. (1983). Assessing alcohol and drug problems among adolescents: Current practice. *Journal of Drug Addiction, 13*, 249–254.

Pandina, R. J., & Schuele, J. A. (1983). Psychosocial correlates of alcohol and drug use of adolescent students and adolescents in treatment. *Journal of Studies on Alcohol, 44*, 950–973.

Shedler, J., & Block, J. (1990). Adolescent drug use and psychological health: A longitudinal inquiry. *American Psychologist, 45*, 612–630.

Skinner, H. A. (1987). A model for the assessment of alcohol use and related problems. *Drugs and Society, 2*, 19–30.

Skinner, H., Steinhauser, P., & Santo-Barbara, J. (1983). The family assessment measure. *Canadian Journal of Community Mental Health, 2*, 91–105.

Stewart, D. G. (1994, August). Antisocial behavior and long term outcome of substance abuse treatment. In S. A. Brown (Chair), *Long term outcomes among adolescents following alcohol and drug treatment*. American Psychological Association annual meeting, Los Angeles.

Stewart , D. G., & Brown, S. A. (1995). Withdrawal and dependency symptoms among adolescent alcohol and drug abusers. *Addiction, 90*, 627–635.

Stewart, M. A., & Brown, S. A. (1993). Family functioning following adolescent substance abuse treatment. *Journal of Substance Abuse, 5*, 327–339.

Tapert, S. F., Stewart, D. G., & Brown, S. A. (in press). Drug abuse in adolescents. In A. J. Goreczny & M. Hersen (Eds.), *Handbook of pediatric and adolescent health psychology*. Needham Heights, MA: Allyn & Bacon.

Tarter, R. E. (1990). Evaluation and treatment of adolescent substance abuse: A decision tree method. *American Journal of Drug and Alcohol Abuse, 16*, 1–46.

Tarter, R. E., Ott, P. J., & Mezzich, A. C. (1991). Psychometric assessment. In R. J. Frances & S. I. Miller (Eds.), *Clinical textbook of addictive disorders* (pp. 237–267). New York: Guilford.

Wallen, J. (1992). A comparison of male and female clients in substance abuse treatment. *Journal of Substance Abuse Treatment, 9,* 243–248.

Wilcox, J. A., & Yates, W. R. (1993). Gender and psychiatric comorbidity in substance-abusing individuals. *American Journal on Addictions, 2,* 202–206.

Winters, K. C. (1990). The need for improved assessment of adolescent substance use involvement. *Journal of Drug Issues, 20,* 487–502.

Winters, K. C. (1991). *The personal experience screening questionnaire.* Los Angeles: Western Psychological Services.

Chapter 12

Anorexia Nervosa

Donald A. Williamson
Louisiana State University

Erich G. Duchmann
Susan E. Barker
Renee M. Bruno
Our Lady of the Lake Eating Disorders Program, Baton Rouge, LA

DESCRIPTION OF ANOREXIA NERVOSA

Anorexia nervosa is an eating disorder with the following symptom profile: refusal to maintain a normal body weight, resulting in emaciation; intense fear of weight gain or fatness; disturbance of body image and/or denial of the seriousness of low body weight; and amenorrhea (absence of menstrual cycle) in females (American Psychiatric Association, 1994). Two types of anorexia nervosa have been described: the *restricting type*, in which the person controls weight by extreme restriction of food intake and exercise, and the *binge eating/purging type*, in which the person engages in binge eating or purging, usually in addition to restrictive eating and exercise.

Many persons presenting for treatment do not report all of the symptoms of anorexia nervosa or bulimia nervosa. For example, the person may be rapidly losing weight, but may not be emaciated or they may not report amenorrhea. Such cases are diagnosed as "subclinical anorexia nervosa" (Eating Disorder Not Otherwise Specified). Nevertheless, these "subclinical" cases are often very disturbed (Williamson, Gleaves, & Savin, 1992) and should be treated aggressively. This chapter, therefore, presents a comprehensive treatment program for anorexia nervosa and "subclinical anorexia nervosa."

STRUCTURE OF THE PROGRAM

Levels of Care

The treatment program described here has three levels of care: inpatient, partial day hospital, and outpatient. Patients are evaluated prior to treatment and are assigned to an appropriate level of care based on the criteria shown in Table 12.1. Presence of any one of these criteria may be used to assign a person to the associated level of care. As treatment progresses, the patient is moved to less restrictive and less intensive levels of care.

TABLE 12.1

Criteria for Admission to Three Levels of Care

Inpatient

1. Extreme emaciation (e.g., body weight is 15% or more below normal).
2. Severe medical complications (e.g., end stage renal disease, diabetes mellitus, extreme dehydration or malnutrition).
3. Repeated failure of less intense levels of treatment.
4. Psychiatric crises (e.g., suicidal attempt or intent).

Partial Day Hospital

1. Moderate level of emaciation (e.g., body weight is 5% to 15% below normal).
2. Rapid weight loss (e.g., patient is losing 2 lbs per week over the past 4 weeks).
3. Repeated failure of outpatient treatment.
4. Denial of need for treatment.
5. Resistance to treatment.

Outpatient

1. Normal body weight status.
2. Low denial regarding need for treatment.
3. Low resistance to treatment.
4. Good family/social support system.

Schedule of Therapeutic Activities

In the inpatient and partial day hospital programs, a 5-day schedule of therapeutic activities is offered. This schedule is shown in Fig. 12.1. Patients in the partial day hospital program return to their homes at night and spend weekends at home. Outpatient groups are held twice per week. Adolescent and adult patients attend separate evening groups for patients and a family group for adolescent and adult patients and their family members. The opportunity is provided for inpatient and day hospital patients to attend these outpatient groups in order to prepare them for long-term outpatient follow-up.

Staffing Requirements

The treatment program is administered across four hospital units: intensive adult psychiatric care, intensive adolescent psychiatric care, open unit psychiatric care for adults, and partial day hospital. In addition to the medical and nursing care for these units, the following staff are required to manage the eating disorders program: psychiatric medical director, internal medicine consultants, clinical psychologist, program director, nurse coordinator, intake counselor, three eating disorder therapists, and clinical dietitian. These staff members manage all aspects of the treatment program described in the remainder of this chapter.

THERAPEUTIC MODALITIES

Pharmacotherapy and Psychiatric/Medical Treatment

Assessment for use of medication is an ongoing process in the treatment of anorexia nervosa. This program advocates the view that effective treatment cannot occur without improvement in nutritional status (and subsequent weight gain). The patients, through the educational and therapeutic processes, are educated that FOOD IS MEDICINE.

TIME	MONDAY	TUESDAY	WEDNESDAY	THURSDAY	FRIDAY
7:30 - 8:30	BREAKFAST AND COMMUNITY ON INDIVIDUAL UNITS				
8:30 - 11:30	SCHOOL FOR ADOLESCENTS ON THE ADOLESCENT UNIT				
9:00 - 9:30	Community Medication Teaching	Community/Questions and Answers w/Physician	Community Medication Teaching	Community/Questions and Answers w/Physician	Community Medication Teaching
9:30 - 10:30	Individual Family Therapy/ Structured Free Time	Structured Free Time/ Extended Evaluation/ Individual Tx w/unit staff	Individual Family Therapy/ Structured Free Time	Structured Free Time Extended Evaluation/ Individual Tx w/unit staff	Individual Family Therapy/ Structured Free Time
10:30 - 11:30	Individual Family Therapy/Structured Free Time	Activity Therapy	Individual Family Therapy/Structured Free Time	Activity Therapy	Individual Family Therapy/Structured Free Time
11:30 - 11:45	Break	Break	Break	Break	Break
11:45 - 12:30	Lunch	Lunch	Lunch	Lunch	Lunch
12:30 - 1:30	Process Group	Process Group	Process Group	Process Group	Process Group
1:30 - 2:00	Break	Break	Break	Break	Break
2:00 - 3:00	Body Image	Assertiveness	Body Image	Assertiveness	Body Image
3:00 - 4:00	Meal Planning	Nutritional Education	Meal Planning	Nutritional Education	Meal Planning
4:00 - 5:00	Exercise and Education	Activity Therapy	Exercise and Education	Activity Therapy	Exercise and Education
5:00 - 5:45	Dinner	Dinner	Dinner	Dinner	Dinner
6:00 - 6:30	Closing Communication	Closing Communication	Closing Communication	Closing Communication	Closing Communication
6:30	RETURN TO UNITS OR ATTEND EVENING EATING DISORDER GROUPS				

FIG. 12.1. Schedule of therapeutic activities for the inpatient and partial day hospital programs.

The assessment of comorbid symptoms and diagnoses begins with the psychiatric history and continues as refeeding occurs. A number of symptoms (i.e., depression, irritability, apathy, sleep disturbance, obsessional thinking) can be the result of undernutrition or may be magnified by undernutrition. Therefore, restoration of body weight and biological function (e.g., return of menses) is a primary focus utilizing food as medicine. Anorexic patients with low to very low body weight are at greater risk for side effects from medication if they are physiologically unstable as the result of self-starvation. Use of psychiatric medications is therefore individualized and introduced gradually to the patient as one possible treatment modality. This form of therapy is accomplished as rapport is established and attempts are made to gain the patient's confidence and trust.

Although there is little scientific evidence that suggests psychotropic medication has clinically significant benefit in anorexic patients, particularly in the initial stages of treatment, there are circumstances in which it is used (Walsh & Devlin, 1992). As positive nutritional balance and weight gain are accomplished, the staff must observe whether depression, anxiety, obsessional thinking, and irritability persist with great intensity. If these symptoms do not remit, medications are strongly considered and are often begun at low doses and gradually increased to a therapeutic range.

Serotonin reuptake inhibitors (e.g., fluoxetine, sertraline, and paroxetine) are often chosen because of the low side effect profile and clinical effectiveness for treating comorbid depression. These pharmacologic properties serve to increase acceptability of pharmacotherapy as one therapeutic component. Antidepressants, such as nortryptiline, imipramine, amytriptiline, and desipramine, are used either alone or in combination with serotonin reuptake inhibitors for treatment of sleep disturbances to augment effects of other medications. Clomipramine may be used to reduce obsessional thinking and may assist with sleep initiation and/or maintenance. Lithium carbonate is used primarily as an adjunct pharmacotherapy to assist in mood stabilization, especially if there is a comorbid diagnosis of bipolar disorder.

Polypharmacy is frequently adopted in patients with recurrent, relapsing symptoms or who have shown poor response to more conventional pharmacologic treatment. Antipsychotic medications are sometimes used in low doses at bedtime to assist in sleep maintenance. As weight is normalized, antipsychotics can be withdrawn or used as needed for their tranquilizing and thought organizing effects. In patients who have failed polypharmacologic trials and have mood disorders in association with anorexia nervosa, electroconvulsive therapy (ECT) has been used. Experience with use of ECT shows that it generally results in improvement of mood. Also, ECT has been beneficial, in some cases, for the treatment of symptoms specific to anorexia (e.g., fear of fatness, overvalued ideas regarding thinness, and resistance to weight gain).

These multiple medication strategies are clearly explained to the patients; education as to expectations for medications and target symptoms are reviewed frequently with patients. Successful utilization, compliance, and effectiveness of medication is influenced by consistent communication, education, and support by the treating psychiatrist and medical staff.

Short acting antianxiety medications (lorazepam, alprazolam) are sometimes used in the early stages of treatment 30 minutes prior to meal time to reduce anticipatory anxiety as caloric requirements are being increased rapidly.

Estrogen replacement directed by a gynecologist for patients with chronic amenorrhea (greater than 1 year) to reduce calcium loss and to reduce the risk of osteoporosis is often recommended. Fiber or bulkagents (Fibercon, Metamucil) are sometimes used during refeeding for regulation of bowel habits.

Behavior Therapy

Behavioral approaches for treating anorexia nervosa have generally focused on modification of eating and purgative behavior (Agras, 1987; Williamson, Cubic, & Fuller, 1992; Williamson, Davis, & Duchmann, 1992). Generally, a primary goal of behavior therapy is weight gain via increasing nutritional intake and decreasing caloric expenditure via extreme weight loss behaviors (e.g., self-induced vomiting, laxative abuse, or extreme exercise). Behavior is modified through meal planning and behavioral contracting. Reinforcement of behavior change is accomplished using a "levels system," whereby access to privileges is made contingent on compliance with the treatment program. Also, staff use social reinforcement to increase healthy eating behavior and to extinguish unhealthy habits. Fear of weight gain causes the anorexic patient to become anxious during and after eating (Williamson, Goreczny, Davis, Ruggiero, & McKenzie, 1988). One technique developed for the purpose of reducing this anxiety is exposure with response prevention (Rosen & Leitenberg, 1982). Using this approach, each meal or snack has therapeutic value because the patient is exposed to the feared stimulus. The patient is not allowed to purge or exercise after eating, in order to prevent extreme weight control behavior, which has previously been reinforced by anxiety reduction (W. G. Johnson, Jarrell, Chupurdia, & Williamson, 1994). Through the process of extinction, anxiety is reduced over the course of treatment. If patients are unable to control the occurrence of extreme weight loss behaviors, this behavior will be strengthened via negative reinforcement (anxiety reduction) and improvement will be unlikely. In such cases, inpatient or partial day hospitalization are generally necessary, in order to modify such behaviors and to reduce anxiety regarding weight gain.

Cognitive Therapy

Recent research has found that cognitive processing of information related to food and body weight/size in patients with eating disorders is biased (Williamson, 1996). This research has shown that patients with eating disorders selectively attend to stimuli associated with fattening foods and to cues of body fatness. Also, they more readily recall this same type of information. Finally, when making judgments about their own body size, or eating behavior, they are more likely to conclude that they are fat or have overeaten (Jackman, Williamson, Netemeyer, & Anderson, 1995; Williamson, 1996). Cognitive therapy is used to directly modify biased information processing. The procedures used for this purpose generally follow those described by Beck, Rush, Shaw, and Emery (1979) for depression. Such procedures have been modified for use with eating disorders (e.g., Fairburn, Marcus, & Wilson, 1993).

The basic cognitive therapy strategy involves education of the patient as to presence of cognitive bias and self-monitoring of automatic thoughts related to biased cognition. Gradually, over the course of therapy, the patient learns to recognize distorted thinking and to replace it with more realistic thoughts and interpretations. In this program, body image disturbances are considered to be a manifestation of cognitive bias, and therapy for body image disturbances generally follows a cognitive model.

Dietary Interventions

A primary goal of dietary therapy is remediation of low body weight associated with anorexia nervosa. However, in addition to possible medical and physical complications associated with very low body weight, starvation and malnutrition can contribute to deficiencies in a patient's mental status and mood (Keys, Brozek, Henschel, Mickelsen, & Taylor, 1950). As noted earlier, other therapies (e.g., pharmacotherapy, cognitive, or behavioral therapies) are frequently unproductive until dietary intervention can result in improved nutritional status. Thus, a second priority of dietary therapy is to improve the anorexic patients' mental and nutritional status so that they may more fully benefit from psychotherapeutic and pharmacologic interventions.

Initially, dietary therapy may involve the consumption of small amounts of food several times per day, increasing food intake daily if tolerated by the patient. If the patient is unable to eat even small amounts of food, nasogastric tube feeding or total parenteral hyperalimentation may be required during the first 1 to 3 days.

In order to establish a consistent pattern of weight increase, between 3,000 and 3,600 kcal per day must be consumed. This level of caloric intake will usually lead to an average weight gain of 1 to 3 lbs per week. It is best to gradually increase the caloric intake over a period of several days to a week. We generally start patients at 1,200 to 1,500 kcal per day and increase by a few hundred calories per day until the target weight gain meal plan can be achieved. This treatment plan allows patients to gradually adapt to the increasing feelings of fullness, and it reduces the risk of edema and other potential medical complications associated with rapid refeeding. One aspect of the syndrome of anorexia nervosa is significant fear associated with eating "fattening" foods. Therefore, a graduated increase in meal plan allows for a graduated exposure to fearful foods and is usually much better tolerated by the patient.

ASSESSMENT METHODS

Psychological

The standard assessment battery is designed to evaluate the symptoms of three clinical syndromes: eating disorders, personality disorders, and affective disorders. Personality disorders (Wonderlich & Mitchell, 1992) and mood disorders (Edelstein & Yager, 1992) have been found in common comorbid diagnoses with the eating disorders. Additional assessment for other problem areas may also be conducted if indicated by information obtained from the clinical interview. The assessment instruments routinely used are described next.

The Interview for the Diagnosis of Eating Disorders–Fourth Revision (IDED–IV) is a structured interview designed to gather information related to eating disorders in a systematic fashion (Williamson, Anderson, & Gleaves, 1996). The questions of the IDED–IV are based on the *DSM–IV* criteria for anorexia nervosa, bulimia nervosa, and binge eating disorder. The IDED–IV has been found to be a reliable and valid method for diagnosing the eating disorders. Self-report inventories that are used to assess eating disorder symptoms are the Eating Attitudes Test (EAT; Garner & Garfinkel, 1979), the Bulimia Test–Revised (BULIT–R; Thelen, Farmer, Wonderlich, & Smith, 1991), and Eating Disorder Inventory–2 (EDI–2; Garner, 1991). Body image disturbances are measured using the Body Image Assessment (BIA; Williamson, Davis, Bennett, Goreczny, & Gleaves, 1989). This is a standardized procedure whereby the therapist can assess the patient's perception of current and ideal body size. The difference between the two measures has been validated as a measure of body size dissatisfaction (Williamson, Gleaves, Watkins, & Schlundt, 1993). The assessment of personality characteristics are assessed using the Structured Clinical Interview for *DSM–III–R* Personality Disorders (SCID–II; Spitzer, Williams, Gibbon, & First, 1990). The Beck Depression Inventory (BDI; Beck, Ward, Mendelson, Mock, & Erbaugh, 1961) is employed in the assessment of mood. Information from the self-report measures is combined with clinical interview information to establish specific diagnoses, to develop an individualized treatment plan, and to assign an appropriate level of care.

Medical Evaluation

It is clearly established that treatment intervention must be first aimed at correction of physiologic and biologic abnormalities related to poor nutrition or malnutrition (*Practice Guidelines for Eating Disorders*, American Psychiatric Association, 1994). Until these physiologic abnormalities are corrected, the patient is at risk for multiple organ system complications that could be life threatening (e.g., cardiovascular collapse, cardiac arrhythmia, renal or hepatic compromise). Therefore, a thorough medical history, review of systems, and a physical exam is obtained with special attention to the endocrine, cardiovascular, and gastrointestinal systems. Weight, height, sexual development, and general physical development are assessed (Kaplan & Garfinkel, 1993). A baseline evaluation is necessary prior to refeeding. Once refeeding is begun, the patient is checked routinely for edema, fluid overload (i.e., congestive heart failure), and adequate gastric motility and bowel function. Patients are informed that they may experience numerous transitory physical changes that will abate with stabilization.

Routine laboratory studies include electrocardiogram, complete blood count, urinalysis, chemistry panel with renal and hepatic function and electrolytes, and thyroid function tests. Further lab studies are determined on an individual basis depending on the patient's condition and as necessary for making treatment decisions.

Assessment of Magnesium, B12, dental erosion, and bone mineral density (to assess risk for pathologic fractures related to osteoporosis in patients who have been amenorrheic for greater than 6 months) are all considered, but not routine. Such laboratory data are often used as objective evidence that is shared with the patient to convey the severity of illness and its harmfulness.

A resting metabolic rate is used to assist in determining the patient's response to refeeding and to clarify nutritional needs if the response to refeeding is atypical.

It is important for the clinician to be aware of the medical effects of poor nutrition to avoid extensive/costly workups for the patient. For example, most undernourished anorexics will have an elevated cholesterol (due to lowered metabolism), which typically returns to normal with refeeding and improved nutritional status.

Results of the medical evaluation are utilized to further guide both the medical and psychological treatment processes.

Dietary Assessment

Nutritional assessment consists of a detailed nutritional history, current nutritional status, anthropometric assessment, estimated ideal body composition, and a hierarchical list of forbidden (i.e., feared) foods or food categories. It is important that the dietitian have prior clinical experience with eating disordered patients, because this population will frequently minimize eating problems and distort reasons for restrictive eating. The dietitian must be able to reliably rule out food allergies/intolerances or other legitimate conditions as possible causes for atypical patterns in dietary consumption, and this information should be incorporated into the dietary therapy. Prescribed dietary intake and goals for weight change are based in large part on the dietitian's estimate of the patient's ideal body composition and weight. The list of forbidden foods is obtained using the form shown in Fig. 12.2. Using this hierarchy of forbidden foods, the patient can be exposed to the fear of eating in a gradual manner. This approach may be described as graduated exposure with response prevention, which was described earlier in the section on behavioral therapy.

Forbidden Food Hierarchy Form

	Food Items	Completed	Date
LEAST FORBIDDEN			
MODESTLY FORBIDDEN			
MODERATELY FORBIDDEN			
VERY FORBIDDEN			

FIG. 12.2. Illustration of Forbidden Food Hierarchy Form.

Psychiatric Evaluation

Routine psychiatric evaluation is conducted by direct clinical interview with the patient and available family members. If the patient is a child or adolescent, parents are interviewed as well as the identified patient. If the patient is an adult, the individual is interviewed as well as other family members closely involved in the patient's life (i.e., spouse, parents, siblings).

The format of the psychiatric evaluation involves obtaining information regarding history of the present illness, past psychiatric history, medical history, family psychiatric history, developmental and social history, and Mental Status Exam.

This information is utilized in association with the psychological assessment tools described earlier to arrive at a multiaxial diagnosis and to devise a treatment plan.

Consensus exists that many psychological symptoms, behaviors, and personality characteristics may result from malnutrition. Awareness of this possibility, at times, results in provisional psychiatric diagnoses with reassessment as malnutrition is reversed.

BASIC TREATMENT PROCEDURES

A primary goal of the treatment program is to provide a high degree of structure and consistency for anorexic patients because they typically require a very structured environment in order to change their eating patterns. The following is a description of standard procedures that are employed in order to provide a consistent treatment program.

Level System

During treatment, it is expected that a patient will advance toward recovery. As the patient advances, it is also expected that the need for therapeutic structure and guidance will decrease until the patient can be safely discharged to outpatient status. In order to adjust therapeutic structure in a systematic manner, a level system has been developed that is described in Table 12.2. As patients improve and are able to meet the requirements of a higher level, they are allowed greater privileges and greater autonomy. In this way, it is possible to assess a patient's ongoing progress and reinforce healthy behaviors by allowing greater privileges.

Weight Monitoring

Anorexic patients have very distorted ideas about body size, shape, and weight. Therefore, discussion about current and ideal body weights should be limited to sessions with the patient's primary therapist. Patients are typically weighed each morning, before breakfast, after voiding, and in a hospital gown. They are usually weighed with their back to the scale (so that they cannot read the recorded weight) and are not told their exact weight status. Care is taken so that they do not peek at their weight or have it observed by other patients who may tell them what it is.

Establishment of Weight Goal and Meal Plan

Hospitalization is typically employed in order to aggressively approach the goal of weight gain in anorexia nervosa. However, the optimal goal for weight change is difficult to determine in a simplistic manner. Determination of a rate of weight change and corresponding dietary intake

TABLE 12.2

Level System

There are a number of behaviors, attitudes, and privileges that are felt to represent each level of recovery from an eating disorder. Following is an explanation of the Eating Disorders Level System, detailed descriptions of each level, and an example of an application for level advancement.

When entering the Eating Disorders Program, each patient will enter on Level I. In order to advance to a higher level, the patient must fill out an application for level advancement, which will then be reviewed by the treatment team. Feedback will be given to the patient regarding the level that has been approved and recommended steps for further recovery. If patients are noncompliant with the general expectations of their current level, a level drop will occur.

Privileges and Parameters of Each Level

Level I:

- The patient will receive an already-prepared meal served on a tray. The foods comprising each meal will be selected by the dietitian in accordance with the patient's nutritional and weight change needs. Input from Level I patients will be used by the dietitian only to deal with nutritional and/or medical complications.
- Patient rooms will be locked for 2 hours after meals, and for 30 minutes after snacks. If the patient needs to go to the bathroom during these times, a staff member must be present to monitor them.
- The patient must eat every meal with a staff member present to monitor food consumption.

Level II:

- Patients will work with the dietitian in meal planning group, making food choices which meet the requirements of their individualized meal plan.
- Patients will go through the line in the cafeteria, asking for foods which are on their meal plan.
- Patients may choose to try therapeutic test meals eaten outside the hospital. These meals must be eaten in the presence of a responsible individual who is capable of monitoring and recording food consumption according to the policy and procedures of the Eating Disorders Program.

Level III:

- Patients may choose their own meals for the day (without a predetermined meal plan), with the goal of meeting their exchanges. Food consumption should continue to be accounted for in accordance with the Eating Disorders Program policy and procedures for monitoring and recording food consumption.

Level III:

- The patients' room will not be locked after meals as postmeal monitoring will not be required.

Expectations for Level Advancement.

From Level I to Level II:

- 100% compliance with meal plan for two consecutive days.
- Compliance with unit and Eating Disorders rules.
- Participation in groups on the unit and in the Eating Disorders program.
- No binge eating, purging, or restrictive eating.

From Level II to Level III:

- Compliance with Level I expectations.
- Planning fear foods on a predetermined basis (daily, 3x per week, etc.) specific to the patient's needs.
- A supportive and cooperative attitude.
- Has identified factors that exacerbate eating disorder symptomatology.

From Level III to Discharge:

- Compliance with Levels I and II expectations.
- Can choose their own meals, meeting their exchanges without problems.
- Is actively engaged in addressing factors that exacerbate eating disorders symptomatology.

pattern is best conducted within a multidisciplinary staffing. It is necessary to take into account factors, such as the degree of medical necessity, the patient's beginning height/weight ratio and body composition, weight history, anticipated length of stay, and the patient's fear of weight gain/tolerance of increases in food consumption. In general, weight gain goal is approximately 2 lbs per week, which usually requires daily caloric consumption of 3,000 kcal or more.

In order to educate and correct irrational/erroneous beliefs regarding food, patients participate in a nutritional education group 3 days per week with a registered dietitian. Preplanning of foods to be eaten is also conducted in this group. With assistance of the dietitian, patients select foods for upcoming meals, with the goal of meeting the dietary exchanges in the prescribed meal plan. These selected foods are recorded on meal planning forms, which are later used to record actual food consumed. The form used for planning and recording meals is shown in Fig. 12.3.

Anorexic patients have a great deal of fear as to weight gain, and discussions about food typically evoke significant anxiety. Therefore, it is crucial that the dietitian have good clinical skills and a good understanding about the role of graduated exposure and response prevention in the process of fear reduction. Depending on the advancement in the level system that the patient has achieved, increasing input into food selection and food handling is allowed. In order to minimize confusion and manipulation of the staff, any changes in the meal plan must be subject to approval by the dietitian.

Dietary Supplementation

The decision to use dietary supplementation is typically made in a multidisciplinary staffing. Dietary supplementation is considered when a patient's current weight level and/or nutritional status are deficient, and the patient is not compliant with the dietary regimen prescribed to

Meal Planning Form

Planned Meal	Changes	% Eaten	Calories	Comments	Initials
Breakfast:					
Snack:					
Lunch:					
Snack:					
Dinner:					
Snack:					

Comments:

Total Calories =

_____
Signature of Dietitian

FIG. 12.3. Illustration of Meal Planning Form.

correct these deficiencies. Supplementation is generally considered following three consecutive days of noncompliance with the prescribed dietary intake, but it may be recommended earlier in cases with medical crises. Patients are supplemented using a hospital-approved, high calorie (1.5 kcal/cc) enteral feeding product. Following each meal or snack, the patient's food consumption is estimated and recorded. The patient is then administered an appropriate amount of supplement in order to replace number of calories missed in the meal. The nutritional supplement regimen is typically continued until the patient demonstrates two consecutive days of 100% compliance with the meal plan, but it may be employed longer if deemed appropriate. If a patient refuses to drink the dietary supplement, nasal-gastric tube feeding is then recommended.

Food Administration

A structured and consistent method of administering food to anorexic patients is very important. Any degree of ambiguity in this procedure may produce increased anxiety in the patients and distrust of staff. It also increases chances for patients to manipulate the therapeutic program and confuse the treatment team. When patients first enter therapy, standard meal trays are ordered and administered without input from the patient. As patients advance toward recovery and graduate to Levels II and III (see Table 12.2), they are given greater responsibility and input into the meal planning and administration process.

Eating and Recording Food Consumption

Eating needs have been found to be a structured event both to increase the patient's sense of control over eating and to prevent behaviors such as the hiding of food that is not consumed. Therefore, patients eat every meal and snack in the company of a staff member. Eating disordered patients eat at a separate table from other patients in order to minimize distractions from eating. Patients are instructed to delay eating until all patients and staff are seated and the prescribed food selections have been verified by the staff member. Thirty minutes are allowed for mealtime and then a record is made of what has been eaten. If a time limit was not used, many patients would sit indefinitely and "pick" at the food on their plate. When the percentage of food eaten is being recorded, the patient is asked to lift all dishes off the tray, tilt drinking glasses/containers, and unfold napkins. If patients are observed eating something that has not been prescribed, they are questioned about the behavior and encouraged to follow the prescribed meal plan. When the dietary supplementation protocol is used, patients who do not consume 100% of their prescribed meal plan are supplemented with an appropriate amount of nourishment to replace that which was not consumed.

Postmeal Monitoring

Many anorexic patients engage in purgative behavior (Garfinkel, Moldofsky, & Garner, 1979; Halmi & Falk, 1982). Therefore, all patients are monitored following eating in order to discourage possible attempts at purging through self-induced vomiting. Patients are monitored by staff when using a bathroom for a period of 2 hours after a major meal and 30 minutes after a snack.

As the patient advances in the level system, the degree of postmeal monitoring is decreased. Patients report such lower level of monitoring to be very reinforcing, and it allows the staff to evaluate the patient's ability to manage anxiety about weight gain without using purgative measures.

Physical Activity Planning

Many anorexic patients have a history of excessive exercise for the purpose of weight control. Therefore, physical activity should be carefully monitored and prescribed. A prescribed activity level is determined via multidisciplinary staffing and is based on factors such as history of exercise abuse, current weight level, and current weight goal. Activity increases are not incorporated into the level system because low weight level and other possible medical factors can preclude increased activity despite the patient's full compliance with the treatment program.

Family Therapy

Family therapy in the treatment of anorexia nervosa is prescribed through an individualized treatment plan. Special consideration is given to the age of the patient, the patient's social/family situation, and so on, as well as the patient's mental and physical status.

Children and adolescents with eating disorders are engaged in family therapy from the start. Because the family is most often the patient's sole or primary social contact, and the eating disorder becomes a focal point for family interaction, therapy starts with support and education of the parents and moves toward exploration of family communication styles via sessions with parents and siblings. Special attention is given to existence of four characteristics of family interaction: overprotectiveness, rigidity, lack of conflict resolution, and involvement of the sick child in unresolved parental conflict (Minuchin, Rosman, & Baker, 1978).

The family therapy then focuses on changing the behavior of all family members, not only the patients, thereby assisting the patients in their struggle for autonomy, self-respect, and identity. Family therapy for anorexia is often difficult and time consuming. The initial phases of treatment (as refeeding proceeds) often require twice-per-week sessions of family therapy, with gradual tapering in accordance with clinical improvement. It is often beneficial to have two therapists in the family sessions because of the demands involved in such work. It is important to attend to what occurs between people—the process of interaction, while following the impact of changes in family interactions on individual family members.

Family therapy for adult patients is often considered secondary as the individual therapy progresses. Couple's therapy is often used with married patients.

GROUP THERAPY PROTOCOLS

Body Image Group

Most anorexic patients experience significant problems with body dissatisfaction and body size overestimation. For this reason, a body image therapy group has been recommended, which is scheduled three times per week. Group content is modeled after the treatment programs described by Rosen and colleagues (Rosen, Cado, Silberg, Srebnik, & Wendt, 1990; Rosen, Reiter, & Orosan, 1995; Rosen, Saltzberg, & Srebnik, 1989) and Cash (Butters & Cash, 1987; Cash, 1991). There are four components in this treatment protocol:

Introduction. A general explanation of the sociocultural, biological, and psychological factors that contribute to weight and body image disturbance is presented, and patients identify the factors that have led to the development and maintenance of their negative body image.

Exercises that are helpful to accomplish this goal include having patients draw "life maps" of significant events that have led to body image and eating disturbance, and constructing collages of pictures from women's magazines that depict current sociocultural pressure for extreme thinness. Patients also identify any avoidance behaviors (e.g., wearing only very loose, baggy clothing) or "body checking behaviors" (e.g., pinching body fat, feeling ribs, etc.), which function to maintain disturbances of body image.

Exposure to Distressing Aspects of Appearance. Patients construct a hierarchy of disliked features of their bodies; exposure to these features can be accomplished imaginally, viewing themselves in a mirror, or by having the patient wear form-fitting clothes. Exposure is typically paired with relaxation. It is important that patients not to be allowed to engage in any body checking behaviors during exposure (e.g., holding in one's stomach while looking in the mirror).

Cognitive Restructuring. Patients are introduced to the concept of cognitive distortions related to body image (Cash, 1991) and are instructed to keep a diary of negative thoughts related to their bodies. They are then taught to recognize maladaptive thoughts related to body image and to replace these thoughts with nonjudgmental and positive statements regarding body size and appearance. For example, the thought "My stomach is sticking out a mile" might be replaced with "My stomach is full because I just ate an hour ago; it will feel smaller after the food is fully digested."

Relapse Prevention. Patients are taught to identify and practice adaptive responses to high-risk situations related to disturbances of body image. For example, patients often respond negatively when family members comment that they are looking "healthier." This is a remark that is often misinterpreted by anorexics as really meaning that they look fat.

Meal Planning/Nutritional Education Group

All inpatients, regardless of their status in the level system, participate in a nutritional education group led by the dietitian. This group is an important part of the patient's therapy because most anorexic patients have inaccurate ideas about healthful eating. For example, the patient may believe that humans do not need to consume any fat in their diets in order to be healthy. When patients reach Level II, they begin to plan their own meals in meal planning group using the American Diabetes Association/American Dietetic Association's dietary exchange system (American Dietetic Association/American Diabetes Association, 1989). Patients receive from the dietitian an individualized plan describing how many exchanges of each type they should eat per day; patients then choose foods from the hospital cafeteria menu based on their exchange plan, and write the choices on a meal planning record. As noted earlier, patients are encouraged to incorporate "forbidden" or feared foods into their diet in a hierarchical fashion (from least feared to most feared). Meal planning occurs well before the actual meal is eaten until the patient reaches Level III, when food choices then are made in the cafeteria at the time of each meal and recorded after the food is eaten. The form that we use for planning and recording food consumption at meals is shown in Fig. 12.3.

Meal planning group can sometimes be a trying experience for both the patient and the dietitian. Many patients do not want to increase either the types or amounts of foods eaten and will try to "bargain" with the dietitian to avoid eating certain types of food. The dietitian leading a meal planning group must have a combination of patience, firm resolve, and clinical skill.

Family Group

Patients and their families should be engaged in the treatment process from the very beginning. The family should be educated about the patients' condition as well as the medical and psychological consequences of semistarvation. Family therapy has been shown to be particularly useful for anorexic patients with early adolescent onset of the disorder (Russell, Szmukler, Dare, & Eisler, 1987). The family group in the program is a blend of a therapeutic support group (where families can express their concerns and frustrations related to having an anorexic family member) and a didactic group (where information related to eating disorders is presented). The weekly group, led by a member of the eating disorder treatment team or an invited guest (e.g., a recovering anorexic patient), runs in 12-week cycles; patients and their family agree to attend the group for 12 weeks. Patients and their families in all levels of care (i.e., inpatient, partial day hospital, and outpatient) participate in this evening group. The didactic topics presented in family group are listed in Table 12.3.

Adolescent Group

A group therapy specifically for adolescents with anorexia nervosa is generally prescribed in the outpatient program. Adolescents who are inpatients attend groups on the Adolescent Unit with the general inpatient population. This outpatient group was developed with two primary goals. One is to offer a supportive peer environment; all patients in the group have been treated for anorexia or bulimia nervosa. The second and primary goal of the group is to assist patients in moving beyond their superficial social competence and to assist them in experiencing comfort with expression of their own emotions, while also assisting others in a similar way. The group is presented as a general process group psychotherapy. Because the focus is not on the eating disorder itself, and the group process requires fairly stable cognitive and emotional functioning, the following criteria are necessary to enter the group:

TABLE 12.3

Family Group Didactic Presentations

Week	Presentation
1	Definitions/theoretical models of anorexia nervosa/bulimia nervosa
2	Psychological characteristics of eating disordered patients
3	Process of recovery from eating disorders/enabling behaviors
4	Open/general meeting
5	Medical aspects and consequences of eating disorders
6	Questions commonly asked by family members/friends of eating disordered patients
7	Current research in eating disorders
8	Family dynamics in eating disorders
9	Recovering eating disorder patient speaks to group
10	Cognitive therapy of eating disorders
11	Nutritional information
12	Assertiveness/effective communication

1. The patient's health is sufficiently good to be maintained on an outpatient status.
2. The patient has shown some capacity or motivation for psychological mindedness, including the ability to reveal feelings and sensitivity to others (Sargent, Liebman, & Silver, 1985).

The group functions best with four to six members. Potential members meet with group leaders individually prior to entering the group to discuss responsibilities of regular attendance. Patients also are informed of the requirement of twice monthly weights and completion of monitoring forms that require honesty in reference to eating behaviors.

New group members are brought in only when there is a space available (i.e., if someone drops out or leaves the group). Members are encouraged to inform the group of their reasons for leaving if they decide to do so.

Twice per year, parents are invited to the group for their own education about the group process. The nutritionist also attends that group to discuss any questions, as most of the patients also receive periodic nutritional counseling.

This group format is a challenging process. The two therapists of the group have generally worked with patients during inpatient treatment, which allows for provision of continuity of care. The formation of group cohesiveness and group dynamics is a slow process with anorexic patients. The most productive and successful work has been done when the group has been closed (no new members) for 4 to 6 months. When new members are brought into the group, existing members are encouraged to openly express their thoughts and feelings about the changes in group membership.

Cotherapy, or use of two therapists, is the chosen method because of the energy required for this work, and to avoid setbacks if one of the therapists is absent. It is important that the therapists be comfortable with each other's style and that mutual support and encouragement be maintained in the therapists' relationship.

Adult Behavior Management Group

This weekly group for adults focuses on helping the patient to identify and change cognitive, behavioral, and emotional factors that have led to development and maintenance of their eating disorder. Adults in the inpatient, partial day hospital, and outpatient programs participate in this evening group. Goal setting through use of behavioral contracts and instruction in problem-solving techniques form the basis of this group. Patients are also taught skills in cognitive restructuring of maladaptive thoughts related to eating disorders. Each week, group members complete a behavioral contract containing goals they agree to carryout during the next week. A typical goal might be "Purge only twice this week instead of four times" or "Follow my meal plan for 5 of 7 days." Patients are encouraged to make small, concrete steps toward larger goals, because lofty goals that are not met may be overwhelming and can result in discouraging emotional reactions. For example, a goal to "Improve self-esteem" is poorly defined and would be difficult to accomplish within 1 week. Patients are instructed to reward themselves (with nonfood rewards) when goals are met. Each week, patients share their successes or failures with other group members, who offer positive and negative feedback along with suggestions about how to accomplish new goals. The behavior management group can be used as a forum for adult patients to share their fears about eating and struggles with recovery with other patients. Doing so fosters a supportive alliance between the group members that is quite therapeutic.

DEVELOPMENT OF A THERAPEUTIC ALLIANCE

A significant impediment to the treatment of anorexia nervosa is denial and resistance to treatment. Without some degree of therapeutic alliance, treatment will quickly develop into a struggle for control between the treatment team and the patient. The determined patient will often win this struggle, if not during hospitalization, then shortly afterward. Therefore, it is important that early treatment efforts be aimed at developing rapport and a therapeutic alliance with the patients and their family.

Several factors are emphasized in the development of therapeutic alliance. First, it is important to impress on the patient that the goals of treatment will extend beyond simple ones such as refeeding and weight gain. Second, the patients and family must be educated about the severity of the medical and psychological symptoms of anorexia nervosa. This form of education should not be presented as a "scare tactic," but instead should describe the legitimate risks of maintaining anorexia nervosa. A third factor is the presentation of realistic expectations for treatment. Having unrealistic expectations of the patient eating in a "normal" manner by the end of hospitalization frequently leads to frustration on everyone's part and distrust of therapy. Finally, the treatment approach and expectations of the patient while in the program should be reviewed. Again, it should be emphasized that refeeding and weight gain will not be the sole treatment goals. However, effects of starvation and malnutrition must be reversed before meaningful therapy can begin. We provide the patient and family an outline of the standard treatment techniques used in the program and review it with them. Afterward, the patient is asked to sign a pretreatment contract (shown in Fig. 12.4) stating an understanding of treatment approaches and expectations, and a willingness to participate in the treatment program. Absolute refusal to sign such a contract is an indication that alliance has not been established and that further work on this problem is necessary.

MAINTENANCE AND GENERALIZATION STRATEGIES

Outpatient treatment lasting 6 to 12 months following discharge from an inpatient or partial day hospital program is very important if improvement is to be maintained and generalized to the natural environment. Also, it is essential for family members to be supportive of the recovery process. It is generally advisable to assign one staff member to function as the case manager for each patient. This person has the responsibility of coordinating all aspects of outpatient care, ranging from group to individual or family therapy. This case management approach can be very useful for preventing premature discontinuation of therapy and relapse.

PROBLEMS IN IMPLEMENTATION

The course of treatment for anorexia nervosa is rarely smooth. Most patients enter treatment with some ambivalence and distrust; at worst, some medically compromised patients are admitted entirely against their will by parents or spouses. Many patients do not refuse treatment outright but seem to sabotage it at every turn (e.g., by refusing to eat). Treatment team members must identify whether noncompliance with treatment recommendations is attributable to resistance, or to the anorexic's extreme fear of weight gain and of losing control. It is often helpful to assist the patients in framing their own attributions about noncompliance in this way as well.

Pretreatment Contract

    I have had a chance to become acquainted with the Eating Disorders Program and have read the Eating Disorders Program Standard Treatment Protocols. I wish to be admitted for treatment. I recognize this program may or may not help me. I am willing to eat all foods as prescribed by the staff (except for three specific foods that I can name), and to accept the goal weight range set by the staff. I will stay as long as necessary as recommended by my treating physician.

    My family agrees to attend family therapy as recommended by the staff. I will not use laxatives, diuretics (water pills), or any other medications unless they have been prescribed for me by your staff. I will be responsible for all expenses associated with my treatment.

Patient Name _____

Parent or Guardian _____
(if patient is a minor)

Telephone Number _____ (Home) _____ (Work)

Address _____

Family Doctor, Internist,
Pediatrician, or Psychiatrist _____

Telephone Number _____

FIG. 12.4. Illustration of Pretreatment Contract.

As noted earlier, the treatment team should form a therapeutic alliance with the patient and the family early in the process. It is helpful to provide patients with clear information about what they should expect in treatment and what expectations of them will be. Families of anorexic patients often present in one of two ways: those who are overly involved with the patient, and those who have become so frustrated with the patient they have become emotionally detached and do not want to participate fully in treatment. Both types of families need to be educated about eating disorders and respond best to clear, consistent messages about how to interact with their family member.

The primary therapeutic goals early in treatment should be refeeding and improved motivation to eat, instead of attempting to effect more substantive psychological changes. Such attempts are likely to lead only to feelings of failure for both the patient and the staff. It is important for staff and family to view recovery from anorexia nervosa as a long, perhaps lifelong process. Staff members (e.g., psychiatric nurses) who do not have extensive experience with eating disorders can become frustrated and overwhelmed by these patients. Personality disorders are common in anorexic patients (Skodol, Oldham, Hyler, Kellman, Doidge, & Davies, 1993) and are associated with negative treatment outcome (C. Johnson, Tobin, & Dennis, 1990). Staff-splitting and other attempts to manipulate the staff are also common and lead to feelings of anger for all concerned. Regular communication and education of the staff about special problems associated with caring for eating disordered patients is essential.

CASE ILLUSTRATION

Melissa B. was a 15-year-old White female who was brought to the program to be evaluated for an eating disorder. On the day of evaluation, she was 67 inches tall and weighed 107 lbs. Anthropometric evaluation determined that she had a medium body frame, and percent body fat was estimated to be 10.5%. Melissa's parents described her as being slightly overweight as a baby. She remained slightly overweight during her childhood and early adolescence. During the summer before she started high school she reportedly weighed about 155 lbs. At this time, Melissa initiated a diet consisting of limiting her fat intake to fewer than 20 grams per day. Her mother, who was concerned about her own weight as well as that of her daughter, initially praised Melissa's weight loss efforts. However, she became concerned when Melissa began to lose weight very rapidly. Upon questioning, Melissa admitted that she was eating only one small, fat-free meal per day, that she had recently begun to experience dizzy spells at school, and that she had been using laxatives at the rate of 15 per day for the past 2 months. She had begun to menstruate at age 14, but had not had a period in nearly 4 months. Melissa was adamant that she would not gain any weight, stating that she would like to weigh below 100 lbs, 7 lbs below her weight at admission.

Melissa was the youngest of three daughters in her family. She was described by her parents as perfectionistic and resistant to change; for example, she had become very upset when her eldest sister had recently moved out of the state. Melissa's parents described their marriage as "rocky." Her father, an attorney, was away from home much of the time. Melissa reported that she believed her mother did not want her to mature.

Melissa's scores on objective questionnaires indicated significant symptoms associated with an eating disorder. In addition, she endorsed symptoms of depression, including anhedonia, lack of motivation, increased social isolation, and difficulty concentrating. She reported sleeping only about 4 hours per night.

Melissa's weight was calculated to be 21% below average for her age and height. She was amenorrheic, did not appear to be concerned about her current low weight, and had intense fears of gaining weight; therefore, she met diagnostic criteria for anorexia nervosa (American Psychiatric Association, 1994). She also was diagnosed as having a major depressive episode; however, many of her depressive symptoms may have been attributable to her state of malnutrition. Because of the severity of her symptoms and reluctance to begin eating more normally, inpatient hospitalization was recommended. On admission, Melissa was placed on a regimen of total bed rest; she could "earn" time out of bed by eating her meals. Although she was initially resistant, she began to eat small portions of food by the second day of hospitalization. In one week's time, she was consistently eating 100% of the prescribed meal plan. She then began to plan her own meals and to participate in meal planning groups. Feared foods were incorporated into her diet in a hierarchical fashion. Melissa participated in body image groups during her inpatient stay, as well as adolescent psychotherapy groups and individual therapy. Her family participated with her in eating disorder family group and in individual family therapy sessions. Melissa's mood improved significantly by the end of the second week of hospitalization. However, she complained of becoming increasingly preoccupied with thoughts of her body size and shape. At the end of 2 weeks of hospitalization, Melissa had reached to 112 lbs and was discharged into the partial day hospital program. Group, individual, and family therapy were continued. She participated in this program for an additional 2 weeks, during which time she reached 115 lbs. She was then discharged to outpatient therapy with the following treatment plan: outpatient individual therapy once per week, outpatient adolescent eating disorder group and family group once per week, and outpatient sessions with a registered dietitian twice per month. Twelve months later she was discharged from outpatient therapy with a weight of 121 lbs. She was much less concerned about body size/shape and was no longer depressed.

CONCLUSIONS

This treatment manual presents a comprehensive program for persons of all ages who are diagnosed with anorexia nervosa. Generally, the course of treatment can be characterized by successes, followed by partial or full relapse, followed by further improvement. Persons who benefit most from treatment are those who remain over a 1- to 2-year period. Patients and their families must form a strong therapeutic alliance with the treatment staff if they are to survive the vicinitudes of a lengthy and difficult period of therapy.

REFERENCES

Agras, W. S. (1987). *Eating disorders: Management of obesity, bulimia, and anorexia nervosa.* New York: Pergamon.

American Dietetic Association/American Diabetes Association (1989). *Exchange lists for weight management.* Chicago: Author.

American Psychiatric Association. (1994). *Practice guideline for eating disorders.* Washington, DC: Author.

American Psychiatric Association. (1994). *Diagnostic and statistical manual of mental disorders* (4th ed.). Washington, DC: Author.

Beck, A. T., Rush, A. J., Shaw, B. F., & Emery, G. (1979). *Cognitive therapy of depression.* New York: Guilford.

Beck, A. T., Ward, C. H., Mendelson, M., Mock, J., & Erbaugh, J. (1961). An inventory for measuring depression. *Archives of General Psychiatry, 4,* 561–571.

Butters, J. W., & Cash, T. F. (1987). Cognitive-behavioral treatment of women's body-image dissatisfaction. *Journal of Consulting and Clinical Psychology, 55,* 889–897.

Cash, T. F. (1991). *Body image therapy: A program for self-directed change.* New York: Guilford.

Edelstein, C. K., & Yager, J. (1992). Eating disorders and affective disorders. In J. Yager, H. E. Gwirtsman, & C. K. Edelstein (Eds.), *Special problems in managing eating disorders* (pp. 15–50). Washington, DC: American Psychiatric Press.

Fairburn, C. G., Marcus, M. D., & Wilson, G. T. (1993). Cognitive-behavioral therapy for binge eating and bulimia nervosa: A comprehensive treatment manual. In C. G. Fairburn & G. T. Wilson (Eds.), *Binge eating* (pp. 361–404). New York: Guilford.

Garfinkel, P. E., Moldofsky, H., & Garner, D. M. (1979). The heterogeneity of anorexia nervosa: Bulimia as a distinct subgroup. *Archives of General Psychiatry, 37,* 1036–1040.

Garner, D. M. (1991). *The Eating Disorder Inventory–2 manual.* Odessa, FL: Psychological Assessment Resources.

Garner, D. M., & Garfinkel, P. E. (1979). The Eating Attitudes Test: An index of the symptoms of anorexia nervosa. *Psychological Medicine, 9,* 273–279.

Halmi, K. A., & Falk, J. R. (1982). Anorexia nervosa: A study of outcome discriminators in exclusive dieters and bulimics. *Journal of the American Academy of Child Psychiatry, 21,* 369–375.

Jackman, L. P., Williamson, D. A., Netemeyer, R. G., & Anderson, D. A. (1995). Do weight preoccupied women misinterpret ambiguous stimuli related to body size? *Cognitive Therapy and Research, 19,* 341–355.

Johnson, C., Tobin, D. L., & Dennis, A. (1990). Differences in treatment outcome between borderline and nonborderline bulimics at 1-year follow-up. *International Journal of Eating Disorders, 9,* 617–627.

Johnson, W. G., Jarrell, M. P., Chupurdia, K. M., & Williamson, D. A. (1994). Repeated binge/purge cycles in bulimia nervosa: The role of glucose and insulin. *International Journal of Eating Disorders, 15,* 331–341.

Kaplan, A., & Garfinkel, P. (1993). Medical complications of anorexia nervosa and bulimia nervosa. In *Medical issues and the eating disorder: An interface* (pp. 26–64). New York: Brunner/Mazel.

Keys, A., Brozek, J., Henschel, A., Mickelsen, O., & Taylor, H. L. (1950). *The biology of human starvation.* Minneapolis: University of Minnesota Press.

Minuchin, S., Rosman, B. L., & Baker, L. (1978). *Psychosomatic families: Anorexia nervosa in context.* Cambridge, MA: Harvard University Press.

Rosen, J. C., Cado, S., Silberg, S., Srebnik, D., & Wendt, S. (1990). Cognitive behavior therapy with and without size perception training for women with body image disturbance. *Behavior Therapy, 21,* 481–498.

Rosen, J. C., & Leitenberg, H. (1982). Bulimia nervosa: Treatment with exposure and response prevention. *Behavior Therapy, 13,* 117–124.

Rosen, J. C., Reiter, J., & Orosan, P. (1995). Cognitive behavioral body image therapy for body dysmorphic disorder. *Journal of Consulting and Clinical Psychology, 63,* 263–269.

Rosen, J. C., Saltzberg, E., & Srebnik, D. (1989). Cognitive behavior therapy for negative body image. *Behavior Therapy, 20,* 393–404.

Russell, G. F., Szmukler, G. I., Dare, C., & Eisler, I. (1987). An evaluation of family therapy in anorexia nervosa and bulimia nervosa. *Archives of General Psychiatry, 44,* 1047–1056.

Sargent, J., Liebman, R., & Silver, M. (1985). Family therapy for anorexia nervosa. In D. M. Garner & P. E. Garfinkel (Eds.), *Handbook of psychotherapy for anorexia nervosa and bulimia* (pp. 257–279). New York: Guilford.

Skodol, A. E., Oldham, J. M., Hyler, S. E., Kellman, H. D., Doidge, N., & Davies, M. (1993). Comorbidity of *DSM–III–R* eating disorders and personality disorders. *International Journal of Eating Disorders, 14,* 403–416.

Spitzer, R. L., Williams, J. W., Gibbon, M., & First, M. B. (1990). *Structured clinical interview for DSM–III–R–personality disorders (SCID–II, Version 1.0).* Washington, DC: American Psychiatric Press.

Thelen, M. H., Farmer, J., Wonderlich, S., & Smith, M. (1991). A revision of the Bulimia Test: The BULIT–R. *Psychological Assessment, 3,* 119–124.

Walsh, B. T., & Devlin, M. J. (1992). The pharmacologic treatment of eating disorders. *Psychiatric Clinics of North America, 15,* 149–161.

Williamson, D. A. (1996). Body image disturbances in eating disorders: A form of cognitive bias? *Eating Disorders: The Journal of Treatment and Prevention, 4,* 47–58.

Williamson, D. A., Anderson, D. A., & Gleaves, D. H. (1996). Anorexia and bulimia nervosa: Structured interview methodologies and psychological assessment. In K. Thompson (Ed.), *Body image, eating disorders and obesity: An integrative guide for assessment and treatment* (pp. 205–223). Washington, DC: American Psychological Association.

Williamson, D. A., Cubic, B. A., & Fuller, R. D. (1992). Eating disorders. In S. M. Turner, K. S. Calhoun, & H. E. Adams (Eds.), *Handbook of clinical behavior therapy* (2nd ed., pp. 355–371). New York: Wiley.

Williamson, D. A., Davis, C. J., Bennett, S. M., Goreczny, A. J., & Gleaves, D. H. (1989). Development of a simple procedure for assessing body image disturbances. *Behavioral Assessment, 11,* 433–446.

Williamson, D. A., Davis, C. J., & Duchmann, E. G. (1992). Anorexia and bulimia nervosa. In V. B. Van Hasselt & D. J. Kolko (Eds.), *Inpatient behavior therapy for children and adolescents* (pp. 341–364). New York: Plenum.

Williamson, D. A., Gleaves, D. H., & Savin, S. M. (1992). Empirical classification of eating disorder NOS: Support for *DSM–IV* changes. *Journal of Psychopathology and Behavioral Assessment, 14,* 201–216.

Williamson, D. A., Gleaves, D. H., Watkins, P. C., & Schlundt, D. G. (1993). Validation of a self-ideal body size discrepancy as a measure of body size dissatisfaction. *Journal of Psychopathology and Behavioral Assessment, 15*(1), 57–68.

Williamson, D. A., Goreczny, A. J., Davis, C. J., Ruggiero, L., & McKenzie, S. J. (1988). Psychophysiological analysis of the anxiety model of bulimia nervosa. *Behavior Therapy, 19,* 1–9.

Wonderlich, S. A., & Mitchell, J. E. (1992). Eating disorders and personality disorders. In J. Yager, H. E. Gwirtsman, & C. K. Edelstein (Eds.), *Special problems in managing eating disorders* (pp. 51–86). Washington, DC: American Psychiatric Press.

Chapter 13

Bulimia Nervosa

Theodore E. Weltzin
University of Wisconsin–Madison Medical School
Burt G. Bolton
Pacific University

DESCRIPTION OF BULIMIA NERVOSA

Bulimia nervosa (BN) belongs to a group of eating disorders that encompasses several subgroups of disorders. The boundaries between subgroups and the terminology used to differentiate these subgroups has been in flux. Nevertheless, considerable literature (Beaumont, George, & Smart, 1976; Casper, Eckert, Halmi, Goldberg, & Davis, 1980; Garfinkel, Moldofsky, & Garner, 1980; Garner, Garfinkel, & O'Shaughnessy, 1985; Halmi & Falk, 1982; Herzog & Copeland, 1985; Strober, Salkin, Burroughs, & Morrell, 1982) suggests that certain factors distinguish subgroups of eating disordered patients. These factors include the amount of weight lost, type of pathological eating behavior, certain psychopathological characteristics, and neurobiological abnormalities.

Bulimia nervosa (American Psychiatric Association, 1994) is at least 10 times more prevalent than anorexia nervosa (Halmi, Falk, & Schwartz, 1981; Pope, Hudson, & Yurgelun-Todd, 1984; Stangler & Printz, 1980). Bulimia nervosa, with the first scientific citation appearing in 1979, only recently has been recognized as a psychiatric problem (Russell, 1979). The lifetime prevalence of bulimia nervosa is approximately 4% in women (Kendler et al., 1991) and, although bulimia may be associated with anorexia or obesity, most women with bulimia nervosa maintain normal weight (Fairburn & Cooper, 1982; Halmi, Falk, & Schwartz, 1981). These patients periodically binge and purge, usually by vomiting, but never become emaciated. That is, they maintain a body weight above 85% of average body weight (Garner et al., 1985). Normal weight bulimics resemble bulimic anorexics in terms of impulsivity and a predisposition to obesity (Garner et al., 1985).

The primary symptom of bulimia nervosa is *binge eating*. Binge eating refers to the "rapid consumption of a large amount of food in a discrete period of time" associated with feeling that such eating is "out of control" (American Psychiatric Association, 1994, p. 545). Binge episodes typically are followed by purging behavior aimed at avoiding real or perceived weight gain after binge eating. Purging can take many forms, including self-induced vomiting, abuse of

435

laxatives and diuretics, and compulsive exercise (Mitchell, Hatsukami, Eckert, & Pyle, 1985). When not binge eating, bulimics frequently restrict intake (Weltzin, Hsu, Pollice, & Kaye, 1991). It has been hypothesized that restrictive eating between binge episodes may result in a malnourished state, even though bulimics remain at a normal body weight (Pirke, Pahl, Schweiger, & Warnhoff, 1985). Other associated symptoms of bulimia nervosa include preoccupation with body size and shape, food, eating, and an exaggerated fear of weight gain even when eating small amounts of food (Hudson, Pope, Jonas, & Yurgelun-Todd, 1983a).

The best-known eating disorder is anorexia nervosa, whose most distinguishing characteristic is severe emaciation. Two types of consummatory behavior are seen in anorexia nervosa. Restrictor, or fasting, anorexics (AN) lose weight by pure dieting. Bulimic anorexics (who qualify for a diagnosis of both anorexia nervosa and bulimia nervosa; AN–BN) also lose weight, but have a periodic disinhibition of restraint and engage in bingeing and purging. Compared with restrictors (AN), the bulimic subgroup (AN–BN) has been characterized as displaying significantly more evidence of premorbid behavioral instability, a higher incidence of premorbid and familial obesity, a greater susceptibility to depression, and a higher incidence of behaviors suggestive of impulse disorders (Beaumont et al., 1976; Casper et al., 1980; Garfinkel et al., 1980; Garner et al., 1985; Halmi & Falk, 1982; Herzog & Copeland, 1985; Strober et al., 1982).

In addition to pathological eating behavior, eating disordered patients report a distortion of body image or body size distress, in which the perceived "ideal body weight" is significantly lower than their actual body weight (Cash & Brown, 1987). A distorted perception of body image occurs in eating disordered patients irrespective of weight. Underweight, or anorexic, bulimic patients will continue to believe that they need to lose more weight even when they are severely underweight. Normal weight patients who binge and purge will frequently attempt to maintain body weight that is unrealistically low. In turn, these attempts at dieting and weight loss lead to states of malnutrition and hunger that increase the likelihood of binge eating. Overweight eating disordered patients also place a greater emphasis on dieting and weight loss than stopping overeating. Body dissatisfaction, a condition in which patients react negatively to their body, is another manifestation. Often, patients will have both body size distortion and body dissatisfaction.

Preoccupation with food and weight, relative to dieting and weight loss and binge eating of "forbidden foods," is prominent in eating disordered patients and suggests a similarity between such symptoms in patients with eating disorders and obsessive compulsive symptoms in Obsessive Compulsive Disorder (OCD). For many patients, compulsive rituals concerning eating, purging, dieting, and exercise are present most of the day. Obsessive thinking about eating, dieting, and exercising also can occur frequently throughout the day. Studies suggest that such symptoms are similar in severity to nonfood- and nonweight-related obsessions and compulsions in OCD (Bastiani, Roa, Weltzin, & Kaye, 1995).

Finally, physical symptoms related to malnutrition and binge eating and purging are present in eating disordered patients. Amenorrhea and other disturbances in menstrual function occur frequently in patients with bulimia (Weltzin, Cameron, Berga, & Kaye, 1994). Most underweight eating disordered patients have a loss of menstrual function, resulting from a combination of weight loss and disordered eating patterns. The condition is manifested as hypothalamic amenorrhea, with reduced pituitary secretion of luteinizing hormone and follicle stimulating hormone, and it appears to be a result of changes at, or above, the level of the hypothalamus. Underweight eating disordered patients have immature gonadotropin secretory patterns, which, in turn, lead to reduced levels of estrogen and progesterone and result in a loss of monthly menstrual bleeding. Such abnormality appears to primarily reflect nutritional disturbance as the majority of patients have a return of normal menstrual bleeding with weight gain.

As many as 50% of patients with bulimia nervosa who are normal weight also have either absent or irregular menstrual bleeding when actively engaging in bulimic behavior. The mechanism of menstrual disturbances appears to be similar to that in underweight eating disordered patients. Normal weight bulimics are more likely to have menstrual disturbances if they have lost a significant amount of weight (Weltzin et al., 1994). With normalization of eating patterns, most patients with bulimia have a return of normal menstrual bleeding.

Binge eating, purging, and malnutrition can lead to a number of medical problems that occur commonly in patients with bulimia (Mitchell, Scim, Colon, & Pomeroy, 1987). In addition to menstrual disturbances, patients with eating disorders have abnormalities of metabolic rate, cortisol secretion, and thyroid functions that normalize with weight gain and a return of normal eating patterns. By the loss of stomach contents, binge eating can lead to reduced serum potassium concentration, which is associated with an increased risk of cardiac arrest and reduced serum sodium concentrations and can increase the risk of seizures and kidney abnormalities. A variety of gastrointestinal symptoms can result from frequent vomiting and laxative abuse, including gastritis, gastric ulcers, esophageal reflux, constipation, diarrhea, and chronic abdominal pain. In general, medical complications correct with recovery from symptoms of the eating disorder in patients who do not develop chronic symptoms.

Bulimia and Comorbid Psychiatric Illness

Several studies have found a high incidence of concurrent depressed mood in patients with bulimia nervosa (Hatsukami, Eckert, Mitchell, & Pyle, 1984; Herzog, 1982; Hudson, Laffer, & Pope, 1982; Hudson et al., 1983b; Gwirtsman, Roy-Byrne, Yager, & Gerner, 1983; Pope, Hudson, Jonas, & Yurgelon-Todd, 1983). In addition, family studies reveal a high prevalence of affective disorders in the relatives of patients with bulimia nervosa. For example, Kassett and colleagues (1986) found that first degree relatives of bulimia nervosa probands had higher rates of major affective disorders than first degree relatives of control subjects. Such findings have led investigators to hypothesize that eating disorders are a variant of major affective disorders (Hudson et al., 1983).

The high incidence of depressive symptoms in bulimic patients has prompted trials of antidepressant medication. Placebo-controlled, double-blind trials of desipramine (A. G. Blouin et al., 1988; Hughes, Wells, Cunningham, & Ilstrupp, 1986), isocarboxazid (Kennedy, Piran, & Garfinkel, 1986), amitriptyline (Mitchell & Groat, 1984), imipramine (Pope et al., 1983), phenelzine (Walsh, Stewart, & Roose, 1984), and fluoxetine (Freeman, Morris, Cheshire, Casper, & Davis, 1988) show that these medications reduce binge eating and purging behavior and/or improve depressive symptoms. Two important points should be made. First, although these medications improve eating behavior, the majority of patients treated with antidepressants continue to exhibit bulimic behavior. Second, antidepressants are associated with improvement of bulimic symptoms in subjects that are not depressed. In summary, data from antidepressant treatment trials suggest some common biological mechanisms between bulimia nervosa and depression, but it cannot be concluded that bulimia nervosa is a subtype of depressive illness.

Recently, investigators have focused on the relation of other psychopathology to bulimia nervosa. Laessle, Wittchen, Fichter, and Pirke (1989) found that 70% of BN patients had a lifetime diagnosis of anxiety disorders, a figure that was greater than the lifetime prevalence (56%) of depression. Hudson, Pope, Jonas, Yurgelun-Todd, and Frankenburgh (1987) found that BN patients had a 43% lifetime prevalence of anxiety disorders in comparison to a 67% prevalence of depression. Studies of bulimia nervosa patients have shown a high incidence of alcohol abuse or dependency, with a range of between 16% and 49% (Beary, Lacey, & Merry, 1986; Bulik, 1987a; Hudson et al., 1983b; Hudson et al., 1987; Laessle et al., 1989). For example, Mitchell and colleagues (1985), in a study of 275 bulimic women, found that 23% acknowledged a history of alcohol abuse and that 18% reported a prior history of treatment for chemical dependency. A high prevalence (between 33% and 83%) of women with bulimia nervosa have at least one close relative with alcoholism (Bulik, 1987b; Herzog, 1982; Mitchell, Hatsukami, Pyle, & Eckert, 1988; Mitchell, & Eckert, 1981; Pyle, Leon, Carroll, Chernyk, & Finn, 1985; Strober et al., 1982). Family epidemiology studies also have found a higher incidence of substance abuse in relatives of patients with bulimia nervosa than in matched controls (Hudson et al., 1987; Kassett et al., 1989).

At best, it remains controversial as to whether eating disorders and major depression share a common diathesis. Critical examination of clinical phenomenology, family history, antidepressant response, biological correlates, course and outcome, and epidemiology yields limited support for this hypothesis (Rothenberg, 1988; Strober & Katz, 1988; Swift, Andrews, & Barklage, 1986). In fact, there is considerable evidence suggesting that eating disorders share some relation with other disorders. That is, anorexia nervosa may have some relationship to obsessive and compulsive behavior and bulimia nervosa may have share some commonality with anxiety disorders or alcoholism and substance abuse.

Epidemiology

Bulimia nervosa is more common than anorexia nervosa. Studies in the United States, England, and Japan report lifetime prevalence of bulimia nervosa in women to be as high as 19.6%; in men, the disease is more rare (Halmi et al., 1981; Pope et al., 1984; Pyle et al., 1983). In college populations, surveys place the prevalence of this disorder at 4% to 13% (Johnson & Larson, 1982) with a distribution of 87% females and 13% males (Halmi et al., 1981). As pointed out by Fairburn and Beslin (1990), much high prevalence may be due to overly inclusive criteria for identifying effected individuals. Using strict criteria, the prevalence is more likely to be closer to 1% in young adult and adolescent females.

Etiology

Although the cause of bulimia nervosa has not been specifically identified, several lines of research point to etiologic factors, such as societal pressures to achieve a slender body, stress in family interactions, and biological abnormalities. For many women, dieting appears to be almost universally a point of entry for development of an eating disorder. Dieting rates for adolescent women are above 50%. Many forces contribute to high rates of dieting in adolescent women. First, societal pressures that contribute to dieting include unrealistic images of females (Striegel-Moore, Silberstein, & Rodin, 1986). The ideal body weight of fashion models has remained unrealistically low, and, in fact, within an anorectic weight range (Garner, Garfinkel, Schwartz, & Thompson, 1980). Publications for women detail weight loss diets and exercise programs that link physical perfection with financial success and interpersonal happiness. Pressures associated with competition for women who participate in athletics and the arts, such as gymnastics and dance, also increase the risk of engaging in pathological eating behaviors. Fasting to maintain a weight that may enhance performance and presentation becomes more important than developing healthy nutritional habits (Smith, 1980). Family pressures to lose weight can also foster pathological eating in patients who develop eating disorders. This may occur particularly if there is a family history of obesity, a tendency for adult family members to diet, or if there are obesity-related health problems in family members, such as cardiovascular disease and diabetes.

Eating disordered patients often report that, during adolescence, dieting and weight loss frequently become ways of dealing with a variety of interpersonal stressors. During the adolescent years, peer interaction and "fitting in" present major developmental steps for all young men and women. Stress that occurs when these developmental steps are not accomplished, or when one's expectations are too high, tends to induce negative feelings of self-image and self-esteem. Through dieting and weight loss, the adolescent may gain a sense of stability, identity, and accomplishment, which may result in short-term well-being due to an unrealistic sense of control, without directly addressing the primary sources of stress in their lives (Hood, Moore, & Garner, 1982; Yates, Leehey, & Shisslak, 1983).

The reason for the increase in incidence of BN in the past decade is not certain. One possible explanation is based on the hypothesis that BN is related to substance abuse, particularly alcohol. BN may serve as a more socially acceptable means, in the current social and cultural climate, of certain women (that have a vulnerability to developing alcohol abuse or dependency) obtaining the same short-term gratification that is found in substance abuse (Bulik, 1987; Kaye et al., 1985).

Several points of evidence (Vandereycken, 1990) suggest a link between BN and substance abuse. Bulimic patients show an addictionlike behavior (craving, preoccupation with obtaining the substance, loss of control, adverse social and medical consequences, ambivalence toward treatment, risk of relapse; Bulik, 1987; Hatsukami et al., 1984; Mitchell et al., 1988), and they often tend to abuse alcohol or drugs. Several authors have noted that bingeing behavior produces a brief reduction in stress and tension that is similar to an intoxicationlike state (Abraham & Beaumont, 1982; Johnson & Larson, 1982; Kaye et al., 1986; Strober, 1984). A higher-than-expected prevalence of substance abuse is reported in relatives of bulimic patients when compared with controls. Studies in humans suggest that the pathophysiology of bulimia nervosa involves alterations of certain central nervous system neurotransmitter systems, such as opioid and monoamine systems (Jonas & Gold, 1986; Kaye, Ballenger et al., 1990; Kaye, Gwirtsman, et al., 1990), which have been implicated in addictive, affective, and anxiety disorders.

Therapeutic strategies for bulimia have been inspired by existing treatments for addictions, although little empirical evidence exists to support this concept. For example, some treatment options, such as the self-help group Overeaters Anonymous (based on the fundamental premises of Alcoholics Anonymous), have gained in popularity.

Neurochemistry and Bulimia

Several neurotransmitter systems that modulate feeding and behavior may contribute to the behavioral disturbances typical of eating disorders (Kaye & Weltzin, 1991). Studies have found reduced plasma and cerebral spinal fluid (CSF) norepinephrine (NE) concentrations (Kaye,

Ballenger et al., 1990) and increased platelet X–2 adrenoceptor activity in bulimia nervosa (Heufelder, Warnhoff, & Pirke, 1985). Other studies have shown that a number of other neuromodulators of feeding may be disturbed in bulimics, including cholecystokinin (Geracioti & Liddle,1988), opioids (Brewerton, Brandt, Lesem, Murphy, & Jimerson, 1990), and peptide YY (Kaye, Berrettini, Gwirtsman, & George, 1990).

Over the past decade, a growing body of data supports a link between reduced central nervous system (CNS) serotonin (5HT) activity and bulimia nervosa (Weltzin, Fernstrom, & Kaye, 1994). First, 5HT is one of several neurotransmitters that modulate appetitive behavior. In animals, reducing transmission across brain 5HT synapses by pharmacologic means stimulates food intake, whereas increasing 5HT activity leads to reduced food intake (Blundell, 1984; Fernstrom, 1992). Second, the majority of clinical studies in patients with eating disorders supports the finding that patients with bulimia nervosa have signs of reduced 5HT activity (Jimerson, Lesem, Hegg, & Brewerton, 1990). Also, antidepressant agents, which increase 5HT activity, have been shown to decrease binge frequency in women with bulimia nervosa (Fluoxetine Bulimia Nervosa Collaborative Study Group, 1992). Data suggest that the "antibulimic effect" of antidepressants may be the result of reduced appetite rather than mood elevation (Fairburn, Agras, & Wilson, 1992). Third, studies suggest that reducing 5HT activity in bulimia leads to reduced satiety, increased eating, and dysphoria in women with bulimia. Finally, animal studies suggest 5HT inhibits X–2 adrenoceptor activation of feeding (Leibowitz, 1988). Thus, binge eating in bulimia could be related to a failure of 5HT to inhibit the NE activation of feeding.

Evidence for Reduced 5HT in Bulimia Nervosa

5HT is synthesized from the essential amino acid L-tryptophan (TRP), which is obtained naturally in the diet. In the brain, TRP is converted to 5HT by the enzyme tryptophan hydroxylase (Green, Greenberg, Erickson, Sawyer, & Ellison, 1962). Rats fed a TRP-deficient diet had significantly lower brain 5HT concentrations compared to animals fed a normal diet (Gal & Drewes, 1962), whereas rats fed a TRP-supplemented diet had an increase in brain 5HT concentrations (J. J. Wurtman & R. J. Wurtman, 1979). Most data in animals suggest the agents that increase 5HT activity, whether injected peripherally (Shor-Posner, Grinker, Marinescu, Brown &, Leibowitz, 1986) or centrally (Lytle, Messing, Fisher, & Phebus, 1975), decrease food intake in rats.

A majority of studies support the hypothesis that reduced 5HT activity occurs in many patients with bulimia nervosa (Weltzin, Fernstrom, & Kaye, 1995). Reduced 5HT activity may then lead to episodes of binge eating through a reduction in satiety, an increase in dysphoria, or both. A disturbance of 5HT activity in bulimia nervosa could be the result of nutritional changes secondary to binge eating and chronic calorie restriction. A second possible explanation could be that a disturbance of 5HT activity in women with bulimia nervosa reflects a state-related risk factor present prior to the onset of bulimia. Finally, in addition to overeating, expression of several other psychiatric symptoms in bulimia nervosa, such as depression, substance abuse, and impulsive behaviors, may be related to a reduced 5HT state.

Of particular interest are recent studies in humans showing that acute tryptophan depletion (ATD), an experimental paradigm that presumably induces a transient state of reduced 5HT activity in humans, appears to be associated with behavioral responses consistent with changes in 5-HT activity. In rats, TRP-deficient diets reduced pain sensitivity (Gibbons, Barr, Bridger, & Leibowitz, 1979), increased mouse killing (Vergnes & Kempf, 1981; Walters, Davis, & Sheard, 1979), and accentuated the acoustic startle reflex (Chamberlain, Ervin, Pihl, &Young, 1987). In nonhuman male primates, ATD increased aggression during competition for food (Young, Smith, Pihl, & Ervin, 1985). In healthy human males, ATD increased dysphoria (Young, Tourjman, Teff, Pihl, & Anderson, 1988) and reduced protein intake (Barr et al., 1994). ATD increased dysphoria in psychiatric patients treated for depression who responded to serotonin specific antidepressants (Delgado et al., 1990; Weltzin, M. Fernstrom, J. Fernstrom, Neuberger, & Kaye, 1996).

To determine whether a disturbance of 5HT activity is relevant to the clinical pathology of bulimia nervosa, a study was planned to examined whether ATD affected "core" bulimic behavior (i.e., appetite and mood) in bulimia nervosa (Weltzin et al., 1996). The ATD treatment consists of an oral mixture of amino acids lacking TRP and including, among others, the LNAA that compete with TRP for brain uptake. ATD decreased plasma TRP by 65% to 76% over a 5-hour period. The study found that short-term food intake after ATD was increased in women with bulimia compared to controls: A majority of bulimics (6/10) had increased food intake whereas the majority of controls (8/10) ate less. In addition, bulimia nervosa women were significantly more irritable and mood labile during ATD compared to controls. Results of this study suggest that altering CNS 5HT activity produces different responses in normal and bulimia nervosa subjects.

Pharmacologic Data

Other indirect evidence that women with bulimia nervosa have reduced 5HT activity comes from studies showing an "antibulimic effect" of antidepressants in most bulimia nervosa patients (Agras, Dorian, Kirkley, Arnow, & Backman, 1987; Barlow, J. Blouin, A. Blouin, & Perez, 1988; Hughes et al., 1986; Mitchell & Groat, 1984; Pope et al., 1983; Walsh et al., 1988). It has been hypothesized that the antibulimic effect of antidepressants occur through a direct effect on the regulation of appetite (Fairburn et al., 1992). This hypothesis is supported by the observation that antidepressants decrease bingeing, but do not affect normal-size meals (Rossiter, Agras, & Losch, 1988), and reduce binge eating without significant improvement in mood (Pope, Keck, McElroy, & Hudson, 1988). Although prevalence of depression is high in bulimia nervosa, studies do not support the claim that the beneficial effects of antidepressants in bulimia nervosa are the result of treating an underlying depression. For example, the antibingeing effect of antidepressants in bulimia nervosa does not depend on the presence of a depressive disorder (Walsh, Steward, Roose, Gladis, & Glassman, 1984) or relate to the severity of depressive symptoms (Walsh, Hadigan, Devlin, Gladis, & Roose, 1991).

5HT and Binge Eating in Bulimia Nervosa

Reduced 5HT activity may contribute to binge eating in bulimia nervosa in several ways. Some data suggest that overeating in bulimia nervosa relates to alterations in satiety. It has been found that overeating in bulimia nervosa patients results from consumption of large meals, rather than eating more often (Weltzin, Hsu, et al., 1991). In animals, food consumption is affected in a similar way when 5HT activity is experimentally reduced (Leibowitz, 1990). To test whether reductions in 5HT mediated satiety may lead to binge eating in bulimia nervosa, studies examining the effects of fenfluramine (a 5HT agonist that inhibits 5HT reuptake, stimulates release of 5HT, and reduces satiety in animals; Leibowitz, 1990) on food intake in bulimia nervosa have been done. The results, however, are equivocal. Although fenfluramine decreased short-term eating in bulimia nervosa (Robinson, Checkley, & Russell, 1985) in one study and led to an improvement in bulimic behavior and mood (A. G. Blouin et al., 1988) in another, two other studies did not find these effects (Fahy, Eisler, & Russell, 1993; Russell, Checkley, Feldman, & Eisler, 1988). Moreover, d-fenfluramine did not appear to impart any additional benefit to bulimia nervosa subjects treated in psychotherapy (Fahy et al., 1993).

If episodes of binge eating are an attempt to "self-medicate" dysphoric moods, alterations in 5HT activity could conceivably contribute to overeating in bulimia. Patients with bulimia nervosa report more negative moods before a binge episode compared to a snack or meal (Davis, Freeman, & Garner, 1988). Some studies suggest that binge eating affects mood, particularly by reducing anxiety in bulimia nervosa (Elmore & de Castro, 1990; Kaye, Gwirtsman, George, Weiss, & Jimerson, 1986). Binge eating may elevate mood and increase satiety through increasing 5HT neurotransmission, as data suggest that TRP/iLNAA ratios change during bingeing (Kaye, Gwirtsman, Brewerton, George, & Wurtman, 1988).

Causes of Reduced 5HT in Bulimia Nervosa

The pathogenesis of reduced 5HT activity in bulimia nervosa is not clear. Perhaps 5HT neurotransmitter disturbances in ill bulimia nervosa patients are a consequence of extremes of dietary intake (Goodwin, Fairburn, & Cowen, 1987). Jimerson and colleagues (1990) proposed a model summarizing the possible relation between nutritional changes occurring before and during active bulimic behavior and altered brain 5HT activity in bulimia nervosa. In this model, prebulimic dieting results in acutely reduced synaptic 5-HT, leading initially to up-regulation of postsynaptic 5HT receptor activity. With development of bulimia, episodes of binge eating stimulate synaptic release of 5HT, with the increase in synaptic 5HT concentration leading to down-regulation of 5HT receptors. Over time, receptor down-regulation remains present between binge episodes when restricting intake is common.

Alternatively, reduced 5HT activity in bulimia nervosa patients may be a trait-related disturbance present in individuals at risk to develop bulimia nervosa. For example, women with bulimia nervosa and their family members have increased rates of depression (Walsh, Roose, Glassman, Gladis, & Sadik, 1985) and substance abuse (Vandereycken, 1990), two disorders linked to reduced 5HT activity. It is possible that this increased risk of developing disorders, with a common link to low 5HT activity, may reflect a persistent disturbance of the 5HT system that predisposes one to develop bulimia nervosa.

Clinical Relevance of Reduced 5-HT Activity in Bulimia

Reduced 5HT activity may also be related to the expression of other clinically relevant behaviors (i.e., mood lability, irritability, and impulsivity) in this disorder. There is evidence that decreased 5HT function is present during depression (Grahame-Smith, 1992; Price, Charney, Delgado, & Heninger, 1990), has a permissive effect on alcohol use in animals and humans (Gill, Fillion, & Amit, 1988; Gorelick, 1988; Sellers, Higgins, & Sobell, 1992), and contributes to anxiety (Charney, Wood, & Henninger, 1987). Furthermore, the most widely replicated set of findings in humans and animals (Coccaro, 1992) suggests a strong link between impulsive/aggressive behaviors and reduced 5HT activity (Broderick & Lynch, 1982; Coccaro, 1989; Copenhaver, Schalock, & Carver, 1978) regardless of psychiatric diagnosis (Brown et al., 1982; Linnoila et al., 1983; Ninan et al., 1984; Roy, Adinoff, & Linnoila, 1988). In bulimia, the relation between depression, substance abuse, and impulsive behaviors and a disturbance of 5HT activity is important because these disorders account for a significant amount of the morbidity associated with this illness.

Standardized clinical interviews (Walsh et al., 1985) have shown that rates of current and lifetime depression in bulimia nervosa are high (21% and 70%, respectively). However, as proposed by Strober and Katz (1988), the character of depressive symptoms in bulimia nervosa may be different than those typical of major depression. For example, fewer than half (40%) of depressive episodes in bulimia nervosa can be characterized as "endogenous depression," whereas a substantial number (35%) is characteristic of "atypical depression" (Cooper & Fairburn, 1986; Johnson & Larson, 1982; Weiss & Ebert, 1983).

Bulimia nervosa patients are often characterized as affectively unstable and impulsive (Hudson, Pope, Yurgelun–Todd, et al., 1987) and commonly have personality disorders that are characterized by mood lability and impulsivity. Rossiter, Agras, Telch, and Schneider (1993) recently reviewed 12 studies and found that they reported a 25% to 48% prevalence rate of borderline personality disorders in bulimia nervosa. Importantly, Rossiter et al. found that 28% of bulimia nervosa patients had a Cluster B personality disorder (histrionic, antisocial, borderline, and narcissistic characteristics). Furthermore, women with bulimia nervosa engage in other impulsive behaviors such as stealing and suicide attempts (Hatsukami, Eckert, Mitchell, & Pyle, 1984; Pyle et al., 1990).

Several lines of evidence suggest a link between bulimia nervosa and substance abuse. First, bulimia nervosa patients show addictionlike behavior (craving, preoccupation with obtaining the substance, loss of control, adverse social and medical consequences, ambivalence toward treatment, risk of relapse; Bulik, 1987a; Mitchell, Pyle, et al., 1988). Second, bingeing behavior produces a brief reduction in stress and tension that may be similar to an intoxication-like state (Kaye, Gwirtsman, George, Weiss, et al., 1986). Third, studies of bulimia nervosa women using contemporary diagnostic criteria, report the incidence of alcohol abuse in bulimia nervosa to be between 23% and 49% (Bulik, 1987; Laessle et al., 1989).

It is important to note that although 5HT activity may be abnormal in all of the disorders already reviewed, there is an overlap in terms of symptom expression within these groups and a high likelihood of the co-occurrence of more than one of these disorders (Reiger et al., 1990). Apter et al. (1990) suggested that the correlation between these symptoms in psychiatric patients may reflect an expression of a dysregulation of the 5HT system, because they found that measures of anxiety, depression, impulsivity, and aggressive dysregulation were all highly correlated.

In summary, a growing body of evidence suggests that a disturbance of 5HT activity may occur in some or all bulimia nervosa patients and may contribute to bulimia nervosa behaviors (i.e., abnormal feeding, mood lability, irritability, and impulsivity). It may be that 5HT neurotransmitter disturbances in ill bulimia nervosa are a consequence of extremes of dietary intake, such as those found in anorexia nervosa. Even if this is the case, bulimia nervosa patients may enter a vicious cycle where pathological feeding sustains and provokes pathological behavior. Few bulimia nervosa patients have any normal meals; they oscillate between restricted eating and bingeing. Such excursions in food intake and restriction could create a vicious cycle that maintains pathological eating. Alternatively, some or all bulimia nervosa patients may have a biological disturbance of 5HT, which contributes to the pathogenesis of this disorder.

METHODS OF ASSESSMENT AND DIAGNOSIS

Overview

The assessment of eating disorders involves a comprehensive evaluation that includes medical and psychological evaluations. The need to make sure that abnormal eating behavior does not lead to potentially life-threatening medical problems cannot be overemphasized. Disease specific mortality rates in anorexia range between 5% and 20% and bulimia nervosa is also associated with potentially life-threatening sequelae. Additional information on assessment is provided in Johnson, Stuckey, Lewis, and Schwartz (1982), who detailed a comprehensive approach to the psychological assessment of eating disorders. Mitchell (1984), Mitchell et al. (1987), and Hsu and Holder (1986) discussed medical complications and medical evaluations of bulimia and anorexia, respectively.

Assessment of Eating Disorder Symptoms

The initial evaluation should include a complete history of weight, eating behavior, psychological functioning, including perceptions of weight and shape, depression, and anxiety, a complete medical history and examination, and family and developmental history.

Body Weight. It is particularly important to document weight at the times of initiation of puberty and onset of abnormal eating behavior. For the adolescent, yearly weights, confirmed by pediatric records if possible, should be obtained. For the adult patient, weights at specific time points including puberty, graduation from high school, college, and coincident with marriage or childbirth should be investigated. Current weight and height and episodes of significant fluctuations in weight should also documented. In underweight bulimics, weighing should be supervised with patients wearing hospital gowns to avoid attempts at artificially increasing weight readings by concealing objects in cloths or taped to their bodies.

Dieting. Frequently, a history of dieting precedes or coincides with development of eating disorder symptoms. Attempts at weight loss by adolescents frequently involves attempts at severe reductions in food intake by skipping meals and eating low calorie foods such as salads and soups. It is not uncommon for a patient's total daily caloric intake to be well below 1,000 calories a day. Nor is it uncommon for patients to avoid eating breakfast or lunch and then have one meal at dinner. This meal pattern allows the patient to conceal severe dieting from family members. Patients often will become vegetarians to avoid the fat content of meats and attempt to not eat meals prepared by other family members. Such severely restricted diets often go unnoticed until a significant weight loss has occurred.

A record of when dieting first began and the regularity of dieting should be detailed, including psychosocial stressors that coincide with dieting behavior. A careful history of the frequency of meals should be recorded, including breakfast, lunch, dinner, and snacks. Types of foods at all meals should be specified, including portion sizes. Also, a list of forbidden foods that typically are percieved as causing weight gain should also be obtained. Frequency with which such foods are consumed and the feeling of guilt associated with eating these foods is often helpful in determining the degree of restrictive eating.

Finally, use of appetite suppressant medication, both over the counter and prescription, should be obtained. Such medication can be associated with increased blood pressure and other cardiovascular symptoms such as headaches, shortness of breath, and rarely, stroke.

Binge Eating.   A careful history of periods of overeating, or binge eating, is essential. This includes an estimate of the number of calories consumed during a binge. Although there is no clear threshold of caloric intake that defines a binge episode, bulimics may not differ from healthy controls by the number of meals they eat. Rather, bulimics tend to eat bigger meals in the afternoon and evening. Studies suggest that a binge episode is characterized by a discreet eating episode in which a large amount of food (usually greater than 1,000 calories) is rapidly eaten and that the types of food consumed are high in fat (i.e., dessert and snack-type foods; Weltzin, Hsu et al., 1991). Some patients will report that a binge may be a small amount of food. In fact, some patients report that they have had a binge when only eating a salad.

Purging.   Patients with an eating disorder engage in a variety of methods to lose weight and counteract the effect of binge eating. Self-induced vomiting is most commonly associated with binge eating in bulimia. Typically, patients self-induce vomiting by manual stimulation of their oral pharynx to stimulate the gag reflex. This can result in injury to their hands, and throat, including severe bleeding. Purging can be particularly dangerous if foreign objects, such as toothbrushes, are used to induce vomiting. Patients with chronic bulimia may be able to vomit spontaneously without manually stimulating the gag reflex.

Laxative abuse is used in as many as a third of patients with eating disorders. Patients typically use over-the-counter stimulant laxatives that contain phenolpthaline (e.g., Correctal or Ex-Lax). Laxative abuse usually begins by using the recommended dose of laxative. As the frequency of use increases, larger numbers of laxatives are needed to cause diarrhea. Laxative use can become severe with patients using as many as 30 to 60 laxatives at once. In severe cases, patients may become incontinent, resulting in social embarrassment and missed days at work and school. In addition, chronic laxative use can lead to bowel dysfunction and chronic constipation. Finally, it is important to document past attempts at stopping laxative use. Frequently stopping laxatives is associated with constipation, water retention with a weight gain of as many as 10 to 20 lbs. and increased anxiety and irritability (Weltzin, Bulik, McConoha, & Kaye, 1995). Although some patients may never have a return of normal bowel function, others can achieve a return of normal bowel function with bowel retraining procedures usually done in conjunction with a gastroenterologist.

Eating disordered patients use other methods of purging, including diuretic abuse, compulsive exercising, use of enemas, thyroid hormone abuse, and other attempts at burning calories or causing diarrhea. A careful history of any such attempts should be obtained.

Menstrual and Sexual History.   Because menstrual dysfunction occurs in 100% of patients with anorexia and approximately 50% of normal weight bulimics, it is important to determine periods of time during which amenorrhea or oligomenorrhea occur. This can serve to support reported periods of recovery or to confirm a more chronic course suggested by long-standing menstrual dysfunction. A menstrual history should include onset of the first episode of menstrual bleeding and the age and duration of regular menstrual bleeding. Loss of menstrual function or onset of irregular menstrual bleeding typically coincides with significant weight loss or an increase in the frequency of binge eating and purging. Attention should be paid to use of birth control medication or presence of other causes of menstrual dysfunction, such as polycystic ovaries. This can help to explain presence of regular menstrual bleeding even when patients are severely underweight or frequently binge eat and purge, as well as the lack of resumption of normal menstrual bleeding with recovery. If questions of other possible causes of menstrual dysfunction exist, a reproductive endocrinologist should be consulted.

Sexual abuse and sexual dysfunction are commonly reported in patients with eating disorders. It is important to include this information in a detailed history, as these issues are likely to impact on patient self-esteem. However, clinicians must use their judgment in the timing of obtaining a detailed sexual history. For some patients, this is best done after an initial period of treatment has occured and a positive therapeutic relationship has been established. It is important to note that when traumatic sexual experiences are not addressed in the course of treatment, they are likely to negatively impact treatment response.

Comorbid Psychiatric Syndromes and Mental Status Examination.   As mentioned earlier, several psychiatric illnesses occur frequently in patients with eating disorders, including depression, social phobia, obsessive compulsive disorder, panic disorder, alcohol and substance abuse, and personality disorders. Identifying past or present occurrence of such disorders is essential in formulating an effective treatment intervention. In addition, impulsive and destructive sexual behaviors are noted in a subgroup of eating disordered patients. This may be an indication of significant impulse control problems or alert the clinician to consider an additional diagnosis of bipolar affective disorder.

It should be determined if the patient meets additional diagnostic criteria, especially for depression, anxiety disorders, and substance abuse disorders, because these occur more frequently in eating disordered patients than the general population and can influence treatment decisions.

A complete mental status examination should be carried out to document any significant affective, anxiety, psychotic, suicidal, or impulse control problems. An adequate assessment of the patients' insight into their problems, judgment, and motivation for change should be conducted because this can influence subsequent treatment decisions.

Social and Developmental History.   A comprehensive assessment should gather information concerning learning disabilities, interpersonal difficulties, coping skills, and peer relationships. Questions should be asked concerning developmental difficulties that relate to self-image. Also, a history of childhood obesity and teasing by peers can often be associated with the onset of eating problems.

Previous Treatment.   The types and extent of previous treatments should be ascertained, including psychotherapeutic approach, family therapy, medication trials, and previous inpatient treatment. Any medical treatment for medical complications of eating disorders should be documented, including hypotension, bradycardia, dizziness or blackouts, electrolyte disturbances, or suicide attempts.

Family History.   Constructing a family genogram, including any significant physical or medical problems, is an essential component of a comprehensive assessment. Special attention should be given to parental opinions concerning weight, eating, and exercise. Also, it is not uncommon for a family crisis to coincide with the onset of an eating disorder or a worsening of symptoms. Use of the genogram has been demonstrated to be a helpful assessment tool, because it clarifies the family constellation of medical and psychiatric illnesses over several generations (McGoldrick, 1985).

Medical History and Physical Exam.   A full physical exam, including neurological assessment and laboratory testing, should be done with underweight anorexics and actively bulimic patients. Laboratory testing should include complete blood counts, serum electrolytes, serum amylase, liver and kidney functions tests, and an electrocardiogram. EEG, CAT, and MRI procedures should be reserved for those patients with suspected neurological illnesses.

TREATMENT AND TRAINING PROCEDURES

Overview

The primary focus of treatment for bulimia nervosa with or without anorexia or obesity should first be the correction of physiological sequelae of abnormal nutrition and the reversal of the psychological problems often associated with eating disorders. Generally speaking, treatment should involve a comprehensive treatment approach that involves nutritional therapy, psychotherapeutic treatment, typically cognitive-behavioral in focus, family interventions, and pharmacotherapy. The following sections present pertinent data supporting this contention.

Nutritional Therapy

In underweight patients with bulimia, weight recovery to at least 90% of average body weight for height should be initiated in addition to attempts at reducing binge eating and vomiting. Initially, calories should be started at 35 calories/kg and increased by 200 to 300 calories every 3 to 5 days to maintain a weight gain of between 1 and 3 lbs per week. This should usually be done in consultation with a registered dietitian, who can help to determine caloric intake, plan calorie increases, and work on incorporating a wide range of food choices into the meal plan. Once a target weight has been obtained, calories should be decreased to a level that will allow patients to maintain their weight (usually between 35 and 50 calories/kg)

For bulimia nervosa patients who do not become emaciated and maintain a body weight above 85% ABW (Fairburn & Cooper, 1982; Garner et al., 1985), nutritional therapy focuses on replacing abnormal or bulimic behaviors with normal eating behavior, which should include regularly scheduled meals without restricting any particular food groups. Dieting should be discouraged during the initial phases of recovery, as food restriction may intensify appetite and increase the likelihood of binge eating. Caloric requirements for weight maintenance (approximately 25 kcal/kg/day) in bulimia are lower than that for anorexia and noneating disordered females (Weltzin, Fernstrom, Hansen, McConaha, & Kaye, 1991).

Psychotherapy

At this point, state-of-the-art treatment of eating disorders involves cognitive-behavioral psychotherapy and interpersonal psychotherapy (Agras, 1991). Techniques of self-monitoring, identifying, and restructuring dysfunctional thinking patterns concerning weight, food, self-image, relationships, problem solving, stress reduction and management, time management, and assertiveness training are all areas that need to be addressed in typical bulimic patients.

Cognitive behavioral therapy (CBT) of bulimia is based on the model that binge eating and purging is the result of society's overemphasis on obtaining a thin figure through dietary restraint and weight loss. The behavioral aim of CBT is to restore normal dietary intake, which will lead to a reduction in binge eating and vomiting. Behavioral changes occur primarily during the initial phase of CBT and rely on a patient's ability to self-monitor food intake to characterize current eating patterns and determine severity of dietary restraint. Self-monitoring involves the patient keeping a daily record of food intake, including time of a meal, types and amounts of foods eaten and their amount, and whether food intake constitutes a meal, snack, or binge episode. The process of keeping a record of food intake presents a difficult task for many eating disordered patients, because they typically feel guilty about the food they have consumed, especially if they have binge eaten. Initially, the treatment focus is to keep an accurate food intake record rather than make attempts to modify food intake. In fact, many times the process of keeping a food record leads to modest improvements in eating, as it makes patients more aware of their behavior. Sessions, especially at the beginning of treatment, should involve reviewing the food records with patients to determine accuracy and overcoming obstacles that they may have with keeping track of their food intake.

The aim of CBT is to challenge distortions of body image and shape; unrealistic expectations about food, meals, and exercise; perfectionism; and self-esteem. Self-image should be dealt with throughout treatment. Because unrealistic expectations about weight and shape often reinforce restrictive eating, it is important to work with patients to formulate realistic expectations of what they should weigh and how much food they should eat to maintain a healthy weight. Restricting intake will increase likelihood of binge eating and purging. Distortions of body image can be identified through behavioral experiments, such as body tracing and video taping (in which the patient and therapist review the discrepancies between real and perceived weight and shape).

Interpersonal psychotherapy appears to be comparable to CBT as an effective treatment for bulimia nervosa (Agras, 1991). Interpersonal stress in eating disorders can relate to problems with self-image, self-esteem, and perfectionism, frequently leading to unrealistic expectations in a variety of areas, such as school, work, and interpersonal functioning. This can result in increased dysphoria and anxiety. Interpersonal therapy, by improving interpersonal functioning reduces binge eating presumably through a reduction in dysphoria.

In addition to pathological eating behavior, bulimic patients tend to have difficulty modulating their reactions and behaviors, which can negatively affect functioning and increase dysphoria. Psychotherapy helps patients to strike an appropriate balance in multiple areas of their lives and may be a general therapeutic theme. With this approach, improvement and reduction in binge eating averages approximately 70% (Oesterhead, McKenna,& Gould, 1987).

Family Involvement

Family treatment in relation to bulimia is less well explored than in anorexia. This is most likely due to the older age of onset and the fact that many patients no longer reside with their family of origin (Hall, 1987; Vandereycken, 1987). Family involvement is important, because many families become frustrated, angry, and hopeless as a result of the chronic course of their child's illness. The secretiveness of the bulimic patient disrupts the sense of trust within the family, and the patient is therefore often met with emotional disapproval (Hall, 1987). Parents typically feel guilty and powerless. The stress of the illness often creates negative change in the family, resulting in emotional distance, withdrawal, and denial. The high rate of sexual abuse and incest found by some authors may certainly contribute to this phenomenology (Oppenheimer, Howells, & Palmer, 1984).

Schwartz, Barrett, and Saba (1984) added to Minuchin, Rosman, and Baker's (1978) psychometric description of the anorectic family to better capture the dynamic picture of the bulimic family. In addition to overprotectiveness, conflict avoidance, rigidity, and enmeshment, there are other factors to be considered—isolation, conscientiousness of appearance, and a special importance placed on food and its meaning (Minuchin, Rosman, & Baker, 1978; Schwartz et al., 1984). It should be emphasized, however, that although many families have some or even all of these characteristics, many have only a few or none. Thus, each family needs to be assessed individually, and an eclectic approach to treatment seems most helpful.

There are several stages of treatment for the bulimic family: motivating the family for differentiation, guiding the differentiation, targeting the symptoms, and teaching patient and family about relapse prevention and preparing them realistically for the continued recovery process (Vanderlinden & Vandereycken, 1988). Consolidating change is the ultimate goal and a multidimensional approach best serves this program.

The primary therapeutic tasks of working with families is to establish a good working alliance, avoid collusion with denial of reality with regard to the severity of the illness, avoid an authoritarian power stance and involve family and patient in decision-making process, resist overidentification with parts of the system (i.e., beware of countertransference issues), restore eating patterns, restore more positive family interactions, help patient become emancipated, and establish a support network for both family and patient as needed (Vanderlinden & Vandereycken, 1988).

Treatment planning should be geared to the goals of reestablishing normal weight and eating patterns as well as the maintenance of these goals. It is important that goals be concrete and achievable, as this will help to minimize both the patient's and family's sense of importance.

The need to empower the family and patient through education about the illness and the treatment must be underscored. Knowledge is power, and it enables family and patient to feel part of the team. It is always easier to work with the system than against it, and involvement tends to diminish resistance. It is also important for the therapist to evaluate the treatment on an ongoing basis. Making use of fellow professionals for supervision and guidance is an essential component toward improving the clinical care of these families.

Pharmacotherapy

Most double-blind, placebo-controlled trials of tricyclic antidepressants, including imipramine (Agras et al., 1987; Pope, Hudson, Jonas, & Yurgelun-Todd, 1983), desipramine (Hughes et al., 1986), and amitriptyline (Mitchell & Groat, 1984), when used at adequate dosages, demonstrate that an active drug is significantly better than a placebo in reducing bingeing and vomiting behavior. Additionally, all studies that reported a significant drug-related reduction in frequency of bingeing also reported an improvement in affective symptoms. Some groups found a correlation between change in binge frequency and mood improvement and other investigators did not. Several studies (Hughes et al., 1986; Walsh et al., 1988) have shown that nondepressed bulimics have similar antibulimic responses to antidepressants. It is worth mentioning that open trials of tricyclic antidepressants have been reported (Brotman, Herzog, & Woods, 1984; Pope et al., 1984) and, in general, findings are similar to controlled trials.

Studies examining the efficacy of MAOIs in bulimia (Kennedy et al., 1986; Walsh et al., 1988) report improvement in bulimic symptoms similar to that with TCAs. In an open trial, Roy-Byrne, Gwirtsman, Edelstein, Yager, and Gerner (1983) reported that only one of eight patients responded favorably to tranylcypromine at dosages of 30 mg or more. All authors recommend careful clinical evaluation of each patient with whom MAOI therapy is initiated, as many bulimic subjects exhibit impulsive behavior patterns and might have great difficulty with adherence to the low tyramine diet necessary for these treatments.

Fluoxitine, a new antidepressant with potent serotonin reuptake blockade characteristics, decreased bulimic symptoms in a severe anorectic patient (Ferguson, 1987) and, in double-blind, placebo-controlled studies, decreased bulimic behavior (Fluoxetine Bulimia Nervosa Collaborative Study Group, 1992).

Trazadone, in a double-blind, placebo-controlled trial (Pope et al., 1988), was found to significantly improve bulimic symptoms when compared with controls, and was well tolerated by the subjects. Other studies have shown moderate benefit (Pope et al., 1984), or in one trial of three patients, a worsening of symptoms using trazadone (Wold, 1983). Reports of lithium being effective in anorexic subjects with bulimic symptoms (Gross et al., 1981) have suggested that it may also be beneficial in bulimia. In a trial in 14 normal weight bulimic subjects, lithium was found to reduce bulimic behavior from 75% to 100% in 12 of the subjects (Hsu, 1984). The efficacy of mianserin, another antidepressant, remains undetermined (Sabine, Yonace, Farrington, Barratt, & Wakeling, 1983).

MAINTENANCE AND GENERALIZATION STRATEGIES

Selecting Optimal Treatment Strategies

Recent data suggest that initial treatment of choice for bulimia nervosa involves a structured program that utilizes cognitive-behavioral, educational, and nutritional interventions in either a group or individual setting (Fairburn, Kir, O'Connor, & Cooper, 1986; Mitchell, Pyle, & Eckert, 1990). For patients resistant to this approach, use of antidepressant medications can help to decrease frequency of binge eating and purging. When outpatient treatment is unable to decrease severe bulimic behavior associated with severe medical instability or disabling depression, anxiety, or impulsive behavior, then a period of inpatient treatment should be implemented.

Relapse Prevention

The concept of relapse prevention in eating disorders involves three main components. First, it must be assumed that there will be continued eating disorder symptoms, either continuously or intermittently during recovery. Patients should assume they will have continued fears of eating and gaining weight, and they will have periods of time when they have urges to restrict, binge eat, use laxatives or diet pills, or exercise. Second, given the inevitability of continued eating disorder symptoms, specific planning should be carried out to determine, in advance, what the patient will do if slips or symptoms occur. This should include determination of the location of support groups, identifying peers and family members that can lend support, seeing continued psychotherapy as important, and having clear meal planning. Third, these plans need to be individualized and implemented. Recovery from anorexia and bulimia must be an active process in which the patient continuously works at maintaining recovery.

It must be emphasized to patients that taking action is critical to recovery. Frequently, fears, low self-esteem, and long-standing isolation make it very difficult for patients to risk new behaviors. For this reason, relapse prevention strategies are more helpful if discussed openly with the individual and tailored to their unique situations and capabilities.

PROBLEMS IN IMPLEMENTING TREATMENT

Poor outcome in eating disorders is associated with longer duration of illness, lower minimum weight, premorbid personality and social difficulties, disturbed relationship with family, and previous treatment (Hsu, 1990).

Clinically, the major obstacle to the treatment of eating disorders is the intense denial of pathological eating behavior as a significant problem. In patients with bulimia and anorexia nervosa this may manifest as a complete denial of weight loss as a problem. Even patients who are able to see that they are underweight cannot tolerate fears of weight gain and becoming "obese." Frequently, bulimic anorexics "bargain" with their family that they will "not lose weight," if they are "not made to gain weight." This may lead the family to support the patient's noncompliance with a weight gain program. Such resistance should be dealt with in terms of improved education as to the unreality of the patient's ability to maintain current weight. Families in this situation should be encouraged to have the patient routinely monitored for weight and electrolyte status to avoid catastrophic medical complications if, in fact, they are unable to maintain their weight. Such monitoring should be carried out by the professionals involved in order to avoid setting up a chronic power struggle within the family. When therapists do not wish to weigh the patient themselves, they should then collaborate closely with a medical professional who will keep close track of the patient, because these data play a critical role in case management. Families frequently go through a phase of "wanting to believe" the patient's intentions, and it is only after they have gone through repeated disappointments that they are able to set limits in terms of necessary weight gain.

In bulimics who remain significantly underweight, experience suggests that patients who are less than 80% to 85% of ABW do not respond as well to "talk therapies" or medication. In the case of psychotherapy, the cognitive rigidity and inability to spend significant time focusing on thoughts that are not unrelated to food and weight interfere with work in psychotherapy. It has found that during weight gain, more frequent sessions of short duration and that are primarily supportive can set the foundation for therapeutic alliance or bonding. The focus may be a casual exploration of possible interests and/or goals not directly related to food, weight, and appearance, which can point toward future psychotherapeutic work. If the patient is unable to present any such themes, simply taking a respectful interest in the patient over and above the eating disorder can set the stage for future work on relationships and self-esteem, because isolation and loneliness are frequently present. In terms of medication response, it is also possible that some of the neurobiological sequelae of malnutrition decrease the effect of medication in these patients.

In patients with bulimia who are normal weight, indicators of poor prognosis include duration of illness, positive family history of alcoholism, and depression (Hsu & Holder, 1986), and higher frequency of binge eating and vomiting (Mitchell, Soll, Eckert, Pyle, & Hatsukami, 1989). Denial is also a problem in normal weight bulimic patient, because they may see binge eating and purging as the problem. Therefore, they will minimize the deleterious effects of pathological eating.

Psychotherapeutically, difficulties may arise in individual sessions with the bulimic if there is a history of troubled relationships, impulsivity, and/or intense feelings of guilt and shame. Consequently, mutually respective relationships should be the goal with realistic expectations being clearly defined. Patients need to be educated about differences between guilt and shame and why keeping these feelings hidden are harmful. They need to be gently encouraged to reveal painful feelings and incidents. Self-destructive and/or deceptive behaviors that lead to authentic guilt need to be confronted respectfully but honestly with a vision toward understanding and changing such behaviors.

CASE ILLUSTRATIONS

Case 1: Bulimia and Anorexia Nervosa

Sarah was a 15-year-old female, the oldest of three children, living at home with their mother and father. Sarah was in good health, did well in school, and was reported by the family to be a "perfectionistic" child who worked hard in school and did not get into trouble.

At the age of 13, she was reported to be increasingly worried about her weight, which had increased about 25 lbs over the last 6 months. This was also a time when she was going through puberty and had begun menstruating. She reported that she began dieting because she did not want to become overweight, and "kids were teasing me at school about my weight." Her dieting consisted of eating low calorie foods. She also started to run 2 to 3 miles a day and bought an aerobics tape, which she used at home alone once a day.

Such activities caused her to lose about 5 lbs over a 1-month period. With this weight loss, she reported feeling a sense of control and accomplishment. It became easier for her to skip meals, usually breakfast and lunch. Sarah also began spending an increasing amount of time either studying or exercising. At this point, she became increasingly self-critical. She would ruminate that she could not make friends because she was not interesting and had nothing to offer. She believed that she was not intelligent, and she would become extremely upset if she did not attain the highest score in her class on a test.

She became more irritable with her family and isolated from her friends. She would not eat with her family, and would spend most of her time in her room where she would argue with her younger sisters and parents. This escalated to the point where her family became relieved when she was in her room because she was so disruptive. They believed that she must be going through an adolescent phase, and hoped things would be back to normal soon.

Sarah's parents began to be concerned about her weight when she began to look "a little too thin" and they could hear her exercising in the middle of the night in her room.

One day Sarah's mother received a call from the school counselor, who was concerned that Sarah might have an "eating disorder." A peer had overheard Sarah vomiting in the school bathroom. Sarah's mother also began to notice certain foods, such as cereal and cookies disappearing at home. Her parents then took her to a therapist recommended by their family physician, who diagnosed her as "bulimic and anorexic."

The therapist began to meet with Sarah on a weekly basis, weighing her prior to each session. Sarah was noted to be quite depressed and angry with her parents. She minimized their concerns about binge eating and weight stating that "my parents think I have a problem with my weight, but I don't." She also dismissed concerns about binge eating by stating that "I don't have problems with overeating because I can get rid of the food by vomiting whenever I want." At home, her parents began to monitor her eating, insisting that she eat with the family. After meals she would go to the bathroom and they could hear her vomiting. At the same time, her weight began to decrease, she continued to exercise 2 to 4 hours a week, and she did not contact her friends.

Her therapist met with the parents and reported that Sarah's weight had continued to decrease. The patient was evaluated by the family physician and was found to have a normal exam except for mildly decreased thyroid function tests, amenorrhea, and parotid swelling. She weighed 85 lbs and had mildly decreased pulse and blood pressure.

Sarah was subsequently admitted to a day program and was found to weigh 80 lbs. She was 5 feet tall, which placed her at 75% ABW. She had normal electrolyte blood counts, but had mildly decreased thyroid hormone levels, and had bradycardia. On physical exam she was noted to have dry skin, prominent definition of her skeletal structure, and increased fine hair on her face and arms.

In addition to a complete physical and neurological exam, she had a complete evaluation including a psychiatric evaluation, nutritional assessment, and family history. She was started on 1,200 kcal a day of meals (35 kcal/kg) and was observed during and 1 hour after all meals and in the bathroom at all times during her time at the day program.

Initial psychiatric evaluation characterized Sarah as a young thin female who made poor eye contact. She was alert and oriented. Formal memory and intellectual testing were normal. She was extremely fidgety and restless during the interview. She reported feeling fat and having a desire to lose weight. She reported a fear of weight gain and panic whenever she would eat and was not be able to vomit because of the fear of "blowing up like a balloon." She reported eating binges when she would rapidly consume 3 to 4 bowls of cereal or as many as a dozen cookies. She reported feeling anxious and out of control when she was eating and would then vomit until she felt that "all the food was out of her stomach." She reported that at times she would eat ketchup at the beginning of a binge so that she would know when she had "vomited all the food out of my stomach." She reported that she spent 99% of her day worrying about weight and food. She at times felt that putting hand lotion or body lotion on would cause her to gain weight. She reported exercising 2 to 4 hours a day and would do a very structured exercise routine that included 100 each of sit ups, jumping jacks, deep knee bends, and pushups. She would time herself, always trying to decrease the amount of time it would take her to complete her exercise routine. She was extremely fearful of eating meats, stating that she had become a vegetarian over the last year and that she was "allergic to sugar." She repeatedly asked if she would have to gain weight in treatment, and commented that all of the other patients were much thinner than she.

She reported a persistent sadness, which was centered around feeling that she was a failure if she gained weight. She also believed the only way she would feel better was if she could diet more and not gain weight. She reported less interest in hobbies that did not relate to dieting or exercising, was not interested in seeing friends, and had difficulty sleeping (characterized by going to bed and waking up at 5 a.m. and not being able to fall back asleep).

She also reported persistent worrying about minor matters usually related to weight and food, but also many important items, such as what college she will go to, and whether she will be able to achieve the success she idealizes.

On further questioning, she also reported a preoccupation with doing things perfectly. This caused her to spend much more time on homework because she would end up recopying the same assignment three or four times to make sure it looked perfect. She also reported spending 2 to 3 hours a day cleaning at home, and would compulsively organize her room so that her books and clothing would be arranged according to size or color. She reported that if things were not clean and organized she would not stop thinking about it until she put them in order or cleaned them. She also reported that she did not like other members of the household to clean because it was not up to her standards.

In addition to reducing frequency of binge eating and purging, the initial treatment focus was on nutritional rehabilitation and weight gain. Sarah was required to eat 100% of a 1,200 kcal diet and when she was able to accomplish this her calories were gradually increased 250 to 300 kcal every 3 to 4 days. Over the first 3 weeks in the day program, she gained very little weight and would lose weight over the weekend at home. However, when her calories were increased to 50 to 60 kcal/kg/day she began to gain 1 to 2 kg a week, and after 10 weeks of treatment she attained her target weight of 102 lbs, or 95% of ABW. Her calories were increased up to 4,000 kcal a day in the week prior to attaining her target weight to maintain weight gain. After attaining target weight, calories were decreased over the course of 1 week to a 2,400 kcal a day for weight maintenance. She then began to prepare her own meals in the day program kitchen, had meals out at restaurants with staff, and went shopping to try on clothes. She would report persistent urges to restrict her intake and lose weight while eating on her own but was able to maintain her weight between 100 and 104 lbs.

The primary treatment was cognitive-behavioral therapy. Its main focus was behaviorally reinforcing healthy eating-patterns as opposed to eating-disordered behavior and identifying pathological thinking patterns that would initiate or perpetuate anorexic behaviors. Thought restructuring techniques were used to help Sarah connect positive results with maintaining a healthy body weight and not engage in anorexic behavior under stress. This was done using a variety of group exercising and a structured treatment manual that Sarah would work on throughout the course of her enrollment in the day program. Taped meal sessions with family and therapist were helpful in exploring dynamics around eating. The simple experience of eating together in a structured setting was anxiety reducing for both patient and family. These tapes were reviewed later to discuss family observations, feelings, and thoughts regarding the exercise. Specific eating tasks were scheduled with staff, such as eating a feared food during the later phases of treatment. Therapeutic meal passes were also scheduled with the family prior to discharge. Eating high-risk, forbidden foods or going to high-risk places like bakeries where she used to binge were also used as behavioral experiments. All of these activities provide experience and information necessary for more complete discharge planning.

In addition, individual therapy was used to identify specific stressful life events and situations that contributed to Sarah's low self-esteem. A move by the family from another city became a focus of treatment. Themes around loss of friends where she previously lived, guilt feelings about how she avoided saying goodbye to them, and anger at her parents about having to move were addressed. This resulted in Sarah renewing some relationships that she found to be rewarding and helpful in transitioning to her new home.

Two major items appeared during the course of a family evaluation that needed to be addressed to facilitate Sarah's recovery. First, mother, who was moderately obese, reported herself to be very fearful that Sarah would become "fat like me." As a result, she reported encouraging Sarah to diet and exercise when her eating disorder began. She would also frequently ask how much Sarah weighed and reward her if her clothes size decreased. She also reported being chronically depressed and felt that she was unattractive to her husband and that her life was going nowhere. Father, on the other hand, was somewhat successful in his job in middle management. However, the family reported significant compulsive behavior at home in terms of cleaning and organizating, and he reported that he had some problems with completing projects on time at work and felt that this had recently kept him from a promotion to a more senior level.

With this information, the focus of family therapy was to identify mother's and father's individual problems and facilitate their working on these. Mother had reported that she had previously attended Overeaters Anonymous and had found this to be quite helpful before they moved. She began attending groups at their new home and reported that this was helping her to control her weight. She also reported an increase in self-esteem. Father was referred to a psychiatrist and was diagnosed as having obsessive compulsive disorder and subsequently responded well to an antiobsessional medication.

After discharge, Sarah was referred back to the therapist who treated her prior to admission. The therapist was notified as to interventions that worked in the day program and treatment recommendation was made for outpatient therapy. These included a contract concerning abstinence from binge eating and purging and weight maintenance that the patient and family signed. This contract stated that if Sarah's weight dropped below 95 lbs, then she would be readmitted to the day program. It was recommended that Sarah be followed by a psychiatrist for monitoring of fluoxetine treatment and psychotherapy focusing on themes that were dealt with in cognitive, individual, and family therapy. The clinicians also remained available for consultation concerning treatment issues that would arise in outpatient therapy.

Follow-up at 1 year after discharge found that Sarah was abstinent from purging and binge ate occasionally when under stress. She was maintaining her weight slightly above her target weight range and was weighing between 105 and 110 lbs. She was able to maintain a regular meal schedule and exercise only 1 hour a day. She did not return to participating in track but was still involved in the school newspaper and had a boyfriend. Her grades continued to be excellent and she was in the process of planning for college. Themes in individual therapy continued to center around rejection sensitivity with a tendency to have an increase in eating disorder symptoms. However, she learned how to identify this pattern and was doing good work in individual therapy by examining possible contributing factors to this problem.

Mother reported that she was happier and involved in volunteer work and spending much more time out of the house and that father was less obsessional and his work was going well. Parents were also able to improve their parenting skills and discuss concerns and proposed interventions with one another before attempting to implement this. This provided more consistency and less opportunity for conflicts over management to develop the diminished stress and conflict over the illness allowed there to focus on their individual problems, which improved their marital communications as well.

Case 1 Summary

This is a typical case history of a patient with bulimia and anorexia. The hallmarks of this case include prominent obsessional and perfectionistic traits that increase as weight decreases. Binge eating is associated with loss of control and guilt. Also, when stress increases, patients typically spend more time involved in anorexic behavior and studying, or binge eating. It is also not uncommon to have compulsive behaviors, such as cleaning and organizing in these patients, and for them to maintain good school or work performance in the setting of poor nutritional low weight.

Denial and resistance to treatment occur in the majority of these patients. Whether patients can see they have anorexia and need to gain weight or do not feel they have a problem, all are extremely fearful of weight gain and typically believe they will binge eat unless in a highly structured setting. If a short-term outpatient treatment does not noticeably improve eating and weight of patients less than 80% of ABW, it is recommended that weight gain in a structured day program be initiated. A weight increase of at least to 80% ABW should be obtained before outpatient treatment is attempted. In highly resistant patients, weight gain to 95% of ABW followed by a period of weight maintenance should be carried out in a hospital or partial hospitalization setting.

Family intervention initially focused on educating the parents about bulimia nervosa, anorexia nervosa, and the process of recovery. Setting firm limits around abstinence from binge eating and purging and weight gain were encouraged; frequent phone contact by the psychiatrist and family therapist served to support the parents in this process. The need for continued treatment following discharge was emphasized. Parents and patients were also realistically prepared for recovery typically including progression, setbacks, and plateaus. Many families and patients hope to be "cured," and this can set up a situation in which they will feel devastated, frustrated, angry, and hopeless if realistic expectations regarding recovery process are a part of the hospitalization experience. As the patient began to improve the parents began to identify marital issues that were contributing to increase stress at home and agreed to a trial of couples therapy to address these.

Although fluoxetine is not FDA approved in the treatment of bulimia or anorexia nervosa, this patient was treated with 40 mg a day, initiated when she reached her target weight. She reported that she had less desire to binge eat, was less anxious about her weight, and had less of an urge to clean and organize with the medication. Her parents and treatment team found her to be less rigid and more flexible on the medication.

Case 2: Normal Weight Bulimia

Lori is a 23-year-old single White woman employed as a salesclerk for a retail store. Her weight at evaluation was 117 pounds with a high weight in the past of 160 pounds and a low weight of 110 pounds. Her height was 5'4". She recounted always having had a "problem" with weight. At age 13 she went on a restrictive diet for 3 weeks and lost 10 pounds, but subsequently she gained all of the weight back.

Lori read about purging techniques (e.g., vomiting and laxatives) in popular magazines, but her first personal experience with vomiting occurred at age 18. Following a large Mexican meal, she developed an upset stomach and subsequently vomited. Vomiting alleviated her feeling of fullness, decreased her dread of putting on weight, and introduced her to a practice that would allow her to eat as much as she wanted without gaining weight.

At first the practice of purging was uncomfortable, but within several months it became a way of life. Food became her "friend," a way to quell anger and reduce depression and anxiety. Prior to binge eating she often felt lonely, empty, and depressed, and had thoughts of failure. During the binge she escaped from her world of immediate cares to a dulled, inner-directed state. As the binge progressed she experienced feelings of fullness, fatness, and loss of control. Tension built and then fell precipitously following the purge. What originally had been a "friend" over time became an uncontrollable habit. Consuming a loaf of bread, a half gallon of ice cream, a plate of spaghetti, and a bowl of cereal several times a day was expensive, time-consuming, and isolating, and often took priority over socializing with friends or going to work. In addition, she had difficulty controlling her alcohol intake and she reported frequent periods of drunkenness.

Lori had a history of relationships with men that were "unhealthy." She tended to be attracted to and date men who abused drugs and alcohol, and she had been physically assaulted on two occasions by two different boyfriends. Her most recent relationship ended when her boyfriend began dating her "best friend." She would deal with her disappointment in these relationships by focusing on her "bad points" and feel that she was not attractive and needed to lose weight so that she would be more attractive and be happy. Dysphoria associated with such disappointments would also be associated with an increase in the frequency of binge eating.

Lori had a very troubled childhood. On the surface her parents were successful and respected in the community. However, her mother was an alcoholic who had frequent episodes of depression and was often unavailable emotionally for the patient. Her father's behavior was unpredictable, ranging from extreme passivity to displays of frightening rage. Lori was frequently in the middle of family disputes and felt responsible for maintaining peace between her parents. Her parents had high expectations of Lori and never seemed satisfied with her accomplishments. On a mental status exam, Lori was attractive, extroverted, and friendly. She described chronic feelings of depression accompanied by intermittent periods of disrupted sleep, crying spells, and suicidal thoughts. Her affect was bright and appeared incongruent with her stated-depressed mood. She spoke of guilt and shame concerning the binge eating and vomiting. She had difficulty verbalizing emotion and would often state that everything was "fine." Physical examination and pertinent laboratory data revealed no physical cause for her vomiting.

Lori reported that she first decided that she wanted to stop bingeing and vomiting at age 21. Typically, she would be able to abstain, with great effort, for a couple of days, but when even a minor stressor would arise she would resume her binge–purge behavior at the same rate or worse than before. She began lying to friends and family about her eating and would steal food and borrow money from friends and family to binge eat.

At age 23, Lori was referred to a private therapist after a suicide attempt precipitated by a period of heavy bingeing. She was seen weekly and initially was able to decrease her frequency of bingeing and purging. However, when unable to stop bingeing, she began feeling guilty and lied to the therapist, telling her she had stopped so as not to disappoint her. As a result of increasing guilt and frustration, she eventually was unable to continue with this therapist and left treatment precipitously. She tried other treatments, including an Overeaters Support Group and a behavioral day treatment program, both of which helped her to stop bingeing initially. With a great deal of effort she could maintain control for up several weeks at a time, but she always resumed bingeing and would subsequently feel guilty and stop treatment. Her self-esteem plummeted and her depression intensified with feelings of sadness, guilt, hopelessness, and helplessness.

On initial evaluation at our program, which included routine psychiatric and physical examinations, Lori was bingeing one to three times a day and had a Hamilton score of 32. She was entered into interpersonal therapy that focused on interpersonal issues related to her relationships. Because of moderate to severe depressive symptoms and some suicidal thoughts she was started on desipramine 10 mg a day, which was increased to 150 mg a day over the next 2 weeks. She reported feeling generally hopeful and was bingeing less but only with much effort. A TCA Level of 98 ng/ml was obtained; her dose was increased up to 250 mg a day, which gave her a level of 198 ng/ml. Over the next 2 weeks she decreased her binge frequency to 1 to 2 binges a week and felt more hopeful that she could have more control over eating. She also felt less depressed as her HAM–D score decreased to less than 10. At this point she was able to recognize certain stressors that precipitated the urge to binge and was referred to a psychotherapist.

At 1 year follow-up, Lori was bingeing one to two times a month and felt less depressed and more in control of her life. She was involved in a new relationship that was "healthy" by her report and was also getting along better with her parents. A trial off desipramine led to an increase in bingeing that she could not tolerate. The desipramine was reinstituted with good results. Her weight at 1 year was 122 lbs. She felt this was too high, but tolerated her mild discomfort as she was afraid she would binge more frequently if she tried to lose weight.

Case 2 Summary

Case 2 is a typical case of bulimia nervosa. The age of onset is typically later than in anorexia because bulimics are aware that their eating is abnormal and they are more likely to conceal their behavior from their family. This case is notable for prominent interpersonal difficulties that are often associated with depressive symptoms, emotional lability, and low self-esteem, and can lead to problems in interpersonal functioning, school performance, and self-destructive behavior (including suicide in addition to binge eating and purging).

Lying and shoplifting are common in bulimia, which can decrease the effectiveness of therapy and be quite frustrating for peer and family members.

Histories of sexual abuse and disruptive home lives, which serve to increase feelings of low self-esteem, are present in this case and are common in bulimia. These are frequent themes in individual and family therapies and need to be addressed if present. The failure to identify and address these issues may result in decreased effectiveness of treatment.

For the majority of bulimics, recovery is a long experience, and short-term goals should include maintaining medical and psychological stability so that patients are able to work effectively in outpatient therapy. Goals in outpatient therapy should be to decrease binge–purge behavior to the point of abstinence. However, many patients continue to have episodic urges to binge eat and/or restrict, especially under periods of stress. Antidepressants typically decrease these urges, and improve mood and emotional stability. However, only rarely do they lead to abstinence. For this reason, antidepressants should be used adjunctively in the setting of ongoing psychotherapy.

CONCLUSIONS

In summary, these two cases of bulimia represent the spectrum of patients that can present with this disorder. The hallmarks of this disorder are pathological eating behavior, with or without weight loss, associated with an intense fear of weight gain. Medical complications, cognitive distortions, depressive and anxiety symptoms, and substance abuse are common and need to be comprehensively assessed in eating disordered patients. Treatment interventions should be multifaceted and involve nutritional rehabilitation, cognitive restructuring, behavioral reinforcement of noneating disordered behavior, interpersonal psychotherapy, and individual, family, and pharmacological therapy. With a comprehensive approach, a majority of patients should improve. However, even at this point, roughly one third of bulimics remain significantly impaired by the illness.

REFERENCES

Abraham, S. F., & Beumont, P. V. (1982). How patients describe bulimia or binge eating. *Psychological Medicine, 12*, 625–635.

Agras, W. (1991). Nonpharmacologic treatment of bulimia nervosa. *Journal of Clinical Psychiatry, 52*, 29–33.

Agras, W. S., Dorian, B., Kirkley, B. G., Arnow, B., & Bachman, J. (1987). Imipramine in the treatment of bulimia: A double-blind controlled study. *International Journal of Eating Disorders, 6*, 29–38.

American Psychiatric Association. (1994). *Diagnostic and statistical manual of mental disorders* (4th ed.). Washington, DC: Author.

Apter, A., van Praag, M., Plutchik, R., Sevy, S., Korn, M., & Brown, S. L.(1990). Interrelationships among anxiety, aggression, impulsivity, and mood: A serotonergically linked cluster? *Psychiatry Research, 32*, 191–199.

Barlow, J., Blouin, J., Blouin, A., & Perez, E. (1988). Treatment of bulimia with desipramine: A double–blind crossover study. *Canadian Journal of Psychiatry, 33*, 129–133.

Barr, L. C., Goodman, W.K., Price, L. H., McDougle, C. J., Delgado, P. L., Heninger, G. R., Charney, D. S., & Price, L. H. (1994). Tryptophan depletion in patients with obsessive–compulsive disorder who response to serotonin reuptake inhibitors. *Archives of General Psychiatry, 51*, 309–317.

Bastiani, A. M., Rao, R., Weltzin, T. E., & Kaye, W. H. (1995). Perfectionism in anorexia. *American Journal of Psychiatry, 151*, 147–152.

Beary, M. D., Lacey, J. H., & Merry, J. (1986). Alcoholism and eating disorders in women of fertile age. *British Journal of Addiction, 81*, 685–689.

Beaumont, P. V., George G. W., & Smart, D. E. (1976). "Dieters" and "vomiters" in anorexia nervosa. *Psychological Medicine, 6*, 617–622.

Blouin, A. G., Blouin J. H., Perez, E. I., Bushnik, T., Zuro, C., & Mulder, E. (1988). Treatment of buliima with fenfluramine and desipramine. *Journal of Clinical Psychopharmacology, 8*, 261–269.

Blundell, J. E. (1984). Serotonin and appetite. *Neuropharmacology, 23*, 1537–1551.

Brewerton T. D., Brandt H. A., Lesem M. D., Murphy D. L., & Jimerson D. C. (1990). Serotonin in eating disorders. In E. Coccaro & D. Murphy (Eds.), *Serotonin in major psychiatric disorders* (pp. 153–184). Washington, DC: APA Press.

Broderick, P., & Lynch, V. (1982). Behavioral and biochemical changes induced by lithium and L-tryptophan in muricidal rats. *Neuropharmacology, 21*, 671–679.

Brotman, A. W., Herzog, D. B., & Woods, S. W. (1984). Antidepressant treatment of bulimia: The relationship between bingeing and depressive symptomatology. *Journal of Clinical Psychiatry, 45*, 7–9.

Brown, G., Ebert, M., Goyer, P. F., Jimerson, D. C., Klein, W. J., Bunney, W. E., & Goodwin, F. K. (1982). Aggression, suicide and serotonin: Relationships to CSF amine metabolites. *American Journal of Psychiatry, 139*, 741–746.

Bulik, C. M. (1987a). Alcohol use and depression in women with bulimia. *American Journal of Drug and Alcohol Abuse, 13*, 343–355.

Bulik, C. M. (1987b). Drug and alcohol abuse by bulimic women and their families. *American Journal of Psychiatry, 144*, 1604–1606.

Cash, T. F., & Brown, T. A. (1987). Body image in anorexia and bulimia nerovsa. *Behavior Modification, 11*, 487–521.

Casper, R. C., Eckert, E. D., Halmi, K. A., Goldberg, S. C., & Davis, J. M. (1980). Bulimia: Its incidence and clinical importance in patients with anorexia nervosa. *Archives of General Psychiatry, 37*, 1030–1035.

Chamberlain, B., Ervin, F. R., Pihl, R. O., Young, S. N. (1987). The effect of raising or lowering tryptophan levels on aggression in vervet monkeys. *Pharmacology Biochemistry and Behavior, 28*, 503–510.

Charney, D. S., Wood, S. W., & Henninger, J. R. (1987). Serotonin function in anxiety: II. Effects of the serotonin agonist MCPP in panic disorder patients and healthy subjects. *Psychopharmacology, 92*, 587–599.

Coccaro, E. F. (1989). Central serotonin and impulsive aggression. *British Journal of Psychiatry, 155*, S52–S62.

Coccaro, E. F. (1992). Impulsive aggression and central serotonergic system function in humans: An example of a dimensional brain-behavioral relationship. *International Journal of Clinical Psychopharmacology, 7*, 3–12.

Cooper, P. J., & Fairburn, C. G. (1986). The depressive symptoms of bulimia nervosa. *British Journal of Psychiatry 148*, 268–274.

Copenhaver, J. H., Schalock, R. L., & Carver, M. J. (1978). Parachloro-D, L-phenylalamine induced suicidal behavior in the female rat. *Psychopharmacology Biochemistry and Behavior, 8*, 263–270.

Davis, R., Freeman, R. J., & Garner, D. M. (1988). A naturalistic investigation of eating behavior in bulimia nervosa. *Journal of Consulting and Clinical Psychology, 2*, 273–279.

Delgado, P. L., Charney, D. S., Price, L. H., Aghajanian, G. K., Landis, H., & Heninger, G. R. (1990). Serotonin function and the mechanism of antidepressant action. *Archives of General Psychiatry, 47*, 411–418.

Elmore, C. K., & de Castro, J. M. (1990). Self-related moods and hunger in relation to spontaneous eating behavior in bulimics, recovered bulimics, and normals. *International Journal of Eating Disorders 9*, 179–190.

Fahy, T. A., Eisler, I., & Russell, G. F. (1993). A placebo-controlled trial of d-fenfluramine in bulimia nervosa. *British Journal of Psychiatry, 162*, 597–603.

Fairburn C. G., Agras W. S., & Wilson G. T. (1992). The research on the treatment of bulimia nervosa: Practical and theoretical implications. In G. H. Anderson & S. H. Kennedy (Eds.), *The biology of feast and famine* (pp. 317–340). San Diego: Academic Press.

Fairburn, C. G., & Beslin, S. J. (1990). Studies of the epidemiology of bulimia nervosa. *American Journal of Pychiatry, 147*, 401–408.

Fairburn, C. G., & Cooper, J. P. (1982). Self induced vomiting and bulimia nervosa: An undetected problem. *British Medical Journal of Clinical Research, 284*, 1153–1155.

Fairburn, C. G., Kir, J., O'Connor, M., & Cooper, R. G. (1986). A comparison of two psychological tratments for bulimia nervosa. *Behavior Research Therapy, 24*, 629–643.

Ferguson, J. M. (1987). Treatment of an anorexia nervosa patient with fluoxetine. *American Journal of Psychiatry, 144*, 1239 (letter).

Fernstrom, J. D. (1992). Diet, food intake regulation and brain serotonin: An overview. In G. Bray & D. Ryan (Eds.), *The science of food regulation* (Vol. 2, pp. 195–209). Baton Rouge, LA: Louisiana State University Press.

Freeman, C. P., Morris, J. E., Cheshire, K. E., Casper, R. C., & Davis, J. M. (1988, April). *A double-blind controlled trial of fluoxetine vs. placebo for bulimia nervosa.* Abstract from the Second International Conference on Eating Disorders, New York City.

Fluoxetine Bulimia Nervosa Collaborative Study Group. (1992). Fluoxetine in the treatment of bulimia nervosa: A multicenter, placebo-controlled, double-blind trial. *Archives of General Psychiatry, 49*, 139–147.

Gal, E. M., & Drewes, P. A. (1962). Studies on the metabolism of 5-hydroxytryptamine (serotonin): II. Effect of tryptophan deficiency in rats. *Procedings of the Society of Experimental Biological Medicine, 110*, 368–371.

Garner, D. M., Garfinkel, P. E., & O'Shaughnessy, M. (1985). The validity of the distinction between bulimia with and without anorexia nervosa. *American Journal of Psychiatry, 142*, 581–587.

Garner, D. M., Garfinkel, P. E., Schwartz, D., & Thompson M. (1980). Cultural expections of thinness in women. *Psychological Reports, 47*, 483–491.

Garfinkel, P. E., Moldofsky, H., & Garner, D. M. (1980). The heterogeneity of anorexia nervosa. *Archives of General Psychiatry, 37*, 1036–1040.

Geracioti, T. D., & Liddle, R. A. (1988). Impaired cholecystokinin secretion in bulimia nervosa. *New England Journal of Medicine, 319*, 683–688.

Gibbons, J. L., Barr, G. A., Bridger, W. H., & Leibowitz, S. F. (1979). Manipulations of dietary tryptophan: Effects on mouse killing and brain serotonin in the rat. *Brain Research, 169*, 139–153.

Gill, K., Fillion, Y., & Amit, Z. (1988). A further examination of the effects of sertraline on voluntary ethanol consumption. *Alcohol, 5*, 355–358.

Goodwin, G. M., Fairburn, C. G., & Cowen, P. J. (1987). Dieting changes serotonergic function in women, not men: Implications for the aetiology of anorexia nervosa? *Psychological Medicine, 17*, 839–842.

Gorelick, D. A. (1988). Serotonin uptake blockers and the treatment of alcoholism. In *Recent developments in alcoholism* (Vol. 7, pp. 267–281). New York: Plenum.

Grahame-Smith, D. G. (1992). Serotonin in affective disorders. *International Journal of Clinical Psychopharmacology, 6*, S5–S13.

Green, H., Greenberg, S. M., Erickson, R. W., Sawyer, J. L., & Ellison, T. (1962). Effects of dietary phenylalanine and tryptophan upon rat brain amine levels. *Journal of Pharmacology and Experimental Therapeutics, 136*, 174–178.

Gross, H. A., Ebert, M. H., Faden, V. B., Goldberg, S. C., Nee, L. E., & Kaye, W. H. (1981). The use of diphenylhydantoin in compulsive eating disorders: Further studies. In R. A. Vigersky (Ed.), *Anorexia nervosa* (pp. 377–385). New York: Raven.

Gwirtsman, H. E., Roy-Byrne, P., Yager, J., & Gerner, R. H. (1983). Neuroendocrine abnormalities in bulimia. *American Journal of Psychiatry, 140*, 550–563.

Hall, A. (1987). The patient and the family. In P. V. Beaumont, E. P. Burrows, & D. C. Casper (Eds.), *Handbook of eating disorders: Part 1. Anorexia and bulimia* (pp. 189–200). The Netherlands: Elsevier Science.

Halmi, K. A., & Falk, J. R. (1982). Anorexia nervosa: A study of outcome discrimination in exclusive dieters and bulimics. *Journal of the American Academy of Child Psychiatry, 21*, 369–375.

Halmi, K. A., Falk, J. R., & Schwartz, E. (1981). Binge-eating and vomiting: A survey of a college population. *Psychological Medicine, 11*, 697–706.

Hatsukami, D. K., Eckert, E. D., Mitchell, J. E., & Pyle, R. L. (1984). Affective disorder and substance abuse among women with bulimia. *Psychological Medicine, 14*, 701–704.

Herzog, D. B. (1982). Bulimia in the adolescent. *American Journal of Disorders in Children, 136*, 985–989.

Herzog, D. B., & Copeland, P. M. (1985). Eating disorders. *New England Journal of Medicine, 313*, 295–303.

Heufelder, A., Warnhoff, M., & Pirke, K. M. (1985). Platelet alpha 2-adrenoceptor and adenylate cyclase in patients with anorexia nervosa and bulimia. Journal of Clinical Endocrinology and Metabolism, 61, 1053–1060.

Hood, J., Moore, T., & Garner, D. (1982). Locus of control as a measure of ineffecitiveness in anorexia nervosa. *Journal of Consulting and Clinical Psychology, 50*, 3–13.

Hsu, L. G. (1984). Treatment of bulimia with lithium. *American Journal of Psychiatry, 141*, 1260–1262.

Hsu, L. G. (1990). *Eating disorders*. New York: Guilford.

Hsu, L. G., & Holder, D. (1986). Bulimia nervosa. Treatment and long-term outcome. *Psychological Medicine, 16*, 65–70.

Hudson, J. I., Laffer, P. S., & Pope, H. G. (1982). Bulimia related to affective disorder by family history and response to the dexamethasone suppression test. *American Journal of Psychiatry, 139*, 685–687.

Hudson, J. I., Pope, H. G., Jonas, J. M., & Yurgelun-Todd, D. (1983a). Family history study of anorexia nervosa and bulimia. *British Journal of Psychiatry 142*, 133–138.

Hudson, J. I., Pope, H. G., Jonas, J. M., & Yurgelun-Todd, D. (1983b). Phenomenologic relationship of eating disorders to major affective disorder. *Psychiatric Research, 9*, 345–354.

Hudson, J. I., Pope, H. G., Jonas, J. M., Yurgelun-Todd, D., & Frankenburg, F. R. (1987). A controlled family history study of bulimia. *Psychological Medicine, 17*, 883–890.

Hudson, J. I., Pope, H. G., Yurgelun–Todd, D., Jonas, J. M., & Frankenburg, F. R. (1987). A controlled study of lifetime prevalence of affective and other psychiatric disorders in bulimic outpatients. *American Journal of Psychiatry, 144,* 1283–1287.

Hughes, P. L., Wells, L. A., Cunningham, C. J., & Ilstrupp, D. M. (1986). Treating bulimia with desipramine: A double-blind, placebo-controlled study. *Archives of General Psychiatry, 43,* 182–186.

Jimerson, D. C., Lesem, M. D., Hegg, A. P., & Brewerton, T. D. (1990). Serotonin in human eating disorders. *Annals of the New York Academy of Science, 60,* 532–544.

Johnson, C., & Larson, R. (1982). Bulimia: An analysis of moods and behavior. *Psychosomatic Medicine, 44,* 341–351.

Johnson, C., Stuckey, M. K., Lewis, L. D., & Schwartz, D. M. (1982). Bulimia: A descriptive study survey on 316 cases. *International Journal of Eating Disorders, 2,* 3–16.

Jonas, J. M., & Gold, M. S. (1986). Naltrexone reverses bulimic symptoms. *Lancet, 8,* 807.

Kassett, J. A., Gershon, E. S., Maxwell, M. E., Guroff, J. J., Kazuba, D. M., Smith, A. L., Brandt, H. A., & Jimerson, D. C. (1986). Psychiatric disorders in the first-degree relatives of probands with bulimia nervosa. *American Journal of Psychiatry, 143,* 1468–1471.

Kaye, W. H., Ballenger, J. C., Lydiard, B., Stuart, G. W., Laraia, M. T., O'Neil, P. Fossey, M., Stevens, V., Lesser, S., & Hsu, L. G. (1990). CSF monoamine levels in normal-weight bulimia: Evidence for abnormal noradrenergic activity. *American Journal of Psychiatry, 147,* 225–229.

Kaye, W. H., Berrettini, W., Gwirtsman, H., & George, D. (1990). Altered cerebrospinal fluid neuropeptide Y and peptide YY immunoreactivity in anorexia and bulimia nervosa. *Archives of General Psychiatry, 47,* 548–556.

Kaye, W. H., Gwirtsman, H. E., Brewerton, T. D., George, D. T., & Wurtman, R. J. (1988). Bingeing behavior and plasma amino acids: A possible involvement of brain serotonin in bulimia nervosa. *Psychiatry Research, 23,* 31–43.

Kaye, W. H., Gwirtsman, H. E., George, D. T., Jimerson, D. C., Ebert, M. H., & Lake, C. R. (1986, May). *Disturbances in noradrenergic systems in normal weight bulimia: Sympathetic activation with bingeing, reduced noradrenergic activity after a month of abstinence from bingeing.* Paper presented at the 139th Annual Meeting of the American Psychiatric Association, Washington, DC.

Kaye, W. H., Gwirtsman, H., George, D. T., Jimerson, D. C., Ebert, M. H., & Lake, C. R. (1990). Disturbances of noradrenergic systems in normal-weight bulimia: Relationship to diet and menses. *Biological Psychiatry, 27,* 4–21.

Kaye, W. H., Gwirtsman, H. E., George, D. T., Weiss, S. R., & Jimerson, D. C. (1986). Relationship of mood alterations to bingeing behavior in bulimia. *British Journal of Psychiatry, 149,* 479–485.

Kaye, W. H., Gwirtsman, H. E., Lake, C. R., Siever, L. J., Jimerson, D. C., Ebert, M. H., & Murphy, D. L. (1985). Disturbances of norepinephrine metabolism and alpha2 adrenergic receptor activity in anorexia nervosa: Relationship to nutritional state. *Psychopharmacology Bulletin, 21,* 419–423.

Kaye, W. H., Weltzin, T. E., Hsu, L. G., & Bulik, C. (1991). An open trial of fluoxetine in patients with anorexia nervosa. *Journal of Clinical Psychiatry, 52,* 464–471.

Kaye, W. H., & Weltzin, T. E. (1991). Neurochemistry of bulimia nervosa. *Journal of Clinical Psychiatry, 52,* 21–28.

Kendler, K. S., MacLean, C., Neale, M., Kessler, R., Heath, A., & Eaves, L. (1991). The genetic epidemiology of bulimia nervosa. *American Journal of Psychiatry, 148,* 1627–1637.

Kennedy, S., Piran, N., & Garfinkel, P.E. (1986). Isocarboxazide in the treatment of bulimia. *American Journal of Psychiatry, 143,* 1495–1496.

Laessle, R. G., Wittchen, H. U., Fichter, M. M., & Pirke, K. M. (1989). The significance of subgroups of bulimia and anorexia nervosa: Lifetime frequency of psychiatric disorders. *International Journal of Eating Disorders, 8,* 569–574.

Leibowitz, S. F. (1988). Hypothalamic paraventricular nucleus: Interaction between alpha 2-noradrenergic system and circulating hormones and nutrients in relation to energy balance. *Neuroscience Biobehavior Review, 12,* 101–109.

Leibowitz, S. F. (1990). The role of serotonin in eating disorders. *Drugs, 39,* 33–48.

Leon, G. R., Carroll, K., Chernyk, B., & Finn, S. (1985). Binge eating and associated habit patterns within college students and identified bulimic populations. *International Journal of Eating Disorders, 4,* 43–57.

Linnoila, M. Virkkunen, M., Scheinin, M., Nuutila A., Rimon, R., & Goodwin, F. K. (1983). Low cerebrospinal fluid 5-HIAA concentration differentiates impulsive from non-impulsive violent behavior. *Life Sciences, 33,* 2609–2614.

Lytle, L. D., Messing, R. B., Fisher, L., & Phebus, L. (1975). Effects of long-term corn consumptions on brain serotonin and the response to electric shock. *Science, 190,* 692–694.

McGoldrick, M. (1985). *Genograms in family assessment.* New York: Norton.

Minuchin, S., Rosman, B. L., & Baker, L. (1987). *Psychosomatic families: Anorexia nervosa in context.* Cambridge, MA: Harvard University Press.

Mitchell, J. E. (1984). Medical complications of anorexia and bulimia nervosa. *Psychiatric Medicine, 1,* 229–255.

Mitchell, J. E., & Groat, R. (1984). A placebo-controlled double-blind trial of amitriptyline in bulimia. *Journal of Clinical Psychopharmacology, 4,* 186–193.

Mitchell, J. E., Hatsukami, D., Eckert, E. D., & Pyle, R. L. (1985). Characteristics of 275 patients with bulimia. *Journal of Clinical Psychopharmacology, 142,* 482–485.

Mitchell, J. E., Hatsukami, D., Pyle, R., & Eckert, E. D. (1988). Bulimia with and without a family history of drug abuse. *Addictive Behaviors, 13,* 245–251.

Mitchell, J. E., Pyle, R. L., & Eckert, E. D. (1990). A comparison study of antidepressants and structured intensive group psychotherapy in the treatment of bulimia nervosa. *Archives of General Psychiatry, 47,* 149–157.

Mitchell, J. E., Pyle, R. L., Hatsukami, D., Goff, G., Glotter, D., & Harper, J. (1988). A 2–5 year follow-up study of patients treated for bulimia. *International Journal of Eating Disorders, 8,* 157–165.

Mitchell, J. E., Scim, H. D., Colon, E., & Pomeroy, C. (1987). Medical complications and medical mangement of bulimia. *Annals of Internal Medicine, 107,* 71–76.

Mitchell, J. E., Soll, E., Eckert, E. D., Pyle, R. L., & Hatsukami, D. (1989). The changing population of bulimia nervosa patients in an eating disorders program. *Hospital and Community Psychiatry, 40,* 1188–1189.

Ninan, P. T., van Kammen, D. P., Scheinin, M., Linnoila, M., Bunney, W. E., & Goodwin, F. K. (1984). CSF 5-hydroxyindoleacetic acid levels in suicidal schizophrenic patients. *American Journal of Psychiatry, 141,* 566–569.

Oesterhed, J. D., McKenna, M. S., & Gould, N. B. (1987). Group psychotherapy of bulimia: A critical review. *International Journal of Group Psychotherapy, 37,* 163–184.

Oppenheimer, R., Howells, K., & Palmer, R. L. (1984). *Adverse sexual experiences and victimization in the histories of patients with clinical eating disorders.* Paper presented at the International Conference on Anorexia Nervosa and Related Disorders, Swansea, UK.

Pirke, K. M., Pahl, J., Schweiger, U., & Warnhoff, M. (1985) Metabolic and endocrine indices of starvation in bulimia: A comparison with anorexia nervosa. *Psychiatry Research, 15,* 33–39.

Pope, H. G., Hudson, J. I, Jonas, J. M., & Yurgelon-Todd, D. (1983). Bulimia treated with imipramine: A placebo-controlled double-blind study. *American Journal of Psychiatry, 140,* 554–558.

Pope, H. G., Hudson, J. I., & Yurgelun-Todd, D. (1984). Anorexia nervosa and bulimia among 300 suburban women shoppers. *American Journal of Psychiatry, 141,* 292–294.

Pope, H. G., Keck P. E., McElroy S. L., & Hudson J. I. (1988). A placebo-controlled study of trazadone in bulimia nervosa. *Journal of Clinical Psychopharmacology, 9,* 254–259.

Price, L. H., Charney, D. S., Delgado, P. L., & Heninger, G. R. (1990). Lithium and serotonin function: Implications for the serotonin hypothesis of depression. *Psychopharmacology, 100,* 3–12.

Pyle, R. L., Mitchell, J. E., & Eckert, E. D. (1981). Bulimia: A report of 34 cases. *Journal of Clinical Psychiatry, 42,* 60–64.

Pyle, R. L., Mitchell, J. E., Eckert, E. D., Halvorson, P. A., Neuman, P. A., & Groff, G. M. (1983). The incidence of bulimia in freshmen college students. *International Journal of Eating Disorders, 2,* 75–85.

Pyle, R. L., Mitchell, J. E., Eckert, E. D., Hatsukami, D., Pomeroy, C., & Zimmerman, R. (1990). Maintenance treatment and 6-month outcome for bulimic patients who respond to initial treatment. *American Journal of Psychiatry 147,* 291–293.

Reiger, D. A., Farmer, M. E., Rae, D. S., Locke, B. Z., Keith, S. J., Judd, L. L., & Goodwin, F. K. (1990). Comorbidity of mental disorders with alcohol and other drug abuse. *Journal of the American Medical Association, 264,* 2511–2518.

Robinson, P. H., Checkley, S. A., & Russell, G. M. (1985). Suppression of eating by fenfluramine in patients with bulimia nervosa. *British Journal of Psychiatry, 146,* 169–176.

Rossiter, E. M., Agras, W. S., & Losch, M. (1988). Binge-eating episodes in bulimia nervosa: The amount and type of food consumed. *International Journal of Eating Disorders, 5*, 255–267.

Rossiter, E. M., Agras, W. S., Telch, C. F., & Schneider, J. A. (1993). Cluster B personality characteristics predict outcome in the treatment of bulimia nervosa. *International Journal of Eating Disorders, 13*, 349–357.

Rothenberg, A. (1988). Differential diagnosis of anorexia nervosa and depressive illness: A review of 11 studies. *Comprehensive Psychiatry, 29*, 427–432.

Roy, A., Adinoff, B., & Linnoila, M. (1988). Acting out hostility in normal volunteers: Negative correlation with levels of 5–HIAA in cerebrospinal fluid. *Psychiatry Research, 24*, 187–194.

Roy-Byrne, P., Gwirtsman, H. E., Edelstein, C. K., Yager, J., & Gerner, R. H. (1983). Response to "The Psychiatrist as Mind Sweeper": Eating disorders and antidepressants. *Journal of Clinical Psychopharmaoclogy, 3*, 60–61.

Russell, G. (1979). Bulimia nervosa: An ominous variant of anorexia nervosa. *Psychological Medicine, 9*, 429–448.

Russell, G. M., Checkley, S. A., Feldman, J., & Eisler, I. (1988). A controlled trial of d-fenfluramine in bulimia nervosa. *Clinical Neuropharmacology, 1*, S146–S159.

Sabine, E. J., Yonace, A., Farrington, A. J., Barratt, K. H., & Wakeling, A. (1983). Bulimia nervosa: A placebo-controlled, double-blind therapeutic trial of mianseren. *British Journal of Clinical Pharmacology, 15*, 195s–20s.

Schwartz, D. M., Barrett, M. J., & Saba, G. (1984). Family therapy for bulimia nervosa. In D. Garner & P. E. Garfinkel (Eds.), *Handbook of psychotherapy for anorexia nervosa and bulimia* (pp. 280–307). New York: Guilford.

Sellers, E. M., Higgins, G. A., & Sobell, M. B. (1992). 5-HT and alcohol abuse. *TiPS, 13*, 69–74.

Shor-Posner, G., Grinker, J. A., Marinescu, C., Brown, O., & Leibowitz, S. F. (1986). Hypothalamic serotonin in the control of meal patterns and macronutrient selection. *Brain Research Bulletin, 17*, 663–671.

Smith, N. J. (1980) Excessive weight loss and food aversion in athletes simulating anorexia nervosa. *Pediatrics, 66*, 139–142.

Stangler, R. S., & Printz, A. M. (1980). *DSM–III* psychiatric diagnosis in a university population. *American Journal of Psychiatry, 137*, 937.

Striegel-Moor, R. H., Silberstein, L. R., & Rodin, J. (1986). Toward an understanding of risk factors for bulimia. *American Psychologist, 41*, 246–263.

Strober, M. (1984). Stressful events associated with bulimia and anorexia nervosa: Empirical findings and theoretical speculations. *International Journal of Eating Disorders, 3*, 3–16.

Strober, M., & Katz, J. L. (1988). Depression in the eating disorders: A review and analysis of descriptive, family, and biological findings. In D. M. Garner & P. E. Garfinkel (Eds.), *Diagnostic issues in anorexia nervosa and bulimia nervosa* (pp. 80–111). New York: Brunner/Mazel.

Strober, M., Salkin, B., Burroughs, J., & Morrell, W. (1982). Validity of the bulimia-restrictor criteria in anorexia nervosa. *Journal of Nervous Mental Disease, 170*, 345–351.

Swift, W. J., Andrews, D., & Barklage, N. E. (1986). The relationship between affective disorder and eating disorders: A review of the literature. *American Journal of Psychiatry, 143*, 290–299.

Vandereycken, W. (1987). The management of patients with anorexia nervosa and bulimia nervosa: Basic principles and general guidelines. In E. P. Burrows & D. C. Casper (Eds.), *Handbook of eating disorders: Part 1. Anorexia and bulimia* (pp. 235–254). The Netherlands: Elsevier Science.

Vandereycken, W. (1990). The addiction model in eating disorders: Some critical remarks and a selected bibliography. *International Journal of Eating Disorders, 9*, 95–102.

Vanderlinden, J., & Vandereycken, W. (1988). Family therapy in bulimia nervosa. In D. Hardoff & E. Chigier (Eds.), *Eating disorders in adolescents and young adults* (pp. 325–334). London: Freund.

Vergnes, M., & Kempf, E. (1981). Tryptophan deprivation: Effects on mouse-killing and reactivity in the rat. *Psychopharm Aggress Social Behavior, 4*, 19–23.

Walters, J. K., Davis, M., & Sheard, M. H. (1979). Tryptophan-free diet: Effects on the acoustic startle reflex in rats. *Psychopharmacology, 62*, 103–109.

Walsh, B. T., Stewart, J.W., Roose, S. P., Gladis, M., & Glassman, A. H. (1984). Treatment of bulimia with phenelzine: A double-blind, placebo controlled study. *Archives of General Psychiatry, 41*, 1105–1109.

Walsh, B. T., Roose, S. P., Glassman, A. H., Gladis, M., & Sadik, C. (1985). Bulimia and depression. *Psychosomatic Medicine, 47*, 123–131.

Walsh, B. T., Gladis, M., Roose, S. P., Stewart, J. W., Stetner, F., & Glassman, A. H. (1988). Phenelzine vs. placebo in 50 patients with bulimia. *Archives of General Psychiatry, 45*, 471–475.

Walsh, B. T., Hadigan, C. M., Devlin, M. J., Gladis, M., & Roose, S. P. (1991). Long-term outcome of antidepressant treatment for bulimia nervosa. *American Journal of Psychiatry, 148,* 1206–1212.

Weiss, S. R., & Ebert, M. H. (1983). Psychological and behavioral characteristics of normal-weight bulimics and normal-weight controls. *Psychosomatic Medicine, 45,* 293–303.

Weltzin, T. E., Bulik, C. M., McConoha, C. W., & Kaye, W. H. (1995). Laxative withdrawal and anxiety in bulimia nervosa. *International Journal of Eating Disorders, 17,* 251–261.

Weltzin, T. E., Cameron, J., Berga, S., & Kaye, W. H. (1994). Prediction of reproductive status in women with bulimia nervosa by previous body weight. *American Journal of Psychiatry, 151,* 136–138.

Weltzin, T. E., Fernstrom, M., Fernstrom, J., Neuberger, S., & Kaye, W. H. (1996). Tryptophan depletion increases binge eating in bulimia nervosa. *American Journal of Psychiatry, 152,* 1668–1671.

Weltzin, T. E., Fernstrom, M. H., Hansen, D., McConaha, C., & Kaye, W. H. (1991). Abnormal caloric requirements for weight maintenance in patients with anorexia and bulimia nervosa. *American Journal of Psychiatry, 148,* 1675–1682.

Weltzin, T. E., Fernstrom, M. H., & Kaye, W. H. (1994). Serotonin and bulimia nervosa. *Nutrition Reviews, 52,* 399–408.

Weltzin, T. E., Hsu, L. G., Pollice, C., & Kaye, W. H. (1991). Feeding patterns of bulimia nervosa. *Biological Psychiatry, 30,* 1093–1110.

Wold, P. (1983). Trazodone in the treatment of bulimia. *Journal of Clinical Psychiatry, 44,* 275–276.

Wurtman, J. J., & Wurtman, R. J. (1979). Drugs that enhance central serotoninergic transmission diminish elective carbohydrate consumption by rats. *Life Science, 24,* 895–903.

Yates, A., Leehey, K., & Shisslak, C. M. (1983). Running as an anolog of anorexia. *New England Journal of Medicine, 308,* 251–255.

Young, S. N., Smith, S. E., Pihl, R. O., & Ervin, F. R. (1985). Tryptophan depletion causes a rapid lowering of mood in normal males. *Psychopharmacology, 87,* 173–177.

Young, S. N., Tourjman, S. V., Teff, K. L., Pihl, R. O., & Anderson, G. H. (1988). The effect of lowering plasma tryptophan on food selection in normal males. *Pharmacology Biochemistry and Behavior, 31,* 149–152.

Chapter 14

Parent Training

John R. Lutzker
University of Judaism, Bel Air, CA

Kim B. Huynen
Behavior Change Associates/Project Ecosystems, Anaheim, CA

Kathryn M. Bigelow
University of Kansas

Behavior modification was born in the mid-1960s. The first recipients of this new form of psychological treatment were children with autism and adults with mental retardation or schizophrenia (i.e., individuals with serious disorders). More successful outcomes with these individuals were shown than had previously been obtained. It soon became apparent that the procedures of this new field could be applied by mediators of treatment other than professionals. Thus, for example, psychiatric staff at mental institutions and teachers were taught to apply these novel treatment strategies. It then became apparent that parents could also be the mediators of behavior change with their children. Thus, parent training soon became a major subfield within behavior modification.

Variously labeled child behavior therapy, child behavior analysis, child behavior management, and child contingency management training, this chapter refers to this field merely as *parent training*, even though there are parent training programs that employ other strategies than the behavioral ones presented here. In part, this label is used because the bulk of parent training and certainly empirically examined parent training has been from a behavioral perspective.

Parent training has been used to treat numerous disorders, such as mealtime problems of children with cystic fibrosis (Stark, Powers, Jelalian, Rapee, & Miller, 1994), withdrawn children (Mokau & Manos, 1989), food refusal (Werle, Murphy, & Budd, 1993), sleep disturbance (France & Hudson, 1990), conduct disorder (Cooper, Wacker, Sasso, Reimers, & Donn, 1990), whining (Endo, Sloane, Hawkes, & Jenson, 1991), noncompliance (Richman, Hagopian, Harrison, Birk, Omerod, Brierley-Bowers, & Mann, 1994), mental retardation (Lowry & Whitman, 1989), child neglect (Feldman, Chase, & Sparks, 1992; Lutzker, 1992), language training (Feldman, Sparks, & Case, 1993), child abuse (MacMillan, Olson, & Hansen, 1991; Lutzker, 1992), autism (Cordisco, Strain, & Depew, 1988; Krantz, MacDuff, & McClannahan, 1993), and attention deficit hyperactivity disorder (ADHD; Anastopoulos, DuPaul, & Barkley, 1991; Erhardt & Baker, 1990; Horn, Ialongo, Greenberg, Packard, & Smith-Winberry, 1991).

In general, there have been three broad approaches to parent training. *Contingency management training* (CMT) has focused on teaching parents to apply consistent consequences and issue clear commands. Although used with a variety of behavioral disorders, the primary use of CMT has been with children who show serious deficits in instruction following (noncompliance) (Graziano & Diament, 1992).

More recently, two additional strategies to parent training have received attention; these are *planned activities training* (PAT) and *behavioral momentum* (Ducharme & Worling, 1994), or *errorless compliance training* (Durcharme & Popynick, 1993). PAT (Sanders & Dadds, 1982; Sanders, 1992) involves a focus on structuring antecedents to increase engagement in activities and prevent challenging child behavior, rather than simply focusing on consequences as with CMT. Behavioral momentum involves gradually fading in more complex and less probable instructions (commands). That is, at first, parents are taught to request behavior from their children to which instruction following is almost certain. Then, gradually, instructions are given that have had a lower probability of instruction following. Each of these approaches has shown considerable promise in parent training.

The focus of this manual is on PAT. The seminal research in this area was conduted with children with conduct disorder (Sanders & Dadds, 1982). It has also been successfully applied with children with developmental disabilities (Harrold, Lutzker, Campbell, & Touchette, 1992; Huynen, Lutzker, Bigelow, Touchette, & Campbell, 1996; Sanders & Plant, 1989) and with ADHD (Huynen et al., 1996).

PAT teaches parents that engagement, (i.e., the planning and structuring of activities with their children) acts to prevent challenging behaviors. PAT involves teaching parents time management, choosing activities, explaining activities and rules, incidental teaching, feedback, and reinforcement. It can be applied to children who have a range of behavioral disorders, and is strongly recommended for families as a preventive tool in everyday child management for children with no apparent disorders.

ASSESSMENT

A thorough assessment is an integral part of parent training and serves several purposes. First, it should allow for the comprehensive examination of the multifaceted factors present within families that influence parent and child behavior. Second, it should provide direction to the development of intervention programs. Finally, assessment should be conducted during, as well as following, intervention in order to evaluate the effects of treatment. Many of the instruments available to clinicians rely on parent report or consist of direct observation. When it is practical, direct observation is the most effective means of evaluating parent–child interactions. Results of parent report measures are, of course, subject to bias due to differences between actual child behavior and parents' perceptions of these behaviors. Further, assessment should be conducted in the natural environment in which the parent and child interact, which may include home and community settings. In-home observation and assessment is preferable to assessment conducted in analogue situations. The constraints inherent to applied settings, however, often preclude such involved and detailed methods. In these cases, parent report measures can still provide much of the information needed to assess behavior and evaluate the effects of treatment. Most importantly, however, the assessment process should be individualized for the family, representing members' specific concerns. In addition to existing assessment devises, use of a functional analysis is an essential element in individualized assessment. Functional analyses, which involve detailed questionnaires, direct observation, and manipulation of environmental variables, provide an understanding of the variables that influence and maintain challenging child behavior.

Several parent report measures for assessing parent report of child behavior problems are available. Two of the most common measures include the Child Behavior Checklist (CBCL; Achenbach & Edelbrock, 1983) and the Eyberg Child Behavior Inventory (ECBI; Eyberg & Ross, 1978). The CBCL (Achenbach & Edelbrock, 1983) consists of ratings of 118 items describing specific behavior problems in children age 2 to 16. The ECBI (Eyberg & Ross, 1978; Eyberg & Colvin, 1994) is a widely used rating scale that measures disruptive behaviors in children age 2 to 16. Furthermore, it is useful in determining whether parents' perceptions of child's behavior are within the range of "normal," and if their perceptions change following treatment (Webster-Stratton, 1988). Thirty-six common child behavior problems are rated on a 7-point scale for intensity. Parents are then asked to rate whether each behavior is a problem, providing a frequency score. Originally, normative data were available for samples of children and adolescents in the northwestern United States. These normative data have been restandardized to include populations in the southeastern United States (Eyberg & Colvin, 1994).

The Daily Child Behavior Checklist (DCBC; Furey & Forehand, 1988) is a 65-item checklist of pleasing and displeasing behaviors. The DCBC is designed to assess behavior problems in the home and requires fewer than 5 minutes to complete. Three scores are derived from the DCBC: the total number of pleasing behaviors, total number of displeasing behaviors, and total child behavior score derived by subtracting number of displeasing behaviors from number of pleasing behaviors. This instrument was developed because of weaknesses of other behavior checklists due to inconsistencies between child behavior and parent perception of such behavior. Items taken directly from several existing instruments, as well as items designed by the authors, are included in this inventory. Additionally, it uses objective terminology and emphasizes factual events rather than attitudes or perceptions.

An integral component to assessment in parent training is the evaluation of a parent's child behavior management skills. Again, observation of actual parent behavior can provide a more thorough indication of the skill level demonstrated by parents. The Home Simulation Assessment (HSA; MacMillan et al., 1991) can be used to assess parent behavior in simulated child management situations and measure the effects of training. An adult actor whose behavior is directed by a clinician observing behind a one-way mirror portrays deviant child behavior in an attempt to assess parents' abilities to apply child management skills. The HSA is especially appropriate for parents with children placed outside of home, and as an alternative to the observation of parents in actual situations (Macmillan, Olson, & Hansen. 1988).

The High-Deviance Home Simulation Assessment, which is an adaptation of and supplement to the Home Simulation Assessment, introduces more demanding child management situations by presenting an additional actor in the simulated situation or by increasing frequency of deviant behaviors displayed by the actor. In addition to coding parental response to child deviance, parent ratings of stress, anger, and anxiousness are collected. Differences between parent scores on the low demand and the high demand assessments may indicate a need for stress reduction or anger control training (MacMillan et al., 1991). Although direct observation is the most desirable method of assessing parent performance, it can often be difficult or unethical to assess child management skills in the home setting with children present. Analogue assessment allows for avoidance of exposure of children to aggression as well as efficiency in assessing specific parent responses to child behavior that may not be demonstrated in actual child management situations with observers present (MacMillan et al., 1991).

The Structured Observation System (Budd, 1988) evaluates parents' use of child management techniques for dealing with common behavior problems. Five brief structured activities are presented that involve specific cues that set the occasion for the assessed skills to be demonstrated. The skills assessed include giving and following through with instructions, differential social attention, use of a token system, teaching new skills, and use of timeout. This measure is applicable for families with children with mental or physical handicaps or without a diagnosis, and is most appropriate for children whose cognitive functioning is within the range of 2 to 5 years. This observational system, although providing a structured situation in which parents are asked to demonstrate their skills, allows for direct observation within the constraints of an applied setting.

The Parent Behavior Checklist (PBC; Fox, 1994), a 100-item questionnaire, can be used to identify parenting strengths and needs based on parents' report of their parenting strategies. The PBC is appropriate for parents of children age 1 to 4 years, and measures three aspects of parenting: developmental expectations, how parents respond to difficult child behaviors, and the strategies parents use to nurture and promote their child's psychological growth.

There are several direct observation measures that evaluate the qualitative and stimulating aspects of the interactions between parents and children utilizing direct observation procedures. Parent–child dyads are observed in semistructured situations, and specifically defined behaviors are observed and coded by a trained observer. S. Z. Lutzker, J. R. Lutzker, Braunling-McMorrow, and Eddleman (1987) measured the quality of affective behaviors demonstrated by parents toward their young children. Behaviors assessed included smiling, affectionate words, guided play, assuming the physical level of the child, affectionate touch, and eye contact. In a similar manner, the Dyadic Parent–Child Interaction Coding System (Eyberg & Robinson, 1981; Eyberg, Bessmer, Newcomb, Edwards, & Robinson, 1994) assesses several positive and negative parent and child behaviors. Some of the parent behaviors measured include commands, descriptive or reflective statements or questions, labeled praise, and critical statements. Child behaviors observed include whine, cry, yell, compliance, noncompliance, and destructive behavior. The Behavioral Coding System (Forehand & McMahon, 1981) assesses the appropriateness of parental antecedents, child behavior, and parental consequences.

In addition to the assessment of child behavior management skills, effectiveness of parents' skill level in teaching their children is also an area that can be assessed. The Training Proficiency Scale–Parent Version is a 13-item rating scale designed to assess parents' competence in using behavioral methods to teach various tasks to their children with developmental disabilities (Hudson, 1988). Items are scored on a 7-point scale and include gaining the child's attention, giving instructions, use of modeling, use of effective prompts, reinforcement contingent on appropriate responses, immediate reinforcement, enthusiastic reinforcement, making trials discrete, making tasks discrete, control of inappropriate responses, showing adequate patience, organizing teaching materials efficiently, and a global rating of teaching ability. This measure can be used to evaluate effectiveness of a parent training program (Hudson, 1988).

Assessment of parental stress and anger are often needed. The Parenting Stress Index (PSI; Abidin, 1986; Loyd & Abidin, 1985) was designed to screen and diagnose the magnitude of stress in the parent–child relationship that may increase the risk of dysfunctional parenting behaviors or behavior problems in the child. Parent characteristics, child characteristics, and other situations directly related to the role of being a parent are assessed (Abidin, 1986). Reliability of this measure has been demonstrated, supporting its use for both preliminary screening and for evaluating the effectiveness of intervention (Abidin, 1986). High scores on the child characteristics domain are often associated with children who display qualities contributing to the overall stress in the parent–child relationship. For parents of children with disabilities (hyperactivity, mental retardation, cerebral palsy, emotionally disturbed, learning disabilities), the child characteristics domain score is usually elevated above the parent characteristics domain (Loyd & Abidin, 1985). Additional research has supported the cross-cultural utility of a Spanish version of the PSI with Hispanic mothers (Solis & Abidin, 1991).

Self-reports of anger related to child behavior is also an area that should be assessed. The Novaco Anger Control Scale (NACS; Novaco, 1975) is a self-report measure designed to evaluate anger and arousal control problems. A brief description of anger provoking situations is presented to parents, who then rate the level of anger this situation would arouse on a 5-point scale. Examples of the situations presented include: "Noise and disorder at the dinner table," and "You are talking to someone and they do not answer you."

The Parental Anger Inventory (PAI; DeRoma & Hansen, 1994), previously known as the MacMillan–Olson–Hansen Anger Control Scale (MacMillan et al., 1988), assesses level of anger experienced by parents in response to difficult child behaviors. Parents are asked to rate 50 child-related situations as problematic or nonproblematic and then indicate the magnitude of anger elicited by each scenario using a 5-point scale. The PAI has been recommended for identifying anger control problems in parents and for evaluating treatment effects for anger reduction interventions.

Problem-solving and coping skills are additional areas that may need to be assessed. The Parent Problem-Solving Instrument is made up of 10 typical childrearing problems presented in the form of a story (Wasik, Bryant, & Fishbein, 1980, cited in Azar, Robinson, Hekimian, & Twentyman, 1984). After the beginning and end of each story is read, parents are asked to provide the middle, which is the solution to the problem. The Parental Problem-Solving Measure (Hansen, Palotta, Tishelman, Conaway, & MacMillan, 1989) evaluates problem-solving abilities in child and nonchild-related situations. This measure is administered by reading problematic situations to the parent and then asking the parent to imagine being in that situation and to "Tell me all of the things you could do to solve the problem, and what you would do." Responses are rated for the number of solutions generated and the effectiveness of the best solutions on a 7-point scale. Two versions have been evaluated: a 25-item version (Hansen et al., 1989) and a 15-item version (Palotta, Conaway, Christopher, & Hansen, 1989).

Wahler (1980) described the lack of social and emotional support and high frequency of negative interactions and contacts as insularity. The extent to which a parent experiences this can be assessed by several measures, such as the Interpersonal Support Evaluation List (Cohen, Mermelstein, Kamarck, & Hoberman, 1985), the Community Interaction Checklist (Wahler, Leske, & Rogers, 1979, as cited in Cerezo, 1988), the 20-Item Network Orientation Scale, and the Perceived Social Support Questionnaire (Procidano & Heller, 1983).

Whereas standardized observation systems and questionnaires can provide valuable information about a variety of relevant factors, a functional analysis allows for an individualized assessment that evaluates the specific function a target behavior fulfills for an individual. By identifying the function of challenging behaviors, interventions can be designed to teach more appropriate and functional alternatives to the undesirable behavior. O'Neill, Horner, Albin, Storey, and Sprague (1990) described three main outcomes that may be derived from a functional assessment: an operational description of the undesirable behavior, a prediction of the times and situations when the undesirable behavior is likely to occur and not occur across a variety of activities, and a description of the function that the undesirable behavior fulfills for the individual.

According to O'Neill et al. (1990), an effective and thorough functional assessment consists of three elements (see Table 14.1). The first is to conduct an interview of the individuals who have frequent contact with the target child or problem. This may include the child, parents, grandparents, teachers, or babysitters, and can serve to identify and define the variables that may be influencing the target behavior. A form designed by O'Neill et al. (1990) provides a format for this interview. Parents are asked to describe the topography, frequency, duration, and intensity of each behavior. Additional variables, such as medications, sleep, diet, communication, activities, and physical settings are evaluated in relation to the target behavior.

The second strategy involves direct observation and the collection of data, and is an essential step in this process. This observation may be conducted by individuals who often interact with the child, and should be done in a simple and time-saving manner. The third strategy involves manipulation of the variables that may be influencing the target behavior, and the observation of the effects of these manipulations on behavior. For instance, if from an interview with the parents and teacher of a child it is found that the child is likely to tantrum when asked to complete certain tasks, this behavior may be observed at various times throughout the day when demands are placed (such as mealtime, bedtime, or after playtime). After data on occurrence and intensity of tantrums have been collected, situations can be manipulated in order to test predictability of this behavior. Various situational factors are presented or changed in order to observe their effects on behavior. This may involve varying level of demands, providing different materials and/or activities, providing different amounts of attention, or leaving the person alone or without attention for varying lengths of time. This process can be difficult and time consuming, but it may be the most effective way to identify the function of the target behavior. Further, in order to develop effective intervention plans, this information is invaluable in teaching functional alternatives to the target behavior (O'Neill et al., 1990).

TABLE 14.1

Three Elements of a Functional Assessment

Strategy	Process	Outcome
Interview	Obtain information about topography, frequency, duration, intensity, and predictability of the target behavior and of the various ecological event that may influence the target behavior through structured interview.	Provides a description of the target behavior and identifies and narrows the range of potential variables that may influence the target behavior.
Direct Observation	Base on interview results, the target behavior is observed and data collected across settings, activities, and times of day. Data should be collected for a minimum of 2 to 5 days.	Provides an actual frequency count of the behavior and information about the times of day, settings, or situations in which the behavior is occurring, and the consequences in effect.
Systematic Manipulations	Various environmental events or situations are repeatedly presented, withdrawn, or changed in order to evaluate the effects of these changes on behavior. Manipulations may include changes in demands, requests, attention, or activities.	Identification of the function of the target behavior. Hypotheses about the variables that are maintaining the target behavior are confirmed or rejected. It may be determined that behavior is maintained by attention, avoidance, stimulation, or access to objects or activities.

Note: From O'Neill, Horner, Albin, Storey, and Sprague (1990).

PLANNED ACTIVITIES TRAINING

Planned Activities Training (PAT) involves six sessions with a family; one session involves assessment and five involve training. The assessment session involves completion of the Problem Setting Questionnaire and a Functional Assessment Questionnaire. During the first session of training, PAT is described and the parent is provided with handouts on PAT, incidental teaching, rule discussions, and minimal prompting. During the second training session, the counselor reviews one home and one community checklist by teaching the parent how to use them during daily activities. During the third training session, a checklist explaining how to structure the environment to teach children to play alone is presented and practiced. During Session 4, the counselor and parent practice the checklist for independent play again, and then are provided with a checklist for getting ready to go out. In Session 5, parents demonstrate PAT to the counselor during a play activity and are asked to evaluate thier own performance.

Assessment Session

The assessment session is an opportunity for the counselor to gather information about the child's behavior and the family. It is also an opportunity for observation of the family and interactions between the parents and child. The counselor must use active listening, reflection, and questions to collect information and develop a working alliance with the family. Active listening involves the counselor using comments and body language that convey listening and empathy to the family. Reflection and empathy involve the counselor acting like a mirror and informing the family what was seen and heard and letting family members know they are understood and accepted. It is important for the counselor to take a position of wanting to work with the family and not act as an expert with all of the answers. This allows the family to be open with the counselor and to begin to learn how to problem solve and feel confident in finding its own answers rather than developing a dependence on the counselor. Asking questions, in a way to gain information, but by using open questions the counselor can also encourage the family to find its own answers. For example, if the family asks what to do when the child tantrums at the grocery store, the counselor can reflect and show empathy by saying, "It can be embarrassing when a child makes a scene in a public place. Many parents report that this is difficult for them. What do you do now?" When the family answers, the counselor can then ask how members feel about what they do now and what friends of theirs do, or what the family has seen other families do. By using this approach, the counselor gains valuable information about the social ecology of the family and its values. The counselor is thus also modeling to the family how to find an intervention for the grocery store that is effective and that is comfortable for that family. This is all critical to an effective intervention.

During the assessment session:

1. Negotiate an Agenda. On arriving at the family's home the counselor greets the parents and child and outlines the activities of the session by explaining that together they will complete a questionnaire, answer several other questions about the child's behavior, and then engage in a play activity with the child. The counselor then emphasizes to parents that the purpose of the first session is to gather information. Parents are asked if they have any questions. Then, the counselor helps engage the child in an independent activity and begins to complete the questionnaire and functional assessment with the parents. It is easier to complete paperwork if

the counselor can arrange to have the first session when the child is not at home so that some private time with parents is possible. Then when the child arrives home, observation of parents and child can be accomplished.

2. Problem Setting Questionnaire. (See later section "Handouts and Assessment Tools Used During the Assessment Session".) The counselor walks through the questions of the problem setting questionnaire with parents in order to gather information about the child's behavior during specific activities.

3. Functional Assessment. The counselor asks questions from the functional assessment handout in order to gather complete information about challenging behaviors. The counselor and parents operationally define challenging behaviors, such as aggression, tantrums, and self-injury. Good operational definitions make the accurate monitoring of progress possible for the family. When a family can track its own progress, the intervention will be more successful. Then, the counselor needs to collect information on the frequency of each challenging behavior, the time of day they occur, if they occur in a chain, under what conditions they are most common, and under what conditions they are least common. The counselor also collects information about medications, diet, sleeping patterns, and daily schedules. Through this assessment, parents begin to understand how to ask questions about challenging behaviors of their children and that they need to look at the entire picture when creating interventions.

4. Observation of Play. The counselor observes the parents and children during a play activity and collects data on their use of PAT, interaction skills of the parents, and behavior of the child. For example, the family may sit down to build with plastic blocks and the counselor will record if the mother explains the activity, uses incidental teaching, interacts with the child at his/her eye level, gives clear instructions, and uses praise. The counselor also records how the child behaves during the observation, noting compliance, language, and any challenging behaviors. This direct observation is used as baseline.

5. Response to PAT. The counselor then plays with the child and records data on the challenging behavior of that child in response to PAT. Noted are any changes in the child's behavior, such as an increase in language, instruction following, or a decrease in challenging behaviors in response to activity explanations, rule discussions, and incidental teaching used by the counselor.

6. Summary. The counselor explains that the purpose of the session was to gather information on the challenging behaviors of the child through use of a questionnaire, structured questions, and direct observation. The counselor then answers any questions the parents may have. Many parents want to know what will happen next and what they should do until the next session. The counselor needs to explain that further evaluation of information collected needs to occur prior to designing an intervention, and that parents should continue doing what they have found successful to this point. Counselors should avoid the temptation to provide parents with interventions at this point because it will undermine the effects of PAT, which involves teaching parents to create their own interventions. The counselor provides the parents with a daily data sheet and explains that tracking challenging behaviors and goals will allow the family to monitor the success of intervention. The counselor then schedules the next session.

PAT Intervention Sessions

The following outline is the training procedure for PAT. Each session is outlined in detail so that a counselor with training, supervision, and practice can use it to provide PAT to a family. The PAT intervention sessions focus on practicing interaction skills in the family's home and in community settings such as bath time, bed time, the grocery store, and play. Session 1 is a general overview of PAT, and Sessions 2 to 5 are practice sessions. Parents learn to use PAT skills during actual activities and learn to evaluate the behavior of their children in relation to their own behavior. The modeling and practicing of the checklists is critical. Each checklist presented should be modeled and rehearsed, and additional information specific to that family should be added to the checklist. Each step of the checklist needs to be individual for each family. On the mealtime checklist, mealtime rules should be written, and consequences and reinforcers decided and written in advance. Specific wording on prompts for coming to the table, and exactly what needs to be on the table prior to the child coming should be written in as well. These additions make the checklist individual and help the parents with follow-through.

Session I

I. Negotiate an agenda. When the counselor arrives, the parent and child are greeted, and an outline of what will occur during the session is presented. The counselor explains that first they will review progress together and they will identify situations where problems are most prevalent. Then, the counselor explains that PAT will be introduced and that several sessions will be needed to review this procedure. The counselor explains that PAT is tailored to the needs of the family and together the counselor and parents will modify the procedure to fit the family.

II. Review Progress

1. Invite parents to comment on how they view progress. The counselor asks them for the data they have collected and then reviews what they see. If there is a decrease in challenging behaviors, then ask about changes in routine or intervention. For example, if the child is hitting others only twice a week now and during baseline was hitting five times a week, then maybe an intervention the family is using has been effective. If there is an increase in challenging behaviors show empathy with the family about how difficult it is to have a child continue to demonstrate challenging behaviors at such a high frequency. If that same child is now hitting others 10 times a week, then maybe there are added stressors, and the family is probably frustrated and exhausted.
2. Prompt the parents to identify any positive or negative changes in their child's behavior.

III. Identify Problem Settings

1. Again, examine data with the family and identify times when challenging behaviors occur at the highest frequency and times when the challenging behaviors do not occur. This provides critical information on which activities are most difficult for the family.
2. Refer to the Problem Setting Questionnaire for more information about settings in which challenging behaviors occur.
3. Ask parents for their opinion as to why they experience these difficulties and what efforts they have made to manage the challenging behaviors they have reported.
4. Rank order the settings from least to most problematic.

IV. Provide Rationale for Planned Activities Training

    1. Mention that you will now begin to discuss ways of dealing with children's behavior in the settings mentioned.

    2. Outline the basic concepts underlying PAT:

        a. Prevention of challenging behavior is the goal. If parents can arrange the environment so that challenging behaviors do not occur, then they do not have to worry about how to deal with such challenging behaviors.

        b. Encouraging children to be involved in activities reduces the opportunity to misbehave and teaches skills. Children who are actively engaged in appropriate tasks are much less likely to display challenging behavior.

V. How to Prepare for Situations by Organizing and Managing Time More Effectively

    1. Discuss issues related to organizing time and avoiding last minute rushing and panic situations. Invite the parent to identify changes in schedule so that time would be available to hold a discussion with the child prior to particular activities.

    2. Parents are reinforced naturally for planning ahead to avoid problems. One family found that if it had a backpack near the door containing sunglasses, sunscreen, a water bottle, extra clothes, babywipes, a small towel, and a few toys, then the mother was able to pick up the bag and go without having to take the time to get supplies ready. The mother said that with her "go out bag" she felt that leaving the home more much smoothly.

VI. How to Discuss Rules Regarding Desired and Undesired Behavior in a Relaxed and Noncoercive Manner

    1. The counselor models appropriate discussion skills that involve the child in the establishment of a rule.

    2. The counselor asks parents what was noticed about the interaction and prompts parents to observe that the counselor was at the child's eye level, gave the child choices, explained the importance of the rule, and discussed it in a positive way. The counselor then prompts the parent to identify the impact of using these skills on the behavior of the child. For example, the child may talk more, follow directions faster, or play longer.

    3. The parent role plays the discussion.

    4. The counselor provides feedback to the parent.

VII. How to Select Activities for Children in Specific Home and Community Settings

    1. Introduce the concept of engagement; when children are busy they are less disruptive.

    2. The counselor provides examples of activities that can be used when in the car, shopping, and visiting. (See the activity lists attached to the parent handouts.)

    3. Parents then add other activities to the list. This may include holiday traditions or special community activities.

VIII. How to Encourage and Extend Children's Engagement in Activities by Use of Incidental Teaching: Handouts are included at the end of Session 1.

   1. Having activities available is no guarantee children will play with them. The goal of incidental teaching is to make interaction with toys and tasks more reinforcing for the child.
   2. The counselor introduces incidental teaching as a way of increasing the child's interest in an activity.
   3. Counselor demonstrates incidental teaching by engaging the children in a discussion about the activity in which they are engaged at the time. If the children are coloring, counselors may ask them what they are making, or counselors may ask to participate by drawing too and then talk out loud about what they are making and what shape and color it is. This will encourage the children to ask questions or make comments. When the children do this, counselors can creatively add to the conversation by following children's interest and adding other information or posing questions.
   4. The parent is prompted to comment on interaction skills displayed by the counselor, the questions used, the answers given, and how the counselor used what was interesting to the child.
   5. The parent role plays by using incidental teaching. Feedback is provided to the parent by the counselor.
   6. Novelty is discussed. Parents are encouraged to introduce a new activity before the child becomes bored with the old one and to reinforce the child's engagement with attention.

IX. How to Select and Apply Practical Procedures for Motivating Children's Behavior in Different Settings

   1. The counselor prompts the parent to identify potential natural or tangible reinforcers.

X. Practical Consequences: Consequences are not a primary focus of PAT. The idea is that if the environment is arranged and skill building is occurring, then artificial consequences are less relevant. Rather, when challenging behaviors occur, parents can problem solve about how to prevent them in the future. Still, parents feel more confident if they know what to do if challenging behaviors do occur.

   1. Ignoring and using terminating instructions are discussed, modeled, and practiced briefly. This may include the instruction to "Stop" or "Listen," or to comment on something else in the environment. If a child is going into the street, the parent can say "Stop" and then direct the child to play ball on the front lawn, and praise the child for playing.
   2. Parents are prompted to use these and to maintain their current method of handling problems.

XI. Discussions With Children Following Activity

   1. The counselor models how to hold a discussion with the child following an activity and to provide constructive feedback on desirable and less desirable behavior.

2. Parents are asked to comment on the interaction and discussion skills they observed the counselor using.

3. The parent practices having a discusssion with the child at the end of an activity and feedback is provided by the counselor.

XII. Summary. Here, the counselor answers questions and provides parents with the summary of the PAT handout, the handout on Incidental Teaching, the handout on Minimal Prompting, and the handout on Rule Discussions. The counselor tells the parents to read each handout and begin to use these skills in play settings. Sometimes the counselor needs to help the parents. Practice the procedures during play and continue to take data without jumping ahead and doing more. The counselor works with the parent to schedule the next session at a convenient time.

Session II

I. First, sit down with the family and outline the session by explaining that homework will be discussed and two checklists will be modeled.

II. Review the homework with parents by asking if they read the handouts on Summary of PAT, Ask Say Do, Incidental Teaching, and Rule Discussions. Then answer any questions they may have. Ask parents to describe a play setting in which they tried some of the skills and how that went.

III. Model Use of a Procedural Checklist:

1. Select one home setting checklist from the handouts provided later. In order to provide an opportunity for success before trying more difficult settings, select a setting in which the parents experience mild difficulty.

2. Give the parent the procedural checklist for that setting and discuss each step relating it to incidental teaching. Be sure to write on the checklist the information specific to the family. Include what supplies the family needs to have ready in advance, what the rules will be for the child, what the reinforcement will be, and how disruptions will be handled. Be sure to answer any questions the parent may have and explain that similar checklists are available and will be used later.

IV. Model a Checklist for a Community Setting:

1. Select a community setting where parents experience mild difficulty.

2. Give the parents the procedural checklist for that setting and discuss each step, relating it to their child. Again, write in the information specific to that family, including specific rules and reinforcements. Answer any questions the family may have and explain that similar checklists are available and will be used later.

V. Establish Goals:

1. Ask parents to implement the procedure in the home and community setting you discussed in the meeting and to record use of each step on the checklist for discussion next week.

VI. Remember to summarize the main points of the session by discussing each checklist. Answer any questions and schedule the next appointment.

Session III

I. First, sit down with the family and outline the session. Explain that in this session you will practice engaging the child in an activity while the counselor and parents talk. Practice incidental teaching and then set homework goals together.

II. Show the parents the checklist for Encouraging Independent Play When Busy. Explain to parents that you would like to practice this checklist together.

1. Prompt parents to identify ground rules and explain them to the child. Help the parent engage the child in an activity close by while you talk to them about how the week went.
2. Cue parents to interrupt their conversation with the counselor to praise the child.
3. After a few minutes, have parents provide the child with behavioral feedback and reinforcement. Prompt parents to review the checklist for encouraging independent play and evaluate use of each step.
4. Prompt the parent to identify solutions to problems encountered.
5. Give parents feedback on their use of procedures.

III. Introduce a general PAT checklist and then practice Incidental Teaching and Structured Play.

1. Ask parents to set the child up in a new activity by getting the supplies ready and explaining the rules to child.
2. Briefly review incidental teaching strategies for extending play, language, and involvement in the activity.
3. Ask parents to use incidental teaching to extend play while you observe for 5 to 15 minutes. Tell parents you are going to watch and record some examples of interaction skills and incidental teaching that can be discussed after observation.
4. Begin the observation and make notes of specific examples of interaction that are correct and incorrect. Try to focus on positive examples. If parents need assistance during play or are having difficulty using incidental teaching, begin to model the skill with specific examples by asking parents to try and join in the activity. Have the parents end the session by providing reinforcement and feedback to the child.

IV. Feedback:

1. Prompt parents to review their performance during the observation.
2. Reinforce correct identification of their strengths and weaknesses.
3. Prompt parents to identify two things they thought they could have done differently.
4. Identify specific steps in incidental teaching parents wish to improve.
5. Summarize the parents; report in steps 2–4. For example: "You feel confident at explaining the rules, and leveling, but you also are having some difficulty with incidental teaching. You seem to talk about what you notice and not what your child is interested in. It is a great idea for you to practice observing your child's interests and commenting on only those items."

V. Establish goals to practice encouraging independent play when busy and one community activity. Give parents the checklist for Encouraging Independent Play and one community checklist. Ask parents to practice the two handouts at least once prior to the next appointment.

Session IV

I. First, sit down with the family and outline the session. Explain that in this session you will practice engaging the child in activity while you talk about the checklists tried last week. Practice incidental teaching and practice getting ready to go out.

II. Practice the Encouraging Independent Play When Busy Checklist: Ask parents to engage the child in an activity using the checklist while the two of you review progress. Prompt parents to explain ground rules to child. Cue parents to interrupt their conversation with the counselor to praise the child. Ask parents to review their use of the checklists selected last week. Have a brief discussion while the child plays. Prompt parents to review child's behavior, and use of PAT. Prompt parents to identify solutions to problems encountered. Give parents feedback on their use of procedures.

III. Practice the Getting Ready to Go Out Checklist: Schedule a shopping trip for the end of the session so that the counselor and parents can practice together. Review the checklist with the parent. Cue the parents to prepare the child in advance by discussing the rules and to follow the checklist. Observe parents as they complete the steps on the Getting Ready to Go Out Checklist. Make notes of how they discuss the rules, how they use interaction skills, and what reinforcers they use.

IV. Feedback: Give parents brief feedback while trying to avoid having the child wait.

V. Goals: Give parents the handout on Getting Ready to Go Out and ask them to practice again during the next week. Ask them to again practice the home and community setting selected the prior week.

Session V

I. Sit down with the family and review progress. Practice using PAT skills with minimal counselor help. Develop problem-solving strategies to handle future problems, and discuss self-management skills parents can use. This may include creating new checklists, posting checklists or rules as reminders, or even taking some breaks alone to make time with the children more productive.

II. Review Progress: Talk to the parents about their feelings of progress in the use of the checklists, and answer any questions they may have.

III. Practice PAT with minimal assistance: Ask parents to interact with the child for 15 minutes while you observe and take note of the parent's discussion skills, incidental teaching, and interaction skills. Also write down specific examples and note how the child responded.

IV. Self-Evaluation: Ask parents to evaluate their own performance. Try using open-ended questions to prompt them to identify what they did well and what specifically they could have done differently. Prompt parents to summarize and write down goals for future practice. For example, if parents have difficulty stating rules positively, or observing the child and asking specfic questions, then the parents can commit to work on these goals.

V. Independent Future Problem Solving: Review with parents the basic steps for designing a PAT intervention checklist and prompt them to identify one remaining problem setting and one possible future problem setting. Give parents a blank behavior checklist and help them to design an intervention for this setting. Ask parents to implement the program for the checklist they have developed.

VI. Goals: Ask parents to review all handouts and to continue to practice the PAT checklists. Summarize the key PAT steps and the progress the parents have made implementing the steps. Remind parents that using the PAT steps will help to decrease children's problem behaviors.

Clinical Accounts

The Brown family was referred for assistance because the 3-year-old daughter, Lucy, displayed temper tantrums and refused to eat at the table. The functional assessment revealed that tantrums occurred primarily during mealtime, showers, and at the grocery store. An observation of Lucy taking a shower was conducted. The mother, Carol, went to Lucy and picked her up without warning and took her into the bathroom while telling her it was time for a shower. She later reported that she had to do this or the child would run away. Lucy screamed when in the bathroom and Carol told her to stop yelling and undressed her. Lucy continued to scream and pull away. Carol put her in the shower and turned on the water. Lucy continued to scream and pull away. Carol washed her hair and took her out of the shower. Lucy continued to scream while dressing and then sat on her mother's lap, sniffling for the next 20 minutes. The counselor showed empathy for Carol about how difficult it must be for her to shower Lucy daily when such challenging behavior occurred each instance. Carol reported that she had tried everything and did not know what to do. The counselor informed Carol about PAT and asked if together they could start the program with Lucy the following week. Carol reported that she would try anything.

In the subsequent 5 weeks, PAT was completed with Carol and Lucy. Carol learned how to use the procedures while Lucy was in the car, when Carol was on the phone, and while at the park. During training, the counselor demonstrated how to use incidental teaching and rule discussions to explain and involve Lucy in the activity. After PAT, the counselor observed shower time again. This time Carol sat down and explained to Lucy that she was going to take a shower in a few minutes. Lucy said she wanted to color one more picture. Carol joined her in coloring the picture and reminded her that when she was done she was going to take a shower. Lucy finished the picture and then they walked into the bathroom together. Once in the bathroom, Lucy started to cry and said she did not want to take a shower. Carol bent down and said she understood her, but that she had to wash her hair because it was very dirty. Lucy stopped crying and took off her clothes. Carol explained that she would wash her hair quickly and that she had to stay calm and help by washing her body. Lucy got into the shower and Carol began asking her questions about some animal stickers on the shower wall. During the next 10 minutes they discussed all the animals and what sounds they made while her hair was washed. She got out of the shower and dressed with no crying.

The Smith family was referred because they could not take their 6-year-old son, Matt, to the grocery store. Matt was diagnosed with autism. He would want to buy an item in the store, and would perseverate on that item until his mother bought it for him or had to leave the store. During an assessment observation, Matt and his mother, Natalie, went to the grocery store. She took Matt into the store and then went down every aisle in the store looking for items she needed. Down each row Matt would also look at the items and then would pick something up and say he wanted her to buy that item. Natalie would say no and tell him to put the item back on the shelf. A few times he followed his mother's direction. Then they came to the breakfast cereal and he wanted a box of "Captain Crunch." Natalie told him no and asked him to put it back. He said he wanted it and began to yell. She yelled at him to put the item back on the shelf. He continued to yell and she took the item and put it back. Natalie then went to the checkout and paid for her items while Matt continued to yell. She told him if he would quiet down she would get the cereal. He became quiet and she purchased the cereal. After the trip, she reported that she did not want to buy the cereal, but did not know how to get him to stop crying.

PAT was conducted with the family during play, meals, and while in the car. After training, another observation was conducted at the grocery store. Before entering the store, Natalie showed a list of items to Matt. She explained that she had to buy these five items and that if he could help her find them, left all the items on the shelf, and used his "inside voice," then he could buy one item for himself. She then gave him a choice of which items he could buy and asked him to choose. He wanted to purchase "Skittles." They then went into the store, and Natalie read the first item on her list; they went looking together for the item. Matt pointed to it and Natalie put it in the basket. He pointed at an item he wanted. She looked and said "yes, that does look very good, but it is not on our list. The next thing we need is eggs," and they went looking for the eggs. When they got the last item she said, "Now you helped me, you left all the items on the shelf, and you used your inside voice so you can get some Skittles." After the trip, Natalie reported that she was gradually making her list longer as Matt got better at helping her find items.

The Gonzales family was referred because they could not go out in public with their 3-year-old son, Jorge, who was diagnosed with autism. His mother, Trina, also had a 12-month-old son. During an assessment observation, counselors accompanied Trina, Jorge, and his brother to the video store. Jorge got out of the car while Trina was trying to get the baby out. Trina somehow held Jorge and the baby, too. Jorge stood at the door of the video store having a tantrum for candy while Trina returned the video. She then took his hand and dragged him back to the car while he yelled.

PAT was conducted during play time and during several activities at home. A follow-up observation was conducted at the video store. When the car pulled into the parking space Jorge said, "Mom, what are the rules at the video store?" Trina said, "What are the rules, Jorge?" Jorge said, "Use my words, and look for letters, and get candy after we're done." Trina said, "that's right," and they went into the store. At the door Trina said, "I am going to return this video, you can look for letters," and then she pointed to a rack and said, "What letter do you see there?" Jorge said, "I see T...TTTT." Trina said, "That's right!! I see J, J for Jorge. You find some more and I will be right back." Jorge continued to look at the rack. Trina returned and said, "What else did you find?" Jorge said, "M." Trina said, "M for mom, and you did great. Would you like some candy?" Jorge picked a yellow candy and they walked to the car. At the car Trina said, "You did a great job looking for letters and using your words."

The Yeng family was referred for services for their 3-year-old daughter, Tram, because she refused to eat food during mealtime. A functional assessment revealed that force feeding had been used during physical therapy when Tram was 6 months old. She had learned to associate eating solid food with an aversive situation. During baseline observations, Mrs. Yeng would carry Tram to the table screaming and yelling while trying to get her to sit. She strapped her in a high chair and Tram continued to try to get up. When food was placed in front of her she closed her mouth and refused to eat. Her mother tried feeding her, but Tram gagged and turned away. After 10 minutes, Mrs. Yeng removed Tram from the table and gave her a bottle.

A combination of PAT and behavioral momentum was used with Tram. Intervention started by training Mrs. Yeng to use a PAT checklist during play with toy dishes. Training then progressed to toy food, and then to cooking food. As Tram became comfortable playing with food and tasting food during play (behavioral momentum), PAT was conducted during mealtime. Tram learned that she could refuse food calmly, but that if she sat at the table with her family she could gain access to a walk to the park, which was something she clearly enjoyed. As Tram began to sit at the table with her family during more meals, they engaged in conversations and incidental teaching about the food present. Tram also began to help with the cooking and clean-up. As her parents focused on PAT and creating a positive eating environment, Tram began to taste food and to gradually eat more solid food. During an observation made 6 months after initial training, Tram sat at the table during a meal and ate a few bites of cantaloupe and some macaroni and cheese. Her parents still wanted her to eat more food, but felt positive that she was gradually improving and would continue to do so with the PAT.

HANDOUTS AND ASSESSMENT TOOLS USED DURING THE ASSESSMENT SESSION

Problem Setting Questionnaire

This questionnaire includes two sections: the home problem checklist (Table 14.2) and the community problem checklist (Table 14.3).

Planned Activity Parent Handouts for Training Session I

Handouts for the first training session include the Planned Activity Training General Handout, Planned Activity Rule Discussions, Guidelines for Incidental Teaching, Minimal Prompting, and Activity List.

Planned Activity Training General Handout

The following information has been found useful in teaching and reminding adults about the important components involved when interacting with children. When conducting activities with children it is important to manage time, be aware of high-risk situations such as times when you are busy with other things, explain the activities and the rules, involve yourself and the children in activities, use incidental teaching, provide reinforcement, and let the children know how they have done.

TABLE 14.2

Home Problem Checklist

MORNING	1	2	3	4	5
Getting out of bed	1	2	3	4	5
Getting dressed	1	2	3	4	5
Brushing teeth	1	2	3	4	5
Brushing hair	1	2	3	4	5
Using toilet	1	2	3	4	5
Preparing breakfast	1	2	3	4	5
Breakfast	1	2	3	4	5
Getting ready to leave	1	2	3	4	5
Inside play	1	2	3	4	5
Outside play	1	2	3	4	5
Telephone rings	1	2	3	4	5
Independent play	1	2	3	4	5
AFTERNOON	1	2	3	4	5
When you are preparing lunch	1	2	3	4	5
Lunch time	1	2	3	4	5
Using toilet	1	2	3	4	5
Getting ready to leave	1	2	3	4	5
When you are busy	1	2	3	4	5
When visitors arrive	1	2	3	4	5
Play inside	1	2	3	4	5
Play outside	1	2	3	4	5
Telephone rings	1	2	3	4	5
Nap time	1	2	3	4	5
Snack time	1	2	3	4	5
When siblings arrive home	1	2	3	4	5
Pick-up from daycare	1	2	3	4	5
EVENINGS	1	2	3	4	5
When you return from work	1	2	3	4	5
While preparing dinner	1	2	3	4	5
Dinner	1	2	3	4	5
Toileting	1	2	3	4	5
Bath time	1	2	3	4	5
Undressing	1	2	3	4	5
Bedtime	1	2	3	4	5
Play with siblings	1	2	3	4	5
Play with parents	1	2	3	4	5
Sleeping	1	2	3	4	5
Other:	1	2	3	4	5

Indicate the extent that this activity is difficult for you and your child. A "1" indicates activity is Okay as is and no changes are needed; "2" indicates that the activity is sometimes difficult; "3" indicates that the activity is often difficult and some change is needed; "4" indicates that the activity is usually difficult and change is needed; "5" indicates that the activity is always difficult and needs great improvement.

Rationale. Many problem behaviors can be avoided completely if adults take steps to ensure that children have interesting and engaging activities available. Bored children are often disruptive. A parent who understands this has activities available for children at all times, and has frequent interactions with the children. Consider the following rules:

TABLE 14.3
Community Problem Checklist

Visiting friends with children	1	2	3	4	5
Visiting friends without children	1	2	3	4	5
Grandparents' house	1	2	3	4	5
Birthday parties	1	2	3	4	5
Weddings	1	2	3	4	5
Holiday parties	1	2	3	4	5
Daycare	1	2	3	4	5
Grocery store	1	2	3	4	5
Mall	1	2	3	4	5
Clothing store	1	2	3	4	5
Bank	1	2	3	4	5
Video store	1	2	3	4	5
Doctor	1	2	3	4	5
Dentist	1	2	3	4	5
Haircuts	1	2	3	4	5
Restaurant–fast food	1	2	3	4	5
Restaurant–sit down	1	2	3	4	5
Travel in parents' car	1	2	3	4	5
Travel in others' car	1	2	3	4	5
Public transport	1	2	3	4	5
Airplane	1	2	3	4	5
Sleep-over	1	2	3	4	5
Other	1	2	3	4	5

Teach adults how to manage children's behavior in specific settings.
It is better to prevent children from misbehaving than to wait until they display inappropriate behavior and then have to institute a consequence.
Children are less likely to misbehave if they are busy in an activity.

Manage Time.   It is possible to keep things moving on track and to avoid problem behavior with the following steps:

Plan your day ahead of time.
Schedule activities so that you plan time to speak with children before and after an activity. To avoid having children wait, make sure you have all the supplies you need before that activity.
You will be reinforced for planning ahead by better child behavior and fewer disruptions.

Pinpoint High-Risk Situations.   Think of situations where children have displayed challenging behavior in the past because there was little for them to do (e.g., shopping trips, traveling in the car, waiting, nap time, mealtime). Then, plan to involve yourself and the children more during these activities to prevent further problems.

Discuss Rules With Children in a Relaxed Manner.   Always try to explain to children what is happening next and what the rules are for the activity. It is helpful to follow these rules:

Explain what the activity is.

Tell the child the rule and explain why. (Try to put rules in the positive: "Don't touch" becomes "keep your hands to yourself." "Don't run" becomes "please walk." "Don't stand on furniture" becomes "please keep you feet on the floor, or your bottom on the chair." "Don't throw crayons" becomes, "please keep the crayons in your hand and on the table.")

Tell the child the consequence of breaking rules. "If you cannot keep the crayons on the table, we will have to put them away." "If you cannot keep your bottom in the chair, you will have to get down from the table."

Tell the child the consequence for following rules. "If you come with me to bed now we will have time to read a story"; "If you help me pick-up the toys, we can listen to music."

Check that the child remembers by asking what the rules are and if they are able to repeat them.

Become Involved in Activities for Children. In each situation, ask yourself what activities you could take with you or arrange that would keep the child amused for at least some of the time. For example, when sitting on bean bags you can look at pictures, and when walking in the community you can talk about the colors of the leaves, the sky, and the houses and then find shapes in all the objects. When arranging activities, always consider the developmental level of the children, and their individual interests. A 2-year-old will be more interested naming objects, whereas a 5-year-old child may want to talk about what letter an object starts with, and read signs in the community. Try to follow the interest of the child by watching them.

Generate an activity list. Involve the children in thinking of activities for particular situations (e.g., rest time, outside time). Ask the children to think of as many activities as possible for the particular event. Encourage them to help you generate a list of 20 to 30 items that include many things they can do on their own, and that do not cost.

Help Children Get Started in Activities. Adults need to start activities by becoming involved in the activity themselves. If you are building with blocks, then start to build something and talk about what you are making, involving the children in what you are doing. You can also help children get started by giving them some ideas on how to interact with the activity, or point out what another child is doing. If you are busy washing dishes and one of your children is playing with the pots, then ask your younger child if he can help his sister.

Attend to Children While They Are Busy. Give children attention periodically while they are busy. Do not wait for them to finish the activity before providing attention. Give attention for brief moments while they are busy. They are more likely to continue if you do this. For example, you might sit down next to a group of children who are working with scissors and paper and talk about what they are making. Offer changes in activities while they are busy rather than waiting until they are bored and start whining.

Use Incidental Teaching. Incidental teaching is a simple procedure that should be used in every activity with children. It is a way to enhance learning and prevent behavior problems. Remember the following guidelines:

The goal is to make play more enjoyable for the child.

Pay attention to what the child is doing or showing interest.

Show interest by looking at the child, smiling, and directing your attention to the child's topic.

Ask the child questions about related subjects.

Provide Reinforcement. Make a list of the objects, activities, places, foods, and people the children enjoy. These may include reading books, going to the park, a special blanket, a glass of juice, or swinging. Provide these things for children during activities. If children do not like bath time, you may add small boats to the bath and then have a cup of juice after the bath to create a more positive bath experience (i.e., if the child likes boats and juice).

Provide Consequences for Problems. A few simple strategies include:

Ignore minor problems.

If problems continue, give a terminating instruction. Use a calm voice. Keep it simple. Try to phrase it positively (e.g., "John, please touch Sally nicely or she will not want to play with you.").

Redirect the child into an activity using incidental teaching.

Discussions Following an Activity. After an activity, let the children know how they followed the rules and helped you. For example:

Tell the child what they did well. "Sarah, you did a great job helping me find the milk and bread at the store. Thank you for your help."

Tell the child what is needed to improve next time. "Sarah, next time I need you to help me put the food on the checkout stand when we pay so that we both have a job."

Check that children remember by asking what they did well and what they need to improve.

Follow-through with consequences for breaking rules and rewards for following rules. "Sam, we cannot go to the park because you did not stay with me in the store, so let's go home and put things away. If you can help me put everything away, maybe we will have time to go to the park."

Planned Activities Rule Discussions

There is more to raising well-adjusted children than reinforcing appropriate behavior. An important part of socializing children involves helping them learn to control their own behavior. It involves learning to regulate impulsive actions, curb inappropriate behaviors, and to manage anger and other emotions. This section discusses the issue of how to effectively discipline and set limits for children's behavior.

Establishing Ground Rules Through Directed Discussion. Children cannot be expected to behave appropriately unless they know what to do. They need some limits to be set for them. Rules help children learn what is expected of them. Homes with only a few rules can be chaotic and homes with too many rules can limit independence. There are five things to remember when establishing rules for children. Rules should be few, fair, easy to follow, enforceable, and positively stated. Also, when possible, children themselves should contribute to decisions about family rules.

1. Have a small number of rules: The more rules there are, the more opportunities children will have for breaking them. This will mean more problems for enforcement. Each parent has to ultimately decide which rules are appropriate for them. There are three general important rules from which most other rules stem: Children should always be safe; children should respect property; children should be nice to others.

2. Rules should be fair: Rules should apply to all children in a family or group. For example, rules relating to the granting of independence (e.g., when children are allowed to do things on their own) should be the same for all children in the family or group. Adults need to use their own judgment in deciding on what rules to insist. Do not be manipulated by children that claim that "everyone else is allowed to." If you do not believe it is a good idea, stand your ground, and explain why. Children ultimately respect adults more if they see you as fair and consistent.

3. Rules should be easy to follow: Children are more likely to follow rules they understand and that are simply stated. They should be able to state the rule themselves and show you exactly what they should do in a particular situation. Some children with limited verbal skills may not be able to do this, but still benefit from this procedure. Adults can check on children's understanding by asking them. "What is the thing you do when you finish your lunch?" They should be able to answer, "Clean up my place."

4. Rules should be enforceable: There is no point having rules if you are unprepared or unable to enforce them. Enforcement should involve praising children when they comply with the rules and having consistent consequences if the rule is broken. All adults need to be consistent in enforcing the rules, otherwise children will not learn to follow them.

5. Rules should be stated positively: Rather than having a long list of "dont's," state rules positively in terms of "do's". Here are some examples of positively stated rules:

"Dont's"	*"Do's"*
Don't run.	Walking feet, please.
Don't hit.	Touch nicely, please.
Don't throw.	Keep the truck on the carpet.
Don't pull on me.	Hands down, please.

Positively stated rules are also specific in that they describe exactly what is expected of the child. Avoid vague expressions like "be good" because they fail to tell the child exactly what to do.

6. Rules for particular situations: It is very useful to explain rules prior to going places (e.g., shopping trips, visiting relatives, air travel), or prior to events (e.g., outside time, rest time, mealtime). The rules are specific to the situations and should be stated prior to the event.

Guideline for Introducing Rules to Children.   When introducing rules to children it is important to ask if the rule is really necessary. Sometimes enforcing an unnecessary rule is not worth the energy and is counterproductive to the development of the child. If you decide the rule is necessary, then proceed as follows:

1. Set the scene: Prior to the activity, gain the attention of the child involved and remind them of the rule.

2. State the reason for the discussion: Tell the child why you have this rule. For example; "Last time we played with paint we had some trouble remembering what paint is for. Today we will all try to follow the rules for paint so we can play with it again next week."

3. State clearly each rule you would like followed: For example, "There are three things we would like you to remember at all times. The first is keep the paint on the table so that we can clean up fast and go outside. Second, stay in your seat while you paint, and third, remember to share the tools so everyone gets a turn."

4. Seek your child's opinion on the rules: If children have strong feelings about the fairness or necessity of the rule, then it is better to discuss this in advance and if necessary work out a compromise. Sometimes children have very good ideas about how to make a rule workable. For example, when a child was told that she needed to keep the water in the bath tub she agreed, but then asked what if she wanted to splash big. The adult answered that is was important to keep the floor dry so we would not have to clean up. The child thought about this for awhile and then said with excitement, "I could close the bath door and the water won't get out!" The parent praised her for using good problem-solving skills and modified the rule.

Ask your children, "What do you thing about that? Is that fair enough? Does that make sense to you?" Sometimes difficult children will not participate in these discussions. It is better in these circumstances to state the rule clearly and end the discussion. Debating and arguing serve no useful purpose.

5. Ask the child to repeat the rule: If they are able, it will help the child remember what is required.

6. Repeat steps 3, 4, and 5 for each additional rule.

7. Summarize the rules: Ask the child to state all the rules covered. "Let's see if you can remember them all."

8. If necessary, write the rules down and put them is a visible place to prompt you and also the child.

9. Decide on specific consequences for complying and breaking rules: Rules are more likely to be followed if they lead to rewards or consequences, particularly in the early stages. Children should be praised for remembering the rules and if they have been particularly good at following them, some appropriate rewards such as an activity they enjoy can be used to give recognition to their effort. Until they understand the rules, frequent rewards are needed to help children learn. As they get better at understanding, success itself becomes the reward.

10. Wind-up the discussion: Close the discussion by making a quick summary of the key issues covered and agreed upon.

Guidelines for Using Incidental Teaching With Children

Incidental teaching is a simple procedure that can be used to prevent behavior problems with children, teach many simple skills, and encourage language development. Development of language in children is an important step in increasing communication skills, their ability to work things out for themselves, and be more independent. Development of these skills provides children with appropriate substitute behavior and eliminates the need for challenging behaviors. Doing this not only helps children express their needs in a more appropriate way, but also increases the children's self-confidence. In time, this will reduce the amount of time spent attending to the child's needs and requests. In the course of a day, adults have many opportunities to use incidental teaching in naturally occurring situations, such as when the child arrives home, during mealtime, bath time, dressing, walks, and play time.

The basic principle of incidental teaching is awareness. This means that when a child initiates a conversation by looking at something, playing with something, or talking about something, the parent notices. Once a child has shown an interest in something, the parent can further the child's learning and involvement with incidental teaching. The parent can enhance the interaction by asking further questions or talking about the item the child has noticed. In this way, the child can learn new words, or new ways to interact with, or think about things.

Incidental teaching can be used with all children, regardless of developmental level. It shows that adults are interested in them, it helps adults to interact with children, and involves children in activities.

Setting. This is any environment that contains materials and activities that are attractive, appropriate, and likely to engage a child. For most children this includes most environments, and if you do not see anything interesting, watch the child because they will surely find something interesting. Children notice the smallest things, from a shadow on the wall to a new black car.

The Adult. Any person interested in the child who is willing to spend time talking to the child about a variety of topics.

Observation. This involves watching and seeing what interests the child. What are they looking at, or pointing to, or talking about?

Responding to the Situation. After the child shows interest in something, the adult then shows interest. First look at the child, have a pleasant facial expression, and direct your attention to the child and what they are interested in.

Checking That You Understand. If you are unsure what the child is interested in, ask the child questions, "What are you pointing to?" or "Do you mean the fire engine?"

Request Elaboration. Show the child you are interested and encourage learning by asking the child questions related the topic. "What color is that car?", "What do you want me to do with this?", or "Do you know where milk comes from?"

Prompting. If the child does not answer or answers incorrectly, the adult can help by reminding the child, or revealing the answer.

Feedback. When the child gives a correct response, confirm the answer. "Blue, that's right, the block is blue just like your dress is blue."

When to Stop Incidental Teaching. Incidental teaching should always be enjoyable for both the adult and the child. It should be a fun exploration of an interest and not a test of how much a child knows. The primary goal is to involve the child in the task by being involved in the task yourself. If an adult becomes angry or irritated, incidental teaching should be terminated. If a child loses interest, incidental teaching should stop and the adult should follow the child to the next area or interest. Consider the following examples:

1. Kate took Nathan to the grocery store. Kate gave Nathan the list and told him he could be her big helper and find the items on the list. Nathan asked, "What first?" Kate read "oranges" from the list and said, "Now where will we find oranges?" Nathan did not know and Kate said, "Well they are a fruit so they are over here." Nathan found the oranges and Kate asked Nathan what color they were. Nathan said, "Orange like the name." Kate said, "That's right, you are so smart, and can you count out 5 oranges and put them in this bag?" Nathan did and Kate praised him again.

2. Spencer was sitting on the floor playing with the wooden logs. Pam approached and said, "What are you making?" Spencer said, "A log cabin." "Wow," said Pam, "Can I play too?" "Sure." Pam started building her own house and said, "I am going to make a Lucky grocery store," because she knew Spencer liked to go to Lucky's. "What will your family buy?" A long discussion about the family, the cabin, and the store continued while they both built their cabins.

Minimal Prompting: Steps to Independence

Many parents with young children want to encourage them to do things for themselves without the need for frequent supervision. For example, children need to learn how to dress themselves, how to play independently, how to care for their possessions, brush their teeth and hair, and use the bathroom. Unfortunately, many times attempts to help children learn these skills are not always effective. In fact, some children always seem to need help, refuse to do things themselves, and can become overly dependent. The following is a simple procedure that any adult can use to encourage independence in a child. Remember, the child is learning and learning takes time.

What Is Ask, Say, Do?   Ask, Say, Do is a way of encouraging children to learn to be more independent in dressing themselves, grooming, and many other skills. It is a procedure that can be used often with children, particularly when you want them to learn a new skill. First you ask them what they should do, than you tell them what to do, and than you help them do it giving them as little assistance as possible. Eventually, children can learn to do tasks before you ask them what they need to do. The procedure follows these steps:

1. Preparation: Get everything you need in advance (clothing, toothbrush).
2. Gain the child's attention: Look into the child's eyes, smile, and try to be cheerful and relaxed.
3. ASK: Ask the child what is the first thing to do in the specific task at hand. "When we brush our teeth, what do we do first?" "When we get undressed what do we take off first?" "When we clean up, what do we do first?"
4. If the child tells you the correct answer, repeat what was said, "Yes, that's right first you take off your shoes." SAY: If the child does not give the correct answer, cheerfully tell her what do: "First, you take off your shoes."

5. If the child complies, give praise for completing the task and move on the next step starting with ASK.

6. DO: If the child still does not perform the task, describe the action, and then use the minimal amount of guidance to help get started. "Alex, let me help you take off your shoes." "Put one hand here, and the other hand here and then pull like this." "Great job! We can do it together."

7. As the action is completed, praise the child describing what was just done. "You just took off your shoes. Great job, Alex!!"

Activity List

The list of activities in Table 14.4 can be used to assess a child's abilities and preferences. The list can then be used to develop the child's schedule and create activity cards.

PLANNED ACTIVITY CHECKLISTS: PARENT HANDOUTS TRAINING SESSIONS 2–5

This is the structure of the checklist for each daily living activity and for a play activity. Each checklist contains steps relevant for the activity.

General Checklist

Follow these guidelines:

1. Identify difficult situations and settings.
2. Prepare in advance for activities by having all materials prepared and ready and taking care of other unrelated activities before beginning an activity.
3. Explain the activity, including what will happen, what can be expected, and how long.
4. Explain the rules.
5. Explain the consequences for following the rules, and for not following the rules.
6. Use incidental teaching: Talk to the child about the activity in which the child is engaged or directing attention; take what the child is showing interest in and talk about it, ask questions, and describe it; provide age-appropriate suggestions for what the child can do to extend play; let child be direct activities, and end when the child stops directing; keep attention to the activity; extend play, language, and involvement; and use elaboration, questions, descriptions, suggestions.
7. Provide engaging activities.
8. Provide feedback following the activity.
9. Provide consequences.

Specific Planned Activity Checklists

The checklists in Table 14.5 can be used with parents to teach them how to use the PAT skills during specific activities.

TABLE 14.4

Activity List

Family Activities	
Make juice	
Set the table	
Wash dishes	
Feed animals	
Dust furniture	
Vacuum	
Plant flowers	
Bake cookies	
Measure items (raisins, cherries)	
Grease cookie sheet	
Make a simple food dish (soup, sandwich, popcorn)	
Arrange crackers for company	
Wipe counters	
Wash clothes (sort, fold, put away)	
Make the bed	
Sweep	
Simple repair jobs (glue, screw, hammer)	
Put groceries away	
Tie newspapers for recycling	
Weed garden	
Wash the car	
Walk the dog	
Help with a younger sibling	
Community Activities	
Grocery shopping	
Short trips to the store (Target, etc.)	
Post office	
Bank	
Rides in the car	
Restaurants	
Fast food places	
Church	
Mall	
Park	
Beach	
Family outings (Disneyland, Knotts, etc.)	
Airport	
Hospital, doctors' office	
Parents' workplace	
Visiting friends	
Language Activities	
Watch how other objects move (cars roll, snails slide)	
Imitate how certain people or objects move	
Try and imitate body movements (swing, jump, turn)	
Find all the colors in a place	
Find all the shapes	
Find all the letters	
Count all of one object in a place	
Sing songs	

Language Activities (cont.)

Collect objects of a certain type (rocks, sticks, leaves, trash)

Compare the sizes of things (big, fat, tall)

Talk about what happens before and after

Listen to the sounds

Find all the smells

Talk about what things feel like to your hands

Look around and see how many objects you can remember when you leave "I'm thinking of" (give hints about and object and see if you can guess it)

Talk about prepositions (what is in, on, under)

"What is missing" (forget something, then try to guess what it is)

Make as many faces as you can

Start a story where each person then adds a line

Other Activities

Coloring

Markers

Cutting, pasting

Glitter

Hole punches

Play dough

Blocks

Sorting objects (buttons, silverware, clothes, socks)

Read books

Read magazines

Look at photo albums

Ask questions about pictures

Cars

Puzzles

Play dress-up

Legos

Dancing to music

Music story books

Dolls

Bubbles

Make a book

Simon says

Treasure hunts (hide an item, then find it)

Play team games

Play ball

Balloon play

Make a tent, car (use boxes, blankets, chairs)

Play in the sand

Play in the bathtub

Note. From Sanders and Dadds (1993). Copyright 1993 by Allyn & Bacon. Reprinted with permission.

PROBLEMS IN IMPLEMENTATION

PAT is easier to teach to parents than more traditional parent training techniques. The likely reason is that PAT is more similar to good parent and teaching practices than other parent training strategies. Parents find it more natural and do not complain that the consequences that are so stressed in other parent training programs are artificial. PAT is not, however, without difficulty in implementing.

TABLE 14.5
Specific Planned Activity Checklists

Mealtime	
Cut down on between-meal snacks.	
Discuss this rule before using it so the child(ren) know what to expect.	
Reduce fluid intake immediately before a meal.	
Gain the child's attention.	
Discuss the rules related to mealtime.	
Rule I:	
Rule II:	
Rule III:	
Discuss the consequences for following the rules.	
Discuss the consequences for not following the rules.	
Give a warning before the meal.	
Get everything ready and on the table before calling the child to the table.	
Encourage conversation during the meal.	
Talk about the food, the day, what the family will do that evening.	
Ask questions about the child's day.	
Offer descriptive praise and encouragement for appropriate mealtime behavior.	
Ignore minor misbehavior, complaints.	
If the child refuses to eat, instruct only a few times to continue eating.	
Then do not offer rewards for appropriate behavior.	
After the meal, offer descriptive feedback on the child's behavior.	
Provide rewards immediately following the meal for good behavior.	
If the child did not behave well, after brief feedback, do not talk about the incident.	
Do not offer additional snacks or drinks.	
Bedtime	
Have a definite and predictable bedtime.	
Discuss this rule beforehand.	
Explain the rules clearly and simply:	
Go to bed when it is time	
Stay in bed	
Remain quiet	
Explain what will happen if the child is cooperative in going to bed.	
Give a warning 20 to 30 minutes prior to bedtime.	
Help the child get ready for bed (brush teeth, put pajamas on, go to toilet).	
Remember to explain what the child is to do.	
Provide child choice of quiet activity.	
Involve the child in a quiet activity.	
Five minutes before bedtime, give a quick reminder that bedtime is in five minutes.	
Get the child into bed, and then spend some time with the child.	
Use incidental teaching.	
Offer praise for cooperating and going to bed well.	
Stay with the child if they are quiet.	
Leave the child quietly.	
Ignore calls from the child (unless you think there is a real problem).	
Return and check on the child when they are quiet.	
If they are awake, tell them they are doing great and you will return to check on them.	
If the child gets out of bed, return him or her to bed with minimal attention.	
Encouraging Independent Play When You Are Necessarily Busy	
Prepare your child by explaining what is going to happen.	
Help your child choose an activity.	

Encouraging Independent Play When You Are Necessarily Busy (cont.)

Enthusiastically help them get started in the activity.

Use incidental teaching.

Explain the rules for when you will be gone.

  Rule I:

  Rule II:

  Rule III:

Let the child know when you will return.

Explain the reward for following the rules.

Set the timer.

Interrupt your activity to praise the child.

Handle disruptions by:

When timer goes off return to child.

Explain how they did.

Spend individual time with child.

Getting Ready to Go Out

Plan your time to avoid last minute rushing.

Have all items prepared to go out.

Explain to your child where you are going.

Explain to your child what they can do where you are going.

Prompt independent getting ready with Ask, Say, Do.

Praise child for getting ready.

Explain rules for where you are going.

Explain rewards.

Make a game out of getting into the car.

Explain how child did once on your way in the car.

Teaching Children to Clean Up

Give your child advance warning of clean-up time.

Explain the clean-up rules.

Explain the rewards.

Enthusiastically start picking up.

Suggest what you can do and what the child can do.

Use incidental teaching while picking up.

Use Ask, Say, Do.

Praise child's attempts.

After clean-up reward child.

Traveling in the Car

Schedule trip to avoid disruptions in routine.

Explain the rules for in the car.

Ask child to repeat the rules.

Explain rewards for following rules.

Allow child to choose car activities.

Use incidental teaching while in car.

Praise child in the car.

Handle disruptions by gaining child's attention and redirecting.

After trip let child know how they did.

Reward the child.

Note. **From Sanders and Dadds (1993). Copyright 1993 by Allyn & Bacon. Reprinted with permission.**

The most common problem is the occasional parent with the expectation that it is the professional who will change the child's behavior as they sit back or leave the home or office. Of course, this is never the case with parent training. The professional teaches the parent, who in turn uses new procedures with the child.

The best way to overcome this obstacle is to clearly inform parents of their role in the first session. That is, it must be made explicit to parents that their active involvement is the key to success in PAT.

Another difficulty in implementing PAT is that some parents feel comfortable with role playing. Again, a first session explanation of what will occur and the importance of role playing goes some way in allaying this concern. Some parents, however, are never completely comfortable with role playing. Again, this can be somewhat overcome by injecting some humor into it and having the trainer take whichever role parents are most uncomfortable playing most of the time.

Having an observer or trainer follow the family in the community is usually cumbersome or uncomfortable for the family during the first few sessions. This can be overcome by making the first one or two community sessions relatively short. It may require taking a ride together as the first session, rather than actually going to a community setting.

Language and cultural issues cannot be overlooked in parent training. It is most useful to try to match ethnicity and race between the family and the trainer, but, of course, this is not always practical or possible. Every staff member should be trained in cultural sensitivity (Lutzker, 1994). Parents should be asked about their reading skills. Sometimes it is necessary to read materials to parents who have reading deficits.

Although it may be possible to conduct PAT in an office, it is strongly recommended that this training be conducted in the home and community. This can present scheduling and logistic difficulties. In part, scheduling difficulties can be overcome by giving parents reminders and prompts about the next visit.

Finally, occassionally PAT is ineffective or it is clear that it will be ineffective because of serious behavioral deficits of the child. Although, PAT has been found to be useful with nonverbal children and with children who display serious challenging behaviors, it may become apparent that communication training or other behavior management strategies may be necessary in some cases before PAT can be implemented.

CONCLUSIONS

PAT is a very effective parent training technique that can normally be conducted in five sessions. It is useful with children of normal intelligence, with children and adults who have developmental disabilities, with children and adults who have head injury, with individuals who have schizophrenia who reside in a state hospital (Gershater, Lutzker, & Kuehnel, 1997), and with families who are involved in or high risk for child abuse and neglect. It is relatively easy to teach and promotes excellent community generalization skills on the parents' and childrens' parts. Frequently, parents apply PAT to other than the child with whom they learned the technique and they most frequently report satisfaction with the process and outcome of their PAT.

Although PAT might not be a panacea, it is the closest behavioral strategy to aspirin in terms of its demonstrated efficacy and ease of implementation.

ACKNOWLEDGMENT

We are grateful for the assistance of Erica Kane and Randi Sherman in the preparation of this chapter.

REFERENCES

Abidin, R. R. (1986). *Parenting Stress Index* (2nd ed.). Charlottesville, VA: Pediatric Psychology Press.

Achenbach, T. M., & Edelbrock, C. (1983). *Manual for the Child Behavior Checklist and Revised Child Behavior Profile.* Burlington, VT: Thomas M. Achenbach.

Anastopoulos, A. D., DuPaul, G. J., & Barkley, R. A. (1991). Stimulant medication and parent training therapies for attention-deficit hyperactivity disorder. *Journal of Learning Disabilities, 24,* 210–218.

Azar, S. T., Robinson, D. R., Hekimian, E., & Twentyman, C. T. (1984). Unrealistic expectations and problem-solving ability in maltreating and comparison mothers. *Journal of Consulting and Clinical Psychology, 52,* 687–691.

Budd, K. S. (1988). Structured Observation System. In M. Hersen & A.S. Bellack (Eds.), *Dictionary of behavioral asssessment techniques* (pp. 452–454). New York: Pergamon.

Cerezo, M. A. (1988). Community interaction checklist. In M. Hersen & A. S. Bellack (Eds.), *Dictionary of behavioral assessment techniques* (pp. 135–138). New York: Pergamon.

Cohen, S., Mermelstein, R., Kamarck, T., & Hoberman, H. M. (1985). Measuring the functional components of social support. In I. G. Sarason & B. R. Sarason (Eds.), *Social support: Theory, research, and applications* (pp. 73–94). The Hague: Martinus Nijhoff.

Cooper, L. J., Wacker, D. P., Sasso, G. M., Reimers, T. M., & Donn, L. K. (1990). Using parents as therapists to evaluate appropriate behavior of their children: Application to a teritary diagnostic clinic. *Journal of Applied Behavior Analysis, 23,* 285–296.

Cordisco, L. K., Strain, P. S., & Depew, N. (1988). Assessment for generalization of parenting skills in home settings. *Journal of Association for Persons with Severe Handicaps, 13,* 202–210.

DeRoma, V. M., & Hansen, D. J. (1994, November). *Development of the parental anger inventory.* Poster presented at the Association for the Advancement of Behavior Therapy Convention, San Diego.

Ducharme, J. M., & Popynick, M. (1993). Errorless compliance to parental requests: Treatment effects and generalization. *Behavior Therapy, 24,* 209–226.

Ducharme, J. M., & Worling, D. E. (1994). Behavioral momentum and stimulus fading in the acquisition and maintenance of child compliance in the home. *Journal of Applied Behavior Analysis, 27,* 639–647.

Endo, G. T., Sloane, H. N., Hawkes, T. W., & Jenson, W. R. (1991). Reducing child whining through self-instructional parent training materials. *Child and Family Behavior Therapy, 13,* 41–57.

Erhardt, D., & Baker, B. L. (1990). The effects of behavioral parent training on families with young hyperactive children. *Journal of Behavior Therapy and Experimental Psychiatry, 21,* 121–132.

Eyberg, S., Bessmer, J., Newcomb, K., Edwards, D., & Robinson, E. (1994). *Dyadic parent–child interaction coding system–II: A manual.* Unpublished manuscript, University of Florida, Gainesville.

Eyberg, S., & Colvin, A. (1994, August). *Restandardization of the Eyberg Child Behavior Inventory.* Poster presented at the annual meeting of the American Psychological Association, Los Angeles.

Eyberg, S. M., & Robinson, E. A. (1981). *Dyadic parent–child interaction coding system: A manual.* Unpublished manuscript, Oregon Health Sciences University.

Eyberg, S. M., & Ross, A. W. (1978). Assessment of child behavior problems: The validation of a new inventory. *Journal of Clinical Child Psychology, 7,* 113–116.

Feldman, M. A., Case, L., & Sparks, B. (1992). Effectiveness of a child-care training program for parents at-risk for child neglect. *Canadian Journal of Behavioral Science, 24,* 14–28.

Feldman, M. A., Sparks, B., & Case, L. (1993). Effectiveness of home-based early intervention on the language development of children of mothers with mental retardation. *Research in Developmental Disabilities, 14,* 387–408.

Forehand, R., & McMahon, R. (1981). *Helping the noncompliant child: A clinician's guide to parent training.* New York: Guilford.

France, K. G., & Hudson, S. M. (1990). Behavior management of infant sleep disturbance. *Journal of Applied Behavior Analysis, 23,* 91–98.

Fox, R. A. (1994). *Parent Behavior Checklist.* Brandon, VT: Clinical Psychology Publishing.

Furey, W., & Forehand, R. (1988). Daily Child Behavior Checklist. In M. Hersen & A. S. Bellack (Eds.), *Dictionary of behavioral assessment techniques* (pp. 161–162). New York: Pergamon.

Gershater, R., Lutzker, J. R., & Kuehnel, T. G. (1997). Activity scheduling to increase staff–patient interactions. *The Clinical Supervisor, 15,* 115–128.

Graziano, A. M., & Diament, D. M. (1992). Parent behavioral training: An examination of the paradigm. *Behavior Modification, 16,* 3–38.

Hansen, D. J., Palotta, G. M., Tishelman, A. C., Conaway, L. P., & MacMillan, V. M. (1989). Parental problem-solving skills and child behavior problems: A comparison for physically abusive, neglectful, clinic, and community families. *Journal of Family Violence, 4,* 353–368.

Harrold, M., Lutzker, J. R., Campbell, R. V., & Touchette, P. E. (1992). Improving parent–child interactions for families of children with developmental disabilties. *Journal of Behavior Therapy and Experimental Psychiatry, 23,* 89–100.

Horn, W. F., Ialongo, N., Greenberg, G., Packard, T., & Smith-Winberry, C. W. (1990). Additive effects of behavioral parent training and self-control therapy with attention deficit hyperactivity disordered children. *Journal of Clinical Child Psychology, 19,* 98–110.

Hudson, A. (1988). Training Proficiency Scale–Parent Version. In M. Hersen & A. S. Bellack (Eds.), *Dictionary of behavioral assessment techniques* (pp. 484–485). New York: Pergamon.

Huynen, K. B., Lutzker, J. R., Bigelow, K. M. Touchette, P. E., & Campbell, R. V. (1996). Planned activities training for families of children with developmental disabilities: Community generalization and follow-up. *Behavior Modification, 20,* 406–427.

Krantz, P. J., MacDuff, M. T., & McClannahan, L. E. (1993). Programming participation in family activities for children with autism: Parents' use of photographic activity schedules. *Journal of Applied Behavior Analysis, 26,* 137–138.

Lowry, M. A., & Whitman, T. L. (1989). Generalization of parenting skills: An early intervention program. *Child and Family Behavior Therapy, 11,* 45–65.

Loyd, B. H., & Abidin, R. R. (1985). Revision of the Parenting Stress Index. *Journal of Pediatric Psychology, 10,* 169–177.

Lutzker, J. R. (1992). Developmental disabilities and child abuse and neglect: The ecobehavioral imperative. *Behaviour Change, 9,* 149–156.

Lutzker, J. R. (1994). Practical issues in delivering broad based ecobehavioral services to families. *Revista, 11,* 87–96.

Lutzker, S. Z., Lutzker, J. R., Braunling-McMorrow, D., & Eddleman, J. (1987). Prompting to increase mother–baby stimulation with single mothers. *Journal of Child and Adolescent Psychotherapy, 4,* 3–12.

MacMillan, V. M., Olson, R. L., & Hansen, D. J. (1988, October). *The development of an anger inventory for use with maltreating parents.* Paper presented at the Association for the Advancement of Behavior Therapy Convention, New York.

MacMillan, V. M., Olson, R. L., & Hansen, D. J. (1991). Low- and high-deviance analogue assessment of parent-training with physically abusive parents. *Journal of Family Violence, 6,* 279–301.

Mokau, N., & Manos, M. J. (1989). A behavioral model for training parents. *Journal of Contemporary Social Work, 70,* 479–487.

Novaco, R. W. (1975). *Anger control: The development and evaluation of an experimental treatment.* Lexington, MA: Lexington Books.

O'Neill, R. E., Horner, R. H., Albin, R. W., Storey, K., & Sprague, J. R. (1990). *Functional analysis of problem behavior: A practical assessment guide.* Sycamore, IL: Sycamore Publishing.

Palotta, G. M., Conaway, R. L., Christopher, J. S., & Hansen, D. J. (1989, October). *The Parental Problem-Solving Measure: Evaluation with maltreating clinical and community parents.* Paper presented at the Association for the Advancement of Behavior Therapy Convention, Washington, DC.

Procidano, M., & Heller, K. (1983). Measures of perceived social support from friends and from family: Three validation studies. *American Journal of Community Psychology, 11,* 1–24.

Richman, G. S., Hagopian, L. P., Harrison, K., Birk, D., Omerod, A., & Brierley, P. B., Mann, L. (1994). Assessing parental response patterns in the treatment of noncompliance in children. *Child and Family Behavior Therapy, 16,* 29–42.

Sanders, M. R. (1992). Every parent: A positive approach to children's behaviour. Sydney: Addison-Wesley.

Sanders, M. R., & Dadds, M. R. (1982). The effects of planned activities and child management procedures in parent training: An analysis of setting generality. *Behavior Therapy, 13,* 452–461.

Sanders, M. R., & Dadds, M. R. (1993). *Behavioral family intervention.* Boston: Allyn & Bacon.

Sanders, M. R., & Plant, K. (1989). Programming for generalization to high and low risk parenting situations in families with oppositional developmentally disabled preschoolers. *Behavior Modification, 13,* 283–305.

Solis, M. L., & Abidin, R. R. (1991). The Spanish version Parenting Stress Index: A psychometric study. *Journal of Clinical Child Psychology, 20,* 372–378.

Stark, L. J., Powers, S. W., Jelalian, E., Rapee, R. N., & Miller, D. L. (1994). Modifying problematic mealtime interactions of children with cystic fibrosis and their parents via behavioral parent training. *Journal of Pediatric Psychology, 19,* 751–768.

Wahler, R. G. (1980). The insular mother: Her problem in parent–child treatment. *Journal of Applied Behavior Analysis, 13,* 207–219.

Webster-Stratton, C. (1988). Eyberg Child Behavior Inventory. In M. Hersen & A. S. Bellack (Eds.), *Dictionary of behavioral assessment techniques* (pp. 205–206). New York: Pergamon.

Werle, M. A., Murphy, T. B., & Budd, K. S. (1993). Treating chronic food refusal in young children: Home-based parent training. *Journal of Applied Behavior Analysis, 26,* 421–433.

Chapter 15

Social Skills Training for Children and Youth With Visual Disabilities

Robert T. Ammerman
Department of Psychiatry and Allegheny Neuropsychiatric Institute
MCP ♦ Hahnemann School of Medicine
Allegheny University of the Health Sciences

Vincent B. Van Hasselt
Nova Southeastern University

Michel Hersen
Pacific University

Despite the consensus among workers in the fields of psychology, psychiatry, special education, and rehabilitation that many visually handicapped children evidence problems in social adaptation, little attention has been directed toward amelioration of these difficulties. This chapter describes the Social Skills Training Program (SSTP), one of the first comprehensive efforts specifically designed to enhance interpersonal effectiveness in visually handicapped children and youth. In SSTP, an assessment battery is first administered to identify areas of social dysfunction. Measurement instruments include role play tests, standardized interviews, self-report questionnaires, and parent and teacher ratings. Assessment data are utilized for intervention in such areas as conversational skills, and positive and negative assertion skills. Within each of these categories, a social skills training package (direct instructions, performance feedback, modeling, behavior rehearsal, manual guidance) is employed to train participants on a number of verbal, nonverbal, and paralinguistic behavioral components. Instruction in social perception skill also is offered in SSTP. The program consists of four stages: skills assessment, skills training, booster sessions, and follow-up. Booster sessions are incorporated to consolidate initial gains and to remediate any posttraining response decrements. Instructions are provided for implementing each aspect of SSTP. Frequently encountered problems are described, and solutions are presented.

A number of clinical and investigative efforts have documented the importance of social skills in the development of normal interpersonal relations in children (see reviews by Hops, 1983; Michelson & Wood, 1981; Van Hasselt, Hersen, Whitehill, & Bellack, 1979). Skill deficits, as well as social withdrawal and isolation, have been associated with low self-esteem and poor academic achievement (Hartup, 1970). Moreover, a considerable body of research has shown that social dysfunction in childhood may lead to adjustment problems later in life (e.g., Cowen, Pederson, Babigian, Izzo, & Trost, 1973; Ullman, 1957). Conversely, children who exhibit high levels of interpersonal effectiveness generally are superior in scholastic endeavors and receive more social reinforcement from their environment relative to socially deficient peers (Gottman, Gonso, & Rasmussen, 1975). Further, a history of adequate interpersonal relationships during the childhood years appears to be a good predictor of adult psychological adjustment (Kohlberg, LeCrosse, & Ricks, 1972). Taken together, the afore-mentioned findings indicate that improving social skills is an important treatment goal for withdrawn or isolated children.

The deleterious effects of poor social adaptation in childhood are perhaps most clearly illustrated in the developmentally and physically disabled. Although attention has been directed to a variety of such populations (e.g., mentally retarded, learning disabled, deaf, orthopedically impaired), considerable research effort has focused on socialization of blind or visually handi-capped children (see Ammerman, Van Hasselt, & Hersen, 1986) relative to sighted controls or children with other disabilities (Bradway, 1937; Maxfield & Fjeld, 1942; McKay, 1936). However, whereas these early endeavors demonstrated that blind children exhibit social dysfunc-tion, the global indices did not permit fine-grained analyses of the specific nature of skill deficiencies.

Recently, Van Hasselt and colleagues (Van Hasselt, Hersen, & Kazdin, 1985; Van Hasselt et al., 1981) conducted empirical evaluations of social skills in visually handicapped children. The primary mode of assessment was the role play test, an instrument involving simulations of social interactions in the laboratory setting (Bellack, 1983; see social skills assessment section). In the first study, Van Hasselt et al. (1981) followed the behavioral-analytic model of test construction (Goldfried & D'Zurilla, 1969) to develop 39 role play situations relevant to the social environ-ment of the blind child. Results of role play assessment revealed that blind children evidenced deficiencies on a number of verbal (speech duration, speech latency, speech disturbances) and nonverbal (smiles, physical gestures, posture, stereotypic behavior) skill components in com-parison to sighted children.

An investigation by Van Hasselt et al. (1985) evaluated social skill in three adolescent populations: visually handicapped students in a residential school, visually handicapped students mainstreamed in public schools, and nonhandicapped students. Assessment instru-ments included role play tests and the parent form of the Child Behavior Checklist (Achen-bach & Edelbrock, 1978). Results indicated that the visually handicapped groups showed deficits on several verbal response indices. In addition, residential blind adolescents showed more deficits in speech duration, speech disturbances, and were more compliant than their mainstreamed counterparts. These data clearly point to the need for skill intervention with blind children and youth.

SOCIAL ADJUSTMENT IN CHILDREN WITH VISUAL DISABILITIES

A major source of difficulty for blind children in developing appropriate social behavior is their obvious inability to utilize visual cues (Farkas, Sherick, Matson, & Loebig, 1981; Van Hasselt, 1983). Many interpersonal skills are acquired through modeling, a process that relies heavily on visual cues. Learning to "look" in the direction of the speaker while engaging in conversation is contingent on adequate modeling of such responses. However, eye contact, as well as some situation-appropriate facial expressions (e.g., smiles) may be impossible for blind children to imitate.

Another integral element in the acquisition of interpersonal skills is performance feedback. Yet, there are indications that blind persons often do not receive accurate or appropriate social feedback. In one study, behaviors of college students in staged interactions with a "normal" and a physically handicapped person were examined (Kleck, Ono, & Hastorf, 1966). Results showed that subjects delivered inaccurate feedback when interacting with the handicapped person. Specifically, they were less variable in their behavior, ended conversations earlier, and expressed notions less representative of their true beliefs. Distorted feedback to the handicapped also has been described by Scott (1969). He reported a subset of parents who continuously dispense positive reinforcement noncontingently, regardless of the child's level of performance. These parents believe their children are completely incapacitated due to their visual handicap and therefore should be rewarded for *any accomplishment*. Scott (1969) contended that such unreliable feedback interferes with the child's ability to assume an appropriate "social role."

There also is evidence to suggest that blind children have fewer social experiences than sighted counterparts. Because of this, they have fewer opportunities to practice and perfect their interpersonal repertoires. One reason for their decreased exposure is the functional limitations imposed by the disability. Blind children cannot take part in many games involving physical activity. Also, the need to attend continuously to verbal cues for information may discourage the blind child from engaging in such activities. Likewise, the impatience of sighted peers may make participation in the game aversive. Given the importance of play interactions in the development of sharing and helping skills (Asher, Oden, & Gottman, 1977), the range and quantity of early social learning experiences is severely restricted for the blind child.

Other explanations may be offered for diminished social interaction of blind children. First, people's attitudes toward the handicapped tend to be negative (Kleck, Richardson, & Ronald, 1974). In particular, a child's facial appearance is an important influence on social popularity (Young & Cooper, 1944). Many blind children have unattractive ocular features, or other salient deformities, and thus they are "at risk" for social rejection and, consequently, fewer interpersonal exchanges.

Several investigators have suggested that blind children may lack knowledge of appropriate interpersonal skills (Richardson, 1969; Scott, 1969). In light of impaired modeling and feedback processes, inadequate knowledge of social behaviors in blind children would not be surprising. Indeed, Lowenfeld (1962) found that blind children are unfamiliar with nonfamilial positions, such as delivery persons, grocers, and so on. This limited social awareness impairs role-taking skill (i.e., the ability to understand and "take" the positions of others during play). Ability in this area has been related to social competence (Feffer & Suchotliff, 1966) and assertiveness (Reardon, Hersen, Bellack, & Foley, 1979) in nonhandicapped child populations.

More recently, researchers have posited that social perception and sensitivity play a critical role in socialization. The ability to detect, understand, and think about the emotions and motivations of others is considered crucial to social development (see discussion by Morrison & Bellack, 1981). Data have been accrued that reveal social perception deficits in learning disabled (Emery, 1975) and emotionally disturbed (Dil, 1972) children. However, only one study has evaluated social perception in blind children. Czerwinski and Tait (1981) read stories of normal, withdrawn, and antisocial characters to 12 congenitally blind children age 5 to 17 years. Children were asked to answer questions concerning character's similarity, desirability, assertiveness, well-being, causality, and changeability. Subjects were able to discriminate between normal and abnormal behaviors. However, methodological shortcomings (lack of sighted controls, unvalidated assessment procedures) mitigate conclusions drawn from this investigate.

The previous data suggest that impaired social sensitivity may contribute to problems in social adaptation. Inadequate social perception may occur in conjunction with social performance deficits, or may be present in children with requisite performance skills. A complete analysis of social adjustment in visually handicapped children must include examination of both specific response deficits and social perception skills.

TREATMENT OF SKILL DEFICITS

Despite the consensus that many visually handicapped children would benefit from social skills intervention, only a few such programs have been reported. In one study, facial expressions, gestures, and postures were targeted in a kinesic training program for seven blind adolescents (Apple, 1972). Treatment consisted of direct instructions, behavior rehearsal, role play, and body conditioning exercises. A second group of blind adolescents and a group of sighted controls received no training. Posttreatment observations of subjects engaged in group discussions unexpectedly showed few nonverbal behaviors in treated subjects. Once again, however, methodological problems (e.g., use of untrained raters, unvalidated assessment instruments) preclude the drawing of any firm conclusions from these findings.

Yarnall (1979) applied tangible and social reinforcement (bright light, food, praise) for appropriate eye contact in a 6½-year-old visually handicapped, deaf girl. Baseline data showed that the subject emitted an average of 3.6 seconds of eye contact per 10-minute period. After 51 ten-minute treatment sessions in a classroom setting, duration of eye contact exceeded 300 seconds for the same observation interval. Yarnall (1979) also attempted to promote generalization to extra-classroom activities by teaching reinforcement procedures to school aides. Although staff members reported substantial increases in the subject's amount of eye contact outside the classroom, no data regarding response generalization were obtained.

Farkas et al. (1981) targeted behaviors presumed to interfere with appropriate social interactions in a 12-year-old blind female. These included inappropriate addressing, stereotyped motor behaviors, and rocking. The subject received 24 treatment sessions involving positive social feedback and token reinforcement (tokens were redeemable for spending time listening to music) contingent on appropriate behavior. A multiple-baseline analysis revealed a substantial decrease in maladaptive responses, with gains maintained at a 1-month follow-up.

Van Hasselt, Hersen, Kazdin, Simon, and Mastantuono (1983) employed a social skills treatment "package" (direct instructions, performance feedback, behavior rehearsal, modeling, and manual guidance) to increase assertive behavior in four blind female adolescents. Each subject exhibited assertion deficits on at least three of the following components: direction of gaze, requests for new behavior, posture, voice tone, and expressive physical gestures. Training consisted of five 15 to 30-minute sessions per week over a 4-week period. A series of multiple-baseline analyses showed positive changes across behaviors in each subject as a function of skills treatment. However, a 1-month follow-up indicated deterioration of some responses. Therefore, four "booster" sessions (i.e., reviews of material covered in formal training) were carried out. These resulted in a return of behaviors to post-treatment levels.

In an effort to enhance social and adaptive living skills in visually handicapped adolescents, Stewart, Van Hasselt, Simon, and Thompson (1985) developed the Community Adjustment Program (CAP). CAP involves training in a number of areas (orientation and mobility, food preparation, home management, clothing care) requisite for independent community living. The social skills component of this program was an adaption of the aforementioned intervention by Van Hasselt et al. (1983). Specifically, five males and five females 13 to 16 years of age ($X =$ 14.5) received 5 weeks of training in assertion and conversational skills. Treatment involved modification of various verbal and nonverbal indices. In addition, subjects received homework assignments to practice newly acquired skills outside of the training setting. Results of pre–post assessments as well as parents' ratings of children's social performance indicated gains for all participants.

It is evident that many blind children demonstrate a variety of social skill deficits. This may be due to poor modeling, inadequate feedback, restricted social experiences, lack of knowledge of appropriate skilled behaviors, or some combination of these factors. With the development of improved assessment techniques (Van Hasselt et al., 1981), targeting of specific skill deficits in this population has become possible. Whereas few treatment outcome studies exist, those conducted have yielded encouraging results. Further, they highlight the heuristic value of social skills training for visually handicapped children.

SOCIAL SKILLS TRAINING PROGRAM

The Social Skills Training Program (SSTP) at the Western Pennsylvania School for Blind Children (WPSBC) is a structured learning package designed to enhance the interpersonal effectiveness of visually handicapped children and youth. The program has received widespread application at WPSBC (see Van Hasselt, Simon, & Mastantuono, 1982), both on a single-case basis and as part of classroom programs in which teachers implement skills training. Training consists of modifying various skill components relevant to the child's social environment.

SSTP is divided into four stages: assessment, treatment, follow-up, and booster sessions. Assessment and follow-up involve evaluation of interpersonal difficulties and specific skill deficits in visually handicapped children. The training stage employs such techniques as direct instructions, modeling, behavior rehearsal, performance feedback, and manual guidance to teach the child more effective social behaviors. Follow-up consists of determining maintenance of improvement in social effectiveness after completion of training. Finally, posttreatment booster sessions are employed to remediate any behavioral decrements that may be evident in follow-up and to consolidate gains made in treatment.

Training Focus

In SSTP, an attempt is made to enhance conversation and assertion skills in visually handicapped children. By subsequently implementing the skills learned in training, the children should be able to maximize their opportunities to obtain positive social reinforcement, while minimizing punishment. Although it is understood that the children will sometimes receive negative feedback for performance of certain social responses (e.g., negative assertion), the goal of training is to maintain a healthy balance. For example, refusing to let other children "cut" in front of a lunchline may elicit immediate anger or social rejection from them. In the long run, however, the visually impaired children will benefit from behaving assertively through increased social effectiveness and heightened confidence in their ability to deal with difficult interpersonal situations. Given that many blind children exhibit extreme behaviors, such as being too hostile or too submissive, establishing and maintaining this balance is of paramount importance.

Social skill implies the coordinated delivery of a variety of verbal and nonverbal components. It consists of what the child says, how it is said, when and where it is said, and how the child appears while saying it. A gestalt is formed by the combination of these elements of social performance. Of course, the components will be differentially weighted in importance and impact as a function of the skill and the situation. In fact, one element may compensate for or neutralize the effect of another. For example, a child who displays appropriate verbal behaviors in the absence of effective nonverbal responses (e.g., direction of gaze, appropriate affect) may find that the deficit negates any positive effects of the skilled elements. Because there are no objective guidelines for determining the relative importance of skill components across situations, trainers must use their best judgment in ascertaining the child's impact on others, as well as targeting behaviors in need of change. This involves an understanding of the target child's effect on other children and adults. Trainers must be tolerant of individual differences in social style, and should be wary of imposing their own style on the child.

Initially, the trainer may have a sense that the child's social style is dysfunctional, but may not know precisely what specific problems exist. Several categories of social functioning are targeted in skills intervention. The first category, *expressive verbal skills*, includes qualitative and quantitative aspects of how the child behaves in social situations. *Speech duration* is the amount of time spent talking during a given interaction. *Speech latency* is the time interval between the end of a statement by the other person and child's response. *Speech disturbances* are those utterances that disrupt the pattern of speech, such as "uh," "uhm," or "well." High rates of these four components often reflect social anxiety, and may communicate discomfort to the other person (Harper, Wiens, & Matarazzo, 1978). *Speech intonation* is a qualitative measure of the amount of vocal affect, ranging on a continuum from a flat, monotonic tone, to a full and lively tone. Intonation is an important aspect of communicating emotion. *Hostile tone* is a separate measure of the degree of hostility present in the child's intonation ranging on a continuum from an abrasive/aggressive to a nonabrasive tone of voice. *Voice volume* is the loudness of the child's speech, ranging from inaudible to overly loud. These three elements are vital in communicating emotion. A loud voice and hostile tone may imply anger, whereas a flat tone and soft voice may suggest disinterest or boredom. Visually handicapped children often exhibit behaviors that are at the extremes of such a continuum, thus diminishing the quality of social interaction.

Verbal content skills are those elements of social interchange that express appropriate and effective meaning to the other person. They are "what" the children say, as opposed to "how" they say it. For example, *compliance* and *requests for new behavior* are aspects of negative assertion. Compliance is the child's acquiescence to the unreasonable request of another person (e.g., lending a quarter to a friend who already owes the child money). Children who are compliant can be "bullied" and manipulated by others. *Requests for new behavior* involve asking the other person to do something different (e.g., refusing to lend the friend a quarter until the money owed is payed back). This is useful to decrease the likelihood of unreasonable demands by other children in the future. *Praise* is an expression of admiration or a compliment toward another person (e.g., the child tells a friend that she did well on a school assignment). *Appreciation* is an expression of gratitude or thanks toward another person (e.g., thanking someone for helping the child across the street). *Spontaneous positive behavior* involves the offering of aid or assistance to another person (e.g., offering to help a visually handicapped friend select appropriately matched clothing). Performance of praise, appreciation, and spontaneous positive behavior provides social reinforcement to others and strengthens interpersonal relationships. These categories are particularly important in light of previous research showing that children who dispense social reinforcement at relatively high rates also receive the most reinforcement from peers (Charlesworth & Hartup, 1967; Keller & Carlson, 1974).

Nonverbal skills consist of what the children do with their body while interacting. *Direction of gaze* is the amount of "eye contact" made by the children with another person in a social situation. In working with visually handicapped children, this category involves turning the head in the direction of the speaker. *Smiles* are defined as an upward movement of the corners of the mouth and some showing of teeth. *Physical gestures* are expressive movements of the hands and arms that are appropriate within the context of the situation. *Posture* is measured on a continuum from poor (head down, slumped over in a chair) to good (shoulders back, head up). These skills are vital to demonstrating interest in the other person. *Proxemics* is the distance between the child and the speaker. Standing too close or too far away increases discomfort and diminishes social effectiveness. Because blind children often have difficulty estimating distance between themselves and other people, proxemics is of particular importance to them. The trainer must practice estimating distance with the child. Reinforcement can be used to shape the child to adjust distance to a socially appropriate level. *Stereotypic behaviors* are movements that are repetitive and inappropriate. These are prevalent in many visually handicapped children, and include rocking, head-weaving, finger-flicking, an so on. Such responses interfere with normal social interaction. Therefore, their elimination is important in improving the child's overall social performance.

Interactive balance does not pertain to a particular behavior per se, but rather refers to the enmeshment and dynamic quality of social interchange. The goal is an appropriate paced "give and take" between the child and the speaker. This involves the coordinated delivery of social skill components. A rapidly paced or halting speech style serves to disrupt the interaction.

There are three primary categories of social skill targeted by SSTP. They are described as skill "repertoires" and have been shown to have particular relevance for blind children (Van Hasselt et al., 1981): positive assertion, negative assertion, and conversational skills.

In *positive assertion*, positive feelings are expressed toward others. This includes giving compliments, communicating affection, making apologies, and offering approval or praise. In addition to being socially reinforcing, these responses reflect concern and consideration for others. This repertoire is vital to the initiation and maintenance of social relationships. Positive assertion also plays a vital role in the reciprocity of social interaction. As mentioned earlier, there is a significant relationship between the giving and receiving of positive reinforcers in children. In addition, peer social status is directly related to the child's emission of social reinforcers (Hartup, Glazer, & Charlesworth, 1967). Thus, acquisition of this repertoire is necessary for adequate social adaptation in childhood as well as later in life.

Negative assertion is the expression of disapproval and displeasure coupled with asking others to change their behavior. Standing up for one's rights is especially problematic for blind children, and has three elements. The first is *refusing unreasonable requests*. Saying "no" to another person's unreasonable demands prevents the child from being manipulated or taken advantage of my others. Noncompliance is most effective when the refusal is accompanied by an explanation. For example, "No, you can't cut in line in front of me because I was here first." The second element, *expressing disapproval and annoyance*, permits the child to directly communicate negative feedback. Failure to do so often results in "pent up" anger, which may be expressed in a hostile or inappropriate manner. Note that assertion does not insure that others will change their behavior, and assertive children will not always "get their way." However, immediate communication of negative feelings is preferable to unexpressed anger. Such skills may prevent future mistreatment, and lessen the effects (e.g., depression) of withholding negative feelings (Bellack, Hersen, & Himmelhoch, 1981).

The third behavioral component of negative assertion is *requests for new behavior*. This involves asking the other person to behave differently in the future. For example, "Why don't you come to lunch earlier if you want to be first in line?" The request is appended to the aforementioned assertion elements. Thus, a complete assertive response consists of a statement of disapproval, a reason for the annoyance, noncompliance, and a request for new behavior.

As mentioned earlier, assertive responses do not always change another person's behavior. Sometimes it is necessary to compromise. *Compromise* involves reaching a solution acceptable to both parties through mutual cooperation. The child must learn to express feelings about an issue, as well as solicit and understand the needs of the other child. Following this, a resolution is offered: "Why don't I use the toy until we finish our game, and then you can play with it." Compromise preserves the rights of the child while bringing about a satisfactory solution to the conflict.

Another skill repertoire is *conversational skills*. The behaviors in this category facilitate the formation and maintenance of relationships. They include initiating and maintaining interactions, displaying appropriate verbal and nonverbal responses, dispensing reinforcement, and terminating conversations. Visually handicapped children often will display deficits in certain situations involving conversational skills. Friendship making is of particular import, especially for younger children. Support for this premise is found in numerous studies showing early social withdrawal in children who evidence adjustment problems as adults (e.g., Waldrop & Halverson, 1975). Visually handicapped children also may exhibit difficulties with specific components of conversational skill. For example, some blind children may rarely initiate interactions with others. This may be partially attributable to their unawareness of others in their immediate environment due to the nature of the visual handicap. Nevertheless, this deficit will have a negative impact on the quality and frequency of social contacts.

Before proceeding, a caveat about training "compound" behaviors is in order. Compound behaviors are those responses composed of several skill elements. For example, an effective positive assertion statement contains audible voice volume, appropriate gaze, lively voice tone, and few speech disturbances. Repertoires such as assertion and conversational skills that are composed of such verbal, nonverbal, and paralinguistic behaviors should be trained first. Mastery of these is a prerequisite to teaching verbal behaviors. The reasons for this are threefold: Nonverbal and paralinguistic skills often are easier to train, verbal skills are rendered ineffective if poorly delivered (e.g., the impact of noncompliance is lessened if it is said in a low monotone as contrasted to an appropriately pitched phrase), and some verbal components of certain repertoires may provide additional problems for the child. For example, many children feel uncomfortable with the concept of negative assertion and its corresponding elements (e.g., noncompliance). They may fear rejection by peers as a result of assertive behavior, and often confuse aggression with appropriate assertion. The trainer must make certain that the child can distinguish between the two. A firm grasp of nonverbal and paralinguistic skills facilitates acquisition of more complex verbal behaviors.

Training Stages

SSTP consists of four stages: skills assessment, skills training, booster sessions, and follow-up. The purpose of assessment is to identify problems and difficulties the child has in particular social situations or with the performance of certain interpersonal skills. A multifaceted battery is administered that includes parents' and teachers' reports of the child's social and emotional adjustment. In addition, the child's self-report is obtained. A role play test of social skill also is administered to each child. The primary purpose of this strategy is to obtain information about the child's interpersonal style. Skills assessment provides data concerning aspects of functioning (e.g., psychological adjustment), which are secondary but may influence the direction of social skills intervention. During the training stage, the following five techniques designed to modify skill deficits (identified through assessment) are employed: direct instruction, behavior rehearsal, modeling, performance feedback, and manual guidance. In addition, social perception training is introduced early in the program. Finally, booster sessions are employed following treatment to maintain and strengthen gains, and remediate any response decrements.

Social Skills Assessment. Prior to skills intervention, an assessment battery is administered to delineate those behaviors and situations that are problematic for the visually handicapped child. To obtain a complete picture of the child's level of functioning, the evaluation includes questionnaires filled out by significant adults (parents and teachers) in the child's environment. The children also complete similar measures about their own behavior. Further, an analysis of the child's social responses is conducted via a role play test. The assessment battery employs teacher ratings, parent ratings, self-report inventories, and role play tests of social skill for children. These measures are described next.

The *Matson Evaluation of Social Skills with Youngsters* (MESSY) is designed to assess social behavior in child populations (Matson, Rotatori, & Helsel, 1983). The children's self-report questionnaire has 62 items and the teacher form has 64 items (both scales in a Likert format). Most items are identical in content across both versions except for a change in tense. Examples of MESSY items include: "I have many friends," and "I like to be alone," "I make other people laugh."

The *Child Behavior Checklist* (Achenbach & Edelbrock, 1978) consists of separate forms for parents (CBCL–P) and teachers (CBCL–T). It is an empirically derived and standardized instrument that yields scores reflecting severity of various social and emotional difficulties. The following categories of psychological functioning are reflected in the scores: somatic complaints, schizoid, uncommunicative, immature, obsessive-compulsive, hostile-withdrawal, delinquent, aggressive, and hyperactive. A social competence scale provides information about interpersonal relationships and social adjustment. A third version of the Child Behavior

Checklist is the Youth Self-Report Form (YSRF). The YSRF is completed by the child, and is available for children and adolescents from 11 to 18 years of age. Scores similar to those already listed are derived.

Michelson and Wood (1982) developed the *Children's Assertive Behavior Scale* (CABS) to provide a quick and efficient measure of assertion in children. It attempts to tap a number of assertion content areas: giving and receiving compliments, making requests for behavior change in others, and delivering empathic statements. This device contains 27 items that describe interpersonal situations requiring assertive responses. Each item is followed by five possible answers that vary along a "passive–assertive–aggressive" continuum. Children are instructed to select one response that best reflects the way they would behave in the situation.

The previous questionnaires are useful in providing a preliminary indication of social functioning in children. However, for a finer-grained analysis, the trainer actually must observe the child's interpersonal interactions. The *role play* test (see Table 15.1) provides the information necessary to target behaviors in need of change, and thus serves as the primary vehicle in skills assessment. In this procedure, a social situation is presented to the child by the trainer. The children then simulate or "act out" what they would do in that situation if it were actually occurring. Where available, a confederate serves as the role play partner, and responds to the children using prearranged prompts. (When it is not possible to include a confederate, the trainer provides the narration and plays the role of the other party in the scenario with the child.) After two interchanges, a new situation is presented. Although some scenarios may be selected from this set for skills intervention, new role play items involving assertion and conversational skills. All role play interactions are videotaped and retrospectively rated on the various verbal and nonverbal skill components described earlier.

The *Standardized Interview* is designed to assess the child's *knowledge* of social skills. Sometimes children may know what to say or do in certain interpersonal situations, but may still fail to respond appropriately due to other factors (e.g., social anxiety). Determining the child's awareness of skills plays an important role in designing an appropriate training package. A child who lacks knowledge of appropriate behavior must learn the "rules" of social interaction. On the other hand, the anxious child will need more practice and possibly adjunctive treatments (e.g., relaxation training) to overcome discomfort. The Standardized Interview

TABLE 15.1

Sample Role Play Test Scenes

Negative Assertion	
Narrator:	You're listening to one of your favorite songs on the radio. Suddenly one of your friends comes over and starts to change the station saying she'd like to listen to something else. She says:
Prompt 1:	"I want to listen to another radio station." (Child's Response 1)
Prompt 2:	"The other station is better and has fewer commercials." (Child's Response 2)
Conversational Skill	
Narrator:	You are walking toward a classroom. The door is partially open and a small group of people is gathered in front of the doorway. Someone says:
Prompt 1:	"Hi, how are you doing?" (Child's Response 1)
Prompt 2:	"Do you want to get through here?" (Child's Response 2)

consists of reading scenarios, such as those employed in role play tests, and then asking the child: "What do you think a person *should* say or do in that situation?" Responses may be audiotaped and scored for compliance, request for new behavior, or additional responses of interest to the trainer.

Social Skills Training.   Based on results of skills assessment, the trainer may develop a preliminary treatment plan consisting of specific goals for skills intervention. This involves construction of a hierarchy of problematic social situations and determination of behaviors requiring modification for each child. The hierarchy consists of two separate listings of scenes and skills arranged in order from least to most difficult for the child to master. For example, goals for one child may include increasing gaze, improving voice tone, increasing frequency of smiles, and teaching the child to initiate social interactions. Goals for another child may be to improve negative assertion skills by increasing the number of requests for new behavior, reducing speech latency, increasing gaze, and decreasing the number of compliant responses. Each session should be devoted to a single behavioral component (e.g., direction of gaze), because children initially find training of multiple components overwhelming. Essentially, skills treatment is conducted in a sequential and cumulative fashion with new behaviors trained only when previously targeted response deficits on the hierarchy have been remediated. A minimum of five role play scenes should be employed during each session to maximize opportunities for behavior rehearsal and to prevent boredom. The trainer should concentrate on those role play situations that are problematic for the particular child receiving skills treatment.

When presenting a component to be modified, a *rationale* for altering the behavior must be provided. The child should learn the importance of changing the behavior, and gain an understanding of its effect on interpersonal interactions. The rationale should be brief; two or three sentences generally are sufficient. For example, "Why don't we work on talking louder. It's important to talk loud enough so that people can hear you without difficulty. They will also know that you are serious about what you're saying. Do you understand why it is important to talk louder? Good." It is imperative that the child understand the rationale, and not simply give "lip service" to the trainer. Sometimes it will be necessary to ask the children to repeat the rationale in their own words. On these occasions, the trainer should reinforce the children's repetition, filling in points that may have been omitted.

Once the children understand the reason for behavior change, the trainer must give *direct instructions* on how to change it. Instructions should be clear and precise. For example, "Try to say 'No, I won't lend you more money' a little louder. See if you can emphasize the 'no' when you say the sentence." Vague instructions, such as "say it louder," will only confuse the children. Also, do not give too many instructions at one time, even if the children exhibit multiple problems when performing the behavior. In addition, instructions should sometimes include what not to do as well as how to improve the skill (e.g., "Be sure not to use an angry tone of voice when you say this, or it will make the other person feel bad or mad at you"). This allows them to discriminate between appropriate and inappropriate responses. However, such qualifications should be added only after the component has been adequately learned. As a rule, once the children can successfully perform the skilled behavior for three successive role plays, training should advance to the next element on the hierarchy.

Social skills have been compared to motor skills, such as swimming (Bellack et al., 1981). They are acquired not only through instruction, but also through *modeling*. By observing or listening to the trainer perform a skilled response, the child can imitate it. Modeling is conducted within the context of the role play format, with the child playing the part of the confederate and the trainer enacting the role of the child. The attention of the child must be focused on relevant aspects of the modeled responses. Without such direction, the children may become confused and their attention may be directed to extraneous aspects of the situation. Once again, brief instructions are recommended: "Now pay attention to how loudly I say 'no, I won't lend you any money.' When you are done, we will do the scene again and I will ask you to say the sentence as loudly as I did." Following the modeled statement, the children should be questioned to see if they attended to the important aspects of the response. It may be necessary to repeat the sequence several times to insure adequate modeling of the behavior.

Role playing can be initiated following the rationale, instructions, and modeling phases. Although parameters of the situation will have been presented earlier in the session, the narration and instructions should be repeated. For example, a role play narration might be as follows: "O.K., let's pretend that you are in the snackbar at 3:30. You run into a friend who has borrowed money from you but hasn't paid you back. He wants to borrow another dollar and promises to pay you back tomorrow. Remember to say, in a loud voice, that you won't lend him any more money until he pays you back. OK?" Notice that the instructions are simple and concentrate on a single target behavior (i.e., loudness of voice). Initially, the trainer should be a cooperative partner, and interchanges should be of short duration. After two or three sessions, when the child has shown improvement on the targeted behavior, the trainer may make the scene more difficult. The second confederate prompt may be changed: "But I really need it (the money) and I promise I'll pay you back tomorrow." However, the rule of thumb during the initial stages of training a behavior is simplicity; more complex exchanges are reserved for later sessions.

Performance feedback and positive reinforcement are dispensed by the trainer after the role played response. Feedback should be specific and succinct, focusing only on one aspect of the child's response. Although other behaviors may be problematic, they should be ignored for the time being. Feedback should always include positive reinforcement. Some aspect of the response, even if it is just the child's motivation and effort, should be praised. Criticism should be avoided. An example of appropriate feedback and positive reinforcement for increasing direction of gaze might be: "That was a really good job. You were looking at my face most of the time while you were talking."

Feedback and positive reinforcement are used to shape the child's behavior. Shaping refers to the differential reinforcement of successive approximations to the desired response. Through this process, the response gradually approaches an acceptable level. For example, a child may speak too rapidly. Through training the child is able to reduce speech rate, although it is still too rapid. After reinforcing the improved responses, the child will receive additional reinforcement only for further decreases in speech rate. Thus, the trainer is "shaping" the behavior toward a desired level.

It often is necessary to use *manual guidance* in modifying certain nonverbal behaviors in visually handicapped children. Totally blind children, in particular, frequently do not know what is meant by proper gaze or physical gestures. By manually guiding the head to the appropriate angle of gaze, the child learns what it feels like to engage in the proper stance. Similarly, for physical gestures, the trainer guides the child's hand and/or arm movements to appropriate positions. The trainer should ask the children to describe what the feeling is like, and how it differs from their usual placement of the head and arms, respectively. The behavior will improve as the children develop their own internal cues for adequate performance of skills.

Repetition is an essential part of skills training. It allows the children to practice what they have learned, and also gives the trainer numerous opportunities to observe the children's behavior. To maximize practice, a given role play scenario should be repeated at least three times, with a maximum of five times. If deficits are still exhibited after five trials, the format must be altered to make it easier for the child. The trainer should return to an earlier level of the hierarchy. Note that some children will not be able to master certain skills. Continued repetition is futile and may be frustrating for both child and trainer. Generally, a reasonable training goal is for the child to perform the *minimum acceptable response*. When this level is attained, advancement to the next hierarchy level should be considered.

Whereas repeated role play interactions provide some practice for the children, it is, of course, necessary for them to apply newly acquired skills in the natural environment. To accomplish this, the SSTP trainer provides *homework assignments* that require the child to practice skills in real-world situations. For example, when working on initiations, the trainer may ask the children to start conversations with two or three children they have never talked to before. Homework assignments in SSTP are less structured than those described in adult skills training programs (see Bellack & Hersen, 1978). This is largely to minimize task complexity for the children and increase the likelihood that assignments will be completed. Also, homework assignments are introduced in an informal manner: "You did a good job starting conversations with me today. Do you think you could begin conversations with two children at school that you have never talked with before? Why don't you try it and you can tell me how it went next time we meet." In the next session, when the children report their efforts to employ newly acquired skills, the trainer should provide reinforcement. Once again, some aspect of the children's behavior (even if it is just an attempt to perform the behavior) should be easy for them to perform successfully. They are designed to provide the children with positive social experiences in vivo, thus increasing their confidence in interpersonal situations. The trainer, therefore, should be certain that the assigned task involves skills in which the children are facile.

Social Perception Training. Social perception refers to the ability to understand social mores, recognize and identify expressed emotions in others, and predict the social consequences of one's interpersonal behavior. Deficits in these skills are likely to result in impaired social interactions (Morrison & Bellack, 1981). Indeed, inaccurate interpretation of feelings and emotions in others will likely result in inappropriate or inadequate social responses to them. Also, knowing *when* to make a certain statement can be just as important as knowing *how* to make that statement.

Social perception training is fairly unstructured relative to other aspects of social skills training. The primary mode of training social perception skills is providing direct instructions concerning social perception skills is providing direct instructions concerning social perception cues. The child is taught to recognize verbal and nonverbal (for partially sighted) cues of emotion (e.g., loud and hostile voice tone reflect anger). The concept should be introduced by the seventh training session, although it may be offered earlier if the child is progressing rapidly. However, the child should achieve mastery of the verbal and nonverbal components of a situation prior to receiving social perception instruction. This is because children often find such information difficult to learn. Further, it may be confusing if introduced while other components are being trained. For example, consider the following role play scenario: "A friend of yours frequently wears mismatched clothing. You would really like to help him."

After training several behavioral components, you may introduce social perception: "O.K. That was good. You spoke loudly, and your voice was very pleasant. Now, when might you say something to your friend about his clothing? You wouldn't want to tell him with other people there, because he might be embarrassed. Maybe you can say something to him after school when the two of you are alone together." Trainers must use their judgment to determine when and how to introduce social perception cues. Some scenarios will involve more social perception information than others. Also, children will vary in their ability to acquire this concept.

Problems in Training

A major difficulty encountered in skills training is adherence to the protocol. Even the most experienced trainers will "drift" in their methods and structure of training, failing to use enough role play repetitions, or advancing to a new component before the first one is mastered. Although there is some latitude in determining the "flow" of sessions (i.e., deciding when to advance to a new behavior or when to concentrate on social perception issues), the trainer should follow the protocol outlined in the manual as closely as possible. Behavior change is achieved only through a full application of the training procedures.

Problems may occur in teaching the child the role play procedure. Bellack (1979) pointed out that people vary in their ability to role play realistically and accurately. Some children may have difficulty imagining themselves in the role play situation. Others may be reticent, self-conscious, or anxious when role playing. Some children may avoid the situation by responding to a prompt with an irrelevant "delaying" statement, such as "I would do..." or "let's see, what should I say." The trainer must discourage these responses and try to make the role playing experience more comfortable for the child. For example, the child can be directed to spend a minute trying to imagine the scene more vividly. This technique coupled with modeling and positive reinforcement by the trainer, will enable the child to adapt to the procedure.

Structure of Training

Skills training is divided into three primary sections: assessment, training, and booster sessions. In addition, follow-up assessments are conducted to ascertain durability of treatment gains. Table 15.2 provides a session-by-session outline of treatment. Note that training consists of up to 20 sessions, depending on the needs of the child.

The first training session should involve establishment of rapport with the child. The trainer should then introduce a skill component (e.g., direction of gaze) to be worked on in the session. The component should be drawn from the pretraining hierarchy developed during the assessment stage. Up to five role play situations may be employed in the session. As mentioned earlier, these scenes may be taken from Van Hasselt et al. (1981), or new situations may be created that are particularly relevant to the child. A choice of situations provides additional information for the trainer and lessens boredom for the child. As the child masters new skills, training should progress through the hierarchy. Social perception training is introduced in Sessions 5–7, following acquisition of several components and situations from the hierarchy.

Following the training stage, *booster sessions* (i.e., reviews of previously trained material) are employed to modify behaviors that may have deteriorated after training and to consolidate

TABLE 15.2

Session-by-Session Plan of Training

Pretraining	Assessment: Self-Report, Parent and Teacher Ratings
Session 1	Role Play Assessment
	Preliminary Treatment Plan
Sessions 2, 3, & 4	Train on first problem area of hierarchy
Sessions 5, 6, & 7	Train on second problem area of hierarchy
	Introduce Social Perception Training
Sessions 8, 9, & 10	Train on third problem area of hierarchy
Sessions 11, 12, & 13	Train on fourth problem area of hierarchy
Sessions 14, 15, & 16	Train on fifth problem area of hierarchy
Session 17	Summarize accomplishments and plan for future problems
Booster Sessions 1, 2, 3, & 4 (4, 6, 8, & 10 weeks following training)	Role play to assess for possible response decrements Remediate skill deficits
Follow-up (12 weeks)	Posttraining assessment to determine maintenance of gains

gains. A number of researchers have advocated the use of such a strategy (see Hersen, 1979). It should not be expected that the child necessarily will retain the level of improvement achieved in training. New problems will arise, and the child may "lose" or "forget" what to do in a situation. Booster sessions serve to reinforce gains and fill in the gaps as new difficulties are encountered by the child. They are held at 4, 6, 8, and 10 weeks posttraining. Format for booster sessions is the same as training sessions: modeling, role play, feedback, and so forth.

As mentioned earlier, follow-up assessment is conducted 12 weeks subsequent to formal termination of training to determine durability of treatment effects. The trainer should readminister those instruments used in the pretraining assessment. These may include role play situations not previously administered to evaluate response generalization. An examination of videotapes of the role played interactions, combined with a comparison of questionnaire scores from pre- to posttraining assessment, provided a gauge through which to measure improvement in social skills.

ACKNOWLEDGMENTS

Preparation of this chapter was facilitated by Grant 12-122 from the March of Dimes Birth Defects Foundation and Grant G008300135 from the National Institute on Disabilities and Rehabilitation Research, U. S. Department of Education. The authors wish to acknowledge the contributions of Louise E. Moore and Jan Twomey.

REFERENCES

Achenbach, T. M., & Edelbrock, C. S. (1978). The classification of child psychopathology: A review and analysis of empirical efforts. *Psychological Bulletin, 85,* 1275–1301.

Ammerman, R. T., Van Hasselt, V. B., & Hersen, M. (1986). Psychological adjustment of visually handicapped children and youth. *Clinical Psychology Review, 6,* 67–85.

Apple, M. M. (1972). Kinesic training for blind persons: A vital means of communication. *The New Outlook for the Blind, 66,* 201–208.

Asher, S. R., Oden, S. L., & Gottman, J. M. (1977). Children's friendships in school settings. In L.G. Katy (Ed.), *Current topics in early childhood education* (Vol.1). Norwood, NJ: Ablex.

Bellack, A. S. (1979). Behavioral assessment of social skills. In A. S. Bellack & M. Hersen (Eds.), *Research and practice in social skills training*. New York: Plenum.

Bellack, A. S. (1983). Recurrent problems in the behavioral assessment of social skill. *Behaviour Research and Therapy, 21*, 29–41.

Bellack, A. S., & Hersen, M. (1978). Chronic psychiatric patients: Social skills training. In M. Hersen & A. S. Bellack (Eds.), *Behavior therapy in the psychiatric setting*. Baltimore: Williams & Wilkins.

Bellack, A. S., Hersen, M., & Himmelhoch, J. M. (1981). Social skills training compared with pharmacotherapy and psychotherapy in the treatment of unipolar depression. *American Journal of Psychiatry, 138*, 1562–1567.

Bradway, K. P. (1937). Social competence of exceptional children: III. The deaf, the blind, and the crippled. *Exceptional Children, 4*, 64–69.

Charlesworth, R., & Hartup, W. W. (1967). Positive social reinforcement in the nursery school peer group. *Child Development, 38,* 993–1002.

Cowen, E. L., Pederson, A., Babigian, H., Izzo, L. D., & Trost, M. A. (1973). Long-term follow-up of early detected vulnerable children. *Journal of Consulting and Clinical Psychology, 41*, 438–446.

Czerwinski, M. H., & Tait, P. E. (1981). Blind children's perceptions of normal withdrawn, and antisocial behavior. *Journal of Visual Impairment and Blindness, 75*, 252–257.

Dil, N. (1972). Sensitivity of emotionally disturbed and emotionally nondisturbed elementary school children to emotional meanings of facial expressions. *Dissertation Abstracts International, 32*, 448A. (University Microfilms No. 72–6652)

Emery, J. E. (1975). Social perception processes in normal and learning disabled children. *Dissertation Abstracts International*, 36, 1942B–1943B. (University Microfilms No. 75–21, 144)

Farkas, G. M., Sherick, R. B., Matson, J. L., & Loebig, M. (1981). Social skills training of a blind child through differential reinforcement. *The Behavior Therapist, 4*, 24–26.

Feffer, M., & Suchotliff, L. (1966). Decentering implications of social interactions. *Journal of Personality and Social Psychology, 4*, 415–422.

Goldfried, M. R., & D'Zurilla, R. J. (1969). A behavioral-analytic model for assessing competence. In C. D. Spielberger (Ed.), *Current topics in clinical and community psychology* (Vol.1). New York: Academic Press.

Gottman, J., Gonso, J., & Rasmussen, B. (1975). Social interaction, social competence, and friendship in children. *Child Development, 46*, 709–718.

Harper, R. G., Wiens, A. N., & Matarazzo, J. D. (1978). *Nonverbal communication: The state of the art.* New York: Wiley.

Hartup, W. W. (1970). Peer interaction and social organization. In P. H. Mussen (Ed.), *Carmichael's manual of child psychology* (Vol. 2). New York: Wiley.

Hartup, W. W., Glazer, J. A., & Charlesworth, R. (1967). Peer reinforcement and sociometric status. *Child Development, 38*, 1017–1024.

Hersen, M. (1979). Limitations and problems in the clinical application of behavioral techniques in psychiatric settings. *Behavior Therapy, 10*, 65–80.

Hops, H. (1983). Children's social competence and skill: Current research practices and future directions. *Behavior Therapy, 14*, 13–18.

Keller, M. F., & Carlson, P. M. (1974). The use of symbolic modeling to promote social skills in preschool children with four levels of social responsiveness. *Child Development, 45*, 912–919.

Kleck, R. E., Ono, H., & Hastorf, A. H. (1966). The effect of physical deviance upon face-to-face interaction. *Human Relations, 19*, 425–436.

Kleck, R. E., Richardson, S. A., & Ronald, L. (1974). Physical appearance cues and interpersonal attraction in children. *Child Development, 45*, 305–310.

Kohlberg, L., LaCrosse, J., & Ricks, D. (1972). The predictability of adult mental health from childhood behavior. In B. Wolman (Ed.), *Manual of child psychopathology*. New York: McGraw-Hill.

Lowenfeld, B. (1962). Psychological foundation of special methods in teaching blind children. In P. A. Zahl (Ed.), *Blindness: Modern approaches to the unseen environment*. New York: Hafner.

Matson, J. L., Rotatori, A. F., & Helsel, W. J. (1983). Development of a rating scale to measure social skills in children: The Matson Evaluation of Social Skills with Youngsters (MESSY). *Behaviour Research and Therapy, 21*, 335–340.

Maxfield, K. E., & Fjeld, H. A. (1942). The social maturity of the visually handicapped preschool child. *Child Development, 13*, 1–27.

McKay, B. E. (1936). Social maturity of the preschool blind child. *Training School Bulletin, 33*, 145–155.

Michelson, L., & Wood, R. (1981). Behavioral assessment and training of children's social skills. In M. Hersen, R. M. Eisler, & P. M. Miller (Eds.), *Progress in behavior modification* (Vol. 9). New York: Academic Press.

Michelson, L., & Wood, R. (1982). Development and psychometric properties of the Children's Assertive Behavior Scale. *Journal of Behavioral Assessment, 4*, 3–13.

Morrison, R. L., & Bellack, A. S. (1981). The role of social perception in social skill. *Behavior Therapy, 12*, 69–79.

Reardon, R. C., Hersen, M., Bellack, A. S., & Foley, J. M. (1979). Measuring social skill in grade school boys. *Journal of Behavioral Assessment, 1*, 87–105.

Richardson, S. A. (1969). The effect of physical disability on the socialization of a child. In D. Goslin (Ed.), *Handbook of socialization theory and research*. Chicago: Rand McNally.

Scott, R. A. (1969). The socialization of blind children. In D. Goslin (Ed.), *Handbook of socialization theory and research*. Chicago: Rand McNally.

Stewart, I. W., Van Hasselt, V. B., Simon, J., & Thompson, W. B. (1985). The Community Adjustment Program (CAP) for visually handicapped adolescents. *Journal of Visual Impairment and Blindness, 79*, 49–54.

Ulman, C. A. (1957). Teachers, peers, and tests of predictors of adjustment. *Journal of Educational Psychology, 48*, 257–267.

Van Hasselt, V. B. (1983). Social adaptation in the blind. *Clinical Psychology Review, 3*, 87–102.

Van Hasselt, V. B., Hersen, M., & Kazdin, A. E. (1985). Assessment of social skills in visually handicapped adolescents. *Behaviour Research and Therapy, 23*, 53–63.

Van Hasselt, V. B., Hersen, M., Kazdin, A. E., Simon, J., & Mastantuono, A. K. (1983). Training blind adolescents in social skills. *Journal of Visual Impairment and Blindness, 77*, 199–203.

Van Hasselt, V. B., Hersen, M., Kazdin, A. E., Sisson, L. A., Simon, J., & Mastantuono, A. K. (1981, November). *A behavioral-analytic model for assessing social skills in blind adolescents*. Paper presented at the Annual Convention of the Association for Advancement of Behavior Therapy, Toronto.

Van Hasselt, V. B., Hersen, M., Whitehill, M. B., & Bellack, A. S. (1979). Social skill assessment and training for children: An evaluative review. *Behaviour Research and Therapy, 17*, 413–437.

Van Hasselt, V. B., Simon, J., & Mastanuono, A. K. (1982). Social skills training for blind children: A program description. *Education of the Visually Handicapped, 14*, 34–40.

Waldrop, M. F., & Halverson, C. F. (1975). Intensive and extensive peer behaviors: Longitudinal and cross-sectional analysis. *Child Development, 46*, 19–26.

Yarnall, G. D. (1979). Developing eye contact in a visually impaired, deaf child. *Education of the Visually Handicapped, 11*, 56–59.

Young, L. L., & Cooper, D. H. (1944). Some factors associated with popularity. *Journal of Educational Psychology, 35*, 513–535.

Chapter 16

Families and the Developmentally Disabled Adolescent

Sandra L. Harris
Beth Glasberg
Lara Delmolino
Rutgers, The State University of New Jersey

Life in a family is complicated. It is good and bad, affirming and distressing, separate and connected. In a healthy family, there can be considerable joy, as well as inevitable tension. In a dysfunctional family, the heartache outweighs the joy, and the entire family suffers. However, pain is not confined to dysfunctional families. Every family, no matter how well functioning, faces moments of sorrow. A grandparent dies, a parent loses a job, or a child has trouble at school. These stressful events take their toll. Nevertheless, in a healthy family they do not destroy the fabric of the family, and the members typically rebound to a more comfortable level of functioning after they cope with the problem.

For some families, there are chronic stressors that impose continuing demands. Such stressors may tug more relentlessly at the strength of the family than do normative and more time limited stressors (e.g., death of a grandparent). One chronic stressor is the presence of a child with a moderate to severe developmental disability such as autism or mental retardation. For both theoretical and pragmatic reasons, researchers have been interested in what it means to a family when an adolescent has a significant developmental disability. A number of investigators have explored whether these families inevitably suffer greater distress than other families.

The purpose of this chapter is to describe the issues faced by families that include an adolescent with a developmental disorder. However, because the teenage years are typically a period of stress for all families, it is important to know something about what it means to be part of any family that includes a teenager. This information may help identify those experiences unique to the family that has a child with a developmental disability. To this end, the impact of adolescence on the young person and some of the developmental tasks of families of normally developing adolescents are discussed first. Then, to help the reader appreciate the unusual demands created by the teenager with a developmental disability, the clinical picture of adolescents with autism or mental retardation are described, and how the symptom picture changes as the child grows up is considered. Next, the special stress is reviewed that accrues in a family, including the siblings, when there is a child with a developmental disability. In particular several specific challenges that face these young people and their parents are examined. Some of these include: sexuality, social development, living arrangements, and job placements. Finally, a case illustration is offered to highlight some issues faced by the family of a teenager with a developmental disability.

NORMATIVE DEVELOPMENT: THE ADOLESCENT AND THE FAMILY

In Western culture, adolescence may be a time of some turmoil for the young person and the family. The biological, cognitive, social, and psychological maturation that accompanies growing up in society generates tensions in the family as the young person adapts to major biological changes, and establishes autonomy. This is a transition of "push and pull" between the young person and the family, and between the adolescent who is becoming and the child who was.

Biological Maturation

The physical changes of adolescence are rivaled only by infancy for the speed and drama of their transforming effects. In a relatively brief period, the body changes in size and shape, and reproductive organs become mature. Although these changes are relatively rapid, there is a moderate age range for initial onset, which means that some youngsters mature physically before others. An example of change is seen in the acceleration of penis growth for males, which, on average, begins at 12.5 years, although it may begin as early as 10.5 years, or as late as 14.5 years (Tanner, 1978). The spontaneous ejaculation of seminal fluid ("wet dreams") begins about a year after the beginning of penis growth. Similarly, for girls, the onset of menarche, which follows the onset of breast development, averages between 12 and 13 years, with a range from 11 to 15 years. Thus, for both girls and boys there is considerable normal age variation in the onset of the development of sexual organs, and of secondary sexual characteristics (Tanner, 1978). The timing of a child's biological maturation carries with it social and psychological consequences. Both early and late maturation can lead to difficulty with self-esteem for girls, and the same consequence is true for late maturing boys (Nottelmann, Inoff-Germain, Susman, & Chrousos, 1990).

Cognitive Changes

There are cognitive as well as physical changes in adolescence. Between the ages of 11 or 12, and 14 or 15, young people become capable of attaining a level of abstract thought that was not possible before. They are able to think about their own thinking (Muuss, 1988). This increased capacity for reflection enables the young person to hold a philosophy about religion, science, politics, and so forth. It is this newly formed ability to think at a more sophisticated conceptual level that is related to the political and social passion shown by many young people as they become concerned about changes in the social order. Another important aspect of this cognitive maturation concerns social cognition, or understanding what other people are thinking or feeling. Not only can adolescents step outside of their skin and understand what another person is feeling, they can more abstractly consider how a third party would think about an interaction (Muuss, 1988).

With the biological, cognitive, and psychological changes of adolescence come new tasks to be mastered by the young person, including appropriate expression of sexual needs, management of increased physical strength, and learning necessary hygiene, as well as adapting to the loss of childhood roles, and handling the demands for a more mature and responsible mode of interacting with others. These physical changes and concomitant psychological and social changes place significant demands on the adolescent and the family.

Psychological and Social Changes

Adolescence is a crucial developmental period. It is a time of challenge and growth for families when both parents and children may find their horizons broadening and their opportunities expanding. In Western culture, the teenage years are a time of increasing autonomy and independence for young people. This is a normative transition from dependence to increased independence that most families handle with reasonable equanimity, but that can create a developmental challenge for some families where the struggle over autonomy is especially fierce.

Ackerman (1980) noted that "the adolescent challenges the family daily with new styles, new language, new mannerisms, and new values for behavior. More than any other family member, the adolescent is not only a conduit to the world at large, but a bridge between old and new" (p. 148). The openness to experimentation of the teenage years leads parents to worry about their child's developing sexuality, the risk of pregnancy, and sexually transmitted diseases including HIV, potential abuse of drugs and alcohol, poor academic performance, and defiance of authority. The extent of the impact of these and similar concerns was reflected in Burr's (1970) observation that adolescence marks one of the lowest points of marital satisfaction for parents.

Although adolescent development makes the adolescent and the family vulnerable to pain and maladaptive behavior, it also offers exciting new adventures for children and parents alike. As teenagers pull away and enters their own world of friendship, dating, school, and work, parents are left increasingly alone to rediscover their own needs, and to explore their intimate relationships. For adults with a healthy marriage and good sense of self, this can be liberating; for those who depended on their children to maintain family stability, it is a time of disorder and potential dissolving of relationships. For single parents, there may be the opportunity to create new intimate relationships, to savor one's singleness, or alternatively to retreat to loneliness.

The Family Life Cycle

The concept of the "family life cycle" has been used to describe the transitional events families face across the entire life span (e.g., Carter & McGoldrick, 1980; McCubbin & Figley, 1983). This cyclic model of family development refers to normative transitions in the lives of children and parents that mark the passage from one life phase to another. Examples of early family life cycle events include marriage, the birth of a first child, and the child's starting school. Each of these events, joyful as they may be, imposes demands on the family to adapt to change. In addition, some life cycle events, such as the death of a parent or a spouse, although normative, are painful and very difficult to accept.

One life cycle event that brings both joy and rigor to most families is the entry of children into adolescence, and later, their launching into young adulthood. Parents of adolescent children, sometimes called the "sandwich generation," may be dealing with more than one transitional event at the same time. As their child enters the teenage years, their own parents may be aging, ill, and may die. These parents must meet the needs of their youngsters, their own parents, and themselves—a series of challenges that can test the most resilient of persons.

Kidwell, Fischer, Dunham, and Baranowski (1983) pointed out that parental development may interact with child development during adolescence. Parents may be confronting a developmental crisis of their own in recognizing that vocational goals—such as becoming CEO of a corporation, principal of a school, or foreperson of a work crew—are beyond one's grasp, and feeling a sense of envy for the young person whose life is just beginning and for whom such dreams are still attainable. Similarly, the young person's budding sexuality may challenge the diminishing sense of sexual attractiveness experienced by some adults. The envy and resentment parents feel in response to these adolescent possibilities can increase tension between generations. It is also, of course, an opportunity for parents to come to a mature understanding of what is important to them, and how they wish to live in the next decades.

Most families are successful in helping their young person navigate the rough waters of adolescence. Although the majority of teenagers in Western culture test the limits of parental authority, and go through a process of separation including arguments and some defiance of parental rules, for the most part this process is mild. Children cut their hair in unusual ways, experiment with alcohol, put a dent in the fender of the car, and stay out too late without permission. These events are transient, respond to limit setting and negotiation, and are counterbalanced by the positive events that follow from entering this new life stage. After effectively completing this transitional phase, the family will find that all of its members have achieved increased autonomy, while still retaining links that allow them to feel enduring bonds.

The Adolescent With a Developmental Disability

This picture of tumult, challenge, growth, and change that is part of normative adolescent development can look quite different when the young person has mental retardation or autism. For these families, adolescence may signify the end of illusion. Parents' hope for a dramatic change in functioning is difficult to sustain as the teenager leaves childhood behind. Those children who were likely to have made major strides toward more normalized functioning are likely to have done so at an earlier age (e.g., Lovaas, 1987), and those children who continue to exhibit significant symptoms are likely to do so into the future. Bristol and Schopler (1983) commented that parents of adolescents with autism have a greater sense of realism and pessimism about their child's eventual outcome than do parents of younger children.

Although children with a developmental disorder grow older, bigger, and physically more mature, they have little capacity to strive for autonomy. Although these young people can continue to acquire new skills in an appropriate educational setting, they remain grossly different from normally developing peers (Mesibov, 1983) and continue to require extensive supervision in basic self-care (Harris, 1984). Realization of the enduring nature of the disability may be a significant stressor for some families in the transition from childhood to adolescence (Harris, Gill, & Alessandri, 1990).

As families confront their enduring sense of loss, they may need formal or informal support in dealing with their grief. The landmarks of adolescence (e.g., learning to drive a car, going out on a first date, or making plans for a first job or college) are not likely to happen to children with a developmental disability. Instead, parents find themselves facing a long-term future of care taking and physical dependence. This long-term dependency must be dealt with on an emotional as well as a pragmatic level. For example, parents and siblings need to begin to talk about who will care for the person with autism or mental retardation when parents are no longer willing or able to do so. As is discussed later, the young people will be able to gain autonomy only to the extent that parents, teachers, and other concerned adults ensure that they are taught the community living and vocational skills essential to such a transition. Unlike their peers, these teenagers are not going to push for the kinds of changes that are part of the normative developmental process of adolescence.

CHANGES IN THE CLINICAL PICTURE

In general, adolescents with developmental disabilities become more "malleable," "adaptable," and "easier to live with" as they grow up (Rutter, 1970). Gillberg (1984) remarked that, in general, the more severe symptoms occur in the early childhood of an individual with autism, followed by somewhat less problematic behaviors in school years, with moderate "crises" surfacing in adolescence. This section reviews some of the areas where changes may occur as children with developmental disabilities enter adolescence. These include: activity level, ritualistic behavior, anxiety and mood, aggression and self-injury, seizures, appearance, and intelligence.

Activity Level

Children with developmental disabilities, like their normally developing peers, show a decline in activity level as they get older. However, unlike their normally developing peers, for some children with developmental disabilities, this may result in underactivity during adolescence (Rutter, 1970). Ando and Yoshimura (1979) compared activity levels of children age 6 to 9, and 11 to 14, with autism or mental retardation. For both diagnoses, the older children had significantly lower levels of activity than the younger ones, including significant underactivity for some children in both diagnostic groups.

Aggression/Self-Injury

Rutter (1970) found no general developmental trends for aggressive or self-injurious behaviors. One obvious consideration is, however, the increased physical strength of mentally retarded or autistic individuals as they grow up. Although there may be no change, or even a decline in the frequency of self-injurious or aggressive behaviors, the consequences of these behaviors, when they do occur, may be more dangerous and create the impression that the behavior is getting worse because the child is stronger (Rutter, 1970; Schopler & Mesibov, 1983).

Compulsive/Ritualistic Behavior

The compulsive, ritualistic, or obsessive behaviors typical of the child with autism tend to lessen in adolescence (Rutter, 1970). There is wide individual variation; however, on average, there is a significant decrease in abnormal preoccupations and obsessive behavior (Garfin,

McCallon, & Cox, 1988). In many cases, it appears that these behaviors continue, but become more manageable and subtle as the individual finds ways to incorporate them into more appropriate or functional aspects of behavior.

Anxiety and Mood

Anxiety and fears, like ritualistic behaviors, decline in adolescence. Rutter (1970) found a decrease in anxiety and fears in his follow-up study of individuals with autism. Similarly, Garfin et al. (1988) observed that if fears continue in adolescence, the individual often has improved skills for coping with them.

There appear to be age-related changes in the mood and affective state of individuals with autism, particularly those children with higher intelligence. Szatmari, Bartolucci, Bremner, and Bond (1989) commented that, in their follow-up study of nonretarded persons with autism, many of the early symptoms disappeared with age. However, these same individuals showed enduring impairment in social interaction and communication. These enduring impairments may have an effect on mood. Gillberg (1984) suggested that people with higher IQs can more readily recognize their residual deficits, and as a result become increasingly aware that they are "different" from typical peers. This awareness is often associated with depression when these individuals enter adolescence. However, the likelihood of the development of depressive symptoms is also related to other genetic components of depression and affective disorders. People who have affected relatives are most likely to be affected themselves (Gillberg, 1984). Gillberg (1984) noted that individuals with mental retardation may also suffer from depression.

Seizures

One of the most devastating changes that may occur is the development of seizures. In most cases, the development of epilepsy at or near the time of puberty has not been preceded by any salient neurological or physiological symptoms associated with seizure activity (Rutter, 1970). Often, the emergence of a seizure disorder is associated with marked cognitive deterioration, but not necessarily by the aggravation of symptoms (Gillberg & Steffenburg, 1987). Schopler and Mesibov (1983) suggested that this is consistent with Rutter's (1970) contention that the development of seizures, much like the underactivity that emerges in adolescence, is related to some physiological aspects of brain maturation.

A number of investigators (Bartak & Rutter, 1976; Gillberg, 1984; Rutter, 1970) have identified those individuals with the lowest IQs to be at higher risk for the onset of seizures. Of the 18 individuals developing seizures in Rutter's (1970) study, only 2 had initial IQs above 65. Schopler and Mesibov (1983) concluded that it is rare to discover individuals with IQs higher than 70 developing seizures after puberty. This is consistent with the general literature suggesting that those who are most severely impaired and affected at the outset have a poorer overall prognosis (Bartak & Rutter, 1976).

Figures estimating the frequency of seizures in individuals with developmental disabilities varies. Gillberg (1984), as well as Schopler and Mesibov (1983), suggested that approximately one third to one quarter of individuals with autism develop epilepsy as adolescents or adults. In the Gillberg and Steffenburg (1987) follow-up study of adolescents diagnosed with autism and other childhood psychoses, 35% of the sample displayed the onset of seizures, in most cases between age 12 and 15. In Rutter's (1970) follow-up investigation, 28% of the participants developed seizures.

Appearance

One of the other physical changes that accompanies adolescence in some people with developmental disabilities is an alteration in appearance. In general, young children with autism appear "normal" (Gillberg, 1984), may be characterized as "intellectual and attractive" (Gillberg & Steffenburg, 1987), and may even be indistinguishable from peers on the basis of physical appearance. During adolescence, it has been observed that often the individual appears more "deviant, coarse, and plump" (Gillberg & Steffenburg, 1987). This change is more noticeable for those individuals with IQs at the lower end of the spectrum, particularly with childhood IQs of less than 50 (Gillberg & Steffenburg, 1987). The "plumpness" may be due to the combination of typical physical changes occuring in puberty in combination with a sharp decline in activity level. Oddities of gait, facial expression, and posture may also contribute to the unusual appearance of the person with a developmental disability.

Intelligence

In assessing changes in intelligence with the onset of adolescence, it is important to remember that children with autism vary widely in intelligence, with some being markedly retarded and others functioning in the normal range. They differ in this respect from other children with mental retardation who, by definition, are all below average in intelligence.

In general, the IQs of individuals with autism remain stable across the lifespan, with no major changes in adolescence (Schopler & Mesibov, 1983). There are specific cases of significant IQ changes in both directions, but these are the exceptions, and the probability of an individual's IQ falling or rising are roughly equivalent (Rutter, 1970). It has been noted by Rutter (1970) that the fluctuations in IQ are "roughly the same magnitude in autistic children as they are in normal children" (p. 441), with the mean change being approximately plus or minus 15 points. Those individuals who develop seizures in adolescence, or show other signs of deterioration often exhibit a measurable decline in IQ as well (Rutter, 1970). Those individuals who are most likely to show gains in IQ are those with initial IQs above 70.

Similar patterns have been observed in other developmentally disabled people. Dykens, Leckman, Paul, and Watson (1988) found no distinct differences in the cognitive profiles of autistic, fragile X, or other individuals with nonspecific mental retardation. The cognitive development of individuals with fragile X, which shares many descriptive features with autism, has also been described as fairly steady through the childhood years followed by a drop or plateau in adolescence (Dykens et al., 1988). There appears to be minimal evidence for persons with fragile X showing increases in IQ after puberty (Dykens, Hodapp, Ort, & Leckman, 1993).

General Trends

Given the variability of behavior characterizing the transition into adolescence for children with developmental disabilities (Gillberg & Steffenburg, 1987), it is not surprising that the "average" profile may appear to be rather stable. The consequences for those individuals who do not progress in a positive direction or who plateau at the onset of puberty can be quite negative. Gillberg and Steffenburg (1987) described two paths for individuals who do not have a positive outcome in adolescence. The first involves a temporary exacerbation of symptoms at the onset of puberty, typically involving greater levels of aggression, destruction, compulsiveness, and some hyperactivity. The second course involves a progressive deterioration of both behavior and skill, often preceded by an aggravation of symptoms.

Gillberg (1984) estimated that deterioration of functioning occurs in approximately one third of adolescents with autism. Rutter (1970) reported that 7 of the 64 individuals with autism in his follow-up sample showed considerable deterioration in adolescence.

Gillberg and Steffenburg (1987) compared people with autism and "other childhood psychoses." This second group consisted of individuals with a range of disorders, including Rett syndrome, hypothyroidism, schizophrenia, and fragile X. The onset of puberty for both groups was marked by a temporary aggravation of symptoms in approximately one half of the cases, and a successive deterioration in 20% of all the cases.

Gender appears to be a factor in deterioration (Gillberg & Steffenburg, 1987) with more females than males declining in functioning. This is consistent with the well-documented finding that the male-to-female ratio of individuals with autism is heavily weighted toward the males (4:1), but that those females affected tend to be more severely impaired, behaviorally and cognitively (Volkmar, Szatmari, & Sparrow, 1993).

STRESS AND COPING IN FAMILIES

This section reviews research on the ways that having an adolescent with mental retardation or autism affects the family. Studies with younger children are introduced for purposes of comparison, or when the only relevant literature involved younger participants.

There is considerable variability in the way families cope with the special needs generated by the disability of a child with autism or mental retardation. Some families appear to cope with relative efficacy, whereas others are so burdened they no longer function effectively. A variety of factors have been linked to this variability in functioning, including the specific diagnosis of the child, the severity of the child's symptoms, the marital relationship, the individual psychological functioning of the parents, and the formal and informal social support networks available to the family. Each of these can impact on how well the family copes with the stressors created by the child's disability. Although there is a moderate body of research looking at how these factors relate to the functioning of families of younger children, relatively little research has looked specifically at how families of adolescents function.

The Effect of Diagnosis on Stress

There is some empirical support for the notion that the adolescent's diagnosis has an impact on parental stress levels. For example, Donovan (1988) studied mothers' reports of family stress levels and methods of coping with their adolescent who had autism or mental retardation. She found that mothers who had a teenager with autism reported higher levels of stress than did mothers of children with mental retardation. However, there were many similarities between the two groups. Both groups of women said they relied a great deal on community resources and professional support in coping with the needs of their teenager. They also did not differ from one another in marital adjustment, with about one third of all mothers reporting significant distress. Donovan's (1988) data supported the notion that "the more pervasive the impact of a handicapping condition on development..., the more stressful the adolescent is on the family" (p. 507).

Further support for the contention that the more severe the child's disability, the greater the toll on the family, was provided by Bristol and Schopler (1983), who reported that families whose child with autism was easier to care for and less profoundly involved were able to cope more effectively than were those parents whose child demonstrated more severe symptoms. In a comparison of stress levels of mothers and fathers of younger and older children with mental retardation, spina bifida, and matched comparison normally developing children, Kazak (1987) found that parents of the older mentally retarded children showed the greatest degree of stress.

In a study of families who had an adolescent with moderate mental retardation, diabetes, or cystic fibrosis, Walker, Van Slyke, and Newbrough (1992) found no differences in overall stress level. There were, however, specific concerns attached to each disability. The mothers of children with mental retardation were more concerned about child management problems, cognitive impairment, and plans for the young person's adulthood than were mothers in the other two groups. It is important to note that these were children with moderate mental retardation, and stress levels for parents of adolescents with severe and profound retardation may be greater than for moderate levels of retardation (e.g., Kazak, 1988).

Changes Across Time

The relation between a child's age and the degree of stress reported by family members is not simple or linear; nor is it constant over time. Rather, some studies suggest stress is a cyclic phenomenon that is intensified at times of major family life cycle transition. Wikler (1986) collected reports of stress from parents of children with mental retardation across several ages including children of latency age, early adolescence, midadolescence, entry to adulthood, and young adulthood. She found the highest levels of stress in families whose children were just entering early adolescence or early adulthood, as compared to those whose children were in latency, later adolescence, or further into young adulthood. Wikler (1986) suggested that the children entering adolescence or adulthood were in periods of significant transition that were accompanied by greater family stress than other periods in the child's life. Her data support the notion that transitions in the family life cycle are a source of special stress for families of children with developmental disabilities.

DeMyer (1979) noted that although the specific kinds of problems a family confronts may change as a child with autism grows older, the sheer demands do not seem to lessen. The parents of children with autism reported problems dealing with sexual development, puberty, finding educational and professional services, worries about long-term care, financial concerns, and distress about other people's responses to their young person with autism. More recently, similar observations were made by Fong, Wilgosh, and Sobsey (1993) in their interviews of parents of adolescents with autism.

In a survey of 23 families of adolescents with autism, DeMyer and Goldberg (1983) found that lack of family recreation time was the most stressful aspect of rearing this child. These families had essentially no time to relax, and many described themselves as reaching the point of "burn out" in their child-care role. Almost all families pointed to the emotional, mental, and physical health of parents as having suffered over the years of childrearing. The large amounts of time required for child care made other activities, such as housekeeping or outside activities, very difficult for most of the women interviewed. Interpersonal relationships were influenced in many respects. For example, parents felt they did not have enough time to devote to their other children, and had concerns about the relationship between the child with autism and the other children. Nonetheless, parental reports suggested that the sibling relationship improved as the children got older.

Parents in the DeMyer and Goldberg (1983) study indicated that their marriages had been more stressed when their child was younger than during the teenage years. Interestingly, the divorce rate for these families was lower than for the general population. Similarly, relationships with relatives seem to have been more problematic early in the child's life than they were later on. Extended family members may have become less critical of the parents over time.

Changes in community acceptance may pose an especially acute problem for the family of an adolescent with a developmental disability (DeMyer & Goldberg, 1983; Suelzle & Keenan, 1981). Their children are no longer "cute" and behavior once accepted as childlike or innocent may now appear increasingly deviant and unacceptable in the eyes of neighbors. Bristol (1984) reported that as children with autism grow up, the family is at greater risk for isolation because of reduced community acceptance of the child. Some families may withdraw from the community when they experience rejection of their adolescent. Rather than be in the public eye, they may avoid going out to dinner, to a movie, or on a family vacation (Akerley, 1984). This isolation runs counter to the stimulation characterizing most families of normally developing adolescents, and may intensify a rigidity of family routines rather than encourage the experimentation that other families attempt at this point in the family life cycle (Harris & Powers, 1984). This diminishing of the informal support network is of great concern because of the vital role such networks play in effective family coping (e.g., Bristol, 1984).

Some investigations have found greater stress for parents of older children as compared to younger ones (Bristol, 1984; Bristol & Schopler, 1983; Donovan, 1988; Holroyd, Brown, Wikler, & Simmons, 1975). Suelzle and Keenan (1981) surveyed 330 parents of children with mental retardation at different stages of the family life cycle, including preschool, elementary school, teenage, and young adult. Parents of younger children reported that they used more professional services and had larger support networks than did parents of older children. Parents of older children described themselves as more isolated, receiving less support, and in need of greater professional services. Bristol and Schopler (1983) noted the lack of services for adolescents, and the increase in parental concern about resources as the child gets older.

Finally, some studies have failed to find consistent differences across age, but rather suggest that stress is sustained over the years. For example, Flynt and his colleagues (Flynt & Wood, 1989; Flynt, Wood, & Scott, 1992) compared the reported stress and social support of mothers of children with mental retardation across three age groups: preschool, school age, and young adult. They found no significant differences in stress levels or coping methods across these three ages.

Among the stressors that appear to persist for parents of children with autism across time are concerns about the welfare of their child when they are no longer able to provide care, the level of the child's cognitive impairment, the child's ability to function independently, and the child's acceptance in the community (Koegel et al., 1992).

There may be several reasons for the variations in timing of reported stress levels from one study to the next. These variables include diagnosis of the child, severity of the child's disorder, age of the child, exact point in the family life cycle when the data are collected, and measures used to assess stress. Use of mothers, or fathers, or both parents as respondents also varies across studies. As an example of a variable that may impact on family stress, Dupont (1986) pointed out that not only is the age of the child important in understanding the family's stress level, so too is the age of the parents. Some parents of adolescents are older than other parents of children of the same age. As a result, parents may be in different stages of personal development. She pointed to older parents who express their frustration as they watch their age peers having a far different life style, free of child care and able to develop their own professional or personal interests. A younger parent of a child the same age might have peers who were still very much absorbed in childrearing and less focused on the next phase of their lives. Thus, although there is support for the notion of increased stress for parents raising a child with a developmental disability, the relationship between stress levels and the child's age has yet to be fully determined.

Financial Factors

Raising an adolescent with autism or mental retardation is expensive. Birenbaum and Cohen (1993), in a 4-year-study of financing care for persons with mental retardation and autism, found that only one third of children with autism between age 10 and 24 could care for themselves alone at home. Less than one fifth of the persons with severe or profound mental retardation could be left alone at home. Only one fourth of all these families reported receiving regular help from someone outside the family. Thus, for most of these families, there were continuing intensive demands for basic child care well beyond the age when most parents would expect to be free of such needs.

The continuing dependency of the child with severe mental retardation has implications for maternal employment. Birenbaum and Cohen (1993) reported that over one half of the women who had a child with a developmental disability were not employed outside of the home, while nationally well over half of all mothers whose youngest child is between 6 and 13 years of age are employed. When these limits on maternal employment are added to the costs of caring for a child whose own long-term employment potential is very limited, it is clear that having an adolescent with a developmental disorder can have a marked impact on a family's financial status. DeMyer and Goldberg (1983) reported that diminished financial resources were a significant issue for most of the families in their study. Worry about family finances has been identified as a special concern for fathers (Lamb, 1983).

Siblings

There is a general agreement in the literature on siblings of children with developmental disabilities that although some children may be at greater risk for discomfort, most children show no significant psychopathology from growing up in a home that includes a child with a disability such as autism or mental retardation (e.g., McHale, Sloan, & Simeonsson, 1986; Rodrigue, Geffken, & Morgan, 1993). There may, however, be subtler, but very real psychological effects from such an experience.

A study by McHale and her colleagues (1986) included children from age 6 to 15 who had a brother or sister with autism, mental retardation, or who was developing without known problems. In general, siblings in all three groups, regardless of age, described their relationship with their brother or sister in positive terms. There was, however, a tendency for the siblings of children with developmental disabilities to be more variable in their responses, with some reporting a very positive relationship, and others a very negative one (McHale et al., 1986). Children with nonhandicapped siblings reported that their families were slightly more cohesive than did the other two groups. Mothers of nonhandicapped children described their children's relationships in more negative terms than did mothers who had a child with autism or mental retardation (McHale et al., 1986).

There are some specific factors that appear to be related to the sibling's responses to a brother or sister with a developmental disability. For example, McHale et al. (1986) found children who saw their parents and peers responding positively to the child with a disability, and who said they understood the nature of the disability, were more likely to respond positively to their brother or sister (McHale et al., 1986). On the other hand, when a child was worried about the future of the child with a disability, or saw parents as favoring that child, there was a more negative sibling relationship.

Consistent with findings mentioned earlier on the impact of diagnosis on parents, there are some data suggesting that children who have a brother or sister with autism are at greater risk for problems than siblings of children with mental retardation. Rodrigue et al. (1993) studied siblings of children with autism, Down's syndrome, or who were developing normally. They found that siblings of children with autism had more internalizing and externalizing problems than the participants in the other two groups. It is important to note, however, that these problems did not reach the level of clinical significance. The three groups did not differ on measures of perceived self-competence, nor their parents' report of the child's social competence. Although age ranges were not reported, the authors found that older children in all three groups were more likely to suffer from internalizing problems than were younger children. The older siblings of the children with autism had more externalizing problems as well.

Although the picture of sibling relationships in adolescence is a generally positive one, there are some variables that put children at higher risk for dysfunction. For example, siblings of children with autism are more likely to have problems of general intelligence, reading, and language (e.g., Folstein & Rutter, 1987). Thus, August, Stewart, and Tsai (1981) tested 41 siblings of children with autism and found that 15 had mental retardation. Similarly, Bartak, Rutter, and Cox (1975) found a family history of reading or language disabilities in 5 of 19 families of children with autism.

In a study of siblings of children with developmental disabilities including mental retardation, and other significant disabilities of early onset, siblings from 8 to 15 years of age whose parents described themselves as more stressed had a lower self-concept than did children whose parents were less stressed (Dyson, Edgar, & Crnic, 1989). Families characterized by free expression of feelings and little interpersonal conflict were more likely to have children with fewer behavior problems than in less supportive, less expressive families (Dyson et al., 1989). However, because the children with disabilities in this study had a variety of diagnoses and because the siblings were from a wide age span, it is difficult to know to what extent these findings would hold true for adolescents who have a brother or sister with autism or moderate to profound mental retardation.

Begun (1989) studied 46 sisters of moderately to profoundly developmentally disabled persons. The participants included 12 adolescent girls, with the remainder being in young or middle adulthood. The adolescent girls reported more conflict in relation to their siblings than did the adults. In general, the picture that emerged was of positive, but not intimate, sibling relationships. The relationships were less intimate and less competitive than between siblings without disabilities.

The formal support network available to the family may help to reduce sibling stress. Mates (1990) studied school-age siblings of children with autism. Although he did not provide detailed information about age range, the mean age for his sample suggests there were a large number in early adolescence. His study did not find significant adjustment problems or academic achievement problems among the siblings of children with autism. He speculated that the extensive network of support available to the families who participated in the study, and the extensive educational services for the child with autism, may serve to attenuate problems of adjustment in siblings.

SEXUALITY

Most families feel challenged by the transformation of their child into a young person with sexual wants and needs. For families of children with developmental disabilities, adolescence poses an even more formidable challenge. Typical adolescents accomplish an age-appropriate degree of social and cognitive development that helps them make sense of bodily changes and urges. By contrast, the adolescent with mental retardation or autism experiences age-appropriate sexual development without the benefit of concomitant social or cognitive development. This leaves the young person with new sexual desires and responsibilities, but without the conceptual tools to accommodate them.

Ignoring Sexuality

The sexual needs of persons with developmental disabilities are often overlooked (Ruble & Dalrymple, 1993). For example, DeMyer (1979) found that most parents of children with autism thought their sons were uninterested in sexual intercourse, and their daughters would only engage in intercourse passively.

Despite the inclination of parents and professionals to believe otherwise (Gath, 1988; Ousley & Mesibov, 1991), people with autism and mental retardation are interested in sexuality (Ford, 1987; Heshusius, 1981). Ousley and Mesibov (1991) compared the sexual knowledge, interest, and experience of people with mental retardation and autism and found that whereas persons with mental retardation were more sexually experienced, the two groups were similar in knowledge and interest. In both groups, IQ was a good predictor of sexual knowledge, and males reported more interest in sex than females.

Skill Deficits

Although there is good evidence that adolescents with autism are interested in sex, personal accounts suggest that autism interferes with the expression of this sexual interest. Ford (1987) noted that higher functioning people with autism have doubts about their capacity to be sexually intimate. Autobiographical works echo this idea with their descriptions of authors having sexual fantasies and frustrated sexual desires (e.g., Grandin & Scariano, 1991). As parents of children with autism, Dewy and Everard (1974) explained that deficits in social skills lead to rejections by love interests that teach the person with autism to remain celibate. Legally, many severely disabled individuals are considered unable to give consent for sexual relations (Kaeser, 1992). Practically, even the most highly functioning individual with autism may be unsuccessful in establishing the intimate relationships that would lead to sex (Ford, 1987). This disappointment can be painful to the individual and to the family as well.

S. S. Cole and T. M. Cole (1993) explained that a child with a developmental disability has less opportunity for appropriate sexual exploration because of a relative lack of privacy compared to other people. An adolescent with a developmental disability may not understand the rules of public and private behavior (Monat, 1982), and, therefore, may engage in sexual self-exploration in public. These young people may expose themselves, masturbate in public, or touch other people's genital regions, behaviors that may offend or embarrass family members (particularly siblings). Fortunately, such behaviors are usually transient and not severe (Gillberg & Schaumann, 1989). They highlight the importance of teaching these young people the rules of public and private behaviors.

Adolescents with developmental disabilities may also have problems with sexual hygiene. For girls, this can pose special problems with the onset of menstruation. Limited receptive communication abilities may prevent a girl from understanding the pain of menstrual cramps or the unexpected blood. Family members may need to assume responsibility for a girl who cannot track her own cycle. Menstrual hygiene may be difficult or unpleasant to teach.

High functioning children with autism face qualitatively different challenges during adolescence than their less cognitively advanced counterparts. Whereas basic concepts, such as privacy or hygiene, may be readily grasped, more subtle social deficits still exist. These young people must learn to deal with the frustration of social rejection (Dewey & Everard, 1974) and manage their sexual and social relationships in a relatively autonomous fashion (Ousely & Mesibov, 1991).

Risks of Sexual Activity

The emergence of sexuality carries certain risks that are common for all adolescents, but are intensified for the person with a developmental disability. First, these adolescents may be at high risk for sexual abuse. Kempton and Kahn (1991) estimated that 85% to 90% of persons with disabilities experience victimization. This may be due in part to what Dewey and Everard (1974) described as guilelessness in the person with autism. Although high functioning adolescents with autism yearn for relationships, they lack social skills, and this combination of circumstances may set them up to be easily duped.

Boundaries for a child with a developmental disability may not be as clear as they are for others. A child with a disability may experience more nudity than other children because of more frequent medical examinations, and because of greater need for physical assistance from others (S. S. Cole & T. M. Cole, 1993).

Another risk for the person with a developmental disability is contracting sexually transmitted diseases, including HIV/AIDS (Kempton & Kahn, 1991). A lack of appreciation of the modes of transmission of these infections may make the person with a developmental disability especially vulnerable to infection. Similarly, there is concern about the risk of unwanted pregnancy for persons who do not understand how to use birth control measures. Gath (1988) noted that parental fears of a developmentally disabled person becoming pregnant may be exaggerated. Using Down's syndrome as an example, she explained that there are very few mothers and no known fathers with Down's syndrome. Although the data do not rule out the risk of unwanted pregnancy, families may worry somewhat more than is warranted.

Sex Education

Families may feel overwhelmed by the number and intensity of dangers associated with the sexuality of their adolescent with developmental disabilities. Fortunately, sex education can effectively address many of these concerns. Sex education programs focus on a range of concerns, including empowering the individual to make appropriate choices (Manilcam & Hensarling, 1990), drawing boundaries around personal space (Champagne & Walker-Hirsch, 1982), developing skills for menstrual hygiene, recognizing privacy, identifying anatomy, and distinguishing appropriate touch (Small, 1989).

Many approaches to sex education involve the family. Ford (1987) advocated teaching family roles as part of sex education in order to help adolescents communicate with their family, and teaching family members to address issues of sexuality proactively rather than reactively. Kempton and Kahn (1991) taught parents how to teach their own child sex education based on the child's level of functioning. Topics suggested include menstrual hygiene, rules of privacy, appropriate touch, resisting exploitation, and masturbation. The use of dolls, models, and drawings is suggested for teaching body parts and sexual activity. These authors argue that the goal of sex education should be to help the adolescent experience pleasure as well as preventing unwanted pregnancies or disease.

Many developmentally disabled youths will never have the social or cognitive skills necessary to forge a relationship with a consenting sexual partner. They face a life of celibacy. Gath (1988) suggested that families and professionals identify appropriate sexual outlets for these young people who may not develop them on their own. Pelling (1989) urged that families and professionals ensure that young people learn the appropriate time and place for masturbation, thus helping to ensure an appropriate outlet for sexual feelings. Robinson, Cohahan, and Brady (1992) dramatically reduced the frequency of severe self-injury by teaching appropriate use of a vibrator. Adolescents with autism or mental retardation also need to learn how to ask for affection, and how to refuse unwanted advances (Champagne & Walker-Hirsch, 1982).

Differing religious, moral, and cultural backgrounds may influence a family's response to sex education. For example, some religions frown on masturbation or birth control. This may result in conflicts between the adolescent's needs, the family's needs, and professional advice. In some families, the matter may be further complicated by parental ignorance about sex (Manilcam & Hensarling, 1990). Kempton and Kahn (1991) suggested that sex educators try to convince parents that their children are indeed sexual beings with needs that should be fulfilled, and that sex education does not stimulate or motivate inappropriate sexual activity.

Because high functioning adolescents with autism or persons with mild to moderate mental retardation face qualitatively different problems than other young people with these disabilities, interventions must occur at a different level. General social skills training, coupled with opportunities to practice and refine these skills with a group of peers, may enable the higher functioning person to lead a sexually satisfying life (Ford, 1987). Valenti-Hein, Yarnold, and Mueser (1994) implemented a dating skills program with people who had mild to moderate mental retardation using role play, group problem solving, and group feedback. After participation in the group, members had increased social and sexual knowledge, improved social skills, spent more time interacting with people of the opposite sex, and spent less time interacting with people of the same sex. Unfortunately, their high level of social anxiety was not diminished in spite of their new skills.

SOCIAL DEVELOPMENT

Social skill deficits may be particularly painful during adolescence. Because expectations for adolescents are more stringent than those for a child, teenagers with a developmental disability may appear to have deteriorated in social behavior when they are just being measured by another yardstick (Elliot, 1990). Although the social skills of adolescence are for the most part a continuation of those available in childhood, regression has been documented in some individuals (e.g., Gillberg & Schaumann, 1989), and improvements in others (e.g., Mesibov, 1988). Families may need considerable assistance in helping their teenager with a developmental disability respond to the increased social pressures of adolescence.

Many young people with developmental disabilities show an increase in social interest, but lack a parallel increase in social skills (Mesibov, 1992). Although they say they would like to have a friend, they do not understand the meaning of that term as used by others (G. Taylor, 1990). Stengel (1987) explained that these youths often refer to mere acquaintances as friends, and cannot discriminate among levels of intimacy, tending to view other people as interchangeable. They may join with their peers around a common interest, but they will be unable to forge deeper emotional ties (G. Taylor, 1990). Even the highest functioning adolescents with autism rarely escape being seen as "loners" or "eccentric" (Volkmar, 1987).

High functioning people with autism frequently express an interest in dating (Dewey & Everard, 1974) as a way to achieve sexual intimacy (Ousley & Mesibov, 1991), adult status (G. Taylor, 1990), or social contact (Volkmar, 1987). Finding a willing partner may also be seen as a victory over one's disability. Despite their skill deficits, a small number of high functioning people with autism do marry, as do some people with mental retardation.

Adolescents with developmental disabilities typically need help learning the social skills that other teenagers learn with little apparent effort. For example, some goals targeted in Mesibov's (1984) social skills group curriculum include paying attention while others speak, sticking to a conversational topic, speaking about things of interest to others, appreciating humor, and learning how to meet another person. Rumsey, Rapoport, and Sceery (1985) viewed the developmentally disabled adolescent's monotone voice and immature beliefs (e.g., there is a Santa Claus) as other noteworthy deficits.

G. Taylor (1990) observed that certain social deficits not only prevent adolescents with developmental disabilities from making friends, but also prevent them from leading autonomous lives. For example, problems with gullibility leave these young people open to abuse, problems with self-organization lead to failed efforts at meetings or deadlines, and difficulties with personal hygiene not only make them unattractive to others, but may endanger their health (G. Taylor, 1990). Mesibov (1992) suggested that an overarching difficulty relating one's actions to consequences, particularly their effect on others, leads to many more specific social deficits.

Baron-Cohen (1992) offered the concept of "mind blindness" to explain the social deficits experienced by persons with autism. This describes the adolescent's lack of sophistication in thinking about what other people are thinking. He found that adolescents with autism who were able to recognize basic facial expressions, such as happy or sad, were unable to sequence a simple picture story leading to these feelings (Baron-Cohen, 1992). Further, these adolescents were adept at visual perspective taking, yet unable to demonstrate conceptual perspective taking in the form of understanding a false belief. Cognitive theorists refer to this inability to think about the thinking of others as a "Theory of Mind Mechanism" deficit (e.g., Baron-Cohen, Leslie, & Frith, 1985).

Patterns of Social Deficits

Wing and Attwood (1987) separated individuals with autism into three social topologies. The first of these is the *aloof* group who fits the general image of persons with autism as in their "own world." Next, the *passive* group includes persons who do not initiate social interaction, but will passively reciprocate another's approach. Third, the *active but odd* group is composed of people who make initiations but in an inappropriate and one-sided manner. Volkmar, Cohen, Bregman, Hooks, and Stevenson (1989) suggested that younger children with developmental disabilities are more commonly aloof, whereas adolescents are more often active but odd. In contrast, Castello and Dawson (1993) found no significant relation between social topology and chronological age.

Self-injurious behaviors and aggression in adolescence stigmatize adolescents with autism and prevent them from integrating successfully with peers. Although biological changes occurring at puberty may trigger these behaviors, Pelling (1989) suggested they sometimes emerge as a result of social deficits. He argued that as individuals with developmental disabilities enter adolescence, both self-imposed and social expectations increase. This, in turn, increases the frustration experienced by the adolescent who cannot meet the perceived demands. This frustration, in an individual with impaired coping skills, may lead to violent behavior.

Pelling (1989) observed that society responds differently to the behavior of a child than an adolescent. Inappropriate behaviors of a child may seem trivial or cute, but in an adolescent they may appear odd or dangerous. Mesibov's (1988) longitudinal assessment of adolescents with autism supports the idea that observers rate adolescents less favorably than children. Although Mesibov (1988) found that children's degree of autistic involvement typically remains constant or improves after puberty, observers' global impressions of the severity of autism increase. Despite this observer bias, some social aspects of developmental disabilities improve at adolescence. For example, adolescents with autism establish more frequent eye contact with their parents than do younger children (Volkmar et al., 1989). Mesibov found communication and activity level improved among many adolescents with autism, and among some higher functioning persons with autism, he found an improvement in relatedness (Mesibov, 1988).

Among the variables that predict improved social skills are the ability to shift strategies when the current one is ineffective (Berger et al., 1993), and recognizing one's self as different from others during early adolescence (Volkmar, 1987). Gender also has an impact on social skills. McLennan, Lord, and Schopler (1993) found that parents described girls with autism as having superior social skills in the preschool years: however, boys were more likely than girls to develop reciprocal social interactions during adolescence.

The anxiety and depression that accompany an awareness of one's disability may intensify social deficits (Wing, 1992). This may be a particular problem for those high functioning youngsters with Autistic Disorder or Aspereger's Disorder who may be mainstreamed, and the victim of peer ridicule (Mesibov, 1984). At a time when these teenagers are beginning to be motivated by the esteem of their peers, teasing can be especially painful.

PLACEMENT

Changes during adolescence are not limited to the child. The rest of the family is passing through this life cycle event as well. Adolescence may be accompanied by changes in the family structure, such as when siblings leave home, or an extended family member becomes ill. In addition, outside influences on the family, such as the community's response to the child with a developmental disability, may change in adolescence. These structural changes and external responses changes may force a family to consider whether or not it is in the child's and the family's best interest to keep their adolescent with a developmental disability at home. In addition, many families regard late adolescence or early adulthood as the normative time to leave home.

Social Expectations

Inherently difficult placement decisions may be complicated by social pressures. Marsh (1992b) explained that, historically, parents were encouraged to place children with atypical development in institutions. If they kept the child at home, they were made to feel guilty. With the normalization movement, deinstitutionalization and placement in the community became popular (Willer & Intagliata, 1982). Because the biological family is the most "normalized" setting, families are now made to feel guilty if they do not keep their child at home (Marsh, 1992b). Even placement in another family's home will not meet societal scrutiny. In her discussion of birthparents who chose adoption for their children with disabilities, Finnegan (1993) explained that siblings, extended family, and professionals may imply that they are "bad parents" who deserted their child.

The "least restrictive alternative" principle is another factor in the choice between in-home versus out-of-home placement. Johnston and Sherman (1993) specified that choosing the least restrictive alternative for a child requires that "when a constitutional right can be legitimately restricted, it should be restricted only to the extent necessary to carry out a valid purpose" (p. 103). This implies that the individual with a disability should have as much independence and freedom as possible. Because most residential placements are more structured and allow less freedom than a family residence, parents are encouraged to keep the child at home whenever possible (Sherman, 1988).

S. J. Taylor, Lakin, and Hill (1989) described a variant of the movement to keep children in a family home as "permanency planning." They explained the emergence of this movement as serendipitous in response to an accidental overestimation of the number of children with developmental disabilities in foster care. As a result, states began a "permanency planning" effort to keep children with their biological families. This led to a 45% decrease in the number of children with developmental disabilities in foster care between 1977 and 1986. S. J. Taylor et al. (1989) cited certain ideals as central to permanency planning. First, supporters of permanency planning believe that all children belong with their biological families. Second, they believe that families need support in handling these children. Third, if for some reason the child needs to leave the family of origin, reunification should be encouraged and contact should be maintained. Finally, if ties are completely broken, adoption should be pursued.

Although keeping children with their biological families is currently the dominant approach, some professionals worry that the field is going too far in this direction. Willer and Intagliata (1982) explained that although many interpret the tenets of normalization to mean that the individual with a disability belongs in the most normative setting, they advocate for an interpretation based on choosing a setting that is most likely to elicit or maintain normative behavior. They warn that one should not assume that a setting is better for an individual solely because it is based in the community. A community environment may be necessary but insufficient for an individual's progress. Similarly, Lettick (1987) supported an individualized approach in which placement is determined by matching client to setting characteristics. By this method, even a more restrictive, institutional setting may sometimes prove to be the best available alternative.

Family Factors

Sherman (1988) explained that caring for a child with a developmental disability at home can cause significant stress for the family. Specifically, Sherman (1988) suggested that the behavioral deficits and excesses of the disabled family member may interfere with family life, pose difficulties in managing behavior, and result in community rejection. Marsh (1992b) added exhausting care responsibilities to the list of possible stressors. Other strains on the family include financial loss, negative effects on the health of the caregiver, time taken away from other children, and a parental longing for an "empty nest" that they know will never arrive (Marsh, 1992a). Because of these factors, having a family member with a disability may act as a chronic stressor, leaving family members with no time to regroup and reinvigorate themselves (Tausig, 1985).

Family life cycle issues and maturation may increase the pressure on families (Blacher & Hanneman, 1992). By adolescence, these issues may intensify to a point where the family questions its resources to cope. For example, many parents seek residential care as a child becomes stronger and more difficult to manage (Luce & Christian, 1989). Problem behaviors may become dangerous when performed by an individual with the strength of an adolescent, and moving an inert adolescent may prove physically overwhelming (Lettick, 1987). As the family ages, siblings who had previously assisted with caregiving may go off to college or to live independently. Similarly, grandparents who had provided support to parents may grow ill or too weak to continue helping. The fact that babysitters for adolescents are hard to find intensifies the loss of familial supports (Cutler & Kozloff, 1987). Thus, it is no surprise that some families with a developmentally disabled family member evidence an increased level of anxiety and depression over time (Marsh, 1992a).

Some family characteristics and outside services may buffer the effects of stress on the family and thereby decrease the probability that the adolescent with a developmental disability will be placed out of the home. Sherman (1988) found that social support from extended family or friends, access to special education facilities and services, emergency care and transportation, homemaker services, and instruction in child management each increases the likelihood that the child would remain at home. Similarly, Marcenko and Smith (1992) found that an intensive family-centered case management approach including stress management, parenting skills, support groups, respite care, financial and transportation help, and advocacy led to increased maternal life satisfaction and decreased maternal depression and anxiety over a 1-year period.

Rimmerman (1989) found that respite care prevents out-of-home placement by decreasing parental and family problems, parental pessimism, parental perception of the child's incapacities, and maternal stress. In fact, 47% of respondents to Rimmerman's questionnaire explained that they would consider out-of-home placement if they were no longer provided respite care services. When comparing users of respite services with nonusers, Factor, Perry, and Freeman (1990) found that children of users exhibited more severe behavior problems and a lower level of functioning than those of nonusers. Further, users reported less social support although their stress levels were equal.

Factors affecting placement decisions typically fall into one of three main categories: characteristics of the disabled individual, characteristics of the family, and outside influences (Tausig, 1985). The severity of the disabled family member's behavior problems, coupled with the individual's level of adaptive functioning, are the most discriminating child characteristics that determine placement (Bromley & Blacher, 1991). Additionally, for individuals with disabilities under 21 years of age, as age increases, the probability of out-of-home placement increases (Tausig, 1985). Family characteristics that predict out-of-home placement include daily stress, parental health, marital status, the presence or absence of support, and family size (Bromley & Blacher, 1991). Sherman (1988) found that families with a lower socioeconomic status and impaired family relations were more likely to place a child out of the home. Finally, outside influences, such as the availability of a day-care program or educational support in the area, may affect placement decisions (Mansell, 1994).

Researchers have attempted to make generalizations about the demographics of those who will remain home and those who will be placed out of the home. Blacher and Hanneman (1992) found that gender exerted no influence on placement decisions: however, Marsh (1992b) found males more frequently placed out of the home than females. Blacher and Hanneman (1992) also reported that more English speaking Caucasian adolescents were placed out of the home than African-American or Latino adolescents. According to Cutler and Kozloff (1987), over 50% of individuals with a pervasive developmental disorder will be placed outside the home for some period of time, and 60% eventually find a permanent residential placement.

At the time of diagnosis, many parents resolve to keep their children at home "forever" (Lettick, 1987). Therefore, the idea of a placement outside the home creates ethical and personal issues. The resulting guilt and ambivalence increase the parents' hefty emotional burden (Marsh, 1992b). Marcus and Schopler (1987) advised those helping families through a placement decision to underscore that a child moving out of the house represents a natural progression toward independence rather than a failure on the part of the family. Similarly, Lettick (1987) explained that moving an adolescent out of the home represents an avenue for improvement. Further, she advocated that parents should try to talk to others who have been through the process before them. If they remain apprehensive, she suggested that they try a placement on a limited basis.

Once a family embarks on finding a residence for a child, needs will center around referral assistance, information gathering, treatment coordination, and emotional support (Marsh,

1992a). Gillberg (1989) described a Swedish example of the process of finding an appropriate residence for a child with autism. The "habilitation chain" begins with a thorough evaluation of the child, including behavioral, medical, and neuropsychological workups. Families are provided with crisis intervention services, practical and financial support including respite, and emotional support. Planning is based on a long-term perspective utilizing an integration of approaches including behavior modification, physical education, basic education, and pharmacotherapy or psychotherapy, if necessary.

McNair and Rusch (1991) viewed parents as the single most important factor in the success of a transition to residential placement. In their experience, parents adopt one of three roles through this process. Some parents act as facilitators, demonstrating commitment to the child and joining the treatment team. Other parents may be seen as nonparticipants. These parents allow the professionals a free hand. Finally, parents may be seen by the team as difficult in that they disagree with the overall treatment approach and therefore with each component. Whereas parental involvement has been shown to predict successful adjustment by the adolescent to her new setting (e.g., Blacher & Baker, 1992), the literature does not separate out the effects of different types of involvement. Although one might hypothesize that antagonistic relations between parents and staff would lead to the child's services suffering, no definitive conclusions can be made.

Living Alternatives

The oldest type of residential placement for adolescents with developmental disabilities is a state institution. As discussed previously, there has been a movement away from this restrictive approach. Additionally, Luce and Christian (1989) claimed that these larger settings promote dependence. Nevertheless, Lettick (1987) argued that for some individuals, the safety features, equipment, and space offered by a large setting may be essential. Further, she noted that institutions are often near cities, which provide a large pool for hiring staff and increased access to the community. Lettick (1987) suggested that institutional settings be judged individually with attention paid to staff–resident ratio, staff turnover, and programming, in addition to location and fit with the individual.

Discontent with the institutional settings led to the emergence of staffed, community-based, group living situations called "group homes." To provide structure, group homes use predictable routines with planned, group activities (Willer & Intagliata, 1982). Luce and Christian (1989) argued that all residential care, even in a less restrictive setting, such as a group home, should be transitional and therefore focus on providing individuals with skills necessary for the next least restrictive setting. Luce and Christian (1989) advised consumers to carefully examine the amount and types of programming offered by each home.

Some adolescents with developmental disabilities need supervision and assistance, but do not require the structure afforded by a group home. For them, a supervised apartment becomes a possibility. In this semi-independent setting, a small number of individuals share an apartment with supervision.

Families of adolescents with developmental disabilities may choose to place their child in a family care home. Family care homes may be chosen when the adolescents' disability is not so severe that they require an intervention more intensive than a family household. Family care homes provide a flexible, individualized environment (Willer & Intagliata, 1982). Ideally, family care homes allow for maintenance of the relationship between the child and the family of origin (Stoneman & Crapps, 1990).

Foster care, usually a short-term placement, presents an alternative similar to family care. There are two major types of foster care. The first focuses on maintenance and daily care for the adolescent and the second focuses on treatment. Treatment foster care providers earn extra money and receive special training for providing approximately 60 hours per month of behavioral programming (Reiss, McKinney, & Napolitan, 1990). In one study of the treatment foster care model, 72% of the children were discharged to home after an average stay of 16.8 days and 70% of them were still at home 3 months later (Mikkelsen, Bereika, & McKenzie, 1993).

Although formal adoption of adolescents is rare, informal separation of the family from the adolescent with a developmental disability is more common. Blacher and Baker (1992) found that one of five residents in care settings had no contact with their families. Stoneman and Crapps (1990) surveyed providers of family home care and found that in over one half of the cases, the family of origin had never visited. Stoneman and Crapps (1990) believed this may be especially damaging because family involvement is correlated with increased success of a placement and improved quality of life. Nevertheless, the same factors that led to an out-of-home placement, such as limited financial resources or ill health, may prevent visits. Other factors that Stoneman and Crapps (1990) found to affect the frequency of visits include the quality of relationship between the caregiver and the family, the involvement of the family in the decision to place the child out of the home, the provider's encouragement of visits, the father's living status, client characteristics, placement length, and the distance between the family residence and the care home. L. R. Simonson and S. M. Simonson (1987) stressed the importance of maintaining the family's identity as the "true family" of the adolescent. To this end, they suggested that residential programs maintain telephone contact with the family, offer liberal visiting hours, and foster positive staff–family relations.

ENTERING THE JOB MARKET

One prominent goal for parents of adolescents with developmental disabilities is the young person's entry to the workforce. Being able to achieve this objective requires personal and vocational skills on the part of the person with a disability, and the availability of appropriate jobs. The technology for both individual skill development and appropriate job placements has improved in recent years.

Within the marketplace, Goldberg, McLean, Lavigne, Fratolillo, and Sullivan (1990) reported that the 1980s saw an increase in programs and services focusing on the integration of individuals with developmental disabilities into the community. This is in contrast to previous years in which the norm was sheltered workshops that did not target eventual competitive employment and community involvement (Goldberg et al., 1990).

Types of Employment

Keirnan, McCaughey, and Schalock (1988) described several employment opportunities for workers with developmental disabilities. These work environments vary from most to least restrictive. At one end of the continuum is sheltered employment involving a highly structured and controlled environment where the individual works for less than minimum wage. Next are supported employment and transitional training/employment where one still receives substantial support, although in transitional employment this is time limited. Finally, competitive employment refers to positions in which an individual with a disability is integrated into a typical work setting with nondisabled coworkers and earns at or above minimum wage (Keirnan et al., 1988).

There are variations on this basic continuum. For example, Wehman, M. Hill, J. M. Hill, Brooke, Pendeleton, and Britt (1985) injected crucial elements of training and supported employment into a competitive setting. These elements include help and support at the job site, an extensive analysis and matching of the working environment to the individual, and assistance for related activities such as travel, interviewing, and social security (Wehman et al., 1985).

Where Are the Jobs?

In a survey of 112,996 persons with developmental disabilities who were receiving vocational training, 65,093 were in sheltered workshops, 6,273 were in transition training/employments, 4,234 were in supported employment, and 12,006 were in competitive jobs (Keirnan et al., 1988). Keirnan et al. (1988) found that the majority of those surveyed worked in areas of food and beverage preparation, janitorial work, assembly and lodging occupations (e.g., maid service). The survey also revealed a movement from more restrictive to less restrictive employment options in recent years.

Predictors of Success

Not surprisingly, Keirnan et al. (1988) found that the number of placements, starting wage, work hours per week, and length of time on the job all increased as function of higher IQ. Age at placement was also significantly related to placement type, with those workers placed in competitive employment being younger than those in more restricted settings (Keirnan et al., 1988).

Although intelligence is a predictor of job outcome, Loveland and Kelley (1988) observed that "managing the social and physical environment...may be much more closely related than academic achievement to vocational success and level of independence" (p. 84). Diagnostic category becomes important when considering social adaptation. For example, Loveland and Kelley (1988) tracked the development of adaptive behavior in children with autism and Down's syndrome over time. They found that the adaptive behavior of individuals with Down's syndrome continues to develop into adulthood while individuals with autism showed relatively stable levels of adaptive behavior after adolescence. Loveland and Kelley (1988) suggested that intensive concentration on adaptive behavior for adolescents with autism may be important to offset this stagnation.

Goldberg et al. (1990) pinpointed job skills that are often problematic for individuals with developmental disabilities. These include lack of productivity, poor social skills, slow performance, and inability to change routine. Targeting these areas during adolescence and into adulthood may help anticipate and diminish job problems. Jacobson and Ackerman (1990) similarly emphasized the importance of teaching social skills, communication skills, and self-control to people with autism.

Support for the importance of adaptive skills was illustrated by Burt, Fuller, and Lewis (1991), who assessed the outcome of competitive employment placement for four workers with autism. Their most useful skills were interpersonal and social appropriateness across a variety of settings and people, and self-management of stereotyped behaviors (Burt et al., 1991). Characteristics that were problematic in the job setting included low motivation to work, lack of flexibility and speed, and persistent inability to make decisions and solve problems. Employer and family support increased the probability of job success (Burt et al., 1991).

Family Issues

McNair and Rusch (1991) surveyed 85 parents of individuals with various learning disabilities, physical handicaps, and mental retardation about parental expectancies and involvement in programs to transition their child into a work setting. The majority of parents said that their preference for their child's employment included earning wages equal to or above the minimum, at a setting in the community. Although this was the shared ideal, only 50% of the parents expected this to occur (McNair & Rusch, 1991).

In general, McNair and Rusch (1991) found that nearly all parents wanted to be involved in the decision making process as their child entered the job market. However, significantly fewer parents were aware that transition programs of this nature existed. Parents also indicated that more specific information about their child's skills, work, and living options would be helpful. McNair and Rusch (1991) pointed out that it remains unclear how increased parent involvement would affect employment outcome, and that further research needs to be done.

THE JOHNSON FAMILY: FROM BOY TO TEEN

By the time Guy Johnson was 2 years old, his parents were worried about his development. Over the course of the next year, they realized something was seriously wrong with him. Shortly after his third birthday, a pediatric neurologist diagnosed Guy as suffering from autism. In the early 1970s, when Guy was a preschooler, there were few resources for very young children with developmental disabilities. As a result, he did not enter a special education program until he turned 5. At that time, his parents enrolled him in a specialized program for children with autism, and Guy made slow but steady progress over the next 7 years. His speech was limited, he became distressed about minor changes in the environment, and he had a broad repertoire of stereotyped behavior, but Guy gradually learned to enjoy being with other people and to be motivated by their approval.

Guy developed seizures when he was 11 years old. Following a period of trial with several different anticonvulsants, one was identified that brought the seizures under control. As he matured physically, the medication had to be continually adjusted. In spite of the seizure activity, Guy became increasingly aware of his environment, and as he approached early adolescence, he seemed to derive greater pleasure from being in the company of other people. He responded well to the school's prevocational curriculum. Nonetheless, he had intermittent periods of aggressive behavior that required an extended behavioral assessment and very sophisticated programming to bring under full control.

Immediately after Guy started school as a little boy, his mother and father participated in a behavioral parent training program. Throughout the early years, they worked hard with him on self-help skills, teaching him to dress, undress, take a shower, and a variety of other essential skills. They also collaborated with the school to ensure that what he learned in school was used at home and in the community.

A few months after Guy turned 12, his teacher approached the school psychologist because she was concerned about the Johnsons' growing reluctance to work with their son. They no longer sent the teacher detailed notes about his home performance, and they appeared to have little interest in taking on new home programs. In addition, the Johnsons were complaining that Guy was getting harder to manage at home.

The school psychologist requested a meeting with Guy's parents. She had worked with them closely over the years, and knew they had always been committed to their son's welfare. The psychologist was puzzled by their shift in attitude. During their conversation, several concerns emerged. Mrs. Johnson was quite frank in saying that she was beginning to feel burned out in her work with Guy. They had put hours and hours into home teaching for their son, and there seemed to be no end to what he needed. She said they were thinking about a residential program as an alternative to the school-based program. Mr. Johnson said that they were also concerned because Guy was masturbating frequently, and had no sense of privacy when he did so. As a result, his 9-year-old sister had several times walked into the living room when Guy had his penis exposed. She was upset by the incidents, and the Johnsons worried that Guy might become sexually aggressive toward her. He had not, however, done so to date.

The school psychologist suggested that the Johnsons might want to join a support group for parents of adolescents with autism. She also talked at length with them about how to help their daughter cope with her worries about Guy. In addition, she developed a program to teach Guy to masturbate in private, rather than in public, so that his sexual conduct would be more appropriate. Perhaps most importantly, she helped the Johnson family apply for respite care to get them some relief from Guy's demands.

This extensive support was helpful to the entire Johnson family. Once the respite care removed some of the physical and emotional burdens from his parents, they were able to be more consistent in working with Guy when he needed them. As a result, his behavior problems decreased. The sexual privacy program written by the school psychologist ensured that his masturbation become a private matter. In the parent support group, the Johnsons began to explore the question of when they would help Guy move into a group home. Having a target date for the move when he became a young adult enabled them to muster the energy they needed to help him through adolescence.

CONCLUSIONS

Although adolescence is a stressful time for many families in Western cultures, there are special stressors that accrue to families who are raising a teenager with autism or mental retardation. The tumult of change that can bring significant developmental benefits to parents and teenagers alike does not occur for families whose child has a significant developmental disability. As a result, these families must make considerable effort to ensure that their young person learns the necessary skills to achieve maximum independence in adulthood. Among the most compelling of these tasks is helping the young person cope with sexuality, social skills, vocational planning, and lifetime living arrangements. The family must also cope with the grief about the child's disability and with the extra financial demands, lack of leisure time, and other burdens that they carry. However, in spite of these demands, it is encouraging to note that most families cope effectively with them.

REFERENCES

Ackerman, N. J. (1980). The family with adolescents. In E. A. Carter & M. McGoldrick (Eds.), *The family life cycle: A framework for family therapy* (pp. 147– 169). New York: Gardner.

Akerley, M. S. (1984). Developmental changes in families. In E. Schopler & G. B. Mesibov (Eds.), *The effects of autism on the family* (pp. 85–98). New York: Plenum.

Ando, H., & Yoshimura, I. (1979). Effects of age on communication skill levels and prevalence of maladaptive behaviors in autistic and mentally retarded children. *Journal of Autism and Developmental Disorders, 9*, 83–93.

August, G. J., Stewart, M.A., & Tsai, L. (1981). The incidence of cognitive disabilities in the siblings of autistic children. *British Journal of Psychiatry, 138*, 416–422.

Baron-Cohen, S. (1992). The girl who liked to shout in church. In R. Campbell (Ed.), *Mental lives: Case studies in cognition* (pp. 11–23). Cambridge, MA: Blackwell.

Baron-Cohen, S., Leslie, A. M., & Frith, U. (1985). Does the autistic child have a "theory of mind"? *Cognition, 21*, 37–46.

Bartak, L., & Rutter, M. (1976). Retarded and intelligent autistic children. *Journal of Autism and Childhood Schizophrenia, 6*, 109–120.

Bartak, L., Rutter, M., & Cox, A. (1975). A comparative study of infantile autism and specific developmental language disorder: I. The children. *British Journal of Psychiatry, 126*, 127–145.

Begun, A. L. (1989). Sibling relationships involving developmentally disabled people. *American Journal on Mental Retardation, 93*, 566–574.

Berger, H. C., VanSpaendonck, K. M., Horstink, M. M., Buytenhuijs, E. L., Lammers, P. M., & Cools, A. R. (1993). Cognitive shifting as a predictor of progress in the social understanding of high functioning adolescents with autism. *Journal of Autism and Developmental Disorders, 23*, 341–359.

Birenbaum, A., & Cohen, H. J. (1993). On the importance of helping families: Policy implications from a national study. *Mental Retardation, 31*, 67–74.

Blacher, J., & Baker, B. L. (1992). Toward meaningful family involvement in out of home placement settings. *Mental Retardation, 30*, 35–43.

Blacher, J. B., & Hanneman, R. A. (1992). Family life cycle issues and mental retardation. *American Journal on Mental Retardation, 96*, 607–616.

Bristol, M. M. (1984). Family resources and successful adaptation to autistic children. In E. Schopler & G. B. Mesibov (Eds.), *The effects of autism on the family* (pp. 289–310). New York: Plenum.

Bristol, M. M., & Schopler, E. (1983). Stress and coping in families of autistic adolescents. In E. Schopler & G. B. Mesibov (Eds.), *Autism in adolescents and adults* (pp. 251–278). New York: Plenum.

Bromley, B. E., & Blacher, J. (1991). Parental reasons for out-of-home placement of children with severe handicaps. *Mental Retardation, 29*, 275–280.

Burr, W. R. (1970). Satisfaction with various aspects of marriage over the life cycle: A random middle-class sample. *Journal of Marriage and the Family, 32*, 29–37.

Burt, D. B., Fuller, P. S., & Lewis, K. R. (1991). Brief report: Competitive employment of adults with autism. *Journal of Autism and Developmental Disorders, 21*, 237–241.

Carter, E. A., & McGoldrick, M. (1980). *The family life cycle. A framework for family therapy.* New York: Gardner.

Castello, P., & Dawson, G. (1993). Subclassification of children with autism and pervasive developmental disorder: A questionnaire based on Wing's subgrouping scheme. *Journal of Autism and Developmental Disorders, 23*, 229–241.

Champagne, M. P., & Walker-Hirsch, L. W. (1982). Circles: A self-organization system for teaching appropriate social/sexual behavior to mentally retarded/developmentally disabled persons. *Sexuality and Disability, 5*, 172–174.

Cole, S. S., & Cole, T. M. (1993). Sexuality, disability, and reproductive issues through the lifespan. *Sexuality and Disability, 11*, 189–205.

Cutler, B. C., & Kozloff, M. A. (1987). Living with autism: Effects on families and family needs. In D. J. Cohen & A. M. Donellan (Eds.), *Handbook of autism and pervasive developmental disorders* (pp. 513–527). New York: Wiley.

DeMyer, M. K. (1979). *Parents and children in autism.* New York: Wiley.

DeMyer, M. K., & Goldberg, P. (1983). Family needs of the autistic adolescent. In E. Schopler & G. B. Mesibov (Eds.), *Autism in adolescents and adults* (pp. 225–250). New York: Plenum.

Dewey, M. A., & Everard, M. P. (1974). The near normal autistic adolescent. *Journal of Autism and Childhood Schizophrenia, 4*, 348–356.

Donovan, A. M. (1988). Family stress and ways of coping with adolescents who have handicaps: Maternal perceptions. *American Journal on Mental Retardation, 92*, 502–509.

Dupont, A. (1986). Socio-psychiatric aspects of the young severely mentally retarded and the family. *British Journal of Psychiatry, 148*, 227–234.

Dykens, E. M., Hodapp, R. M., Ort, S. I., & Leckman, J. F. (1993). Trajectory of adaptive behavior in males with fragile x syndrome. *Journal of Autism and Developmental Disorders, 23*, 135–145.

Dykens, E., Leckman, J., Paul, R., & Watson, M. (1988). Cognitive behavioral and adaptive functioning in fragile x and non-fragile x retarded men. *Journal of Autism and Developmental Disorders, 18*, 41–52.

Dyson, L., Edgar, E., & Crnic, K. (1989). Psychological predictors of adjustment by siblings of developmentally disabled children. *American Journal on Mental Retardation, 94*, 292–302.

Elliot, A. (1990). Adolescence and early adulthood: The needs of the young adult with severe difficulties. In K. Ellis (Ed.), *Autism: Professional perspectives and practice* (pp. 105–122). London: Chapman & Hall.

Factor, D. C., Perry, A., & Freeman, N. (1990). Brief report: Stress, social support and respite care use in families with autistic children. *Journal of Autism and Developmental Disorders, 20*, 139–146.

Finnegan, J. (1993). *Shattered dreams—lonely choices: Birth parents of babies with disabilities talk about adoption.* Westport, CT: Bergin & Garvey.

Flynt, S. W., & Wood, T. A. (1989). Stress and coping of mothers of children with moderate mental retardation. *American Journal on Mental Retardation, 94*, 278–283.

Flynt, S. W., Wood, T. A., & Scott, R. L. (1992). Social support of mothers of children with mental retardation. *Mental Retardation, 30*, 233–236.

Folstein, S. E., & Rutter, M. L. (1987). Autism. Familial aggregation and genetic implications. In E. Schopler & G. B. Mesibov (Eds.), *Neurobiological issues in autism* (pp. 83–105). New York: Plenum.

Fong, L., Wilgosh, L., & Sobsey, D. (1993). The experience of parenting an adolescent with autism. *International Journal of Disability, Development and Education, 40*, 105–113.

Ford, A. (1987). Sex education for individuals with autism: Structuring information and opportunity. In D. J. Cohen & A. M. Donellan (Eds.), *Handbook of autism and pervasive developmental disabilities* (pp. 430–439). New York: Wiley.

Garfin, D. G., McCallon, D., & Cox, R. (1988). Validity and reliability of the childhood autism rating scale with autistic adolescents. *Journal of Autism and Developmental Disorders, 18*, 367–378.

Gath, A. (1988). Mentally handicapped people as parents. *Journal of Child Psychology and Psychiatry and Allied Disciplines, 29*, 739–744.

Gillberg, C. (1984). Autistic children growing up: Problems during puberty and adolescence. *Developmental Medicine and Child Neurology, 26*, 125– 129.

Gillberg, C. (1989). Habilitation for children with autism: A Swedish example. In C. Gillberg (Ed.), *Diagnosis and treatment of autism* (pp. 329–346). New York: Plenum.

Gillberg, C., & Schaumann, H. (1989). Autism: Specific problems of adolescence. In C. Gillberg (Ed.), *Diagnosis and treatment of autism* (pp. 375– 382). New York: Plenum.

Gillberg, C., & Steffenburg, S. (1987). Outcome and prognostic factors in infantile autism and similar conditions: A population-based study of 46 cases followed through puberty. *Journal of Autism and Developmental Disorders, 17*, 273–287.

Goldberg, R. T., McClean, M. M., LaVigne, R., Fratolillo, J., & Sullivan, R. T. (1990). Transition of persons with developmental disability from sheltered employment to competitive employment. *Mental Retardation, 28*, 299–304.

Grandin, T., & Scariano. M. M. (1991). *Emergence: Labeled autistic.* Novato, CA: Arena Press.

Harris, S. L. (1984). The family of the autistic child: A behavioral-systems view. *Clinical Psychology Review, 4*, 227–239.

Harris, S. L., Gill, M. J., & Alessandri, M. (1990). The family with an autistic child. In M. Seligman (Ed.), *The family with a handicapped child* (2nd ed., pp. 269–294). Boston: Allyn & Bacon.

Heshusius, L. (1981). *Meaning in life as experienced by persons labeled mentally retarded in a group home: A participant observation study*. Springfield, IL: Thomas.

Holroyd, J., Brown, N., Wikler, L., & Simmons, J. (1975). Stress in the families of institutionalized and noninstitutionalized autistic children. *Journal of Community Psychology, 3*, 26–31.

Jacobson, J. W., & Ackerman, L. J. (1990). Differences in adaptive functioning among people with autism or mental retardation. *Journal of Autism and Developmental Disorders, 20*, 205–219.

Johnston, J. M., & Sherman, R. A. (1993). Applying the least restrictive alternative principle to treatment decisions: A legal and behavioral analysis. *The Behavior Analyst, 16*, 103–115.

Kaeser, F. (1992). Can people with severe mental retardation consent to mutual sex? *Sexuality and Disability, 10*, 33–42.

Kazak, A. E. (1987). Families with disabled children: Stress and social networks in three samples. *Journal of Abnormal Child Psychology, 15*, 137–146.

Kazak, A. E. (1988). Stress and social networks in families with older institutionalized retarded children. *Journal of Social and Clinical Psychology, 6*, 448–461.

Kempton, W., & Kahn, E. (1991). Sexuality and people with intellectual disabilities: A historical perspective. *Sexuality and Disability, 9*, 93–111.

Keirnan, W. E., McGaughey, M. J., & Schalock, R. L. (1988). Employment environments and outcome for adults with developmental disabilities. *Mental Retardation, 26*, 279–288.

Kidwell, J., Fischer, J. L., Dunham, R. M., & Baranowski, M. (1983). Parents and adolescents: Push and pull of change. In H. I. McCubbin & C. R. Figley (Eds.), *Stress and the family: Vol. 1. Coping with normative transitions* (pp. 74–89). New York: Brunner/Mazel.

Koegel, R. L., Schreibman, L., Loos, L. M., Dirlich-Wilhelm, H., Dunlap, G., Robbins, F. R., & Plienis, A. J. (1992). Consistent stress predictors in mothers of children with autism. *Journal of Autism and Developmental Disorders, 22*, 205–216.

Lamb, M. E. (1983). Fathers of exceptional children. In M. Seligman (Ed.), *The family with a handicapped child: Understanding and treatment* (pp. 125–146). New York: Grune & Stratton.

Lettick, A. L. (1987). Educational and residential placement: Difficulties, decisions, and issues. In D. J. Cohen & A. M. Donellan (Eds.), *Handbook of autism and pervasive developmental disorders* (pp. 722– 734). New York: Wiley.

Lovaas, O. I. (1987). Behavioral treatment and normal educational and intellectual functioning in young autistic children. *Journal of Consulting and Clinical Psychology, 55*, 3–9.

Loveland, K. A., & Kelley, M. L. (1988). Development of adaptive behavior in adolescents and young adults with autism and Down's syndrome. *American Journal on Mental Retardation, 93*, 84–92.

Luce, S. C., & Christian, W. P. (1989). State of the art programming in Massachusetts: A brief description of the May Institute. In C. Gillberg (Ed.), *Diagnosis and treatment in autism* (pp. 363–374). New York: Plenum.

Manilcam, R., & Hensarling, D. S. (1990). Sexual behavior. In J. L. Matson (Ed.), *Handbook of behavior modification with the mentally retarded* (pp. 503–522). New York: Plenum.

Mansell, J. (1994). Specialized group homes for persons with severe or profound mental retardation and serious problem behavior in England. *Research in Developmental Disabilities, 15*, 371–388.

Marcenko, M. O., & Smith, L. K. (1992). The impact of a family-centered case management approach. *Social Work in Health Care, 17*, 87–100.

Marcus, L. M., & Schopler, E. (1987). Working with families: A developmental perspective. In D. J. Cohen & A. M. Donellan (Eds.), *Handbook of autism and pervasive developmental disorders* (pp. 499–512). New York: Wiley.

Marsh, D. (1992a). *Families and mental illness*. New York: Praeger.

Marsh, D. (1992b). *Families and mental retardation: New directions in professional practice*. New York: Praeger.

Mates, T. E. (1990). Siblings of autistic children: Their adjustment and performance at home and in school. *Journal of Autism and Developmental Disorders, 20*, 545–553.

McCubbin, H. I., & Figley C. R. (Eds.). (1983). Stress *and the family: Vol. 1. Coping with normative transitions*. New York: Brunner/Mazel.

McHale, S. M., Sloan, J., & Simeonsson, R. J. (1986). Sibling relationships of children with autistic, mentally retarded, and nonhandicapped brothers and sisters. *Journal of Autism and Developmental Disorders, 16*, 399–413.

McLennan, J. D., Lord, C., & Schopler, E. (1993). Sex differences in higher functioning people with autism. *Journal of Autism and Developmental Disorders, 23*, 217–227.

McNair, J., & Rusch, F. R. (1991). Parent involvement in transitional programs. *Mental Retardation, 29*, 93–101.

Mesibov, G. B. (1983). Current perspectives and issues in autism and adolescence. In E. Schopler & G. B. Mesibov (Eds.), *Autism in adolescents and adults* (pp. 37–53). New York: Plenum.

Mesibov, G. B. (1984). Social skills training with verbal autistic adolescents and adults: A program model. *Journal of Autism and Developmental Disorders, 14*, 395–404.

Mesibov, G. B. (1988). Diagnosis and assessment of autistic adolescents and adults. In E. Schopler & G. B. Mesibov (Eds.), *Diagnosis and assessment of autism* (pp. 227–230). New York: Plenum.

Mesibov, G. B. (1992). Treatment issues with high functioning adolescents and adults with autism. In E. Schopler & G. B. Mesibov (Eds.), *High functioning individuals with autism* (pp. 143–156). New York: Plenum.

Mikkelsen, E. J., Bereika, G. M., & McKenzie, J. C. (1993). Short-term family-based residential treatment: An alternative to psychiatric hospitalization for children. *American Journal of Orthopsychiatry, 63*, 28–33.

Monat, R. K. (1982). *Sexuality and the mentally retarded.* San Diego: College Hill Press.

Muuss, R. E. (1988). *Theories of adolescence.* New York: Random House.

Nottelmann, E. D., Inoff-Germain, G., Susman, E. J., & Chrousos, G. P. (1990). Hormones and behavior at puberty. In J. Bancroft & J. M. Reinisch (Eds.), *Adolescence and puberty* (pp. 88–123). New York: Oxford University Press.

Ousley, O. Y., & Mesibov, G. B. (1991). Sexual attitudes and knowledge of high functioning adolescents and adults with autism. *Journal of Autism and Developmental Disorders, 21*, 471–481.

Pelling, H. (1989). Psychotherapeutical help in adolescents. In C. Gillberg (Ed.), *Diagnosis and treatment of autism* (pp. 413–418). New York: Plenum.

Reiss, S., McKinney, B. E., & Napolitan, J. T. (1990). New mental retardation service models: Implications for behavior modification. In J. L. Matson (Ed.), *Handbook of behavior modification with the mentally retarded* (2nd ed., pp. 51–70). New York: Plenum.

Rimmerman, A. (1989). Provision of respite care for children with developmental disabilities: Changes in maternal coping and stress over time. *Mental Retardation, 27*, 99–103.

Robinson, C. P., Cohahan, F., & Brady, W. (1992). Reducing self-injurious masturbation using a least intrusive model and adaptive equipment. *Sexuality and Disability, 10*, 43–55.

Rodrigue, J. R., Geffken, G. R., & Morgan, S. B. (1993). Perceived competence and behavioral adjustment of siblings of children with autism. *Journal of Autism and Developmental Disorders, 23*, 665–674.

Ruble, L. A., & Dalrymple, N. J. (1993). Social sexual awareness of persons with autism: A parental perspective. *Archives of Sexual Behavior, 22*, 229–240.

Rumsey, J. M., Rapoport, J. L., & Sceery, W. R. (1985). Autistic children as adults: Psychiatric, social, and behavioral outcomes. *Journal of American Academy of Child Psychiatry, 24*, 465–473.

Rutter, M. (1970). Autistic children: Infancy to adulthood. *Seminars in Psychiatry, 2*, 435–450.

Schopler, E., & Mesibov, G. B. (1983). *Autism in adolescents and adults.* New York: Plenum.

Sherman, B. R. (1988). Predictors of the decision to place developmentally disabled family members in residential care. *American Journal on Mental Retardation, 92*, 344–351.

Simonson, L. R., & Simonson, S. M. (1987). Residential programming at Benhaven. In D. J. Cohen & A. M. Donellan (Eds.), *Handbook of autism and pervasive developmental disorders* (pp. 384–395). New York: Wiley.

Small, A., (1989). Mental retardation. In L. G. Hsu & M. Hersen (Eds.), *Recent developments in adolescent psychiatry* (pp. 367–392). New York: Wiley.

Stengel, B. E. (1987). Developmental group therapy with autistic and other severely psychosocially handicapped adolescents. *International Journal of Group Psychotherapy, 37*, 417–431.

Stoneman, Z., & Crapps, J. M. (1990). Mentally retarded individuals in family care homes: Relationships with family of origin. *American Journal on Mental Retardation, 94*, 420–430.

Suelzle, M., & Keenan, V. (1981). Changes in family support networks over the life cycle of mentally retarded persons. *American Journal on Mental Deficiency, 86*, 267–274.

Szatmari, P., Bartolucci, G., Bremner, R., & Bond, S. (1989). A follow-up study of high functioning autistic children. *Journal of Autism and Developmental Disorders, 19*, 213–225.

Tanner, J. M. (1978). *Fetus into man. Physical growth from conception to maturity*. Cambridge, MA: Harvard University Press.

Tausig, M. (1985). Factors in family decision-making for developmentally disabled individuals. *American Journal of Mental Deficiency, 89*, 352–361.

Taylor, G. (1990). Adolescence and early adulthood: The needs of the more able young adult. In K. Ellis (Ed.), *Autism: Professional perspectives and practice* (pp. 78–104). London: Chapman & Hall.

Taylor, S. J., Lakin, K. C., & Hill, B. K. (1989). Permanency planning for children and youth: Out of home placement decisions. *Exceptional Children, 55*, 541–549.

Valenti-Hein, D. C., Yarnold , P. R., & Mueser, M. T. (1994). Evaluation of the dating skills program for improving heterosexual interactions in people with mental retardation. *Behavior Modification, 18*, 32– 46.

Volkmar, F. R. (1987). Social development. In D. J. Cohen & A. M. Donellan (Eds.), *Handbook of autism and pervasive developmental disorders* (pp. 41–60). New York: Wiley.

Volkmar, F. R., Cohen, D. J., Bregman, J. D., Hooks, M. V., & Stevenson, J. M. (1989). An examination of social typologies in autism. *Journal of the American Academy of Child and Adolescent Psychiatry, 28*, 82–86.

Volkmar, F. R., Szatmari, P., & Sparrow, S. S. (1993). Sex differences in pervasive developmental disorders. *Journal of Autism and Developmental Disorders, 23*, 579–591.

Walker, L. S., Van Slyke, D. A., & Newbrough, J. R. (1992) Family resources and stress: A comparison of families of children with cystic fibrosis, diabetes, and mental retardation. *Journal of Pediatric Psychology, 17*, 327–343.

Wehman, P., Hill, M., Hill, J. M., Brooke, V., Pendleton, P., & Britt, C. (1985). Competitive employment for persons with mental retardation: A follow up 6 years later. *Mental Retardation, 23*, 274–281.

Wikler, L. M. (1986). Periodic stresses of families of older mentally retarded children: An exploratory study. *American Journal on Mental Deficiency, 90*, 703–706.

Willer, B., & Intagliata, J. (1982). Comparison of family-care and group homes as alternatives to institutions. *American Journal of Mental Deficiency, 86*, 588–595.

Wing, L. (1992). Manifestations of social problems in high functioning autistic people. In E. Schopler & G. B. Mesibov (Eds.), *High functioning individuals with autism* (pp. 129–142). New York: Plenum.

Wing, L., & Attwood, A. (1987). Syndromes of autism and atypical development. In D. J. Cohen & A. M. Donellan (Eds.), *Handbook of autism and pervasive developmental disorders* (pp. 3–19). New York: Wiley.

Author Index

Subject Index